Rural India Facing the 21st Century

Rural India Facing the 21st Century

BARBARA HARRISS-WHITE

&

S JANAKARAJAN

Anthem Press

Anthem Press is an imprint of
Wimbledon Publishing Company
75–76 Blackfriars Road
London SE1 8HA

First published by Wimbledon Publishing Company 2004

British Library Cataloguing in Publication Data
Data available

Library of Congress in Publication Data
A catalogue record has been applied for

ISBN 184331 087 2 (hbk)
      184331 088 0 (pbk)

Designed by Abe Aboody
Typeset by Alliance Interactive Technology, Pondicherry, India
Printed in India

Contents

List of Tables

Appendix 2

1–5: LABOUR, GENDER RELATIONS AND THE RURAL ECONOMY

1–6: SOCIAL INSTITUTIONS AND THE STRUCTURAL TRANSFORMATION OF THE NON-FARM ECONOMY

List of Figures

Preface, Acknowledgements and Dedication

THIS project has grown from an enquiry into the spread of the Green Revolution in the 1970s, through one into the regional upstream and downstream linkages of agriculture ten years later, to one examining long-term changes in the rural economy and the impact of development policy on rural people in the 1990s. Research networks and interests have meant that it has evolved from a project run jointly by teams from the Centre for South Asian Studies, Cambridge University, and the Department of Economics of Madras University; through one run jointly by the International Food Policy Research Institute in Washington DC (IFPRI) and Tamil Nadu Agricultural University (TNAU); to one run from the Madras Institute of Development Studies (MIDS) jointly with Queen Elizabeth House (QEH), Oxford University.

North Arcot District in Tamil Nadu was originally selected because it was a relatively poor region, with a semi-arid tropical climate and an agrarian structure dominated numerically by small-scale *ryotwari* producers, often called – without derogatory intent – 'peasants'. (In these research projects they have also been called 'cultivators', 'farmers' and 'petty commodity producers', just as 'landless agricultural labourers' are also referred to as 'wage workers', 'landless peasants' and even 'proletarians' and 'direct producers', since the theoretical worlds informing this research over the last three decades have been many and various.) Tenancy in North Arcot District was and is negligible. Along with the Kaveri Delta, North Arcot was one of Tamil Nadu's rice bowls. Eleven villages on the eastern Coromandel Plain side of the district were randomly selected in 1973, stratified by physical accessibility, population size and the ratio of agricultural labourers to cultivators. One of the villages – Dusi – studied at much wider intervals ever since 1916, when Gilbert Slater, teaching at Madras University, insisted that his economics students had field experience, was also included as it is sited on North Arcot's eastern edge. Another of the villages was the site of detailed economic anthropological fieldwork in 1973. Agricultural markets over the entire district also came under scrutiny. A core of data collected in 1973 was collected again in 11 villages in 1982–3 and also in a subset of 5 (recovering from severe drought) in 1983–4 as part of the TNAU/IFPRI database for a regional social accounting matrix, thereby enabling agrarian economic change to be tracked in a systematic way over two decades. We replicated the field study in 1993–4, recensusing the 11 villages and studying 3 in which the central core of information was updated and our own enquiries were given expression.

In 1972 the region was famous in scholarly circles for the epidemiological field studies run from Christian Medical College, Vellore. Now of course several books on aspects of the rural economy exist[1] and papers from the three rounds of projects published in journals and edited collections can be counted in the hundreds. A selection is published in the companion volume. *The Green Revolution and After: Studies in the Political Economy of Rural Development in South India,* edited by Barbara Harriss-White and John Harriss, Anthem, 2004. A major intellectual spin-off, not reported in this book (because not part of the project funded by DFID – the UK's Department for International Development – under the 1993–4 round) has been the study of business in Arni town each decade.[2] Thus the project has not only grown, it has been fertile and multiplied. The region is now famous. But this fame has its own ironies. The most developed village has been favoured with attention from a fertilizer company and now has a teacher training institute on its dry land. In 1993–4, the wealthiest household there had an estimated US$150,000 of assets, while the poorest had $6.[3] The least developed village is neglected by the state and has changed little over 20 years.

The two agricultural policy issues which focused the research in 1973–4 were the extent of adoption of high-yielding varieties (HYVs) of rice and their social impact. The adoption of HYVs was found to be one third of what was officially claimed in government statistics.[4] The project also obtained important hydrological evidence of a secular lowering of the water tables.[5] It warned of increases in income inequality already brought about by HYVs[6] (which may have been among the many forces which led both state and central government to take various kinds of preemptive action). And it gave a warning of the indirect control over production by traders' credit (against which the official credit plans for the district have subsequently pitted themselves).

From 1973 to 1983/4 rice production had doubled, due both to yield intensification and to multiple cropping. Whereas, in 1973, only 13 per cent of paddy area was under HYVs and adopted by the largest farmers, by 1983 adoption was generalized and scale-neutral. But HYVs did little to increase agricultural employment; wages had certainly risen, but those for women by only half as much as male wages.[7] HYV adoption increased the incomes – and the real consumption expenditure – of agricultural producers and labourers by 30 per cent and indirectly raised those of producers in the non-farm economy by 20 per cent.[8] By then it had also become clear that intervillage diversity had led to intervillage differentiation in development over the first decade, 1973–83/4. The distribution of land showed complex and contradictory patterns, challenging any one theory of social mobility, though the concentration of land ownership was greatest in the poorest villages.[9]

In 1983–4 the policy issues concerned not only the direct impact of technical change but also its indirect multiplier effects: notably the capacity of agriculture to generate local non-farm production and consumption linkages. Using a social accounting matrix, the project found linkages from agriculture to the local non-farm economy that were much weaker than expected and to government and agrobusiness that were much stronger than expected.[10] It was predicted that real rice prices would remain stable, that both within agriculture and in the non-farm economy the trend towards diversification would continue (the project predicted increased output of vegetables, flowers, fruit, milk production and sericulture), and that water supply would become increasingly constraining.[11]

In 1991, North Arcot District was split horizontally and the new, southern, Tiruvannamalai District found itself underindustrialized and relatively underdeveloped with a relatively impoverished, predominantly agrarian resource base. After the droughts of the mid-1980s, and beset by environmental problems caused by hydrological stress, growth in the agricultural economy was believed to have faltered and the rural economy was known to have diversified but – contrary to what had been predicted – in the direction of rain-fed cereals and labour-sparing crops. However, the degree of experimentation with water-conserving technology (percolation tanks, check dams, tank repair and maintenance) was unknown. The northern split district (initially known as Ambedkar but now as Vellore) straddles one of the most infrastructurally, commercially, agriculturally and industrially advanced zones in India with a dense reticulation of towns and strong rural–urban linkages. The market town of Arni, serving a hinterland of some 100 villages (including 3 of those randomly selected for our project), has grown from 39,000 people in 1973 to 49,500 in 1983 and from 56,000 in 1991 to an estimated 80,000 now. Well south of the dynamic Madras–Bangalore corridor, not connected by rail and poorly served by road and other hard and soft infrastructure, it nevertheless magnetizes investment from its rural environs and elsewhere.

We set out to track agrarian change for 1993 as it had been tracked for 1982–4, but with three differences:

i) The 1993–4 research round had a more limited spatial focus, excluding the villages in Ambedkar District and those in Tiruvannamalai District *outside* the retail hinterland of Arni. This left us with 3 of the original 11 villages, now not randomly selected but representing varied levels of development within Arni's region: Nesal (John Harriss's 'Randam') – large, accessible, developed and well-irrigated; Vinayagapuram – medium, remote, agrarian with canal irrigation; and Veerasambanur – small, remote, underdeveloped and poorly irrigated.

ii) The agricultural economy had been undergoing diversification, while the surveys had hitherto focused on rice cultivation (and to a lesser extent on groundnuts). A record of agrarian change could now not avoid studying diversification. We expected to find three types: occupational diversity in households; cropping patterns on land; and rural but non-agricultural sectors of the economy. We proposed to examine the roles played by poverty in forcing diversification and by wealth in inviting it.

iii) Village-level studies would be put to use to examine the impact of the macro-economic reforms on the semi-subsistence rural economy and the micro level. By late 1992, structural adjustment had affected taxation reform, the public, financial and corporate sectors, trade and exchange rate policies.[12] With respect to agriculture, the unfavourable economic environment inherited from the 1980s was characterized by declining agricultural growth rates, declining employment elasticities and a movement away from public investment in agriculture towards subsidy-based development. Structural adjustment had been predicted to affect the rural economy through a reduction in inputs and infrastructural subsidies, the evolution of a less (if not de-) regulated price structure towards that of 'the world market', and a reduction in social expenditure, involving the provision of a more highly targeted safety net of social welfare interventions for the rural poor. Last but not least, the rural sector was predicted to be *residualized*, both through 'rural–urban interaction' and through urban biases in public expenditure and the sequencing of public policy.

And by 1993 structural adjustment had indeed already had an impact on price structures in Tiruvannamalai District. From 1992 to 1993 the price of coarse rice (previously taxed in relation to world market prices) had shot up by 33 per cent to Rs 6.5 per kg,[13] groundnuts (previously protected) had slumped by a similar proportion to Rs 18 per kg; the partial lifting of fertilizer subsidies had resulted in a trebling of potash prices (to Rs 255/50kg in 1993) and a doubling of the phosphatic fertilizer price (to Rs 360). Subsidies on pesticides, production credit and electricity (the latter free of cost to producers) and on publicly distributed rice (retailed at Rs 2.75/kg) were being threatened with reductions or removal.

Yet although DFID had funded our project as being relevant to the agenda of structural adjustment in India, we had to face the fact that the anticipated policy adjustments had not materialized by the time of fieldwork. As the reader will already know, the predictions of – and the arguments for – radical policy change had not reckoned with the obstinate resistance of state governments to measures threatening rural votes. No big bangs in India. By 1993–4, fertilizer subsidies had had to be partially reimposed. Agricultural credit was slowly being deregulated. Electricity remained free to agricultural producers. The public distribution system (PDS) of subsidized foodgrains had not been streamlined and targeted, nor had its issue prices changed very greatly.

So where policy had *not* 'adjusted' by 1993–4, where there was no 'impact' to trace, we made an audit of existing policies on the economies and societies of these villages. Some policies, such as credit, antipoverty interventions, food and nutrition and education policies have been well studied in villages elsewhere.[14] Others have not. The villages also offered surprises: village land and paths stinking like latrines as never before,[15] stagnant agriculture, tragic declines in female status, the role of disabling incapacity in downward mobility and poverty, the enduring control of merchants' capital despite economic diversification. A number of policies affecting people's safety and security commended themselves. These interventions are all particularly vulnerable to the incremental expenditure cuts which states are under such extreme pressure to make – to which the local state government has put up opposition. We looked at 'infrastructure': in this case not roads but drinking water and sanitation, without which neither economic nor social/human development can take place. We evaluated the skeletal social security system targeted at poor people, which Tamil Nadu governments have made especially their own. We looked at how the state responds to the worryingly large proportion of adults who become incapacitated from work and disabled, and what it does about the increasingly antifemale bias in life chances in what used to be a region where women had relatively high status. We nested our village-level research in debates on policy at the state and national level.

The resulting book shows the kind of achievements and problems that rural India faces in the twenty-first century. It has three parts: in the first we look at long-term changes, in the second at policies affecting production and in the third at policies affecting social welfare. The busy reader will get the gist of its contents from the first and last chapters and from Chapter 2–1, which forms the introduction to parts Two and Three.

The contents of this book are essays – attempts and compositions – using approaches from development economics and political economy. As compositions they are varied. Some are prescriptive, like the essays on poverty-targeting and on social security and its reform. Others are critical (water and infrastructure, electricity, the life chances of girls, education, corruption). They experiment, particularly with approaches to evaluating policy, given the nature of findings and the hands and minds which have joined the team and helped.

Our essays suffer from not having been written after months at a stretch spent by the writers in these villages, for which there is absolutely no substitute. Even the field investigators had to commute at times from local towns, though the richness of their village diaries amply testifies to their commitment. The division of labour between those running the project was as follows. S Janakarajan was responsible overall for the three phases of the detailed field survey in three villages and the later censuses in eight more, trained and managed the field team, watched over data entry in Chennai, visited the fieldworkers regularly in the course of his own field research into rural contractual arrangements, which forms a separate study,[16] and developed spin-off research into water-table depletion and water management. Barbara Harriss-White ran the administration from QEH, Oxford, collaborated there with Dr Theo Palaskas on a longitudinal study of the price behaviour of staple foodgrains,[17] drafted the field questionnaires, collaborated on the instructions to field investigators, made regular visits to Chennai and the field, initiated one spin-off village study into the consequences of disability (Chapter 3–3), a second spin-off case study of silk weaving in the region,[18] and a third into the paradox of liberalization and the rise in corruption.[19]

For their contributions to the making of this research and the writing of this book we wish to offer our sincerest thanks to many people, while absolving them from any responsibility for error:

To the patient women and men of Nesal, Veerasambanur and Vinayagapuram, who have put up each decade with days of detailed questions lasting over the period of a year; to those of Duli, Kalpattu, Sirungathur, Vegamangalam and Vengodu of Vellore District; of Amudur, Meppathurai and Vayalur in Tiruvanna-malai District (all of which villages were subjected to a detailed socio-economic census) and to those of Thammanur, Kalur and Vitchanthangal in Chenglepet District, where the consequences of incapacity and disability were researched; and also to many village, block and *taluk* officials.

To ESCOR of the Department for International Development (DFID, formerly ODA), UK Government, for having funded the second resurvey of three villages and the recensus of the eight others, the extra small research project on disability and the further period of data-checking and of preparation of this book, and in particular Dr Charles Clift and Dr Susanna Moorehead for their patience and counsel, though neither they nor DFID are implicated in the conclusions of our research; also to Queen Elizabeth House, to Wolfson College and to the Social Studies Faculty's Webb Medley Fund, Oxford University, for useful smaller grants to top up the resources we needed.

To Prof. Peter Hazell of IFPRI, Prof. C Ramasamy of Tamil Nadu Agricultural University and Prof. John Harriss of the London School of Economics for making available data from earlier rounds.

To other members of the research team in the Madras Institute of Development Studies, Dr D Jayaraj and Prof. K Nagaraj; and also to Prof. S Subramanian; to field researchers I Ambalavanan, M Arunachalam, Chitra, E Innocent, G Jothi, S Mariasusai, M Nageswaran, P Pandian, Dr S Ramachandran and M V Srinivasan (who also took responsibility for the dissemination workshop), data inputter Ms U Archana Arunachalan, computer lab supremo R Dharmaperumal and accountant R Robinson; last but not least in his base in Arni, to 'muse', teacher and translator P J Krishnamurthy, whose help was vital to the project.

To other co-researchers in Oxford, Susan Erb, N Narayanan, Indian Administrative Service (IAS) (on a Visiting South Asian Fellowship), and Dr Theo Palaskas; to masters, students and other research assistants and officers Vishal Agarwal, Dr Shukri Ahmed, Aziz Arya, Paul Barbour, John Cahill, Alexandra Couto, Trevor Crowe, James Dunmore, Lisa Gold, Taimur Hyat, Lara Legassick, Matthew McCartney, Paul Nilleson, Hemani Saigal, Dr Ruhi Saith, Dr Jean Sargent, Dr Balihar Sanghera and last, but certainly not least, Diego Colatei, who so competently grasped the project's reins when it was needed; to administrators Julia Knight, Rosemary Francis, Wendy Grist; to QEH's Information Technology Officer Roger Crawford and secretaries Mary Quirke and Maria Moreno, whose commitment far exceeded the call of duty.

To discussants at the dissemination workshop held at MIDS in 1996 for their constructive criticism and comments, Prof. Venkatesh Athreya, Prof. Elisabetta Basile, Prof. G S Bhalla, Dr Neal Bliven, Prof. Terry Byres, Ms S R Chunkath, IAS, Mr Asvin Dayal, Dr Mridul Eapen, Dr Martin Greeley, Dr Judith Heyer, Dr Anuradha Khati, IAS, Dr R Krishnasamy, IAS, Prof. C T Kurien, Dr K R John, Dr Manabi Majumdar, Dr D Narayana, Emeritus Prof. S Neelakanthan, Dr Wendy Olsen, Mr R C Panda, IAS, Mr N Ram, Prof. C Ramasamy, Mr S Ramasundaram, IAS, Mr Gilbert Rodrigo, Prof. Padmini Swaminathan, Prof. U Shankar, Dr K Skandan, IAS, Prof. A Vaidyanathan, Ms R Vasantha, Dr Davaluri Venkateshwarlu and Prof. S Wanmali; and there are others, thanked in the chapters with which they helped. We wish to thank Tom Penn and Anthem for their highly professional contribution to the book's publication.

Finally, we remember two centrally important formative influences, sadly no longer with us: Dr B H (Ben) Farmer, founder–director of the Centre of South Asian Studies, Cambridge University, who had the idea for this project in 1971 and directed the first investigation in 1972–4, who died in 1996; and Prof. S Guhan at MIDS, who guided the work on social security[20] and always kept us on our toes, asking sharp questions throughout about the relevance of all this to public policy and helpfully providing documentation and policy-making contacts when he thought we passed muster, who died in 1998. We wish to dedicate this book to their memory.

Bringing to a conclusion the third round of a complicated project stretching over three decades and involving many people is inevitably a protracted process, but we hope the results – in several respects unique – afford a basis for understanding rural development in India and for future policy-making. Even so, the final stages have been affected by more than the normal and expected incidences of misfortune. Not to put too fine a point on it, in the late 1990s the grim reaper went harvesting in the families and among the friends of those directing this research and the consequences delayed our work, reduced its scope and without doubt cut its value. We have done our best and look forward to others developing some of the themes neglected[21] – as well as those celebrated here – in the future. For in what follows we hope to show that village studies are far too important to our understanding of economy and society to have atrophied in the way they seem to have done over the last decade.

Barbara Harriss-White, Oxford
S Janakarajan, Chennai

Glossary

Aathu kaalvai:	spring water channel.
Alfisols:	rain-fed red soil, often leached, on granite.
Agamudayan:	see next entry.
Agamudaiyar Mudaliar:	locally dominant agricultural and trading caste.
Ambedkar Iyakkam:	local NGO for scheduled castes.
Anicut:	barrage or diversion dam.
Ari:	'handful of paddy on the stalk', = 1.3 kg.
Arrack:	locally distilled alcoholic spirit.
Avani:	Tamil month, mid-August to mid-September.
Ayacut:	wet land below a tank.
Beedi:	local cigarette.
Boga cheetu:	seasonal chit fund (rotating credit association).
Brahmin:	highest ranking, priestly caste.
Caste:	social grouping defined by ritual ranking, endogamy, commensality and sometimes still by occupational specialization.
Ceri:	Scheduled-caste hamlet.
Coolie:	day payment for casual labour, or a casual labourer.
Crore:	10,000,000.
Dhoti:	cloth worn by men over lower part of body.
Etram:	water lifting device – beam with a bucket, lifted and lowered by human effort.
Gounder:	see Vanniar.
Grama sevak:	village-level worker (government official).
Jaggery:	unrefined sugar.
Jagir:	literally 'place-holding' – an hereditary assignment of land and its rents.

Jajmani:	system of hereditary service relationships.
Kacai Payanam:	'folk' theatre.
Kai ari:	payment to irrigation worker for assistance with agricultural operations.
Kammukutti:	(low-status) irrigation labourer.
Kani or *kaani:*	1.32 acres.
Kani ari:	payment to irrigation worker for assistance with work related to irrigation (see *kai ari* and *kumbidu ari* for his other obligations)
Kanthu vaddi:	exploitative loans to scheduled-caste people.
Karnam:	village accountant.
Kavai maniyam:	tank irrigation overlord or supervisor
Kavalai:	lift irrigation device, operated with bullocks walking up and down a ramp beside a well.
Khadi:	domestic crafts 'cottage industry'.
Kharif:	Monsoon, Summer season, June–December.
Koottalis:	agricultural manager; supervisor of cultivation operations, tenant farmer, sometimes also an attached labourer.
Kumbidu ari:	payment to irrigation worker for his menial and servile work.
Lakh:	100,000.
Machcha maghasul:	fishery rights in tank.
Maligai:	master weaver and silk merchant.
Maniyakkarar:	(high-status) irrigation overseer or manager.
Maniyakkaran veettu:	water manager's 'house' or lineage.
Mannakkaran vetu vagayara:	water manager's family's share of tank irrigation water.
Marakkal:	3 padis.
Mudaliars:	see Agamudayan.
Murai:	literally 'order' – in this case of shares of tank water.
Naattamaikarar veetu:	water manager's house.
Naidus:	trading caste (originating from Andhra Pradesh).
Nanjai:	wetland, tank-irrigated land.
Narikai:	unit of time for irrigation – 24 minutes.
Nattamai:	tank irrigation manager.
Navarai:	dry agricultural season from December–January to May.
Nazhigai:	4-hourly share of tank water.

Neerkatti:	(low-status) tank irrigation labourer.
Padi:	(volumetric unit) a 'Madras Measure': 64 padis per 75 kg bag (*muutai*) of paddy, 1.6 kg of rice, 1.15 kg of paddy.
Padial:	attached labourer.
Pala madagu:	deepest sluice in tank.
Panchayat:	unit of local governance.
Panguni:	Tamil month – mid-March to mid-April.
Pongal:	main harvest festival celebrated in mid-January; also a rice porridge.
Punjai:	dry land, rain-fed land.
Rabi:	dry, winter season, December to May.
Ragi kanji:	gruel or porridge made from a small black millet.
Ragi:	small black millet, *Eleusine coracana*, also known as *keelvaraku*.
Ryotwari:	owner occupancy of land.
Samba:	main agricultural (rainy) season from July–August to December–January.
Saree:	cloth, at least 5 m long, worn by women.
Scheduled caste:	low caste, 'dalits', 'Harijans', designated as eligible for positive discrimination ('reservations') in the public sector and in education.
Sengunda Mudaliar:	'backward' caste of 'weavers'.
Seru:	deep black ooze; flooded wetland soil.
Siruvadu:	small loan of up to Rs 300.
Sornavari:	lightly rainy agricultural season from May or June to September.
Thasildar:	official responsible for a *tehsil* or *taluk* subdivision of a district.
Thotti:	watchman and herald, overseer of water from the tank, person responsible for drummers at festival and funerals.
Toddy:	alcoholic brew fermented from palm juice.
Ur:	caste village.
Vanniar:	also known as Gounder, 'backward' agricultural caste.
Yadava:	'backward' agricultural caste.
Zari:	gold thread (used for embroidered borders of sarees).

Notes on Land Measures and Exchange Rate

Notes on Land Measures

1. In this book, land is measured in hectares, acres and kaani:
   1 hectare = 2.45 acres
   1 acre = 0.41 hectares
   1 kaani = 1.32 acres = 0.54 hectares
2. In Chapter 1-1 the text uses hectares throughout, while certain tables are in acres.
3. Standard acres, incorporating differences in the productivity of land of different quality, are expressed in wetland equivalents. We have used productivity (where approximately two units of dry land equals one unit of wetland). If the Rs value of land were used for standardization, the correction factors would need to be village-specific and would approximate five units of dry land for one unit of wetland.

Notes on Exchange Rate

During the period of the resurvey (1993–5) the Rupee was about 33 to the US$ and about 47 to the £.

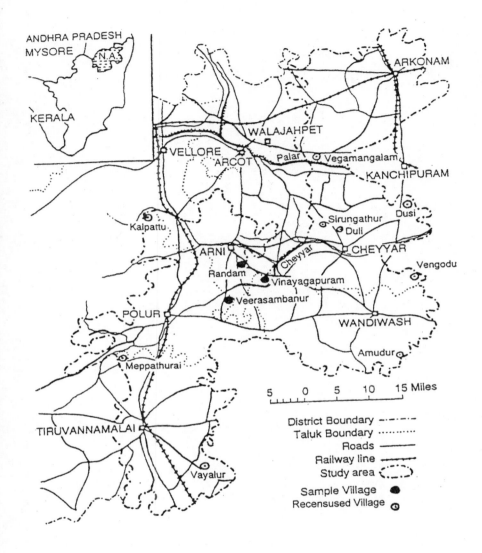

Map of Study Villages

Source: Farmer 1977, p. 8. © 1977 The Macmillan Press Ltd. See also Hazell and Ramasamy 1991, fig 2.3, p. 24.

PART ONE

Long-Term Change

Introduction: Heavy Agriculture and Light Industry in South Indian Villages

BARBARA HARRISS-WHITE, S JANAKARAJAN AND DIEGO COLATEI

THE 'Green Revolution' was introduced to the Indian subcontinent about thirty years ago in the wake of an influential report from the Ford Foundation, followed by a period of experimentation and planned diffusion and then two years of serious, generalized drought.[1] Its features are well known and combined a mixture of market incentives, heavily regulated market provision and state-administered, non-market distribution. This process of heavy agriculturalization required long-term state subsidies and coordinated planning. The transfer, adaptation and development of high yielding varieties of wheat and rice from Mexico and the Philippines to the plains of Punjab in the north and the rice deltas of the southeast required assured irrigation and consolidated plots large enough to take machinery; on top of which production credit, subsidized input prices, stable output prices and state-funded infrastructure (ranging from electricity and water to roads, market sites, research and development and extension) all had to be developed.

Of some 300 Indian districts, 20 were selected for intensive agriculture along lines that were later copied, with lags, idiosyncrasies and less abundant resources, in less advantaged regions. As a result, while the area cropped in India grew by 8 per cent between 1960 and 1987, yields increased by 51 per cent and total production rose (by 81 per cent).[2]

But by the mid-1990s it had become evident that this 'green revolution' had faltered. While foodgrains production grew at 3.5 per cent per annum during the 1980s, it had decelerated to 1.5 per cent from 1990 to 1996 despite a run of very good, well distributed rainfall. This was lower than the rate of population growth (although that too is decelerating). The policy environment is a more likely candidate than the physical environment to account for this recent mediocre performance, although the physical environment is continually being modified by policy.[3] In particular, the terms and conditions of fertilizer provision affect soil quality, and those of electricity affect the availability of irrigation water. It was in precisely these policy areas that the new era of liberalization was expected to define itself. The Indian state was poised to privatize state electricity boards and to remove the considerable subsidies for agricultural electrification. Meanwhile subsidies on fertilizer had been partially removed, and its price structure had been reorganized. Rural banking was to be deregulated and concessional credit more tightly targeted. The price bias against agricultural products, particularly the quiet taxation of rice, was being rectified, with increases in the prices at which food was purchased by state agencies, though there was little sign then of any more radical change in the provisioning role of the state.[4]

In otherwise neglecting agriculture, the economic reforms reinforced reactionary agrarian politics and supported an anti-agricultural policy that is now difficult to reverse. An example of the former is the fact of increasing inter-regional disparities in absolute yields between the revolutionary heartlands of Punjab, Haryana and western Uttar Pradesh in the northwest, and the underdeveloped peripheries of Bihar, Orissa and Assam in the north and east, despite catch-up growth in the latter region.[5] A 'reverse land reform' advocacy is another case in point. An influential body of opinion is now on record arguing for the lifting of land ceilings in the interest of 'efficiency' and corporate agrocommercial capital.[6]

Examples of this anti-agricultural policy are the stagnation of state outlays on research and development and infrastructure (especially irrigation and other capital expenditure) and proposals to reduce other agricultural subsidies.[7] Reforms affecting food and agriculture are administered outside the agriculture ministry and departments proper: for example irrigation works and rural roads, electricity, credit, rural development, food and social welfare. Cuts in any of these departmental budgets affect agriculture. And while the central government controls the food sector, each constituent state is constitutionally responsible for 'agriculture'. So state-level political forces independently affect agricultural policy. In many of the constituent states, the food and agricultural sector reforms have been strenuously resisted by the expedient of borrowing. By 1996, many states approached their credit limits.

Yet agriculture still directly provides the livelihoods of two thirds of the Indian population. If agriculture fails to release labour and capital, if it fails to provide food, other basic wage goods and industrial raw materials and if agrarian demand is not created for non-agricultural products, a wide-based economic development does not take place.[8] Agriculture's nosedive down the policy agenda of the 1990s therefore has ramifications for the entire economy and polity.

In this introductory chapter, we summarize our main findings about the social impact of the transformative agricultural technologies from the early 1970s to the turn of the millennium in one region of northern Tamil Nadu, a rice-growing state in South India. Tamil Nadu governments have a long established, distinctive and competitive politics of rural development and welfarist redistribution.[9] As outlined in the Preface, these have been tracked at close quarters since 1972 in a series of 3 studies of 11 villages.[10] The history of the fieldwork and the selection of villages and households is summarized in Appendix 1. What follows are the highlights of our findings, divided into five sections: the impact of the Green Revolution; from Green Revolution to rural reaction; trends in real incomes and poverty; rural industrialization; and the rural impact of India's economic reforms. In the first section, some material on long-term changes which is not presented in other chapters of Part One is treated in greater detail than in a normal introduction. Conclusions have been italicized to help the busy reader, who is also directed to the introduction to parts Two and Three (i.e. Chapter 2-1) and to the concluding chapter (Chapter 4-1).

1. THE IMPACT OF THE GREEN REVOLUTION, 1972–94

The Coromandel Plains region lies squarely in the large agroclimatic zone of the semi-arid tropics, which constitutes about 42 per cent of India's area and accounts for the same proportion of its production of foodgrains. It is characterized by rainfall dependence and is subject to periodic droughts which may last for more than one year. Rainfall varies between 850 and 1,000 mm, distributed roughly equally between the southwest and northeast monsoons (though the latter precipitation is much more intense and concentrated than the former). Historically, the region's agricultural population has protected itself against the seasonal vagaries of rainfall and against longer periods of drought by systems of tank irrigation, collectively maintained, which also served to recharge underground aquifers.[11] The latter were reached by open wells. In 1972–3 a significant minority of these were still operated by human (*etram*) or bullock (*kavalai*) power. A combination of investible agricultural surplus, nationalized bank credit and state-funded rural electrification had enabled these wells to be expanded in number, electrified and deepened. Maddumma Bandara writes of there already being 229,394 wells in the North Arcot District in 1971.[12] This was among the highest density of wells in Tamil Nadu, which in turn had the highest density of open wells in India. Most of the army of electrified open wells was sited in the wetland, but the stark contrast in soils between the dark, sticky, anaerobic *seru* of the predominantly tank, and well-irrigated wetland and the lighter red alfisols of the predominantly rain-fed dry land, was beginning to be blurred as a result of the dispersion of pump sets out onto rain-fed watersheds.

Nevertheless, in the early 1970s agriculture was still quite highly seasonal, with production concentrated in the rainy *samba* season (plantings in July/August; harvestings in December/January) and with the most rapid adoption of early high-yielding varieties of rice in the well-irrigated, hot and dry *navarai* season (plantings in December/January; harvestings in May). The third season, *sornavari*, with plantings in May/June and harvests in September under the less reliable rainfall distributions of the fading south-west monsoon, was of lesser importance (Table 1).

In other agrarian respects, the region was not very distinguished. Though land holdings were very far from being equal, North Arcot has always been known as a region of smallholder agriculture. In 1973, the average land holding in the plains region was 1.43 ha. Tenancy was rare, at 5 per cent of holdings. The rural population depended overwhelmingly on agriculture. Among rural households, 50 per cent were small-scale landed cultivators and 80 per cent of these cultivated two crops, paddy and groundnuts: paddy for subsistence – mainly on the wetland – and groundnuts as the cash crop – mainly on the dry land. A further 35 per cent of rural households had agricultural labour as their primary occupation.[13] So the fortunes of 85 per cent of rural households were bound up with agriculture.

The region provided 10 per cent of Tamil Nadu's rice: half a million tonnes. Yields were comparatively low. The agricultural economy was simple: rice was grown on 32 per cent of the total cropped area and groundnut on 32 per cent. The main objective of the first phase of this long-term research project was to investigate the rate – and the socio-economic context – of adoption of the generation of high-yielding varieties (HYV) of rice which emanated from the International Rice Research Institute (IRRI) in the Philippines.[14] The rate of adoption was revealed to be low (covering 13 per cent of cropped area), much lower than suggested by official estimates (39 per cent). The reasons were not to do with yields and returns, for HYV yields, though low compared with their apparent potential, were higher than those of local varieties, as were their financial returns.

TABLE 1 Seasonality of paddy cultivation, 1972–3 to 1993–4

| Season | Per cent total paddy area cultivated | | |
	Samba	Navarai	Sornavari
1972–3	47	38	15
1973–4	56	20	24
1993–4	40	36	24

Source: Chinnappa 1977, p. 99. Field survey, 1993–4.

The main constraints on adoption were rather – at the 'meso' level – the non-availability of varieties appropriate to the rainy and pesty conditions of the *samba* season when post-harvest prices were lower (because the *samba* harvest provides the main marketing glut); and – at the micro level – the non-availability of assured water and fertilizer supplies.

Paddy yields in 1973–4 are found in Table 2, which shows that the average weighed in at 2.7 tonnes per hectare.[15] HYV yields were 45 per cent greater than those of local varieties, and average yields even for the *navarai* and *sornavari* seasons were 10 per cent greater than the three-season, all-variety average. In 1973–4 there was a rainfall of 732 mm: 35 per cent below average, a serious drought in fact.

As early as 1976, both of the technical constraints identified in 1973–4 had been relaxed. The short supply phase of the fertilizer 'hog cycle' was over and a set of IRRI rices (IR8 and 20) was found appropriate to the *samba* season.[16] By the time of the second survey in 1982–4 there had been a rapid rise in fertilizer use, particularly on HYVs and in the *navarai* season. New IRRI varieties had been adopted: IR36 and 50 and a generation of IRRI/TNAU crosses were widely available. Adoption had spread to small producers and the social extent of HYV adoption was no longer an interesting question. Over the decade from 1973–4 to 1983–4 rice production had increased by 38 per cent.[17]

For the most part this was due to yields, which appeared to have increased by 30 per cent (see Table 3). While Chinnappa disaggregated yields by season, Hazell and Ramasamy disaggregated yield by farm size, distinguishing those under and those over one hectare.[18] Their findings are very interesting. While the yields of small farmers had increased by 43 per cent from 2.1 to 3.04 tonnes per hectare (tph) in the nine years from 1973–4 to 1982–3, those of producers with more than one ha had increased only by 7 per cent, bringing them up to the same average level. Indeed the aggregate increase recorded by Hazell and Ramasamy may be misleadingly large because 1982–3 was the third year of another notorious drought (with 751 mm in 1982–3), such that paddy production was confined to well-irrigated land and the two highest yielding minor seasons. In

TABLE 2 Paddy yields, kg/ha, 1973–4 to 1993–4 by season

Season	Samba	Navarai	Sornavari	Av
1973–4				
HYVs	3347	3729	4089	3555
Others	2292	2597	2877	2459
Total	2525	2939	2931	2676
1993–4	3388	4326	3953	3881

Source: Chinnappa 1977, p. 103. Field survey, 1993–4.

TABLE 3 Paddy and groundnut yields, kg/ha, 1973–4 to 1993–4 by holding size

	1973–4	1981–2	1982–3	1983–4 5 (poorest) resurvey villages	1993–4 3 villages
Paddy					
<1ha	2123		3043	2777	3622
		3409			
>1ha	2845		3045	2176	4283
Groundnut					
<1ha	1280		897	1760	727
		1000			
>1ha	1495		969	1309	964

Source: Hazell and Ramasamy 1991, p. 32. Field survey, 1993–4.

the following year, when rainfall (1,272 mm) was above the average, another survey of a subset of the five villages most affected by drought showed much lower paddy yields: 2.7 tph for small farmers and 2.2 tph for those over one hectare.[19]

Hazell and Ramasamy also recorded groundnut yields in the same way. Groundnuts were still overwhelmingly rain-fed in the early 1980s. Unsurprisingly Hazell and Ramasamy found that there were small class differences in the yields in 1973–4 (favouring those operating with wage labour on a larger scale). These differences were maintained nine years later, but yields in 1982–3 were substantially lower. By contrast, in the recovery year they showed a 38 per cent expansion over the decade on smallholdings but a 13 per cent *decline* on larger farms.

The themes of mediocre, 'unrevolutionary' growth[20] and instability were confirmed by the analysis of growth rates over the 23-year period from 1961/2, which showed a yield-driven growth of 1.5 per cent per year in production of paddy and an area-driven growth of 1.04 per cent per year in groundnut production.[21] Paddy production had declined between 1973–4 and 1982–3 (by 5 per cent on smallholdings and 33 per cent on larger farms). At the district level there was a 42 per cent decline, caused by drought, which made evaluation of the medium-term trends in production difficult. If the data are compared over the decade from 1973–4, then smallholder production had increased by 82 per cent (due mainly to yield) while larger farm production had increased by 143 per cent, due to area expansion. What the drought of the early 1980s highlighted was, firstly, an instability in production and, secondly, the brisk substitution of paddy for groundnut production and vice versa according to rainfall conditions.[22] But Hazell and Ramasamy conclude that paddy and groundnut still, on trend, occupied a third of total cropped area each.[23]

In the village agrarian economy of the early 1980s, 58 per cent of gross cultivated area was irrigated. 71,722 wells had been dug between 1971 and 1982, bringing their number for the North Arcot District to 301,116. These were increasingly
greedy of electricity as well depth was extended downwards, bringing electricity
into sharp focus in agrarian politics; yet they demonstrably could not protect
production against drought. Significantly, the average holding size had declined
to 1 ha (though mobility matrices revealed contradictory upward and downward trends in land holdings and indicated a combination of both concentration and pauperization.[24]

The regional accounts showed 'manufacturing' at 20 per cent of net domestic
regional product, while agriculture registered 40 per cent. While the ratio of
agricultural labourers to cultivators in the villages had risen (from 7 to 10 in the
1970s to 9.5 to 10 in the 1980s – (33 per cent being landless labourers and 35 per
cent of households being cultivators in 1982–3), 10 per cent of rural households
had manufacturing as their primary occupation. This rural region was witnessing expansion in agroprocessing, leather tanneries, silk and cotton textiles and
metal working. To analyse the technologies and social relations of the agricultural sector alone risks giving an increasingly incomplete and arbitrary account
of the region's development.

2. FROM GREEN REVOLUTION TO RURAL REACTION: 1984–94[25]

The decade from 1983–4 to 1993–4 was alarming on many fronts in the former
North Arcot District. Instead of expanding, and despite heavy subsidies, local
rice production fluctuated wildly (varying between 280,000 and 658,000 tonnes
of paddy) but was generally stagnant in terms of trend.[26] The same was true of
yields, which varied between 1.5 and 3.9 tonnes;[27] the number of wells was virtually static (between 297,000 and 303,000). The energization of open wells continued apace (between 5,000 and 7,000 per year), which meant that the expansion
of lift irrigation was roughly counterbalanced by well fatigue and abandonment
(discussed by Janakarajan in Chapter 1–2 below). The state and collective management of tanks and canals, and the sharing of their water, both definitively
collapsed because of the consequences for collective obligations of the changes
in the caste ownership of land from upper to lower castes, and because of the
evolving domination of private incentives as groundwater went critical for production.[28] Tank irrigation water was often polluted by agrochemical effluents
and tanks came to serve the residual purposes of water table recharge and dry-
season drinking water and sites for defecation (see Chapter 2–3). Tank beds also
provided silt deposits for brickmaking.

Agriculture became heavily dependent on private lift irrigation. Competitive deepening (with prevalent violation of spacing norms) led to a well failure rate of 20–30 per cent. On village wetland, well depths increased on average by 6.5 metres (and on dry land by 9.5 metres) from their average original depth. The impact of the secular lowering of the water table is far-reaching. It includes the irremediable drying of drinking-water wells and rising investment in wells both for drinking and for irrigation, together with increases in operating costs. According to the *Report of the Working Group on Major and Medium Irrigation Programme for the Eighth Plan*,[29] surface irrigation investment during the Seventh Plan period (1985–90) was computed at Rs 36,240 per hectare irrigated, whereas field data pertaining to well investment suggested that Rs 80,500 was required per net hectare irrigated on either wet or dry land. The latter is about 2.25 times the amount spent to create one hectare of surface irrigation potential.[30]

Then the electricity consumed per pump set increased by 73 per cent between 1982–3 and 1992–3 (see Table 4) and is reputed to have doubled by 1996. As a result, there was increased waste of water and electricity, a decline in HYV paddy yields, increased indebtedness, the emergence of water market monopolies, conflicts over shared well water, pauperization, landlessness and agrarian differentiation, irreversible changes in private irrigation technology and unknown costs to future generations (due to saline incursion risks).[31] Virtually free agricultural electricity from 1990 accentuated rationing and supervision failures. The

TABLE 4 Electricity consumption per electric well in Tamil Nadu

Year	Total Energy Consumed for Ag Purposes (mn units)	No. of Electric Pumpsets	Energy Consumed per Electric Well (units)
1980–81	2299	919162(100)	2501(100)
1981–2	2354	945520(103)	2490(100)
1982–3	2230	965017(105)	2311(92)
1983–4	2200	982606(107)	2239(90)
1984–5	2415	982606(107)	2458(98)
1985–6	2840	1033533(112)	2748(110)
1986–7	3114	1074184(117)	2899(116)
1987–8	3135	1116177(121)	2810(112)
1988–9	3524	1184450(129)	2975(119)
1989–90	3740	1235941(134)	3026(121)
1992–3	5635	1445951(157)	3897(156)

Note: Index nos are bracketed. 1980–81 = 100.

Source: Tamil Nadu Electricity Board, *Tamil Nadu Electricity Board Statistics at a Glance*, various years.

governments of Tamil Nadu resisted (and to this day resist) strong aid-donor and loaner pressure to reintroduce volumetric pricing.

The region now produced only 5 per cent of Tamil Nadu's rice,[32] half its contribution of two decades earlier. Production, averaging 450,000 tonnes per annum over the decade, became increasingly unstable from year to year (see Appendix 2, Table 1). The exception to this picture of stagnation concerns the provision of nitrogenous fertilizer, the use of which expanded from 29,500 to 39,022 tonnes between 1986–87 and 1991–2, after which the rate of growth slackened. But the use of the other two major nutrients (phosphorus and potash) contracted after 1991, when subsidies were lifted. The elasticity of yield to fertilizer varied from 0.07 for phosphorus to 0.36 for nitrogen and was greater for small peasants than for the larger enterprises which supplied the bulk of the marketed surplus (discussed in Chapter 2–6). On aggregate, and despite the trumpeted potential of HYVs for the minor seasons, the relative importance of the seasons remained much as it was two decades earlier (see Table 1), though there was extreme intervillage variation.[33] The two more developed villages – Nesal (big, differentiated, accessible and diversified) and Vinayagapuram (remote, least unequal, agrarian) – were expanding production based upon groundwater in the two dry seasons, which between them accounted for 70 per cent of the gross cropped area. By contrast, in Veerasambanur (small, poor, differentiated, remote), dry season cultivation amounted to only 45 per cent.

2.1 Trends in land concentration

By the early 1990s a combination of sale and partition had halved average land holdings to 0.7 ha. The proportion of farm households cultivating less than 1 ha had increased from 58 per cent in 1973 to 72 per cent in 1993–5. The average holding sizes of those working under and over one hectare were 0.45 and 2.03 respectively (see Appendix 2, Table 4).

Land has been and continues to be considered as one of if not the most, important productive assets, accounting for between 43 and 55 per cent of the total value of assets in the three villages (see Table 5). This alone would be a natural reason to analyse how land is distributed in the villages. But there is more. The distribution of land ownership among households of the same communities was investigated in earlier projects.[34] To a certain extent, it is possible to make comparisons with those results and to look at changes in the 3 villages over the last 20 years.

The inequality of distribution of assets is chiefly a question of land distribution.[35] Table 6 presents Gini coefficients for the distributions of the total value of assets, land, other agricultural assets and non-agricultural assets. For all three

TABLE 5 Assets by village (Rs), 1993

Assets		Village					
		Nesal		Vinayagapuram		Veerasambanur	
All Assets		**66071**	*100%*	**83104**	*100%*	**50016**	*100%*
	Std Dev.	150370		118072		63156	
Land		28375	*43%*	45595	*55%*	25236	*50%*
	Std Dev.	81450		74806		37238	
Other agricultural assets		16090	*24%*	21285	*26%*	12680	*25%*
	Std Dev.	43804		35641		18480	
Non-agricultural assets		21606	*33%*	16224	*20%*	12099	*24%*
	Std Dev.	46502		21398		18452	

TABLE 6 Gini coefficients for the ownership of land and the value of assets

Gini Coefficients		Village					
		Nesal		Vinayagapuram		Veerasambanur	
		including zero values		including zero values		including zero values	
Land ownership		**0.51**	**0.81**	**0.46**	**0.62**	**0.46**	**0.66**
	nos.	208		79		51	
Assets value		**0.75**	**0.76**	**0.63**	**0.63**	**0.62**	**0.63**
	nos.	11				4	
Land		0.61	0.85	0.55	0.69	0.53	0.71
	nos.	208		79		52	
Other agricultural assets		0.81	0.84	0.71	0.72	0.66	0.71
	nos.	48		15		18	
Non-agricultural assets		0.67	0.70	0.55	0.55	0.59	0.61
	nos.	24		4		7	

Note: Zero values correspond to landless and/or assetless household observations.
Gini ratios for land in standard acres for households with land in the other eight villages censused in 1995 are as follows: Amudur 0.49, Duli 0.45, Kalpattu 0.43, Meppathurai 0.44, Sirungathur 0.58, Vayalur 0.58, Vengodu 0.49 and Vegamangalam 0.54.

villages, the distribution of land (whether in quantity or in value terms) and other agricultural assets is more unequal than the distribution of non-agricultural assets, and most unequal in Nesal.[36]

Gini coefficients for land ownership were calculated by Hazell and Ramasamy for the years 1973 and 1983,[37] and presented after having classified villages into rich and poor. Their conclusions were of a 'clear worsening – albeit a modest one – in the equity of the distribution of land in the poor villages that is not evident in the rich villages' (confirmed by Gini coefficients declining modestly in the rich villages from 0.697 to 0.663 but increasing in the poor villages from 0.652 to 0.665).[38] However, both the trend and the conclusion differ if we consider our (reduced) 1993 data. It is not clear whether the distribution of land worsened or not in the rich villages, because it is not known whether landless households were included in the computation for 1983.[39] However, a Gini coefficient of 0.81 in Nesal not only contradicts the declining trend for 1973–83 but also is highly inequitable. In our one 'poor village' (including the landless) the long-term trend at worst is static; at best (excluding them) land holding has become more equitable.

But when they produce interesting findings, summary statistics such as the Gini still need to be interpreted with caution, for they conceal a great deal of detail;[40] so it is then worth looking at the size distribution of land holding for the three villages, and trying to make some comparisons with more disaggregated data.

The distribution of land ownership in the three villages can be found in Table 7. In Nesal, while 75 per cent of households are either landless or own less than 0.4 ha (1 acre), the top 16 households (5 per cent) with over 2.25 ha own 43 per cent of total land. In Vinayagapuram, 61 per cent of the village – landless or with less than 0.4 ha – own 14.5 per cent of land, while those with holdings larger than 2.25 ha control almost a third of the land owned in the village. In Veerasambanur, 65 per cent of households have less than 0.4 ha, while the 6 per cent which owns over 2.25 ha control 28 per cent of total land.

The highly skewed distribution of land in Nesal had been already stressed by John Harriss in 1982.[41] What is new, however, is the 'clear worsening in the equity of the distribution of land' in this rich village that was not evident from the previous studies.[42] From Table 8, we see that landlessness has increased considerably in all three villages and that the total extent of land owned by the top decile of households has also increased in Nesal and Veerasambanur.

If we then analyse the land ownership distribution of landed households (see Table 9), we find that the average farm size declined in Nesal and Veerasambanur, but remained the same as in 1983 in Vinayagapuram. In the first two villages, *the average farm size declined in all quartiles.* But while in Nesal it declined most in the two quartiles of largest holdings, in Veerasambanur the greatest reduction occurred in the two quartiles of smallest holdings. In Vinayagapuram, the average farm size only decreases for the bottom quartile. While stressing considerable variations in the changes over time by village, Table 9 also shows that *the average area owned per farm by quartile, in 1993, is much closer than it was 10 and 20 years before. Concentration and convergence coexist.*[43]

The economic significance of land is affected by both its type and its quality. In these villages, land is classified into the three categories of 'wet', 'dry' and '*punjai* (dry land) with wells'.[44]

The 1993 census found the total area owned by the households of Nesal to be

TABLE 7 Size distributions of land ownership (acres)

Size Category (acres)	Village Nesal No. of households	% of total	Extent of land (acres)	% of land	Vinayagapuram No. of households	% of total	Extent of land (acres)	% of land	Veerasambanur No. of households	% of total	Extent of land (acres)	% of land
Landless	20	61.3			79	30			51	37		
0.01–0.5	16	4.72	5.1	1.4	23	8.8	8.4	2.2	22	16	6.2	4
0.51–1	36	10.6	31	9.2	54	20	48	12	15	11	12	7.9
1.01–1.50	14	4.13	18	5.5	26	10	35	9.3	8	5.8	11	7.2
1.51–2	24	7.08	47	13	18	6.9	33	8.8	12	8.8	21	14
2.01–2.50	2	0.59	4.8	1.4	10	3.8	23	6	6	4.4	14	9.5
2.51–3	7	2.06	20	5.8	14	5.4	40	10	8	5.8	23	15
3.01–4	8	2.36	32	9.2	15	5.7	56	14	6	4.4	21	14
4.01–5	8	2.36	37	10	5	1.9	23	6.1	6	4.4	28	18
5.01–7	6	1.77	38	11	8	3	48	12	1	0.7	6	3.9
7.01–10	6	1.77	54	15	5	1.9	41	10	1	0.7	7.5	4.9
10.01–12.50	2	0.59	22	6.5								
12.5–15	1	0.29	15	4.3	2	0.7	24	6.2				
>15	1	0.29	17	4.9								
Total	33		344		259		384		136		152	
Gini	0.5		0.8		0.4		0.6		0.4		0.6	

* Landless households are excluded from the Gini coefficients calculation.

TABLE 8 Changes in distribution of land ownership

	Village								
	Nesal			Vinayagapuram			Veerasambanur		
	1973	1984	1993	1973	1984	1993	1973	1984	1993
Landless households (% total households)	41	44	61.36	11	11	30.50	23	21	37.50
Percentage of total land area owned by:									
Lower half	1.70	1.20		3.40	10.40	7.76	11	12.80	2.56
Top size decile	55.20	51.70	64.53	54	49	42.07	32.30	30.70	40.49

The size distribution includes the landless.

Source: J Harriss 1991c, p. 68 and census data, 1993.

TABLE 9 Average land area owned by quartile of landed households (ha) (from smallest at top to largest at foot of table)

Village	Nesal					Vinayagapuram					Veerasambanur				
				% Change					% Change					% Change	
	1973	1982	1993	73–81	82–92	1973	1982	1993	73–81	82–92	1973	1982	1993	73–81	82–92
1st Quartile	0.30	0.26	0.21	−13.3	−19.2	0.22	0.23	0.22	4.5	−4.3	0.26	0.30	0.11	15.4	−62.4
2nd Quartile	0.64	0.58	0.45	−9.4	−21.8	0.54	0.42	0.43	−22.2	2.4	0.74	0.67	0.38	−9.5	−42.8
3rd Quartile	1.54	1.25	0.86	−18.8	−31.2	0.97	0.79	0.79	−18.6		1.24	1	0.79	−19.4	−20.8
4th Quartile	5.23	3.50	2.66	−33.1	−24.1	2.27	1.96	1.99	−13.7	1.5	2.19	2.03	1.60	−7.3	−20.9
All Farmers	1.98	1.40	1.05	−29.3	−25	1	0.86	0.86	−14		1.09	1.01	0.72	−7.3	−28.7

The size distribution excludes landless households.

Source: Hazell and Ramasamy 1991, p. 50, and census data, 1993.

154.9 hectares (see Table 10). The proportions of wet and dry land are quite similar (29.8 per cent wet and 31.7 per cent dry), while the extent of *punjai* land with wells is greater (38.5 per cent). Over the latest decade, well-digging allowed the relative extent of wet and especially garden land to increase considerably at the expense of dry land.[45] In Vinayagapuram, 157.7 ha of land are owned by the villagers. There are 41 ha of wet land, 45.3 ha of dry land and 71.5 ha of *punjai* land irrigated with wells. In Veerasambanur, the total land ownership amounts to 62.4 ha, 37.6 per cent of which is wetland while dry land counts for another 36 per cent. The proportion of *punjai* land irrigated with wells is only 26.4 per cent of total land, which is much lower than in the other two villages. Considering all the households in the village, land ownership per household is lowest in Nesal (0.42 ha/1.02 acres) and highest in Vinayagapuram (0.61 ha/1.49 acres). However, because more households are landless in Nesal the average land holding is greater there (1.08 ha/2.63 acres).

2.2 Diversification of crop varieties

Whereas early HYVs maximized environment–genotype interaction and were designed to be appropriate for a wide range of paddy growing conditions, the next generation of so-called high yielding varieties sought to minimize environment–genotype interaction, i.e. to specialize for particular agro-ecological niches. Other varieties were bred so as to substitute plant architecture and physiology for commercial input requirements such as water and pesticides. In the

TABLE 10 Land classification (acres)

	Village					
	Nesal			*Vinayagapuram*	*Veerasambanur*	
Total Land	344.42	100%	384.70	100%	152.2	100%
per household	1.02		1.49		1.12	
per landed household	2.63		2.14		1.79	
no. of landed households	131		180		85	
Wet	102.60	29.8%	99.93	26%	57.23	37.6%
per household	0.30		0.39		0.42	
per landed household	0.78		0.56		0.67	
Punjai with wells	132.73	38.5%	174.27	45.3%	40.18	26.4%
per household	0.39		0.67		0.30	
per landed household	1.01		0.97		0.47	
Dry	109.09	31.7%	110.50	28.7%	54.79	36%
per household	0.32		0.43		0.40	
per landed household	0.83		0.61		0.64	

Note: 1 acre = 0.41 ha; 1 ha = 2.45 acres.

1990s there were more new varieties and their rate of obsolescence increased. Table 11 lists 23 HYVs according to their precise season of cultivation for the specific conditions of northern Tamil Nadu, and Appendix 2, Table 2, displays their use. In the *samba* season, new varieties have higher yields than older ones and 75 per cent of the land is cropped with newer varieties. In *navarai*, the older varieties have higher yields and 50 per cent of the land down to paddy grows older varieties. The three paddy varieties from IRRI (IR20, IR36 and IR50) have been proved to be very robust, had already been introduced in the mid-1970s and were widely adopted by the early 1980s. Thirteen recommended varieties are local/IRRI crosses and seven are entirely the results of local seed breeding. On aggregate the newer HYVs averaged 3.6 tonnes per hectare, while *older HYVs did much better* – at 4.7 tonnes per ha (see Table 12).

2.3 Diversification of cropping patterns

With respect to agricultural diversification, the theory of growth linkages which informed the research in 1982–4 (in which the consumption linkages from agricultural production fed back, through higher incomes and demand for income elastic food and other agricultural products, to agricultural production) is but one among several well theorized pathways. Von Thunen argued that the diversity of land use would be maximized in peri-urban rings and would give way to monocropping and then livestock rearing with increasing distance from a town.[46] The expansion of towns (and a real reduction in transport costs) would therefore lead to a linear expansion of the width of the zone of diversified land use and an exponential expansion of its production. Further causes of crop diversification, intercropping, a wide range of varieties of a given crop, agropastoral mixes, crop diversity and farm/non-farm activity mixes are all long-standing responses to environmental hazards, particularly to high variances in the annual and/or monthly distribution of rainfall such as characterize the semi-arid tropics.[47] A change in the vector of agricultural hazards in a semisubsistent agricultural economy could thus lead to diversification.

While paddy is still grown on 51 per cent of the total cropped area and groundnuts are grown on 37 per cent, there is no doubt that land use has diversified over the last 40 years, though finding data is very difficult. The records of the Nesal village *karnam's* (accountant) show that the category of 'other' uses of land increased from 3 to 10 per cent of cultivated area between 1959–60 and 1972–3,[48] but the land-holding distribution was not given. Hazell and Ramasamy's project survey data reveals that a good proportion of 'other' is rain-fed sorghum and millets and that whereas 'other' doubled between 1973–4 and 1982–3 as a proportion of the cultivated lands of smallholders, it increased by a factor of five on the

TABLE 11 HYVs of rice and groundnuts recommended for northern Tamil Nadu

HYVs of Rice

Season										
Sornavari	IR64	IET1441	TKM9	ADT36	IR50	CO37	ADT37	ASD16	ASD17	ASD18
Samba	Ponumani	ADT40	Bhavani	IR20	White Ponni	CO43	CO44	Paijuri	PY4	CR1009
Navarai	ADT36	IR20	CO37	ADT39	CO43	IR64	ASD16	ASD18		

HYVs of Groundnut

Rain-fed									
Adi (early June–July)	TMV2	TMV7	TMV12	TMV10	VR3				
Irrigated									
Summer (April–July)	TMV2	TMV7	CO1	CO2	JL24	TMV12	VR2	VR11	V13
Winter (December–January)	TMV2	TMV7	CO1	CO2	JL24	VR11	VR12	VR3	

TABLE 12 Weighted[1] mean paddy yields (kg/ha), 1993–4, by villages, seasons and generations of HYVs

	Total no. landed hh	av. size (ha)	Nesal	Vinayaga-puram	Veera-sambanur	Total
Farm size						
< 1 ha	286	0.45	4061	3271	3837	3622
(valid n)			(22)	(33)	(10)	(64)
> 1 ha	110	2.03	4824	4190	3991	4283
(valid n)			(9)	(25)	(8)	(41)
Total	396	0.7	4278	3665	3907	3881
(valid n)			(30)	(58)	(18)	(106)
Season						
samba 93			4441	3111	3023	3388
navarai 94			4572	4027	5074	4326
sornavari 94			3937	3879	4252	3953
Generation of HYVs						
Newer						3611
Older						4689
Other						3621

Note: [1] For details of weighting, see Appendix 1.

Source: Field survey, 1993–4.

land of those owning more than one hectare (see Table 13).[49] Their findings are certainly consistent with the working hypotheses, though we still do not know whether the residual 'other' in 1982–3 included income-elastic, high-value products. By 1993–4 the picture is clearer: there had been widespread land-use diversification with crops other than rice and groundnuts occupying 30 per cent of cultivated land. In the poor village of Veerasambanur the major change was the arrival of sugar cane, a high-income, agro-industrial product, no respecter of rural classes, occupying about 40 per cent of the standard cropped acres. Water-sparing sorghum and millet occupied about 5 per cent of land. In Vinayagapuram, only 4 per cent of standard acres had come under crops other than paddy and groundnuts, but the crops in question illustrated a range of reasons for diversification. Some crops were income-elastic, as predicted by the TNAU/IFPRI project (vegetables and chilli), some were water-sparing (grams and *ragi*) and some were labour cost-minimizing (casuarina) – see Table 14. Nesal also had a diverse cropping pattern, with sugar cane, banana and coarse grains occupying roughly 40 per cent of cropped land. All agrarian classes practised crop diversification, but it was most advanced among the elite households and remarkably so in the village nearest town.

TABLE 13   Cropping patterns by farm size group (ha)

	Small farms				Large farms			
	1973/4	1982/3	1983/4	1993/4	1973/4	1982/3	1983/4	1993/4
All villages								
Paddy	0.53	0.35	n.a.	n.a.	1.41	0.89	n.a.	n.a.
Groundnuts	0.3	0.33	n.a.	n.a.	1.19	1.21	n.a.	n.a.
Sorghum/ millets	0.05	0.06	n.a.	n.a.	0.1	0.34	n.a.	n.a.
Other crops	0.05	0.09	n.a.	n.a.	0.05	0.54	n.a.	n.a.
Total	0.93	0.83	n.a.	n.a.	2.74	2.99	n.a.	n.a.
Operated farm size	0.59	0.61	n.a.	n.a.	2.42	2.68	n.a.	n.a.
Crop intensity index	1.57	1.36	n.a.	n.a.	1.13	1.11	n.a.	n.a.
Resurvey villages				*3 villages*				*3 villages*
Paddy	0.55	0.31	0.64	0.36	0.75	0.79	2.11	0.61
Groundnuts	0.48	0.28	0.15	0.38	1.08	1.1	0.86	1.15
Sorghum/ millets	0.01	0.14	0.08	0.13	0.24	0.45	0.01	0.38
Other crops	0.03	0.06	0.02	0.72		0.33	0.2	1.59
Total	1.07	0.8	0.89	1.59	2.08	2.68	3.18	3.7

Note: In the *3 villages* survey, 'other crops' refers to sugar cane for small farms; for large farms, 'other' is composed of sugar cane (0.81) and banana (0.78).

Source: Hazell and Ramasamy 1991, p. 34; survey data, 1993–4.

TABLE 14   Land use, three villages, 1993–4 (Per cent total cropped area [SAS] by class)

	Paddy	Ground- nut	Sugar cane	Sorghum/ Ragi Other[1]	Banana	Total Standard Acres[2]
Veerasambanur						
Poor peasant	35	18	42	4	–	11.1
Elite households	48	10	37	5	–	13.5
Vinayagapuram						
Poor peasant	60	36	–	4	–	36
Elite households	74	22	–	4	–	27
Nesal						
Poor peasant	48	35	8	7	–	12
Elite households	45	27	13	–	14	88.7

Note: [1] 'Other' in Vinayagapuram includes green gram, red gram, casuarina and chilli.
[2] On weights for standard acres, see notes to Table 5, Chapter 2–4.

Source: Field survey.

2.4 Yields

Paddy yields were analysed for the three seasons between *samba* 1993–4 and *sor-navari* 1994. If the results for the 3 villages in 1993–4 are compared with those for 11 villages 20 years earlier, HYV paddy yields remained virtually static (averaging 3.6 tonnes 20 years before and 3.9 tonnes in the later period – an increase of only 8 per cent). *Navarai* season had much the highest yields (28 per cent above those of *samba*, which is the season watered by both the southwest monsoon and pump sets): see Table 12. In 1993–4, yields on dry land with wells were higher than those on traditional *seru* paddy land: wetland with surface water. As in 1973–4, but unlike in the 1980s, *there was a strong positive relationship between size and productivity.* While producers operating below one hectare had yields 7 per cent below the weighted mean, larger producers had yields 10 per cent above it (Table 12).

Turning to groundnuts, *yields declined,* fluctuating from 1.4 tonnes per hectare in 1973–4 to 1 tph in 1981–2, 1.5 tph in the recovery year of 1983–4 but only 0.994 tph in 1993–4 (see Tables 3 and 15). Traditional groundnut varieties still dominated production and it was only in one developed village (Nesal, where groundnuts were grown under irrigated conditions) that new varieties were adopted, that too on only 8 per cent of the land down to groundnuts. The 'new' varieties of groundnut grown were not up-to-date and did not appear among those officially recommended.[50] While the difference in groundnut yields between farm-size categories is statistically significant, if yield is statistically controlled for the type of land, irrigation status and variety, then *the relationship between size and productivity becomes insignificant.*

2.5 Production

As with yields, there is *persistent, consistent and often statistically significant variation between the poor peasants and elite agricultural households in factor use and costs as well as in the prices received for their products.* While the real rupees intensity of fertilizer and agrochemicals was static for poor producers, for rich agricultural households it increased by a factor of 3 over 20 years. Groundnut prices were some 43 per cent higher for elite households than they were for poor producers, although the class difference in prices quoted was much less – 6 per cent – for paddy sales. Returns to both paddy and groundnut production were thus differentiated in favour of nascent capitalist households.[51] Significant intervillage variations accentuated class-specific differentiation in production conditions (see Chapter 1–3). For comparison, we keep to the size classification of Hazell and Ramasamy, though it masks some of these differences.

TABLE 15 Average cropped area, yield and production of paddy and groundnuts by farm size group

		Area (ha)				Yield (kg/ha)				Production (kg)			
		1973–4	1982–3	1983–4	1993–4 (plot size)	1973–4	1982–3	1983–4	1993–4 kg/ha	1973–4	1982–3	1983–4	1993–4
Paddy													
Small farm		0.53	0.35	0.64	**0.32**	2123	3043	2777	3622	1125	1065	1777	**1159**
	obs				55								
Large farm		1.41	0.89	2.11	**0.58**	2854	3045	2176	4883	4024	2710	4592	**2832**
	obs				51								
ALL					**0.44**				3881				1708
	obs				106								
Groundnuts													
Small farm		0.3	0.33	0.15	**0.34**	1280	897	1760	736	384	296	264	**248**
	obs												32
Large farm		1.19	1.21	0.86	1	1495	969	1309	988	1779	1172	1126	**981**
	obs												28
ALL					**0.61**								551
	obs												60

Source: Hazell and Ramasamy 1991, p. 32; survey data, 1993–4.

Details of production are given in Table 15. Some 76 per cent of landed house-holds produced paddy, while 67 per cent produced groundnuts. However while, during the 1970s, about 80 per cent of cultivators grew both crops, by 1993–4 the proportion growing both crops had dropped to 43 per cent.[52] Hazell and Rama-samy's costs of production data for the period 1972–3 to 1982–3 (Table 16) are not derived from the sample villages and are also not disaggregated in the way ours are for 1993–4 (Tables 17 to 19).[53]

Average real costs per hectare have more than doubled since 1973–4. *The real costs of paddy per unit output have also increased by 63 per cent.* Furthermore, the ratio of gross to net returns, *the profitability index, has dropped* from a range of 3.2 to 5 in the early 1970s to 1.9 by 1993–4 (Table 19). By contrast, *the cost structure has been remarkably stable,* labour amounting to just under half of all paid-out costs and fertilizer a quarter (Tables 17 and 18). *The biggest change over the period is the share of costs taken by pesticides:* up from 1 per cent to 11 per cent. The struc-ture of labour and employment costs are summarized later. With respect to agrochemical inputs (Table 18), fertilizer is used with equal intensity by small and large farmers, but most intensively on wetland. It is pesticides which are used disproportionately by large farmers, not only on wetland but equally through all seasons. Organic manure is spread for preference on rain-fed land. Groundnuts have a similar intensity of application of organic manure, but fer-tilizer and pesticides are used at a mere 14 per cent of the intensity of paddy and intensely focused on HYVs.[54]

2.6 Credit

Partially deregulated institutional credit, with an average interest rate of 12.2 per cent, was almost entirely captured by the most propertied classes; the excluded mass of poor producers relied on non-institutional sources (where interest rates averaged 28 per cent) (see Chapter 2–4). *The 25 per cent of households with total assets in excess of Rs 1 lakh (US$3,000) borrowed 85 per cent of total formal credit,* but 48 per cent of total informal credit. The bottom third of households with assets under Rs 15,000 (US$450) had 5 per cent of formal debt and 11 per cent of informal debt. Of the latter, there was a great variety, access to which was highly segmented by caste and kinship, by purpose and by social class. Special-ized chit funds (rotating credit groups) had proliferated for scheduled-caste people, women and agricultural labourers. Women took semi-secret loans from the wives of money-lending farmers and traders. Traders' credit persisted as the single most quantitatively important source. Institutional credit had not cracked the prevalent interlocked contracts of the informal sector. However, *whereas two decades earlier it had been agricultural traders' credit which exercised an*

TABLE 16 Costs and returns from HYV paddy (1973–4 prices)

	1972/3	1973/4	1974/5	1975/6	1976/7	1977/8	1978/9	1979/80	1980/1	1981/2	1982/3	1993/4
Yield (kg/ha)	2588	2747	3637	3239	3746	3022	2772	2835	3234	3249	3035	3978
Price (Rs/kg)	1.02	0.94	1.21	1.02	1.02	1.02	1.06	0.99	1.07	0.9	1.04	3.6
Value output (Rs/ha)	2647	2581	4389	3292	3805	3101	2941	2805	3453	2908	3168	14260
Variable costs (Rs/ha)[B]	1179	817	845	1067	1986	1175	1240	969	1114	1246	1068	7781
Seed	113	90	103	126	203	118	133	114	89	138	139	747
Manure	73	66	38	88	153	116	104	90	85	50	31	490
Fertilizers	242	184	219	340	600	284	325	199	347	463	384	1742
Pesticides	14	12	15	29	55	22	24	15	23	33	7	894
Hired labour	483	401	409	417	578	486	447	451	506	399	460	3763
Hired bullocks	52	25	37	40	43	41	34	36	25	10	30	
Hired machines	182	15	8	9	318	85	157	50	19	149	14	
Other	20	24	16	18	36	23	16	14	20	4	3	582
Gross margin (Rs/ha)	1468	1764	3544	2225	1819	1926	1701	1836	2339	1662	2100	

Note. Costs and returns based on planted area and averaged over seasons.

[B] Real 1993–4 variable costs = Rs. 1945 approx. in 1973–4 prices.

Source: 1972–83, Cost of cultivation of principal crops data, TNAU; 1993–4, field survey.

TABLE 17   Paddy, groundnuts: labour inputs and costs per ha, 1993–4

	Labour days/ha									Labour costs (Rs/ha)					Casual labour costs		
	Family			Casual			Per-manent All	Ex-change All	ALL	Casual			All labour (not Family)	Other costs	Male (Rs/day)	Female (Rs/day)	Ratio Male/female wage
	Male	Female	All	Male	Female	All				Male	Female	All					
Paddy	137	90	228	68	150	218	6	3	454	1600	1694	3296	3701	412	24	11.5	2.2
by village																	
Nesal	17	7	24	70	155	225	6	0	255	1879	2043	3922	4627	484	26.5	13.3	
Vinay	182	144	326	63	126	189	8	0	524	1438	1464	2903	3270	343	23.7	11.6	2
Veera	188	52	240	79	221	302	0	15	557	1665	1860	3534	3563	515	21.6	8.6	2.2
by farm size																	2.6
small farms	123	269	74	136	136	210	2	3	483	1735	1607	3345	3562	400	23.6	11.9	
large farms	50	177	61	167	167	228	11	3	419	1442	1795	3238	3865	425	24.5	11.1	2.1
by land type																	2.3
nanjai	125	67	192	75	176	252	9	6	459	1485	1506	2997	3317	364	23.8	10.9	
pww	127	100	226	61	127	188	4	0	418	1623	1710	3332	3753	416	24.1	11.7	2.4
rainfed	583	350	933	55	90	145	0	0	1078	1696	1867	3562	4038	455	24.2	12	2.1
by variety																	2.1
newer HYV	191	116	907	70	146	217	4	2	530								
older HYV	49	45	93	72	160	231	14	6	345								

TABLE 17 (*cont.*):

Groundnut																
Groundnut	29	34	65	22	59	81	3	1	150	650	745	1396	1403	182	25.1	10.69	2.6
by village																
Nesal	5	4	9	35	101	136	6	0	151	1118	1540	2659	2694	297	32.6	15.3	2.2
Vinay	38	46	86	14	37	51	3	1	141	481	454	935	935	2	24.1	9	3
Veera	25	29	61	31	82	115	0	0	177	480	938	1422	1430	616	19.1	8.9	2.2
by farm size																
small farms	37	46	86	22	51	73	0	0	159	586	665	1254	1258	215	23.7	10.6	2.4
large farms	17	17	34	21	71	93	8	1	137	407	457	864	866	4	22.3	8.4	2.8
by land type																
nanjai	33	38	71	21	61	82	13	3	170	1181	1386	2567	2593	319	31.5	13.5	2.7
pww	15	16	31	25	74	100	1	0	132								
rainfed	39	49	92	19	45	65	2	0	158								
by variety																
newer HYV	1	0	1	17	144	161	28	0	189								
local/traditional	30	36	67	22	55	78	2	1	148								

Source: Field survey, 1993–4.

TABLE 18 Average agrochemicals inputs and costs per ha, 1993–4

| | Inputs | | | | | Manure (kg/ha) | | | | Fertilizer (kg/ha) | | | | ratio all | | | ratio chemical | | |
| | Rs/ha | | | kg/ha | | | | | | | | | | | | | | | |
Paddy	Man-ure	Ferti-lizer	Pesti-cide	Man-ure	Ferti-lizer	N	P	K	PK	N	P	K	PK	N	P	K	N	P	K
by village	**490**	**1748**	**394**	**5317**	**369**	**53.2**	**31.9**	**63.8**	**148.9**	**79.8**	**56.8**	**51.2**	**187.8**	**1.2**	**0.8**	**1**	**1.6**	**1.1**	**1**
Vinay	256	2041	413	4679	435	46.8	28.1	56.1	131	88.9	65.6	61	215.6	1.2	0.8	1	1.5	1.1	1
Veera	626	1430	390	6373	307	63.7	38.2	76.5	178.4	66.5	47.9	44.7	159	1.1	0.7	1	1.5	1.1	1
Nesal	453	2273	372	2989	457	29.9	17.9	35.9	83.7	107.5	70.3	55.5	233.3	1.5	1	1	1.9	1.3	1
by farm size																			
small	434	1755	375	5282	366	52.8	31.7	63.4	147.9	79.3	62.3	46.8	188.3	1.2	0.9	1	1.7	1.3	1
large	557	1740	418	5359	373	53.6	32.2	64.3	150.1	80.5	50.2	56.5	187.2	1.1	0.7	1	1.4	0.9	1
by season																			
Samba	378	1663	395	4690	353	46.9	28.1	56.3	131.3	77	52.7	46.2	175.9	1.2	0.8	1	1.7	1.1	1
Navarai	548	1844	388	5452	380	54.5	32.7	65.4	152.7	87.2	52.9	48.6	188.7	1.2	0.8	1	1.8	1.1	1
Somavari	544	1739	399	5815	375	58.1	34.9	69.8	162.8	75.3	64.8	58.9	199	1	0.8	1	1.3	1.1	1
by land type																			
nanjai	540	2027	418	5524	430	55.2	33.1	66.3	154.7	94.4	65.5	58	217.9	1.2	0.8	1	1.6	1.1	1
pww	420	1510	374	4992	318	49.9	30	59.9	139.8	67	49.4	45.9	162.3	1.1	0.8	1	1.5	1.1	1
rainfed	833	685	312	7500	128	75	45	90	210	31.3	22.5	15.7	69.5	1	0.6	1	2	1.4	1
by variety																			
newer HYV	501	1762	383	5402	358	54	32.4	64.8	151.2	78.3	56.4	47.7	182.4	1.2	0.8	1	1.6	1.2	1
older HYV	542	1849	464	5832	415	58.3	35	70	163.3	86.9	58.8	59.1	204.8	1.1	0.7	1	1.5	1	1

TABLE 18 (*cont.*):

Groundnut	333	253	52
by village			
Nesal	176	400	203
Vinay	314	115	11
Veera	564	517	14
by farm size			
small	275	90	30
large	416	489	84
by season			
Samba	416	285	52
Navarai	241	307	6
Somavari	190	77	87
by land type			
nanjai	475	262	104
pww	109	489	79
rainfed	477	36	7
by variety			
newer HYV	452	1239	502
older HYV	328	211	33

Source. Field survey, 1993–4.

TABLE 19 Paddy production, costs and marketed surplus

Paddy	Yield kg/ha	Price Rs/kg	Value output Rs/ha	Variable costs (Rs/ha) Hired labour	Seed	Manure	Ferti-lizer	Pesti-cides	Other	Total	Profitability index average	weighted	Quantity sold kg/ha	Rs/ha	Market surplus share of production
All	3978	3.6	14260	3763	747	503	1784	401	582	7781	1.83	1.92	1901	6798	0.44
by village															
Nesal	4239	3.5	14803	4584	620	261	2088	411	521	8485	1.74	1.76	2265	7902	0.48
Vinay	3806	3.7	13878	3270	779	626	1430	390	574	7069	1.96	2.02	1566	5727	0.39
Veera	4098	3.6	14582	3613	823	449	2341	372	631	8229	1.77	1.88	2292	8137	0.56
by farm size (H-R)															
small farms	3761	3.6	13284	3652	764	455	1816	387	651	7724	1.72	1.77	1676	5812	0.39
large farms	4228	3.6	15379	3891	728	558	1748	418	504	7847	1.96	2.09	2142	7853	0.51
by season															
Samba	3386	3.4	12269	3276	760	369	1669	390	426	6890	1.78	1.86	1974	6700	0.52
Navarai	4325	3.7	15659	3753	746	569	1872	390	422	7752	2.02	2.1	2137	7777	0.47
Somavari	3875	3.7	14483	4038	719	544	1739	399	843	8282	1.75	1.8	1622	6000	0.35
by variety															
newer variety	3602	3.4	12566	3525	795	514	1794	387	590	7605	1.65	1.77	1555	5178	0.38
older variety	4627	3.9	17713	4603	644	570	4885	470	624	8796	2.01	2.05	2606	9941	0.54
by land type															
Nanjai	4296	3.6	15586	4248	778	555	2066	420	543	8610	1.81	1.88	2249	8117	0.5
Punjai	3434	3.6	12996	3329	692	431	1546	386	641	7025	1.85	1.95	1555	5481	0.39
by cluster															
poor	3510	3.6	12611	3337	783	541	1685	336	782	7443	1.69	1.77	1194	4110	0.35
middle	3865	3.7	14063	3495	707	478	1774	345	452	7252	1.94	2.02	2058	7551	0.48
elite	4728	3.5	16526	4775	779	505	1917	581	591	9148	1.81	1.9	2370	8288	0.48
by land size															
landless	3104	3.6	10910	3940	729	238	2089	273	276	7546	1.45	1.42	493	1766	0.16
marginal	3790	3.4	12848	3539	805	527	1636	376	475	7357	1.75	1.9	1608	5401	0.4
small	3864	3.6	13889	3589	756	448	1912	368	751	7824	1.78	1.79	1909	6706	0.44
medium	4171	3.7	15253	3656	778	560	1537	448	508	7487	2.04	2.08	2010	7446	0.48
large	4463	3.6	16263	4724	586	607	2039	476	518	8950	1.82	2.14	2563	9379	0.55

Source: Field survey, 1993–4.

indirect control over petty production and market supplies, by the 1990s it was a combination of agricultural and non-agricultural commercial credit which played this role with respect to the more diversified agricultural and non-agricultural base of petty production.

2.7 Marketed surplus

The marketed surplus (as a weighed aggregate proportion of paddy output) has increased by a third over the last 20 years from 33 to 44 per cent, testifying to the persistence of subsistence production (Table 19). Large farms[55] had a marketed surplus one third greater than did small farms. Old HYVs in the *samba* season dominate supplies to market. The per hectare net profitability of the paddy surpluses of large farms exceeded those for small farm sales by 18 per cent.

The marketed surplus of groundnuts, an inedible agro-industrial oilseed, was low at 60 per cent due to the fact that quality on the open market for groundnut oil was so unreliable that producers made their own. One third was kept for seed and for custom-milling for home consumption, where quality and non-adulteration could be assured.

For the vast majority of the population who were small cultivators and landless agricultural labourers, more of their consumption consisted of products received as wages in kind than of crops they themselves grew. In contrast, in the minority of elite households, the grain payments they received from others for water supplied by them and the produce from their own land, constitute their grain stock, a small proportion of which needed to be retained for consumption while the rest was marketed. While what poor households consume is the residual after meeting their immediate cash payments and settling loans, for the elite, what is sold in the market is the residual above seed and consumption needs. The marketed surplus thus has two components, the former price unresponsive and a function of debt and the latter price responsive and a function of scale and of distance from market.[56]

2.8 Agricultural employment

While two thirds of the total rural workforce remained in agriculture, over the 20 years the ratio of cultivators to agricultural labourers had reversed itself to stand at 10 to 10.5. *Agricultural labour increased by 50 per cent over the two decades.* Yet the growth rate of the agricultural labour force and the labour-absorptive capacity of agriculture slackened (see Table 20). Total labour inputs on small paddy farms were to all intents and purposes unchanged from 1973: up

TABLE 20   Adult employment per paddy farm in crop production by type of labour (days)

	1973/7		1982/3		1983/4		1993/4	
	Small farms	Large farms	Small farms	Large farms	Small farms	Large farms	Small farms	Large farms
Family Labour	129.7	207	64.1	115	147.8	303	112.5	143.4
Male	34.3	148.5	52.2	96.7	104.8	191.9	65.1	90.3
Female	95.4	58.5	64.1	18.3	43	111.1	47.4	52.8
Casual Labour	138.1	360.2	76.2	287.5	77.3	244.3	190.2	357.9
Male	39.2	125.5	19.2	72.5	28.7	100.6	63.9	93.9
Female	98.9	234.7	57	215	48.6	143.7	126.3	264
Attached Labour	6	46.6	3	31.5	22	83.6	1.8	30
Male	5.6		3	31.1	21.7	68.3	1.8	
Female	0.4	46.6		0.4	0.3	15.3		30
Exchange Labour	21.3	50.1	0.5	3.8	0.5	17	1.5	3.6
Male	3.9	12.8	0.1	0.6	0.2	13.7	0.3	0.6
Female	17.4	37.3	0.4	3.2	0.3	3.3	1.2	3
Total	295.1	663.9	143.8	437.8	225.6	647.9	306	535.8

TABLE 20 (*cont.*):

Labour								
Male	144.1	333.4	74.5	200.9	133.7	374.5	131.4	214.5
Female	151	330.5	69.3	236.9	91.9	273.4	174.9	319.8
Total Labour/ha	557	471	411	492	353	307	483	419
(for operated ha	500	274	234	163	410	269		
gross cropped area)	317	242	173	146	253	204		
Total Casual	261	255	218	323	121	116	210	228
Labour/operated ha	234	149	125	107	141	101		
gross cropped area	148	131	92	96	87	77		

Note: Small farms are cultivators holding (operating) less than 1 hectare of land. The labour/ha ratios for the years 1973–4, 1982–3 and 1983–4 have been calculated considering the average plot size per paddy cultivation reported in Hazell and Ramasamy 1991 (table 3.2, p. 34).

Source: Hazell and Ramasamy 1991, p. 38; survey data 1993–4.

from 295 to 306 days. By contrast on large farms – accounting for most of the area and most of the output dominating the marketed surplus – *in the 1990s there was a 20 per cent decline in the average labour inputs of the 1980s and 1970s.* Per hectare, as noted in the 1980s, small farms remained some 15 per cent more labour-intensive than large ones,[57] but over the two decades *total labour per hectare had dropped by 15 per cent on small farms and by 12 per cent on large farms.* The continued mechanization of ploughing, irrigation and threshing accounts for this process of labour shedding.

It is not only the total quantity and intensity of 'labour' in the abstract which varies over time, it is also the labour process. Its components have changed remarkably over time. While in 1993–4 the *exchange of labour* had been all but obliterated from production, what is left of it is every bit as female as it had been in the 1970s, when it was more important (though less noticed in the literature) than attached/permanent labour. On small farms, *attached contracts* had accounted for 2 per cent of labour-days in 1973–4 but were negligible in the 1990s.[58] But on large farms they were virtually unchanged, at 6 per cent, down from 7 per cent two decades earlier. The most striking long-term trend, however, is the *substitution of casual labour for family labour*, both on small farms (where family labour was down 14 per cent from 1973 levels) and on large ones (down by 30 per cent, mostly accounted for by the withdrawal of male family labour), most dramatically on the large farms in Nesal, the most developed village.[59] On small farms, the casual labour component had increased by 38 per cent: a significant trend in the miniaturization of the wage-labour form of production. If on large farms *casual labour* was static in terms of the absolute number of days, put another way: it *rose by 22 per cent to two thirds of all labour*. In Table 20, data for the periods of drought and recovery in the 1980s show that labour contracts can be quite contingent on circumstance. While, during the extreme drought, there was a marked drop in all forms of labour, the period of recovery in the truncated set of villages was marked by dependence on male labour forced into attached contracts.

In the exceptional circumstances of the 1980s, Hazell and Ramasamy observed a marked masculinization of labour, but the long-term trend over the two decades 1973–93 goes in the opposite direction: from equal inputs of male and female labour regardless of farm size in 1973 to a situation in 1993 where women worked 57 per cent of the total days of labour worked on small farms and 60 per cent of that on large ones. Some 80 per cent of this female labour is casual wage work, an increase of 15 per cent over the two decades. On small farms, 72 per cent of female labour is casual, an 11 per cent increase. Table 20 also reveals that, while on small farms the component of family labour is being masculinized, on large farms even family labour is being feminized. In a nutshell, although per hectare employment and livelihoods declined, *agricultural production depended increasingly on female and casual labour* (see also Chapter 1–5).

Trends in real casual wages are found in Table 21, showing that the 'labour market' is a spread of rates specific to gender, task and village. Though real pay for all tasks has risen, there is no obvious trend towards convergence. Rates have tightened most in Vinayagapuram and least in Nesal; most for men ploughing, least for women harvesting; in general, more for men and less for women. Male wages are at least twice and in some instances three times greater than female wages (see Table 17). In two villages, where women formed three quarters of the agricultural labour force, their real wages actually declined over the last 20 years.

Rates, terms and conditions, contractual forms, tasks and trends vary from village to village, according to the production technology, the size of land holdings of employers, the caste and gender of labour and the availability of seasonally specific non-farm employment alternatives for it (see Chapter 1–5). *On the average, in 1993–4, paddy required 450 labour-days per hectare.* There were marked seasonal variations in labour requirements; other things being equal, the rainy season required 30 per cent fewer days' work. Massive inputs of family labour were necessary for the small area of unirrigated land down to paddy. Newer HYVs are 50 per cent more labour-intensive for – as seen earlier – lower yields

TABLE 21 Real casual wage rates by gender and village[1] 1973–93.

		1973–4	1983–4	1993–4	*Index*
				(1973–4=100)	
Women's wages					
Transplanting (Rs)[2]	N	1.3	1.6	2	153
	Vi	0.7	1.4	2.3	329
	Ve	1.3	1.4	1.8	128
Harvesting (kg)	N	4.3	5	5	116
	Vi	3	4	6.4	213
	Ve	4.3	4.3	6.4	149
Men's wages					
Ploughing with bullocks (Rs)	N	1.5	3.3	6.3	420
	Vi	0.7	1.4	2.3	329
	Ve	0.8	2.8	5	625
Threshing (kg)	N	8.5	10	10	118
	Vi	3	4	12	400
	Ve	8.5	8.5	12	141

[1] N: Nesal, Vi: Vinayagapuram, Ve: Veerasambanur.
[2] Small farms are cultivators holding (operating) less than 1 hectare of land. The labour/ha ratios for the years 1973–4, 1982–3 and 1983–4 have been calculated considering the average plot size per paddy cultivation reported in Hazell and Ramasamy 1991 (table 3.2, p. 34).

Source: Field survey, 1993–4.

than older HYVs (see Table 17). By contrast, *groundnuts required 150 labour-days per hectare*. Fluctuations in labour demand according to season or irrigation status were of much lower amplitude than for paddy. HYVs required 33 per cent more labour than traditional varieties. There were markedly different tendencies in the organization of labour by village: while the labour process in Nesal was dominated by female casual labour, in Vinayagapuram female family labour was the biggest single component.

At this stage, our conclusions are sobering. Despite the developmental effort put into agriculture, before, during and after the first generation 'green revolution', the impact on yields is disappointing. Agricultural production remains extremely vulnerable to its physical environment and its trend is flat. The farm size/productivity relationship is positive. Despite the universal adoption of new varieties, it is the larger land holdings on which the highest yields are obtained. The agricultural population is increasingly differentiated and its factor environment persistently unequal in class terms. In this region of India, the 'green revolution' has dissipated into a not particularly 'green' reaction.

3. TRENDS IN REAL INCOMES AND POVERTY

Table 22 summarizes income, expenditure and poverty in the three villages. Between 20 and 30 per cent of households, throughout the income distribution, declared total expenditure in excess of income. In such households, expenditures therefore relied on debt. Another subset of households – around a third – were still under the Planning Commission's poverty line for an average-sized

TABLE 22 Income, expenditure and poverty, 1993–4

	n	(a)	(b)	(c)	(d)	(e)
Village						
Nesal	55	34	27	47	9	100
Vinayagapuram	35	29	29	60	17	100
Veerasambanur	25	36	20	100	16	100

n: number of sampled households
(a): households below poverty line (%)
(b): households where expenditure exceeds income (%)
(c): proportion of (b) below poverty line (%)
(d): households where food expenditure exceeds income (%)
(e): proportion of (d) below poverty line (%)

Note: The poverty line is calculated at Rs 195 per person per month in 1993–4 prices: Rs 819 per average household.

Source: Field survey 1993–4.

household. A weighted average of 60 per cent of 'indebted' households were under the poverty line. One in ten households had *food* expenditures which exceeded their stated income – all being below the poverty line.

A very major developmental achievement, however, is that between 1973 and 1994 *average real expenditure* increased by a factor of 6 for elite producers, 4.5 for poor producers and 2.8 for landless agricultural labourers (see Chapter 3–4). The sixfold increase in the spending of the agrarian elite masks its internal differentiation, the top of the elite in terms of assets distribution achieving much higher real increases in income than its base.

This increase in real incomes is due in part to the state. The achievement of a threefold increase in the real incomes of wage labourers had more to do with the controlled prices of wage goods under the Essential Commodities Acts and nutrition interventions than it had to do with the minimum wages legislation, which is not enforced. Table 23 shows that in these villages *open-market coarse rice prices have been held roughly constant in real terms over the two decades,* while male wages have more than doubled and female wages almost doubled. *Furthermore, the casual wage can purchase from the Fair Price Shop (which issues rice from the PDS) more than twice the amount of rice it will buy on the open market.*

While the proportion of households in nutritional stress had halved over the

TABLE 23 Wage–price relations for agricultural labour in the three villages, 1973–4 to 1993–4

	1973–4	1982–3	1993–4
A. Current Rs			
Wages			
(a) ploughing (men)	2.27	3.99	22
(b) transplanting (women)	1.13	2.45	8
(c) price of coarse parboiled rice	1.27	2.14	5.5
(rural retail price Rs/kg)			
(d) PDS (Rs/kg)			2.5
issue price			
B. Constant 1993–4 prices			
(a)	9.1	7.5	22
(b)	4.5	4.6	8
(c)	5.1	4	5.5
C. Wage–price ratios			
(a)/(c)	1.8	1.8	4
(b)/(c)	0.9	1.1	1.45
(a)/(d)			9
(b)/(d)			3.2

Source: Field material plus data in Hazell and Ramasamy 1991, pp. 89, 116.

last two decades, it averaged 26 per cent of the households of poor peasants and landless agricultural labourers. Calorie consumption had remained stable over the 20-year span at 1,900 calories per adult equivalent. Meanwhile, the diet of the elite had diversified to a high-income, 'metropolitan' nutritional pattern. Access to the public distribution scheme, making rice available at controlled prices, and to the noon meals scheme (providing one third of daily calorie requirements to pre-school and school-aged children) both proved to be socially redistributive and, despite leakages and marked intervillage variations, these two schemes protected the nutritional security and enhanced the real incomes of the poorest households.[60]

Drowning the effect of direct state welfare interventions, however, was the tightening impact on agricultural wages of the increased spatial mobility of labour, in particular daily commuting and both seasonal and permanent out-migration of male labour, which increasingly avoided agricultural work, and of the in-migration of investment in the non-farm rural economy (which, in 3 out of the 11 villages amounted to 'suburbanization'). This process of reorientation of livelihoods, physical work and the economic structuring of space has been termed 'de-agrarianization'. Calls have been made to reformulate the agrarian question (by which is meant the relation of agrarian classes to national capitalist development) in order to encompass the ubiquitous expansion of non-agricultural economic activity under a variety of forms of production relations.[61] The main features of the way this change affected the villages we studied are outlined in the following section.

4. FROM GREEN REVOLUTION TO RURAL INDUSTRIALIZATION

Historically, agriculture has declined in relative importance over time, containing, as it does, the components of its own decline: capital, labour, wage goods and raw materials. All of these need to be shed in order for the non-agricultural sectors of an economy to grow. It has been an important planning objective since Indian Independence to hasten this process.[62] Rural economies are expected to *diversify* as agriculture *grows* in absolute terms but declines in relative terms.[63] Increased real agricultural incomes consequent to the Green Revolution will in turn create increased demand for income-elastic goods and services.[64] Such incremental demand will be met by small-scale, local, labour-intensive non-agricultural production which will mop up surplus labour from the agricultural sector.[65] It will be the *cause* of such industrialization. The argument about intersectoral resource transfers by means of agricultural growth linkages has been conducted without reference to spatial factors and the presumption is that local diversification is rural.[66] Rural non-farm employment in India did indeed expand at the rate of 4.6 per cent over the period 1972–3 to 1987–8.[67]

Others, however, have argued that the evolution of the non-farm economy is a function of changing production conditions and the forms in which surplus is generated and redistributed. It might be the product of agrarian pauperization and of a deterioration in the terms and conditions of work of the rising share of the workforce which is not self-employed.[68] It could be a long-standing, risk-minimizing response to economic and/or environmental hazards in agricultural production conditions;[69] or a more recent response to non-local demand (whether agrarian or non-agrarian), to (more or less targeted) state-led employment creation,[70] state-subsidized and/or regulated (foreign) investment,[71] or even to industrial downsizing.[72]

Given the sparse nature of the existing database on non-farm assets and employment, Visaria commented:[73]

> We need to understand the pace and processes of growth or decay of different activities in our villages and towns, with due account taken of the place of usual residence as well as place of work of workers. Such mundane research, which may not offer scope for the use of sophisticated quantitative techniques, is imperative to validate, document and analyse the ongoing changes suggested by macro-data provided by the censuses and national surveys.

What light do our data shed on this issue?

4.1. Employment

The debate about the dynamics of rural diversification can be illuminated by empirical material from the three villages which were subject to intensive study. While only 10 per cent of households gave 'manufacturing' as their primary occupation, apparently disposing of the idea that the non-farm economy has expanded, this figure conceals what we believe to be *a significant change over the previous decade.* For 41 per cent of male labour and 8 per cent of female labour were employed in the rural non-farm economy, *and half the landed agricultural households reported at least one adult in non-agricultural activity* (see Chapter 1–6, Table 9). And, when we look at individuals rather than households, we find not only the agricultural proletarianization of women and the emergence of weaving as a major form of rural livelihood but a massive increase in yet another miscellaneous category of 'other' activity (from 20 per cent in 1982–4 – gender unspecified – to 36 per cent for men and 18 per cent for women in 1993–4). 'Other' activities include petty or household manufacturing, construction, trade, transport, storage and 'other services', which is itself a quite large, unspecified category. Caste and gender are strong filters of entry into, and stratifiers of returns from, this non-farm sector. *Scheduled caste workers tend to be screened out of the activities with the highest returns* and are thus restricted to agriculture, to mud and construction work and to work outside the locality of their settlement. In this process, and subject to the market-mediated screening of caste, women are also at a distinct disadvantage compared with men. Women gained but 8 per cent of all non-agricultural earnings and earned less than men per unit of time, even when tasks were not gender-specific. *In silk weaving, womens' average daily earnings were Rs 6.5, contrasted with Rs 34 for men. Girl assistants were paid nothing, while boys got Rs 5 a day.*[74] Silk weaving takes a putting-out, household form based upon a technologically retrogressive shift (from fly to throw shuttle and using child labour) that is unlikely to develop into a factory industry.[75] From our evidence, the evolution of the rural non-farm economy is clearly a function of changing village-specific production conditions and the forms in which agricultural surplus is generated and redistributed. It may be as much the product of relative agrarian pauperization – and of the rising share of the workforce which is not self-employed – as it is the product of the process of rural accumulation. At the same time, the poorest people are excluded.

4.2. Assets

For employment to be created either in agriculture or in the rural non-farm economy, investment is a prior requirement. From the patterns of assets distribution and from the nature of these investments it is then possible to comment on the assumption that (local) agricultural growth linkages were their cause. Assets are the 'fossils' of investment histories. In 1993–4, inequality in assets was impressive. Table 24, which shows the detailed disaggregations of means and standard deviations of total assets for the three intensively studied villages, suggests not only the extent of intervillage variation but also that assets ownership is highly socially differentiated in village-specific, fractal patterns.[76]

At the same time the composition of these assets was overwhelmingly agricultural, throughout the rural class structure. Land still accounted for the largest share among the different components that make up the asset structure: 40 per cent of total assets and 56 per cent of productive ones. Agricultural assets ranged from 74 per cent of total assets in the poorest village to 65 per cent in the richest one. Among the class of poor households (with an average of Rs 60,000 of assets), two thirds of total assets were in land, a quarter in buildings and transport, and the rest took the form of jewellery and informal finance. The village elites had very highly capitalized land of the best quality, farm machinery and livestock, rice mills and informal sector financial investments. Even so,

TABLE 24 Asset holding in the three villages

| Village | Land | Live-stock | Average EMV of the Asset per Household | | | | | | Non-prod. assets | Total EMV of the asset per household | Percentage of non-agricultural employment | | |
| | | | Productive assets | | | Financial assets | | | | | | | |
			In agri.	In non-agri.	Total	Inst	Non-inst.	Total			Total	Male	Female
A Nesal (n=57)	49126 (49.1)	1628 (1.6)	22904 (22.9)	6 (neg.)	22910 (22.9)	661	3420	4081 (4.1)	22313 (22.3)	100,058 (100)	27.9	41.7	14
Vinayagapuram (n=36)	62371 (46.7)	3772 (2.8)	41548 (31.1)	1978 (1.5)	43526 (32.6)	1083	1486	2569 (1.9)	21282 (15.9)	133,520 (100)	28.5	39.9	16.2
Veerasambanur (n=25)	73693 (35.9)	3492 (1.7)	20222 (9.9)	38592 (18.8)	58814 (28.7)	13387	3512	16899 (18.2)	52335 (25.5)	205,234 (100)	33.2	44.7	16.6
All 3 villages	65043 (40.4)	3183 (2)	27296 (16.9)	19247 (11.9)	46543 (28.9)	6937	2874	9811 (6.1)	36501 (22.7)	161,072 (100)	30.4	42.5	16
B Nesal	76	51	84	Neg.	49	10	119	42	61	62	92	98	88
Vinayagapuram	96	119	152	10	94	16	52	26	58	83	94	94	101
Veerasambanur	113	110	74	201	126	193	122	172	143	127	109	105	104
All 3 Villages	100	100	100	100	100	100	100	100	100	100	100	100	100

EMV = Estimated market value

A = Rs; B = % of 3 village average.

finance was but 7 per cent, buildings and transport 20 per cent and rice mills, looms etc. 15 per cent. *The entire local rural non-farm economy* (including construction and transport) *appears to operate from one third of total rural assets and one tenth of total productive assets.*

While 29 per cent of the households in our sample were without land, no landless household was without assets.[77] The total assets of landless households varied from a mean of Rs 2,665 in Veerasambanur, through Rs 14,408 in Vinayagapuram, to Rs 21,093 in Nesal. Being landless in a village is no longer to be associated with the most dire poverty, although the poorest are certainly landless. Non-land assets mitigate agricultural poverty, just as non-agricultural salaried employment differentiates wage labour. Non-land assets mainly take the form of dwellings. In Veerasambanur, the non-building, non-transport, non-agricultural assets of the landless are tiny: up to Rs 25 for farm tools, up to Rs 150 for artisanal tools, up to Rs 350 in non-institutional credit, the same in jewellery and Rs 5 in livestock. In Vinayagapuram, there are some significant differences: up to Rs 1,315 in handlooms, up to Rs 2,500 in non-institutional finance, the same in jewellery and up to Rs 1,000 in livestock. In Nesal, financial assets substitute for looms, otherwise the pattern is similar.

The difference between the total assets of the richest household (with approximately Rs 43 lakhs) and the five poorest households in our rural sample (each with total assets under Rs 2,000) is a factor of 2,150.

The narrow base of non-agricultural investment may have resulted from the mediocre performance of agriculture; in other words, there may be a simple explanation that there are few growth linkages from agriculture. Non-farm assets tended to be highly socially restricted (though not as socially restricted and concentrated as land). The classes with the greatest agricultural assets were precisely those with the greatest non-agricultural assets. The link between the sectors was direct, by means of household accumulation. But this was not the whole story.

Non-agricultural investment was highly socially concentrated, while non-farm employment was far less socially restricted. Productive investment in the non-farm economy shows far more intervillage variation than does employment in the non-farm economy. The latter took the labour of 41 per cent of men but only 8 per cent of women – for whom agricultural wage work was the fallback. Either men commuted away from the locality or they worked inside these villages using assets which were not theirs.[78] For this to have occurred when there is so little evidence for assets-holding in such sectors we must be observing *contraflows of capital.*[79] *Capital is emigrating from – and at the same time a certain amount is migrating into – these rural sites.* We have little exact data, but we used reasonable assumptions to make a conservative estimate of capital emigration.[80]

While 1 to 2 per cent of two villages' assets were outside the village, the proportion of Nesal's assets that is invested outside was a striking 54.5 per cent.

Theories of labour migration can be adapted to apply to capital migration. Hart (1996) has talked of urban push and rural pull, arguing with empirical evidence from Malaysia and Taiwan that, rather than rural industrialization being an immediate local response to agricultural growth linkages (which she calls rural pull), it is rural–urban differentials in rents, infrastructure and the existence of dispersed and cheap labour that repel industries from urban locations into rural ones (which she calls 'urban push'). Our field research would lead us to add to this list of forces the better opportunities for tax evasion in rural locations, and for the exploitation of unwaged female and child labour.[81] But whereas Hart's analysis focuses on export-led rural industrialization, what we observed in the villages we studied is a production process for a rapidly emerging national market. Some of this market is rural (a little local, but *most non-local*), but the vast bulk is *urban/metropolitan* in origin. It is evident that capital is far from fungible, that those exporting assets from villages and investing in land, rice mills, trade and finance are unable to finance much of the non-farm employment growing within these villages because of factors connected to the social profile of capital ownership – most notably restrictions on entry due to caste. Those exporting capital from *urban* sites to these villages and investing in silk weaving are unwilling or unable for the same reason to invest in the activities of *rural* capital exporters. While the ownership of assets is increasingly concentrated, the locations of the propertied elite are increasingly dispersed, and the village is increasingly a unit of residence and less and less one of production and consumption.

We would expect that increasing rural economic diversity – whatever the causes – would mean that agricultural and non-agricultural diversification would take shape according to locale, caste, class and gender. Households' responses to changes in the balance between the different economic and ecological forces they confront would also be facilitated and constrained by these factors. This in turn means – contrary to the assumptions of the liberal reform agenda – that the ability of agricultural prices *per se* to explain and elicit supply is considerably qualified (see Chapter 2-2).

5. THE INDIAN REFORMS AND RURAL DEVELOPMENT

For structural adjustment to accelerate diversification by reducing barriers to mobility and by relaxing regulations which previously inhibited rural non-farm productive activity,[82] markets must be capable of wrenching capital from its social moorings. This is not what is taking place in the area we studied. Market exchange, while increasingly dominant, is heavily embedded in, and constitutive of, relations of class, caste, locality and gender – as is the local state. The modalities by which the combined activities of state and market might dissolve the social foundations of accumulation are not well understood. Education is often cited as a dissolving force. While Jayaraj shows that higher education is associated with greater diversity of, and higher returns to, employment, we have yet to understand how education might challenge the distribution, composition and location of assets holdings, and every reason to suppose that it currently reinforces it.[83]

The trends we found in two-way urban–rural, farm–non-farm capital migration may be observed throughout Tamil Nadu, not merely in the trade and services, the agroprocessing and construction activities which are to be found everywhere, but in the regional specialities: matches around Sivakasi, *korai* and gem cutting around Tiruchirapalli, cotton textiles diffusing out from Tiruppur, leather tanning in and around the Palar Basin,[84] metalwork and engineering in rural settlements around Coimbatore. The non-agricultural rural economy is no longer marginal, it is of central importance to the reproduction of rural society. In the region we have studied, the new wave of capitalist development is sucking certain castes that are preponderant in small-scale agricultural production and in agricultural labour into dependent, small-scale commodity production controlled by non-agricultural merchants' capital, deploying household labour (including children withdrawn from school) under conditions of technological retrogression. The macro-economic policies creating and skewing consumer demand are encouraging urban capital 'flight' to these rural sites. The stage being observed in northern Tamil Nadu could be a precondition to a phase of export production, not necessarily by foreign capital, but by local or national capital. *Diversity is the hallmark of the expansion of rural capitalism here.* It is agrarian households with the larger land holdings and hired labour forces which not only diversify into both income-elastic and water-sparing agricultural products but also (because of the ceiling on the absorptive capacity of agriculture and because of higher rates of return) into the non-farm economy. Such assets accumulation, both within the village economy and directly and indirectly outside it, renders these households doubly diversified. When combined with salaried employment in the state or the urban economy (as happens in these households), they are trebly diversified. Such diversification is a close associate of agrarian differentiation. At the micro-economic scale, it enables the capital-accumulating class to manage a uniquely varied portfolio using the joint family form of household. In turn, this class is endowed with a risk-resisting economic plasticity.

In sum, the Green Revolution has succeeded in keeping rice production at a medium-term constant, while a third of cultivated area has been diverted to other crops. This has been achieved at the cost of increasing instability of output, stagnant yields and plunder of the water table. It relies on an increasingly feminized casual labour force. It is evidently now the non-agricultural economy which is providing developmental dynamism to the region – drawing in capital, shifting capital intersectorally and providing employment (but in a way that is biased against women, against the lowest castes and the poorest classes). While the food needs of the local population and the agro-industrial raw materials can both be (and increasingly are) supplied from elsewhere in a lengthening and thickening mesh of interregional trade flows, the process of capital formation and the private intersectoral transfer of capital are still intensely localized. Yet agricultural production has reached the stage of severely diminishing marginal returns among the most landed class, which has historically controlled the shedding of capital and labour. This is an unprecedentedly grim scenario. *With local per caput consumption of rice stagnant and food scarcity still affecting 26 per cent of poor households, with production stagnant and (despite a rapid fertility decline) population still growing, the roles of the local and central state in guaranteeing the transfer of low-price grain from long distant or local grain bowls to regions such as this one are of enduring importance to people's welfare.*

By 2001, agriculture provided only 17 per cent of state domestic product. The rice economy was growing at 0.8 per cent per annum.[85] Little more can now be expected of this highly differentiated agriculture in the absence of a new wave of agricultural research and development and in the absence of the public provision of physical infrastructure. The latter is known to work in sync with private capital formation and agricultural production. In the further very hostile policy context of i) a mediocre record from the 1980s of research and infrastructural investment in the agricultural sector, ii) pressing requirements (moving from the phase of the rhetorical to that of the actual) for public expenditure to be cut, and iii) the funding cuts to the Consultative Group for International Agricultural Research (hereafter CGIAR) system of international seed-breeding institutions for foodgrains (which is the only one the world has),[86] such investments are no longer on the horizon. The local developmental baton has been seized by rural industrialization. But to assume that 'de-agrarianization' or rural industrialization can answer the agrarian question or solve the many persistent, technical and social problems of agriculture would be, from our evidence, to err.

ACKNOWLEDGEMENTS

We are grateful for their discussants' comments at the 1996 workshop, MIDS, to G S Bhalla, Neil Bliven, Martin Greeley, Judith Heyer, R Krishnaswamy,

S Neelakanthan, K Nagaraj, Wendy K Olsen, R C Panda, C Ramasamy, K Skandan, Padmini Swaminathan and A Vaidyanathan; and to Colin Leys and Matthew McCartney for help with the final draft. We are also grateful for discussion at presentations at the British High Commission, New Delhi; at the Institute of Social Studies, The Hague (especially to Haroun Vikram-Lodi and Jos Mooij); at Reading University; and at the 1999 Conference of the British Association of Agricultural Economists, Belfast. We are responsible for any remaining errors.

Appendix 1

The Selection of Villages and Sampled Households

North Arcot District was selected for study by Madras University in 1973:

i) because of being both a rice bowl and yet not an Intensive Agricultural District Programme (IADP) District;

ii) because its agricultural economy was simple – based then on rice and groundnut;

iii) because its semi-subsistence production was undergoing rapid commercialization;

iv) because poverty was widespread;

v) because its semi-arid agro-ecology was not only representative of conditions widespread in peninsular India but was also similar to that of a district in Sri Lanka's Dry Zone with which the original project did comparative research; and

vi) because at the time little applied research had been carried out there apart from sociomedical and epidemiological work based on Christian Medical College (CMC) Hospital.

Eleven villages on the Coromandel Plain of North Arcot District were randomly selected in 1973 from the 989 villages listed in the 1971 census. The systematic sample was stratified by physical accessibility, population size and the ratio of agricultural labourers to cultivators. One of the Slater villages (studied at much wider intervals from 1916) – Dusi – was also included. Another of the villages was the site of detailed economic anthropological fieldwork in 1973 (J Harriss 1982).

From village household censuses, after classifying the population of paddy farms over 1/4 acre by HYV status and ranking these farms by farm size and the maximum area planted to paddy, a sample of 161 paddy-cultivating households was selected for a detailed farm management survey. A second sample of 137 households (of which 57 were paddy-cultivating, 3 non-paddy-cultivating and 77 non-cultivating households) was drawn systematically from subsamples of the paddy households, non-cultivating households and from households cultivating only dry land for investigations of income, consumption and expenditure (Chinnappa 1977).

In 1983, the 11 villages were resurveyed by TNAU/IFPRI. The surveys began in 1982–3 but, this being a severe drought year, the survey was repeated in 1983–4 in poorly irrigated villages recovering from drought (Hazell and Ramasamy 1991, p. 5). Selection of 160 paddy-cultivating households was done by systematic random sampling, the census population having been grouped according to pump-set possession and tenurial status and ranked by operational holding size; 25 non-paddy-cultivating households were selected by simple random sampling; and 160 non-cultivating households were selected, the census populations having first been grouped by primary occupations (9 types) and ranked according to household size. Between opening and closing inventories, detailed monthly income and expenditure surveys were carried out (see Hazell and Ramasamy 1991, pp. 262–4 and 267–9, for a detailed discussion).[1]

The 1993 census resurvey of three villages sought details of assets, land tenure, well ownership, type of house, consumer durables, food stores, debt, income, family size and composition, occupation, work in the previous month, education and some details of incapacity. Then a set of 18 variables was chosen to form the basis of a cluster analysis, the classes of which were used as the basis of sampling (see Chapter 1–4 for the theoretical background to this approach).

The cluster analysis was carried out by village on account of the long-apparent phenomenon of intervillage variation, which itself has been subjected to a variety of attempts at systematic classification (Chambers and Harriss 1977; Hazell and Ramasamy 1991; and see Chapter 1–2). Clusters are therefore village-specific. The pooling of subsamples of households derived from the clusters does not permit generalization beyond the households. However, because these three villages represent archetypes, pooled data for these three villages would represent those types of agrarian conditions. It is commonly the case that, in a multipurpose survey, samples selected on one basis are subsequently used for other research objectives, which provoke similar problems of representivity as does the pooling of subsamples taken according to different criteria. Multivariate clusters of different populations (villages) have the advantage of being as broadly based as their vector of variables, which in the current case is a) carefully justified and b) wide-ranging. There are two further responses to the question of pooling data obtained on different bases, both more expedient. First, the International Crops Research Institute for the Semi-Arid Tropics (ICRISAT) village laboratory studies have set a precedent in pooling data derived from village-specific classifications (Walker and Ryan 1990; Ryan, Bidinger *et al.* 1984 – in their case widely varying acreage thresholds for classifications of small, medium and large farmers). Second, it turns out that the characteristics of the principal multivariate clusters identified here are extremely similar (see discussion in Chapter 1–4). We then took a systematic random sample of households stratified by cluster, with sample sizes proportionate to the share of each village cluster to the census population total, subject to the constraint of a total sample size being 120, a size which was determined by the number of field investigators and by supervisory capacity. Two households refused, so the sample was 118 households. The sample is two thirds the size of that drawn for 1973 and 1982–4, but since we studied 3 of the 11 villages the sampling fraction is much higher.

The selected households were visited three times during 1993–4. On each occasion, the costs and returns to all productive agricultural and non-agricultural activity and all forms of labour were recorded for the previous season. In the first round, extra questions on water management were asked. In the second round, a detailed consumption survey was canvassed. In the third, we asked for people's experience of social welfare and its cost, health, the public distribution system, nutritious noon meal for children and social security scheme.

A second cluster analysis was conducted to evaluate the relevance of certain errors in the census data and mistakes committed in the computation of the variables used for the first cluster analysis, which had been encountered only at a later stage (three years after the survey). Three households had to be dropped from the sample because of missing data (in two cases the original questionnaire schedule had vanished from the shelves in Chennai). Tables 2 and 3 report the number of households from census and sample, classified by village and cluster. It is easy to see that certain household groups are over-represented (such as the elite of Nesal), while others are under-represented (such as the middle peasants with land in Veerasambanur).

To the extent that the various household groups identified in the two cluster analyses differ, the sample means will then be biased estimators of the total population and the village population means. The only means which would not be unbiased are those relative to the cluster means within each village. Weights which are inversely proportional to the probability of a household being selected have then been used to correct the bias in subsequent analysis.

Over 1994–5 the remaining eight villages were visited, households were listed and the demographic, economic and social census previously applied to the three villages was extended to them. The information gathered has been used in Chapter 1–3 on intervillage variation, Chapter 3–1 on poverty and Chapter 3–2 on life chances.

TABLE 1 Census households classified by village and cluster

Population	Village				
		Nesal	Vinayaga-puram	Veera-sambanur	All
Elite		26	27	20	73
	Col%	7.67	10.42	14.71	9.95
	Row%	35.62	36.99	27.40	100
Middle landed peasants		69	76	27	172
	Col%	20.35	29.34	19.85	23.43
	Row%	40.12	44.19	15.70	100
Middle landless peasant		47	17	4	68
	Col%	13.86	6.56	2.94	9.26
	Row%	69.12	25	5.88	100
Poor landed peasants		36	77	39	152
	Col%	10.62	29.73	28.68	20.71
	Row%	23.68	50.66	25.66	100
Poor landless peasants		161	62	46	269
	Col%	47.49	23.94	33.82	36.65
	Row%	59.85	23.05	17.10	100
Total Households		339	259	136	734
	Col%	100	100	100	100
	Row%	46.19	35.29	18.53	100

TABLE 2 Sampled households by village and cluster

Population	Village				
		Nesal	Vinayaga-puram	Veera-sambanur	All
Elite		9	2	3	14
	Col%	16.36	5.71	12	12.17
	Row%	64.29	14.29	21.43	100
Middle landed peasants		8	12	3	23
	Col%	14.55	34.29	12	20
	Row%	34.78	52.17	13.04	100
Middle landless peasant		4	5	1	10
	Col%	7.27	14.29	4	8.70
	Row%	40	50	10	100
Poor landed peasants		10	7	9	26
	Col%	18.18	20	36	22.61
	Row%	38.46	26.92	34.62	100
Poor landless peasants		24	9	9	42
	Col%	43.64	25.71	36	36.52
	Row%	57.14	21.43	21.43	100
Total Households		55	35	25	115
	Col%	100	100	100	100
	Row%	47.83	30.43	21.74	100

TABLE 3 Weights for sample

Population	Village			
		Nesal	Vinayaga-puram	Veera-sambanur	All
Elite		2.889	13.500	6.667	5.214
	Col%	7.67	10.42	14.71	9.95
	Row%	35.62	36.99	27.40	100
Middle landed peasants		8.625	6.333	9	7.478
	Col%	20.35	29.34	19.85	23.43
	Row%	40.12	44.19	15.70	100
Middle landless peasant		11.750	3.400	4	6.800
	Col%	13.86	6.56	2.94	9.26
	Row%	69.12	25	5.88	100
Poor landed peasants		3.600	11	4.333	5.846
	Col%	10.62	29.73	28.68	20.71
	Row%	23.68	50.66	25.66	100
Poor landless peasants		6.708	6.889	5.111	6.405
	Col%	47.49	23.94	33.82	36.65
	Row%	59.85	23.05	17.10	100

Appendix 2:
Production Statistics

TABLE 1 Basic statistics on agricultural production in former North Arcot District, 1982–3 to 1992–3

| | PADDY | | | Post harvest Paddy price Jan Rs/Q | Post harvest Gnut price June Rs/Q | Fertilizer (tonnes) | | | Area ('oooha) | Prodn (Kernel) ('ooomt) | Yield (kg) |
	Area ('oooha)	Prodn ('ooomt)	Yield kg/ha			N	P	Q			
1982–3	118.3	231	2452	200	450	21758	8621	8761	232	83	350
1983–4	753.5	533	2106	139	397	25435	11668	10890	280	112	400
1984–5	289.8	580.0	2001	145	636	37027	12906	14539	194	39	200
1985–6	255.0	510.0	2000	157	654	37135	17685	16575	240	60	250
1986–7	277.1	554.3	2000	246	715	29159	15599	15269	194	48	247
1987–8	150.6	280	1859	479	922	29701	13987	14592	186	37	200
1988–9	271.8	488	1795	400	990	35504	14181	15983	249	49	196
1989–90[2]	297.0	440	1481	250	962	34595	15069	17507	195	90	460
[4] 1990–1[2]	220.8	387	1753	275	1062	38645	17487	17544	203	81	394
1991–2[2]	302	658	2179	260	1020	39022	1366	14689	254	102	402
1992–3[2]	270	388	1437	313	819	—	—	—	256	103	402
Source	(2)	(1)	(1)	(1)	(2)	(2)	(2)	(2)	(1)	(1)	(1)

TABLE 1 (*cont.*):

	Pumpsets Energized	Total Wells	Elec to[5] AG (m units)	Rainfall	CPAIL (price deflator) (1960–61=100)
1982–3	4108	290506	530	693	515
1983–4	4210	302400	387	1365	518
1984–5	9967	301547	432	819	516
1985–6	4197	297669	504	1233	559
1986–7	7028	298697	548	709	603
1987–8	7464	302765	541	1062	664
1988–9	6609	303683	543	820	710
1989–90[2]	5216	303814	629	946	745
[4] 1990–1	5216	303862[3]	628	608[3]	851
1991–2	6000	303363[3]	605	1157[3]	1002
1992–3	5280	303832[3]	—	818[3]	1026
Source	(2)	(2) (3)	(2)	(2)	(3)

Notes on sources and data:

1 Arni regulated market records (unpublished Annual Report)

2 Tamil Nadu Economic Appraisals (various years)

3 TN Dept of Statistics, Tiruvannamalai office

4 From 1990–1 the data for Ambedkar and Tiruvannamalai

5 Elec to Ag for NADT is calculated from Table qty elec (in TN) to

$$\text{ag} \times \frac{\text{total energized pumpsets in NA}}{\text{total energized pumpsets in TN}}$$

TABLE 2 Paddy production by variety, village and season

a) Nesal

Village	Season	Measure	Newer: IR 38	IR 50	IR 39	ADT 39	Older: Ponni	IR 20	IR 36	ADT 36	HYVs Non Classified*	Total All Varieties
N	Samba	Row % of number of plots	7	63.3	5.6	—	5.6	—	12.7	—	5.6	100
		Average plot size (ha)	0.26	0.80	0.80	—	0.80	—	0.31	—	1.20	0.72
		Row % of operated land	2.5	70.1	6.3	—	6.3	—	5.5	—	9.4	100
		Average Yield per hectare	3577	4822	6033	—	4288	—	3240	—	2500	4441
E		Row % of total production	1.9	75.6	8.1	—	5.8	—	3.5	—	5	100
	Navarai	Row % of number of plots	—	38.6	—	—	4	4	32.2	21.1	—	100
		Average plot size (ha)	—	0.62	—	—	0.80	1.20	0.87	0.45	—	0.69
S		Row % of operated land	—	34.5	—	—	4.7	7	40.3	13.6	—	100
		Average Yield per hectare	—	4022	—	—	5128	4277	3776	6288	—	4573
		Row % of total production	—	42.6	—	—	6.5	8.1	19.4	23.3	—	100
	Sornavari	Row % of number of plots	—	63.8	—	3.8	—	—	19.1	4.9	6.4	100
		Average plot size (ha)	—	0.51	—	0.40	—	—	0.43	0.25	0.80	0.48
A		Row % of operated land	—	68.2	—	3.2	—	—	17.3	6.3	6.4	100
		Average Yield per hectare	—	3293	—	2610	—	—	4758	5267	6096	3841
		Row % of total production	—	62.9	—	2	—	—	19.3	6.3	9.5	100
	All seasons	Row % of number of plots	1.8	54.6	1.5	0.9	2.9	1.5	22.2	11.3	2.9	100
		Average plot size (ha)	0.26	0.62	0.80	0.40	0.80	1.20	0.64	0.38	1	0.62
L		Row % of operated land	0.8	55.1	1.9	0.9	3.8	2.8	23	6.9	4.7	100
		Average Yield per hectare	3577	3937	6033	2610	4708	4277	4078	5959	4298	4246
		Row % of total production	0.7	59.9	2.8	0.6	4.3	2.9	13.9	10.3	4.7	100

*Other: HYVs for which no variety was reported.

TABLE 1 (cont.):

b) Vinayagapuram

Village	Season	Metric	Newer				Older				HYVs Non Classified*	Total All Varieties
			IR 38	IR 50	IR 39	ADT 39	Ponni	IR 20	IR 36	ADT 36		
V I N A Y	Samba	Row % of number of plots	—	68.8	—	—	—	—	—	5.4	25.7	100
		Average plot size (ha)	—	0.50	—	—	—	—	—	0.30	0.42	0.47
		Row % of operated land	—	73.3	—	—	—	—	—	3.5	23.2	100
		Average Yield per hectare	—	3388	—	—	—	—	—	2260	2534	3107
		Row % of total production	—	73.7	—	—	—	—	—	3	23.3	100
A G A	Navarai	Row % of number of plots	—	50	—	—	17.3	—	10.8	8.8	13.1	100
		Average plot size (ha)	—	0.35	—	—	0.77	—	0.40	0.12	0.24	0.39
		Row % of operated land	—	44.6	—	—	33.8	—	11	2.7	7.9	100
		Average Yield per hectare	—	3592	—	—	3586	—	5625	6250	3467	4027
		Row % of total production	—	34.2	—	—	35.1	—	17.9	4.9	8	100
P U R	Sornavari	Row % of number of plots	—	69.1	—	—	—	—	26.3	4.6	—	100
		Average plot size (ha)	—	0.15	—	—	—	—	0.47	0.12	—	0.23
		Row % of operated land	—	43.6	—	—	—	—	54.1	2.4	—	100
		Average Yield per hectare	—	3221	—	—	—	—	5388	3208	—	3791
		Row % of total production	—	33.1	—	—	—	—	65.1	1.9	—	100
A A M	All seasons	Row % of number of plots	—	62.5	—	—	5.9	—	12.1	6.3	13.2	100
		Average plot size (ha)	—	0.33	—	—	0.77	—	0.45	0.17	0.36	0.37
		Row % of operated land	—	56.9	—	—	12.3	—	14.9	3	13	100
		Average Yield per hectare	—	3384	—	—	3586	—	5460	4363	2846	3637
		Row % of total production	—	47.9	—	—	13.6	—	23.7	3.4	11.3	100

*Other: HYVs for which no variety was reported.

TABLE 2 (cont.):

c) Veerasambanur

Village	Season		Newer				Older				HYVs Non Classified*	Total All Varieties
			IR 38	IR 50	IR 39	ADT 39	Ponni	IR 20	IR 36	ADT 36		
V		Row % of number of plots	—	56.5	—	13	17.5	—	—	—	13	100
E		Average plot size (ha)	—	0.47	—	0.93	0.16	—	—	—	0.86	0.53
E	Samba	Row % of operated land	—	50.4	—	22.9	5.3	—	—	—	21.3	100
		Average Yield per hectare	—	2691	—	3543	3281	—	—	—	3602	3023
R		Row % of total production	—	45.2	—	25.4	5.5	—	—	—	24	100
A		Average plot size (ha)	—	0.35	—	—	—	—	—	—	—	0.35
	Navarai	Row % of operated land	—	100	—	—	—	—	—	—	—	100
S		Average Yield per hectare	—	5074	—	—	—	—	—	—	—	5074
A		Row % of total production	—	100	—	—	—	—	—	—	—	100
		Row % of number of plots	—	40	—	—	—	—	—	—	60	100
M		Average plot size (ha)	—	0.19	—	—	—	—	—	—	0.39	0.31
B	Sornavari	Row % of operated land	—	24.4	—	—	—	—	—	—	75.6	100
A		Average Yield per hectare	—	3193	—	—	—	—	—	—	4958	3637
		Row % of total production	—	17	—	—	—	—	—	—	83	100
N		Row % of number of plots	—	62.8	—	5.9	7.9	—	—	—	23.5	100
		Average plot size (ha)	—	0.37	—	0.93	0.16	—	—	—	0.51	0.42
U	All	Row % of operated land	—	55.5	—	13	3	—	—	—	28.4	100
R	seasons	Average Yield per hectare	—	3753	—	3543	3281	—	—	—	4619	3907
		Row % of total production	—	52.5	—	12.2	2.6	—	—	—	32.6	100

*Other: HYVs for which no variety was reported.

TABLE 3 Agricultural production by village and season, 1993–4

		Nesal				Vinayagapuram				Veerasambanur				All Villages			
		Samba	Nava-rai	Sorna-vari	All Seasons	Samba	Nava-rai	Sorna-vari	All Seasons	Samba	Nava-rai	Sorna-vari	All Seasons	Samba	Nava-rai	Sorna-vari	All Seasons
% of ag. producers																	
Paddy producers		79	95	71	85	69	88	91	75	66	76	100	68	70	88	84	76
	obs	13	15	14	19	17	16	16	19	7	4	5	8	37	35	35	46
Groundnut producers		34	4	47	51	68	52	11	74	77	24		73	63	34	24	67
	obs	7	1	12	14	17	10	2	20	10	1		10	34	12	14	44
Other producers		4	16	3	16	4	15	8	11		24	27	11	0	17	9	13
	obs	1	4	1	6	1	4	2	4		1	1	1	1	9	4	11

Note: Column totals sum to more than 100 since farmers may produce more than one crop.

Source: 1993–4 field survey.

TABLE 4 Average holding size (ha) by village per landed household

		Village			
		Nesal	Vinaya-gapuram	Veera sambanur	All Villages
	no. of village households	339	259	136	734
	no. of landed households	131	180	85	396
	no. of landed households <=1ha	92	131	63	286
	no. of landed households >1ha	39	49	22	110
Total Land					
	households <=1ha	0.47	0.46	0.41	0.45
	households > 1ha	2.43	1.92	1.58	2.03
Wet					
	households <=1ha	0.15	0.11	0.15	0.13
	households >1ha	0.70	0.52	0.60	0.60
Punjai with wells					
	households <=1ha	0.21	0.18	0.12	0.18
	households >1ha	0.87	0.94	0.38	0.80
Dry					
	households <=1ha	0.11	0.17	0.14	0.14
	households >1ha	0.86	0.46	0.60	0.63

Irrigation: The Development of an Agro-Ecological Crisis

S JANAKARAJAN

1. INTRODUCTION

IRRIGATION has historically played a very important role in India's agriculture. The technology of gravity-flow irrigation in particular has been used from time immemorial. In the southern part of India, in such states as Tamil Nadu and Andhra Pradesh, the hot summer months followed by a vigorous monsoon season meant that farmers had to store surface run-off. 'Tanks' (reservoirs with an embankment on one side) were constructed for this purpose, connected to each other through channels called surplus courses, feeding water downstream to a tank below. Some tanks are also fed through rivers by means of *anicuts* (diversion channels) and canals. Tanks vary in size. Some irrigate a few thousand acres, while others feed less than ten. Farmers have also used gravity-flow irrigation by bringing spring water from rivers and mountains through open-cut canals some 5 to 7 km long. Tanks, springs and other traditional rainwater-harvesting systems were the only surface irrigation sources in South India until the advent of the post-Independence dams and canals. Tanks are still one of the main sources of irrigation in many parts of India.

According to the Minor Irrigation Census conducted by the Government of India in 1985, the total number of tanks in the country was estimated as 200,000 to 250,000 with a combined water spread area of 3 million hectares and a command area of 4.5 million hectares. Tanks being shallow reservoirs, the ratio of the area under submergence to the area irrigated tends to be high, in this case 0.66. In the state of Tamil Nadu, there are reported to be about 39,000 tanks, besides numerous spring channels originating from rivers. However, many of these tanks are in a state of decay, while others are defunct. Spring channels are in an even more pathetic state, as most have either been encroached upon and de facto privatized or their water supply has seized up completely. Over the past five or six decades, the net area irrigated under tanks has been declining steadily, whereas the area irrigated by open wells has been rising.[1]

The condition of tanks has been deteriorating for at least 150 years.[2] In 1947, Krishnaswami wrote:[3]

> There is a general consensus of opinion among officers who have dealt with the maintenance of minor irrigation works and among the intelligent lay public that there has been systematic deterioration, showing itself in the neglected conditions of the supply channel and unremitting silting up of the bed level of the water for the *ayacut* determined by the Tank Restoration Scheme party.

So the symptoms of the degeneration of tanks have been silt accumulation, encroachment in the catchment area, neglect of the supply channels and lack of incentives for the users of tanks to maintain tanks and channels and collectively to manage water. The main reason for these symptoms is groundwater irrigation. Private access to subterranean water has destroyed the incentives for collective action to maintain tanks.

A recent study of 15 tanks of the age-old Palar Anicut System in North Arcot District suggests that *it is the complex interaction of several institutional, technical and physical factors which have contributed to the decaying condition of the tanks,*[4] such as the rapid shift in the land ownership from Brahmins and other upper castes to the cultivating castes, the emergence of owner cultivation as the dominant mode of production and the development of groundwater as the most critical source of irrigation both in the tank commands and in the dry lands (which accompanied the introduction of the high-yielding biochemical technology for rice). In 6 of the 15 tanks studied, the traditional irrigation institutions were defunct. These were also the villages in which the density of wells was highest. In the seven villages in which the irrigation institutions were effective, well densities were found to be either much lower or else the tanks were in an advantageous position at the head of a canal system with an assured supply of water. So one of the most significant factors to affect the functioning of tanks has been the rapid growth of well irrigation.

Groundwater exploitation, however, has led to the secular lowering of the water table in several parts of the state.[5] Maddumma Bandara, geographer and hydrologist, another member of the 1973 survey team, concluded at that time that the expansion of groundwater irrigation had reached a stage in North Arcot District when any further development would have serious hydrological consequences:[6]

> ...Further expansion of lift irrigation may lead in the near future to unwelcome hydrological consequences such as lowering of water tables and dwindling

surface-water resources, unless suitable preventive measures are introduced in time. If the present trend continues, extraction of surface water may, before long, become a form of self-defeating 'agricultural mining'.

This analysis was based on rainfall patterns and their association with river-water flows as well as water table readings recorded from wells. Monthly rainfall data for 12 stations for the period from 1920 to 1974 was used to arrive at the important conclusions that the incidence of rainfall in North Arcot District has the characteristic of secular fluctuations; rainfall has a tendency towards 'persistent trends' in which declining or increasing trends have persisted for several years. These trends then correspond with the flow of water in rivers and tanks. However, when the flow of water in the Cheyyar River, measured at Uthiramerur for the period from 1958 to 1970, is related to rainfall over its catchment area for the corresponding period, an increasing gap between rainfall and flow of water is discovered. Since the period covered for this analysis was not long enough for a meaningful time series analysis, Maddumma Bandara was not very sure of the reason for the gap between rainfall and surface water flow. If the gap is real (and not random), it could occur either because of the overuse of water in the upper reaches, or because a larger proportion of the rainfall at the beginning of the rainy season replenishes the lowered ground water table, or both. One important point emerges from this analysis: a persistent declining trend in rainfall, under continuous drought conditions, will have a more damaging effect – both on the surface and the subsurface waters – for a more prolonged period than has been observed before. Furthermore, it was also clearly demonstrated that access to well irrigation was found to be the most essential condition for the adoption of the HYV technology.[7]

Given this hydro-ecological history, three aspects of water management will be updated in this chapter: the traditional tank irrigation system (sections 2 and 3); the extraction of groundwater (section 4); and the impact of irrigation on the agrarian economy of the study villages (section 5). The resurvey conducted during 1993–5 in three villages (Nesal, Vinayagapuram and Veerasambanur) in the present Tiruvannamalai District (the southern part of the previously undivided North Arcot District) had a special focus on water and its use. This is the source of information for this chapter.[8]

2. THE TRADITIONAL IRRIGATION SYSTEMS OF THE STUDY VILLAGES

Table 1 lists the traditional irrigation sources with their respective registered command areas in each village. Except in Veerasambanur, tanks are fed by the

TABLE 1 Traditional sources of irrigation in the selected villages[a]

Village	Name of the tank	Ayacut (acres)	Source of supply	Surplus goes to
Nesal[b]	Nesal big tank	100.00	Kamantala aaru	
Vinayagapuram	1. Peria Eri	69.03	Cheyyar river	Nariyam tank
	2. SK Thangal	10.37	Surplus from AK Thangal	Peria Eri
	3. AK Thangal	12.76	Cheyyar river	Peria Eri
	4. Spring Channel	76.64	Cheyyar river	Peria Eri
Veerasambanur	1. Peria Eri	74.01	Rain-fed	Not available
	2. Malavan Eri	36.05	Rain-fed	Not available
	3. Palayateri[c]	1.03	Rain-fed	Not available

Notes:

a) There is discrepancy in the *ayacut* details collected from various sources. *Ayacut* is the land below a tank irrigated from it.

b) Nesal revenue village has two other tanks which do not serve the Nesal hamlet.

c) Palayateri has now disappeared.

Source: Village records.

NB: 1 acre is 0.41 hectares

River Cheyyar. The agrarian economy of Veerasambanur is less developed than that of the other villages. However, the present condition of the tanks in all three villages is remarkably similar. There is clear evidence of the complete neglect not only of the tanks and the associated earthworks but also of the inlet channels (which are either encroached upon or completely silted up).

2.1 *Traditional Irrigation Institutions*

2.1.1 *History*

The irrigation institutions seem to have functioned effectively in all the villages until the early 1970s. There were two layers of irrigation functionaries, one to enforce the rules and the other to execute the work. While the high-caste landlords invariably constituted the first category, which is a high-status position, the scheduled-caste labourers were employed in rotation (from among selected families who had a right to such work) for the second type, which involved heavy manual work. The dignified managers of the system were generally known as *nattamai, maniyakkarar, oor gounder* or *kavaimaniayam* when solely designated to supervise the irrigation work. The irrigation workers were called *neerkatti, kammukutti* or *thotti*. These irrigation workers were paid in kind at the end of each season by the community of water users according to the area commanded under the tank. There are clear indications that, in the past, the irrigation institutions were quite effective in all three villages. Let us quickly go over the manner in which the critical functions of water management were organized.

2.1.2 *Maintenance*

In all the villages, there was a standard procedure to mobilize users of tank water: as soon as the upstream tank received water, the *maniyakkarar* announced this fact to the tank community by the beat of the *neerkatti*'s drum. He also announced the labour requirement for work. This was usually fixed on the basis of one person per acre or per *kani* (1 kani = 1.32 acres or 0.54 ha). Those who abstained from the work for whatever reason had to compensate for their labour either with a cash equivalent of a forfeited day's wage or by providing substitute labour. Those who failed to do both were fined.

In Vinayagapuram, where the spring channel was an important source of irrigation water, maintenance work was organized slightly differently. Although it passes through at least one other village upstream, the water in this spring channel is the exclusive right of this village. For 5 km, the channel runs beside and slightly below the bed of the Cheyyar River so as to tap the water seeping from the river. When the water started flowing in the river, the first work done by irrigation workers was to lie down in a line in the river bed so that sand built up against their bodies, making a diversion bund which facilitated the flow of water into the channel. The next day, a *neerkatti* announced through the beat of the drum at 6.00 a.m. that the *aathu kaalvai* (spring channel) work would begin that day. Then he departed to inspect the channel. At 9.00 a.m. another *neerkatti* would beat the drum for people to follow him and the *maniyakkarar*. Normally, the work obligation for a farmer with – say – 2.5 acres of land receiving irrigation water either directly from the channel or from the tank was to dig, broaden and deweed the 3-feet-channel (ca. 1 m) each day (himself or using a proxy worker). If a farmer had five acres of land, he would be required to undertake a 6-feet-length (ca. 2 m) channel each day and so on. In normal years, the work used to begin during the Tamil month of Avani (early August) and went on until Panguni (early April) every day except during the Pongal festival. The spring channel had its own direct irrigation *ayacut* as well as feeding that of the tank. Until the end of January, it fed the tank, after which it irrigated the *ayacut* directly. Users of water from both sources were required to join in maintenance work. Many Brahmin landowners and other well-to-do farmers used to hire *koottalis* (permanent labourers) specifically for this purpose.

On many occasions, the village had taken collective action to assert its rights over water. In the early 1950s, for instance, the spring channel was completely silted up with river sand after heavy flooding. The people of Vinayagapuram could not clear it unaided. In the upstream village (Konayur), through which the channel passes, people approached the *thasildar* to allow them to take over the channel. The people of Vinayagapuram were provoked to approach the government for funds (Rs 20,000) to desilt the channel and instal a permanent structure at the head to reduce silt flow. On another occasion, in the late 1960s, a major dispute was triggered between these villages when a farmer belonging to Konayur pilfered water from the channel. The people of Vinayagapuram caught the pilferer, tied him to a tree and beat him severely. The *eetram* equipment which he used for lifting water was seized and auctioned off. By way of retaliation, the infuriated people of Konayur beat five of Vinayagapuram's men: sufficient enough cause for police intervention. In order to meet the court expenses, even those who did not benefit from the channel water contributed liberally since the pride of the village was at stake. In the end, however, everything was patched up. As late as the 1960s, the entire responsibility for irrigation management was in the hands of Brahmin landlords. Their good rapport with government officials helped to secure the rights of the village on several occasions.[9]

2.1.3 *System of water sharing*

In all the villages, the opening and closure of sluices was dictated by the *maniyakkarar*. As a rule, the deepest sluice was opened for irrigation first. Only when the water level receded below the level of the deepest sluice were other sluices opened. When tanks were full, which was rare, no rotation of water rights was needed. More usually, the system of water allocation (*murai*) was based upon a rotation system in which the entire tank command area was broken into divisions and a ration of one hour's water supply per acre was allowed. Since the *maniyakkarar*'s land was always in the head reach under the deepest sluice, the rotation started with the segment of the *ayacut* in which the *maniyakkarar* possessed land. In the big tank of Nesal the *ayacut* was divided into 4 divisions,[10] in Vinayagapuram 18 and in Veerasambanur 4.

2.2 *Neerkattis/thotti (irrigation workers)*

The *neerkatti* has had a unique role in the traditional irrigation institution, critical for irrigation maintenance as well as for water sharing. His primary responsibilities were: to protect the inlet channel during the monsoon months; to guard against any breaches in the channel or pilferage of water; to watch the bunds and surplus weirs, in particular during floods; to open and close the sluices; to irrigate the plots of land in rotation, in particular during scarcity periods; and, above all, to organize cultivators for collective maintenance work. In some villages, such as Veerasambanur, the *neerkatti* also assisted in key agricultural operations as well as in community activities like drum-beating during marriages and village festivals.

In Nesal, the irrigation worker is called *thotti* and selected in rotation. His wages were paid in the form of *ari*, or 'paddy on the stalk', at the end of each harvest by the community of water users. The *thotti* in Nesal used to receive 12 *aris*, which is equivalent to about 20 kg per *kani* (1.32 acres). On average, the *thotti* used to collect about 18 to 20 bags of paddy at the time of the *samba* harvest (the major season) plus some groundnut harvested during the summer months. In Vinayagapuram, the wage payment was also 12 *aris* per *kani*, but this wage had to be shared between two *thottis*. However, since the area irrigated was larger in this village than in Nesal, each *thotti* used to collect at least 15 bags of paddy at the *samba* harvest, besides about 2 bags of groundnut each in the month of April.

The case of Veerasambanur differed from the other two villages as the responsibilities of the *thotti* were quite diverse and heavy. In addition to the irrigation-related operations, they also assisted farmers in certain agricultural operations such as uprooting the paddy nursery, distributing the paddy seedlings to various parts of the field, spreading the news of a death to other villages, disposal of dead animals, beating drums on all important occasions and so on. The wage payment was made in the form of *ari*, as in other villages, but there were three types. First, *kumbidu ari* was a payment made to him for all the menial and servile work: at the time of harvest, the *thotti* would go to the field, salute the landowner by bowing or prostrating and pick up a small bundle of paddy on the stalk which would be granted by the landowner. Second, *kani ari* constituted the major part of his payment and was paid for all the irrigation-related work. Third, *kani ari* was paid for assisting farmers with agricultural operations. Altogether, the *thotti* used to receive 12 *aris* per *kani* (16 kg of paddy) or a total of about 20 to 24 bags of paddy per annum.

On the whole, these irrigation institutions have now become history, but the manner in which they functioned illustrates the social relations of production as they existed. That the managers of the system had a vested interest in tank management is clear from the rules by which the tank water was shared. For instance, in Nesal, there seems to have existed a water-sharing system during times of scarcity. The entire land under the tank command was divided into four parts, each associated with a leading landowner. Each part was given a time-slot of water once every 24 hours in rotation. The biggest part was called the *maniyakkaran veettu vagayara* (meaning the *maniyakkarar's* close family circle). This family held all the good-quality land, having access to the *palla madagu* (the deepest sluice), and this part received water for 30 *nazhigai* or 12 hours. All the other three parts received water for 10 *nazhigai* (or 4 hours). John Harriss, in his account from 1973, notes that the *maniyakkaran veettu vagayara* was one of 10 parts of the tank command area which received water for 12 hours in rotation, once in 48 hours. Though the information about rotation varies over time, the fact remains that the managers of the system were the principal users of the tank water. Thus Harriss writes about Nesal:[11]

> Two channels lead from the central sluice (the deepest sluice) and they irrigate principally land which belongs to Agamudayans, whereas land belonging to Yadavas is irrigated from the secondary sluices. This surely reflects the Agamudayans' dominance of the village and their control of more than 60 percent of the village lands. Further, the major part of the land which is most favourable situated in relation to the main sluice belongs to the naattamaikarar viiTu.

2.3 *Traditional irrigation institutions: present status*

2.3.1 *Physical condition*

At present, irrigation institutions are more or less defunct, which is characteristic of the post-Green Revolution agrarian scene in many parts of Tamil Nadu. The system is reported to have functioned reasonably well until the early 1970s but failed afterwards. *The tanks and feeder channels in all the villages are completely silted up.* Absolutely no maintenance work has been carried out in Nesal and Veerasambanur during the past 20 years, except during the drought of 1982–3, when two weeks of desilting of the tank bed was carried out by the Public Works Department. In Vinayagapuram, however, unsuccessful efforts were made as late as 1990 to desilt the feeder channel. The regulatory structures are in a sad state in Nesal, while in the other two villages they are reasonably good. In all the villages, *the tank foreshore areas have been encroached upon.* In Veerasambanur, for instance, about 10 acres of tank foreshore area has been cultivated by a few farmers from the adjacent village for the past 20 years. The revenue authorities have apparently taken no action against them. The major distributaries from the sluices are also silted up and encroached upon. After 1970, in Nesal, there is no evidence of a full crop cultivated with tank water. In Veerasambanur, the tank last received water almost to capacity in 1989, after which it has remained dry. The picture is the same in Vinayagapuram, except that monsoon water flowing in the spring channel has kept the channel active until recent times. In all three tanks, however, some water is stored during the monsoon months (though water levels are well below the sluices). *At least tanks provide drinking water to cattle.*

2.3.2 *Status of the irrigation organizations*

The traditional organizations for irrigation-related operations have either disappeared (as in Nesal and Veerasambanur) or remain inactive. In Nesal, there is no evidence of the existence of any irrigation official. Even the last *oor maniyak-karar* who managed the system 25 years ago (who is still alive) has lost interest in the tank. In Vinayagapuram, the *kavai maniyam* and *nattamaikarar* exist but are inactive and not respected as they were in the past. The existing *kavai maniyam* (who has held the post since 1980) is unable to mobilize cultivators for channel maintenance work. The irrigation organization in Vinayagapuram (which until the 1960s remained very powerful under Brahmin landlords) is too weak to prevent clashes in the village and the *kavai maniyam* has been taken to task for swindling public money. In 1991, the *kavai maniyam*-cum-*nattamai* took a unilateral decision to fell a tree in the middle of the village to construct a Panchayat building, in the fall-out from which he was comprehensively humiliated and factions were intensified. In Veerasambanur, as in Nesal, the *nattamai* is powerless and has no role to play in water management.

However, the lowest-grade irrigation functionaries, *neerkatti/thotti*, continue to exist and to receive customary payments. Certain key operations – drum-beating on occasions such as village festivals, death ceremonies and so on, removing dead animals, providing a courier service to other villages on occasions such as death etc. – are still performed by the *thotti*. However, the customary payments to this village worker have been considerably reduced. While in Nesal the *neerkatti* collects hardly 2 *aris* per *kani* or a total of 2 bags of paddy per annum (during the *samba* season), in Vinayagapuram and Veerasamabanur the *neerkattis* receive better payments. In Vinayagapuram the two *neerkattis* together collect about eight bags of paddy per annum, while in Veerasambanur the *thotti* receives about ten bags.

3. REASONS FOR THE DECAY OF TRADITIONAL IRRIGATION INSTITUTIONS

A detailed study of 15 other tanks in the undivided North Arcot District has revealed the reasons for the disintegration of the traditional irrigation institutions.[12] The first consists of changes in land ownership from the upper castes to the lower castes. This has also resulted in the emergence of owner cultivation as the primary mode of cultivation. When the upper-caste landlords such as Brahmins and Mudaliars were the dominant landowners, they operated land principally by means of share-cropping tenancy, which gave them access to the labour of their tenants for operations such as tank maintenance and so on. These landlords played a crucial role in enforcing tank maintenance and providing leadership, for the simple reason that they had the largest stake in the tank water. After the changes in the land-ownership pattern, which triggered changes in the mode of cultivation (particularly the casualization of labour, crop technology and the lack of authority of those who purchased the land), the traditional irrigation institutions broke down.

The second factor is the widespread use of groundwater irrigation and the rising density of wells in the tank command area. In the three villages of the resurvey, we do not have much evidence to suggest that changes in the land-ownership pattern have contributed to the decline of the system, except in Vinayagapuram, where the village was predominantly in the hands of Brahmin landlords until the 1960s. Field notes for Vinayagapuram written in 1973–4 by Robert Chambers and John Harriss recorded that ten big Brahmin land-owning families had left the village in 1950, and many more Brahmin landlords were leaving the village in the 1970s. Even as late as 1982–3, Brahmin families held about one fifth of the prime wetlands under the tank command, and 5 of the 18 shares of the tank water and the fishery rights were still in the names of Brahmin landlords. In the other two villages, Agamudaya Mudaliars remain the major landowners, although in recent times Yadavas in Nesal and Vanniars (gounders) in Veerasambanur have purchased considerable amounts of land.

However, in all three villages, groundwater extraction has grown rapidly. In Nesal, as early as 1973, John Harriss found an association between the rapid spread of mechanized lift irrigation and the declining fortunes of the tank irrigation system. He wrote:[13]

> . . . we have seen that although well irrigation has long been 'traditional' in Randam [his pseudonym for Nesal], it has undergone a substantial expansion in the last fifteen years; and the agricultural system of the village is now heavily dependent upon it. The question that arises as to whether the supply of water in the tank was more reliable in the past, and further whether its present unreliability might be due in some way to expanded exploitation of groundwater, or to a failure of local or official organisation. . .

Elsewhere, he emphasizes the utter lack of interest and non-cooperation in tank management of the large landowners whose lands have better access to groundwater irrigation. To quote:[14]

> . . . the tank is of slight importance in village agriculture today, however, the fact that five of the richest farmers in the village own lands which are mainly well-irrigated and are remote from the tank, compared with only two from the group of 'magnates' whose lands lie near the main sluice, shows how groundwater irrigation has now reduced the importance of control of tank water.

The spurt in mechanized lift irrigation should not be viewed as an isolated event. If we look at statistics for the number of wells for the North Arcot District, there is a sharp rise in the mid 1960s, which was the period of the introduction of HYV technology – a precondition for which was a reliable, assured and controllable source of irrigation. Moreover, tank water was adequate for only one crop, whereas the HYV seeds had the potential for three short-duration crops. In addition to that, the application of HYV technology presupposes the timely availability of water, so that chemical inputs could be applied with precision. Moreover, it was around this time that most of the villages in North Arcot District were electrified. So a combination of all these factors facilitated the rapid growth of well irrigation. The expansion of lift irrigation on such a massive scale reduced the collective interest in tank maintenance.

4. THE GROUNDWATER STATUS OF THE STUDY VILLAGES

Table 2, showing wells in the study village since 1973, confirms a tremendous expansion of lift irrigation after the introduction of HYV technology. Nesal witnessed the most rapid increase in the number of wells, registering a 78 per cent rise over the period of the past two decades. While Veerasambanur registered an increase of 39 per cent, Vinayagapuram registered a modest increase of 15 per cent since 1973. Similarly, the density of wells in the respective villages shows an increase of 0.11 wells per acre in 1973 to 0.19 in 1993 in Nesal; of 0.17 to 0.23 in Veerasambanur; and of 0.17 to 0.19 in Vinayagapuram.

While Nesal has virtually given up on tank irrigation, in the other two villages tank irrigation was active until recently – in particular in Vinayagapuram, where the spring channel was yielding a reasonably good water supply until the

TABLE 2   Number of wells in the villages, 1973–93

Particulars/Year		Villages		
		Nesal	Vinayagapuram	Veerasambanur
Number of wells				
	1973	73(100)	124 (100)	89 (100)
	1993	130 (100)	142(115)	124 (139)
Wells per acre[a]				
	1973	0.11	0.17	0.17
	1993	0.19	0.19	0.23
Wells not in use[b]				
	1973	NA	NA	NA
	1993	28	25	32

Notes:
a) Well density is calculated for the total area under wet and dry land in each village.
b) 'Wells not in use' are those which have not been used for irrigation in the last five years.

Source: Ramasamy *et. al.* 1991. and survey, 1993–4.

1980s. Table 2 shows that while, in the 1970s, the farmers of these villages were drawing water for irrigation from conventional surface sources, these villages are now completely dependent upon lift irrigation. The density of wells is so high that there is one well for each five acres of combined wet and dry lands. The incidence of abandoned wells in the 1993 survey is quite high: 26 per cent in Veerasambanur, 21 per cent in Nesal and 18 per cent in Vinayagapuram. Although we do not have a comparative picture of the wells not in use in 1973, there is every reason to believe that wells were increasingly abandoned from 1973 to 1993.[15] There is no comparative data with which to examine this issue. Nevertheless, in 1993–4 we conducted a (random) sample study of one sixth of the total wells (covering wells located both in wet and dry lands) in the three villages to quantify the decline of the water table. Two simple questions were posed to all the sample well owners: i) what was the original depth of the well at the time the well was first dug? ii) what is the current depth of the well? The answers have been tabulated and are presented in Tables 3 to 5 separately for each village.

It is evident that *the gap between the original and the current depths is quite significant*, more so in the dry-land wells than in wells located in the wetland. From Table 3 for Nesal, at least one sample well in the wetland and five in the dry land were originally in the shallowest depth band (of less than 20 feet – ca. 6 m), whereas by 1993 no wetland wells and four dry-land wells were so shallow. All these shallow wells have been abandoned. In the higher depth ranges, wells have

TABLE 3 Distribution of the wells in Nesal by depth, 1995

Depth Range (feet)	WET				DRY			
	Original Depth		Current Depth		Original Depth		Current Depth	
	No. of Wells	%	No. of Wells	%	No. of Wells	%	No. of Wells	%
<20	1	12.5	0		5	33.4	4	26.7
20–30	3	37.5	1	12.5	6	40	0	
30–40	1	12.5	2	25	1	6.7	2	13.3
40–50	2	25	2	25	2	13.3	3	20
50–60	0		1	12.5	1	6.7	2	13.3
60–70	1	12.5	0		0		0	
70+	0		2	25	0		4	26.7
TOTAL	8	100	8	100	15	100	15	100
Av. Depth in Feet		34.8		45.2		27.2		56.5

Notes: The four dry-land wells recorded in the <20 feet current depth range are disused.

Source: Survey, 1993–5.

been deepened. The picture is the same in the other two villages (see Tables 4 and 5). In all the villages, *the difference between the wet and dry-land wells is quite significant*, which indicates that the water table is falling much faster under the dry land than under the wetland. A similar picture has been obtained in other

TABLE 4 Distribution of the wells in Vinayagapuram by depth, 1995

Depth Range (feet)	WET				DRY			
	Original Depth		Current Depth		Original Depth		Current Depth	
	No. of Wells	%	No. of Wells	%	No. of Wells	%	No. of Wells	%
<20	6	60	0	0	8	61.6	0	0
20–30	4	40	0	0	5	38.5	0	0
30–40	0	0	0	60	0	0	4	30.8
40–50	0	0	4	40	0	0	5	38.5
50–60	0	0	0	0	0	0	4	30.8
60–70	0	0	0	0	0	0	0	0
70+	0	0	0	0	0	0	0	0
Total	10	100	10	100	13	100	13	100
Av. Depth in Feet		17.1		38.9		18.8		45.4

Source: Survey, 1993–5.

TABLE 5 Distribution of the wells in Veerasambanur by depth, 1995

Depth Range (feet)	WET				DRY			
	Original Depth		Current Depth		Original Depth		Current Depth	
	No. of Wells	%	No. of Wells	%	No. of Wells	%	No. of Wells	%
<20	6	75	0	0	9	75	3	25
20–30	2	25	1	12.5	2	16.7	1	8.3
30–40	0	0	2	25	1	8.3	1	8.3
40–50	0	0	2	25	0	0	3	25
50–60	0	0	3	37.5	0	0	3	25
60–70	0	0	0	0	0	0	1	8.3
70+	0	0	0	0	0	0	0	0
Total	8	0	8	0	12	100	12	100
Av. Depth in Feet		16.1		42.9		17.6		46.9

Notes: The three dry land wells recorded in the <20 feet current depth range are disused.

Source: Survey, 1993–5.

hard-rock regions in Tamil Nadu.[16] The average original and current depths of the sample wells, however, are the most crucial information, clearly pointing to a secular lowering of the water table. For instance, in Nesal village, the average original depth of the sample wells in the wetland was 34.8 feet (10.6 m), but for the same set of sample wells the average current depth is 45.2 feet (13.77 m). *In the dry land, the difference between the average original and the current depths is more than double.* In the other two villages, both in the wet and the dry-land wells, the difference between the average original and the current depths is even more striking and significant.

The rate at which the water table has fallen is found in Table 6. While the water table is deepest in Nesal, the rate at which it has been falling is highest in Veerasambanur, followed by Vinayagapuram.

Nevertheless, comparison of the original and the current depths of wells dug before 1975 throws up much more striking results. Of the total of 23 sample wells in Nesal, 23 in Vinayagapuram and 20 in Veerasambanur, 18, 16 and 17 respectively were dug before 1975. Of those wells which were dug before 1975 however, 7, 2 and 4 wells have been completely abandoned owing to low or non-existent water yields. Table 7 pertains to those wells which were dug before 1975 and those which continue to yield water to this day. The table clearly shows that there has been a competitive deepening of wells, resulting in the secular lowering of the water table. The rate at which groundwater is extracted seems much more than the rate of subsurface replenishment by way of infiltration.

TABLE 6 Extent of decline in the water table (in feet)

Village	Wet		Dry	
	AOD[A]	ACD[B]	AOD	ACD
Nesal	34.8	45.2	27.2	56.5
	(100)[c]	(129)	(100)	(211)
Vinayagapuram	17.1	38.9	18.8	45.4
	(100)	(229)	(100)	(237)
Veerasambanur	16.1	42.9	17.6	46.9
	(100)	(269)	(100)	(261)

Notes:

(A) AOD refers to the average original depth–average of the sample wells.

(B) COD refers to the average current depth.

(C) Figures in brackets denote the percentage variation between the average original and the current depths.

Source: Survey, 1993–5.

5. THE IMPACT OF THE SECULAR LOWERING OF THE WATER TABLE ON THE AGRARIAN ECONOMY

The impact of the competitive deepening of the wells and the progressive lowering of the water table can be broadly identified under the following three heads: i) the effect on agriculture; ii) the costs involved; and iii) the institutional implications.

5.1 *Effect on agriculture*

The yield of paddy reflects the impact of the falling water table conditions on agriculture. In 1973, it was 2.66 tonnes per hectare, but it includes more than 50 per cent of the area cultivated under the traditional varieties whose yield – at 2.5 tonnes – was considerably less than the yield of HYVs at 3.56 tonnes. In 1993, however, the area under HYVs was almost 100 per cent. Therefore, a simple comparison of the HYV yield in 1993 (which was 3.88 tonnes) shows that yields have increased by only 8 per cent. The yields of paddy in the three villages may be compared in Table 8. The yield in Nesal is highest (4.2 tonnes) followed by Vinayagapuram (3.1 tonnes) and Veerasambanur (3 tonnes). Such yields corroborate the general irrigation scenario and in particular the steeper decline of the groundwater table in Veerasambanur.[17] Comparison of the area irrigated by the sample wells when originally dug and the area irrigated in 1993 also indicates a high incidence of wells irrigating a reduced area.

TABLE 7 The average original and the current depths of the sample wells which were dug before 1975

Village	Wet			Dry		
	No. of wells	AOD[A]	ACD[B]	No. of wells	AOD	ACD
Nesal	6	32.5 (100)[c]	47.3 (146)	5	31.8 (100)	56 (176)
V'Puram	8	19.5 (100)	46.9 (241)	6	15 (100)	47.7 (318)
V'sambanur	6	14 (100)	44.5 (318)	7	14.3 (100)	43.7 (306)

Notes:
[A] AOD refers to the average original depth–average of the sample wells;
[B] COD refers to the average current depth;
[c] Figures in brackets denote the percentage variation between the average original and the current depths.

Source: Survey, 1993–5

TABLE 8 Yield of paddy in the study villages, 1993–4
(in kilograms per hectare)

Village	Season		
Nesal	4278	samba	3388
Vinayagapuram	3111	navarai	4326
Veerasambanur	3023	sornavari	3953
Weighted av. yield			3881

Source: Survey, 1993–4.

The development of non-farm employment in silk weaving is yet another important change, which is the direct off-shoot of distress in agriculture caused by the combination of factors such as the continuous falling of the water table and the persistent drought conditions of the 1980s.[18] Although the art of silk weaving is considered to be the occupation of a particular group of castes, in recent times many agricultural castes such as Agamudaya Mudaliars, Vanniars and Yadavas have also entered the field. From our census, weaving has been reported to be the main occupation of 8 per cent (63 people in Nesal), 16 per cent (106 people in Vinayagapuram) and 9 per cent (26 people in Veerasambanur). Since 1993, the number of weavers appears to have gone up considerably. Practically none had reported weaving as the main occupation in earlier surveys. Weaving provides a buffer during times of agrarian crisis.[19] The agrarian crisis in the state generally, and in the study villages in particular, has been caused by the persistent drought conditions of the 1980s:

> The obverse of this phenomenon, viz., the possibility that weaving provides the buffer in a period of agrarian crisis – points to an important dimension of the agriculture – weaving linkages, viz., the role played by agrarian distress – of agrarian differentiation more generally – in the emergence and growth of silk weaving in and around Arni. Our village survey revealed that the overwhelming proportion of weavers who had some links with agriculture were from the poorer strata of the peasantry. This points to the possibility that agrarian distress would have played a role in the shift to silk weaving made by these households. Our general enquires in the village revealed that this indeed was the case, particularly in the first half of the eighties. While a spell of bad monsoons in the early eighties was the proximate factor behind the distress in agriculture – and hence the shift to weaving – the longer term of process of agrarian differentiation appears to have played a major role here.[20]

5.2 *Cost implications*

The competitive deepening resulting in the progressive lowering of the water table has enormous implications for costs, not only for individual farmers but for society as a whole. First, consider the social costs involved. Future generations are badly affected as there exists a danger of complete loss of access to groundwater due to over-pumping and to the increasing mismatch between the rate of water extraction and recharge. Moreover, over-pumping may cause underground sea water intrusion in coastal areas, a fate already looming over the southern coastal regions of Tamil Nadu. Most important of all is the rising unit cost of water pumped to the surface. Another major social cost incurred by society is expenditure on energy generation and distribution for agricultural purposes. In the state of Tamil Nadu, the electricity consumed per electrified pump set has gone up from 2,501 units in 1980–81 to 3,897 units in the year 1992–3 (a rise of 56 per cent over a period of 12 years). This cost is entirely born by the state, in other words by taxpayers.

The cost incurred by an individual well owner is ever rising in real terms. The investment in well-digging, in the construction of pump-set sheds, the installation of pump sets, pipelines, further improvements to the wells, such as deepening, installing vertical and horizontal bores and so on, is all on the increase. In recent times, considerable investment has gone into laying pipelines, a technique which the farmers are forced to adopt to preserve wastage from seeping and evaporation. In Vinayagapuram, 12 farmers had invested in pipelines. Elsewhere, hose pipes are mostly used for water conveyance. This is a phenomenon of the 1990s. Although we have not investigated the costs of the various components of well irrigation as incurred by an individual well owner, research elsewhere in Tamil Nadu shows that it exceeds the per unit area of surface irrigation by major and medium irrigation schemes.[21] According to the *Report of the Working Group on Major and Medium Irrigation Programme for the Eighth Plan*, Government of India (1989), the amount spent per acre of irrigation potential created during the Seventh Plan (1985–90) is Rs 14,700 (Rs 36,240 per hectare), whereas according to the study on wells conducted in the Vaigai Basin it is Rs 32,600 per acre or Rs 80,000 per hectare of net area irrigated. *Private well irrigation is about two and a quarter times more costly per unit area than is surface irrigation.* If we also add the costs incurred on failed wells the multiple would increase. According to Nagaraj *et al.* (1994), the probability of well failure is 0.4 in the hard-rock zones such as those of our study region.

5.3 *Institutional implications*

The process of differentiation is the most important institutional implication. Available evidence suggests that differentiation is intensified by competitive well-deepening and the secular lowering of the water table. As more and more resource-poor well owners are excluded from the race of competitive deepening, a few emerge to monopolize the precious groundwater. The conditions of such resource-poor well owners is precarious. The process of differentiation is accelerated by competition for water in at least two ways. First, a significant number of producers have lost access to land through debt due to their expenditure on wells. We have recorded a good number of cases of those who have lost their land – either fully or in major part – as a result of heavy investments in wells. Second, many of those who failed in the race of competitive deepening resort to the purchase of water at high rates. They also enter into complex contracts mediated by both price and non-price means. The nexus between water sellers and water purchasers and the manner in which the water market is interlocked with the labour and product markets has been documented by Janakarajan.[22] Apart from charging a price for the water supplied, there are two other measures used to extract surplus: i) by commanding the underpaid and unpaid labour services of water purchasers; and ii) by compelling water purchasers to lease out their parcels of land in favour of water sellers on arbitrary terms (the case of 'reverse tenancy'). Some have been forced to sell tiny parcels of land. The incidence of reverse tenancy and forced sale is significant in Vinayagapuram and Veerasambanur.

The consequences of the secular lowering of the water table and of the competitive deepening for a given well owner depend at least partly on the emergence of non-farm employment mediated by agrarian distress. The escalating cost of wells, however, was the most striking proximate impact. The process of differentiation is accelerated due to the ever rising investment in wells.

6. SUMMARY AND CONCLUSIONS

This paper traces the development of an agro-ecological crisis in the agrarian economies of three villages over two decades. Though 1973 (the year of the first survey) has been kept as a reference period for the sake of comparison, we have traced the events as far back as possible. The present status of the traditional irrigation institutions (tanks and springs) is discouraging, as they are in disuse or decay in all the villages. It is the complex interaction of several technical, socio-economic and institutional factors which is responsible for the disintegration of the traditional irrigation institutions. The introduction of HYV technology and the concomitant spread of well irrigation are the two crucial factors contributing to the decay of traditional irrigation sources.

The massive spread of mechanized private lift irrigation over the past two decades has to a great extent been facilitated by the electrification of the villages, and though it contributed significantly to agricultural production, it has had adverse impacts on the lowering of the water table. As a consequence, there have been escalating investments in wells, increasing social costs and depressed returns to agriculture. The combined effect of all these events has accelerated differentiation in these villages.

ACKNOWLEDGEMENTS

I am indebted to respondents in the villages who generously gave their time whenever we wanted. The insights we obtained from the village irrigation workers were remarkable. This paper is indebted in great measure to the untiring efforts of the project assistants, namely Mr G Jothi, Mr S Mariasusai and Dr S Ramachandran. My sincere thanks to all of them.

Time and Space: Intervillage Variation in the North Arcot Region and its Dynamics, 1973–95

M V SRINIVASAN

1. INTRODUCTION

PLANNING based on aggregate data at the national or regional level frequently conceals important lower-level variations and underplays the complex relationships among a multitude of social, economic and political factors.[1] The factors of development identified at the macro level are of hardly any use in initiating economic change in smaller spatial units such as villages or groups of villages.[2]

The specific conditions of individual villages will determine how development policies are implemented. Understanding the reasons for variation among villages helps us to know more about critical variables in rural development[3] – something that is of particular importance in the context of decentralization of powers through *panchayati raj* (local government) institutions.

Yet no specific theory that explains change in the *village* economy has been developed for India. The village was for years seen by many economists – erroneously, as it turned out – as a closed subsistence economy. More recently, it has been analysed as a unit for the exercise of power: the power of social norms and the power of the propertied class over labour, and even sometimes the power of labour over property.[4] This power is mediated by information and threats and expressed in contracts and transactions at rates and prices varying drastically from village to village, such that the spatial integration of agrarian markets becomes something which cannot be assumed to exist.[5] Village class structure needs to be examined, not just for an understanding of agricultural policy but also as an analytical category in order to understand economic behaviour. Though there is an abundance of micro-level data from village-level studies, higher-order statements about the developmental experience of villages is notable for its absence.[6] The major limitation of existing attempts to generalize is their inadequate theorization of dynamics.[7] Yet theorizing change in the rural economy through descriptive modelling could serve as a basis for planning the development of villages.

The longitudinal study reported here sprang from a need to trace the impact of the 'green revolution' in South Asia. Eleven villages[8] were selected by stratified random sampling according to two criteria: (a) villages with populations ranging from 50 to 5,000; and (b) locations in *non*-hilly and *non*-reserved forest (RF) areas.[9] Between 1993 and 1995, the 11 villages were house-listed and subjected to a detailed census which is used here. In this chapter we look critically at existing village typologies and justify this fresh enquiry. We then explore the methodological problems generated by it. This section is followed by an analysis of changes in the study region: in demography, agriculture, employment and wages. The final section attempts a classification of villages using factor analysis and cluster analysis and makes a move towards theorizing intervillage variation.

2. VILLAGE TYPOLOGIES: A REVIEW

Several attempts have been made to systematize the classification of villages.[10] In the first survey conducted in 1973 it was found that continuity in the production process, particularly in agriculture, was the key factor accounting for inter-village variation (IVV) in development.[11] Villages with better-quality irrigation had continuous production, supported an increase in population and met a higher demand for labour with higher wage rates.

Two types of factors, causative and derivative, were identified as responsible for inter-village variation. The former included location, resources in relation to population and the nature of the production process. The latter comprised demographic trends, farming practices, aspects of labour relations and wages. Based on a classification according to such factors, the villages were grouped into three sets: (a) 'quasi-industrial' villages (Kalpattu, Nesal, Vinayagapuram and Vegamangalam) which showed symptoms of labour shortages, high or modest wage rates and semi-permanent contracts; (b) 'seasonally expanding' villages (Duli and Meppathurai) with modest wages, few regular labourers and continuous labour shortages; and (c) 'seasonal production process' villages (Sirungathur, Veerasambanur, Vengodu, Vayalur and Amudur) where there were strong surpluses of labour, low wage rates, few perquisites and little opportunity for regular labour contracts.

The classification was based solely on agricultural jobs. Non-agricultural jobs, which were developing slowly, were not included. Social institutions (such as caste and gender) and their influence on the village economy and rural labour markets were peripheral to the classification. The connections between the quality of irrigation infrastructure, the continuity of demand for labour, levels of wages and the incidence of semipermanent labour contracts were the analytical focus.

In the first resurvey in 1982–4, John Harriss tried to improve this classification. He identified the emergence of segmented labour markets owing their existence to the development of labour relations in non-farm employment as a major factor in causing intervillage variation. Harriss classified the villages on the basis of irrigation facilities, availability of employment and prevailing wage rates (see Table 1).[12]

Harriss stressed that growth linkages from agriculture were responsible for the spread of non-farm employment opportunities into the rural economy. Entry into non-farm employment was limited by discrimination against depressed classes (particularly scheduled-caste households, which were forced to remain in the villages with agriculture as their mainstay. The production of silk sarees, a newly growing market-oriented commodity, was closed to the depressed classes.

Though it was an improvement over the first typology, Harriss did not explain why there could be radical intervillage variation in the relation between labour use in agriculture and non-agriculture, in the casualization of labour and in wages. Moreover, as in the previous survey, he stressed some variables and neglected others – such as demographic factors. There was no systematic enquiry taking into account a multiplicity of factors or one using statistical tools.

Biplab Dasgupta had earlier made such an effort using larger sets of variables to identify variations in the types of village.[13] He analysed data collected from 126 villages by various agro-economic research centres between 1954 and 1961. Using principal component analysis and discriminant analysis, he classified the

TABLE 1 Intervillage variation [12]

Villages	Irrigation	Wage rates	Use of Labour (employment)
Nesal & Vegamangalam	Good	High	Low
Kalpattu, Meppathurai	Good	Relatively high	High
Vinayagapuram	Good	Low	High
Veerasambanur, Amudur & Meppathurai	Poor	Low	High
Vengodu, Sirungattur & Amudur	Poor	Low	Low
Vayalur & Duli	Poor	High	Low

villages into two types. Type A are advanced or modern villages and Type B are the obverse. Some villages, belonging to neither category or having characteristics of both, were classified as Type AB villages. One of the limitations of Dasgupta's study was the exclusive emphasis on variables relating to employment. Both the early village typologies, based on simple classification, and those using advanced statistical tools excluded institutional factors now known to be significant for development. Rising to the challenges caused by the different objectives of previous attempts, we faced major problems with data and method.

3. METHODOLOGICAL PROBLEMS IN THE CURRENT STUDY

The first problem concerned the boundary defining a village. Though the previous surveys used the census list of villages as the sampling frame for the study, they did not adhere strictly to the definition of a census village. More often, they used the village as a social unit[14], which in many cases differed from the boundaries of the census village. So we decided to adhere strictly to the revenue administration boundary of the villages, which is also comparable with census boundaries. This enabled us to include all the households within the boundary of the revenue village in our census listing. In other words, we have considered the socio-economic conditions of those households residing within the revenue boundary of the respective villages regardless of the location of their assets, both agricultural and non-agricultural. This means that comparison of change over the years is very difficult. For instance, by 1993–4 in some villages (Sirungathur and Meppathurai),[15] the extent of absentee landownership was very high, up to 40–50 per cent of the total land holdings. By contrast, in other villages (Vegamangalam, Vayalur and Duli), many households owned lands outside the revenue village.

For three villages (Nesal, Vinayagapuram and Veerasambanur), wages were studied in detail. For the remaining villages, the wage data were collected by recall from agricultural labourers and well-informed farmers.

We also use official census data for the study villages. Using the duration of work, the Census of India classifies workers into two groups: main workers and marginal workers. The 1991 Census defined a main worker as 'one who has worked for the major part of the year (183 days or more)'. Those who worked for less than 183 days were considered marginal workers (consistent with definitions in the 1981 Census). The 'main workers' of 1981 and 1991 may not be consistent with definitions for previous decades. Though data for main and marginal workers could in theory be combined, the occupational distributions of marginal workers are not available at the village level.

The next problem concerns categories. The 1981 Census divided the main workers into four categories: cultivators, agricultural labourers, household industry and a catch-all category of 'other workers', which includes main workers in animal husbandry and plantation, mining and quarrying, non-household industry and service, construction, trade and commerce, transport, storage and communication and other services. Censuses prior to and after 1981 provide a nine-category data of workers, including those in services. For 1981, such data is available for districts alone. For this reason, a comparison of nine categories of workers is not possible for all the three census years, 1971, 1981 and 1991. This restricted our analyses to three categories.

The 1991 census data on the villages of Kalpattu, Vayalur and Veerasambanur provided us with such exorbitantly high or low figures that they raise suspicion about the official census data. Only for two years, 1971 and 1981, can the data be compared across all the villages. Similarly, the official census data on literacy in 1981 for Vengodu seem anomalous. Due to such problems, we were unable to do a complete analysis of census data for all 11 villages over the years.

4. DEMOGRAPHIC TRENDS

Generally, it appears that the population in our sample villages grew slowly in the first decade, 1973–83, and faster in the second decade, 1983–93. When population grew slowly, it was at lower rates than the state and national trend, and when it grew faster, its rate was higher than the state and national trend (see Table 2). The average size of the sample villages increased from 895 in 1973 and 959 in 1983 to 1,195 in 1995. Census figures for our villages in 1971, 1981 and 1991 are not only higher than those from our surveys, but their growth trends are also quite the opposite of those from our surveys.

According to the latter in 1973–83, Meppathurai was growing very rapidly, followed by Duli and Vengodu (Table 2). During this decade, Kalpattu had a negative growth rate of 0.94 per cent. In the second decade, however, Veerasambanur was the only village where the population showed a negative growth rate (−0.56 per cent). Two villages, Sirungattur and Nesal, showed positive but declining trends. The other villages increased their population. Kalpattu, in particular, had an extraordinarily high growth of 5.25 per cent in this period, followed by Duli and Vinayagapuram. Over two decades, Duli was the fastest growing village, followed by Meppathurai, Kalpattu and Vinayagapuram. Villages like Vegamangalam and Amudur were stagnating or showed sluggish growth. It is difficult to explain the wide variation between growth trends of sample villages from the official census data and from our surveys.

What could be the reasons for the growing population? Can field observation explain these changes and identify factors causing or hindering growth? Our

TABLE 2 Population from survey and census

Village	Survey			Census			Survey			Annual Growth Census		
	1973	1983	1995	1971	1981	1991	73–83	83–95	73–95	71–81	81–91	71–91
Amudur	942	986	1165	934	1121	1255	0.47	1.51	1.04	2	1.20	1.60
Duli	456	538	824	450	617	726	1.80	4.43	3.23	3.71	1.77	2.74
Kalpattu	1537	1393	2271	1942	2228	na	-0.94	5.25	2.44	1.47	na	na
Meppathurai	551	747	932	583	784	913	3.56	2.06	2.74	3.45	1.65	2.55
Nesal	1388	1487	1551	3155	3701	3920	0.71	0.36	0.52	1.73	0.59	1.16
Sirungathur	948	1049	1303	813	1172	1392	1.07	2.02	1.58	4.42	1.88	3.15
Vayalur	639	692	810	672	739	na	0.83	1.42	1.15	1	na	na
Veerasambanur	565	620	578	540	560	na	0.97	-0.56	0.13	0.37	na	na
Vegamangalam	1023	1062	1167	1028	1214	1311	0.38	0.82	0.62	1.81	0.80	1.30
Vengodu	1046	1165	1396	1061	1274	1364	1.14	1.65	1.42	2.01	0.71	1.36
Vinayagapuram	750	814	1153	784	846	1254	0.85	3.47	2.28	0.79	4.82	2.81
Average*	895	959	1195	1101	1341	1517	0.72	2.05	1.44	2.49	1.68	2.08
INDIA(Rural)										1.93	2	
Tamil Nadu(Rural)										1.30	1.33	

Note=*-Average of 8 villages for census data and 11 villages for survey data.

Source: District Primary Census Abstract, Census of India for years 1971, 1981 and 1991, Houselisting Survey, 1995, and J Harriss 1991b.

experience in the villages suggests the following comments on the trends in population growth.

4.1 *In-migration*

This is one of the major reasons for the expansion of the populations of Kalpattu and Duli. By 1995, new hamlets had been founded in both villages. Kalpattu is located on the flank of the hills bounding the region. A nearby village, Keelarasampattu, is developing as an agricultural market place. A few years ago, homeless wage labourers in Keelarasampattu squatted on government land in Kalpattu and so formed a hamlet. A similar process has enlarged Duli, located near Cheyyar. Carpenters and other artisan families from surrounding villages who had lost their jobs migrated to Duli's new hamlet, where they eke out their livelihoods.

4.2 *Human development*

According to the official census, literacy increased from 26.3 per cent (11 villages) in 1971 to 35.3 per cent (11 villages) in 1981 and 43.2 per cent (8 villages) in 1991 (see Table 3). The growth was even throughout both decades. *Surprisingly, literacy rates have grown much faster for females than for males.*

In the period in which we conducted our resurvey (1993–5), literacy rates were higher than the census figures for the year 1991. Among the villages, Vegamangalam (71.9), Duli (63.2), Kalpattu (60.7) and Vayalur had literacy rates much

TABLE 3 Decadel growth of literacy rates by sex and village, 1971–91

Village	71–81			81–91			71–91		
	male	*female*	*total*	*male*	*female*	*total*	*male*	*female*	*total*
Amudur	0.62	65.91	14.61	8.79	40.69	21.08	9.47	133.41	38.77
Duli	50.66	103.91	61.81	−14.80	32.63	−4.18	35.77	158.05	57.02
Kalpattu	80.44	236.82	108.93						
Meppathurai	44.19	78.93	53.84	−1.25	16.10	1.86	42.93	105.64	55.97
Nesal	18.20	96.55	33.58	24.83	83.43	42.56	43.19	234.96	82.36
Sirungathur	38.08	25.79	38.50	39.74	125.42	65.40	78.07	233.86	113.46
Vayalur	5.53	99.81	22.49						
Veerasambanur	6.72	142.56	27.51						
Vegamangalam	30.08	154.78	57.20	2.95	2.41	2.31	33.04	158.77	59.84
Vengodu	−43.29	−77.56	−53.45	87.14	174.49	113.18	44.38	211.93	76.26
Vinayagapuram	42.34	97.96	54.31	−0.40	111.64	29.50	41.93	283.18	88.12
Average	22.61	68.28	32.55	18.37	73.35	33.96	41.10	189.97	71.47

Source: District Primary Census Abstract, Census of India for years 1971, 1981 and 1991.

higher than the region's average of 56.8 per cent. Generally, male literacy exceeded its female counterpart by about 50 per cent. The highest gender differences were found in Vinayagapuram (where male literacy exceeded female literacy by 84.4 per cent) and Veerasambanur (82.6 per cent). The lowest gender differences were found in Vegamangalam[16] (34.8 per cent) and Vayalur (37.9 per cent). Similar data are not available for previous surveys.

When we correlated literacy with the sex ratio (SR), fertility and infant mortality rates (IMR) for all the villages, we found some interesting trends (see Tables 4 and 5). *Villages with high IMR tend to have relatively low levels of literacy and highly male-biased sex ratios.* Variations in the village-level child sex ratios (under six years) are closely associated with literacy in both genders, infant mortality and fertility. *Where girls are being culled, IMR is relatively high, fertility is high and literacy is low.* Although no generalization outside this region is warranted from these results, the correlations confirm the findings of others. Sabu George and colleagues (1992), in their study of 12 villages in western North Arcot District, found that in 6 villages female infanticide was practised, a major cause of the decline in the sex ratio. These villages were generally remote and poorly supplied with education. Moreover, female infanticide was widely practised by Vanniars, an upwardly mobile agricultural caste (though classified by the state as 'Most Backward'). Another study using 1991 census data found a positive relation between literacy and the sex ratio.[17] By using data from the sample registration and census for the 1980s and 1990s, Basu (1999) concludes that gender inequality has been increasing in the southern states of India, particularly in Tamil Nadu, with its lead in lower fertility. Though she argued that increasing female infanticide results in such a trend, elsewhere in India sex-selective abortion is practised, and in many of the villages we took for our case study the mechanism of culling is neglect in health care during infancy and childhood (see Chapter 3–2).

5. VARIATION IN AGRICULTURE

Earlier studies examined the impact of the Green Revolution on the agrarian economy and used aspects of the agricultural economy to classify the villages. Chambers and Harriss (1977) observed change in the following factors: (i) the scale neutrality of the area under high-yielding varieties (HYV) among various classes of farmer (which was increasing); (ii) crop diversification; (iii) the extent of exploitation of groundwater for irrigation purposes; (iv) the impact of high-yielding varieties; and (v) trends in non-farm employment.

TABLE 4 Other demographic trends in NA District

Village	Sex Ratio (census)			Survey (1995)			Literacy Rates (1995)			Differences (in %)
	1971	1981	1991	Sex Ratio	Fertility Ratio	IMR	Male	Female	Total	
Amudur	1066	1053	910	879	40.65	45.45	64.68	40.73	53.48	−58.78
Duli	860	910	1000	957	17.54	—	75.30	50.62	63.23	−48.75
Kalpattu	925	944	na	908	50.66	80.0	72.02	48.29	60.72	−49.14
Meppathurai	937	908	968	902	76.92	176.47	64.08	42.53	53.86	−50.66
Nesal	994	1029	1019	1030	na	na	65.18	44.98	54.93	−44.91
Sirungathur	1007	921	902	928	29.3	214.29	62.87	42.26	52.95	−48.75
Vayalur	965	1070	na	929	22.47	—	68.57	49.74	59.51	−37.85
Veerasambanur	1045	1162	na	1035	na	na	68.31	37.41	52.60	−82.57
Vegamangalam	1000	955	977	1009	26.02	615.38	82.62	61.26	71.89	−34.86
Vengodu	875	951	1003	969	32.05	235.29	60.23	39.30	49.93	−53.24
Vinayagapuram	912	927	987	974	n.a.	na	66.10	35.85	51.17	−84.36
Average	956	957	971	956	36.95	170.86	68.03	45.11	56.75	−50.80

Notes: Nation and State sex ratios estimated for the census year 1991.
Averages estimated for the villages for which data is available.

Source: District Primary Census Abstract for years 1971, 1981 and 1991 and Houselisting survey, 1995.

TABLE 5 Correlation matrix of some demographic variables in the study villages

Variables	Sex Ratio	<6 Sex Ratio	Fertility Rate	Male Literacy	Female Literacy	Infant Mortality Rate	Total popu- lation
Sex Ratio	1						
<6 Sex Ratio	0.084	1					
Fertility Rate	−0.555	−0.500	1				
Male Literacy	0.238	0.457	−0.351	1			
Female Literacy	0.052	0.541	−0.384	0.846	1		
Infant Mortality	0.702	0.317	−0.045	0.427	0.484	1	
Total population	−0.208	−0.096	0.249	−0.037	0.092	0.058	1

Note: The number of cases (villages) is 11 for all variables but fertility rate and infant mortality rates. The details of these variables for three villages are not included in the correlation.

5.1 *Trends in agrarian class composition*

The North Arcot region was originally selected for its high proportion of small farmers. By 1993–5 we find: (a) an increase in the proportion of landless labourers, accompanied by increasing members of absentee landowners and a decline in tenancies; and (b) an increase in non-agricultural employment (see Table 6) (developed by Jayaraj in Chapter 1–6 here). *But neither trend is visible at the level of the household*, when it is classified by the main source of income and ownership of assets. Both proletarianization and economic diversification are processes that take shape inside households, through individual members, as components of the household's income stream.

In 1993–5, landless *households* accounted for 38 per cent of households in the region. They had been 36 per cent in 1973. However, there are dramatic IVV in trends in landlessness. For instance, while in 1973 in Vinayagapuram 16 per cent of total households were landless agricultural labourers, they were 37.23 per cent in 1993–5. Amudur increased its share of landless households from 24 to 37 per cent. However, in four villages (Vendogu, Vegamangalam, Veerasambanur and Kalpattu), the proportion of landless households was reduced over time.

The proportion of non-cultivating owners increased from 1.6 per cent in 1973 to 3 per cent in 1993–5. Amudur and Nesal had about 5 per cent of households in this category. In Sirungathur no such households were found.[18] Owing to the absence of village land data on tenancy from previous surveys, we can make no conclusions about historical trends. Though we will analyse the changing dynamics of non-farm employment in the study region later, we note here that households depending on non-agriculture as their main source of income increased from 9.6 per cent in 1973 to 15.85 per cent in 1993–5.

Since 1973 farming households have been classified into two categories: (a)

TABLE 6 Composition of households in the study villages, 1995

Village	Total House-holds	Farmer Households (in %)				Others		Landless hhds (in %)		difference (in %)	% of small farmers
		Owner Culti-vators	Non-culti-vating owners	Tenant Culti-vators	Total Far-mers	Agri. Lab. Hhds	Rest	1973	1993-5		
Amudhur	246	54.47	5.28	3.25	63.01	24.80	12.20	24	36.99	54.13	65
Duli	161	62.73	1.86	0.62	65.22	9.94	24.84	28	34.78	24.22	41
Kalpattu	507	56.41	2.56	2.76	61.74	25.05	13.21	40	38.26	-4.34	78
Meppathurai	189	63.49	1.59	0.53	65.61	24.34	10.05	27	34.39	27.38	46
Nesal	346	34.39	4.91	3.18	42.49	39.31	18.21	48	57.51	19.82	68
Sirungathur	263	50.19		0.76	50.95	23.57	25.48	37	49.05	32.57	80
Vayalur	165	48.48	3.03	6.67	58.18	21.21	20.61	34	41.82	22.99	64
Veerasambanur	262	67.18	2.67	0.38	70.23	20.23	9.54	33	29.77	-9.78	71
Vegamangalam	246	63.41	4.07	3.25	70.73	19.51	9.76	35	29.27	-16.38	66
Vengodu	290	66.55	1.38	3.45	71.38	12.76	15.86	45	28.62	-36.40	58
Vinayagapuram	137	59.12	3.65		62.77	22.63	14.60	16	37.23	132.66	71
All Villages 1993-5	2812	56.95	2.82	2.26	62.03	22.12	15.85		37.23	132.66	64
All Villages 1973		62.30	1.6	3.5	63.90	23	9.60	36.10			

Sources: House listing Survey, 1993–5; Farmer (ed.) 1977.

TABLE 7 Details about land holdings by villages (in percentages)

Village	Total Holdings (in acres)	Within the village	Outside the village	No. of Land-owning Hhds.	Average Farm Size	Percentage of	
						Big Farmers	Small Farmers
Amudhur	369.27	78.88	21.12	147	2.51	34.69	65.31
Duli	413.07	73.78	26.22	104	3.97	58.65	41.35
Kalpattu	580.43	89.39	10.61	304	1.91	22.04	77.96
Meppathurai	417.2	98.92	1.08	123	2.91	54.47	45.53
Nesal	437.96	83.21	16.79	136	3.24	31.62	68.38
Sirungathur	257.35	97.56	2.44	133	1.93	24.06	75.94
Vayalur	227.5	72.70	27.30	87	2.61	35.63	64.37
Veerasambanur	158.25	96.90	3.10	86	1.84	29.07	70.93
Vegamangalam	425.18	70.42	29.58	161	2.63	34.16	65.84
Vengodu	560.04	93.15	6.85	198	2.82	42.42	57.58
Vinayagapuram	395.74	96.34	3.66	183	2.16	28.96	71.04
Total	4182.19			1662			
Average (1993)	385.64	86.48	13.52	151.09	2.52	35.98	64.02
(1973)						48.00	52.00
(1982)						42.00	58.00

Sources: (a) Village Administrative Officers of the respective villages.
(b) Houselisting survey.

small farmers – those who own less than one hectare (or 2.47 acres); and (b) big farmers – those who own more than one hectare.[19] Despite the crudity of such a classification, we have followed it in order to trace the changes over the years. Table 7 shows that there has been an increase in the proportion of small farmers from 52 per cent in 1973 to 58 per cent in 1982, and further to 64 per cent in 1993–5. Except for Duli (41.35 per cent), Meppathurai (45.53 per cent) and Vengodu (57.58 per cent), the villages have always had a proportion of small farmers that was higher than the region's average. Small farmers account for more than three quarters of the farm households in Kalpattu and Sirungathur. *The distribution of ownership of land is increasingly unequal.* Small farmers (64 per cent of households) owned only 29 per cent of the total lands in the study region. Against this, large farmers who account for 36 per cent of total households owned 71 per cent of the total lands. Land ownership was most unequal in Nesal, Sirungathur and Vegamangalam (see Table 6). While the average land-holding size was 2.52 acres in 1993–5, Duli and Nesal had average holdings of 3.97 and 3.24 acres respectively. Average land holdings were lowest in Kalpattu, Sirungathur and Veerasambanur.

5.2 Cropping intensities

There are two types of indicator of cropping intensity. The first is normal crop-ping intensity (NCI), defined as the proportion of total area under various crops to total operational holdings. The higher the NCI, the more intensively the land is being cultivated. However, one of the limitations of this method is that it gives equal weights to all crops – irrespective of how many seasons they take to produce. So sugar cane, a one-year crop, is given equal weight to ground-nut, which needs a maximum of five months. In order to overcome this problem we estimated adjusted cropping intensity (ACI), defined as the proportion of total area under all crops (area under long-term crops times 2 or 3 + area under other crops) to total operational holdings. Among the villages, the average NCI was 117 per cent. Vegamangalam had a higher NCI (see Table 8); Meppathurai had the lowest (79 per cent), followed by Sirungathur. Using the ACI, we ob-served that the cropping intensity improved from 117 to 142. Except for Duli, *all the villages have improved their cropping intensities.* In Duli, farmers cannot cul-tivate long-term crops such as sugar cane owing to the unsuitable quality of the soil. The difference between the two cropping intensities exposed a set of vil-lages (Kalpattu, Nesal and Vegamangalam) in which long-term crops are now cultivated. The prosperity of agriculture can also be seen in the variation of

TABLE 8 Details of cropping intensities

Village	Total Opera-tional Hold-ings	Gross Cropped Area	Crop-ping Inten-sity (normal)	Area Under Long-Term crops	Adjusted GCA	Crop-ping Intensity (adjusted)	Inten-sity Vari-ation (in%)
Amudhur	361.64	629.91	1.74	182.97	751.89	2.08	19.36
Duli	407.73	454.96	1.12	0	454.96	1.12	0
Kalpattu	600.41	622.23	1.04	628.44	1041.19	1.73	67.33
Meppathurai	355.12	280.92	0.79	64.56	323.96	0.91	15.32
Nesal	423.63	447.25	1.06	196.20	578.05	1.36	29.25
Sirungathur	288.48	251.35	0.87	61.35	292.25	1.01	16.27
Vayalur	216.52	234.26	1.08	61.98	275.58	1.27	17.64
Veerasambanur	160.19	181.71	1.13	58.80	220.91	1.38	21.57
Vegamangalam	388.12	632.15	1.63	307.62	837.23	2.16	32.44
Vengodu	598.94	668.75	1.12	155.55	772.45	1.29	15.51
Vinayagapuram	386.22	502.46	1.30	27	520.46	1.35	3.58
Average	380.64	446	1.17	158.59	6068.93	1.42	21.66

Note: All the holdings and areas are measured in acres.

Source: Houselisting Survey.

cropping intensity according to the two definitions (Table 8). Using a formula of simple growth rates, the difference between ACI and NCI in percentage terms is (ACI-NCI)/NCI* 100. Kalpattu, Nesal and Vegamangalam are the villages in which the difference in measures greatly exceeds the average of 21.66 per cent. Kalpattu's is 67.33 per cent and Vegamangalam's 32.44 per cent. Kalpattu is surrounded by hills collecting rain that recharge the groundwater table, so that farmers are able to cultivate over the entire agricultural year. As a result of the construction of a large overhead tank to supply water to Kancheepuram (the town near Vegamangalam village), the natural spring which supplied water to this village in the 1970s and 1980s now dries up frequently. Previously, it used to get water for irrigation for 9–10 months a year. While paddy was cultivated three times a year earlier, now a single crop is grown. There are no groundwater resources in the village and the terrain below is impermeable. When multiple cropping stopped being possible, land where water was available was purchased outside the village for the cultivation of perennial and annual crops. Nearly 30 per cent of the land owned by Vegamangalam farmers is outside the village (see Table 7).

5.3 *Irrigation intensity*

The cropping intensity is determined by the irrigation potential of the area. Changes in irrigation infrastructure underlie changes in the agricultural economy. The irrigation infrastructure has stagnated over the years (see Table 9). The ten-year growth rate of the number of wells (in use) fell from 8.4 per cent in 1973–83 to 1.34 per cent in 1983–93. The growth of electrified pump sets also declined in similar fashion.[20] In 1973–83, the absolute number of wells increased in all villages but Amudur and Sirungathur. During this earlier period, Duli and Nesal trebled their wells.

In 1983–95, in four villages (Duli, Nesal, Sirungathur and Veerasambanur), growth had become negative. *Many wells have been abandoned.* The irrigation intensity defined as the proportion of total area irrigated to total cropped area tells us about IVV in the intensity of current irrigation sources. It reveals that Vegamangalam, Meppathurai and Amudur have a high irrigation potential with around 90 per cent of the gross cropped area irrigated. Kalpattu and Vayalur had an intensity of around 80 per cent.

5.4 *Cropping pattern*

Paddy remains the predominant crop, covering 47.01 per cent of the total cropped area in the region on average (see Table 10). It was 74.24 per cent in

TABLE 9 Trends in irrigation infrastructure in NA District

Village	1974		1982–3		1993–5		Growth rate			
							Pumpsets		Wells	
	Pump-sets	Wells	Pump-sets	Wells	Pump-sets	Wells	73–83	83–95	73–83	83–95
Amudhur	56	90	59	86	86	114	0.67	3.81	–4.44	3.26
Duli	9	12	23	38	27	28	19.44	1.45	216.67	–2.63
Kalpattu	116	173	124	194	85	232	0.86	–2.62	12.14	1.96
Meppathurai	57	148	69	159	156	219	2.63	10.51	7.43	3.77
Nesal	63	73	161	227	N.A.	130	19.44	N.A.	210.96	–4.27
Sirungathur	51	130	75	98	79	83	5.88	0.44	–24.62	–1.53
Vayalur	34	85	37	87	39	99	1.10	0.45	2.35	1.38
Veerasambanur	38	89	41	130	N.A.	124	0.99	N.A.	46.07	–0.46
Vegamangalam	38	45	60	69	65	83	7.24	0.69	53.33	2.03
Vengodu	39	80	75	134	N.A.	N.A.	11.54	N.A.	67.50	N.A.
Vinayagapuram	26	124	73	109	N.A.	142	22.60	N.A.	–12.10	3.03
Average	48	95	72	121	77	125	8.40	1.34	52.30	0.65

Sources: Houselisting Survey, 1993–5, Farmer (ed.) 1977.

TABLE 10 Cropping pattern in the study villages (area in acres)

Village	Total Cropped Area	Paddy	Groundnut	Sugarcane	Others
Amudhur	629.91	74.24	15.45	9.68	0.63
Duli	454.96	39.74	51.43	0	8.84
Kalpattu	622.23	31.81	21.79	3.40	42.53
Meppathurai	280.92	58.72	20.44	15.32	5.52
Nesal	894.5	46.19	37.18	7.31	9.32
Sirungathur	251.35	35.29	47.12	8.14	8.27
Vayalur	234.26	36.75	35.19	8.82	19.24
Veerasambanur	363.42	50.36	43.19	5.39	1.06
Vegamangalam	632.15	54.67	27.82	16.22	1.39
Vengodu	668.75	46.88	34.69	15.51	2.92
Vinayagapuram	1004.92	42.48	49.65	0.90	6.98
Total	6037.37	2868.29	2213.81	466.52	575.81
Average	548.85	47.01	36.23	8.24	9.70

Source: Houselisting survey.

Amudur, 58.72 per cent in Meppathurai and 50.36 per cent in Veerasambanur, while it was considerably lower in Kalpattu (31.81 per cent) and Vayalur (36.75 per cent), where non-staple commercial crops are cultivated. The former is a dry-land village where there is insufficient water and the latter is an irrigation-rich village where a particular variety of cotton suited for both dry-land and wetland farming is being cultivated. By contrast, plantain, turmeric and Indian kale (yam) are commercial crops that were cultivated in Kalpattu from as early as 1973. The second major crop in the region, groundnut, is cultivated mostly on unirrigated lands. In Duli and Vinayagapuram nearly half the total cropped area is put to groundnut. Sugar cane, recently introduced in the region, occupies third place. It is cultivated mainly in three villages – Vegamangalam, Vengodu and Meppathurai. The first two villages sell cane to new sugar mills nearby, whereas Meppathurai, which does not have surfaced road facilities, is prevented from milling sugar. Instead, farmers manufacture *jaggery* and export it to Andhra Pradesh, where it is used in the rural distillation of arrack liquor.

5.5 *Employment patterns*

Earlier studies found that the use of high-yielding varieties (HYVs) of paddy had increased employment in the study region on a seasonal basis – during harvesting and threshing. Among the conclusions for policy were widening the irrigation potential and bringing more land under cultivation.[21] However, the development of non-farm employment has changed the set of livelihood possibilities in nearby towns and distant cities (particularly Chennai/Madras and Bangalore). These non-farm jobs have not benefited all castes. *The labour markets in nearby urban areas where non-farm jobs are available and expanding are highly segmented and discriminate particularly against scheduled castes and women* (see chapters 1–5 and 1–6).

Over the years, the proportion of households engaged in agricultural labour has fluctuated. It was 21.8 per cent of the total population in 1973; it increased to 23.77 per cent in 1983 and then declined to 18.71 per cent in 1993–5 (see Table 11). In Amudur, the proportion of agricultural labourers was highest. *Agricultural wage work appears to be a highly unstable process.* Other villages have seen fluctuations and have changed their rankings considerably. For instance, Vinayagapuram employed the lowest proportion of agricultural labourers in 1973. It suddenly jumped to second rank in 1983 and then again declined to fifth position. In Nesal and Veerasambanur, the proportion of households working as agricultural labourers has declined over the years. In some villages this increased in the first decade and declined in the second decade (Amudur, Duli, Vegamangalam and Vinayagapuram) or vice versa (Kalpattu and Vayalur). Meppathurai was the only village where the proportion of agricultural labourers grew positively but with a declining rate.

TABLE 11 Agricultural labourers by village, 1973–95

Village	Work Participation			% of Agr. Labourers		% Change (Annual)		
	1971	1981	1991	1973	1983	1994	1973–83	1983–95
Amudhur	28.91	48.17	51.08	29.20	36	22.20	2.33	−3.19
Duli	56.67	72.29	60.47	19.80	25.50	11.40	2.88	−4.61
Kalpattu	33.42	44.25	na	19.40	16.70	21.30	−1.39	2.30
Meppathurai	43.22	42.60	51.15	16.20	17.10	19.50	0.56	1.17
Nesal	45.51	44.44	49.15	25.60	25.30	17.10	−0.12	−2.70
Sirungathur	28.04	52.22	46.98	18.90	29.60	21.50	5.66	−2.28
Vayalur	32.89	58.86	na	26	15.60	18.30	−4	1.44
Veerasambanur	55.74	60.54	na	28	21.10	18.50	−2.46	−1.03
Vegamangalam	46.60	48.02	40.27	21.10	23.20	18.90	1	−1.54
Vengodu	39.30	60.52	36	20.40	20.20	17.90	−0.10	−0.95
Vinayagapuram	59.95	32.27	42.26	15.20	31.20	19.20	10.53	−3.21
Average*	43.53	50.07	47.17	21.80	23.77	18.71	1.35	−1.33

Note: * 8 villages for census data (1971, 1981 and 1991) and 11 villages for our surveys.

Source: District Primary Census Abstracts for various years and Houselisting Survey.

Due to differences in the methodology of classification, the official census revealed a different picture (Table 12). The proportion of agricultural labourers was increasing as that of direct producers declined, and non-farm employment hardly rose. Non-farm employment stagnated at 10 per cent in 1971 and 1981, increasing to 18 per cent in 1991. Vinayagapuram, with only 3.83 per cent of non-farm jobs in 1971, increased its share to 39.25 per cent in 1991. The development of artisan work – silk saree weaving and related activities – was responsible for the trend. Other villages (Nesal, Vayalur, Vegamangalam and Vengodu) have been industrialized. However, due to inconsistencies in data availability, we found it difficult to come to any definite conclusion, except on the two following points: (a) *agricultural livelihoods have been transformed progressively into wage labour* on farm and in non-farm jobs; and (b) *the growth of non-farm employment has profoundly affected the rural economy.*

Changes in the agricultural labour force may be the product of diversification to less labour-intensive crops. Amudur has the highest cropped area under paddy, which may be the reason for the higher proportion of the labour force in agriculture. Here, male agricultural labourers also get seasonal employment in the sugar-cane fields, migrating to Andhra Pradesh every October/November and returning in June/July. In the case of Kalpattu, commercial crops are grown more extensively both on a long-term and a short-term basis, requiring a continuous supply of labour. Our house-listing survey did not allow us to probe further into the issues, except in the three villages taken for detailed study.[22]

By 1993–5, while villages far removed from urban centres (such as Amudur, Kalpattu, Vegamangalam, Vengodu and Meppathurai) have less than one fifth of their total workforce in non-farm jobs (Tables 13 and 14), more than one third in all the other villages worked outside agriculture. Silk saree weaving has arrived at Sirungathur, Duli, Amudur, Meppathurai, Veerasambanur, Vinayagapuram and Nesal. Employment in Duli, Nesal, Sirungattur[23] and Vayalur includes a considerable proportion in trade and services, owing to their proximity to towns. Other linkages to agriculture also play a considerable role in employment generation. For instance, animal husbandry gave employment to 11 per cent of the workforce in Nesal (in milk cooperatives and other related activities).

With regard to gender differences in the workforce distribution, the proportion of women in employment was 29.5 per cent in Amudur, 30.7 per cent in Vegamangalam and 24.4 per cent in Vayalur (see Table 14). Female participation was lowest in Vinayagapuram and Veerasambanur. The proportion of women in agriculture (as labourers) exceeds that of men everywhere.

TABLE 12 Distribution of workers in North Arcot, 1971–91

Village	1971					1981					1991				
	Total Workers	Culti-vators	Agri-cultural La-boureres	House-hold Indus-try	Non-House-hold, other indus-tries, & ser-vices	Total Workers	Culti-vators	Agri-cultural La-boureres	House-hold Indus-try	Non-House-hold, other indus-tries, & ser-vices	Total Workers	Culti-vators	Agri-cultural La-boureres	House-hold Indus-try	Non-House-hold, other indus-tries, & ser-vices
Amudhur	270	58.15	37.41	0	4.44	540	30.56	59.26	0.56	9.63	641	36.19	54.76	0.94	8.11
Duli	255	90.98	5.10	0.39	3.53	446	29.82	67.26	0.22	2.69	439	25.28	72.21	1.14	1.37
Kalpattu	649	62.25	25.58	4.01	8.17	986	61.87	31.54	0.51	6.09					
Meppathurai	252	39.68	48.41	0.40	11.51	278	49.28	47.84	0	2.88	467	77.09	14.56	1.28	7.07
Nesal	1474	34.96	40.94	2.14	21.96	1705	37.64	35.50	5.46	21.40	1840	22.58	46.32	8.92	22.18
Sirungathur	228	79.82	11.84	2.63	5.70	394	39.59	49.75	3.81	6.85	566	33.57	50.35	0.71	15.37
Vayalur	221	58.82	33.03	0	8.14	269	60.22	25.65	6.69	7.43					
Veerasambanur	301	54.49	43.85	0.33	1.33	328	27.44	70.43	0	2.13	517	17.60	65.18	4.84	12.38
Vegamangalam	479	33.19	60.54	3.34	2.92	232	37.07	48.28	0	14.66					
Vengodu	417	50.12	32.61	7.43	9.83	703	59.03	36.56	0	4.41	491	39.31	40.33	5.50	14.87
Vinayagapuram	470	80.85	14.26	0.43	3.40	273	73.26	12.82	6.59	7.33	530	27.55	33.21	24.53	14.72
Average		54.86	33.50	1.95	9.61		44.70	42.76	2.67	9.87					
Eight Villages	480.6	58.47	31.39	2.09	7.91	571	44.53	44.66	2.08	8.73	686	34.90	47.11	5.98	12.01

Source: District Primary Census Abstract, Census of India for years 1971, 1981 and 1991.

TABLE 13 Distribution of workforce by sex and major industrial categories, 1993–5

Village	Total	Culti- vators	Agrl. Lb.	Ani-. mal Hus- bandry	Indus- try	Ser- vice	Others	% of Non- farm	% Ser- vices
Amudhur	484	27.27	53.51	4.96	2.07	4.96	7.23	14.26	12.19
Duli	422	44.31	22.27	2.84	7.58	9.95	13.03	30.57	22.99
Kalpattu	1306	41.88	37.06	2.30	0.84	3.29	14.62	18.76	17.92
Meppathurai	453	41.72	40.18	5.08	1.32	3.97	7.73	13.02	11.70
Nesal	776	21.39	34.15	11.21	13.79	7.47	11.98	33.25	19.46
Sirungathur	657	19.48	42.62	3.04	8.98	6.85	19.48	35.31	26.33
Vayalur	418	28.23	35.41	5.98	3.83	7.42	19.14	30.38	26.56
Veerasambanur	302	32.78	35.43	3.64	12.58	8.28	7.28	28.15	15.56
Vegamangalam	528	33.52	41.67	3.79	2.46	3.41	14.39	20.27	17.80
Vengodu	754	43.63	33.16	3.98	2.65	7.03	9.55	19.23	16.58
Vinayagapuram	689	35.12	32.08	4.21	18.72	3.63	6.24	28.59	9.87
Average		33.58	37.05	4.64	6.80	6.02	11.88	24.71	17.90
INDIA(1991)		48.15	32.17	1.96	6.27	5.53	5.92	17.72	11.45
TAMILNADU(1991)		32.76	44.73	1.86	8.64	6.09	5.92	20.65	12.01
INDIA(1981)		50.95	30.09	2.37	6.95	4.91	4.73	16.59	9.64
TAMILNADU(1981)		38.28	40.27	2.44	9.00	5.7	4.31	19.01	10.01

Sources: Houselisting Survey.
Primary Census Abstract for the years 1981 and 1991, Govt of India.

5.6 Trends in Wages and Earnings

In the early 1970s, the introduction of HYVs in North Arcot villages increased employment, which also widened income inequality. The income of cultivators of HYVs increased by 75 per cent over producers of traditional varieties, whereas that of agricultural labourers increased by only 33 per cent. Moreover, this employment was not sufficient to absorb the total underemployment in the area.[24] However, it was optimistically predicted that better irrigation endowments would lead to more intensive cultivation, generate a higher and more continuous demand for labour and thereby higher wage rates. Nevertheless John Harriss found in 1983 that labour markets were not strictly market-driven, as hypothesized earlier, but were instead significantly influenced by institutional factors, notably caste. He argued that one vector of IVV involved wages and labour use.[25]

In 1993–5, *wages prevailing in the study villages were far from homogeneous for all operations* (see Table 15). For instance, although an agricultural labourer ploughing a farmer's land and providing labour services alone was paid Rs 10 per day, if he went with plough and bullocks he got Rs 30 per day in Duli, Rs 25 in Vegamangalam and Rs 50 in Kalpattu. The agricultural labourer does not always need equipment to earn a reasonable wage. In the harvesting and threshing of paddy, for example, the labourer works with her bare hands.

TABLE 14 Distribution of workers by major classification and sex (in %), 1995

Village	Category	Culti- vators	Ag. Labour	Animal Hus- bandry	Agri- culture	Indus- try	Services	Others	Total (in %)
AMUDUR	Male	41.16	38.91	4.18	84.24	1.29	6.75	7.72	64.26
	Female	2.31	79.77	6.36	88.44	3.47	1.73	6.36	35.74
	Total	27.27	53.51	4.96	85.74	2.07	4.96	7.23	100
DULI	Male	47.22	6.75	1.59	55.56	10.71	15.08	18.65	59.72
	Female	40	45.29	4.71	90	2.94	2.35	4.71	40.28
	Total	44.31	22.27	2.84	69.43	7.58	9.95	13.03	100
KALPATTU	Male	43.09	24.45	2.76	70.30	0.97	4.70	24.03	55.44
	Female	40.38	52.75	1.72	94.85	0.69	1.55	2.92	44.56
	Total	41.88	37.06	2.30	81.24	0.84	3.29	14.62	100
MEPPATHURAI	Male	48.08	28.08	6.54	82.69	1.92	5.77	9.62	57.40
	Female	33.16	56.48	3.11	92.75	0.52	1.55	5.18	42.60
	Total	41.72	40.18	5.08	86.98	1.32	3.97	7.73	100
NESAL	Male	23.85	21.44	9.85	55.14	19.26	12.25	13.35	58.89
	Female	17.87	52.35	13.17	83.39	5.96	0.63	10.03	41.11
	Total	21.39	34.15	11.21	66.75	13.79	7.47	11.98	100
SIRUNGATHUR	Male	21.35	26.22	2.43	50	12.43	11.08	26.49	56.32
	Female	17.07	63.76	3.83	84.67	4.53	1.39	10.45	43.68
	Total	19.48	42.62	3.04	65.14	8.98	6.85	19.48	100

TABLE 14 (*cont.*):

VAYALUR	Male	32.31	20	6.15	58.46	6.15	11.15	24.23	62.20
	Female	21.52	60.76	5.70	87.97	0	1.27	10.76	37.80
	Total	28.23	35.41	5.98	69.62	3.83	7.42	19.14	100
VEERASAMBANUR	Male	34.21	19.74	3.95	57.89	15.79	15.79	10.53	50.33
	Female	31.33	51.33	3.33	86	9.33	0.67	4	49.67
	Total	32.78	35.43	3.64	71.85	12.58	8.28	7.28	100
VEGAMANGALAM	Male	44.64	25.22	3.77	73.62	3.19	5.22	16.81	65.34
	Female	12.57	72.68	3.83	89.07	1.09	0	9.84	34.66
	Total	33.52	41.67	3.79	78.98	2.46	3.41	14.39	100
VENGODU	Male	52.72	17.73	3.31	73.76	4.49	9.69	12.06	56.10
	Female	32.02	52.87	4.83	89.73	0.30	3.63	6.34	43.90
	Total	43.63	33.16	3.98	80.77	2.65	7.03	9.55	100
VINAYAGAPURAM	Male	39.27	16.38	4.52	60.17	25.99	5.37	8.47	51.38
	Female	30.75	48.66	3.88	83.28	11.04	1.79	3.88	48.62
	Total	35.12	32.08	4.21	71.41	18.72	3.63	6.24	100
All Villages	Male	38.90	22.26	4.46	65.62	9.29	9.35	15.63	57.94
	Female	25.36	57.88	4.95	88.19	3.62	1.51	6.77	42.06
	Total	33.58	37.05	4.64	75.26	6.80	6.02	11.88	100

Source: Houselisting Survey.

TABLE 15　Wage data, 1994–5
(Details of wages prevailing in the study villages (Rs per day))

Name of village	Ploughing	Groundnut Weeding	Transplantation / Weeding of paddy	Harvesting	Threshing	Cane Harvesting	Cane Lifting
Sirungathur	Rs 25–wp Rs 10–wop	na	Rs 10–12 (7.30 a.m.–2 p.m.) or Rs 240 / acre	3 padis of paddy	6 padis with meal / 5 kg. of rice or Rs 40 for both female and male	Rs 65–80 / tonne and Rs 2.50 for broth expenses / person	Rs 15 or 7–10 paise / bundle (for child labourers)
Vegamangalam	Rs 25–wp Rs 15–20–wop	na	na	45 marakkals per acre or ½–2 marakkals / person (8 a.m.–4 p.m.)	na	na	Rs 10–20
Duli	Rs 30–wp Rs 10–wop	na	Rs 10 (8 a.m.–2 p.m.) Rs 12 (8 a.m.–4 p.m.) and a meal	4 padis (8 a.m.–4 p.m.) 6 padis (8 a.m.–6 p.m.)	2 marakkals or 6 padis	not cultivated	not cultivated
Vengodu	Rs 25 (3 a.m.–7 a.m.)	Rs 7	Rs 6 and meal (10 a.m.–4 p.m.) Rs 7 and meal (9 a.m.–5 p.m.) Rs 9 and meal (7 a.m.–5 p.m.)	6–7 araipadis or 3–3½ araipadis	10–12 araipadis and two meals	Rs 65–75 / tonne and rice equivalent to one meal per day per person or Rs 2 for broth expenses	Rs 7 (one bundle a time) Rs 14 (two bundle a time)

TABLE 15 (*cont.*):

Vayalur	Rs 30 (6 or 7 a.m.–12 noon) for evening Rs 50 (only in busy season)	Rs 7–8	Rs 7–8 (if morning only) and Rs 5 (for evening)	6 araipadis 2½ kg of rice and bran or 1¼ marakkals	8 arai padis 6–12 bundles of sheaves or 3 marakkals	Rs 90 / tonne and ½ padi rice and Rs 2.50 for broth expenses	na
Meppathurai	Rs 30–wp Rs 15–wop (5 a.m.–1 p.m.)	Rs 6 (6 a.m.–1 p.m.)	3–4 padis or one marakkal and a meal		4 bundles / 100 bundles of sheaves threshed or 3 marakkals	Rs 25 / day For gur making Rs 2000 acre or Rs 65–105 tonne	Rs 10
Amudur	Rs 25–2p (6 a.m.–12 noon) Rs 10–wop	Rs 10	Rs 10 and a meal (8 or 9 a.m.–5 or 6 p.m.) Rs 5 (8 or 9 a.m.–1 p.m.)	3–4 padis, one kurunee / marakkal 6–8 araipadis (9 a.m.–5 p.m.)	4–6 padis and two meals or 8–12 araipadis (4 a.m.–6 p.m.)	Rs 15 / tonne and a meal	na
Kalpattu	Rs 50	Rs 8–10 and a meal (8 a.m.–2 or 3 p.m.)	Rs 4 (6–9 a.m.) Rs 6 (7 a.m.–1 p.m.) Rs 10 (7 a.m.–5 p.m.)	na	3 marakkals (1 a.m.–6 p.m.)	na	na

Notes: 1. wp = with plough, wop = without plough. 2. See glossary for volumetric measurements. 3. 'Broth expenses' = food or gruel.

Wages varied according to operation, gender and working hours (Table 15). In some villages, work started in the early morning, in others not until 9 or 10 a.m. Wages were not fixed but varied with the size of specific land holdings, hours of work and season. The perquisites provided during the work were also not standardized but were determined mainly by the distance of the work from the houses of the labourers and by the labourers' preferences. For example, in Kalpattu, labourers preferred to have a meal from the house of their employer because their own houses were located in the main village, whereas in Vayalur labourers preferred to be paid extra wages instead of food. Wages are still paid in kind for all harvesting operations, except those for commercial crops such as plantain, cotton, turmeric and sugar cane (see Table 16). For these crops labourers are paid either on a fixed contract basis or via piece rate wages in cash along with perquisites. Detailed research in 3 of the 11 villages found that, besides gender discrimination against women in the growth of real wages, most of the earnings of women goes to household income, unlike that of men which is for private consumption (see Chapter 1–5).

Gender discrimination in wages is severest in commercial crop cultivation, particularly sugar cane. Though it provides higher wages for both genders, it fails to give employment throughout the year. Wages are generally fixed on a contract basis (Rs 65–100 per tonne), along with food expenses. During the harvest season, women worked alongside men in bundling sugar cane and carrying it from the field to the main roads, from where it would be transported to the sugar mills by lorries or tractors. While all male labourers shared the income from the

TABLE 16 Changes in wages paid in kind

Village	HARVESTING (WOMEN)			THRESHING(MEN)		
	1973–4	1983–4	1994–5	1973–4	1983–4	1994–5
Amudhur	2.5	6	4	3.5	8	4–6
Duli	3.5	2.5	4	1	6	7–10
Kalpattu	3.5	3.5	5–6	3.5	3.5	15
Meppathurai	3	3–4	3–5	4.5	4.5–6	15
Nesal	3	3	5 KGS.	6	6	10 KGS.
Sirungathur	4	4	3	4	4	6
Vayalur	2.5	3 KGS.	3–6	5	6 KGS.	12
Veerasambanur	3	3	6.4	6	6	12
Vegamangalam	4	N.A.	2.5–5	4	N.A.	8
Vengodu	3.5	5 Ltrs	3–3.5	3	6 Ltrs	5–6
Vinayagapuram	2.1	4 KGS.	6.4	2.3	6 KGS.	12

Notes: Wages in kind are given local measures. They vary by villages. Generally they were converted into padi (the common measure), equivalent to 1.6 kg of paddy.

Source: Observations during the Houselisting survey and J Harriss 1991.

contract payment for the harvest, fixed wages were given to women labourers (along with perquisites). The share of male labourers was 2 to 2.5 times higher than that of female labourers. This was not so in other crops, such as paddy, where women workers predominate and male labourers are paid the same rates as women.

The real wages for women in Vengodu are low and have been declining over the years (see Table 17). In this village, family labour is involved in such operations as transplantation and harvesting. Certain tasks are also performed through mutual 'exchange of labour'. It appears that frequent caste conflicts between two dominant middle castes, Vanniyars and Yadavas, is the reason why the exchange labour system is sustained among their kith and kin. During the peak seasons, it was difficult to find sufficient willing labourers, the number of scheduled-caste agricultural labour households being minimal. Thus, limited dependence on scheduled-caste landless agricultural labourers kept wages low over the years.

Wages for the harvesting and threshing of paddy were unexpectedly high in Veerasambanur and Vinayagapuram, but the wages for other operations compensated by being relatively low. Over the period 1973–95, the real wages for harvesting declined in Vengodu and Amudur. In Amudur, the decline of area under paddy probably accounts for this disaster for agricultural labourers.

The wages for threshing were double or treble the wages for harvesting. Working hours for this operation ranged within and between villages from 8 to 16 hours per day without a break. In some villages, agricultural labourers were tied to work for farmers who gave them credit, as a result of which they received wages which were less than 'market' rates. Normally, peak season wages would be slightly higher than those during the rest of the year. Farmers give interest-free loans to some labourers to tie them to work for lower wages regardless of the season. Indebted labourers are not exactly at the beck and call of their employer-creditors. They may work for others when there is no work in their fields. Certain farmers kept labourers under an implicit contract whereby they were given less than the going wage but employed more frequently. When compared with the minimum wages fixed by the state government, men, except for ploughmen, were earning above the statutory minimum wage but women earned well below it.[26]

5.7 *Per capita income and liabilities*

An approximate per capita income per annum was calculated on the basis of the complete census enumeration of households. The average annual per capita income was Rs 2,742. The top-ranking three villages (Vegamangalam, Amudur

TABLE 17 Trends in wages for major agriculture operations, 1973–95

Village	Ploughing (men)					Weeding and Uprooting (both men & women)					Transplanting (women)				
	1973–4	Inf. to 1982–3	1982–3	1983–4	1994–5	1973–4	Inf. to 1982–3	1982–3	1983–4	1994–5	1973–4	Inf. to 1982–3	1982–3	1983–4	1994–5
Amudhur	2	3.67	2.75	5.5	25	1.8	3.3	N.A.	6	35	1.3	2.4	2	2.37	13
Duli	2	3.67	3	7.2	30	1	1.84	N.A.	5	25	1.5	2.75	2.5	3	11
Kalpattu	3.5	6.44	5	N.A.	50	1	1.84	N.A.	N.A.	30	1	1.84	2	N.A.	13
Meppathurai	2.8	5.14	5	3.22	35	2	3.67	3	4.3	27.5	1.5	2.75	2.1	3.18	9
Nesal	2.5	4.6	4.62	N.A.	N.A.	2.5	4.6	5.5	5	N.A.	1.5	2.75	2.74	3	N.A.
Sirungathur	2.5	4.6	5	N.A.	25	2	3.67	N.A.	N.A.	30	1	1.84	2.25	N.A.	8
Vayalur	2	3.67	6.33	5.6	30	2	3.67	7.5	8	30	1	1.84	2.66	4	11
Veerasambanur	2.33	4.28	3	2.83	25	2	3.67	2.83	3	N.A.	1.2	2.2	2	2	N.A.
Vegamangalam	3	5.5	5	N.A.	28	3	5.5	5.37	N.A.	20	1	1.84	3.16	N.A.	9
Vengodu	2	3.67	4.1	N.A.	25	1	1.84	3	N.A.	25	1.57	2.87	2.13	N.A.	N.A.
Vinayagapuram	2	3.67	3	4.37	N.A.	1.7	3.12	3	4	N.A.	0.7	1.29	2	2	N.A.

Sources: Observations during the houselisting and J Harriss 1991b.

Note: The column 'Inf. to 1982–3' represents 1973–4 wages in 1982–3 prices.

and Kalpattu) had an average of Rs 3,506, nearly 60 per cent greater than the average for the lowest three (Veerasambanur, Meppathurai and Sirungattur) at Rs 2,228 (see Table 18).

Cultivators everywhere had higher incomes on the average than agricultural labourers and non-farm households. Non-agricultural households had higher average earnings than landless agricultural labourer (LAL) households. *LAL households earned only 37.3 per cent of the average income of cultivators, whereas non-farm household members earned 62 per cent of those cultivators' incomes.* Cultivators in Nesal and Vegamangalam earned a higher per capita income than those elsewhere. Sirungattur and Veerasambanur's cultivators earned the lowest incomes. In the case of agricultural labourers within their respective villages, those in Nesal, Meppathurai and Vegamangalam earned between 23 and 27 per cent of the income earned by cultivators. In Vinayagapuram and Sirungattur, agricultural labourers earned more than 50 per cent of the cultivators in their villages. In four villages (Veerasambanur, Sirungathur, Vinayagapuram and Amudur), they earned more than 75 per cent of cultivators' incomes.

If we presume that sources of liabilities signify sources of credit, we find that many of these villages depend little on formal sources of credit (see Chapter 2–4). Less than one third of the reported liabilities are from such sources (see

TABLE 18 Per capita income of village households by category (in Rs)

Village / Category	Per capita income (PCI)			% to village PCI			Proportion of cultivators income to		
	Culti-vators	Land-less Agri. La-bourers	Non-farm Hhds.	Culti-vators	Land-less Agri. La-bourers	Non-farm Hhds.	Land-less agri. la-bourers	Non-farm hhds
Amudur	4130	1373	3119	47.90	15.92	36.18	33.23	75.53
Duli	3468	1610	2574	45.32	21.04	33.64	46.43	74.22
Kalpattu	4889	2161	3178	47.80	21.13	31.07	44.21	65.01
Meppathurai	3753	893	2069	55.89	13.30	30.81	23.79	55.13
Nesal	4409	1159	1836	59.54	15.66	24.80	26.30	41.65
Sirungathur	2974	1607	2528	41.83	22.61	35.56	54.06	85
Vayalur	3821	1568	2040	51.44	21.10	27.46	41.03	53.38
Veerasambanur	2640	1180	2416	42.33	18.92	38.75	44.69	91.53
Vegamangalam	7582	2063	3064	59.66	16.23	24.11	27.21	40.41
Vengodu	4388	1444	2647	51.75	17.04	31.22	32.92	60.33
Vinayagapuram	3387	1929	2609	42.74	24.34	32.92	56.95	77.04
All villages	4131	1544	2553	50.21	18.77	31.02	37.38	61.79

Source: Houselisting survey.

Table 19). When we compared this trend with the previous decade, for which we have data for four villages, we find that *the role of the formal sector is not only low but also declining* (from 44.75 to 33.19 per cent). While 47.45 per cent of the total liabilities of landed households in the 11 villages was from formal sources, only 33 per cent of landless agricultural labourers' debt was from the banks and in non-agricultural households it was down to a quarter.

Formal credit ranged in penetration from Vengodu, where 61 per cent of total debt was owed to formal sources, to Kalpattu, Veerasambanur, Sirungathur and Vinayagapuram, where the figure was only 20–30 per cent.

What is the reason for IVV in types of credit? We can answer using examples. Due to the prevalence of local chit fund savings, borrowers in Kalpattu depended more on informal sources. Most of the households were involved in at least one chit fund. Chit fund organizers were either wealthy, educated farmers or government employees. There was fierce competition among the members who bid for the chit at each auction, a process by which bidders can find themselves further indebted. In Duli, non-agricultural households did not have any institutional liabilities, due to lack of access to institutional credit and sufficient regular income from service jobs (carting and loading) to depress demand for consumption loans. Most scheduled-caste labourers could in principle gain access to institutional credit, especially that of the Integrated Rural Development Programme. Yet, despite repeated loans, they were able neither to generate assets (see Table 20) nor to improve their standards of consumption.[27]

6. IDENTIFYING DIMENSIONS OF INTERVILLAGE VARIATION AND CLASSIFICATION OF VILLAGES

6.1 *Factor analysis*

So far we have analysed IVV in terms of trajectories of change over two decades: in demographic factors, agriculture, employment and earnings. We have not looked into the relationships between these dimensions. There are evidently intractable difficulties in identifying factors causing intervillage variation. We can however use statistical tools – in particular factor analysis – to identify variables or groups of variables which cause intervillage variation. This technique has been used widely by social and behavioural scientists to identify a relatively small number of factors that could be used to represent relationships among bundles of many inter-related variables. Here, from the set of different methods of factor analysis, we selected principal component analysis, because components or factors loaded using this method can explain greater variations than other methods.

TABLE 19 Liabilities of village households and per capita income by category, 1995

Village/ Category	Non-institutional Sources			Institutional Sources			Per capita income	Liabilities (in %)	
	Culti-vators	Land-Agrl. La-bourers	Non-farm Hhds.	Culti-vators	Land-Agrl. La-bourers	Non-farm Hhds.		Non Institu-tional	Institu-tional
Amudur	37.69	70.29	65.31	62.31	29.71	34.69	2874.11	57.76	42.24
Duli	43.02	28.37	100	56.98	71.63	–	2550.99	57.13	42.87(61)
Kalpattu	79.54	79.26	90.55	20.46	20.74	9.45	3409.25	83.12	16.88
Meppathurai	47.11	62.24	86.89	52.89	37.76	13.11	2238.03	65.41	34.59
Nesal	55.19	65.20	60.91	44.81	34.80	39.09	2468.15	60.43	39.56(46)
Sirungathur	61.22	70.56	84.04	38.78	29.44	15.96	2369.50	71.94	28
Vayalur	48.04	83.21	75.53	51.96	16.79	24.47	2476.29	68.93	31
Veerasambanur	59.78	85.89	89.13	40.22	14.11	10.87	2078.50	78.27	21.73(44)
Vegamangalam	32.53	91.85	59.91	67.47	8.15	40.09	4236.17	61.43	39
Vengodu	32.95	24.26	59.74	67.05	75.74	40.26	2826.33	38.98	61
Vinayagapuram	63.01	80.70	70.51	36.99	19.30	29.49	2641.78	71.40	28.59(28)
All villages	52.51	66.98	76.19	47.49	33.02	23.81	2742.65	58.72	32.19(44.75)

Source: Houselisting survey.

TABLE 20 Distribution of assets in the North Arcot villages (recensus)

Village	total assets	top 25%	bottom 25%	% owned by top 25%	% owned by bottom 25%
Amudur	12101984	9513817	121110	78.61	1
Nesal	12101984	5499209	2703520	45.44	22.34
Duli	7952212	5767298	106300	72.52	1.34
Kalpattu	28402599	21360442	434775	75.21	1.53
Meppathurai	9247148	6954756	112428	75.21	1.22
Nesal	27038773	23450237	98053	86.73	0.36
Sirungathur	6706242	5977092	56847	89.13	0.85
Vayalur	5787796	4095873	145360	70.77	2.51
Veerasambanur	15032952	12709790	130280	84.55	0.87
Vengodu	13127087	9957985	224577	75.86	1.71
Vinayagapuram	22084657	14637770	295432	66.28	1.34

Apart from our census of households, the information given by village administrative officers has also been used. To start with, a correlation matrix was constructed for 42 variables with the objective of removing some variables in order to avoid multicollinearity. We have used two criteria for removing variables: (a) the size of correlation coefficients; and (b) variables with abnormally high negative coefficients. Low correlations make it unlikely that variables share common features. The second criterion is used to take one variable to represent the set of two variables in which one would be the residual of the other. In our model, only one variable (normal cropping intensity [NCI]) had low or zero coefficients with all the other variables and four variables (the proportion of large farmer households, the land owned by large farmers, the percentage of other/backward classes and the percentage of non-agricultural assets including gold and savings) had high negative correlations. So we removed five variables and extracted factor loadings. The missing values for two variables (fertility ratio and wells per acre) were replaced with mean values to avoid the total cases being reduced to seven.

Four factors exhibit similar kinds of correlations in the model. The number of factors was determined as the minimum that could explain the larger part of the variations in the sector of villages. In our case, the first four factors explained nearly 72 per cent of the variation. Another six factors explained only 28 per cent of the total variation.

Though the factor matrix indicated some relation between variables and factors, the next analytical stage – providing an explanation for the factors – was difficult. If several factors have high loadings on the same variables, it is difficult to ascertain how the factors differ. In our model, seven variables have had high loadings on three factors.

Using the varimax method of orthogonal rotation, we derived a rotated factor matrix. The varimax method is most commonly used and can minimize the number of variables that have high loadings on a factor, which helps interpretation of the factors.[28] In this process, two commonalities and the total variance did not change, but there was a slight change in the distribution of variance accounted for by each of the factors.

It appears that the first factor represents the variables relating to *wet and dry agriculture and the development of non-farm employment*. This factor relates positively with: i) the area under groundnut, the principal dry-land crop in the region; ii) non-farm employment for males; iii) the per capita income of landless agricultural labourers; iv) work participation rates; v) the sex ratio; vi) the work participation of women and female cultivators; vii) male landless agricultural labourers; viii) irrigation intensity; ix) the area under paddy; x) female landless agricultural labourers; xi) population per acre; and xii) the fertility ratio.[29] In this factor, non-farm linkages are associated with wet and dry agriculture. More males were engaged in non-agricultural activities, fewer women were engaged in agriculture as their main occupation, economic participation rates were higher, fertility rates were lower and sex ratios higher.

The second factor reflects *backwardness*. Though having a high positive correlation with the incomes of non-farm households, variables such as female literacy, male literacy, the sex ratio of children below the age of 6 and income earned by cultivators correlated negatively in this factor. The extent of work participation of females, the dependence on a few wells, the ownership of lands outside the village are characteristics of villages which have scored positively on this factor. Lower rates of literacy, a sex ratio biased against women, which could be due to excess female infant mortality, and low incomes from agriculture feature in this factor.

The role of social and institutional factors has not been studied in earlier attempts to typologize villages. They are difficult to quantify. We collected information on caste in the study villages and included it in the model. The proportion of scheduled castes (SCs) is important to the third factor. The characteristics of villages which scored positively on this factor are: a high proportion of female non-agricultural labour, a low proportion of cultivators, a high proportion of SCs, proximity to urban locations, lower acreage under crops other than paddy and groundnut, lower dependence on informal sources of credit and higher involvement in agriculture-allied activities such as animal husbandry. We call this factor *gender and caste sensitivity* due to the fact that the variables with the highest coefficients related to gender and caste. Among non-farm workers and cultivators, it was women who had higher coefficients than men.

The fourth factor clearly identifies the *distribution of means of production and liabilities*. All the factors show the relative poverty of a subset of villages. This factor is construed by the proportion of small farmers, the area owned and cultivated by small farmers, informal-sector liabilities of landless agricultural labourers and cultivators, and cultivation of crops other than groundnut and paddy. Two variables, agricultural assets and male cultivators, had negative relationships.

The relationship among the variables causing intervillage variation is highly complex. However, their influence in the form of different factors is evident. One factor, non-farm linkages with dry-land farming, affected intervillage variation very strongly. The first two factors also were strong in demographic and human capital variables.

6.2 *Hierarchical cluster analysis*

Though we have identified four factors that account for the bulk of variation in the village economy, the work of classifying these villages remains. Due to the inter-relationship of many variables, the factor scores of villages are inadequate for a classification of villages. For instance, the village of Duli scored positively on one factor but negatively on another. Since the factors can also be used as variables representing the set of other inter-related variables, by using these factors it is possible to classify the villages using another multivariate technique – hierarchical cluster analysis (see discussion of cluster analysis in Chapter 1–4, pp. 215–18).

In order to combine clusters, we use the 'average linkage between groups' method (in which the distance between two clusters is the average of the distances between all pairs of villages in which one member of the pair is from each of the clusters). Once the distance matrix is calculated, the clusters can be computed. Table 21 summarizes clusters using the method of average links between various groups. From the clustering coefficients, it appears that a five-cluster solution is appropriate for explaining the intervillage variation of the study region.

The clustering of villages is based on the factor scores of each village. Villages in *cluster 1* have a higher proportion of agricultural assets with moderate cropping intensity and higher irrigation intensity. They are generally far from towns, with lower economic participation rates. Their sex ratios are highly biased against women in general and children in particular, accompanied by higher fertility. Nearly three quarters of the population are from depressed communities

TABLE 21 Village classification, 1993–5

Cluster Number	Villages	Type
Cluster 1	Amadur, Meppathurai and Vengodu	ag. underdevd
Cluster 2	Duli	suburban
Cluster 3	Kalpattu	remote, ag., commercialized
Cluster 4	Nesal, Vayalur and Vegamangalam	developed
Cluster 5	Sirungathur, Veerasambanur and Vinayagapuram	SC, poor.

(SCs). Over half the farmers are small farmers and owned only 23 per cent of the total land.

Duli is an isolated village represented by *cluster 2*. As mentioned earlier, this village has a dry agriculture and is being suburbanized. Kalpattu (*cluster 3*) is also a unique and advanced agricultural village. It is far from urban centres and all the variables relating to agriculture show prosperity, including per capita income. In terms of demographic indicators we observe a perplexing trend. Both villages have strongly anti-female sex ratios, though that of children for Kalpattu is higher than for Duli.

Villages in *cluster 4* are ahead of the other villages in providing more literacy for women, having a low fertility rate and less biased sex ratios for general population as well as for children. They are close to towns (the average distance being 10 km). In agriculture they have a higher irrigation intensity and cropping intensity with more small farmers. *Cluster 5* represents villages where social institutions such as gender and caste are reflected most strongly in the economy. The villages are on average 15 km from town. More than 43 per cent of male workers are engaged in non-agriculture employment. These villages have low levels of female literacy, but their male and female work-participation rates are highest. The sex ratio remains biased against women but less so than in other clusters with the exception of cluster 4. Work participation is also high. We found the highest proportion of SCs residing in this cluster, accounting for 46 per cent of the total population.

7. CONCLUSION

In what way is this classification superior to previous typologies? Is it possible to theorize from the above analysis? Or is it simply another five-fold classification similar to the three-fold classification of 1973 and the six-fold classification of the 1983 surveys?

Given the increasing complexity of the rural economy, we attempted a fresh typology which takes into account other characteristics of villages than those considered in the 1970s. This typology permits analysis of the relations of each factor with others. Methodologically, the present study suffers from intractable difficulties if used for the tracking of *trends*. However, we can summarize broad changes in the region from this detailed analysis of the censuses of 11 villages.

Population growth has accelerated, not only through high fertility but also through selective in-migration. Female literacy has increased over both the decades, but this has not improved the survival chances of girls. The sex ratio in general and for children aged below 6 in particular has moved against females (see Chapter 3–2).

There has been a general feminization of agricultural employment, but this has not improved female earnings. The pattern of ownership of land reveals a rapid increase in petty holdings and in the casualization of the workforce. Crop diversification has further intensified, with an increase in the seasonal demand for labourers for less water-sparing crops. Diversification is mainly due to a decline in the growth of irrigation infrastructure, dating from the second decade of the study period.

Agricultural employment has declined, while non-farm jobs have increased. In 1993–5, nearly one quarter of the economically active population was engaged in non-farm activity. When compared with state and national trends, this is quite striking. However, this growth is still structured by proximity to urban locations and other social factors such as caste.

Wage determination in the region is a complex phenomenon influenced by many institutional factors. Gender discrimination prevails, with denial of statutory minimum wages to women workers. Earning differences across different classes vary substantially. Those households depending on non-farm employment are better off than the agricultural labouring classes. The dependence on informal sources of credit has increased over the years. On the one hand, new forms of informal credit have evolved. On the other hand, state-directed credit institutions are on the retreat.

Multivariate analyses of the village-level data reduced variables into four factors and grouped the villages into five types. The present typology is not based on any of the other preconceived classifications but on the careful measurement of relationships among the major variables causing intervillage variation in levels of productive and human development. The factors influence the variables relating to non-farm employment, irrigation infrastructure, proximity to urban locations, demographic factors and distribution of the means of production. However, a major feature of this venture is the close relations between the variables which render the classification of villages watertight. *Key variables such as the sex ratio, female literacy, intensity of irrigation, proportion of small farmers, extent of non-farm employment for males and proximity to urban locations are the main dimensions of intervillage variation and need to be investigated further in future.*

ACKNOWLEDGEMENTS

The author wishes to acknowledge the help of Barbara Harriss-White, Archana, Praveena and Zarin in writing this paper.

Appendix

Analysis of Clusters

THE clustering procedure is based on the distance or nearness of all variables to each other for every village. The steps for clustering are: (a) using all the variables, a matrix called squared Euclidean dissimilarity (SED) which is the sum of the squared differences over all the variables is constructed; (b) using SED to form clusters using agglomerative hierarchical clustering, one of the common methods of cluster formation; (c) an icicle plot is drawn using the agglomeration schedule. Using (b) and (c), the number of clusters and villages in each cluster will be identified. Now it may be appropriate to explain the steps.

In agglomerative hierarchical clustering, clusters are formed by grouping villages into bigger and bigger clusters until all villages become members of a single cluster. At the first step all villages are considered separate clusters; there are as many clusters as there are villages. At the second step, two of the villages are combined into a single cluster. At the third step, either a third village is added to the cluster already containing two villages or else two additional villages are merged into a new cluster. At every step, either an individual village is added to clusters or already existing clusters are combined. Once a cluster is formed, it cannot be split; it can only be combined with other clusters. Thus, in this method, villages are not allowed to separate from clusters to which they have been allocated.

Social Stratification and Rural Households

DIEGO COLATEI AND BARBARA HARRISS-WHITE

1. INTRODUCTION

AGRICULTURAL households in South Asia are notorious not only for being extremely unequal across a range of dimensions but also for not being politically organized in coherent strata based on their relationship to the means of production. Consequently, they have been classified in many different ways, according to a bewildering variety of attributes and variables which have been more or less grounded in theories of stratification, class formation and economic mobility or in the state's land-holding categories. Further, as Olsen says, '. . . the current transition to a capitalist economy and the growth of formal-sector employment makes the classification of whole households the more difficult'.[1] In a situation in which the economy of agrarian households is diversifying, we have to search for a method of classification that formalizes the identification of relatively homogeneous and socially meaningful groups.

Peter Hazell and others,[2] in their quantification of the economic linkages of the 'green revolution' among the villages we have resurveyed, used land holding and paddy farming as the basis for the classification of households. Separate results were reported for farms smaller or larger than 1 hectare. The use of land holding alone, however, does not allow for any consideration of differences in irrigation status, productivity or value of the land. Furthermore, even if these are taken into account (by using land values or productivity in order to 'standardize' land), standardized holdings would ignore differences in objectives and in the organization of production. These might not be related to farm size yet are significant shapers of agrarian outcomes. Janakarajan has gone further and has concluded that water rather than land is the stratifier and differentiater of production relations.[3] He divides households into groups of water sellers and water buyers. However, it is then difficult to locate farms doing neither, or to map scale or land holding off water relations.

Other studies have classified agrarian households according to tenurial status.[4] This criterion may also lead to a crude division of households, especially when tenure categories conceal different types of tenancy and a range of extent of total operational holding. Moreover, classifications based on tenurial status can lump together radically different types of enterprises, as in the case of reverse tenancy.[5]

Income and, more rarely, wealth have also been used to classify agrarian societies.[6] The derivation of income as well as the productivity of own assets, however, is often ignored. Sources of income such as wage labour in cash or in kind, trade, rents, interest, agriculture, livestock, rental of tools or premises and non-farm activity have specific and different impacts on growth and well-being. Assets may be differentiated into productive ones such as agricultural land ownership, tools and animals, on the one hand, and non-productive assets such as consumer durables and jewellery, on the other.

Other classifications have been based on the relations of labour in production.[7] Such a criterion, however, requires a large amount of information on both family labour and labour hired in and out. Single indices conceal the fact that many households both hire in and hire out labour. Without an indicator of land ownership, inferences about agrarian classes are nonetheless risky. A multidimensional index is needed to provide a more reliable method of classification.[8]

Modes of appropriation of surplus and market dependence, usually for staples and for credit, have also been used to delineate social strata.[9] Yet the definition of surplus is often contested because of its arbitrariness, depending as it does on a consensus about the definition of the product necessary for social reproduction; or on sales (usually of staple grain) net of preharvest buy-back, neglecting forms of exchange and market dependence specific to non-staple crops.[10]

Another body of research has championed classifications of peasant households according to their demographic composition, not merely their size but also the relationships between active workers and dependants. Regardless of differentiation arising from size, scale, tenure, mode of organization, complexity and diversification, it is argued that economic inequality and mobility may be due, independently, to changes in dependency burdens and workforce capacity arising from the family life cycle.[11] Allowing for the possibility of demographic differentiation requires, in its crudest formulations, the incorporation of data on household composition, age structures and individual work status. At their most sophisticated, such studies have incorporated sets of forces externalized by those classifications which result from the privileging of the process of capitalist commodification. Redistributive exchange,[12] redistributive policy,[13] population growth,[14] and even the growth of the non-farm economy[15] have been theorized as factors which counter the centrifugal form of capitalist differentiation – and which therefore structure inequality. An even more ambitious concept of agrarian structure would include the structures of exchange and commerce and of key policy interventions, as well as ideologies of social rank, which all condition the range of inequality, the type of differentiation and its distributional consequences.[16]

The debate over the classification of agrarian households has simmered for three reasons: technical difficulties, disagreement about methodologies and differences in the implications for measurement of various bodies of theory. Although some criteria are empirically harder to measure than others, each has its own theoretical merits and each approach aims at: i) distinguishing homogeneous groups; and ii) allowing generalization about the groups and their socially relevant interactions.[17]

The evidence from Indian applied research over the last two decades shows that the rural economy is diversifying.[18] This process takes a number of forms. In Tiruvannamalai District, the increase in crop varieties, the introduction of perennial crops, the new crops brought under cultivation, new combinations of crops, the colonization of wetland by dry-land crops, the intensification of irrigation, electrification and mechanization are all manifestations of agricultural diversification. The increasing range of occupations undertaken by family members and the range of types as well as scales of assets ownership is testimony enough to household diversification. The expansion of non-farm activities such as silk weaving and petty trading, transport and construction work, employment in government or in the service sector are evidence of non-agricultural diversification. The latter may occasionally appear in the form of household diversification or may, at times, involve the complete departure of entire households from the agricultural sector or from the village.

Given this complicated set of possibilities, a classification of rural households based only on agricultural criteria is inappropriately selective. At worst, it leads to the omission from research of non-agricultural households;[19] at best, to the need to develop elaborate classification schemes accounting for non-agricultural attributes. In such a context, a classification of households based on a wider range of both agricultural and non-agricultural variables which can group together relatively homogeneous households is the need of the hour. Cluster analysis is such a procedure.

2. THE CHARACTERISTICS OF CLUSTERING TECHNIQUES

Cluster analysis is a technique used to classify observations, or variables, into categories. It has been widely used in the biological sciences to classify animals and plants or in the medical field to identify diseases and their stages. However, there are also precedents for its use in social science and, in particular, for classifications of rural households in Malawi[20] and slum households in Bangladesh.[21] Srinivasan has used the method here to classify villages (see Chapter 1–3).

The idea behind a cluster analysis is that a bulk of observations, which are usually intractable when considered as single units, can be classified into manageable groups provided that characterizing variables or attributes have been specified.[22] Given n households and p variables according to which the n households can be measured, it is possible to define a procedure for classifying the observations into g groups. In this way, households with similar characteristics are identified and grouped together into homogeneous clusters.

The way clusters are generated differs according to the procedures adopted in the analysis. *Tree hierarchical clustering* and *k-means clustering* are two methods commonly used for cluster analysis.[23] We have adopted the tree hierarchical clustering method. Although there was some *a priori* expectation (derived from the literature on classification and on the dynamics of peasant society)[24] about the types and range of household categories, we preferred not to impose any assumption on the number of clusters at the outset. Instead we use the method to analyse village society at various levels of resolution.

A great advantage of hierarchical techniques is the possibility of showing the outcome of the analysis through a graphical representation. The dendrogram indicates the clusters which are identified and combined at every step of the fusion process, as well as their distance. In this way, the researcher can exercise judgement over the number of distinct groups it would be desirable to conceive of and tractable to analyse. The greater the distance between clusters, the more dissimilar the clusters and therefore the greater the loss of information in their fusion. A common way to proceed is then to determine the number of clusters according to the loss of information which derives from fusing dissimilar groups of households.[25] But it is also possible, and sometimes very useful, especially in policy analysis, to decide on a classification based on a few general groups, which can always be disaggregated into subgroups later for specific purposes. In hierarchical clustering, observations are combined in a stepwise progression. An index commonly used for measuring dissimilarities (or distances) between observations is the squared Euclidean distance, which is the sum of the squared differences over all of the selected variables. In order to carry out a tree hierarchical analysis, however, it is also necessary to specify a rule for linking clusters at every step. In other words, we need a criterion to establish when two clusters are sufficiently similar to be combined. Although many procedures exist, all of them are always based on a matrix of similarity or dissimilarity between pairs of cases. Ward's method is the rule which has been adopted in the following study.[26]

3. THE CLUSTER ANALYSIS OF THE 1993 VILLAGE RECENSUS OF HOUSEHOLDS

The 1993 census of three villages generated the data upon which the cluster analysis has been carried out. Despite being located within the hinterland of the same market town of Arni, these villages nevertheless represent different agro-economic micro-environments. Nesal is a large, accessible and well-irrigated village: in Srinivasan's classification it is a developed village. Vinayagapuram is fairly large and well irrigated, but it is not accessible by surfaced roads. By contrast, Veerasambanur is a small, remote and poorly irrigated village. Both are classed as villages in which the social institutions of caste and gender have a strong impact on the economy (see Chapter 1–3).

The three villages are thus no longer randomly selected and generalization of the results to regional conditions, therefore, needs to be treated with due reserve. In contrast to the earlier two rounds of research in which households and villages were 'pooled', the analyses of agrarian change conducted in the 1993–4 study and presented in this book are mainly village-specific. Nevertheless, an attempt has been made to generalize for the archetypal agricultural conditions represented by the three villages in the analysis of agricultural production and a basic economic census was conducted on the remaining villages in 1994–5 (analysed in Chapter 1–3).

4. VARIABLES AND METHOD

The selection of the household sample surveyed in the agricultural year 1993–4 proceeded along a multistage design involving the selection of the villages, the identification of homogeneous household groups within the villages and the selection of representative households within each group.

Since the variables included in a cluster analysis constitute the frame of reference within which household groups are formed, their choice is critical for the final outcome of the analysis. Given the variety of characteristics that have been used to classify agrarian households, in this study we attempted to define a set of variables which could reflect the eclectic classifications reviewed in the introductory section. Eighteen variables were used for the cluster analysis, grouped as follows.

- Land variables
    1. Acres of wetland operated by the household.
    2. Acres of dry land operated by the household.
    3. Total operational holding size, standardizing acreage for productivity.
- Tenurial variables
    4. Proportion of total operational land leased and mortgaged in.
    5. Proportion of total operational land leased and mortgaged out.
- Income and wealth variables
    6. Gross household annual income from all sources.
    7. Total value of assets.
    8. Total value of livestock.
- Variables revealing the organization of production[27]
    9. Total family labour days in own agricultural production in the last month.
    10. Total family labour days in non-agricultural production in the last month.
    11. Total labour days hired in for work in own agricultural production in the last month.
    12. Total labour days hired in for work in own non-agricultural production in the last month.
    13. Total labour days hired out for agricultural production in the last month.
    14. Total labour days hired out for non-agricultural production in the last month.
- Market dependence variables
    15. Average number of months of consumption of cereals produced on own land holding (or received as wage payments in kind).
    16. Total liabilities.
- Household demographic variables
    17. Household size.
    18. Dependency ratio.

Apart from the category based on the organization of production, each group is thus represented by between two and three variables. The decision of using six variables for the labour relations subset, however, has two objectives: one to indicate the modes of organization of production and the other the extent and social distribution of diversification into non-agricultural activities.[28]

The cluster analysis was then performed according to the following steps:

Step 1: The 18 continuous variables were standardized to solve the problem of differences in scales and units of measurement.

Step 2: The matrix of distances was computed adopting the squared Euclidean distance measure.

Step 3: The stepwise fusion of observations and clusters was conducted using Ward's method.

Step 4: The results of the tree hierarchical progression were interpreted by analysing the dendrogram and the loss of information at various steps.

5. THE STRUCTURE OF THE FUSION PROCESS

The n initial observations, for each village, are identified by n horizontal lines. The results of the stepwise progressions are indicated by the merging of the lines representing individual clusters into new agglomerated clusters. The horizontal side of the dendrogram shows the loss in variance of the whole data-set resulting from the combination of clusters. A small loss of variance (or distance between clusters) indicates that clusters being joined are fairly similar. As the process continues, however, increasingly dissimilar clusters are linked together, implying that at every further step of the fusion process a greater amount of information about differences between households is lost. There is a clear trade off-between the number of clusters and the loss in households' heterogeneity. We then have to decide to what extent we are willing to lose household details in order to get a small and manageable number of household groups. Figure 1 shows, for example, the loss of information resulting at every step of the fusion process for Nesal.

For all three villages, the relative increase in the loss of information, with respect to immediately preceding stages, becomes significant only at the very last steps of the fusion process. This means that the households can be classified

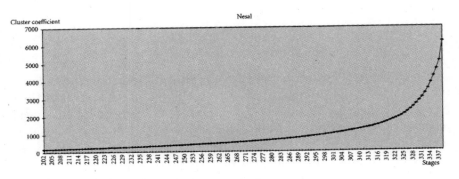

FIG. 1 Stepwise fusion Nesal: loss of information.

according to a relatively small number of clusters. However, there is no objective means by which to decide the optimal number of clusters. For practical and cognitive reasons, we know it is not worth having a large set of household groups. But what is the limit and how do we decide?

The outcome of the fusion process itself helps to suggest a given range within which it would be reasonable to select the groups – in the steeper range of the curves. For reasons explained later (p. 134), a five-cluster scheme, recommends itself.[29] Prior to working with this scheme, it is worth considering the results of increasingly detailed clusters located on the steeper part of the curves, since we can distinguish groups of households which are quantitatively important from those which are qualitatively interesting. We have decided to start by presenting the results of a two-cluster solution for the three villages, because it is the most simple disaggregation of households we can obtain and therefore relatively easy to grasp. We then decompose the agrarian structures of the villages by reversing the fusion process, and we discuss the outcome for the six- and ten-cluster solutions, respectively. The choice of describing the solutions for six and ten clusters is related to the fact that these represent stages located at one third and two thirds of the steeper range of the fusion process.

6. THE ANALYTICAL ZOOM LENS

When a cluster is considered as the unit of reference, any kind of distributional issue within the cluster itself has to be ignored. Since a cluster represents relatively homogeneous households, by observing the characteristics which pool together similar households within a village we can identify types of socioeconomic differentiation. Then, if we compare clusters between villages, we can also evaluate intervillage variation. In what follows, we will interpret the results obtained by the cluster analysis in a way which can facilitate comparisons within and between the three villages.

6.1 *The two-clusters classification*

A two-cluster solution divides each village into two groups of households. From the dendrogram shown in Fig. 1, it is easy to see that Nesal can be described by a very large group, representing about 90 per cent of the households, and a small one, which describes the remaining 10 per cent of the households. Vinayagapuram is similar to Nesal, but in Veerasambanur the proportion of households assigned to each group is 62.5 and 37.5 per cent, respectively.

In Table 1, three columns of values, divided into three different sets, are reported for each village. The first columns summarize the village means of the 18

TABLE 1 Two-cluster classification

	Nesal			Vinayagapuram			Veerasambanur		
	Village	Peasants	Elite	Village	Peasants	Elite	Village	Peasants	Elite
Households (1)	339	313	26	259	232	27	136	85	51
A) Average levels									
Household members	4.46	4.27	6.85	4.38	4.19	6.04	4.25	3.91	4.82
Dependency ratio	0.68	0.70	0.52	0.61	0.62	0.54	0.74	0.91	0.55
Family labour agriculture	7.42	4.65	40.81	12.59	8.16	50.70	9.38	1.13	23.14
Family labour non agriculture	12.41	11.91	18.38	14.86	14.54	17.59	11.10	4.98	21.29
Hired in labour agriculture	8.85	3.81	69.58	9.29	5.21	44.33	8.81	1	21.82
Hired in labour non agriculture	1.10	0.05	13.69	2.55	2.72	1.11	1.07	0	2.84
Hired out labour agriculture	9.06	9.58	2.73	13	13.85	5.63	13.07	14.75	10.25
Hired out labour non agriculture	14.19	14.02	16.23	10.31	9.50	17.22	7.77	3.25	15.31
Income (Rs)	11358	7647	56043	11689	8225	41456	8530	4189	15765
Wet land (acres)	0.67	0.36	4.38	1.03	0.58	4.95	0.74	0.11	1.81
Dry land (acres)	0.36	0.22	2.08	0.43	0.36	0.99	0.41	0.18	0.79
Total operational land	0.74	0.41	4.80	1.12	0.65	5.15	0.83	0.14	1.96
leased and Mortgaged out land	0.06	0.06	0.08	0.01	0.01	0.01	0.03	0	0.07
leased and Mortgaged in land	0.06	0.06	0.05	0.04	0.05	0	0.04	0.06	0
Assets (Rs)	66071	38357	399710	83104	50552	362812	50016	12927	111830
Livestock (Rs)	1592	1154	6862	2171	1452	8352	1614	572	3351
Debt (Rs)	5572	4011	24365	6461	4227	25659	5033	1604	10747
Cereal consumption	1.29	1.23	2.04	2.13	1.30	9.22	1.69	0.15	4.26
B) % to village total									
Households		0.92	0.08		0.90	0.10		0.63	0.38
Household members		0.88	0.12		0.86	0.14		0.57	0.43
Dependency ratio		0.95	0.05		0.91	0.09		0.74	0.26
Family labour agriculture		0.58	0.42		0.58	0.42		0.08	0.92
Family labour non agriculture		0.89	0.11		0.88	0.12		0.28	0.72
Hired in labour agriculture		0.40	0.60		0.50	0.50		0.07	0.93

TABLE 1 (*cont.*):

Hired in labour non agriculture	0.05	0.95	0.95	0.05	0	1
Hired out labour agriculture	0.98	0.02	0.95	0.05	0.71	0.29
Hired out labour non agriculture	0.91	0.09	0.83	0.17	0.26	0.74
Income	0.62	0.38	0.63	0.37	0.31	0.69
Wet land	0.50	0.50	0.50	0.50	0.09	0.91
Dry land	0.56	0.44	0.76	0.24	0.27	0.73
Total operational land	0.51	0.49	0.52	0.48	0.11	0.89
leased and Mortgaged out land	0.90	0.10	0.91	0.09	0	1
leased and Mortgaged in land	0.93	0.07	1	0	1	0
Assets	0.54	0.46	0.54	0.46	0.16	0.84
Livestock	0.67	0.33	0.60	0.40	0.22	0.78
Debt	0.66	0.34	0.59	0.41	0.20	0.80
Cereal consumption	0.88	0.12	0.55	0.45	0.06	0.94
C) %ages to village averages						
Household members	0.96	1.53	0.96	1.38	0.92	1.13
Dependency ratio	1.03	0.77	1.02	0.88	1.23	0.74
Family labour agriculture	0.63	5.50	0.65	4.03	0.12	2.47
Family labour non agriculture	0.96	1.48	0.98	1.18	0.45	1.92
Hired in labour agriculture	0.43	7.86	0.56	4.77	0.11	2.48
Hired in labour non agriculture	0.05	12.44	1.07	0.44	0	2.67
Hired out labour agriculture	1.06	0.30	1.07	0.43	1.13	0.78
Hired out labour non agriculture	0.99	1.14	0.92	1.67	0.42	1.97
Income	0.67	4.93	0.70	3.55	0.49	1.85
Wet land	0.54	6.52	0.55	4.83	0.14	2.43
Dry land	0.61	5.71	0.85	2.31	0.44	1.94
Total operational land	0.55	6.44	0.58	4.63	0.17	2.38
leased and Mortgaged out land	0.98	1.25	1.02	0.83	0	2.67
leased and Mortgaged in land	1.01	0.85	1.12	0	1.60	0
Assets	0.58	6.05	0.61	4.37	0.26	2.24
Livestock	0.73	4.31	0.67	3.85	0.35	2.08
Debt	0.72	4.37	0.65	3.97	0.32	2.14
Cereal consumption	0.95	1.58	0.61	4.34	0.09	2.52

Note: (1) see page 120 for definitions of variables and units of measurement.

variables. The second and third columns show the characteristics of the two clusters. Set A) reports the actual mean values of the clusters. In set B) we have calculated the percentage shares of the clusters with respect to the village values, for each variable. In set C) the clusters are described in terms of the ratios of the group means to the village means.

For all the villages, the first group of households is characterized for the most part by values below the village means. The only values above, but still close to, the village averages and higher than the values reported for the second group are those for dependency ratio, labour hired out in agriculture and land leased – or mortgaged – out. The second cluster is composed of relatively wealthy households, with a large extent of operated land (both wet and dry), comparatively high levels of income, debt and own cereal consumption, and high values of assets and livestock. Families in this group are also characterized by a higher number of household members and a bigger amount of both family and hired labour for own agricultural and non-farm activities.

We have labelled the two clusters *peasants* and *elite* respectively. Peasant households are mostly agricultural workers but have a comparatively higher number of members of non-working age (either young or old). Contrary to expectations, it is not the elite which leases out land. Big landlords are rare here, and households lease out because they are unable – for reasons of absence, poverty or incapacity – to cultivate land or because they are engaged in non-agricultural activity.

Although the *elite* of Veerasambanur is relatively larger, the gap between *peasants* and the *elite* is relatively smaller than in the two other villages.[30] Veerasambanur is both smaller and poorer than Vinayagapuram and Nesal, and it contradicts the idea that 'poorly endowed villages tend to be less equitable'.[31] However, the breakdown of village society into two classes ignores a great deal of heterogeneity within the two groups. A finer grain of resolution provides us with more interesting information about the structure of agrarian society. For this reason, it is worth moving backwards and analysing the outcome of the preceding stages of the hierarchical progression.

6.2 *The six-clusters classification*

Table 2 shows the results of the six-clusters solution for each village, both in terms of actual means and ratios of the group means to the village means, with respect to every variable. For Nesal and Vinayagapuram, the cluster of *peasants* is now broken down into four groups, while the cluster of the *elite* is split into two groups. Although a substantial proportion of households is still described in terms of only one cluster in both villages (75.6 per cent for Nesal and 74.9 per

TABLE 2   Six-cluster analysis

Nesal	Peasants				Elite		Peasants				Elite	
	A) Average levels						B) %ages to village averages					
	Dependent	Peasants	Lease out	Lease in	Elite 1	Elite 2	Dependent	Peasants	Lease out	Lease in	Elite 1	Elite 2
Households	14	263	19	17	23	3	4.13	77.58	5.60	5.01	6.78	0.88
Household members	1.21	4.41	3.68	5.24	6.96	6	0.27	0.99	0.83	1.17	1.56	1.34
Dependency ratio	#DIV/o!	0.68	0.63	0.75	0.54	0.38	#DIV/o!	1	0.92	1.10	0.79	0.57
Family labour agriculture	0	3.82	2.37	23.76	40.70	41.67	0	0.52	0.32	3.20	5.49	5.62
Family labour non agriculture	2.14	12.56	12.37	9.35	18.43	18	0.17	1.01	1	0.75	1.49	1.45
Hired in labour agriculture	0	3.25	1.26	18.29	32.57	353.33	0	0.37	0.14	2.07	3.68	39.93
Hired in labour non agriculture	0	0.05	0	0.18	15.17	2.33	0	0.05	0	0.16	13.79	2.12
Hired out labour agriculture	0.64	10.32	4.05	11.71	3.09	0	0.07	1.14	0.45	1.29	0.34	0
Hired out labour non agriculture	2.71	14.49	19.84	9.47	15.74	20	0.19	1.02	1.40	0.67	1.11	1.41
Income	1388	7567	12682	8403	46979	125533	0.12	0.67	1.12	0.74	4.14	11.05
Wet land	0	0.32	0	1.71	3.39	12	0	0.48	0	2.55	5.05	17.86
Dry land	0	0.23	0.09	0.44	2.35	0	0	0.63	0.25	1.21	6.45	0
Total operational land	0	0.37	0.02	1.80	3.86	12	0	0.49	0.02	2.42	5.18	16.11
leased and Mortgaged out land	0	0.01	0	0.98	0.09	0	0	0.13	0	16.08	1.41	0
leased and Mortgaged in land	0	0	0.98	0	0.06	0	0	0.03	16.29	0	0.97	0
Assets	3447	33485	147588	20398	305442	1122433	0.05	0.51	2.23	0.31	4.62	16.99
Livestock	0	1066	1711	2853	6322	11000	0	0.67	1.07	1.79	3.97	6.91
Debt	286	3700	7107	8429	21065	49667	0.05	0.66	1.28	1.51	3.78	8.91
Cereal consumption	1.79	1.16	2.34	0.53	2.28	0.17	1.39	0.90	1.82	0.41	1.77	0.13

Vinayagapuram

	Dependent	Peasants	Lease out	Lease in	Elite 1	Elite 2	Dependent	Peasants	Lease out	Lease in	Elite 1	Elite 2
Households	10	194	12	16	26	1	3.86	74.90	4.63	6.18	10.04	0.39
Household members	1.40	4.26	4.75	4.63	6.08	5	0.32	0.97	1.08	1.06	1.39	1.14
Dependency ratio	#DIV/o!	0.61	0.58	0.48	0.55	0.25	#DIV/o!	1	0.96	0.79	0.90	0.41
Family labour agriculture	0.50	8.54	3.92	11.56	52.66	5	0	0.04	0.68	0.31	0.92	4.180
Family labour non agriculture	0	13.31	10	41.88	18.27	0	0	0.90	0.67	2.82	1.23	0
Hired in labour agriculture	0	5.84	1.75	3.44	41.42	120	0	0.63	0.19	0.37	4.46	12.92
Hired in labour non agriculture	0	0	1.67	38.19	1.15	0	0	0	0.65	14.96	0.45	0
Hired out labour agriculture	2.40	14.56	16	10.88	5.85	0	0.18	1.12	1.23	0.84	0.45	0
Hired out labour non agriculture	0	10.08	9.58	8.31	15.58	60	0	0.98	0.93	0.81	1.51	5.82
Income	2000	8157	6307	14374	32398	276975	0.17	0.70	0.54	1.23	2.77	23.70
Wet land	0.10	0.62	0.28	0.63	4.83	8	0.10	0.60	0.27	0.61	4.67	7.73
Dry land	0	0.41	0.29	0.15	1.03	0	0	0.94	0.68	0.34	2.39	0
Total operational land	0.10	0.70	0.34	0.66	5.04	8	0.09	0.62	0.30	0.59	4.50	7.14
leased and Mortgaged out land	0	0.02	0	0.03	0.01	0	0	1.07	0	1.79	0.86	0
leased and Mortgaged in land	0.10	0	0.79	0	0	0	2.33	0.08	18.35	0	0	0
Assets	22861	50555	73750	50416	350785	675500	0.28	0.61	0.89	0.61	4.22	8.13
Livestock	0	1550	250	2063	8327	9000	0	0.71	0.12	0.95	3.84	4.15
Debt	300	4013	4979	8719	21569	132000	0.05	0.62	0.77	1.35	3.34	20.43
Cereal consumption	0.05	1.41	0.79	1.16	9.12	12	0.02	0.66	0.37	0.54	4.29	5.65

TABLE 2 (cont.):

Veerasambanur

	Depend-ent	Peas-ants	Lease out	Lease in	Elite 1	Elite 2	Depend-ent	Peas-ants	Lease out	Lease in	Elite 1	Elite 2
Households	8	72	5	27	23	1	5.88	52.94	3.68	19.85	16.91	0.74
Household members	1.38	4.19	3.80	4.74	4.91	5	0.32	0.99	0.89	1.12	1.16	1.18
Dependency ratio	#DIV/o!	0.84	0.90	0.66	0.41	1.50	#DIV/o!	1.14	1.22	0.90	0.56	2.04
Family labour agriculture	0	1.33	0	14.19	33.78	20	0	0.14	0	1.51	3.60	2.13
Family labour non agriculture	0	5.04	12	4.07	40.91	35	0	0.45	1.08	0.37	3.69	3.15
Hired in labour agriculture	0	1.18	0	12.93	30.61	60	0	0.13	0	1.47	3.47	6.81
Hired in labour non agriculture	0	0	0	0	2.39	90	0	0	0	0	2.24	84.41
Hired out labour agriculture	1.88	15.81	20.20	8.19	13.13	0	0.14	1.21	1.55	0.63	1	0
Hired out labour non agriculture	0	3.83	0	20.30	10.13	0	0	0.49	0	2.61	1.30	0
Income	593	4579	4340	9705	22962	13850	0.07	0.54	0.51	1.14	2.69	1.62
Wet land	0.04	0.12	0	1.65	2.03	0.80	0.05	0.16	0	2.22	2.73	1.08
Dry land	0.04	0.21	0	0.30	1.38	0.50	0.10	0.50	0	0.74	3.38	1.22
Total operational land	0.05	0.16	0	1.71	2.31	0.90	0.06	0.20	0	2.07	2.79	1.09
leased and Mortgaged out land	0	0	0	0.01	0.13	0.44	0	0	0	0.24	4.89	17.08
leased and Mortgaged in land	0	0.01	1	0	0	0	0	0.17	24.73	0	0	0
Assets	8969	11328	42281	91347	139245	34333	0.18	0.23	0.85	1.83	2.78	0.69
Livestock	0	622	760	1896	5204	0	0	0.39	0.47	1.17	3.22	0
Debt	38	1734	2240	5652	16441	17350	0.01	0.34	0.45	1.12	3.27	3.45
Cereal consumption	0	0.18	0	2.87	5.89	4.50	0	0.11	0	1.69	3.48	2.66

Note: The symbol #DIV/o! has been used for households which are entirely dependent. These are households whose members are all over 60 years of age. Some such people occasionally work on their own plots or hire out labour (see note 33).

Source: Field survey, 1993.

cent for Vinayagapuram), the breakdown of the group of *peasants* produces noteworthy results.

Some 4 per cent of the households of both villages is grouped into a cluster of *shattered households*,[32] consisting of one or two members either of non-working age or only very occasionally employed.[33] Their household income levels for 1993 average Rs 1,388 in Nesal and Rs 2,000 in Vinayagapuram (12 and 17 per cent of the respective village means). Such households do not own livestock and most of them do not operate any land. The value of their assets is also extremely low when compared to the village averages. This cluster has been labelled *dependent* families.

By contrast a second small cluster, composed of about 6 per cent of the households, is strongly characterized by *leasing out* land. These households deploy most of their own labour in non-agricultural business. Some members are also employed in non-farm activities. The two groups of *dependent* households and those *leasing out* land are also captured, and with similar village proportions, when we break down the cluster of *peasants* in Veerasambanur.

As far as the *elite* of the villages is concerned, there are two similar and tiny clusters, one in Vinayagapuram and the other in Nesal, composed of one and three wealthy households, respectively. These agricultural households operate relatively large land holdings and hire in a large amount of labour. They are also deeply indebted (having the easy access to credit that comes with land collateral). The *elite* of Veerasambanur is comprised of three groups. The first (Elite 1) is a relatively rich group with assets, income, landholding, cereal stocks and debt between 2.5 and 3 times the respective village averages. The second (Elite 2) is a unique household (quantitatively unimportant but interesting!) which leases in land, is engaged in both agricultural and non-agricultural activities and hires a great deal of non-agricultural labour. The third is characterized by households hiring in agricultural labour and hiring labour out into non-farm activities, with income and debt levels and value of livestock very close to the village averages. More than a real elite, this last group most closely approximates *middle* peasants, not self-sufficient as in the classical definition but deeply involved in labour markets in a balanced manner.

There are also some village-specific groups. A cluster characterized by households *leasing in* land, for example, can be clearly distinguished in Nesal, but not elsewhere. In Vinayagapuram, instead, there is a group of households not appearing elsewhere which *hire in* a large amount of labour for non-agricultural activities.[34] The fact that clusters strongly characterized by some particular variable are not found in all villages might be interpreted as clear evidence of intervillage variation. But certain groups conceal heterogeneity and the structure can be disaggregated further.

6.3 *Fine-grained Stratification*

The ratios of the group means to the village means, for the ten-clusters solution, are reported in Table 3. The group of village *peasants* that was defined in the two-clusters classification is now split into six groups in Nesal, seven in Vinayagapuram and four in Veerasambanur. The *elite* is instead split into four, three and six groups for the respective villages.

At this most detailed resolution, in each village, the group of *dependent* families and the cluster of households *leasing out* land, discovered with a six-cluster classification, remain strongly consolidated and homogeneous groups. A cluster of households *leasing in* land, which earlier seemed representative only of a very specific and peculiar group of households in Nesal, now appears also in Vinayagapuram and Veerasambanur.

The extremely large clusters of peasants in Nesal and Vinayagapuram, representative of 78 and 75 per cent of the households of the two villages, are now split into three groups in both villages. Two of them (Medium 1 and Medium 2), although diversified in terms of labour organization, have characteristics quite similar to the *middle* class of Veerasambanur, which incidentally has now split into two new groups. The third is instead a cluster of *poor peasants*, characterized by hiring out agricultural labour.

Turning to the elite of Nesal, we can now find a cluster (E1a) of households hiring in labour for non-farm activities and which are not committed to farm production. Although much wealthier, this cluster can be considered similar, in terms of organization of production, to the group of households hiring in non-agricultural labour in Vinayagapuram.

Though the villages were chosen as varied archetypes, *these results actually reveal their structural similarities.*[35] Furthermore, *rural diversification is proceeding in ways which seem to differentiate households in such diverse ways* that any analysis of agrarian societies based on highly aggregated household classifications (ignoring heterogeneity within household groups) will most likely gloss over this significant developmental trajectory.

A 15-cluster analysis was carried out. Its outstanding features will be summarized here. The group of *dependent households* – 32 of them (4.5 per cent) – appeared in the six-clusters classification. Recall that they are the poorest households in terms of income, assets, livestock and land. *Closer scrutiny reveals that 20 of these households are constituted by a single woman aged over 61. So a third of the households composed only of female members are among the very poorest families. A further 60 per cent of these entirely female households are found in the next poorest cluster.* All-female families, which are often the result of death or abandonment, are among the poorest rural people. In Veerasambanur, *their*

TABLE 3 Ten-cluster analysis

Nesal

	Peasants						Elite			
	B) %ages to village averages									
	Dependent	Poor	Medium1	Medium2	Lease in	Lease out	E1a	E1b	E2a	E2b
Households	4.13	53.98	16.52	7.08	5.01	5.60	1.47	5.31	0.59	0.29
Household members	0.27	0.89	1.38	0.82	1.17	0.83	1.48	1.58	1.34	1.34
Dependency ratio	#DIV/0!	0.98	1.09	0.88	1.10	0.92	1.08	0.73	1.05	0
Family labour agriculture	0	0.25	1.31	0.69	3.20	0.32	0.38	6.90	6.07	4.72
Family labour non agriculture	0.17	0.90	1.17	1.48	0.75	1.00	2.42	1.23	1.21	1.93
Hired in labour agriculture	0	0.16	0.90	0.73	2.07	0.14	1.36	4.33	50.85	18.08
Hired in labour non agriculture	0	0.02	0	0.38	0.16	0	57.98	1.51	3.18	0
Hired out labour agriculture	0.07	1.42	0.46	0.60	1.29	0.45	0.66	0.25	0	0
Hired out labour non agriculture	0.19	0.64	2.31	0.92	0.67	1.40	0.76	1.21	2.11	0
Income	0.12	0.44	1.43	0.64	0.74	1.12	3.70	4.26	7.60	17.96
Wet land	0	0.18	1.41	0.59	2.55	0	2.84	5.66	14.14	25.30
Dry land	0	0.23	1.94	0.57	1.21	0.25	3.30	7.33	0	0
Total operational land	0	0.18	1.46	0.59	2.42	0.02	2.88	5.82	12.76	22.83
leased and Mortgaged out land	0	0.13	0.17	0	16.08	0	0	1.81	0	0
leased and Mortgaged in land	0	0.04	0	0	0	16.29	0	1.23	0	0
Assets	0.05	0.24	1.29	0.75	0.31	2.23	3.57	4.92	14.13	22.70
Livestock	0	0.43	1.52	0.48	1.79	1.07	2.01	4.52	10.36	0
Debt	0.05	0.48	1.16	0.89	1.51	1.28	2.62	4.10	2.15	22.43
Cereal consumption	1.39	0.17	0.55	7.32	0.41	1.82	2.25	1.64	0.19	0

Table 3 (*cont.*):

Vinayagapuram

	Dependent	Poor	Medium1	Medium2	Lease in	Lease out	Hire in na	E1a	E1b	E2
Households	3.86	45.17	22.39	6.18	1.16	4.63	6.18	8.88	1.16	0.39
Household members	0.32	0.85	1.11	1.33	1.14	1.08	1.06	1.41	1.22	1.14
Dependency ratio	#DIV/o!	0.98	1.16	0.78	0.60	0.96	0.79	0.89	0.98	0.41
Family labour agriculture	0.04	0.31	1.21	1.04	2.65	0.31	0.92	3.69	7.94	0
Family labour non agriculture	0	0.42	1.90	0.96	0	0.67	2.82	1.30	0.67	0
Hired in labour agriculture	0	0.23	1.43	0.34	2.15	0.19	0.37	3.29	13.46	12.92
Hired in labour non agriculture	0	0	0	0	0	0.65	14.96	0.51	0	0
Hired out labour agriculture	0.18	1.33	0.56	1.70	0.77	1.23	0.84	0.51	0	0
Hired out labour non agriculture	0	0.47	0.58	5.60	3.88	0.93	0.81	1.58	0.97	5.82
Income	0.17	0.47	1.06	0.87	1.63	0.54	1.23	2.53	4.62	23.70
Wet land	0.10	0.24	1.21	0.67	2.37	0.27	0.61	4.57	5.85	7.80
Dry land	0	0.98	0.71	1.30	2.17	0.68	0.34	1.60	8.52	0
Total operational land	0.09	0.29	1.17	0.72	2.35	0.30	0.59	4.34	6.06	7.20
leased and Mortgaged out land	0	0.41	0	0.33	51.64	0	1.79	0.97	0	0
leased and Mortgaged in land	2.33	0.11	0.05	0	0	18.35	0	0	0	0
Assets	0.28	0.34	1.10	0.66	1.11	0.89	0.61	3.97	6.12	8.13
Livestock	0	0.28	1.31	1.38	2.61	0.12	0.95	3.25	8.29	4.15
Debt	0.05	0.35	1.14	0.81	0.17	0.77	1.35	3.45	2.50	20.43
Cereal consumption	0.02	0.20	1.54	0.60	1.96	0.37	0.54	4.11	5.65	5.65

Veerasambanur

	Dependent	Poor1	Poor2	Lease out	Me-dium1	Me-dium2	Lease in	E1b	E1c	E2
Households	5.88	32.35	20.59	3.68	8.09	11.76	4.41	9.56	2.94	0.74
Household members	0.32	0.70	1.44	0.89	1.22	1.04	1.06	1.12	1.41	1.18
Dependency ratio	#DIV/0!	0.87	1.41	1.22	0.79	0.99	0.68	0.65	0.27	2.04
Family labour agriculture	0	0.03	0.32	0	1.41	1.58	4.16	3.98	1.52	2.13
Family labour non agriculture	0	0.64	0.16	1.08	0.25	0.45	2.03	2.50	10.05	3.15
Hired in labour agriculture	0	0.10	0.19	0	1.53	1.43	2.84	4.51	1.05	6.81
Hired in labour non agriculture	0	0	0	0	0	0	0	3.97	0	84.41
Hired out labour agriculture	0.14	0.70	2.01	1.55	0.51	0.70	1.21	1.22	0	0
Hired out labour non agriculture	0	0.42	0.61	0	5.77	0.44	0.75	1.96	0	0
Income	0.07	0.46	0.66	0.51	1.19	1.10	2.71	2.37	3.72	1.62
Wet land	0.05	0.11	0.25	0	1.35	2.82	2.50	3.12	1.82	1.08
Dry land	0.10	0.29	0.84	0	0.93	0.60	1.92	4.93	0.55	1.22
Total operational land	0.06	0.12	0.31	0	1.31	2.60	2.44	3.30	1.69	1.09
leased and Mortgaged out land	0	0	0	24.73	0	0	17.47	0.59	0	17.08
leased and Mortgaged in land	0	0	0.44	0	0	0	0	0	0	0
Assets	0.18	0.20	0.27	0.85	1.21	2.25	1.77	3.54	1.84	0.69
Livestock	0	0.46	0.27	0.47	0.28	1.79	2.27	4.01	2.09	0
Debt	0.01	0.20	0.57	0.45	1.10	1.14	1.68	3.79	3.94	3.45
Cereal consumption	0	0.06	0.18	0	1.05	2.14	3.44	4.02	1.77	2.66

annual average income is Rs 593: 7 per cent of this rather poor village's average. They should therefore be considered as a 'target' for social transfers.

Only at the 15-clusters level does landlessness emerge as the defining feature of clusters of very poor households. Nesal's landless households have incomes, at Rs 4,924, of 43 per cent of the village average. These are very poor, uncreditworthy, *agricultural labourers.* Poor and middle peasants are further disaggregated along the lines of: i) land; ii) income poverty; iii) the extent of de-agrarianization and employment in the non-farm economy; and iv) tenancy status. In the latter case, reverse tenancy between small, poor landholders and relatively wealthy tenants who are also hiring out their own labour can be found. Middle peasants are not self-sufficient but deeply engaged in labour markets, both as hirers in and hirers out, and in the non-farm economy as well as in agriculture. *The elite turns out to be characterized by extreme differentiation along many axes*: i) wealth; ii) family size (up to 17 members); iii) heavy debt; iv) degree of economic diversification both within agriculture (by type, scale and the role of livestock) and in the non-farm economy – not only in terms of employment as in poorer clusters but also in terms of investment and ownership; v) the degree of self-sufficiency in cereals (all clusters selling and buying rice leaving a residual of own-produced rice for on-farm consumption).

6.4 *A reclassification of the village households*

The most detailed 15-household grouping, although illuminating the characteristics of an increasingly diversified village economy, is not tractable for statistical analysis. When we described the various clusters, we saw that groups of households can be linked together into bigger groups because of similarities either in the levels of income and debt, the value of assets, or in the way they organize labour or production. It is both possible, manageable and useful, especially for intervillage comparisons, to regroup the 15 clusters into the 3 categories of poor peasants, middle peasants and elite, further stratifying the poor and the middle peasants according to landlessness, as shown in Fig. 2.

The five re-classified household groups are presented in Table 4. The elite constitutes between 8 and 15 per cent of the village households. Middle peasants with land are between 20 and 30 per cent, while those without land are between 3 and 14 per cent. In Nesal, most of the poor peasants do not own any land (47.5 per cent of village households). In Vinayagapuram, 30 per cent of households are poor peasants with land, while 24 per cent are poor without land. In Veerasambanur, poor peasants with land include 29 per cent of households, and 34 per cent are without land. These are the classes which will be used wherever possible in the rest of the analysis.

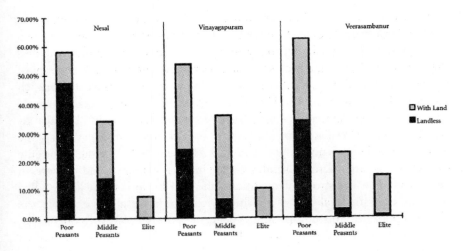

FIG. 2 Landlessness within household groups

TABLE 4 The reclassified household groups

Household groups		VILLAGE			
		Nesal	Vinayaga-puram	Veera-sambanur	All Villages
Elite	n.hhs	26	27	20	73
	Col %	7.7%	10.4%	14.7%	9.9%
Middle peasants with land	n.hhs	69	76	27	172
	Col %	20.4%	29.3%	19.9%	23.4%
Middle peasants without land	n.hhs	47	17	4	68
	Col %	13.9%	6.6%	29%	9.3%
Poor peasants with land	n.hhs	36	77	39	152
	Col %	10.6%	29.7%	28.7%	20.7%
Poor peasants without land	hhs	161	62	46	269
	Col %	47.5%	23.9%	33.8%	36.6%
Village households		339	259	136	734
	Col %	100%	100%	100%	100%

7. LAND RELATIONS AND ECONOMIC STRATIFICATION

In all the villages, the percentage of households without land is very high among the poor peasants. For the elite, by contrast, landlessness is not an issue. Only one household, in Veerasambanur, among the elite of the three villages does not own any land.

If we then look at both the extent and the quality of land which households in different groups are endowed with, we find that poor peasants, when they own land, generally have more dry than wet or well-irrigated land and mostly less than 1 acre. In Table 5, the 15 clusters have been aggregated into the 3 groups of poor peasants, middle peasants and the elite in the same way as we did for each village in the previous section. The farm size of poor peasants averages around 0.76 acres in Veerasambanur, 0.97 acres in Nesal and 1.28 acres in Vinayagapuram. In the first two villages, dry land contributes to more than 50 per cent of the total extent of land owned by poor peasants. Households belonging to the elite own, on average, 6.10 acres in Nesal, 5.91 acres in Vinayagapuram and 3.53 acres in Veerasambanur. The strong inequalities in the distribution of land are revealed when we examine total land ownership by cluster. In Nesal, for example, the group of poor peasants, comprising 58 per cent of households, own only 10 per cent of land. When we break down land into its various types, poor peasants own 12 per cent of total dry land, 10.3 per cent of well-irrigated land and less than 8 per cent of the total wetland. For the elite, these percentages change drastically. The six better-off clusters in Nesal, which represent 7.7 per cent of households, own 40.3, 52.9 and 45.4 per cent, respectively, of total dry, wet and well-irrigated *punjai*.

8. INTRAVILLAGE DIVERSIFICATION AND INTERVILLAGE VARIATION

We can now turn to the comparison of household groups across villages. The most interesting outcome of the detailed cluster analysis is that *the three villages appear to be very similar in terms of the structure of their societies*. Firstly, clusters strongly characterized by specific variables, such as shattered and dependent households or those reverse-leasing-in or reverse-leasing-out land, are found in all three villages, though they are quantitatively unimportant everywhere. Second, *in all three villages we have also recognized common elements*: clusters of poor and middle peasants, and the elite, and we have seen that these groups can be broken down further. Within the set of poor peasants we have discovered clusters of agricultural workers, and groups of households mainly engaged in non-farm activities or with a diversified supply of labour. Among the middle peasants we have found groups of farmers, of households employed in non-agricultural activities and of households with diversified production. Among the elite we have detected those households which are highly indebted, those operating a very large extent of land and those in non-agricultural businesses. Third, in all the villages, the fact that the elite is split into a large number of groups confirms that richer households are highly diverse as far as production and the organization of labour are concerned.

TABLE 5 Land distribution by household groups

Nesal

Nesal	Poor Peasants without land			Poor Peasants with land			Middle Peasants without land			Middle Peasants with land			Elite		
		col%	row%		col%	row%		co%	row%		co%	row%		co%	row%
Households	161		47.5%	36		10.6%	47		13.9%	69		20.4%	26		7.7%
Landless	161		77.4%				47		22.6%						
With Land				36	100%	27.5%				69		52.7%	26		19.8%
Total Land (acres)				34.93	100%	10.1%				150.87	100%	43.8%	158.62	100%	46.1%
per landed household				0.97						2.19			6.10		
Wet land				7.93	22.7%	7.7%				40.35	26.7%	39.3%	54.32	34.2%	52.9%
per landed household				0.22						0.58			2.09		
Punjai land with wells				13.77	39.4%	10.4%				58.66	38.9%	44.2%	60.30	38%	45.4%
per landed household				0.38						0.85			2.32		
Dry land				13.23	37.9%	12.1%				51.86	34.4%	47.5%	44	27.7%	40.3%
per landed household				0.37						0.75			1.69		

Vinayagapuram

Vinayagapuram	Poor Peasants without land			Poor Peasants with land			Middle Peasants without land			Middle Peasants with land			Elite		
		col%	row%		col%	row%		co%	row%		co%	row%		co%	row%
Households	62		23.9%	77		29.7%	17		6.6%	76		29.3%	27		10.4%
Landless	62		78.5%				17		21.5%				0		0
With Land				77	100%	42.8%				76		42.2%	27		15%
Total Land (acres)				98.51	100%	25.6%				126.74	100%	32.9%	159.45	100%	41.4%
per landed household				1.28						1.67			5.91		
Wet land				22.40	22.7%	22.4%				22.83	18%	22.8%	54.70	34.3%	54.7%
per landed household				0.29						0.30			2.03		
Punjai land with wells				23.68	24%	13.6%				72.64	57.3%	41.7%	77.95	48.9%	44.7%
per landed household				0.31						0.96			2.89		
Dry land				52.43	53.2%	47.4%				31.27	24.7%	28.3%	26.80	16.8%	24.3%
per landed household				0.68						0.41			0.99		

TABLE 5 (cont.):

Veerasambanur	Poor Peasants without land			Poor Peasants with land			Middle Peasants without land			Middle Peasants with land			Elite		
		col%	row%		col%	row%		co%	row%		co%	row%		co%	row%
Households															
Landless	46		33.8%	39		28.7%	4		2.9%	27		19.9%	20		14.7%
With Land	46		90.2%			45.9%	4		7.8%	27	100%	31.8%	1	5%	20%
Total Land (acres)				39	100%	19.6%				27	100%	36.4%	19	95%	22.4%
per landed household				29.83						55.33			67.04	100%	44%
Wet land				0.76						2.05			3.53		
per landed household				6.63	22.2%	11.6%				23.41	42.3%	40.9%	27.19	40.6%	47.5%
Punjai land with wells				0.17						0.87			1.43		
per landed household				5.21	17.5%	13%				23.77	43%	59.2%	11.20	16.7%	27.9%
Dry land				0.13						0.88			0.59		
per landed household				17.99	60.3%	32.8%				8.15	14.7%	14.9%	28.65	42.7%	52.3%
				0.46						0.30			1.51		

The process of *diversification* in an agrarian society can then be analysed in terms of differences in the organization of labour and production between the various clusters. Households engaged in productive activity – whether agricultural, non-agricultural or both – can be found among all the clusters (the only exception being the group of dependent households in Veerasambanur). The *richest* households, however, are often those with the highest number of family days devoted to the household's own activities and which also hire in most agricultural and non-farm labour. The *poorest* groups are mainly net sellers of labour, particularly in agriculture. Middle peasants, instead, are employed (rather more than the poor households) in the non-farm economy. Some members of elite households also work on, or manage, non-farm activities.

Lastly, intervillage variation emerges from the ratios of the village means to the three-village averages (see Fig. 3).

The diagram clearly shows that households in Vinayagapuram spend a higher number of family labour days on own-farm and non-farm activities. They also hire in a larger amount of labour, specially for non-agricultural business. Households in Nesal participate more intensively in wage work in the non-farm economy. Family labour in agriculture and the extent of operated land are also lower in Nesal than they are in the other villages. Labour hired out for non-farm

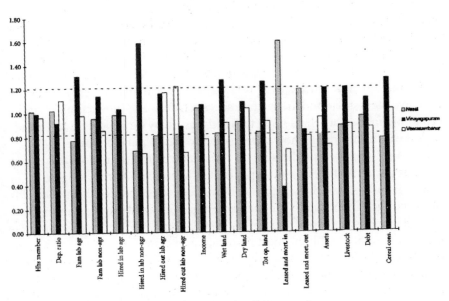

FIG. 3 Intervillage variations: village average (% of 3-village means)

activities is lowest in Veerasambanur. The average values of income, assets and debt are also lower in Veerasambanur than in the other villages. The extent of land leased in by households in Vinayagapuram is very low when compared to the other villages, especially with respect to Nesal.

Having classified households, we can turn to examine the relationships between social institutions other than class (caste and gender) and resources (land and non-land assets).

9. CASTE AND FEMALE-HEADED HOUSEHOLDS

9.1 *Caste and household clusters*

Caste was not included among the defining characteristics of the clusters for three reasons. First, the theoretical referents concerned with differentiation and dynamics in peasant society have for the most part been blind to stratification by ethnicity and in India have excluded caste. The theoretical situation is beginning to change[36] as the privileging of class over other forms of stratification and political mobilization has been questioned,[37] as caste grows ever more laden with economic content and as liberalization reworks the social institutions in which markets, old and new, are embedded.[38] Second, from a statistical point of view, a quantitative variable should have been used to represent caste in the analysis. Although nominal values can distinguish different castes, assumptions may be needed, and therefore problems may arise once castes have to be ordered.[39] As the social and economic ranking of caste differs, the very concept of rank is awkward. Furthermore, we would have also needed to address the issue of distance: by how much a caste is higher or lower than another. Third, even though caste is still found to structure social relations and interactions in India, economic and social behaviour within each caste may vary widely.[40] It is nevertheless worth considering how caste maps into the household groups.

The Agamudayan Mudaliars are the dominant caste in the region, making up some 23 per cent of Nesal and 37 per cent of Veerasambanur (see Table 6). In Vinayagapuram, two castes represent more than 90 per cent of the households in the village. The Vanniars are the highest in status and the most numerous. They alone constitute 70 per cent of the population. Scheduled castes, comprising a set of what are still the most disadvantaged castes, are the second biggest community. In Veerasambanur, scheduled-caste Christians are most numerous, representing 45 per cent of the village. In Nesal, Christians are about 7 per cent of the households, while other scheduled castes constitute 36 per cent of the village.

TABLE 6 Caste groups in the villages

CASTE		Village		
		Nesal	Vinayaga-puram	Veera-sambanur
A.Mudaliar	No. hhs	78		50
	hhs % (col)	23%		36.8%
Naidu	No. hhs	10		
	hhs % (col)	2.9%		
Vanniar	No. hhs	1	185	18
	hhs % (col)	0.3%	71.4%	13.2%
Yadava	No. hhs	59		
	hhs % (col)	17.4%		
S.Caste	No. hhs	122	50	1
	hhs % (col)	36%	19.3%	0.7%
S.C.Christian	No. hhs	23	1	61
	hhs % (col)	6.8%	0.4%	44.9%
Other	No. hhs	46	23	6
	hhs % (col)	13.6%	8.9%	4.4%
Total households		339	259	136
		100%	100%	100%

Tables 7, 8 and 9 report the mapping of caste onto clusters. These tables can be read in two ways: either in terms of clusters by caste (by looking at the column per cent), or in terms of castes by cluster (by looking at the row per cent). If we look at how castes map onto the five household clusters, we see that in all three villages the column percentages follow a decreasing path. Two patterns are evident. First, perhaps contrary to expectations, the highest castes such as the A. Mudaliars, the Naidu and the Vanniars are found everywhere in the social strata. In Nesal, for example, there are 18 households from the dominant caste which are poor peasants without land. Second, however, when we concentrate on the lower castes, we find that, apart from one Christian household in Nesal, none of the scheduled-caste households are part of the economic elite of the three villages.

9.2 Distribution of assets by caste

The socially dominant castes also dominate the assets distribution. In Veera-sambanur, the A. Mudaliars and the Vanniars together have command over 90 per cent of the total value of assets (see Table 10). The A. Mudaliars of Nesal are endowed with 55 per cent of the total value of village assets, while in Vinayaga-puram the Vanniars control almost 90 per cent.

Although caste and economic status usually co-vary, neither can be simply read from the other. On the other hand, poverty and scheduled-caste status are

TABLE 7 Nesal: caste by household groups

NESAL	Elite	Middle with land	Middle without land	Poor with land	Poor without land	All House-holds
A. Mudaliar	13	28	11	8	18	78
Col %	50%	40.6%	23.4%	22.2%	11.2%	23%
Row %	16.7%	35.9%	14.1%	10.3%	23.1%	100%
Naidu	1	2	2	3	2	10
Col %	3.8%	2.9%	4.3%	8.3%	1.2%	2.9%
Row %	10%	20%	20%	30%	20%	100%
Vannier					1	1
Col %					0.62%	0.29%
Row %					100%	100%
Yadava	8	17	7	14	13	59
Col %	30.8%	24.6%	14.9%	38.9%	8.1%	17.4%
Row %	13.6%	28.8%	11.9%	23.7%	22%	100%
S.Caste		8	12	4	98	122
Col %		11.59%	25.53%	11.11%	60.87%	35.99%
Row %		6.56%	9.84%	3.28%	80.33%	100%
S.C. Christian	1	3	5	2	12	23
Col %	3.8%	4.3%	10.6%	5.6%	7.5%	6.8%
Row %	4.3%	13%	21.7%	8.7%	52.2%	100%
Other	3	11	10	5	17	46
Col %	11.5%	15.9%	21.3%	13.9%	10.6%	13.6%
Row %	6.5%	23.9%	21.7%	10.9%	37%	100%
All Households	26	69	47	36	161	339
Col %		100%	100%	100%	100%	100%
Row %	7.7%	20.4%	13.9%	10.6%	47.5%	100%

still closely related. This is confirmed when we look at how assets are distributed across castes (again, see Table 10). Lorenz curves for the total assets distribution within the villages have been disaggregated according to higher caste and scheduled-caste households (see Fig. 4). While higher-caste households are spread throughout the Lorenz curve, scheduled-caste households are mostly to be found in the bottom part of the curve.

9.3 *Distribution of land by caste*

The land distribution expresses the same relationship with caste (see Tables 11–13). The highest castes own the greatest bulk of the land and in particular they own land of better quality. In Nesal, A. Mudaliars own 40 per cent of *punjai* (dry) land with wells and 65.5 per cent of wetland. In Vinayagapuram, Vanniars

TABLE 8 Vinayagapuram: caste by household groups

Vinayagapuram	Elite	Middle with land	Middle without land	Poor with land	Poor without land	All House-holds
A. Mudaliar						
Col %						
Row %						
Naidu						
Col %						
Row %						
Vanniar	25	69	15	45	31	185
Col %	92.59%	90.79%	88.24%	58.44%	50%	71.43%
Row %	13.51%	37.30%	8.11%	24.32%	16.76%	100%
Yadava						
Col %						
Row %						
S. Caste		4		26	20	50
Col %		5.26%		33.77%	32.26%	19.31%
Row %		8%		52%	40%	100%
S.C.Christian					1	1
Col %					1.6%	0.4%
Row %					100%	100%
Other	2	3	2	6	10	23
Col %	7.4%	3.9%	11.8%	7.8%	16.1%	8.9%
Row %	8.7%	13%	8.7%	26.1%	43.5%	100%
All Households	27	76	17	77	62	259
Col %	100%	100%	100%	100%	100%	100%
Row %	10.4%	29.3%	6.6%	29.7%	23.9%	100%

own 86 per cent of wetland and 92 per cent of *punjai* land with wells. In Veera-sambanur, A. Mudaliars own 78 per cent of wetland and 84 per cent of *punjai* land with wells.

The proportion of landlessness is much higher among the scheduled castes, and lower among the other communities. In Nesal, 90 per cent of households belonging to the scheduled castes and 74 per cent of scheduled-caste Christians do not have any land. In addition, 40 per cent of the scheduled castes in Vinaya-gapuram and 57 per cent of scheduled-caste Christians in Veerasambanur are landless. Moreover, apart from three cases (one for each village), those who have land do not own more than 2 acres, and usually this is either dry land or *punjai* land irrigated with wells. Very rarely do we find households of the scheduled castes owning wetland. It is abundantly evident that caste still plays an import-ant role in the stratification of rural societies.

TABLE 9 Veerasambanur: caste by household groups

Veerasambanur	Elite	Middle with land	Middle without land	Poor with land	Poor without land	All House-holds
A.Mudaliar	15	22		9	4	50
Col %	75%	81.5%		23.1%	8.7%	36.8%
Row %	30%	44%		18%	8%	100%
Naidu						
Col %						
Row %						
Vanniar	3	5	1	2	7	18
Col %	15%	18.52%	25%	5.13%	15.22%	13.24%
Row %	16.67%	27.78%	5.56%	11.11%	38.89%	100%
Yadava						
Col %						
Row %						
S.Caste				1		1
Col %						0.74%
Row %						100%
S.C.Christian			2	26	33	61
Col %			50%	66.7%	71.7%	44.9%
Row %			3.3%	42.6%	54.1%	100%
Other	2		1	1	2	6
Col %	10%		25%	2.6%	4.3%	4.4%
Row %	33.3%		16.7%	16.7%	33.3%	100%
All Households	20	27	4	39	46	136
Col %	100%	100%	100%	100%	100%	100%
Row %	14.7%	19.9%	2.9%	28.7%	33.8%	100%

10. GENDER AND ECONOMIC RESOURCES

While we will elaborate gender relations in the next chapter, we need to antici-pate some of the argument here. South Indian women have had higher eco-nomic status than elsewhere in the subcontinent due in material terms to their economic participation in agricultural production,[41] to supportive patterns of cross-cousin, short-distance marriages and low marriage expenses. This rela-tively higher status has been reflected in aspects of female well-being: life expec-tation, nutrition etc.[42] In recent years, this status has started to change.[43] Tamil Nadu is a microcosm of India itself, the southern districts of the state bearing a distinct similarity to the conditions in Kerala, which are the most advantageous to women in the subcontinent and a 'model' for Third World countries (which is not to say that deleterious change is not taking place in Kerala).[44] The region under our spotlight, in the northern part of Tamil Nadu, bears some resemblance

TABLE 10 Average value of assets by caste (Rs)

Total Assets		Village		
	Nesal	Vinayaga puram	Veera- sambanur	All Villages
A. Mudaliar	156636	.	102593	135525
hhs%	23.01		36.76	17.44
tot. ass%	54.55	.	75.41	34.20
Naidu	22447	.	.	22447
hhs%	2.95			1.36
tot. ass%	1.00	.	.	0.44
Vanniar	5015	103945	53779	99033
hhs%	0.29	71.43	13.24	27.79
tot. ass%	0.02	89.34	14.23	39.83
Yadava	77613	.	.	77613
hhs%	17.40			8.04
tot. ass%	20.44	.	.	9.03
S.Caste	12229	20045	3150	14436
hhs%	35.99	19.31	0.74	23.57
tot. ass%	6.66	4.66	0.05	4.92
S.C.Christian	40829	4500	8610	17280
hhs%	6.78	0.39	44.85	11.58
tot. ass%	4.19	0.02	7.72	2.90
Other	63930	55973	29352	58724
hhs%	13.57	8.88	4.41	10.22
tot. ass%	13.13	5.98	2.59	8.68
Village mean	**66071**	**83104**	**50016**	**69106**
hhs%	100	100	100	100
Tot Ass%	100	100	100	100

to northern parts of the subcontinent. Declining fertility is accompanying changes in marriage practices which both raise the cost of girls and reduce the support to and from women. The possession of property is leading to increased discrimination against them (see Chapter 3–4 for nutrition and Chapter 3–2 for life itself). Liberalization is predicted to lead to a dissolution of primordial structures, gender being possibly the most primordial of all. Yet precisely the opposite seems to be happening. Here we examine how the assets distribution is gendered.

10.1 *Female-headed households*

Analysing the outcome of the cluster analysis, we noticed dependent households and found that the highest proportion of them were female households. We then searched out all-female households, mapped them onto clusters and have to report that most of these households were among the poorest in these villages.

Households composed of females are by definition female-headed.[45] If we

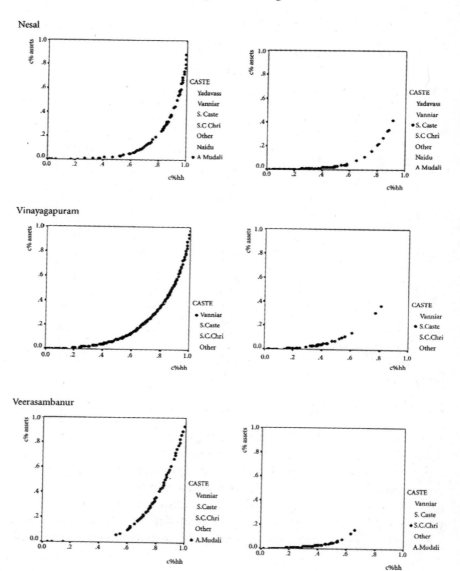

Fɪɢ. 4 Lorenz curves for assets distribution by caste

TABLE 11 Nesal: distribution of land by caste

NESAL	A.Muda-liar	Naidu	Vanniar	Yadava	S.Caste	S.C Christian	Others	ALL
Total	78	10	1	59	122	23	46	339
Households								
Landless	29	4	1	20	110	17	27	208
With land	49	6	0	39	12	6	19	131
% of total households	23%	2.9%	0.3%	17.4%	36%	6.8%	13.6%	100%
% of landlessness within caste groups	37.2%	40%	100%	33.9%	90.2%	73.9%	58.7%	61.4%
Total extent of land (acres)	155.91	5.04		99.38	19.25	6.83	58.01	344.42
of which:								
Dry land	35.11	3		43.32	2.00	1.00	24.66	109.09
Wet land	67.19	0.72		18.85	0.20		15.64	102.60
Pww land	53.61	1.32		37.21	17.05	5.83	17.71	132.73
%of total land	45.3%	1.5%		28.9%	5.6%	2.0%	16.8%	
%of dry land	32.2%	2.8%		39.7%	1.8%	0.9%	22.6%	
%of wet land	65.5%	0.7%		18.4%	0.2%	0.0%	15.2%	
%of punjai land with wells	40.4%	1.0%		28.0%	12.8%	4.4%	13.3%	

TABLE II (*cont.*):

Landholding size groups (acres)	number of households							
Landless	29	4	1	20	110	17	27	208
0.01–0.50	5	2		6	2	1		16
0.51–1.00	11	3		10	2	3	7	36
1.01–1.50	5			6	1	1	1	14
1.51–2.00	5	1		7	6	1	4	24
2.01–2.50				2				2
2.51–3.00	6						1	7
3.01–4.00	4				1		3	8
4.01–5.00	6			2				8
5.01–7.00	2			3			1	6
7.01–10.0	3			2			1	6
10.01–12.5	1			1				2
12.50–15.0							1	1
>15	1							1

Table 12 Vinayagapuram: distribution of land by caste

VINAYAGAPURAM	*A.Muda-liar*	*Naidu*	*Vanniar*	*Yadava*	*S.Caste*	*S.C Christian*	*Others*	*ALL*
Total	—	—	185	—	50	1	23	259
Households								
Landless			46		20	1	12	79
With land			139		30	0	11	180
%of total households			71.4%		19.3%	0.4%	8.9%	100%
% o f landlessness within caste groups			24.9%		40%	100.0%	52.2%	30.5%
Total extent of land (acres)			334.85		29.50		20.35	384.70
of which:								
Dry land			88.81		17.94		3.75	110.50
Wet land			85.93		3.40		10.60	99.93
Pww land			160.11		8.16		6	174.27
%of total land			87%		7.7%		5.3%	
%of dry land			80.4%		16.2%		3.4%	
%of wet land			86%		3.4%		10.6%	
%of punjai land			91.9%		4.7%		3.4%	

TABLE 12 (*cont.*):

Landholding size groups (acres)	number of households				
Landless	46	20	1	12	79
0.01–0.50	11	10		2	23
0.51–1.00	38	13		3	54
1.01–1.50	21	2		3	26
1.51–2.00	13	4		1	18
2.01–2.50	10				10
2.51–3.00	14				14
3.01–4.00	14	1	1		15
4.01–5.00	4			1	5
5.01–7.00	7			1	8
7.01–10.0	5				5
>10	2				2

TABLE 13 Veerasambanur: distribution of land by caste

VEERASAMBANUR	A.Muda-liar	Naidu	Vanniar	Yadava	S.Caste	S.C Christian	Others	ALL
Total	50	—	18	—	1	61	6	136
Landless	4		8		1	35	4	51
With land	46		10			26	2	85
% of total households	36.8%		13.2%		0.7%	44.9%	4.4%	100%
% of landlessness within caste groups	8%		44.4%		—	57.4%	66.7%	37.5%
Total extent of land (acres)	109.96		23.60		0.25	17.59	0.80	152.20
of which:								
Dry land	31.56		9.40		0.25	13.58		54.79
Wet land	44.83		12.40			4.01	0.80	57.23
Pww land	33.57		1.80					40.18
%of total land	72.2%		15.5%		0.2%	11.6%	0.5%	
%of dry land	57.6%		17.2%		0.5%	24.8%	—	
%of wet land	78.3%		21.7%		—	—	—	
%of punjai land	83.5%		4.5%		—	10%	2%	

TABLE 13 (cont.):

Landholding size groups (acres)		number of households				
Landless	4	8		35	4	51
0.01–0.50	4		1	15	2	22
0.51–1.00	5	4		6		15
1.01–1.50	6	1		1		8
1.51–2.00	9			3		12
2.01–2.50	4	2				6
2.51–3.00	6	1		1		8
3.01–4.00	6					6
4.01–5.00	5	1				6
5.01–7.00		1				1
>7	1					1

restrict our analysis of the gendered control over economic resources to completely female households, not only would we underestimate the total number of female-headed households but we may also make misleading inferences, since not all female-headed households are assetless. However, problems arise in defining the head of the house when families include people of both sexes. A definition commonly used in household surveys is based on the sex of the respondent, who is usually that person whom the other members of the household recognize as the head. Other definitions of headship emphasize economic responsibility or the exercise of authority and decision-making. The determination of economic support and authority is nevertheless difficult when there are multiple earners and multiple decision makers.[46] An indicator based on the amount of work, or income, of the different household members, even if able to highlight the effective 'breadwinner', will not necessarily indicate anything about the process of decision-taking within the family.[47] On the other hand, for an indicator based on the sex of the respondent or on authority, relative economic contributions will be irrelevant. It is possible to find cases where the head of the household is an economically inactive person, an elderly male.[48]

Because of data limitations, we decided to adopt the definition of headship in terms of the respondent (since investigators were asked to try to obtain the census information from the 'household head'). In Nesal, there are 49 female-headed households (FHH) – 14.5 per cent of the total. Among them there are 31 households composed only of female members (FH), 10 of which include only women aged over 61 (these being dependent households). The other 21 households have at least 1 member of working age. These are mostly poor families, although three of them are in the cluster of middle peasants. There are then 18 households with members of both sexes. In seven of these, women are the actual breadwinners, since male members are either inactive, or unemployed, or students. If we look at the clusters into which they are grouped, five are poor families and two are middle peasants. There are finally 11 households where both males and females work. Only one of these belongs to the elite (see Table 14).

Landlessness in female-headed households is much higher than that for the total population of households. Four fifths of FHH and 90 per cent of FH do not own any land. Of the nine FHH owning land, six have members of both sexes – and in five of them both males and females are workers (see Table 15).

In Vinayagapuram, 12.4 per cent of the village live in female-headed households, of which half are FH. Five families are identified as dependent households (all members being over 61), while 22 other households are poor peasants: four fifths of the FHH are among the poorest of the village. Three households are middle peasants and two others are part of the elite (see Table 16).

In contrast to Nesal, in Vinayagapuram only 47 per cent of the FHH are

TABLE 14 Nesal: female-headed households and clusters

NESAL	Poor without land	Poor with land	Middle without land	Middle with land	Elite	ALL
Female-headed households	35	3	5	5	1	49
only female members	26	2	2	1	–	31
all aged >61	10					10
with at least 1 member in working age	16	2	2	1		21
males and females only female members	9	1	3	4	1	18
work	4	1	2	–	–	7
male members are students	4		1			5
male members are inactive		1	1			2
both males and females work	5	–	1	4	1	11

TABLE 15 Nesal: female-headed households and land ownership

NESAL		Land ownership				
	Landless	0.01–1.00	1.01–2.00 Number of households	>2	ALL	Landless %
Female-headed households	40	4	2	3	49	82%
only female members	28	1	1	1	31	90%
all aged >61	10				10	100%
with at least 1 member in working age	18	1	1	1	21	86%
males and females	12	3	1	2	18	67%
only female members work	6	1			7	86%
male members are students	5				5	100%
male members are inactive	1	1			2	50%
both males and females work	6	2	1	2	11	55%

TABLE 16 Vinayagapuram: Female-headed households and clusters

VINAYAGAPURAM	Poor without land	Poor with land	Middle without land	Middle with land	Elite	ALL
Female-headed households	15	12	—	3	2	32
only female members	12	5	—	—		17
all aged>61	3	2				5
with at least 1 member in working age	9	3				12
males and females	3	7		3	2	15
only female members work	1	1	2	—		4
male members are students	1	1	2			3
male members are inactive	1					1
both males and females work	2	6		1	2	11

TABLE 17 Vinayagapuram: female-headed households and land ownership

VINAYAGAPURAM	Land ownership				ALL	Landless %
	Landless	0.01–1.00	1.01–2.00	>2	Number of households	
Female-headed households	15	7	5	5	32	47%
only female members	12	3	2		17	71%
all aged >61	3	1	1		5	60%
with at least 1 member in working age	9	2	1		12	75%
males and females	3	4	3	5	15	20%
only female members work	1	1	1	1	4	25%
male members are students		1	1	1	3	—
male members are inactive	1				1	100%
both males and females work	2	3	2	4	11	18%

landless (see Table 17), although 71 per cent of the FH are deprived of land and none of the five households with land owns more than 2 acres.

In Veerasambanur, 18 per cent of households are female-headed (see Table 18). In their ranks are 17 FHH. Five of these families are dependent households. Fourteen households are poor landed peasants and eight more, although landed, are still poor peasants. Only two households are middle peasants, while not a single female-headed household is part of the village elite. About 90 per cent of female-headed households are among the poorest families of Veerasambanur.

If we look at ownership of land by FHH (see Table 19), we find 63 per cent not owning any land. Of the nine households with land, seven own 1 acre or less.

TABLE 18 Veerasambanur: female-headed households and clusters

VINAYAGAPURAM	Poor without land	Poor with land	Middle without land	Middle with land	Elite	ALL
Female-headed households	14	8	1	1	–	24
only female members	12	4	–	1		17
all aged >61	4	1				5
with at least 1 member in working age	8	3		1		12
males and females	2	4	1	–		7
only female members work	1	2	–			3
male members are students	1	1				2
male members are inactive		1				1
both males and females work	1	2	1			4

TABLE 19 Veerasambanur: female-headed households and land ownership

VEERASAMBANUR	Land-less	Land ownership			ALL	Land-less %
		0.01– Number of households	1.01–	2.01–3		
Female-headed households	15	7	1	1	24	63%
only female members	12	4	1		17	71%
all aged >61	4	1			5	80%
with at least 1 member in working age	8	3	1		12	67%
males and females	3	3		1	7	43%
only female members work	1	1		1	3	33%
male members are students	1			1	2	50%
male members are inactive		1			1	0%
both males and females work	2	2			4	50%

Only one household owns more than 3 acres. The proportion of landlessness among FHH exceeds 70 per cent.

There are some rare and extreme exceptions to the tendency of FHH to be poor and landless (see Table 20). In Nesal and Vinayagapuram, a small minority is in the top 10 per cent of richest families. For the most part, FHH control 6–8 per cent of total village assets in units between 35 and 60 per cent smaller than those controlled by men. The distribution bears a strong family resemblance to the land distribution of scheduled castes (see Fig. 5).

11. SUMMARY AND CONCLUSIONS

Village society is highly stratified. Given that the survey method made it impossible either to establish households' own social ranking (which would have

Nesal

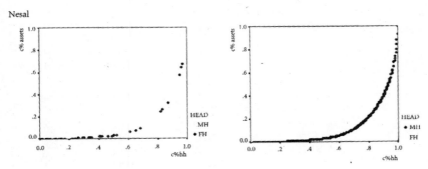

Vinayagapuram

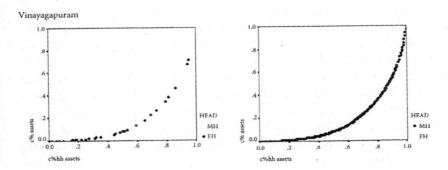

Veerasambanur

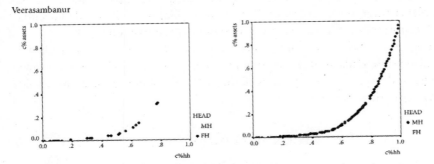

Fig. 5 Lorenz curves for assets distribution by household head

TABLE 20 Average value of assets by household head (Rs)

Household Head		VILLAGE		
		Nesal	Vinayaga-puram	Veera sambanur
	Total Assets			
Female Head		32360	52778	17797
	hhs % (col)	14.45	12.36	17.65
	tot. ass %	7.08	7.85	6.28
Male Head		71767	87379	56920
	hhs % (col)	85.55	87.64	82.35
	tot. ass %	92.92	92.15	93.72
	Village mean	**66071**	**83104**	**50016**

required an unprecedentedly massive process of participation) or to situate households in their political dynamic (which might have been possible after many months of participant observation), we have classified rural households using criteria drawn from several contested theories of mobility and differentiation, adapted for the existence of the agrarian non-farm economy. Cluster analyses isolated three classes of poor peasants (with and without land), middle peasants and an elite. Although the villages differ from each other in significant ways,[49] they have deep continuities in social structure. Each has a massive bloc of peasants – 70 to 80 per cent – who are agricultural workers with less than about an acre of (dry) land or entirely landless; 4–5 per cent of households consist of a single elderly person. Each has a minority of elite households with the largest (irrigated) land holdings, which are diversifying assets and occupations in idiosyncratic and diverse ways. These households dominate the ownership of non-agricultural assets.

Mapping caste onto these classes, we found the dominant agrarian castes to be distributed throughout the classes. By contrast, there are no scheduled castes among the elite classes anywhere and scheduled-caste people dominate the landless labour force. Recent research on these villages also shows that occupation is still stratified by caste in a way that is statistically significant.[50]

Mapping gender onto the classes was more difficult. We found female-headed households in all classes, though concentrated among the poor. Female households were poorer than female-headed ones. Single female households were the poorest of all.

ACKNOWLEDGEMENTS

We are grateful to Venkatesh Athreya, S Janakarajan, Wendy Olsen and S Nee-lakanthan for their comments at the 1996 workshop.

Labour, Gender Relations and the Rural Economy

BARBARA HARRISS-WHITE

1. INTRODUCTION

R URAL labour relations have long been observed to be heavily socially embedded: wage rates are determined by custom – non-market allegiances of patronage and clientship structure rates and non-contractual obligations; labour markets are segmented by caste, ethnicity, age, locality and gender.[1] The great range of contracts (by no means all voluntary) are also found to be more affected by social institutions than they are by transaction costs.[2] Scholars watching the interplay between the economy and institutions such as caste and gender expect that, with liberalization, the significance of the social factors which structure economic behaviour will diminish relative to that of economic factors.[3] Elsewhere we have presented ethnographic evidence from the local urban economy which shows that, far from diminishing, social institutions are being refashioned by market exchange, becoming more economic in their content and roles, but still shaping economic action in ways which are quite distinctive to these institutions.[4] In this chapter we examine some of the ways in which gender is embedded in the rural economy of northern Tamil Nadu and vice versa, and some of the ways these relationships have changed.

There are at least seven ways in which gender is reported to affect economic behaviour.

First, gender ideologies assign responsibility for domestic productive and (socially) reproductive work to women: not only child care but also the gathering of fuel, water and food and handicrafts.[5] So, women's labour-market participation may be constrained by price-unresponsive work.

Second, the work burden of women is heavier than that of men.[6] According to Walker and Ryan (1990), in villages of the Indian semi-arid tropics, women work 10 to 30 per cent longer than do men, with the latter averaging 7–8 hours.

Third, production is marked by strong gender divisions. Ploughing, working bullocks and seed drills, the application of water, fertilizer and pesticide, transport, mechanical milling and the repair of machinery are typically or exclusively male jobs. Harvesting, threshing and winnowing are performed by both men and women. Weeding, transplanting and most of the unmechanized tasks of post-harvest processing are the domain of women.[7] While inelastic in a given locality, there is considerable regional variation in the way tasks are gendered. In Tamil Nadu, Mencher and Saradamoni (1982) found localities where paddy harvesting was done exclusively by women, while elsewhere these operations were performed by mixed-gender pairs. Gender segmentation has been explained with reference to concepts of light and heavy work.[8] But much of the work regarded as light and therefore female (for example, transplanting paddy) is in fact arduous, intensive and skilled,[9] while work observed as heavy (for example carrying water), though it could never be claimed to be light, may be performed with great energy economy.

Fourth, labour market returns are lower for women than men. Either the labour market is neutral with respect to gender and labour-market participation by women is residual and necessarily confined to work of low productivity (which fits in with the priorities of domestic work), or the labour market is as patriarchal as the household and women are paid low wages not as a result of their productivity but as a result of ideologies associating female gender with inferiority. The latter is consistent with evidence that, whenever operations are comparable, women are paid less than men.[10] Research distinguishing the roles of demand for labour from those of so-called 'human capital' variables, (education, age and experience, nutritional status) in the determination of wages has confirmed the gender-specificity of this process, but in contradictory ways. Ryan and Wallace found 'human capital' variables important to the explanation of variations in male wages and 'demand' variables for that in female wages. But Rosenzweig, 1984 and Ryan and Ghodake, found human capital effects overwhelmed by demand variables, particularly for women.[11]

Fifth, despite wage and other kinds of discrimination, women contribute significantly to household income. In 28 villages scattered through Kerala, Tamil Nadu and West Bengal, the minimum amount contributed to household income by women was larger than the minimum contributed by men.[12]

Sixth, women, lacking control over resources, also lack collateral for loans or may only gain access to loans through the relations of clientelage of male family members.[13]

Seventh, female labour-market participation or income-earning production may be a *necessary* condition for women to have an impact on the intrahouse-hold distribution of control over resources or decisions, but it is not *sufficient*.[14] A conscious political struggle in the domestic arena also appears to be required for changes in the balance of control over resources and decisions.[15] While the evidence for gender inequality in nutrients consumption does not necessarily indicate gender bias, the access of women to health care, education and re-sources for private consumption is generally inferior to that of men.[16]

Technical change in agriculture and the penetration of the non-farm econ-omy into rural areas can be expected not only to have different impacts on the genders but also to be intertwined with changes in gender relations resulting from other kinds of social development. From 1983–4 to 1993–4 we would ex-pect to find increased wage work, declines in the gender differences in wage rates and increases in real wage rates and in the elasticity of the gender divisions of tasks. The literature does not permit a simple conclusion on the gendered im-pact of technical change in agriculture. In part, this is because its impact is also caste- and class-specific.[17] In part, it is because of the gendering of labour dis-placement due to mechanization in a given locality. This will depend on the exact tasks mechanized, the prior gender division of labour and that associated with any change in cropping patterns.[18] Both our earlier projects and the field research by Mencher and Saradamoni in northern Tamil Nadu showed demand for female labour increasing in agricultural production and declining in post-harvest processing as a result of the early phases of the Green Revolution.[19] Women were therefore restricted to villages for their livelihoods. Our earlier studies have also shown there to be non-trivial intervillage variation in labour relations, particularly the relative roles of family, permanent and casual labour.[20]

2. LABOUR IN AGRICULTURAL PRODUCTION

Agriculture uses combinations of male and female household labour and hired wage labour, of which there are in turn two types: permanent and casual (the ex-change of labour now being very rare). The focus on gender in this chapter leads us to disaggregate labour in terms of shares or proportions of total labour time. The analysis of 'absolute quantities' of labour has been presented in chapters 1–1 and 1–3. In all three villages in 1993–4 the permanent labour force was composed solely of men, all employed as agricultural labourers. Family labour inputs were also male-biased, while women tended to be casual labourers (see Chapter 1–1 for details). Overall, women worked more days in agricultural production than men. In both the poor peasant and the elite households, women contributed on aggregate more than the 50 per cent of total farm production time that is quoted by Ghodake and Ryan for South India in the 1980s.[21]

From the discussion in Chapter 1–1 we saw that, even within the same class, there are intervillage variations in the type of labour employed in agricultural work. In Nesal, there is a massive contrast between the low agricultural labour input of female family labour and the high input of female hired casual labour. In Veerasambanur the contrast is less marked. In Vinayagapuram, however, male family labour contributes by a hair's breadth the larger number of days to agricultural production. Of the female labour used for farm work, family labour plays a greater role than hired labour.[22]

A gendered comparison between poor and 'elite' households in each of the villages shows consistent class-specific patterns in the labour process.[23] The proportion of total labour from casual female labour on the agricultural land of richer households is some 39 per cent greater than that on poor peasant holdings. By contrast, male casual labour remains at almost the same proportion on rich households' land as on that of poor households.

Results from this truncated sample of 3 villages are in sharp contrast to those from the 11 villages in 1973 and 1983 (see Table 1). In 1973, male and female labour were equally employed in crop production, while men dominated the labour-days in 1983. Hired labour was as important as family labour in 1973, but its share in total labour use had fallen by 25 per cent on the average farm a decade later.[24]

By 1993–4, hired labour was 60 per cent of all labour inputs on small peasant holdings and 70 per cent on those of the agrarian elite. The second decade witnessed an intensification of the class differences observable for 1983: a doubling of female casual labour inputs on the land of elite households (from 27 to 54 per cent) and the halving of the proportion of labour supplied by female family workers in rich peasant households.

Pace predictions about the female-labour-displacing impact of mechanization

TABLE 1 Percentage of labour days spent in crop production by male and female labour, 1973–93

	1973 (11 Villages)		1983 (11 Villages)		1993 (3 Villages)	
	Small Farms	Large Farms	Small Farms	Large Farms	Small Farms	Large Farms
Family Labour:						
Male	36	33	47	35	25	18
Female	14	16	19	20	17	7
Casual Labour:						
Male	16	18	13	18	18	19
Female	34	32	21	27	42	54

Source: 1973 and 1983: summary data adapted from Hazell and Ramasamy 1991; 1993–4: field survey. 'Small' farms are under 1ha, 'large' farms over 1ha.

in paddy cultivation,[25] the agricultural labour force appears now to be being feminized. The earlier trend is being reversed and it is male labour that is displaced. Da Corta and Venkateshwarku (1999) have observed exactly the same trends not far away in Chittoor District, Andhra Pradesh. Such a feminization may be due to the male-labour-displacing impact of mechanization in lift irrigation, ploughing and harvesting; to male withdrawal from joint tasks performed by both genders; to increasing local off-farm income-earning opportunities for men; or the tendency for men temporarily to migrate in search of work (women being prevented by child care and other gender-inelastic, domestic work).

2.1 *The gender division of agricultural labour*

In an agricultural production process characterized, as here, by sex-sequential tasking, rigid gender divisions are expected, where ploughing is done almost exclusively by men and the transplanting of paddy and weeding is done predominantly by women. The gender exclusivity of tasks and the importance of the various agricultural operations in contributing to agricultural labour income are presented by class. Table 2 shows that for labouring poor peasants (landed and non-landed) the gender exclusivity of tasks is as expected. Ploughing forms

TABLE 2 Percentage of income earned by 'poor peasant' cluster in agricultural wage work, by operation

Operation	Nesal		Veerasambanur		Vinayagapuram	
	% of Men's Income from Agric. Wage Work	% of Women's Income from Agric. Wage Work	% of Men's Income from Agric. Wage Work	% of Women's Income from Agric. Wage Work	% of Men's Income from Agric. Wage Work	% of Women's Income from Agric. Wage Work
Ploughing	57	0	36	0	67	0
Contourbunding	5	0	0	0	0.5	0
Planting	5	0	0.5	3	2.5	4.5
Sowing	4	4	2	4	0	2.3
Uprooting	5	2	4	1	11	0
Transplanting	0	12	0	10	0	13
Weeding	2	29	14	21	0.8	18
Harvesting	9	33	7	20	4	33
Threshing	13	18	7	20	4	33

Source: Field survey, 1993–4.

the bulk of the agricultural wage income of men. Transplanting is performed only by women and weeding contributes relatively far more to female income than it does to male income. Once again, there is intervillage variation in the gender specificity of tasks even within the same socio-economic group. In Veerasambanur, weeding contributes 13 per cent to male income, whereas in Nesal this contribution is negligible and no weeding is done by men in Vinayagapuram. In Nesal and Vinayagapuram, men earn very little of their income from harvesting (which used to be a joint task). In these villages, harvesting has been mechanized.

By contrast, among the rural elite, the gender divisions in tasks are slightly less rigid (see Table 3). Some income (albeit very little) is earned by women in ploughing, possibly through the supervision of ploughing, while men participate in transplanting and weeding in Nesal and Veerasambanur, where they gain a comparatively high proportion of income from transplanting. Transplanting is reported to be a 'female' task. The relaxation in task rigidity in the direction of masculinization found in Veerasambanur is not a common phenomenon. This substitution of male for female labour may be due to the fact that, with increased income, female household members are being withdrawn from field work. As in the poor peasant cluster, the mechanization of harvesting in Nesal and Vinayagapuram appears to have displaced male labour.

TABLE 3 Percentage of income earned by elite cluster in agricultural wage work, by operation

Operation	Nesal		Veerasambanur		Vinayagapuram	
	% of Men's Income from Agric. Wage Work	% of Women's Income from Agric. Wage Work	% of Men's Income from Agric. Wage Work	% of Women's Income from Agric. Wage Work	% of Men's Income from Agric. Wage Work	% of Women's Income from Agric. Wage Work
Ploughing	42	2.5	38	0	64	0
Contourbunding	3	0	0	0	0	0
Planting	2	6	1	0	0	13
Sowing	0	0.6	0	0	0	2
Uprooting	12	1	12	0	16	0
Transplanting	2	20	17	21	0	9
Weeding	8	20	5	28	0	22
Harvesting	9.5	37	16	39	5	31
Threshing	10	11	11	12	14	24

Source: Field survey, 1993–4.

While the segmentation of tasks by gender varies by village and by socio-economic group, and while tasks are more gender-elastic than they used to be, the restriction of women to the lower-paid tasks is solidly institutionalized.

2.2 *Agricultural wages*

There are five features of the market for agricultural labour. First, rates are both village- and task-specific. In 1993–4, over the set of 11 villages (if Table 4 here is compared with Table 15 in Chapter 1–3) the daily rates for ploughing varied from Rs 20 to Rs 50, the rate for weeding groundnut was only Rs 7, while those for weeding paddy varied from Rs 7 to Rs 12. Second, kind components of wages mean that payment varies even more. Measures for raw kind-payments vary. Cooked meals range from gruel to rice and dhal. By-products are sometimes included in payments in kind. Third, contracts are moving ineluctably towards piece rate and payments per unit of land for an entire operation such as transplanting or harvesting – so that labour organizes itself by group, reducing transaction costs for employers. Fourth, there is great specificity in the length of the working day. Ploughing shifts range by village from 3 a.m. to 7 a.m., through 5 a.m. to 1 p.m., to 7 a.m. to midday. Similarly, transplanting can last from 6 a.m. to 9 a.m., from 10 a.m. to 4 p.m., 7 a.m. to 5 p.m., 8 a.m. to 3 p.m. and so on. Village conventions still structure agricultural labour, making the returns per hour of labour both indeterminate and uncomparable.

But fifth, the overriding inequality in payment is by gender. Women's wages can be down to half those paid to men for ploughing. This difference in remuneration cannot easily be attributed to differences in productivity. It must result from the operation of gender ideologies. Table 4 shows the average daily wage rates for different tasks and modes of payment in the three villages, and the 1993 wage has been deflated to be compared with real wages in 1983 and 1973. Over the two decades, while real, average male wage rates have increased by 20 per cent, those for women have increased by 15 per cent. This masks a tightening in the casual female labour market in Vinayagapuram and declines in real female wages for transplanting and weeding in both Nesal and Veerasambanur. Gender differentials in agricultural wages are widening. In the decade from 1983–4, while the real male *cash* wage has increased by 85 per cent and the kind wage by 80 per cent, the figures for women have increased by 38 and 37 per cent respectively.[26]

2.3 *Gendered contributions to household income*

Despite the fact that women are paid lower wages than men, women work more days and longer hours in agricultural production than men, and they contribute

TABLE 4 Daily agricultural wages and trends, 1973–93 (constant 1973 Rs)

	1993 Current	Constant (1)	1983 Constant	1973 Constant
NESAL				
Ploughing with bullocks (M: 6 hr day)	Rs 25	4.25	3.25	1.5
Transplanting / Weeding (F)	Rs 8 (2)	1.36	1.63	1.3
Harvesting (F) in kg (3)	5	5	5	4.25
Threshing (M) kg	10	10	10	8.5
VEERASAMBANUR				
Ploughing with bullocks (M: 6 hr day)	20	3.4	2.75	0.75
Transplanting / Weeding (F)	7	1.19	1.36	1.25
Harvesting (F) in kg (3)	6.4 (4)	6.4	4.25	4.25
Threshing (M) kg	12 (5)	12	8.5	8.5
VINAYAKAPURAM				
Ploughing with bullocks (M: 6 hr day)	20	3.4	2.7	2
Transplanting / Weeding (F)	9	1.53	1.36	0.7
Harvesting (F) in kg (3)	6.4(4)	6.4	4	3
Threshing (M) kg	12 (5)	12	4	3

Notes:

(1) The deflator using the CPIAL is 0.17 for 1993–1973.

(2) This is actually Rs 7, plus a meal. Meals are of *ragi kanji*, worth Rs 1.

(3) Actually paid in *padi*, which is approximately 1.6 kg.

(4) Harvesting and threshing rates are net of meals. A meal is estimated at Rs 6.

(5) This rate is now for harvesting and threshing together. See note 4.

(6) The daily rates are village averages per task, per day.

Source of 1983 and 1973 data: Hazell and Ramasamy 1991.

more in earnings to household income. Again, villages and classes produce systematic variations. While in Veerasambanur, among poor peasants, men contribute more to household earnings from agriculture and elite men and women contribute about equally, in Vinayagapuram and Nesal women contribute more in wage income.[27]

3. LABOUR IN NON-AGRICULTURAL PRODUCTION

As in agriculture, so in non-farm activity, the labour input is both paid and unpaid.

3.1 *Wage work*

In 1983, non-agriculture and non-farm business constituted 37 per cent of total male employment and 25 per cent of female employment in Nesal and 11 per

cent of total male employment in Veerasambanur. There was no female participation in non-farm wage work in Veerasambanur and no male or female participation in Vinayagapuram.[28] Since 1983, the non-farm economy in all three
villages has grown considerably, particularly as a result of the expansion of the
silk-weaving industry (see Chapter 1–6 here).

If women dominate the work of crop production, the non-agricultural sector
gives livelihood opportunities biased towards men. That this is not an exclusive
phenomenon can be judged from the relatively high proportion of women employed in the non-farm sector in Veerasambanur. Table 5 shows the percentage
of total days worked in non-farm activity and Table 6 the respective percentage
of total earnings by gender. The differences between the two tables reflect gender differences in rates of pay and in the returns to household-based production. From these a high level of village-specific idiosyncrasy in the non-farm
activity of richer households can be seen. In Nesal (with the most advanced capitalist production relations), two thirds of the labour is from male wage workers
and the rest from male household members. In Vinayagapuram the proportions are reversed, while in Veerasambanur non-farm activity is confined to the
poor. Among poor households, while in Veerasambanur the labour process is
based predominantly on male family labour, in Vinayagapuram and Veerasambanur labour is more evenly distributed between domestic and wage workers.
*For the three villages, women bring in only 8 per cent of all income earned from
non-farm wage work.* If we compare earnings with days of work in non-farm activity, men earn more per unit of time than women, although the differential

TABLE 5 Gender division of the proportion of total days spent working
in non-agricultural production, by village and cluster

Village and Cluster	% of Total Days in Non-Farm Work by Gender and Labour Type			
	Family Labour Male	Family Labour Female	Casual Labour Male	Casual Labour Female
NESAL				
Elite	29	0	71	0
Poor Peasant	49	5	46	0
VEERASAMBANUR				
Elite	0	0	0	0
Poor Peasant	81	19	0	0
VINAYAGAPURAM				
Elite	87	0	13	0
Poor Peasant	28	9	43	20

Source: Field survey, 1993–4.

TABLE 6 Gender differentials in proportion of total household wage earnings from non-agricultural work

Village and Cluster	% of Total Non-Farm Earnings	
	Male	Female
NESAL		
Elite	100	0
Poor Peasant	94	6
VEERASAMBANUR		
Elite	100	0
Poor Peasant	94	6
VINAYAGAPURAM		
Elite	100	0
Poor Peasant	72	28

Source: Field survey, 1993–4.

TABLE 7 Wage differentials by gender and occupation for non-agricultural wage work

	Average Daily Wage (Rupees)	
Activity	Male	Female
Food Collection	5.5	6.6
Firewood Collection	32	8
Mosaic Work	38	10
Wood Cutting	25	10
Silk Coolie	34	6.5
Silk Apprentice	5	0
Dhobi (Clothes Washing)	1	0.3

Source: Field survey, 1993–4.

varies between villages. In particular, when the 'joint' tasks are performed by both men and women, the pro-male gender bias in wages is strikingly greater than it is in agriculture (see Table 7).

3.2 *Unwaged work*

Our survey could not include a study of the time allocation of men and women for unpaid labour input into the maintenance of the household. Table 8 shows the results from a time allocation study near Gudiyatham in North Arcot (Ambedkar) District, where the time spent by women in domestic activities is compared with that spent by men in income-earning activity. Women spend a far higher proportion of time in household maintenance, production and

TABLE 8 Activity patterns (mins/day) by gender

Activity	Men	Women
Personal	701	766
Domestic and child care	16	290
Social	237	151
Field Supervision	22	3
Field Work	151	120
Animal Care	95	52
Travel	112	35
Leisure	39	8
Business and Trade	17	4
Other Occupations	50	11

Source: Gillespie and McNeill 1992.

TABLE 9 Gender distribution of labour input time for livestock upkeep, by village and cluster

Village	% Total Livestock Labour Input			
	Poor Cluster		Elite Cluster	
	Male	Female	Male	Female
Nesal	51	49	36	64
Veerasambanur	18	82	74	26
Vinayagapuram	64	100	100	0

Source: Field survey, 1993–4.

reproduction than men do. It has also been reported that women spend much unwaged work time looking after livestock. Rogaly (1994) in his study of two villages in West Bengal, for instance, found that women spent twice as much time as men in the upkeep of livestock. The evidence from these three villages, however, is different. There is intervillage variation (significant at the 5 per cent level) in the time input of men and women (see Table 9). In Nesal, the care of livestock is more feminized than elsewhere. And this crosses classes. There is also significant class variation. Poor peasant women put a 27 per cent greater time input into livestock rearing than do men. In rich households, men spent an average of twice the time of women on the care of animals.

As was the case in crop production, there is considerable elasticity in the gendered tasks involved in livestock rearing, none being completely exclusive (see Table 10). While the collection of fodder tends to be a female task and the washing of livestock is a male task, grazing and watering are more evenly shared by the genders. Class differences characterize milking (a male task for the poor and a female task for the rich) and feeding (the reverse).

TABLE 10 The gender division of tasks in livestock upkeep

Operation	% Livestock Labour Input Time by Operation			
	Males Poor Cluster	Males Elite Cluster	Females Poor Cluster	Females Elite Cluster
Grazing/Rearing	60	34	40	66
Grass Cutting	6	0	94	100
Washing	77	75	23	25
Feeding	22	76	78	24
Grass Collection	16	10	84	90
Cleaning	6	0	94	0
Watering	58	66	42	34
Milking	63	17	37	83

Source: Field survey, 1993–4.

4. THE PRIVATE GENDERED APPROPRIATION OF INCOME

The material subordination of women is widely thought to extend to highly unequal access to household income appropriable for individual consumption. But the overwhelming majority of studies on intrahousehold expenditure biases failed to find them, even when the welfare outcomes of expenditure are biased by gender. Most work has used data on food intake and makes statistical inferences from household expenditure and gendered composition. However, Asadullah has used National Council for Applied Economic Research (NCAER) data for the 1990s on individual direct expenditure to examine intrahousehold disparities and non-compensated discrimination between the genders in medical and educational expenditure in Tamil Nadu.[29] Males consistently receive a greater expenditure on all aspects of education than do females across all age bands to ages well beyond secondary school. Male children get 30 per cent greater medical expenditure than do girls. He concludes that there is strong evidence of gender discrimination in expenditure. To assess gendered expenditure disparities, household expenditure on 'adult items' which (according to Mencher and Saradamoni's 1982 research) are generally or exclusively for male consumption (alcohol, tobacco, cigars, betelnut and income spent in tea houses) was calculated as a percentage of total food expenditure.[30] In the same way, expenditure on cosmetics – which are generally (although certainly not exclusively) female items – was calculated.

Tables 11 and 12 show that expenditure on male items relative to total expenditure on food is comparatively higher in poor households than in rich households. In the poor peasant cluster, expenditure on 'male items' is significant in

TABLE 11 Expenditure on 'male' goods and on cosmetics as a percentage of total food expenditure (TFE), by season and village–'poor peasant' cluster

Season	Nesal		Veerasambanur		Vinayagapuram	
	Male % of TFE	Cosmetic % of TFE	Male % of TFE	Cosmetic % of TFE	Male % of TFE	Cosmetic % of TFE
1	6	0.2	5	0.3	2.3	0.2
2	34	1.5	29	0	17	0.2
3	35	1	29	0	14	0.7
Average	13	0.6	8	0.2	4	0.3

Note: TFE = total food expenditure.

Source: Field survey, 1993–4.

TABLE 12 Expenditure on 'male' goods and on cosmetics as a percentage of total food expenditure (TFE), by season and village–'elite' cluster

Season	Nesal		Veerasambanur		Vinayagapuram	
	Male % of TFE	Cosmetic % of TFE	Male % of TFE	Cosmetic % of TFE	Male % of TFE	Cosmetic % of TFE
1	2	0.2	2	0.3	2.4	0.3
2	15	1	25	0	19	0
3	13	1	25	0	14	1
Average	4	0.4	3.4	0.2	4	0.3

Source: Field survey, 1993–4.

proportion to household food expenditure and is many multiples (13–20) of estimated female private expenditure. In particular, in the seasons where absolute expenditure on food is low, the amount spent on male goods does not fall, and so the proportion increases markedly (an inelasticity which was also observed a decade earlier[31]). The behaviour of rich households is different from that of poor ones. It is also unexpected. Gillespie found in a nearby locality that richer households spent significantly more throughout the year on tobacco and alcohol than did poor ones.[32] Since according to Engel's Law the proportion spent on food relative to other goods falls with rising income, it is surprising that in relative terms the proportion spent on 'male' goods (at ten times the expenditure on female goods) is not even higher relative to food expenditure in rich households. It is also surprising that the proportion of private expenditure in richer households rises and that the antifemale gender bias increases in the 'minor' seasons of *navarai* and *sornavari*.

5. CONCLUSIONS

The evolution of the relations between gender and the labour market is much more complex than allowed for by the notion of liberalization and 'marketization' as social solvents.

5.1 *Plus ça change: The more things change...*

Whereas, 20 years ago, the agricultural labour process was incipiently capitalist, now casual wage labour relations dominate small holder agriculture. Hired labour is now 60–70 per cent of all labour input to agriculture. Women have not been marginalized. On the contrary, *women have come to dominate the labour input into agriculture and provide over half of all farm labour, largely as casual wage workers. Despite significantly lower wage rates,[33] they contribute more to household income than do men.*

Wide class differences are now visible: female casual labour is employed disproportionately in the labour process of richer households. From 1983 to 1993, female family inputs in the households of the rural elite halved, whereas there was but a slight drop in poor households. *Mechanization appears to be displacing men, confirming one of the original expectations.* The process of proletarianization and the degree of consolidation of female labour markets shows intervillage variation, as might be expected, since labour relations are distinctively localized.[34] In Veerasambanur, transplanting is being masculinized. Whereas in Nesal agriculture is dominated by female casual labour and the non-farm economy by male casual labour, in the other two villages the non-farm economy is less developed and family labour is more significant to both sectors.

The non-farm economy is emerging at a rapid pace, but entry is biased towards men. Women in richer households are completely excluded from non-farm activity, although they still have a significant role in the care of livestock. *Rigidities in the gender divisions of labour are being relaxed, but increasing gender-elasticity appears first in the enterprise mix of richer households, where tasks such as transplanting (and even the supervision of ploughing) are less fiercely gender-rigid than either they used to be or than they still are in poor peasant production.*

5.2 *Plus c'est la même chose: the more things stay the same...*

The village is still a significant unit for the understanding of labour relations, despite wage rates showing greater regional integration than a decade previously. *The operation of these three village economies remains very biased against women.* Real wage rates for the majority of women's tasks have been stagnant or have declined over the last decade. Personal, private consumption is heavily biased against women, more so in poor households than in rich ones. We saw earlier that female households and female-headed ones are most consistently associated with poverty (and also see Chapters 2–4 on credit and 3–1 on poverty). Gender differences in wage rates in the non-farm economy greatly exceed those in agriculture. The labour process, though increasingly differentiated, is still strongly segmented by gender. Women earn less than men, *even* for joint tasks which may be performed by either sex and irrespective of their productivity.

While we have recorded a pervasive antifemale bias in agriculture, non-agriculture, household production and personal consumption, the extent of that bias varies between and within localities and socio-economic classes. So while we cannot argue in an essentialist way that 'liberalization is good for men', we appear to be witnessing here what has been noted generally: the feminization of poverty.[35]

The effects of markets on gender relations are ambivalent. Their capacity to dissolve can be seen in the increasing gender-elasticity of the divisions of tasks and in the exploitation of female labour in agriculture in order to keep down the costs of production. The accumulating classes are segmenting the casual labour market along gender lines, allotting women to agriculture and men to the non-farm economy. We can also see markets remaining embedded in (the product of) gender relations and ideologies to the extent that the best paid segments of work are captured by men. In the rapidly developing labour markets in the non-farm economy, gender differentials in wages for comparable tasks exceed those in agriculture. Female income does not translate itself into increased female control over domestic resources and decisions. Where work in the non-farm economy sometimes requires spatial mobility, women's (still mostly) non-negotiable 'prior' domestic work physically constrains their participation and forces them into longer working days than men. Rather than eroding gender as a factor affecting the operation of markets, markets are reworking gender here. If such processes are reproduced more widely, then market reforms can be expected to be mediated by gender. In such circumstances, gender equity cannot be left to market forces but will have to be fought for by determined political action inside and outside the market domain, both to regulate labour relations and to create and defend equitable non-market principles of exchange.

A female agricultural proletariat has been created. But there is no evidence of any mobilization to counter gender discrimination across classes, over a wider region or even within socio-economic groups and small localities. There is no evidence from these villages that the increasingly important contribution of female earnings to household income, particularly in poor households, has been translated into increased female control of resources or decisions domestically.

Women have had wage work superimposed upon their domestic economy. The outlook for most women is one of drudgery.

ACKNOWLEDGEMENTS

The descriptive analysis is drawn from the unpublished M.Sc. thesis of Lara Legassick, to whom I am very grateful. Thanks are due to S Janakarajan for field direction and to A Dayal and A Vaidyanathan for their discussants' comments at the MIDS workshop in 1996.

Social Institutions and the Structural Transformation of the Non-Farm Economy

1. INTRODUCTION

Employment in the rural non-farm sector increased strikingly over the two decades studied. In the case of male workers, it has increased from 16.7 per cent of total employment in 1972–73 to 29 per cent in 1990–91, though the corresponding shares for women workers are 11.2 and 15.1 per cent. This expansion in rural non-farm employment[1] may be viewed with relief as a solution to the problems of increasing agricultural unemployment and underemployment and of the rural exodus to towns and cities in search of livelihoods, with consequent increases in the pressure on urban infrastructure.[2] There is therefore a literature documenting the growth and spatial variation in the incidence of rural non-agricultural employment,[3] as well as a literature analysing the causes of growth and of spatial variations in it.[4] These studies have been influenced a great deal by Mellor's *New Economics of Growth* (1976), his theory of growth linkages from agriculture,[5] and the 'coincidence' observed between the increase in agricultural production and productivity (the result of the 'green revolution' introduced in the mid-1960s) and the expansion in rural non-agricultural employment.[6] The growth in rural non-agricultural employment was assumed to be induced by agricultural growth linkages or agrarian prosperity, powered by changes in purchased inputs, the expansion of marketing and processing activities and consumption patterns involving demand for local non-farm products.[7]

A contrary view attributes the growth in rural non-agricultural employment to agrarian distress, by which is meant acute poverty in the agricultural sector.[8] The contrast has been posed as being between choice and necessity.[9] But each of these views is extreme, partial and restrictive, not recognizing the importance either of seasonality or of social and cultural factors, whether as determinants of demand for non-farm-produced goods or as constraints to skill accumulation. In this chapter, a broad framework which accommodates a wider range of analytical perspectives and empirical conditions will be developed and special attention will be paid to social institutions in shaping the expansion of rural non-farm employment.

2. AN ANALYTICAL FRAMEWORK[10]

A simple model is provided in Fig. 1 in which the structural transformation of the workforce is viewed as one component of the process of socio-economic transformation. Urbanization and the growth of rural non-farm employment may be seen as spatial manifestations of this structural transformation. Urbanization has two components: a) the growth of existing urban centres; and b) the emergence of new urban centres.[11] The expansion of existing urban centres, apart from being due to urban population growth, is powered by migration. If the structural transformation of the workforce occurs on a large enough scale to change the character of the village economy from agrarian to non-agrarian, new

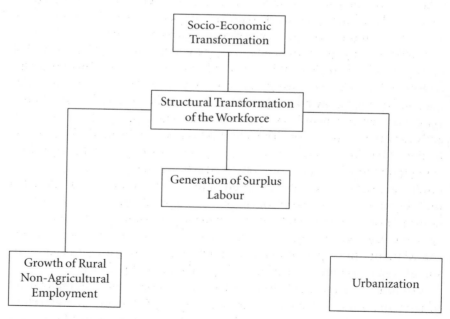

FIG. 1 Structural transformations

urban centres emerge. So the growth of employment in the rural non-farm sector can be viewed either as a structural transformation without non-farm production being scaled up or as a prelude to the transformation of rural areas into urban space. Rural and urban can be seen as inter-related spaces in a process of transformation in which the generation of 'surplus labour', which is central to the structural transformation of the workforce, takes place.[12]

Figure 2 summarizes the factors that can affect the 'generation of surplus labour'. The latter can be theorized to result from the result of the technological transformation of agriculture,[13] or alternatively be a consequence of 'distress', by which is meant conditions of acute poverty with or without technological transformation.[14] But Figure 2 shows how labour surpluses can develop for a variety of reasons other than the mechanization of agriculture or agrarian poverty, the nature of which determines the character and extent of diversification in the rural non-farm sector. Population growth and the consequent increase in the labour force are straightforward to understand. Social sector development, particularly the growth of education, results in the generation of surplus labour because educated people generally look for employment outside agriculture, in particular for white-collar jobs. The commercialization of agriculture and institutional changes in the labour market (e.g. the breakdown of the *jajmani* system and the decline in permanent/attached labourers) lead to casualization of the workforce and freer mobility of labourers.[15] Caste is an institution under which the scope for alternative skill accumulation and occupational mobility has been restricted. Education has helped to break down such restrictions.

Conventional growth theory and the urbanization literature stress the generation of surplus labour only from the agricultural sector. But surplus labour may be extended from the urban, industrial and rural non-farm sectors. For instance, the decline in rural household industries (e.g. cotton handloom and mat weaving) leads to the release of surplus labour. The closure of sick, modern, small-scale industries (e.g. the closure of eight TANSI (Tamil Nadu Small Industries) units, BHEL (Bharat Heavy Electricals Ltd) ancillaries, Mettur Textiles and Standard motors in Tamil Nadu) also contributes to surplus labour. Apart from these factors the state's structural adjustment policies, downsizing employment in public-sector enterprises, generates surplus labour.

Conventional growth theory is flawed for yet another reason. Technological transformation in the agricultural sector, which accompanies agrarian prosperity, is assumed to be labour-displacing.[16] The possibility that labour-absorbing technological transformation could accompany agrarian prosperity is discounted.[17] This neglect has resulted in the hypothesis of a direct relationship between agrarian prosperity and 'surplus labour generation'.

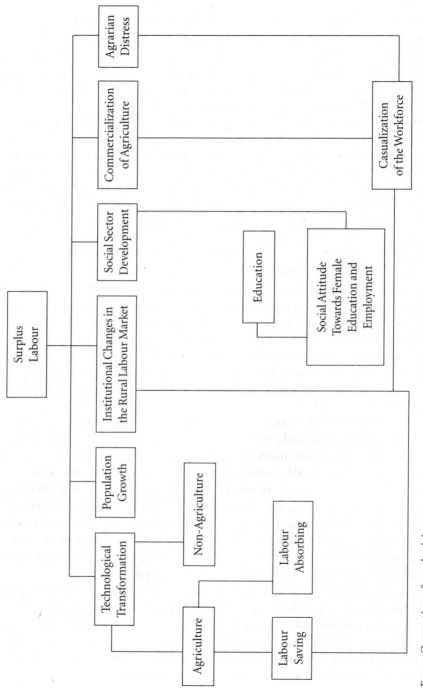

FIG. 2 Generation of surplus labour

The generation of surplus labour, while necessary for the structural transformation of the workforce, is not a sufficient condition. Factors affecting the demand for the goods and services of the rural non-farm sector play a crucial role. Figure 3 lists the factors affecting the demand for rural non-farm goods and services. The forward and backward linkages generated by agricultural growth or agrarian prosperity are well documented.[18] Here, a direct relationship between agrarian prosperity and the rural demand for rural non-farm-produced goods and services is hypothesized. Increases in income in the agricultural sector are expected to be spent on rural non-farm-produced goods. But agroprocessing industries are largely located in urban areas.[19] Consumption patterns are affected by demonstration effects, social sector development, particularly education, by upward social mobility[20] and by the introduction of new goods (say, synthetic fibres, which accelerated the destruction of the rural-based cotton handloom industry). Thus the direct relationship is simplistic and incomplete.

Even if demand shifted in favour of urban manufactured goods, which employment in trade and transport will increase, the net impact of such changes depends on the scale of decline in employment in the handloom and other household manufacturing industries that are destroyed in the villages and on the scale of absorption of labour in new activities. Demand for housing, for the growth of modern industries and for services in urban areas will affect the extent of employment in the rural non-farm sector. The extent and nature of growth in the rural non-farm sector depends on the nature of the urban centre to which the village is connected and the distance between the urban centre and the village.[21] Commuting results in an increase in the number of rural residents reporting non-farm employment, though the activity pursued is actually outside the rural area. Conversely, the ancillarization or subcontracting of production leads to the growth of ancillary industries in villages close to industrial centres. These location patterns lead to underestimates of urban employment multipliers.

Quite apart from these factors, government expenditure on rural employment generation programmes, on the promotion of *khadi* and village industries (including the subsidies given to consumers as sales promotion measures on occasions of festivals), on government purchases of consumer goods and on expenditure on rural health, on antipoverty schemes, on the public distribution system and on education and physical infrastructure affect the growth of the rural non-farm sector. Government employees in rural and semi-urban areas create their own local consumption multipliers.[22]

The spatial distribution of non-agricultural activities is also influenced by government policies[23] such as the establishment of industrial estates in backward

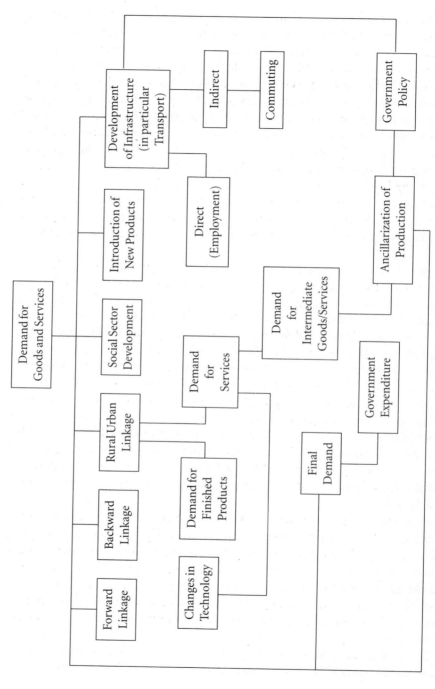

FIG. 3 Factors affecting demand for goods and services of rural origin

districts, credit policy, investments in infrastructural facilities and subsidies given to industries in backward regions. The location of rural industries is also path-dependent. The local history of industrialization, the availability of natural resources, climatic conditions and the development of skills affect their sites.

If, as is assumed in the empirical literature on the growth of rural non-farm employment, the rural non-farm sector is homogeneous and market forces alone determine access to employment in the rural non-agricultural sector, social institutions, particularly caste and gender, will not affect the probability or chances of employment. But if these institutions are found to affect rural classes differently and hence differentially affect the chances of entry into non-agricultural sectors, then it follows that the rural non-farm sector is *not* homogenous and market forces by themselves do *not* determine access to non-farm activity. Our particular concern, which arises from a consideration for equity, is the relationship between access to land and access to non-agricultural employment. If the members of landed households enjoy relatively better access to non-agricultural employment than do landless agricultural labour households, then inequality in the distribution of income will increase. The objectives of this chapter are to examine: 1) the influence of caste and gender on access to non-farm employment; and 2) the importance of access to the means of production, particularly land, as a determinant of access to non-agricultural employment.

3. SOURCES OF DATA

Census schedules canvassed in the three villages of Nesal, Vinayagapuram and Veerasambanur provided detailed information on caste, education, land holdings and occupational details of members of households. Apart from the data collected from the village census house listing, information obtained from knowledgeable village informants was also used. We examine first the distribution of households by major occupation of household members and then the distribution of workers according to their industrial classification by caste and sex.

There are 745 households in the 3 selected villages. These households are classified into households with a) at least one earning member (703) and b) no earning member (42). The distribution of these households by caste and by access to land is presented in Table 1.

4. THE NON-FARM VILLAGE ECONOMY

The 703 households with at least one earning member have been classified into agricultural and non-agricultural households. Four different distributions of

TABLE 1 Distribution of households by access to land and access to non-agricultural employment

	Classifications			
	I	II	III	IV
Agricultural Households				
Own/Operate Land	102 (50.50)	177 (59)	177 (57.10)	206 (57.70)
Landless Agricultural	100 (49.50)	123 (41)	129 (41.61)	146 (40.90)
Other Labour	0	0	4 (1.29)	5 (1.40)
Sub-Total	202 (28.73)	300 (42.67)	310 (44.10)	357 (50.78)
Non-Agricultural Households				
Own/Operate Land	307 (61.28)	232 (57.57)	232 (59.03)	203 (58.67)
Landless Agricultural	121 (24.15)	98 (24.32)	92 (23.41)	75 (21.68)
Other Labour	73 (14.57)	73 (18.11)	69 (17.56)	68 (19.65)
Sub-Total	501 (71.27)	403 (57.33)	393 (55.90)	346 (49.22)
Total	703 (100)	703 (100)	703 (100)	703 (100)

I = Animal husbandry is a non-agricultural activity
II = Animal husbandry is agricultural
III = One member with secondary occupation as non-agricultural
IV = At least one worker with primary occupation as non-agricultural

the households are obtained. About 58 per cent of the total households have access to land. About 50 per cent of these households have at least one worker reporting his/her primary occupation to be a non-agricultural activity other than animal husbandry. Around 75 per cent of the households with access to land have at least one working member reporting the secondary occupation as a non-agricultural activity, including animal husbandry. Equivalent figures for the landless households are 33.94 per cent (with a non-agricultural primary occupation) and 54.75 per cent (with a non-agricultural secondary occupation).[24]

Households with access to land enjoy relatively better access to non-agricultural employment.

In the past, caste determined occupation, access to resources and education. Despite constitutional provisions to safeguard the interests of the backward and deprived sections of India's population, the situation seems to have changed but little. Table 2 provides, for each caste, the distribution of households obtained for classification I in Table 1. Based on the data provided in Table 2, an index of excess access to land and non-agricultural occupation has been constructed.[25] This index is defined for each category.

Table 3 provides information on: 1) excess access to land by each caste; 2) excess access to non-agricultural employment by caste, controlling for access to land; 3) excess access to non-agricultural employment by caste, controlling for landlessness and presence of at least one agricultural labour; and 4) excess access to non-agricultural employment by caste, controlling for all other characteristics (specialized non-agricultural households). Agamudhya Mudaliars, who are at the top of the caste hierarchy in these villages, enjoy relatively better access to both land and non-agricultural employment. Similarly, Naidus, who are placed next to Agamudhya Mudaliars in the caste hierarchy, enjoy disproportionately

TABLE 2 Distribution of agricultural and non-agricultural households by access to land and by caste

Caste	Agriculture		Non-agriculture		Others	Total
	Own/ Operate	Landless	Own/ Operate	Landless		
A. Mudaliar	17 (16.67)	1 (1)	75 (24.43)	8 (6.61)	17 (23.29)	118 (16.79)
Naidu	– –	1 (1)	6 (1.95)	2 (1.65)	1 (1.37)	10 (1.42)
Vanniar	46 (45.10)	16 (16)	106 (34.53)	18 (14.88)	14 (19.18)	200 (28.45)
Yadava	6 (5.88)	4 (4)	34 (11.08)	7 (5.79)	8 (10.96)	59 (8.39)
Scheduled Caste	20 (19.61)	57 (57)	32 (10.42)	52 (42.98)	8 (10.96)	169 (24.04)
Scheduled Caste (Christian)	11 (10.78)	15 (15)	24 (7.82)	22 (18.18)	4 (5.48)	76 (10.81)
Others	2 (1.96)	6 (6)	30 (9.77)	12 (9.92)	21 (28.77)	71 (10.10)
Total	102 (14.51)	100 (14.23)	307 (43.67)	121 (17.22)	73 (10.38)	703 (100)

TABLE 3 Indices of excess access to land and non-agricultural employment by caste

Caste	Land	Indices Of Access Non-Agricultural Employment		
		Own/ Operated	Landless	Others
A. Mudaliar	33.95	8.61	62.35	38.70
Naidu	3.52	33.22	21.76	−3.53
Vanniar	30.61	−7.09	−3.31	−32.59
Yadava	16.57	13.24	16.23	30.62
Scheduled Caste	−47.13	−18.02	−12.87	−54.41
Scheduled Caste (Christian)	−20.81	−8.65	8.60	−49.31
Others	−22.57	24.90	21.76	184.82

better access to land and non-agricultural employment. The Vanniars are the single largest caste in these villages, accounting for 28.45 per cent of all households. The value of the index of excess access to land, at 30.61, suggests that they have disproportionate access to land compared with any other caste except the Agamudhya Mudaliars. However, their access to non-agricultural employment is relatively low compared to their share to total households. Not surprisingly, the Yadavas, who are not different from the Vanniars either in their caste position or in terms of economic status, enjoy a greater access to non-agricultural employment as their traditional occupation was animal husbandry. Tables 2 and 3 show that the scheduled castes, those most deprived, still have not gained much from the protective measures of the government. Their access to both land and non-agricultural employment is very low. Nor have scheduled-caste converts to Christianity fared better than their Hindu counterparts.

Two major communities, Vanniars and scheduled castes (including scheduled-caste Christians) supply the agricultural labour force. The excess access to non-agricultural employment is the highest for those designated as 'Others', including service castes.

5. DISTRIBUTION OF WORKERS BY INDUSTRIAL CLASSIFICATION

The distribution of workers by primary occupation according to industrial classification is provided in Tables 4 and 5 for males and females respectively. Gender limits the access to non-agricultural employment. The non-agricultural sector, while accounting for a little less than half the total male employment,

TABLE 4 Industrial distribution of male workers by primary occupation

Caste	Cultivators	Agric Labour	Live Stock	Weaving	Other Hh Ind	Manu-facturing	Con-struction	Trade Commerc	Transport Storage	Other Services	Total
A. Mudaliar	76 (25.25)	6 (3.21)	11 (16.42)	26 (19.12)	1 (6.25)	23 (46.94)	4 (10.81)	9 (31.03)	13 (39.39)	13 (11.93)	182 (18.88)
Naidu	0	0	2 (2.99)	4 (2.94)	0	1 (2.04)	0	2 (6.90)	0	5 (4.59)	14 (1.45)
Vanniar	131 (43.52)	34 (18.18)	12 (17.91)	74 (54.41)	0	7 (14.29)	3 (8.11)	3 (10.35)	7 (21.21)	20 (18.35)	291 (30.19)
Yadava	39 (12.96)	6 (3.21)	13 (19.40)	15 (11.03)	0	3 (6.12)	4 (10.81)	2 (6.9)	7 (21.21)	5 (4.59)	94 (9.75)
Scheduled Caste	30 (9.97)	98 (52.41)	19 (28.36)	3 (2.21)	0	6 (12.24)	12 (32.43)	1 (3.44)	3 (9.09)	25 (22.94)	197 (20.44)
Scheduled Caste Christian	8 (2.66)	35 (18.72)	6 (8.96)	0	3 (18.75)	3 (6.12)	13 (35.13)	3 (10.35)	2 (6.06)	13 (11.93)	86 (8.92)
Others	17 (5.65)	8 (4.28)	4 (5.97)	14 (10.29)	12 (75)	6 (12.24)	1 (2.70)	9 (31.03)	1 (3.03)	28 (25.69)	100 (10.37)
Total	301 (100) (31.22)	187 (100) (19.40)	67 (100) (6.95)	136 (100) (14.11)	16 (100) (1.66)	49 (100) (5.08)	37 (100) (3.84)	29 (100) (3.01)	33 (100) (3.42)	109 (100) (11.31)	964 (100) (100)

TABLE 5 Industrial distribution of female workers by primary occupation

Caste	Cultivators	Agric Labour	Live Stock	Weaving	Other Hh Ind	Manu-facturing	Con-struction	Trade Commerc	Transport Storage	Other Services	Total
A. Mudaliar	55 (26.57)	29 (7.13)	8 (13.33)	17 (28.81)	1 (50)	4 (44.45)	0	1 (16.67)	0	12 (23.53)	127 (15.84)
Nadu	3 (1.45)	6 (1.47)	2 (3.33)	1 (1.69)	0	1 (11.11)	0	0	0	0	13 (1.62)
Vanniar	100 (48.31)	107 (26.29)	9 (15)	32 (54.24)	0	0	0	3 (50)	0	6 (11.77)	257 (32.04)
Yadava	20 (9.66)	23 (5.65)	14 (23.33)	5 (8.48)	0	0	0	0	0	4 (7.84)	66 (8.23)
Scheduled Caste	14 (6.76)	149 (36.61)	10 (16.67)	0	0	3 (33.33)	1 (100)	0	0	9 (17.65)	186 (23.19)
Scheduled Caste Christian	4 (1.93)	69 (16.95)	5 (8.33)	0	0	0	0	0	0	5 (9.80)	83 (10.35)
Others	11 (5.32)	24 (5.90)	12 (20)	4 (6.78)	1 (50)	1 (11.11)	0	2 (33.33)	0	15 (29.41)	70 (8.73)
Total	207 (100) (25.81)	407 (100) (50.75)	60 (100) (7.48)	59 (100) (7.36)	2 (100) (0.25)	9 (100) (1.12)	1 (100) (0.12)	6 (100) (0.75)	0	51 (100) (6.36)	802 (100) (100)

accounts for only 23.44 per cent of the total female employment. Household industry other than weaving, manufacturing, trade and commerce accounts for a negligible proportion of women workers; in particular there are no women employed in the transport and storage industry. With respect to caste, Agamudhya Mudaliars specialize in manufacturing, accounting for about 47 and 45 per cent, respectively, of the male and female manufacturing workers. Similarly, Vanniars specialize in weaving. Nearly 69 per cent of all male workers in the industrial category and more than 71 per cent of agricultural labour are either from scheduled castes or from scheduled-caste Christians. Thus until now, despite all protective measures by the government, scheduled-caste workers are largely found in physically demanding wage work.

Education also affects access to the non-farm economy particularly sharply for women (see Table 6).

The relationship is also much modified by caste. Agamudhya Mudaliars are at a disadvantage compared with Vanniars, at (higher) equivalent levels of education. Poorly educated or illiterate members of backward or most backward castes have all been able to enter weaving. While members of scheduled castes and scheduled-caste Christians have a greater probability of work in the non-farm economy as their educational level rises, this dips dramatically after secondary education. Illiterate scheduled-caste workers are unable to enter weaving.

Weaving emerged as an occupation in these villages from 1985 onwards. There are about 63 looms in Vinayagapuram, 50 in Nesal and 22 in Veerasambanur. The sudden emergence and growth of this activity calls for some scrutiny. In the region of Arni, as is the case in the whole of northern Tamil Nadu and in particular in the old North Arcot District, the 'pump-set revolution' has displaced traditional irrigation sources, denying tank water to small and marginal farmers (see Chapter 1–2 here). The pump-set revolution and the consequent extension of irrigation to dry land has resulted in changes in cropping patterns. Sugar cane has been cultivated since the mid 1980s. In the garden land or the irrigated *punjai* (rain-fed land), vegetables are being produced. Since the beginning of the 1980s tractors have been used, particularly for tilling.

These changes associated with the overall growth of rural non-agricultural

TABLE 6 Employment in the non-agricultural sector (% of total population)

	Male	Female
Illiterate	42	18
Higher than Secondary	63	80

activity appear to support the agricultural growth-linkage hypothesis. But analysis of the distributions of workers by industrial classification reveals the fallacy of such an inference. Weaving, particularly silk saree weaving, which has emerged as the major activity in these villages, is *not* directly related to agricultural production in these particular villages or in this region, either through backward linkages to raw materials (cocoons from Bangalore and *zari* (gold thread) from Ahmedabad), or through forward linkages to markets (urban and metropolitan). The looms do not produce commodities for local consumption. None of the weavers are independent petty producers. Instead, all the weavers work as disguised wage labour for the silk *maligais* (big silk merchants/master weavers). The *maligais* and master weavers, who control information about the markets for different types of local silk sarees throughout Tamil Nadu and India, have acted as catalytic agents by advancing loans for the installation of looms and for the provision of raw materials.

In the mid-1970s and at the beginning of the 1980s, there were years of poor rainfall. The competitive deepening of wells intensified in this period.[26] In the process, small and marginal farmers have lost out, while the upper sections of

TABLE 7 Distribution of workers literate and having completed primary education by sector of employment

Caste	Male Workers			Female Workers		
	Agri-cultural	Non-Agri-cultural	Total	Agri-cultural	Non-Agri-cultural	Total
A. Mudaliar	38 (48.72)	40 (51.28)	78 (100)	18 (46.15)	21 (53.85)	39 (100)
Naidu	0 0	5 (100)	5 (100)	1 (50)	1 (50)	2 (100)
Vanniar	69 (61.61)	43 (39.39)	112 (100)	27 (69.23)	12 (30.77)	39 (100)
Yadava	22 (61.11)	14 (38.89)	36 (100)	2 (25)	6 (75)	8 (100)
Scheduled Caste	43 (64.18)	24 (35.82)	67 (100)	22 (88)	3 (12)	25 (100)
Scheduled Caste Christian	11 (42.31)	15 (57.69)	26 (10)	9 (90)	1 (10)	10 (10)
Others	7 (17.95)	32 (82.05)	39 (100)	11 (64.71)	6 (35.29)	17 (100)
Total	190 (52.34)	173 (47.66)	363 (100)	90 (64.29)	50 (35.71)	140 (100)

the peasantry have gained.[27] As a consequence, members of small and marginal farm households (particularly those who belonged to the Agamudhya Mudaliar caste) in Nesal and Veerasambanur and landless agricultural labour households (particularly those who belonged to the Vanniar caste) in Vinayagapuram entered weaving. The Sengunda Mudaliars in the region of Arni, who had been historically engaged in cotton weaving, shifted to silk and expanded into villages. This expansion led to an increase in the demand for child labour to assist weaving both in the town of Arni and in villages around Arni. Children belonging to middle and lower middle castes acquired weaving skills. But children from scheduled-caste households were not allowed entry into the caste-Hindu households and hence did not learn weaving skills. We see here: i) the role of agrarian distress in the emergence of silk weaving in these villages; and ii) the role of caste in restricting skill acquisition. So the labour market is deeply segmented by caste. We see that the causes of the growth of the non-farm economy will vary according to the circumstances of each precise sector.

TABLE 8 Distribution of workers who have completed middle school by sector of employment

Caste	Male Workers			Female Workers		
	Agri-cultural	Non-Agri-cultural	Total	Agri-cultural	Non-Agri-cultural	Total
A. Mudaliar	19 (44.19)	24 (55.81)	43 (100)	11 (68.75)	5 (31.25)	16 (100)
Naidu	0 0	3 (100)	3 (100)	1 (33.33)	2 (66.67)	3 (100)
Vanniar	28 (63.64)	16 (36.36)	44 (100)	8 (66.67)	4 (33.33)	12 (100)
Yadava	5 (38.46)	8 (61.54)	13 (100)	2 (50)	2 (50)	4 (100)
Scheduled Caste	9 (40.91)	13 (59.09)	22 (100)	8 (72.73)	3 (27.27)	11 (100)
Scheduled Caste Christian	5 (26.32)	14 (73.68)	19 (100)	4 (80)	1 (20)	5 (100)
Others	6 (24)	19 (76)	25 (100)	4 (50)	4 (50)	8 (100)
Total	72 (42.60)	97 (57.40)	169 (100)	38 (64.41)	21 (35.59)	59 (100)

TABLE 9 Distribution of workers who have completed secondary school by sector of employment

Caste	Male Workers			Female Workers		
	Agri-cultural	*Non-Agri-cultural*	*Total*	*Agri-cultural*	*Non-Agri-cultural*	*Total*
A. Mudaliar	5 (23.81)	16 (76.19)	21 (100)	1 (20)	4 (80)	5 (100)
Naidu	0 0	1 (100)	1 (100)	0 0	0 0	0 (100)
Vanniar	13 (54.17)	11 (45.83)	24 (100)	0 0	1 (100)	1 (100)
Yadava	2 (22.22)	7 (77.78)	9 (100)	0 0	0 0	0 0
Scheduled Caste	8 (54.14)	6 (42.86)	14 (100)	1 (100)	0 0	1 (100)
Scheduled Caste Christian	1 (50)	1 (50)	2 (100)	0 0	1 (100)	1 (100)
Others	1 (12.50)	7 (87.50)	8 (100)	0 0	2 (100)	2 (100)
Total	30 (37.97)	49 (62.03)	79 (100)	2 (20)	8 (80)	10 (100)

TABLE 10 Distribution of workers who have education above secondary by sector of employment

Caste	Male Workers			Female Workers		
	Agri-cultural	*Non-Agri-cultural*	*Total*	*Agri-cultural*	*Non-Agri-cultural*	*Total*
A. Mudaliar	8 (53.33)	7 (46.67)	15 (100)	1 (50)	1 (50)	2 (100)
Naidu	0 0	1 (100)	1 (100)	0 0	0 0	0 0
Vanniar	7 (43.75)	9 (56.25)	16 (100)	0 0	0 0	0 0
Yadava	0 0	1 (100)	1 (100)	0 0	0 0	0 0
Scheduled Caste	1 (33.33)	2 (66.67)	3 (100)	0 0	0 0	0 0
Scheduled Caste Christian	0 0	6 (100)	6 (100)	0 0	2 (100)	2 (100)
Others	1 (25)	3 (75)	4 (100)	0 0	1 (100)	1 (100)
Total	17 (36.96)	29 (63.04)	46 (100)	1 (20)	4 (80)	5 (100)

6. CONCLUSION

A coherent framework has been developed to analyse spatial and temporal variations in the incidence of rural non-agricultural employment, in which the development of the rural non-agricultural sector is viewed as one component in a process of structural transformation. The growth of rural non-agricultural employment, which is a spatial manifestation of this structural transformation, is affected by factors such as caste, gender and access to land (which in general have been neglected). Here we have shown both the usefulness of the framework and the importance of social institutions as determinants of access to employment in the rural non-agricultural sector. Gender and caste, in particular, limit access to *non*-agricultural employment.

The case of silk weaving in these villages demonstrates the fallacy of hypothesizing the growth of rural non-agricultural employment as being induced either by agrarian distress or by prosperity alone. The roles of agrarian distress, of gender, caste and caste-based social exclusion, of the history of skill formation in the region and of the development of a national market for Arni-style silk sarees all play a part in accounting for this remarkable phenomenon.

ACKNOWLEDGEMENTS

Grateful thanks are due to Dr S Janakarajan for giving access to the village survey data used for tables 2 to 10, to Prof. Barbara Harriss-White for her useful comments on an earlier version of the paper and to Prof. A Vaidyanathan for his discussant's comments.

PART TWO

Production Policy and Village Perspectives

Policy and the Agricultural Development Agenda

Barbara Harriss-White

ROSENCRANTZ: Take you me for a spunge my lord?
HAMLET: Ay, sir; that soaks up the king's countenance, his rewards, his authorities. But such officers do the king best service in the end; he keeps them like
an ape doth nuts, in the corner of his jaw; first mouthed, to be last swallowed;
when he needs what you have gleaned, it is but squeezing you, and, spunge,
you shall be dry again.
ROSENCRANTZ: I understand you not my lord.

William Shakespeare, Hamlet, *Act IV, Scene II*

'The *status quo* is an option for partial participation in reforms. One wonders
if it stands any chance at this juncture?'

Randhawa 1994, p. 361

1. WHAT IS POLICY?

PARTS Two and Three of this book are devoted to the impact of development
policy for production and distribution in South Indian villages in the mid-
1990s. They are largely about the 'status quo' in agricultural and welfare policy
and the reasons for the considerable 'chance' it had – for good or ill – throughout the last decade of the twentieth century.

The study of development policy suffers acutely from its exclusion from theories of development whose *raison d'être* would seem to be their presumed policy relevance. 'Policy' is missing from the indexes of most major textbooks on
development, development theories and the politics of development.[1] While

the *Oxford English Dictionary* defines policy as '*the course of action adopted* by government' (my italics) to achieve certain objectives, policy in the discipline of economics is commonly presented and understood as meaning the course of action that ought to follow. It is based on the results of hypothesis-testing or a set of deductions from economic theory. Policy is seen in terms of 'implications' – and neither the character of the state nor the operating costs of the policy implications are usually considered. In rational choice theory, policy is seen as the product of social interests. The metaphors of policy as a 'commodity', of lobbies as 'interests' or 'purchasers' and of votes as 'currency' are abstracted from any history – and the history of the evolution of the deep social forces shaping the volatile 'epiphenomena' of policy is outside the frame.[2] In Foucauldian analysis, development agencies generate discourse, creating in turn a structure of knowledge which, while failing in its own terms, has effects including the entrenchment of bureaucratic power and the denial of politics.[3] James Ferguson's conclusion that 'development' is an 'anti-politics machine' is more realistic, yet, while he points out that development policy threatens domestic political mobilization by depoliticizing what it contacts, he nevertheless avoids the question of the very real resources and politics generated by development policy itself, forces which strongly influence distributive outcomes.

The mainstream understanding of the policy process tends to be instrumentalist and positivist. Policy is a rational activity carried out by technical experts in and out of the state, using objective methods in a transparent way.[4] Problems are identified, generally as deficits; their scope is sectoralized; data are organized for a process of dispassionate consideration; a selection known as policy-making takes place; decisions are made known; thereafter 'other and different (non policy) things, known as implementation occur'.[5] At best, but rather rarely, monitoring and evaluation complete a feedback loop and, as is all too well known, when evaluated against statements of intention policy is almost always unsuccessful. Obstacles – either 'in society' or of 'political will' – then serve as scapegoats which enable failed policies to be replicated or the responsibilities of officials to be avoided.

The English language is one of the few to distinguish policy from politics. This distinction enables the depoliticization of policy. As a result, crucial political factors shaping the mobilization and allocation of public-sector resources are excluded from consideration. If policy 'is what it does', it has to be recognized that the entire process bristles with politics. The question is what sort. Unless this question is asked, the history of policy will be banal and misleading. Commonly the scope of policy reform is exaggerated by experts, in their 'exemplary positions' of authority.[6] Opposition, if considered at all, is conceived in terms of the economic costs of suboptimal decision-making (the 'lack of political will').

Paradoxes, in which intended beneficiaries of a policy become its victims (and vice versa) when the policy is implemented (or in which the costs of the ineligible but included [E errors] are deplored while those of the eligible but excluded [F errors] get neglected), then become routine. The suppression of the fact that policy is messy is itself part of the ways in which those with a stake in 'policy technique' defend their vested interests.

The most useful alternative framework to those considered above for teasing out the constellation of power relations generated by development policy remains that of Bernard Schaffer (1984), though his credo does not make light reading. Summarizing and developing Schaffer, we see that the policy process involves four kinds of overlapping politics. They may be separated for the purpose of analysis, but in practice they operate simultaneously. The first is that of *agenda*: the power relations involved in the creation, negotiation and ordering of sets of themes about which statements of intention are made. The second is that of the translation of policy discourse into *procedure*: the enacting and internalizing of laws and informal rules of procedure and of access. The third is the power relations by means of which *public resources are raised and allocated*, tax is resisted and expenditure challenged. The fourth is the politics of *access* to bureaucratically distributed goods.[7] In the whole set of processes, party politics and bureaucratic politics are meshed with the politics of social institutions and material interests, and the neat boundary between state and society is blurred.[8]

It is through the politics of *agenda-setting* that issues are labelled, contested and ranked. In the analysis of policy not only is this kind of politics uniquely privileged (as though the rest did not exist), it is commonly reduced to a 'distanced' technical sphere – one occupied increasingly by experts in international banks and their client aid agencies and by client academics, consultancy firms and local technical advisory cells. It is carried out in a lingua franca of markets, profit, efficiency and conditionality, and with the use of statistics. Hamlet's 'spunges' may be found here. Evidence expressed in any other paradigmatic, disciplinary – or even real – language is rejected and excluded (or, as the World Bank sometimes does, it may be published as a device to distract attention from the real business of banking). In practice, however, many other interests with different and unequal powers are pitted together in agenda-setting. There are of course individual bureaucrats interested in the perpetuation of their jobs. The interests of collective, departmental or part-privatized quango and public corporative bodies come into contention, as do structures of patronage and social networks (ethnic, religious, regional, gendered) operating inside the state. Then there are the media, in which certain kinds of evidence dismissed by technical experts may be considered valid and important (for instance particular individual cases) and where other kinds of evidence are neglected or censored.[9] In electoral democracies such as India's, political parties are arenas in which ideas about policy can seethe creatively, although the individual politician in a given party may be ignorant of development policies or understand his or her party's position on specific issues in ways that flatly contradict the understanding of other party members.[10] There may be party coalitions in government and opposition in which matters which are low on the agendas of individual parties shoot upwards as a result of their significance in consensus-making. Agendas are also shaped by organized national and international lobbies representing material interests (trades unions, family businesses, corporations, banks, 'farmers', members of advisory committees and councils) for which the politics of agendas is important only in so far as they can be used to mask the competition over the creation and protection of rents that is taking place elsewhere. There are also civil society institutions, non-governmental organizations (NGOs) and social movements which work on agendas, sometimes without any material interest but deploying information and persuasion ('advocacy').

Inside and outside the state, in struggles around the agenda, development is *sectoralized* as a specific set of actions (for example nutrition policy excludes *food* policy, let alone alcohol policy). 'Terms of art' (and their acronyms) are created and become imbued with very specific and exclusive meanings (take for example 'safety net', 'TRYSEM Training for Self Employment', 'social exclusion', 'gender and development (GAD)', 'the environment', even 'the reform period'). These special meanings are understood in development agencies; they structure what is researched, taught and debated in universities and research institutions. Routines also persist, even when leached of their original purpose (e.g., often, 'participation'). People are then labelled (for example as 'pregnant and lactating mothers', 'small farmers', 'BPLs' [people below the poverty line], the micro-creditworthy, 'SC/ST' [those eligible for positive discrimination in India] etc.), although in reality people will belong to several such categories.[11] Some of these labels set people up as targets, making them doubly objectified. Entitlements follow from these terms ('nominee directors', 'informal livelihoods', 'small-scale industry', 'desert development'). This is the language of Hamlet's 'spunges', people who hang around in management consultancies and bureaucracies and wait upon politicians to this day. By these means some policies are excluded and some people are rejected, silenced and made invisible. Meanwhile forces entirely outside a given agenda, or excluded from it in the process of sectoralizing, may determine policy priorities. Equally, these labels create categories around which those labelled may develop their own political mobilization. Technique may not always triumph; decisions may never be formalized; but most crucially of all, stated intention may never be taken at face value.

In the process of *proceduralization* (the means whereby a policy objective is operationalized), components of the agenda – scholarly papers, policy notes, manifestos, project appraisals, plans etc. – are translated into patterned behaviour through legislation, departmental orders and informal procedural norms. Sometimes breaking the rules is rewarded, as in public-sector food storage and processing, where outdated technologies are specified but performance is improved by ignoring the rules. Procedure is the least visible arena of policy. The power to introduce discrepancies between the intentions expressed in agendas and what procedures really imply may mean that procedure contains internal contradictions and inconsistencies. These become more and more inconsistent as amendments are made over time, or as officials change posts and newcomers interpret the rules differently. Formal procedures may even prevent implementation altogether (for example, the international convention on freedom from hunger where it has not yet been possible to codify 'hunger').[12] More than one form of procedure often coexist[13] and the very *idea* of what procedure involves may mutate inside bureaucracies or in civil society.

Procedure is a resource to be captured: the administration of procedure is a 'field of power'.[14] These 'complex systems of power . . . codify social norms and values, and articulate fundamental organising principles of society, they also contain implicit (and sometimes explicit) models of society'.[15] In legally plural societies like that of India, for example, combinations of parts of different legal systems – juridical and customary – may be opportunistically deployed. They may be the objects of attempts at capture. Judgements of breaches of procedure come into conflict, as a result of which there are further discrepancies between procedural norms and actual practice. Informal systems of regulation and sanction develop in response. The Essential Commodities Act is a case in point, with 59 amendments, highly varied local understandings of its scope, informalized implementation and socially codified norms of corruption.[16]

Most policy analysis also pays scant attention to the third set of political forces shaping the policy process, except in the technical fields of public finance and corruption theory. These are the power relations shaping *the mobilization of resources* for the implementation of policy. Policies have economic costs. Resource mobilization through taxation, loans and grants of aid may take a range of forms and is subject to the other kinds of bureaucratic politics too. The seasonality and timing of revenue flows, and the social composition of the forces resisting and those complying, result in patterns in the supply of tax revenue that are the truest reflection of the structure of accountability of a society. Fiscal resources pour into a convection system to be allocated between current and capital expenditure, between departments and projects, between sectors and subsidies, centre and states. The seeming deadweight of past patterns of allocation should not blind us to the fact that political forces keep these allocations in place. They also determine the extent to which individual departments are co-ordinated; for *every* department of government has a role in the regulation of markets and most have a role in the development of agriculture.

The fourth aspect of the politics of policy concerns the power relations through which rules of *access* are enforced and challenged: those of the '*counter*' (how many points of distribution or registration are there? When are they active? Where are they located and with what implications? What are the volumes of administered goods and services flowing over them?); *eligibility* (who qualifies? Who is excluded? Who decides?); *queues and their discipline* (among those who qualify who gets the goods and services? In what order?); *voice* (who [eligible or non-eligible] can intermediate or manipulate the rules of access to their own advantage?); and *exit*[17] (who drops out? Who does not benefit? Who finds ways other than those ruled in order to obtain the benefit to which they are entitled?). In accounts of access to bureaucratically distributed goods and services, people are frequently referred to as 'beneficiaries' or 'targets'. They are seen as passive recipients. Of late, 'participation' has been popularized with a view to incorporating beneficiaries actively into the process of access, and to a more limited extent into allocation.[18] (It has also become an end in itself.) How far 'participation' has changed the power relations of access is not well understood.

Not only is the four-fold nature of development policy revealed in its intrinsic richness (and orthodox notions in their politically selective simplicity), but the process of implementation is also seen to transform policy utterance 'out of all recognition'.[19] These transformed relations of authority then *actively conceal* developmental possibilities.[20] Development policy must therefore be understood in terms of complex layers of politics. To analyse them is an ambitious undertaking. Indeed, it has never been attempted in its entirety. For this, it would be necessary to stand outside the knowledge structure and the constituent disciplines created for development in order to perceive the power relations masked by its discourse. But the language in which one carries out the operation is inevitably part of this structure of knowledge. This analysis would also call for evidence to be found in many different places, evidence requiring expert interpretation (for example, the cost-benefit and welfare economics paradigms or legal texts) as well as evidence from verbal accounts, not excluding anecdotes and rumour, which is extremely hard to collect and is considered of doubtful legitimacy in social science;[21] Schaffer himself observed that '(s)uch data is decentralised, humble and dirty'. The collection of such evidence calls for the participant observation of an anthropologist, the critical methods of the historian and the professional expertise of economists, political scientists and lawyers, and its analysis requires efforts of deconstruction. No single scholar has these skills. No discipline encourages their development. However, if the analysis of policy is not to connive with one small part of the process (that of technique) to the exclusion of all the rest of it (which continues to shape the policy process, despite our ignoring it and whatever our judgement of its desirability), then we somehow have to make the attempt.[22]

It goes almost without saying that our studies of policy do not rise especially well to this challenge. They are best understood as first attempts to find some of the pieces of a large jigsaw puzzle. There are good methodological reasons for the small number and wide scatter of these jigsaw pieces. They reflect disciplinary tyrannies and resource constraints, not to mention the geographical positioning of the field research in villages and their local urban environs. It isn't necessary to espouse the view that villages and states are separate entities to point out that villages are not good sites from which to observe the national and international forces bearing on policy agendas. Village-level evidence will not reveal much about the legal framework of policy implementation or the power relations at play in the way resources are raised by the state, especially loans and aid, even if the power relations around villages help to informalize procedure – and to require fiscal deficits. Villages are excellent sites, however, from which to observe *access*. Most of the essays in parts Two and Three make connections between the wider policy agendas and access in villages. If this book makes a contribution to the understanding of policy, it is through the wide range of policies examined simultaneously in these villages. The second half of this chapter moves to consider the agricultural policy agenda, first in general and then in the villages.

2. THE COMPOSITE AGRICULTURAL POLICY AGENDA

In India, agricultural policy is the responsibility of constituent states. However, both the Planning Commission and the central government ministries in New Delhi influence state policy agendas. They also affect state-level resource mobilization, allocation and access. The politics of agricultural policy – operating at different scales – may involve different agendas, procedures, resources and rules of access.[23] The composite nature of the agenda, the regulative framework and the sources of funding may themselves become resources in the competition over surplus that lies at the heart of development. Here, we explore these propositions with special reference to the state of Tamil Nadu.

Already by the mid-1990s there were two worked-out policy packages for agriculture with material resources to back them. One, the liberalization paradigm, had and still has a highly influential reach. This was the paradigm being debated by administrators and scholars alike in Washington, London, New

Delhi and metropolitan India, as though there were no other kind of agricultural policy. It is the one taught to students all over the world. The other paradigm, discovered much later through interviews with local agricultural officials in Tamil Nadu and evident in the reports of the Agriculture Department, is grounded in the science-based paradigms of the local state bureaucracy and the politics of patronage. By 2001, however, there were at the very least three paradigms.[24] At the risk of some arbitrary simplification, the assumption of just three agricultural policy paradigms helps us understand the role of agendas in the politics of agricultural policy and then the role of composite, interlocking agendas in the politics of reform.

2.1 *Fast-track liberalization*

We start out from the justified and critical statement on policy options for economic liberalization made from N S Randhawa's review of papers to the New Delhi conference on 'Agricultural Policy in the New Economic Environment', sponsored by the FAO (Food and Agriculture Organization) and held in September 1993.[25] 'To be phased over 3 to 4 years', the controls over the agricultural sector needed to be eliminated in order for markets to function efficiently and for the economic distortions caused – for reasons of private interest – by bureaucrats and politicians to be eliminated. At least 20 major agricultural commodities would be involved, notably foodgrains (whose domestic prices would rise to the level of world markets), together with oilseeds and sugar (should the OECD countries fulfil their treaty obligations under GATT and reduce their agricultural protection). For India, this was an agenda for the deregulation of commodity and factor markets. It involved the elimination of movement restrictions, the unbiased operation of freight transport, the privatization of storage, the deregulation of agroprocessing from its special (protected or restricted) status as a 'small-scale industry', the dismantling of subsidies on fertilizer and electricity, with increased exports compensating for the production disincentives resulting from the price squeeze from raised costs of production. It involved either dismantling or privatizing most of the activities of the public distribution system, the liberalization of the land market – starting with land lease deregulation – and permission for corporate investment in 'wasteland' and degraded forest.

The fast-track agenda was far from being a policy for wholesale privatization. The conception of public goods and services embodied in fast-track policy required investment in port infrastructure for agricultural exports and imports, irrigation infrastructure in the deprived regions of the north-east and east, research and development for the crops of these regions, universal safety nets for the poor, who would get food stamps, a much reduced buffer stock of foodgrains and, more controversially, the protection of targeted and subsidized credit for small-scale agricultural production.

The people who made this input into the agricultural policy agenda were not only national economic policy elites but also international technical advisers able to impose conditions on international loans.[26] Their criteria were based on benefit-cost paradigms and a disembedded conception of efficiency. The discourse was (macro)economic, with the consequence that institutional change was conceived as 'engineerable' – and indeed friction-free. Since then, ongoing debate has concerned means or instruments for such change rather than its principles. What is excluded is significant. There is practically no concern for the agro-ecological environment, and the only concern expressed concerning the mass of small producers and labourers in agriculture is that they are a threat to the smooth running of the new policies and to be assuaged with a safety net. Markets are assumed to operate neutrally with respect to society. This agenda is thus crudely 'antipolitics', both in the sense of not arising from party politics or being associated with any single party and in the sense that it depoliticizes development by its discourse. Indeed, it is openly said by economists to 'remove politics from the economy'.

2.2 *Critical globalization*

Here the key text is the report of, and comments on, a detailed interview with the agricultural scientist M S Swaminathan, under whose charge HYV seeds were introduced to India. He is an ex-Secretary of Agriculture to the Government of India and an ex-Director of the International Rice Research Institute (IRRI) in the Philippines, who now directs in Chennai a state-of-the-art, private agricultural research institute that is named after him.[27]

The globalized agricultural trade and investment regime has provoked a new and critical agricultural agenda. Three policies have particular urgency.

The first results from the establishment in 1994 of the World Trade Organization which regulates, *inter alia*, global agricultural trade. Compliance with its rules has been unbalanced: it has been forced on developing countries but resisted by the OECD block. For OECD countries, formal exceptions have been created, by the mechanism of policy 'boxes', to protect incomes and even raise the level of farm support. Hence there needs to be a counterpart 'Livelihood Box': a set of quantitative restrictions on imports for countries such as India in cases threatening the mass of agricultural livelihoods.

The second policy proposal results from the proprietary control of the biosphere where international procedure is both inappropriate and inconsistent.

Trade-related intellectual property rights (TRIPS) are already at variance with the legally binding provisions of the International Convention on Biological Diversity (their global signatories coming from different domestic ministries). So there needs to be protection for the rights of Indian farmers to retain seed between seasons and to protect new varieties developed by themselves.

Third, the genetic modification (GM) of agricultural products poses two further kinds of currently unresolvable policy problems. The first is the relation between GM crops and the environment. On the one hand, GM crops may constitute a technical solution to production in agronomic environments (notably saline and dry land) for which policies of conventional biotechnological change have had little success. On the other hand, GM crops are certain to be biochemically unstable, to create gene pollution and to risk unpredictable and irreversible environmental impacts. The second problem is the relation between the control and goals of GM science and the material practices and outcomes actually associated with it. Although publicly funded research will always be 'distorted' (meaning it will be moulded by the agendas of funders, the career interests of scientists, peer pressure etc., rather than induced by factor scarcities), it may nonetheless have some social goals and long-term horizons, whereas privately funded research is first and last for profit and dividends. There is therefore an urgent need for a National Commission on Genetic Modification.

Policy-makers engaging critically with agricultural globalization are drawn from the agricultural science elite in state-funded research institutions and the scientific civil service, from NGOs and social movements and from certain political parties.[28] Their positions and priorities range from a resistance to global capital on both the right and left (based variously on nationalism, socialism or participative forms of democracy) to a concern for mass livelihoods and/or the environment. All aspects of this agenda presuppose a strong domestic regulative role for a state that is strong enough in turn to alter or to resist the global rules for agrocapital.

2.3 *Tamil Nadu's agricultural policy agenda – the garden*

Here we start out from the four Annual Policy Notes and data on Agricultural Department expenditure published under the names of the Tamil Nadu Agricultural Ministers K P Krishnan and V S Arumugham from 1994 to 1997 (during a change of ruling party), backed up by the Budget Speeches for this period.[29] These texts exemplify non-metropolitan agricultural development policy.

Tamil Nadu's agenda in the early reform period shows a substantial degree of autonomy, as does its defence of the scope and price parameters of the public distribution system together with the noon meal nutrition scheme. Since it is so different from the liberalization agenda, from textbook agricultural policy and from the critical agenda,[30] and so far less well analysed, we will consider this one at greater length. Tamil Nadu's stated policies for agriculture are as follows:

i) environmental protection, focusing on wastelands, soil conservation and watershed development;

ii) sustainability (organic farming, biofertilizer development, integrated pests management, bioconversion of agricultural and urban waste);

iii) improved water management at the micro scale, using a variety of participative, collective and (semi) state institutions and scientific techniques;

iv) 'scientific implements' for agricultural production;

v) seed patenting for biodiversity, focusing on horticulture, oil palm etc.;

vi) diversification in production: an active role for the state via demonstration plots and extension in horticulture, sericulture, dairying, poultry and fisheries;

vii) logistical, technical and financial support to increase exports, particularly of horticultural and floricultural products with upstream production linkages to agroprocessing plants;

viii) increased vegetable production;

ix) 'reasonable' prices regulated through the streamlining of marketing infrastructure (extension staff are to shed their inputs-trading activities, but agricultural wholesale Regulated Market Committees are to expand the pledge-loan facility based on produce stored at regulated market sites; a continued effort is to be made to systematize quality grades across a wide range of products [a necessary precondition for long-distance trade]); and

x) the creation of new forms of active economic management (direct trading by the Agriculture Department to be hived off to state corporations; new parastatal trading agencies and seed inspectorates for plantation crops to be created; new laws regulating horticulture to be passed).

This agenda is advanced by politicians and administrators and expressed in a combination of science-derived and triumphalist language that is greatly at variance with that of fast-track liberalization. The territorial state is envisioned as a very large garden. The political state is unavoidably engaged in creating the collective preconditions for the 'gardeners' to go to market and in reducing the unequal terms of bargaining they can expect once they get there. Table 1 shows that, throughout the period of heavy pressure to cut public expenditure, capital and current expenditure by the Agriculture Department exceeded estimates.[31] Expenditure was on an expansion path and attempts to contain it failed.

TABLE 1 Agriculture Department spending, Tamil Nadu
(Rs crores [10 million])

		1994–5	1995–6	1996–7	1997–8
Current	Estimated	665	253	744	689
	Revised	717	786	789	719
Capital	Estimated	679	765	754	
	Revised	730	795	802	

Source: Government of Tamil Nadu, 1995 to 1998, *Policy Notes on Agriculture*.

Much is made of ecological diversity, which implicitly justifies modes of procedure and allocation that work through a mass of projects and micro-schemes. Their description uses a language of decentralization, scientific technique and specificity. Huge emphasis is also placed on the category of 'small farmers', with contradictory mixes of individual incentives and rewards (packages of high-tech and green-tech inputs [see Table 2]) and of collective action to enhance economies of scale.[32] Entire districts are selected for special attention, for crop-specific projects, wasteland cultivation, soil conservation or watershed development. Immense possibilities for patronage are generated by configuring agricultural policy in this way. At the same time, the proliferation of small schemes for small producers depends in part on the political interests of project funders from outside India. The agendas and resources of aid agencies have a direct influence upon the state government: the FAO trains farmers in 'biocontrol'; the World Bank trains district-level planners in planning and agricultural professionals in IT; DANIDA (Danish Agency for Development Assistance)

TABLE 2 Patronage of small farmers, 1995

Heavily Subsidized or free provision of rationed goods and services:-
Agricultural kits to farm women
Coconut seedlings to children
Storage bins
Tarpaulines
Tyred bullock carts
Power tillers, threshers, trailers
Micro minerals
Green manure seeds
Biofertilizer packs
Power pesticide sprayers
Raticide
Petromax light traps

Source: Government of Tamil Nadu, 1995, *Policy Notes on Agriculture*, pp. 18–22.

develops the skills of agricultural women and encourages watershed development; SIDA (Swedish Agency for Development Assistance) dynamizes agroforestry and dry-land agriculture; while the Government of Israel helps to transfer technology for high-value crops. The state's capacity to absorb these project funds is saturated. Year by year, the policy notes record incomplete uptake and delays. Ecological diversity, external project funding and the politics of patronage are mutually reinforcing here. The result is a striking inertia in both discourse and resource allocation.

Over precisely the kind of time span in which the fast-track liberalizers expected deregulation to penetrate the entire economy, the Tamil Nadu Agriculture Department showed how little it needed to change. At the margins in fact, a populist form of agricultural patronage was exchanged for corporate patronage in 1996 when Jayalalitha's All-India Anna Dravida Munnetra Kazagham (AIADMK) regime was replaced by Karunanidhi's Dravida Munnetra Kazagham (DMK). Grants for temple gardens and for the beautification of Ooty Lake for filmsets, and prizes to exemplary extension officers and farmers, were suddenly stopped.[33] Instead new resources were made available to subsidize corporate capital to develop wastelands for floriculture and undertake joint ventures in agroprocessing. Infrastructure for agroprocessing and specialized physical market sites (for *jaggery*, for flowers) was promised, along with subsidized transport for farmers.[34] Above all, the state agenda expresses continuity, complexity and expansion. It reflects solid bureaucratic interests, a nexus structured around patronage and the application of scientific techniques, together with the needs of a diverse but powerful political constituency.[35]

Major parts of the agricultural economy are strikingly marginalized on this agenda. The foodgrains economy of rice and groundnuts, in which a state with fabled grain bowls has lost rank and where growth has faltered,[36] are not the central concerns of local agricultural policy.

Although the agricultural policy agendas are distinct, they are implemented in ways which make them mesh not just with one another but with non-agricultural policy too. Indeed, not only is the local policy agenda different from fast-track liberalization but also the main policies that affect agriculture are not administered through the Agriculture Department. They are administered through a range of other departments (Public Works for road and irrigation infrastructure; Food and Civil Supplies for food; Industry for fertilizer; Social Welfare for labour; Cooperatives and Finance for credit) and parastatal corporations (Electricity Boards; the All-India Food Corporation and the State Civil Supplies Corporation for food; the Cotton Corporation, Storage and Warehouse Corporation etc.). The regulation of agrarian markets is administered through combinations of state and central government departments and corporations. Most of these departments and corporations are also doing non-agricultural things. As a result, the priorities of the agricultural agenda and the ranking of agricultural policy as a whole in the priorities of each institution implementing agricultural policy will be quite specific. In implementation as well as in theory, agricultural policy will be affected by non-agricultural policy. Agricultural policy (as is the case with other kinds of policy[37]) is also supported by non-agricultural justifications. A new parastatal for agro-engineering services is justified not only for agriculture but also as a component in the state's policy to give livelihoods to unemployed engineers. The state does not simply – and conventionally – sectoralize agriculture. It splits agriculture up into micro-sectors and distributes it across almost all formal institutions of government. Only in the year 2000 did 'bureaucratic co-ordination' appear in the state's agricultural policy notes.[38] No acknowledgement of the idiosyncracy of what is labelled agricultural has ever appeared there.

2.4 *Interpretations*

Although three quite separate policy agendas can be discerned, each with their histories (fast-track liberalization, creative globalization and Tamil Nadu's garden programme), all of them intertwine – not just because they coexist in time but because of overlapping institutions and interests. Although far from exhaustive, our description of them is detailed enough to show the influence of agricultural research on the idioms of both the global and the state agenda, and of macro-economic context on liberalization and globalization policy. Both the global and state agendas are also characterized by a paternalistic populism. The interests of international aid agencies pervade all three agendas: financial aid in the first case, social movements in the second and bi- and multilateral development agencies in the third. While the global and state agendas each embody contradictory positions on capital (and by implication on labour and petty production), the first agenda encourages capital while depoliticizing it discursively. The agendas are also at different stages of formation, that at the state level being most deeply settled while the other two are in contention. Agricultural policy vividly illustrates the dynamic nature of this political process.

Agriculture is slow to be reformed. The state's involvement in agriculture expanded in the first phase of liberalization. By the mid-1990s, fertilizer had been partially decontrolled and subsidies had been rapidly restored. Agricultural credit had not been touched. Product prices were moving towards world market levels: the price of rice rose, while that of groundnuts sank. Movement restrictions on agricultural trade were lifted in 1993 (but lorry drivers still had to bribe checkpost guards to let them through and Indian railways still favoured public corporations over private trade). The structure of subsidies (on credit, agricultural cooperatives, fertilizer, food, electricity, diesel, kerosene and irrigation) was intact and remained so throughout most of the 1990s (see Table 3). The redistributive operations of the Food Corporation of India supplying the public distribution system (PDS) was lethargically revamped so as to target areas as well as income categories. The movement of groundnuts had not been deregulated. Local states still regulated markets in order to enable state procurement of a range of commodities. Agroprocessing was still reserved for 'small-scale industry' until 2001.[39]

The low relative priority given to agricultural reform can be explained in a number of persuasive ways. In Pranab Bardhan's political economy, for instance, where policy is the outcome of clashes between three proprietary classes, the relative speed of reform is dictated by the nature of the costs and benefits to interests in opposition to it.[40] In the case of agriculture, we have to explain why states have been so reluctant to acquiesce to fast-track liberalization. A massive array of political forces have interests opposed to liberalization. First, while agrocommercial capitalist elites and potential exporters could be expected to be the main downstream beneficiaries of agricultural liberalization, in practice these are the powerful interests which have for decades benefited from rents derived from the structure of state regulation of the agricultural sector. So these elites have contradictory interests. Second, the price structure of basic wage goods for the agrarian workforce – including people selling foodgrains after harvest and buying some back before the next – is at stake. A substantial part of the electorate has an interest in low and controlled prices for essential

TABLE 3 Agricultural and welfare subsidies

All-India 1993–4 Rs bn crores	Fertilizer	Electri-city	Irrigation[(1)]	Credit	Food	Total Ag. +Non-Ag.
	2.7	3.5	2.6	1.8	3	127

Tamil Nadu Rs crores	Rs crores	Electricity	Social Security	Noon Meal	Food	
1990–91		175.7		235.3	257.8	
1991–2		4.3		255.6	332.2	
1992–3		826.3		272.3	473.1	
1993–4		890.2	62.4	282.5	359	
1994–5		653.8	66.5	365.2	440	
1995–6		354.8	85.9	356.9	800	

Note: Agricultural subsidies as % of total government subsidies: 13%.
Agriculture as % of total GDP (1990): 32%.

Sources: Randhawa 1994, p. 368; Bardhan 1998, p. 147; Government of Tamil Nadu raw data.
(1) Including the annualized cost of the book value of capital costs.

commodities. Third, the agro-engineering sector exerts heavy pressure on policy elites (and exploits the physical proximity of its lobbying organizations to these elites, sharing all but the last digit of the latter's postal codes). This is also an interest that has profited from the structure of partial regulation, or state control, of intermediate goods to agriculture.[41]

Then Rob Jenkins' controversial hypothesis that successful reform has occurred by stealth – whatever its relevance to industry – carries the powerful implication for agriculture that, since reforms touching mass livelihoods cannot under any circumstances be stealthy, they will be delayed.[42] Bardhan's depiction of the central government 'chipping away',[43] piecemeal, but not necessarily by stealth, has had little purchase on agricultural policy in the 1990s. Even though one sure way in which the central state has 'chipped away' is through reducing its subsidies to states, states have borrowed heavily so as not to disturb their agricultural policies: a 'mere' transfer of the financial burden from the centre to the states, rather than a set of policy responses. Even the argument about the need to reduce the contribution of total subsidies to the fiscal deficit may work curiously in favour of agricultural subsidies, since they are not the largest element. Total food and agricultural subsidies in 1993 were about 13 per cent of total government subsidies, while agriculture was 32 per cent of GDP (Table 3). Until bankruptcy requires a response, agricultural policy can be predicted to resist reform.

In addition to these several explanations based on material interests, the analysis of the agricultural agenda presented here reveals another simple and obvious reason for delayed reform. Agricultural policy is very complex. It operates simultaneously in several policy paradigms. The range of interests in it are justified in many ways. Policy is inconsistent, path-dependent and contested. It involves most departments of government and links the jurisdictions of centre and state. Laws and administrative procedure mirror this complexity. Agricultural development turns out to be regulated by project and by patronage as well as by price and subsidy. Organizing the dismantling of existing agricultural policy would require the coordination of most departments of government. This bureaucracy is also an interest in its own right. So the interlocking complexity of policy for agriculture also defies reform.

3. SITUATING OUR POLICY RESEARCH IN THE POLICY FRAMEWORK

During the 1990s the Indian State all but ignored the case of pro-liberalization moderates that resources currently devoted to subsidies should be switched to investment in infrastructure, without which markets cannot function. Despite the proven synergy between public and private investment in agriculture, despite the fact that infrastructure is essential to the blossoming of crucial agro-processing and agribusiness linkages from agriculture, despite the fact that the supply of both paddy and groundnuts in Tamil Nadu over the period from 1950–1 to 1992 responded with higher elasticities to irrigation than to fertilizer and had a low response to own price and cross prices,[44] infrastructure is on the track of long-term decline.[45] As a result we explored institutional aspects of under-researched parts of the infrastructure policy agenda, where deregulation and privatization have been advocated.

In Chapter 2–2 we examine the institutions through which drinking water and sanitation and water-using utilities are provided to these villages. Technologies which are appropriate when privately acquired are so inappropriate when supplied through state institutions (to precisely those people unable to purchase them or gain access to them privately) that access is effectively debarred. The egregious neglect of repair and maintenance (as is the case with both sanitation and drinking-water supply) has a similar social impact on access. Collective action, responding to failures of provision, is deeply socially divisive. Despite its failure and flying in the face of privatization advocacy, the public provision of sanitation and drinking water is expanding, with benefits to suppliers and officials.

Chapter 2–3 on 'power' (electricity) exposes the key role of party-political competition: first in conceding free electricity for the private pumping of irrigation water in the face of a militant farmers' movement; and second in maintaining resistance to the reintroduction of user fees (a policy reflecting the consensus of analysts using cost-benefit techniques), pressed by international banks and aid agencies. Given the irreversible and unequalizing impact of a decade of free electricity, it is argued that the policy of introducing user fees would now bolster economic differentiation and accelerate the environmental catastrophe. The immediate beneficiaries of the stalemate during the entire course of the 1990s were not only the water-selling upper strata of agricultural producers but also the entire workforce for whom rice is the basic wage good.

Chapter 2–4 on rural credit examines the history of the close relation between research and policy, culminating in the policy recommendations of the Narasimhan and Khusro commissions: to liberate interest on loans and deposits, phase out subsidies to rural banks and target production credit on the smallest farmers. Village credit markets are found to be already dominated by unregulated credit. Institutions such as rotating credit associations (chit funds) proliferate in the space created by state neglect. Informal credit (meaning money not regulated by the state) is fuelled in part by the onward lending of formal credit, a practice not apparently intended in credit policy and, provided formal loans are repaid, one which there are no incentives to trace. Women have separate credit institutions whose existence is often hidden from their men, let alone from the state. Areas of policy which have been captured by vested interests and are inequitable and inefficient are shown to be resistant to adjustment; the targeting of credit on the smallest farmers would be a radical reversal of the current pattern of access. A policy possibility which has been studiously avoided – distributing credit to small and landless producers to enable them to purchase land – is explored. Its likely consequences for formal creditworthiness suggest that formal credit is quite intentionally supporting local elites rather than small-scale production.

Chapter 2–5 turns to fertilizer policy in the early reform period. Controlled by central government and implemented through heavily regulated public and private corporate enterprises, reform was not resisted. Instead the removal of subsidies (the benefits of which were spread 50:50 between the few manufacturers and the dispersed final users) was partially implemented and provoked unintended consequences which are tracked here at state and village levels. The crucial importance of non-price factors in yield responses to fertilizer, and of low-tech organic manure (invisible in policy-making) in assuring a soil structure conducive to the yield-fertilizer elasticities, make the impact of fertilizer policy dependent on access to factors outside the fertilizer sector.

Although the Indian state sector is about half the size of its Western counterparts in term of its share of GDP,[46] it permeates agricultural production and is the only institution of any significance engaged in redistribution. Agricultural policy is a thickly tangled skein of power. Together with the interests involved in the sheer size of the subsidies, interests which also derive rents from the nexus of partial interventions, the composite nature of agricultural policy may be an additional important factor delaying liberalization.

ACKNOWLEDGEMENTS

I am grateful to N Narayanan, IAS, for helping me locate budget speeches and policy notes and to Nitya Rao and Colin Leys for fruitful discussions.

Rural Infrastructure and Local Utilities: Institutions and Access

Barbara Harriss-White

1. INTRODUCTION

VILLAGE-LEVEL studies rarely examine infrastructure or utilities: electricity, water, drainage, sewerage, garbage disposal, public hygiene and physical security. This 'hard infrastructure' is all fundamental to the functioning of any market economy. So also is certain 'soft infrastructure' (also known as 'basic needs'): shelter, health, education and food. Together, hard and soft infrastructure shape not only the public health environment and the private quality and distribution of 'human capital', but also the capital and transactions costs of the market economy and the terms and conditions on which labour is supplied – and thus production. This study of policies for production starts with infrastructure and is concerned with rural infrastructure previously neglected, even in the literature on infrastructure: drinking water, sanitation, waste disposal and other water-using utilities. Research as far apart as Nairobi and Los Angeles[1] has confirmed not only the existence of extreme social and spatial differentials in people's access to infrastructure but also wide differences in the ways that ownership and organization contribute to the supply of such services and to performance.

How is infrastructure provided? Both the hard infrastructure and basic needs *may* be provided by the state, 'the market' and 'the community'. The state is indispensable to the other two. Market provision is generally a hybrid form with the state playing a significant regulatory role. Voluntary provision through NGOs, user groups or community development is also thought to have to be accountable – by regulation and inspection – to the state.[2] It is generally assumed that demand for such infrastructure exceeds supply, so that rationing is inevitable.[3] In many Third World settlements the rationing of provision is unequal, those last served, or tail-enders, having disproportionately small and unreliable actual entitlements. Highly specific problems also arise from environmental pollution,[4] the close proximity of hazardous waste to residential areas, inadequate and ageing equipment.[5] While all these characteristics call for public provision, the Washington consensus argues for the competitive privatization of infrastructure.[6] And the Eighth Five-Year Plan (1992–7) covering the period of our village resurvey calls for the freeing of activity 'from any unnecessary controls and regulations and withdrawing state intervention' while also acknowledging the necessity of dovetailing 'the market mechanism and planning . . . so that they are complementary to one another'.[7] In this chapter we will review the characteristics of infrastructural institutions as presented in the literature and then examine how infrastructure is provided in the three villages and the market town in whose hinterland they are sited.

1.1. *Planned provision*

The planned provision of civic services and infrastructure faces extreme uncertainty, monitoring and information problems, all in the context of 'market failure':

> We simply do not know enough to be able to allocate resources efficiently. It is difficult to substitute the decisions of thousands of people as they live, work and play . . ., by the decisions of a planning authority.[8]

It is unsurprising then that one characteristic of public provisioning is its great *unevenness*. Kundu (1991) documents wide variation in the public provision of water and sanitation to the urban poor by local authorities across India. There are two features: local variation in and lack of access to these services. Wanmali and Ramasamy, using data for the 1980s, show how local infrastructural provision in the former North Arcot District varies spatially and how staggering the budget variations are by subsector and over time.[9] Poor access to hard infrastructure is shown to have a negative impact on rural soft infrastructure.[10]

The *finance* of utilities and services is another significant problem for local administration. Bagchi (1992) shows that the budget constraint arising from free-riding curtailed the type and extent of services that could be provided by a local authority. Local urban governments have to obtain state and central government funds. Yet such budgets are in turn constrained, not only by the structure of taxation but also increasingly by conditions on expenditure prescribed by Bretton Woods Institutions. Kothari and Kothari write:

The IMF – World Bank (insistence) on increasing government efficiency by cutting spending is of particular concern . . . [since] countries under SAP conditionalities invariably end up chopping allocations for those social or 'soft' sectors which cannot show immediate tangible returns.[11]

The danger is then that the weakest and neediest social strata are deprived of services,[12] while the most powerful sections of society are well provided for.

1.2 *Market provision*

Private infrastructure also requires finance. Funding depends on collateral and is therefore biased against the poor.[13] Collateral is required to tide institutional lenders over an uncertain period during which the infrastructure developers require money to obtain clearance while the lenders require clear title and permissions. When developers are contracted to cooperatives, the ownership of land or property is not easily established. Thus 'working capital is available only to established developers who generally operate in the up-market segment'.[14] And private developers catering for downmarket purchasers or clients are unable to accumulate the creditworthiness to obtain loans.

Vested interests and lack of trust combine to constrain and compartmentalize the development of infrastructure and privately to appropriate territory for the non-poor. The question arises whether that lack of access to finance results from the lenders' knowledge of risk or from their experience of uncertainty and is in some sense 'real' or whether it is an excuse to prop up repeated financial transactions in a set of vested interests? If the former, then the state has a role in forms of regulation which provide 'the market' with safety-net services. If the latter, then governments might, through regulative sanctions, coerce institutions into altering their repeated and self-interested behaviour.

Either way, those who benefit privately from private provision may be expected, first, to espouse forms of politics seeking the private appropriation of benefits of infrastructure, second, to avoid the negative externalities of the market-based provision they solicit and, third, to minimize contributions to the local public sector resource base.

1.3 *Community and household provision*

Many analysts[15] argue that the management of resources ought to be organized on a decentralized level because this will ensure greater distributional equity:

. . . the true alternative to the economic crisis lies in getting away from both an overcentralised system, which has been the case since Independence, and an excessively privatised one, which is looming on the horizon. Community management of resources needs to be revived, with a clear set of rights and obligations for local communities, governmental agencies and voluntary organisations.[16]

However, these polemicists neglect three important issues:

i)   The self-reinforcing inequity of decentralized revenue-raising without redistribution from rich to poor localities and the uncongruent relationship between institutions of revenue and expenditure.

ii) The class specificity of community-managed space and the tendency towards 'group privatization' under conditions of 'state failure'. With respect to physical security, collective privatization is accompanied by a politics of 'radical conservatism' (radical because organized at the grass roots and rejecting conventional political expression, but conservative because confined to reactionary ['NIMBY'[17]] values or easily 'winnable' issues).

iii) The politics of the creation of institutional authority.

Kumar and Mukherjee (1993) see the last two emerging from a more powerful engagement of voluntary organizations in the participative monitoring of both public sector and market provisioning. The literature therefore suggests – not without its moments of irony – that, for different reasons, all forms of provision are prone to be differentiating: the state sector according to the locations of political support, the market according to demand rather than need, and community action according to the opportunistic processes of NGO articulacy and scope.

1.4 *Institutional combinations*

It is clear that the public sector, while desirable, is not *essential* for all infrastructure.[18] Public provision is least controversial for those 'public goods'[19] where provision has to be on a large scale, where both positive and negative externalities are high and visible, where scale economies are manifest and where cross-subsidy is possible for the purposes of the politically endorsed 'social inclusion' of poor and marginalized people. In practice, composite combinations of institutional provision are very common. The extent to which composite provision is coordinated seems an entirely separate issue. In one example, health services were most institutionally diverse (involving a variety of public sector institutions, private, voluntary and 'traditional' non-modern health care, not always supplied on the basis of market exchange). The system was poorly coordinated, revealing that composite systems of service provision can coexist with the underutilization of capacity. With respect to drinking water and sewerage there was institutional substitution, but the different types of provision were better coordinated.[20] Baru (1993) for India reveals the wide spatial variation of health provision furnished by combinations of the public, private and voluntary sectors. There is a positive association between economic development, market provision, public provision and voluntary provision. The three modes of provision are synergistic complements rather than substitutes. Yet the central-place nature of such services cannot explain these wide variations in the provision of services. If health institutions are synergistic, then inter-regional differences in the quantity and quality of provision of civic services can be predicted to increase.[21]

It has been suggested in the context of structural adjustment: i) that the coordination of service provision between state and market and that within state and market can be improved (though the mechanisms by which increased coordination might take place are unexplored); and ii) that the state can play a facilitating role for the private system of provision in conditions where the state has been forced out or has been unable to contain private provision (though the mechanism by which a weak interventionist state can turn into a strong regulating state is not specified).[22]

1.5 *Resourcing infrastructure*

While revenue constraints have pitched many local administrations into the arms of central government grants and subventions to maintain minimal services, it is possible to charge residents without sacrificing a political mandate. The municipality of Barrackpore in Calcutta has succeeded in doubling its revenues over an 11-year period. Bagchi comments:

> It would be simplistic to explain the behaviour of Barrackpore residents in terms of rational 'public choice' given the universal 'free rider' instinct of tax payers and the deep distrust of politicians so prevalent in this part of the world. Apparently what counts . . . is nothing but the ability of those in charge of the civic body to overcome that distrust and to persuade their constituencies to take their word that they meant business and that they could be counted upon to deliver what they had promised . . . this was no mean task.[23]

One of the mechanisms by means of which trust was won was through residents noting immediate tangible changes in their urban environment as 'effective control of the utilities staff' by local elected councillors ensured better public hygiene and garbage removal. Another mechanism was the use of example. Residents saw councillors taking a lead by raising the rateable values of their own properties and by paying promptly. Their expression of accountability then spread to the electorate.

2. RURAL INFRASTRUCTURE

In this and the following section we examine some of the hard infrastructure in the rural economy.

2.1 *Drinking water*[24]

In the short run drinking water is more important than food. Its supply is the stuff of village politics. In 1990–1, according to Wanmali and Ramasamy, approximately 70 per cent of villages in the old North Arcot District had adequate supplies of drinking water.[25] Our three villages would count in this 70 per cent.

Provision
Twenty years ago, drinking water was got from tanks or hauled from unprotected irrigation wells, from private wells or from public drinking wells, access to which was strictly screened by caste. The idea that drinking water was a public good developed very slowly. That this public good could then be privatized and that its provision could also be differentiated according to use are still contested notions. In 1982–3, roughly 90 per cent of rural households in the old North Arcot District lacked access to tap water.[26] Many drinking-water wells had already been abandoned in the 1970s because of water table depletion (see Chapter 1–2). In the 1980s, during the prolonged and severe drought, the state invested in bore wells (separately for caste Hindus and for scheduled castes) and deepened and desilted existing drinking wells. In Veerasambanur, there are two bore wells and five public taps. In Vinayagapuram, there are no private taps. The village is supplied inadequately by public taps from an overhead tank built in 1991 with water pumped from the Cheyyar 'river'. Wells dug in the early 1960s by the Panchayat, one for each street, are now not fit for drinking from. In Nesal, the Panchayat Union invested in three wells as early as 1971–3. After the drought of the 1980s a deep bore well was constructed, 1 overhead tank was built and 146 houses were given drinking-water connections. Of these, only 12 were in the scheduled-caste 'colony', in part because poverty prevented them from making the initial fixed investments. By 1994, 90 per cent of houses in the caste part of Nesal village had their own tap connections. Public action by scheduled-caste residents through the Ambedkar Peoples' Movement had resulted in a deep bore well and a public hand pump in the 'colony'.

By the mid 1990s, in all three villages 'free' public provision played a key role (see Table 1). But the density and quality of public infrastructure varied enormously. It exhibits synergy with village size, accessibility and wealth but, above all, with the micro-geography of caste. In Veerasambanur, the tap water had to

TABLE 1 Drinking water: sources and collection

A: Drinking Water Sources (% sources)

		Public Well	Private Well[1]	Public Water Tap	House Tap	Own Well	Public Hand pump	Pond/Tank	Irrigation Well	Shared Private Tap
Nesal	A	3	11	33	44	3	7	–	–	–
	B	47	31	–	–	3	11	–	–	–
Vinayagapuram	A	–	–	100	–	–	–	–	–	–
	B	44	27	–	–	–	22	5	–	–
Veerasambanur	A	–	–	100	–	–	–	–	–	–
	B	–	8	42	–	–	21	–	13	17

B: Collector of Water (% instances)

	Wife	Female hhh	Sister/ Daughter	Grand-daughter	Daughter-in-law	Son	Grand-mother
Nesal	85	4	5	2	2	–	2
Vinayagapuram	44	19	14	3	11	3	6
Veerasambanur	76	–	20	4	–	–	–

Note: [1] either own or other's

A Normal conditions
B Scarce water conditions
hhh = household head

be pumped three miles from a substation sited outside the jurisdiction of the village and frequently needing repair. Only in Nesal were public taps not the only source under normal conditions. In Nesal, water provision reaches urban standards. Yet a minority of houses in this village still had to use wells and public hand pumps. All the public taps in the scheduled-caste colony were out of order during our fieldwork. Their bore well and public well had saline, undrinkable water and their overhead tank was broken down.

Water is often scarce. Inadequate supplies are the result of electricity failures in the summer months, failures which can still last up to 10 consecutive days. Pumping equipment frequently breaks down and pipes are blocked or burst. Waste also results in scarcity. Missing control valves are common enough to require the building of ditches for overflow water in parts of villages suffering seasonal scarcity. Under scarce water conditions, recourse is taken to sources radically different from those used normally. Public wells and hand pumps are reverted to and, in a minority of cases, poor-quality, unprotected sources such as tanks, ponds and irrigation wells are used. Scarce water conditions are reported as general. But in fact *scheduled-caste households face scarcity, while caste households experience normal conditions*. It is scheduled-caste households which have to draw water from unprotected public sources. Scarce conditions result as much from technical failures (equipment, electricity) as from hydrological or rainfall failure. In Veerasambanur in the hot season, while a public supply of water is needed for 3–4 hours each day, electricity failures and rationing result in the village's actually receiving a half to one hour of water every two days. Then, both caste and scheduled-caste women have to use the hand pump of a bore well *in an adjacent village*. In Nesal 'colony', in 1995, when all the public drinking taps were out of order, scheduled-caste women had routinely to beg well-water from caste households. In Vinayagapuram, scheduled-caste people still used the pond at dry times of year.

Maintenance

The system of tanks which supplied water for all purposes was of such fundamental importance that villages defined themselves as social units through contributions to collective labour or to the payment of village servants who maintained tanks and channels (see Chapter 1–2). The arrival of state-provided drinking water and the privatization of irrigation put paid to the kinds of 'community action' that are being called for now. Instead the state, through its Public Works Department, maintains the tank system irregularly and fails to regulate tank levels, discharges and uses. Tail-end villages now not only suffer water scarcity but also serious pollution.

The state-provided drinking-water infrastructure suffers poor maintenance, frequent breakdowns and is reported to be inadequate to needs, as well as poorly or wrongly sited. It deteriorated over the last two decades of the twentieth century and wastes water as a result of poor siting, poor design and lack of maintenance.

In 1993–4, Block Development Officers were charged with the maintenance of public wells, overhead tanks, pipes and taps. As a result of delays[27] and incompetence, ad hoc private collective maintenance arrangements went into operation in Veerasambanur, maintenance costs were borne by a public/private mixture in Nesal and ad hoc supplementary collective arrangements were tried in Vinayagapuram. These amount to informal user fees. Such voluntary collective action rarely works for long and households refuse to pay a fee – even one as low as Rs 1–2 per month – for the maintenance of drinking water. The Christian Church and the Ambedkar Peoples' movement have been instrumental in sinking 'private' wells and installing public hand pumps in certain 'colonies'. These are collectively maintained. However, this collective maintenance generates severe conflict between cost bearers and free riders. In addition, 'scheduled-caste wells' have been vandalized by caste Hindus and scheduled-caste users are unable and/or unwilling to cooperate to repair the damage. As a result, drinking water is of unreliable quality and its provision may be associated with waste and with micro-environments delightful for water-borne diseases.

Access

Those with responsibility for access are almost always adult women (sons and elderly women in a tiny minority of instances). Water collection from public taps is still a strenuous activity (Table 1). Sheer human strength affects access. There is no difference in the division of tasks under scarce conditions, though quarrels and fights over queues and quantities are much more frequent at times of scarcity.

Table 2 summarizes the results of these relations of access. There is little intervillage variation in the average time: between 37 and 45 minutes a day under normal conditions and between 1 and 1.5 hours when water is scarce. That still represents a substantial female burden, both in energy and in time. Volumetric estimates of water utilization were obtained. These show small average intervillage variations, water consumption in Nesal (307 litres [l] per household per day) being 25 per cent greater than that in Vinayagapuram (234 l), with Veerasambanur intermediate (272 l). But Nesal's landless labour households use more than Vinayagapuram's elite. The three village elites use 40 per cent more water (averaging 358 l) than do landless agricultural labour households (223 l). We also find in Nesal's use of water exactly what is found with their assets and their diet, namely that the agrarian elite now has a quantitatively and qualitatively

TABLE 2 Access to drinking water in the three villages

Class	% hh	Aver. Water collection litres per day hh	Aver. collection time, normal conditions (hrs)	Aver. collection time, scarce conditions (hrs)
A Nesal n=				
richer, non-ag.	2	500	2.5	2.5
richer agricultural	7	509	1.13	1.75
poor peasants	16	400	0.72	1.39
hardly landed/landless peasants	75	263	0.62	0.80
B Vinayagapuram n=36				
richer, non-ag.	8	250	0.89	1.78
richer agricultural	25	276	0.75	1
poor peasants landless peasants	67	217	0.71	1.3
C Veerasambanur n=25				
richer, non-ag.	8	300	1.5	2.5
richer agricultural	16	189	0.53	1.4
poor peasants	24	150	0.75	1.5
hardly landed/landless peasants	52	190	0.69	1.38

different pattern of resource use. In the case of drinking water, this elite on average uses 3.4 times the water used by poor peasants in Veerasambanur. *The same public provision that has widened social access has also enabled this social differentiation in access to develop.*

Not only class and locality structure access but so does caste. The density of public taps is lower in the 'colonies' than in the caste villages. Where there are cross-caste queues at public sources, caste structures access and scheduled-caste people are prevented from obtaining water until caste households have satisfied their needs. Caste conflicts over water are common. It is scheduled-caste households which experience the impact of conflict of uses: for irrigation, personal hygiene, drinking, cattle-watering and clothes washing. It is scheduled-caste households which are forcibly denied access to irrigation wells for drinking water in times of scarcity and prevented from taking drinking water from tanks and ponds. It is scheduled-caste households which are forced to beg for water from caste households with private connections.

2.2. *Sanitation*

Provision
State policy is to provide public latrines free of charge. Each Panchayat Union has had one or two public toilets constructed separately in the villages for caste households and in the 'colonies' for scheduled-caste people. The latrines are caste-segregated. Their use is as gendered as is the use of public space for defecation. Private latrines (six in Nesal, one in Vinayagapuram) are only used by women, and then only in cases of urgency.[28]

Access
Public sanitation infrastructure is inappropriate. It is not used, for several reasons. First, the facilities provided are so inadequate for potential need that access is avoided altogether. Then there are either no maintenance personnel or those appointed do not carry out the work required of them. General water scarcity prevents the routine cleaning of public facilities. No water is provided for users. Instead, public sanitation is used for entirely different purposes: as shelter for cattle and goats or as a sleeping space for children or adults.

As a result, rural people continue to use common land, or agricultural land where common land is not to hand. Such territory is invisibly marked by space and time so that the genders and castes use specific locations at specific times of day. Men use the tank beds, tank littorals, irrigation channels and fields. Women have access to common or waste lands near their homes. Children are allowed to defecate beside roads and paths[29] and often do this near taps and water sources. Excreta are left to be eaten and recycled by pigs and dogs or to decompose. Domestic rubbish and cowdung is generally taken to the fields. But the area of public space in front of houses is often cleaned, because it is used as a drying area for harvested grains, vegetables and by-products.

As the population grows and as water sources diffuse, the 'negative externalities' of this form of sanitation become all the more acute. Common lands provide epicentres for fly- and mosquito-borne diseases, while public sources may be polluted by the faeces and urine of children. Lack of drainage around public water sources exacerbates these health hazards.

3. LOCAL URBAN UTILITIES

Beede and Bloom (1995) have noted from global research a positive association between income, consumption, waste and public health hazards – and a collective negative association with levels of political awareness of these relationships! The contrast between rural and urban locations rams home this point. The local town of Arni acts as a central place for the three villages and at least a hundred more. It is 150 km south-west of Madras, with an economic base consisting of administration, commerce (increasingly wholesale), paddy trading and milling and silk saree weaving. According to the censuses, its population has grown from some 39,000 in 1972 to 49,000 in 1981 and 55,000 in 1991. The municipality, created in 1951 and converted to grade 2 status in 1971, has already engulfed 11 revenue villages. In fact the population directly associated with Arni's urban economy is around 100,000, the census population being inflated by transients and by regular commuting from a ring of villages. The latter resist incorporation into the municipality in view of the increases this would make to local taxation – a fact which makes the town's administration chronically underfunded. Arni has also lost out in the political scramble for services,[30] and for a town of its size it is relatively poorly endowed with infrastructure.[31] There are 7 slums, each having between 70 and 400 huts and accommodating 15 per cent of households. Arni is a good example of access to infrastructure under conditions of high inequality. By contrast, its town plan document declares that Arni 'is well served by utilities'.[32] The plan, while detailed on land use zoning, makes no mention of utilities at all.

3.1 *Drinking water*

Protected water has been supplied on a mass basis since 1974.[33] But by 1982–3, three quarters of the residents still lacked access to tap water.[34] Water has been diverted for unplanned industrial use, including the dyeing of silk yarn and the parboiling of paddy. Conditions have radically changed. There are now major infiltration wells in the Cheyyar and Arni riverbeds and one other at Kamandanaganathi. From these water is pumped to 3 overhead tanks and drawn thereafter by gravity to tap connections in 42 per cent of houses and to 152 public drinking fountains. Access to domestic tap water in Arni is therefore almost on a par with that in Nesal village. The facility is screened by ability to pay (Rs 20 per month for domestic connections and Rs 50 per month for commercial premises). The water table is not particularly high, at 9 metres, supplying 23 per cent of houses directly via private drinking wells. During the late 1980s, a World Bank loan was used to remedy the acute shortages of the drought years and 160 bore wells were sunk, which households share (privately). The poorest 30 per cent have access to some 112 public hand pumps (the installation of which has sometimes been triggered by local collective subscription) and 94 public wells. Clothes can be washed in the 4 public tanks, but within the last 20 years these have become extremely polluted and are avoided. In Table 3, certain public utilities of Arni are compared with those of Thanjavur (where Elango and

TABLE 3 Water, sanitation, drainage and garbage: Arni and Thanjavur compared

	Thanjavur official population 1991 234,000	*Arni official population 1991* 55,000
Drinking water		
popn. per house tap connection	44	14
litres of water per cap per day	100	60
Sanitation		
popn. per private power flush latrine	17	11
popn. per private dry latrine	40	14
popn. per public flush latrine	3,966	3,928
popn. per public urinal	58,500	55,000
Drainage		
popn. per km of open drain	4,775	3,552
popn. per km of underground drain	234,000	15,277
Garbage		
annual manure composted per head (kg)	100	4
total (tonnes)	23520	233
price/tonne Rs.	8.7 (1992)	21.5 (1994)

Sources: Arni, *Municipal Abstract 1993–4*.
Thanjavur: Elango and Ramachandran, 1993.

Ramachandran conducted a similar study into infrastructure [1993]). Here it can be seen that Arni is considerably less developed than Thanjavur with respect to drinking water.

3.2 *Drainage and sanitation*

When fine roads were surfaced 40–50 years ago, part of the elite residential area and the central business area were provided with an underground drainage system which flows to a drainage tank (Paiyur Eri) on the edge of town. For the rest, open drains lead to 96 drain pits. Not only does rainwater accumulate, but all manner of organic waste, street waste and dead animals are shovelled and swept into these congested ditches. They are physically dangerous and constitute a public health hazard which the municipality has a responsibility to clean once a week.

Visibly worsening public squalor is the product of Arni's political history. As a *jagir*, Arni was outside the jurisdiction of the Municipal Act. Little was done about sanitation until relatively recently. The built-up area of the town was interspersed with open spaces used systematically (rather like the village commons) for purposes of defecation (as were the outer limits of temples), the product being recycled by pigs and dogs. These areas have been encroached upon and the dense population has induced certain changes in site and in technology. Now sections of alleys in the congested central business area and residential wards are intensively deployed for defecation, no longer well recycled by animals, but accumulating and slowly decomposing. Also, the paucity of public latrines (Table 3) allows no option to the vast population of daily visitors (the cinemas alone being able to give 'doses' of film to 20,000 incomers per day). There has been a rapid change in domestic sanitary technologies: 55 per cent of houses have flush latrines and 43 per cent (most of the remainder) dry latrines. Few, however, are connected to septic tanks, so untreated human sewage joins drain water and untreated chemical effluent from the dyeing of silk yarn. This heady brew seeps, via semi-closed drains, to an open tank, originally positioned on the southern extremity of the small nineteenth-century village[35] but now engulfed and centrally sited in the twenty-first-century settlement.

3.3 *The fire service*

This also requires water. Despite a substantial population increase in the urban region and rurally within a radius of 30 km, the fire service, established in 1974, has seen no commensurate increase in fires. This is just as well because water-table depletion robbed the fire service of its well and, starved of resources, it was dependent on the private patronage of rice mill owners for its most crucial raw material until 1999. It is largely a rural service, and the state of rural roads and the unpredictable barriers of level crossings on the railways inevitably make it slow and cumbersome for such a purpose. The fires are mostly agricultural. Hot-season fires occur in sugar-cane fields. Rainy seasons provoke electrical fires both in the fields and in huts. As in the case of public latrines in villages, so here, the fire service is used for purposes other than these intended – notably as an ambulance in case of accidents.

3.4 *Garbage and waste*

This is a story of public provision selectively privatized with private incentives. The municipality is charged with the daily sweeping of the central business area. This is done twice a week. In response to the tide of filth, shopkeepers organize and supplement this service privately and/or collectively. But such action displaces garbage rather than removes it. Three groups of municipal scavengers police the garbage, 160 people aged between 23 and 58, of whom 30 are women. The municipality allows these jobs to be inherited. Conditions are relatively privileged. The pay is Rs 1,800 per month (twice that of rice mill work, seven times that of male agricultural labour), hours are strictly regulated, a rest day is allowed, provident fund and pensions are paid and these gangs are solidly unionized. Standing by is an army of 200 reserves who take temporary employment at Rs 40 per day. Scavengers live in four slums and a set of quarters managed by the municipality. There is a gender division of labour, women doing the latrines and men the drains and solid refuse. The labour force supplements its pay (by Rs 600–1,000 per month[36]) through private contracts and by supplying raw materials to recyclers. The municipality is widely alleged to delay wages, to appropriate the provident fund and to take ages to provide pensions. In return, the passive resistance of this reluctant labour aristocracy of social outcasts leads to a systemic deterioration in the quality of public service and thus to private provision by the urban elite.

Three zones can become dangerously foul if not cleaned regularly. These are the environs of the three slaughterhouses. The slaughter area west of Suriyakulam, specializing in goats, sheep and chickens, produces 21.3 tonnes of meat per year, while the slaughter of cows and buffalo produces 181 tonnes.[37]

Organic manure is heaped in great piles in the central business area to be transferred, when it reaches a critical mass, to landfill and to compost pits east of the town which are auctioned off to farmers four times a year and refilled. It is the use of solid waste as landfill that may explain the significant difference between Arni (low) and Thanjavur (high) in the amount of manure produced per head of population.

While in the early 1970s all the waste from the business area was organic (and packaging used leaves) and while, in the early 1980s, paper had replaced leaves, most was recycled by the large populations of pigs, dogs, donkeys and goats roaming the town. In the 1990s, however, a substantial amount of inorganic, non-biodegradable waste was generated. It took the form of metal, polythene, plastic and glass. The municipality is charged with providing cement bins in each street for such waste. But a continual stream of bribes is necessary to ensure these bins are placed and then kept in position. A private cottage industry of scavenging competes with the municipal scavengers to pick and sort this refuse (while the municipal scavengers remove what remains). These itinerants are the true destitutes of Arni. About 100 tribal and scheduled-caste adult and child labourers, organized loosely in gangs, move between wards of the town and local villages collecting non-biodegradable waste for sale to recyclers. Of these there are about 20, closely clustered in a mainly Muslim Suriyakulam ward, near to the central business area. Recyclers specialize by type (glass, metal, cardboard, plastic, polythene) in sets of firms organized so as to preempt commercial taxation. Large-scale, metropolitan recycling factories are supplied by these means. In Arni, the trades are collectively self-regulated and provide credit to recyclers for whom this low-status trade is highly profitable. Meanwhile a scavenging family with two adults will make about Rs 2,400 per annum.

The degradation of the urban habitat is a global phenomenon. As Elango and Ramachandran have concluded (1993), its nature and pace vary according to location, class and caste. These social institutions are at work within the town. We would add gender to them. It seems that private domestic fastidiousness is combined with a disregard for increasingly dangerous public squalor. This paradox has been explained by the gendering of space (the domestic is female and clean, the public is male and filthy) and by the operation of caste (scavenging and the clearing of what historically were modest levels of refuse being the domain of untouchables).[38] These factors make sanitation quite literally an untouchable policy issue.

4. CONCLUSIONS

Wanmali and Ramasamy recorded a wave of infrastructural provision in both urban and rural locations during the 1980s and relate this to agricultural/economic development.[39] No doubt there has been a decentralization of hitherto urban central place functions and infrastructure, but their quality, once installed, is inadequate, particularly with respect to public provision.[40]

Free public provision of infrastructure is recognized as being especially important for poor people. Yet maintenance costs are the first to be squeezed.[41] The breakdown of public infrastructure exacerbates class, gender and caste differentiation in access and use. It also provokes a variety of institutions, small commercial firms, collective action and NGOs to compensate for the gross deficiencies in maintenance. However, this institutional plurality is not coordinated nor does it demonstrate synergy. Nor is it stable or effective. The community institutions advocated as favourable forms of governance at the rural-community level during the reform period[42] are seen here to be ad hoc and by no stretch of the imagination necessarily efficient or equitable solutions to problems of access. Rather they are a response that creates conflict and accentuates gender, caste and class differences, which the state is unable to regulate.

The proliferation of civic associations certainly works towards the enforcement of municipal accountability, but in ways which serve sectional interests.[43] So-called communitarian organizations are in fact highly socially exclusive. Private action, private patronage and modest levels of group action guarantee the safety of the elite business class, which controls commodity, money and labour markets in the region. But mass hygiene and public health depend on the work of a few hundred social outcasts.

The Eighth Five-Year Plan not only called for community involvement in self-sustaining maintenance; it also advocated full-cost recovery unless infrastructure is demonstrably for the poor. From our account, it is plain that such a policy would be predatory in the absence of a marked improvement in service. Water poverty is a special kind of poverty, depending on the one hand on sites and technologies which are state-provided and on the other on the physical capacities of women.

The plan also advocates the extension of sanitation (with user charges where appropriate) to SC/ST households.[44] Our account reveals a massive clash of culture with respect to sanitation, such that no attempt to institutionalize the use of latrines has a chance of success without a mass education campaign and improvements in maintenance. In fact latrines are likely to be used as latrines only if they are provided as private property and with the resources to maintain them; and even then they are less likely to be used by men than by women.

The provision of infrastructure is replete with *paradoxes of entitlement*:

i)   between a wide range of legal entitlements translated into planning objectives and the meagre, uneven and inappropriate infrastructure biased against women and low-caste people;

ii)   for the commercial and agrarian elites, between their superior claim on the state's obligations and their simultaneous deployment of exit options and a plurality of state, private and collective modes of provision;

iii) for the poor, between their flawed entitlement and their need for state provision.

The local municipal administration varies in the efficiency with which it provides infrastructure to different classes. Water is far from being a developmental success and refuse disposal is a dangerous failure. A preoccupation with forms of ownership and finance may have diverted policy-makers' attention from much more important and 'prior' issues. Public property rights and obligations are fuzzy and contested; both providers and beneficiaries are alienated and communitarian institutions are riven with conflict.

Kumar and Mukherjee conclude for health provision – but with much wider relevance:

> In the field of public health services there is a lack of incentive for efficient provisioning. Improvements in management and administration . . . are essential . . . (but so also are the) ethics of management. There is a need for a new consciousness among public service managers . . . not only to encourage improved publicprovisioning but also to monitor performance and ensure accountability.[45]

That this conclusion is deeply unfashionable does not invalidate it.

ACKNOWLEDGEMENTS

The assistance from Elizabetta Basile, S Janakarajan, G Jothi, S Mariasusai, G Murugan, N Narayanan, S Ramachandran, Helen Rosenfeld, Ruhi Saith, B S Sanghera, M V Srinivasan, S Wanmali and Elinor Harriss is very gratefully acknowledged.

Populism and Electricity in Rural Tamil Nadu

S JANAKARAJAN

1. INTRODUCTION

O NE of the striking features of India's economy has been indiscriminate subsidies of various kinds offered by governments both at the centre and at state level. The total value of the subsidies extended both by the central and all the state governments amounted to a staggering Rs 137,000 crores in the year 1994–5, which is 14.5 per cent of GDP. Some of this subsidy goes to agricultural inputs such as chemical fertilizers, farm equipment, support prices for agricultural output, irrigation water, electricity for groundwater and so on. While many of these subsidies are centrally sponsored, the most important among those sponsored by the local states are the public distribution system (PDS), irrigation and electricity (for pumping water) (see Chapter 2–1). These are critical because of the large number of users involved and for that reason, over and above developmental reasons, they are of cardinal interest to politicians.

The Indian Government has already spent more than Rs 600 billion at 1988–9 prices on canal networks in the last 40 years, creating an irrigation potential of 22 million hectares. Recoveries from users of irrigation water constitute only a small fraction of the operation and maintenance costs incurred by the government, let alone the capital costs involved. While the 1972 Irrigation Commission recommended the recovery for canal water charges of at least 5 per cent and 12 per cent of the gross revenue of farmers from food and commercial crops respectively, actual recoveries constitute barely 1 per cent of their gross revenue.[1] The recently constituted Committee on the Pricing of Irrigation Water observes in its 1992 report: 'The gross receipts of major and medium irrigation and multi purpose projects fell short of their working expenses by about Rs. 168 million a year on an average during the three years 1974–77; the gap rose to Rs. 2,775 million a year during the period from about Rs. 1,737 million a year to Rs. 9,867 million a year' by 1990.[2] Although the pricing of irrigation water has been one of the major issues that has preoccupied successive central and state governments, very little has been done so far towards the recovery of costs and the redressing of water rates. On the contrary, state governments have effectively resisted the implementation of the recommendations of the Irrigation Commission, as well as the recommendations of the Committee on the Pricing of Irrigation Water.

In addition to irrigation water, power has also been supplied at a subsidized price to run agricultural pump sets. This is the subsidy which is the subject of this chapter. In fact, many State Electricity Boards (SEBs) have sought refuge in the subsidized power supply extended to agricultural pump sets, as an excuse to cover up many of the technical and distributional shortcomings that have led to substantial losses to these boards. The policy issues of the revision of surface water rates and electricity tariffs for pumping groundwater have lately been much politicized, although in a state like Tamil Nadu they have a long history. Against this background, two issues will be examined here: (a) the rationale of supplying electricity at zero price; and (b) the impact on different sections of agrarian society if the electricity supplied to the agricultural pump sets were to be priced.

The argument is organized as follows. Section 2 takes stock of the power sector in the state and the consumption pattern among users. The use of electricity by the agricultural sector and the subsidy provided to it is discussed in Section 3. Section 4 deals with the policy issue of free electricity, while the final section provides a summary and suggests policy implications.

2. POWER SCENARIO AND CONSUMPTION PATTERN OF ELECTRICITY IN TAMIL NADU

Installed power-generation capacity in the country has increased from a meagre 1,400 megawatts (MW) in 1947 to 89,167 MW at the end of 1997–8.[3] Power generation in the state of Tamil Nadu has also come a long way (see Table 1). During the First Plan period (1951–6), installed capacity by the Tamil Nadu State Electricity Board (TNEB) was only 256 MW and, with the purchases from other states and from the central grid, total power availability amounted to 1,058 million units. Per capita consumption was a bare minimum of 21 units. Since then, there has been remarkable progress in the extent of power generated in the state. Towards the end of the Eighth Plan (1992–7), the installed capacity at the command of the TNEB was 6,908 MW, with a peak demand at 4,875 MW. This is no mean achievement. However, by 1998–9 there was still a deficit of 1,059 MW

TABLE 1 Installed capacity, peak demand and per capita consumption of power in Tamil Nadu as seen in the plan period, 1950–51 to 1996–7

Plan Period (As at the end of)	Installed Capacity At the command of the TNEB (MW)	Peak Demand (MW)	Gross Power availability (generation + Purchases) (mu)	Per capita Consumption (units or Kwh)
Pre-plan March 1951	156	110	630	12
First Plan 1951–56	256	172	1058	21
Second Plan 1956–61	571	381	2243	60
Third Plan 1961–66	1370	717	4041	92
Annual Plans 1966–69	1470	997	5260	116
Fourth Plan 1969–74	2254	1287	6948	127
Fifth Plan 1974–78	2424	1641	9453	157
Annual Plans 1978–80	2719	1710	10414	183
Sixth Plan 1980–85	3344	2154	13731	195
Seventh Plan 1985–90	5473	2929	18273	295
Annual Plan 1990–91	5744	3094	20794	332
Annual Plan 1991–92	6019	3501	21920	360
Eighth Plan 1992–97	6908	4875	32700	420

Source: *Tamil Nadu–An Economic Appraisal, 1996–97*, Government of Tamil Nadu, Chennai.

between power availability and requirement, a deficit expected to be wiped out by the end of the Ninth Five-Year plan.[4] The per capita consumption of electricity also rated high at 420 units, ranking fifth in the country after Punjab (786 units), Haryana (601 units), Gujarat (549 units) and Maharashtra (483 units).[5] Apart from the first five, only two other states (Karnataka and Andhra Pradesh) have a per capita consumption more than the all-India average of 319 units.[6] As may be seen from Table 1, the peak demand generation has also gone up by many times, from 172 MW at the end of the First Plan period to 4,875 MW at the end of the Eighth Plan period.

The consumption of electricity reflects differentials in sectoral development. Industry has been the biggest consumer of electricity in the state, using over 40 per cent of total power. Although there has been a steady increase in the power consumed by this sector, a certain sluggishness in the mid-1990s is attributable to the general industrial stagnation.

Rural electrification has been one of the most important rural infrastructural programmes undertaken by both the Government of India and state governments, for it enabled the development of groundwater (pump-set) irrigation. As a matter of fact, it is now acknowledged that the success of the Indian 'green revolution' is due to the rapid growth of modern lift irrigation technology. As of March 1998, 11.8 million pump sets had been energized.

Tamil Nadu has been ahead of other states in rural electrification. Even during the Sixth Plan period, Tamil Nadu had achieved almost complete electrification of its countryside. The agricultural sector has been one of the major consumers of electricity since the 1960s. In 1970–71, about a quarter of the total power availability in the state (1,275 million units [mu]) was consumed by this sector in order to operate agricultural pumps. In 1974–5, the power consumed by this sector had gone up to one third of the total power availability in the state (1,850 mu). Since the mechanization of water lifting devices was given utmost importance, this sector continued to expand in absolute terms, but its share declined steadily afterwards until the 1990s (see Table 2), when it rose from 21 per cent to 27 per cent (from 3,233 mu in 1989–90 to 6,730 mu in 1995–6). This reversal is largely due to the policy of free electricity supplied to agriculture by the Government of Tamil Nadu.

One of the biggest problems of the Indian power system has been the very high and increasing losses incurred in the process of transmission and distribution (T&D). While, in 1980, T&D losses were at a level of 20.6 per cent, by the end of 1990 they had increased to 22.4 per cent and settled at 21 per cent in 1995–6. Contrast this with the T&D losses of five major Asian countries for the year 1990: China 7.1 per cent, Indonesia 16.4 per cent, Korea 5.6 per cent, Thailand 10.9 per cent and Japan 5.7 per cent.[7] In terms of kilowatt-hours (kWh) lost in T&D, Tata Energy Research Institute (TERI) has calculated an aggregate figure of 75 billion kWh for 1996–7. The government is reported to be 'making efforts to reduce these losses at the rate of 1 per cent per year (resulting in a saving of approximately 800 MW) to about 15 per cent through technical innovations as well as stricter enforcement of electricity laws'.[8] In Tamil Nadu, T&D losses are comparatively low. In 1996–7, the total T&D losses stood at 16.9 per

TABLE 2 Consumer category-wise energy consumption in Tamil Nadu, 1970–71 to 1995–6 (in million units–mu)

Year	Domestic	Commercial	Agriculture	Industries	Others
1970–71	336 (6.5)	411 (8)	1275 (24.8)	2931 (57)	193 (3.8)
1974–75	425 (7.6)	417 (7.5)	1850 (33.3)	2674 (48.1)	194 (3.5)
1979–80	777 (9.5)	650 (8)	2178 (26.8)	4187 (51.4)	350 (4.3)
1984–85	1405 (12.8)	890 (8.1)	2424 (22.3)	5779 (52.8)	457 (4.2)
1989–90	2649 (17.5)	1160 (7.7)	3233 (21.4)	7261 (48.1)	807 (5.3)
1995–96	4184 (16.5)	1734 (6.8)	6730 (26.6)	10981 (43.4)	1701 (6.7)
1996–97	4181 (16.2)	1776 (6.9)	6910 (26.8)	10617 (41.1)	2321 (9)

Note: Figures in parentheses are row percentages.

Source: *Economic Intelligence Service*, 'Energy', March–April 1999, CMIE. *Tamil Nadu–An Economic Appraisal, 1996–97*, Government of Tamil Nadu (only for the year 1996–7).

cent. This was significantly less than in 1990 (19 per cent) and much lower than the all-India average.

The relative efficiency of T&D in Tamil Nadu needs setting in the context of the level of unmetered consumption of electricity in the state. Electricity for agricultural pump sets was about 27 per cent of the net power available for T&D for the year 1995–6. Since power has been supplied free to agricultural pump sets since 1991, the electricity consumed in this sector is not metered. The T&D losses in the same year stood at 16.9 per cent of gross power available in the state,[9] or 5,530 million kWh units. The total unmetered consumption plus losses in the state amounts to 12,472 million units in 1996–7 (Rs 2,494 crores, or about Rs 25 billion). The TNEB uses the category of unmetered consumption to account for corruption, pilferage and operational inefficiency. This issue becomes much more meaningful if we take into account the cross-subsidies provided by the other users such as high and low tension consumers (industries) and other commercial categories.

In Tamil Nadu, the unit cost of power in 1997–8 was 192.28 paise[10] per kWh. But there is a big variation in the tariff charged for different users. For instance, domestic users are charged (on average) 123.6 paise with a subsidy element of 68.68 paise. The agricultural sector (for pump sets) is charged nothing, so the subsidy element involved is 192.28 paise. Commercial users, on the other hand, are charged 286.7 paise and the cross-subsidy provided by this sector is 94.42 paise per kWh. Industries are charged (on average) 278.9 paise and the cross-subsidy provided by this sector is 86.62 paise.[11] It would be worth exploring the extent to which the subsidy provided for certain sections of the population is the root cause for the losses incurred by the TNEB, as often claimed by TNEB's bureaucracy, or if inefficient management and corruption are responsible.[12]

All the states of India have physical deficits in the electricity sector that have been increasing over time, mainly because of the increasing state subsidies on the operation of agricultural pump sets. The net power supply position in the state of Tamil Nadu since 1990–91 is presented in Table 3.

Tamil Nadu's deficit has been increasing over time, due in part to free supply of power to agricultural pump sets, which encourages farmers to use electricity inefficiently, and in part to the mismatch between supply and demand.

3. THE STATE SUBSIDY TO THE AGRICULTURAL SECTOR (FOR AGRICULTURAL PUMP SETS) IN TAMIL NADU

Energy consumption per electric pump set has been on the rise. A comparison of the consumption of power by agriculture and industrial sectors estimated in the Fifteenth Electric Power Survey of India, published by the Central Electricity Authority, with those actually consumed by these sectors in the year 1994–5 indicates that the agricultural sector consumed 5 per cent more than the forecast. By contrast, the industrial sector's consumption was less by 10 per cent. 'If this trend is not reversed, a major percentage of power generation from new power stations during the ninth Five Year Plan may well go towards meeting the requirements of losses, agricultural consumption and the pilferage of electricity'.[13] As of 31 March 1998, 11.8 million pump sets have been energized in India and the total electricity subsidy extended to the agricultural sector in

TABLE 3 Electricity balance in Tamil Nadu

Year	Supply over demand Surplus (+) or Deficit (—)
1990–91	−6.4
1991–92	−4.8
1992–93	−1.8
1993–94	−3.9
1994–95	−2.8
1995–96	−10.9
1996–97	−13.8

Source: TERI Energy Data Directory and Year Book, 1998–99, TERI, New Delhi.

the year 1996–7 was a jolting Rs 15,329 crores. In 1991–2, it had been Rs 5,938 crores.

The then Finance Minister of the Government of Tamil Nadu, Mr V R Neduncgezhian, in his budget speech in the State Legislature for the financial year 1995–6, made the following remarks to highlight the losses incurred by the TNEB due to the supply of free electricity to agricultural pump sets:

> Even after revision of tariffs, the Tamil Nadu Electricity Board is confronted with a total resources shortfall of Rs. 522.32 crores in 1995–96. The continued supply of electricity to farm pump sets free of cost has imposed a major financial burden on the Tamil Nadu Electricity Board. It is estimated that the total cost of supplying free electricity is Rs. 1112.40 crores in 1994–95. As the costs continue to rise, and the Government cannot provide more than Rs. 350 crores as cash subsidy and other categories of consumers cannot be charged more, the situation has become quite complex. The Tenth Finance Commission has also completely disallowed provision of cash subsidy to the Tamil Nadu Electricity Board to cover the cost of free supply of electricity to farm pump sets. A long term solution will have to be found in due course.[14]

The increases in energy consumed by the agricultural sector, the number of electric pump sets and the electricity consumed per pump set may be understood from Table 4. In particular, a substantial increase in consumption per electric pump set indicates the secular decline in the water table and the competitive deepening of wells by farmers (see Chapter 1–2).[15] The increase in per-pump-set consumption of this extent might be justified if the area irrigated per well also shows a corresponding increase. But the available data indicates that there is only a marginal increase in the area irrigated per well over the last two decades (Table 4). It is particularly interesting to see the association between electricity consumed per electrified well and the type of electricity tariff prescribed by the state. When tariffs were imposed or raised, consumption increased quite rapidly. Since farmers' use of energy is driven by incentives, the efficiency of use of free groundwater and electricity may be doubted.

The electricity subsidy for agricultural pump sets in Tamil Nadu has a political history and a political rationale. Free electricity, introduced in the year 1991, is the result of a militant farmers movement in the state, dating back to the 1970s. This farmers' movement originated in the dry tracts of Coimbatore, Erode and Salem districts and later spread to other parts of the state. Agriculture in the dry tracts depends almost entirely upon well irrigation. The water problem was aggravated by a series of droughts during the period 1965 to 1976 in which the water table declined, necessitating a great deal of investment by farmers. Even a small change in the electricity tariff affected the pumping costs considerably. When the State Government decided to raise the electricity tariff from 8 paise to

TABLE 4 Electricity consumption per pump set and changes in the tariff structure in Tamil Nadu 1970–71–1996–7

Year	Total energy consumed for ag. pump sets (mu)	Total Number of electric pump sets	Energy consumed per pump set (units)	Area irrigated per well (hectare)	Tariff charged for agricultural pump sets
1970–71	1,241 (100)	5,29,932 (100)	2,342	0.63	8 paise / unit
1971–72	1,269 (102)	5,94,169 (112)	2,136	0.63	9 paise / unit
1972–73	1,430 (115)	6,49,241 (122)	2,203	0.66	11 paise / unit
1973–74	1,576 (127)	6,81,205 (128)	2,314	0.69	11 paise / unit
1974–75	1,847 (149)	7,06,914 (133)	2,613	0.63	11 paise / unit
1975–76	1,675 (135)	7,42,745 (140)	2,255	0.55	16 paise / unit
1976–77	1,697 (137)	7,73,702 (146)	2,193	0.52	16 paise / unit
1977–78	1,786 (144)	8,09,606 (153)	2,206	0.60	Big farmers – 16 paise/unit; Small——14 paise/unit
1978–79	2,104 (170)	8,40,557 (159)	2,503	0.67	Big farmers – 14 paise/unit; Small——12 paise/unit
1979–80	2,186 (176)	8,87,227 (167)	2,464	0.69	Big farmers – 14 paise/unit; Small——12 paise/unit
1980–81	2,299 (185)	9,19,162 (173)	2,501	0.66	Big farmers – 14 paise/unit; Small——12 paise/unit
1981–82	2,354 (190)	9,45,520 (178)	2,490	0.64	Big farmers – 15 paise/unit; Small——12 paise/unit
1982–83	2,230 (180)	9,65,017 (182)	2,311	0.50	Big farmers – 15 paise/unit; Small——12 paise/unit
1983–84	2,200 (177)	9,82,606 (185)	2,239	0.56	Big farmers – 15 paise/unit; Small——12 paise/unit
1984–85	2,415 (195)	9,82,606 (185)	2,458	0.61	Big Farmers: Rs.75/HP/year; Small:Rs.50/HP per year

TABLE 5 (cont.):

Year					
1985–86	2,840 (229)	10,33,533 (198)	2,748	0.62	Big Farmers: Rs.75/HP/year Small:Rs.50/HP per year
1986–87	3,114 (251)	10,74,184 (203)	2,899	0.60	Big Farmers: Rs.75/HP/year Small:Rs.50/HP per year
1987–88	3,136 (253)	11,16,177 (211)	2,810	0.66	Big Farmers: Rs.75/HP/ year Small: Rs.50/ HP per year
1988–89	3,524 (284)	11,84,450 (223)	2,975	0.65	Big Farmers: Rs. 75/HP/year Small:Rs.50/HP/year
1989–90	3,740 (301)	12,35,941 (233)	3,026	NA	Big Farmers: Rs.75/HP/year Small Rs.50/HP per year
1990–91	3,974 (320)	13,18,671 (249)	3,014	0.63	Rs.50 / HP / annum for £ 10 HP and Rs.75 / HP/ per annum for >10 HP
1991–92	4,451 (359)	13,59,748 (257)	3,273	0.69	Since 1991 free supply for all
1992–93	5,160 (416)	14,03,673 (265)	3,676	NA	
1993–94	5,618 (453)	14,45,951 (273)	3,885	0.77	
1994–95	6,228 (502)	14,88,469 (281)	4,184	0.80	
1995–96	6,626 (534)	15,28,807 (288)	4,334	NA	
1996–97	6,910 (557)	15,67,317 (296)	4,409	NA	

Source: TNEB, *Tamil Nadu Electricity Board at a Glance* (various years), and Government of Tamil Nadu (various years), *Season and Crop Reports.*

10 paise per unit (kWh) (see Table 3), the costs/price scissors laid the ground for a movement in which farmers mobilized over two issues: a reduction in the electricity tariff and the remission of loans for well digging and deepening. The State Government arrested several hundred agitating farmers in Coimbatore District. Finally, after a month-long struggle, the tariff was reduced from 10 paise to 9 paise per unit. In 1972, the DMK ministry headed by Mr M K Karunanidhi raised the tariff from 9 to 12 paise per unit. This time the agitation spread to other districts of the state. Opposition parties also supported the farmers' protest. The state police organized strong measures to suppress the movement. In the process, 15 people were killed. At the end of this particular episode, the government, after holding talks with the farmers' leaders, decided to reduce the tariff from 12 to 11 paise per unit. During the emergency period (1976), when the state was under the President's rule again, the tariff was raised from 11 to 16 paise per unit. However, farmers' protests were stifled, since any form of rallies was prohibited under the state of emergency. After the emergency period, the AIADMK party (which contested the state election for the first time) promised to reduce the tariff but, even though the party swept into power, it failed to fulfil its promises. As a result, the farmers' agitation intensified all over the state. Police firing led to the killing of three people. Finally, the government was forced to reduce the tariff from 16 to 14 paise. From that time onwards, the political parties in the state understood the strength of the farmers' movement, realized the potential vote bank in the countryside and tried to attract farmers by promising liberal concessions. Thus in 1980, the AIADMK ministry introduced differential electricity rates of 14 and 12 paise, respectively, to big and small farmers. This was opposed by the farmers' leaders whose agitation picked up sufficient momentum for the State Government to resort to measures such as disconnecting electricity and the auctioning of properties of farmers in default. It again raised the tariff in 1981 from 14 to 16 paise per unit. But around this time the farmers' movement was weakened by a split in their organization and by a change in state pricing policy. In 1982, a political party called the Indian Farmers' and Toilers' Party was launched and contested a by-election. It was miserably defeated, securing only around 3 per cent of votes. Again in 1984, when this party contested the State Assembly elections, it failed. Faced with a weakening of this pressure group, the State Government could have raised the tariff. Instead, it introduced a flat tariff of Rs 75 per horsepower (HP) per annum. As sections of the farming community found that acceptable, the movement was threatened. Nevertheless, in 1988, when the state was under the President's rule, the government was able to take tough measures to collect the dues from defaulting farmers. When the state Assembly elections were held in 1989, almost all the political parties promised to waive dues; but the DMK went several steps further and

promised to introduce free electricity to all sections of the farming community. When the DMK won the 1989 election, it implemented its promise. It is ironical that the party which resorted to periods of repression to check the militant farmers' movement finally capitulated.[16] This is a clear manifestation of the 'competitive populism' of the local political parties, in which short-term advantage overruled the serious economic and ecological consequences.

4. THE RATIONALITY OF FREE SUPPLY OF ELECTRICITY TO FARM PUMP SETS: SOME VILLAGE-LEVEL EVIDENCE

As part of the resurvey of villages in Tiruvannamalai District, data relating to groundwater irrigation (the number of hours pumped, the area irrigated by wells, productivity, costs of cultivation and so forth) were collected in Nesal, Vinayagapuram and Veerasambanur. There has been a progressive lowering of the water table over a period of time in all three villages. In particular, the wells dug after 1975 have been drastically deepened in the last couple of decades (see Chapter 1–2),[17] and pumping depths and pumping costs are positively associated). In this context, it is interesting to examine gross receipts and costs of cultivation with and without electricity charges (see Table 5).

The area irrigated per well has a systematic positive association with the holding size class. Larger size classes irrigate a larger area per well compared to lower size classes. The wells owned by larger farmers are of better quality (in terms of water yields). If electricity charges are reintroduced, the distribution of costs will be retrogressive. Let us consider the first size class, <1.00 acres. The gross irrigated area (GIA) per well in this size class is 1.26 acres and the imputed electricity cost per acre of GIA is Rs 995. (Energy consumed is also 955 units, since we assumed Rs 1 per unit as the imputed cost).[18] Gross receipts and costs per acre of GIA in this size class are Rs 3,919 and 2,974 respectively. Gross costs work out to Rs 3,929 if the imputed electricity cost is included. This size class makes a profit of Rs 945 per acre of GIA, if the imputed electricity cost is excluded. Otherwise, a loss of Rs 10.30 is incurred. In other words, the imputed electricity cost constitutes a very high proportion – one quarter – of total receipts obtained from one acre of GIA by well. The GIA per well in the second size class (1.01–2.50) is 1.90 acres. The imputed electricity cost for this size class per acre of GIA is Rs 572. This size class makes a profit of Rs 1,150.50 per acre of GIA even if imputed electricity cost is included in the gross payments. The electricity cost constitutes only 13.5 per cent of total receipts obtained from one acre of GIA by well.

As the size of land holding increases, this trend continues. The gross receipts

TABLE 5 Gross receipts and net of payments (in Rupees)—well-owning farmers (total for three villages—Nesal, Vinayagapuram and Veerasambanur), 1993–5

Size Class -acres	No of sample farmers (a)	Land owned (Std. Acres) (a)	Gross irrigated area (GIA) (e)	No. of wells in use	Gross receipts per acre of GIA (Rs) (b)	Gross payments /acre of GIA (Rs) (c)	Imputed electr. cost/ acre of GIA (Rs) (d)	Total of all paymets /acre of GIA (7+8) (Rs)	Gross receipts –minus payments (6–7) (Rs)	Elect. cost as % of gross receipts 8 as % of 6	Elect. cost as % of total payments 8 as % of 9	Gross receipts minus total payments 6–9 (Rs)
1	2	3	4	5	6	7	8	9	10	11	12	13
<1.00	4	2.97	5.04	4	3919	2974	955	3929	945	24.4	24.3	–10.30
1.01–2.50	11	19.30	24.82	13	4254	2531	572	3103	1722	13.5	18.4	1150.50
Sub-total	15	22.27	29.86	17	4197	2606	637	3243	1591	15.2	19.6	954.60
2.51–5	14	50.02	40.79	18	4926	2272	621	2894	2654	12.6	21.5	2032.85
5.01–7.50	5	30.06	30.00	7	5261	2283	281	2664	2878	5.3	10.5	2597.46
Sub-total	19	80.08	70.79	25	5068	2319	477	2796	2749	9.4	17.1	2272.12
7.51–10	4	34.15	39.20	8	4703	3026	919	3945	1677	19.6	23.3	757.78
10.01–15	0	0	0	0	0			0	0	0	0	0
Sub-total	4	34.15	39.20	8	4703	3026	919	3945	1677	19.6	23.3	757.78
15.01–2	1	19.50	24.50	3	22549	4730	673	5403	17819	3.0	12.5	17145.73
>2	0	0	0	0	0	0	0	0	0	0	0	0
Sub-total	1	19.50	24.50	3	22549	4730	673	5403	17819	3.0	12.5	17145.73
Grand Total	39	156.00	164.35	53	7429	2899	641	3540	4530	8.6	18.1	3888.79

net of all costs (including that of electricity) increase with holding size. The imputed electricity cost as a proportion of total receipts declines inversely with holding size.

A note of caution is needed. These cost and returns data cover all crops grown. While crops such as paddy are water-intensive and require regular irrigation once every two or three days depending upon the soil type, many commercial crops – oilseeds, cotton, vegetables and so forth – require wetting only about once every ten days. So their electricity consumption is lower. Irrespective of size class, since paddy-cultivating farmers consume relatively more electricity compared to farmers growing other crops, profits to paddy would be lower. But while a smallholder would have the constraint of land availability to prevent him from growing crops other than paddy, bigger landholders are free to allocate land to a range of crops. Even if paddy is found to be unprofitable (if an electricity tariff is reimposed), a larger landholder's overall profit, which he may obtain by cultivating combination of other less water-intensive commercial crops, may not be as greatly reduced as that of a monocultivating small producer.

What do we learn from this exercise? How far is it justifiable to continue with the present 100 per cent subsidy to farmers? Should the electricity tariff be imposed on farmers? If yes, should the tariff be the same for all sections of farmers or should differential rates be charged?

Before passing judgment on whether an electricity tariff could be imposed, let us study a few other issues: the ownership of wells across different size classes

---

Notes to Table 5:

(a) *Land owned in standard acres:* Land owned by the sample farmers is differentiated into several categories, such as those plots of land which are solely irrigated by surface sources, those which are irrigated by surface and groundwater, plots which are irrigated only by well water and those which are dependent entirely upon rainfall. According to the productivity of land, scores were given to these plots in order to arrive at the standard acres owned by the sample farmers.

(b) *Total receipts per acre:* Total receipts include gross value of yield, market value of by-products, land rent received and water charges received (by way of selling groundwater).

(c) *Total gross payments:* Gross payments include all labour payments towards crop operations (cash and kind), cost of physical inputs such as chemical fertilizers, pesticides, farmyard manure, cost of hiring farm equipment, land rent paid and water charges paid.

(d) *Imputed electricity cost per acre:* We have collected data on number of wells (in use), number of electric pump sets which are operated, and number of hours each pump set was operated per day and in each season by the sample farmers. If a 1 HP motor is operated, electricity consumption will be 0.75 unit per hour. With this information, we arrived at the total energy consumed by the sample farmers who have operated electric pump sets. One Rupee per unit of energy consumed has been assumed to arrive at the imputed electricity cost. This data may not be 100 per cent accurate, but it certainly gives a useful estimate of the extent of energy consumed by farmers.

(e) Gross irrigated area is the irrigated area cropped over three seasons.

Source: Field survey, 1993–5.

of farmers, the extent of competitive deepening of wells by farmers and the extent to which individual farmers have invested in well irrigation. The results presented in Table 5 are based upon 53 sample wells (which are in use), randomly selected from all three villages. Roughly one third of the sample wells are owned by farmers whose holding size is less than or equal to 2.50 acres, and the GIA from these wells accounts for only 18 per cent of the total GIA irrigated by all the sample wells. And two thirds of the sample wells are owned by farmers whose holding size is less than or equal to 5 acres, amounting to 43 per cent of the GIA. Around 21 per cent of the sample wells, owned by farmers whose holding size is more than 7.50 acres, contribute 39 per cent of the GIA. Similar results were obtained in a study of well irrigation in the Vaigai river basin in southern Tamil Nadu.[19] Two points are clear from these data. First, contrary to the general notion that well irrigation is accessible only to the larger farmers, small farmers indeed own the larger number of wells. Second, the mere ownership of wells is not very informative, because those owned by the larger farmers are of better quality in terms of yield. The area irrigated per well is much higher. So, for the larger farmers, the marginal cost of pumping will be lower than that for smaller farmers.

This inequity is exacerbated by the secular lowering of the water table. Many studies confirm that there has been a progressive lowering of the water table in several parts of the country, in particular during the post-Green Revolution period.[20] To get a feel for the extent of competitive well deepening and the declining water table in the three villages (Nesal, Vinayagapuram and Veerasambanur), the original and current depths of the sample wells which were dug before 1975 were compared. The original depth refers to the actual depth up to which the well was first commissioned and the current depth refers to the depth of the well as recorded at the time of the survey. There is a big difference between the original and current depths of the sample wells, implying a rapid decline in the groundwater table during the last two decades (see Chapter 1–2). In Veerasambanur, until 1971, the wells were so shallow that they could be operated with *kavalai* (bullock-driven lifting apparatus) and *yetram* (human lift). Electricity was introduced in this village as late as 1971. But while the average original depth of the sample wells dug before 1975 was 14 feet, the current depth is 44 feet. Large differences between original and current depths are seen in the other two villages as well.[21] Similar results were obtained in a study of the southern Vaigai Basin, which involved 1,200 wells distributed over 27 villages in different parts of the river basin, where the average original depth was 30 feet (9.15 m) and the current depth is 41 feet (12.5 m) in wetland and 34 feet (10.36 m) and 51 feet (15.5 m) respectively in dry land.[22] This secular lowering of the water table is clearly due to the expansion of the area under groundwater irrigation and the resultant competitive deepening of wells. This has implications for resource-poor well owners. While the threat of getting eliminated from the race of competitive deepening is very real for resource-poor farmers, large farmers are able to sustain the adverse effects of competitive deepening.

In other parts of Tamil Nadu (such as the Vaigai and Noyyal river basins), even though the water table has dropped a considerable extent over time and even though the yield of water per well is extremely low, farmers still continue to pump, using new water-extraction and irrigation techniques. In the Vaigai Basin for instance, in some of the water-scarce villages, in order to cope with the dropping water table contiguous well owners (involving three to five wells) jointly pump and irrigate a plot of land. This is practised when water from an individually operated well is so low that irrigation is not possible.[23] Furthermore, in both these river basins it is common to find two motors set at intervals in the deepened well, with compressors installed in the deep bores (to cope with the low water yields). In the Noyyal river basin, water is sometimes pumped from a well or a deep bore to be stored in another well and pumped again for irrigation. In other words, the same water is pumped twice for irrigating a plot of land. *In a sample of 146 wells in use, spread over 4 villages in the Noyyal Basin, in as many as 46 per cent of them water is twice pumped for irrigation.*[24] Thus the energy consumed is doubled, which under market circumstances (when a tariff is charged) farmers would hesitate to do.

The competitive deepening of wells and the progressive lowering of the water table has also resulted in a big hike in the investment required for well digging, construction, lifting and water conveyance. A further survey of eight villages, in connection with the ongoing study of conflicts in the use of groundwater in the Palar river basin (erstwhile North Arcot District), gives information on costs incurred by well owners on the components of well irrigation (well digging, construction, installation of water-extracting and conveyance mechanisms, installation of vertical and horizontal bores and further deepening of wells.[25] Using this information, the amounts invested per hectare of gross (GIA) and net area irrigated (NIA) per well have been calculated. A very liberal definition of the extraction of groundwater for one watering in a year from a sample well has been used to arrive at the area irrigated by wells. The average amount invested (for all the eight villages surveyed), measured in terms of per hectare of GIA and NIA by the sample wells, is Rs 30,000 and 50,000 respectively. If the costs incurred and lost in the failed and abandoned wells are also included in this calculation, the figure is Rs 36,000 and 59,000 respectively per hectare of GIA and NIA. Across villages it varies a great deal, as may be seen from Table 6.

In fact, information for two other low-rainfall, hard-rock river basins, those of the Vaigai (in the region of Madurai and Ramanathapuram) and Noyyal (in

TABLE 6 Investment in well irrigation calculated per hectare of GIA and NIA by sample wells in the Palar Basin, 1997–8

Name of Village	Number of sample wells		Investment per hectare (taking into account only wells in use) (Rupees in thousands)		Investment per hectare (taking into account all wells) (Rupees in thousands)	
	In Use	Not in use	Per hect. of GIA (Rs)	Per hect. of NIA (Rs)	Per hect. of GIA (Rs)	Per hect. of NIA (Rs)
Kathiavadi	34	6	54	75	59	81
Poondi	20	2	39	65	40	67
Gudimallur	13	6	36	72	42	84
Damal	36	13	20	22	24	26
Periavarigam	14	16	26	67	37	97
Solur	9	12	28	77	40	108
Ramanayakkan pettai	26	16	36	98	49	135
Nariampattu	23	3	22	44	22	45
Total	175	74	30	50	36	59

Source: Field survey, 1997–8.

the region of Coimbatore and Tiruppur), is arresting. In the Noyyal Basin,[26] the average amount invested in the wells (for 144 wells in use and 37 not in use sampled from four villages) comes to Rs 104,000 and 164,000 per hectare of GIA and NIA respectively. If abandoned wells are also included in the calculation, then the amount invested rises to Rs 120,000 and 190,000 respectively per hectare of GIA and NIA. In the Vaigai Basin,[27] it amounts to Rs 80,000 per hectare of NIA by wells. According to the Government of India's 1989 *Report of the Working Group on the Major and Medium Irrigation Programme for the Eighth Plan,* the amount spent per hectare of irrigation potential created by canal during the Seventh Plan (1985–90) works out at Rs 36,240. But the survey results indicate that the amount spent to create one hectare of irrigation potential by wells is several times higher than what has been spent on surface irrigation potential.

So it is clear that reintroduction of an electricity tariff would adversely affect small and marginal landholders. There is also reason to believe that, as two thirds of the wells are owned by small and marginal landowners, the additional cost by way of an electricity tariff would provide such a severe burden that it could result in abandonment of many such wells. On the other hand, large landowners would easily sustain the tariff, for not only are they better off, many of them currently also make use of the free supply of electricity to sell water at profit to other farmers as well as to urban industrial consumers.[28] Furthermore, it would be erroneous to club all well owners into one category, because the re-source-rich farmers, being the first to invest in well irrigation, have not only exploited groundwater earlier but have damaged aquifers irreversibly by draining them. Poor farm households, while owning wells in large numbers, are late-comers to the exploitation of groundwater. They are now faced with a hydrological regime in which groundwater is declining too fast for them to sustain competitive deepening. In the process, many of them have fallen into debt. The reintroduction of an electricity tariff to farmers is therefore not a simple and straightforward matter. It is contingent upon several deeply rooted socio-economic and political issues.

5. SUMMING UP

The most important policy issues which need to be recapitulated in this section are: i) the present state of Tamil Nadu Electricity Board (TNEB) in the particular context of the state's liberal policy of supplying free electricity to farm pump sets; ii) the use and misuse of free electricity supply by different sections of farmers; and iii) their potential capacity to pay a tariff.

The state supplies free electricity to farm pump sets, which constitutes roughly one third of the power available in the state for distribution. This power is not metered. Further, there is a loss of around 17 per cent of the gross power available in the state by way of transmission and distribution. Therefore, there is a total unmetered consumption / energy loss of 12,472 million units (or Rs 2,494 crores [Rs 25 bn]) per annum. The TNEB may take refuge in the free electricity supply to farmers and T&D losses as an excuse to mask all its inefficiencies and pilferage of power.

In other words, whether it is the subsidy and/or other unmetered consumption that is the root cause of losses incurred by the TNEB needs substantiating. The *Economic Survey* published for the year 1998–9 by the Government of India's Ministry of Finance, took a serious view of the T&D losses incurred by the State Electricity Boards (SEBs). To quote:

> The SEBs have continued to suffer from high T&D losses, which stood at 22.3 per cent in 1995–96, have increased to 23.4 per cent in 1996–97. The losses are extremely high when compared with the international average of less than 10 per cent for the advanced countries of the world. These T&D losses are due to the sparsely distributed loads over large rural areas, substantial energy sold at low voltage levels, inadequate investment in distribution systems, improper billing and high pilferage.[29]

As of 1994–5, except for four states (West Bengal, Kerala, Maharashtra and Himachal Pradesh), all the rest have incurred an annual loss to the tune of Rs 4,696 crores. This figure stood at Rs 2,719 crores in 1990–91. The main reason for the loss is argued to be the bad financial condition and management of the boards.[30] Indeed, the restoration to financial health of the SEBs and an improvement in their operational performance continues to remain the most crucial issue in the power sector. Thus, the Draft Approach Paper to the Ninth Five-Year Plan (1997–2002) states, 'The deteriorating financial health of the State Electricity Boards has been one of the most critical factors constraining power development in the country'.[31] In terms of Section 59 of the Electricity (Supply) Act of 1948, SEBs are required to earn a minimum rate of return (RoR) of 3 per cent of their net fixed assets in service after providing for depreciation and interest charges. But in reality most SEBs do not comply with this regulation. There were only three SEBs which had a positive RoR in 1996–7 including the subsidy. The main contributing factors are low tariffs, sociopolitical compulsions and operating inefficiencies in the SEBs. The average RoR (with subsidy) for SEBs was as low as –12.1 per cent in 1996–7 and further plunged to –17.6 per cent in 1997–8.[32]

A process of restructuring of the SEBs has been initiated in several states. The restructuring aims at decentralizing the power industry by separating generation, transmission and distribution; at bringing in competition by allowing private participation in generation and distribution; and by developing a regulatory framework. The Orissa SEB was the first to be restructured in April 1996, being replaced by two corporations to look after the functions of generation and distribution. The Haryana Electricity Reforms Bill has already become an Act after receiving the Presidential assent. Rajasthan, Goa and Gujarat have drafted their bills. The Andhra Pradesh Electricity Reforms Bill awaits Presidential assent. The governments of Madhya Pradesh, Karnataka, Kerala, Uttar Pradesh, Maharashtra, Bihar and West Bengal are also in the various stages of reforming their respective SEBs.

In order to retrieve Tamil Nadu State Electricity Board from the grip of heavy losses, the Government of India has suggested certain policies, such as the creation of a separate entity for hydro and thermal power generation, the setting up of an independent tariff regulatory commission with judicial authority and changes in the organization of power distribution. But the state of Tamil Nadu has not yielded to any pressure from the centre.

Another problem that the Tamil Nadu Government is encountering in the process of revamping its TNEB is the resistance put forward by its employees. The State Government has set up an independent consultant to restructure the TNEB with a view to decentralize the functions hitherto carried out by it. All the employees' unions have refused to cooperate with the independent consultants appointed by the state. The unions claim 'any new approach of dismantling the power sector with the aim of privatisation will engender disruption'.[33] The unions are agitated about the announcement made by the state in July 1999 in which the TNEB was designated the State Transmission Utility (STU). Power generation hitherto handled by the TNEB would be transferred to another organization as a subsidiary of TNEB.[34] The TNEB employees' non-cooperation and boycott call cannot be ignored and it remains to be seen how this dimension of the problem is going to be handled by the state.

Meanwhile a new ordinance, the Electricity Regulatory Commissions Ordinance, 1998, was promulgated on 25 April 1998. After a considerable debate, the Lok Sabha passed the bill with drastic amendments to some of the provisions. The amendments completely reduced the rigour of the ordinance, making it *optional* for the state governments to establish State Electricity Regulatory Commissions. Moreover, the bench mark for tariff fixation of 50 per cent of the average cost of supply of electricity has been dropped. The bill, thus amended, has received Presidential approval.

One of the main factors which hamper the functioning of the SEBs has been interference by respective state governments in fixing the electricity tariffs for various categories of users. In particular, as we have seen here, considerable political popularity is achieved by supplying highly subsidized electricity to the agricultural sector. According to the Government of India's *Economic Survey*, 1998–9, the gross subsidy involved in the sale of electricity to the agricultural sector was Rs 5,938 crores (Rs 59.38 billion) in the year 1991–2. It went up to Rs 19,091 crores (Rs 190.91 billion) in 1997–8. The estimated and the anticipated subsidy for the years 1998–9 and 1999–2000 were in the order of Rs 21,322 crores (Rs 213.22 billion) and Rs 23,847 crores (Rs 238.47 billion) respectively.

It is argued that a highly subsidized power supply encourages farmers to mis-use and overuse both power and groundwater. It is advocated that the electricity tariff should be used to manage and regulate groundwater extraction.[35] Thus Tushaar Shah argues, '. . . it can even be argued that State Electricity Boards which are responsible for pricing and management of power have a more central, powerful and far-reaching influence on groundwater development than even the groundwater departments and corporations'.[36] Moreover, there is reason to believe that the free supply of power has induced farmers to deepen their wells in a competitive manner, even though the yield of water is very low and is not commensurate with the marginal operating cost of pumping under normal circumstances of pricing.

Electricity is sometimes said to constitute a low proportion of costs compared to other agricultural inputs.[37] It is argued that since the cost of electricity constitutes only a small proportion of total cost of cultivation, even if a pro-rata tariff is introduced, it would not greatly alter electricity consumption. We have seen in section 3 above and in Table 4 that this view is incorrect. There has been a steady increase in the electricity consumed per pump set. When electricity was made free in 1991, there was a jump in per capita power consumption (see Table 1). From Table 5, the cost of electricity constitutes over 18 per cent of the total cost of cultivation. Moreover, what is important is not what an individual farmer incurs or does not incur by way of pumping cost, it is the cumulative social cost incurred, which imposes a very high burden on the state. This burden varies across regions. For instance, in the low-rainfall, hard-rock regions of Tamil Nadu, such as Coimbatore, Erode, Salem, Dharmapuri, Ramanatha-puram, Madurai and Vellore, the groundwater table has retreated to deep levels and in many places groundwater is seriously depleted. In these areas, the cost of electricity as a proportion of the total cost of cultivation is relatively large. Moreover, the proportion of pumping cost to the total cost of cultivation depends upon several technical factors, such as the depth of the water table, the subsoil structure, the type of well and the type of water-lifting device used, the volume of water delivered per hour (the yield of water), the area irrigated per well, the type of crops cultivated and so forth. A paddy-producing farmer, having to irrigate at least thrice a week, has a relatively high electricity con-sumption. In contrast, those who grow high value-commercial crops such as banana, turmeric, cotton, flowers, chilli etc. have lower crop water requirement and power consumption, since these crops need watering only once in ten days.

The prime reason that triggered off a vibrant and militant farmers' move-ment in Tamil Nadu, which shook up all the political parties in the late 1970s and in the 1980s, was small increases in the electricity tariff (from 8 to 11 paise per unit). Subsequently, the ruling parties in the state, after putting up considerable resistance and after the loss of many lives, were compelled to lower the tariff in a politically competitive manner until it was reduced to zero in 1991 by the DMK ministry.

The introduction of new agricultural biochemical technology and the neglect of traditional surface sources of irrigation have contributed to a rapid growth of well irrigation in the state, as well as in other parts of the country. As a con-sequence, wells were deepened in a competitive manner in order to get access to assured, timely and better quality irrigation. Free and unrationed electricity has also contributed to indiscriminate and unregulated pumping. About two thirds of the wells are owned by farmers who have less than or equal to five acres. And one third of wells are owned by small and marginal farmers who have less than 2.5 acres of land (see section 4 above). This is a paradoxical situation in which there seems to be equity in access to groundwater. But in practice it reinforces a new class of farmers. Those who have struck good aquifers quite early on, large landowners who are better endowed with resources and potential water sel-lers, have all prospered (see Table 5). But for small and marginal farmers, late exploiters of groundwater, there is a high probability of being displaced in the process of competitive deepening.

While large operators of land can sustain an unsuccessful investment in well digging and deepening or survive persistent drought conditions (as occurred in the 1980s), a small farmer finds these shocks unsurmountable. Further, the very high incidence of joint well ownership (sharing a well) complicates matters. In all the river basins studied, 40–50 per cent of wells are jointly owned. The problem gets further compounded because the incidence of joint well ownership is most frequent among small and marginal categories of farmers. For these farmers, the reintroduction of an electricity tariff would be a severe blow. Without a compensation in product prices, they can be expected to abandon or sell their wells. If these farmers go out of orbit, there would be unemployment, loss of production and so on.

Ruling parties, through their short-sighted vision, discovered the potential of capitalizing on the vote bank in rural areas by supplying free electricity. However, these subsidies have coincided with, if not caused, unacceptable levels of public-sector debt, pressure to reduce which requires a reduction in subsidies or an increase in fiscal resources. In the absence of interest in the latter, reform is focused on the former. But as the foregoing discussion indicates, it is not going to be possible to lift the subsidy on electricity, since over 60 per cent of the wells are owned by small and marginal farmers who would not find it viable to operate their pump sets if tariffs were reintroduced. This is a situation of political deadlock which the state cannot simply afford to overlook. Is there a way out?

Rural Credit and the Collateral Question

BARBARA HARRISS-WHITE AND DIEGO COLATEI

Two questions are considered in this chapter. One concerns the role of state-regulated or formal credit in the rural economy. It can be explored through the evolution of the policy agenda and through access in the villages. We can then use village studies to address a specific policy question. Given moves to deregulate credit and remove subsidies, should the state target concessional credit to small, marginally landed and landless producers for the express purpose of purchasing land? We call this the collateral question. In other sectors of the economy, notably food distribution, attempts to drop general subsidies have been accompanied by the protection of subsidies to vulnerable people. The collateral question is consistent with these trends in India's economic reforms.

1. STATE-REGULATED CREDIT

1.1 *The context: waves of rural credit policy*

State-regulated rural credit was originally justified by a set of developmental objectives: the need to displace informal finance[1] on the grounds of the kind of monopolistic and exploitive practices excoriated in the All-India Rural Credit Survey of 1954; the need to penetrate regions as yet thinly and imperfectly provisioned with credit, the need to counter the concentrated, oligopolistic and thinly dispersed character of private banking and to encourage a wider social dispersal of increased incomes in order to achieve higher levels of output and growth.[2] The instruments of this 'needs-based' credit policy are very well known:

- state ownership of 14 banks (nationalized in 1969);
- segmentation among banks (Cooperatives [for rural short-term credit], land development banks, nationalized banks [for urban long-term credit], commercial banks);
- refinance from the IMF and World Bank by means of the National Apex Bank for Agriculture and Rural Development (NABARD);
- spatial and sectoral targets (organized by Lead Banks) with differentials in interest rates;
- quotas for credit disbursement on concessional terms (e.g. 40 per cent of credit directed to priority sectors and 18 per cent to agriculture); and
- regulation under the Banking Regulation Act by the Reserve Bank of India.

In the early 1980s (given the failure of poor people to gain access to formal sector credit and that of the seed–fertilizer–water technology to diffuse to the social base or to regions of rain-fed agriculture and provide widespread employment or real wage increases), the Integrated Rural Development Policy (IRDP) was inaugurated to alleviate poverty by means of credit for non-land assets endowments. Forty per cent of IRDP loans were supposed to be targeted at women.[3] These layered policies endured into the 1990s, when they were threatened by a battery of theoretical critiques and refinements, policy changes and critical evaluations of the way they had been implemented.

While the reduction in the general distance between people and banks helped to raise the share of rural deposits (savings) from 3 per cent in 1969 to 15 per cent in 1996,[4] and a quantitative expansion in formal credit took place at the expense of private moneylender-credit (from 7 per cent in 1951 to 63 per cent in 1981),[5] 'the quality of lending' deteriorated.[6] The structure of credit policy contained its own debilities. First, formal sector administration costs were higher than those of the informal sector. Second, interest rate ceilings not only reduced incentives to save, they reduced incentives both to repay and to recover loans,[7] so that overdues increased. Third, the recovery process was also vulnerable to the power of agricultural interest groups at elections and dotted with loan waivers and write-offs.[8] Fourth, the profitability of dispersed rural banks had been acutely sensitive to the competence of management.[9]

Be that as it may, an econometric study at the all-India level of the returns to state-regulated agricultural credit from 1972–3 to 1980–1 shows (on generous assumptions) that the policy led to '*modest increases in aggregate crop output*; sharp increases in the use of fertilizers and in investment in physical capital and substantial *reductions in agricultural employment*' (our emphases). The net additional agricultural income exceeded the cost to the state of its agricultural credit policy by 13 per cent.[10]

Other criticism had also alerted policy-makers to the 'multiplier effects' of their credit. The assumptions about the directibility of credit were exposed as naive. First, formal loans were fungible (directly or through onward lending for unintended and unsupervisable purposes – notably 'consumption' for which the formal sector is prevented from lending).[11] Second, rationed credit was captured by agrarian elites by means of its prohibitively high transactions costs (which repelled small producers) and rent-seeking by bank officials (which screened small producers out).[12] By the late 1980s, 60–70 per cent of rural credit was going to farmers owning in excess of 5 acres.[13] Binswanger and Khandker quote Rath (1987) to the effect that 'only about a quarter of cultivators borrow, and long-term loans are received by no more than two per cent. The majority of small cultivators have little access to credit'.[14] Presumably this referred to formal credit, because Rao has evidence for the mid-1980s showing that producers with assets under Rs 10,000 obtained between 68 and 90 per cent of their credit from informal sources.[15] It is nevertheless hardly surprising that the *indirect* impact of state-regulated credit is found to be significant: an elasticity of 0.24 in *non*-agricultural employment over the first ten years of agricultural credit expansion.[16]

The anti-poverty thrust of IRDP got ambivalent reviews: on the one hand, 57 per cent of beneficiaries received incremental incomes of Rs 2,000 plus and a similar percentage were heaved over a very conservative poverty line. On the other hand, 43 per cent of borrowers were 'wilful defaulters' and effectively received a politically motivated grant, which had knock-on effects on other loan repayments to the 'formal sector'.

As the directed credit policy consolidated itself, another 'deformity' came to light, which is the backcloth to our village study. This is that the southern states grew to be relatively oversupplied with directed credit. By 1985, the southern states – with 19 per cent of India's total cultivated area – had 28 per cent of bank offices, 44 per cent of directed agricultural credit, average loan sizes over twice bigger than those in the eastern region and 73 per cent of the outstanding debt. What is perhaps less well known is that Tamil Nadu (though better supplied with banks and credit than elsewhere in India) bucked this trend. It was the only one of the southern states to see a *decline* in the percentage of short-term loans supplied by the formal sector between 1973 and 1985.[17]

As late as the time of our field survey in 1993–4, it was still possible to write that the impact of India's credit policy on the informal credit market was unknown;[18] attention had shifted so markedly to the formal sector. Two influential evaluations, the Khusro Committee (reporting in 1989) and the Narasimhan Committee (in 1991/1998), concluded that wide-ranging reforms to rural credit were overdue: interest rates on loans and deposits should be market-determined, subsidies to private capital cut, rural banking deregulated, concessional targeted credit confined to small and marginal farmers (Khusro) or increased in scope to include (private/regional banks in) a wide range of activities in rural marketing and the non-farm sector (Narasimhan). Meanwhile the Reserve Bank of India continued to regulate such parameters as interest on deposits and loans, the capital/asset ratios of banks, directed credit (but less ambitiously than before) and reporting requirements. Private and international banks expanded operations and work on (global) commercial principles.[19] The policy debate between deregulation (responding to the structural weaknesses of formal credit by abolishing it) and reform (responding to its problems by lowering transactions costs and administration, changing incentives, widening scope and experimenting with new forms – particularly with micro-credit and group credit) continues unabated.[20]

1.2 *Evolving credit relations in the region*

Just as the region has been dominated by paddy production, so the credit market has been dominated by personalized contracts between paddy traders and producers, interlocking money and product markets. Informal lending long pre-dated state involvement. J Harriss argued, from conditions in the early 1970s, that traders' credit was crucial in financing the agricultural cycle which reproduced the small peasantry.[21] B Harriss concluded that the interlocked contract enabled the rates of profit from trade greatly to exceed that from production proper. Further, foreclosure on the fragmented land plots which supplied collateral for overdue loans was unattractive to traders on grounds of the transaction costs of taking over ownership and the supervision costs of production thereafter.[22] So petty production was maintained by traders and the development of capitalist land relations was constrained. In 1973, formal credit was underdeveloped – a mere 12 per cent of the total volume of credit in 11 randomly selected villages.

A decade later, in the heyday of directed credit and IRDP and the state's sustained attempt to disperse petty capital formation, the thesis that traders' credit reproduced small-scale production was jettisoned.[23] While traders' credit certainly remained important (the data actually do not identify traders' credit, but in 1983 'informal credit' still amounted to 53 per cent in the three villages we re-surveyed in 1993–4), formal credit had expanded to 42 per cent of debt, of which IRDP made up between 6 and 15 per cent. J Harriss found that the great majority of producers had a permanent personalized relation with a paddy trader, but that, while the contract was still an important means of syphoning resources away from agriculture, an element of option had entered the relationship because of the existence of alternative sources of credit. These alternatives were thought to have contributed to a decline in usury (also noted in Athreya *et al*'s research much to the south [1990])[24] and were part of a much wider trend of increasing agrarian dependence upon the state.[25] The state had replaced grain traders in supplying the means whereby the process of differentiation through land relations could be constrained. Yet it would not actively allow IRDP credit, or any other loans, to small or landless peasants for the purchase of land.

A decade later the story, which we will tell more fully, twisted again. Our data come from village diaries, from census information collected in late 1993 and the detailed follow-up survey of 1994 which concerned the previous agricultural year. In this study the detailed data for *loans taken out*[26] in that year alone are analysed. Households took out up to four loans per season, for each of the three seasons. To make this research directly comparable with others', credit is analysed according to asset ownership groups.

1.3 *Local planned credit*

In 1993–4, the year of our study, some Rs 77 crores of state-regulated credit was available for Tiruvannamalai–Sambuvarayar District. This money was very highly directed with physical or financial targets, as appropriate, for every bank and for every one of 66 government schemes. The region we study was remarkable on an All India scale for the share of its formal sector loans to the priority sector. At 85 per cent, this was double the 40 per cent national target![27] The latter, in any case, had not been achieved during the 1991–6 period of the Eighth Plan.[28] The share of formal loans allocated to 'weaker sections' (scheduled castes and tribes), at 36 per cent, was also considerably above the national average and target. But loans outstanding were also double the target! While targets for agriculture in general, for biogas and other state schemes were reached over the period 1990–92, they mask *underachievement by commercial banks and overachievement by nationalized banks.*[29] Short-term agricultural production loans are dominated by the finance of sugar cane and other commercial crops quite disproportionately to the number of producers and are biased particularly away from groundnuts, but even away from paddy/rice (see Table 1). *The components of overachievement are not agricultural* but in 'artisanal' activity, small-scale industry and most notably 'trade and services'. Loans for rural industrialization doubled in the early 1990s – but from an extremely small base to 7 per cent of formal loans. Loans specifically for *trade* were targeted at some 20,000 borrowers – four times the number for non-farm production. *Lending is trade-heavy.* Around Arni, Rs 7.2 crores were available for lending, of which government grants amounted to Rs 1 crore.

TABLE 1 Crop loans, 1991–2 (Rs lakhs)

	Accounts		Loans	
	n	%	*n*	%
Crop				
Paddy/rice	69823	43	761	32
Groundnut	52785	32	309	13
Sugar cane	27490	17	898	38
Other (Comm. Crop)	13079	8	384	16
TOTAL	163177		2352	

Source: Indian Bank 1993, p. 2.4.

1.4 *Moneylending in the villages, 1993–4*

Before we turn to the survey data, there is much to be learned about credit in the three villages which is completely invisible from the conventional and bland form in which the data set has been coded for analysis. For the colour, the field investigators' village diaries are invaluable. These reveal a huge range of uniquely combined credit arrangements in each village.

1.4.1 *Vinayagapuram*

This is a remote but developed agricultural village with a relatively egalitarian land-holding structure. Dominating the informal credit arrangements of this village is a family-based moneylending cascade controlling about Rs 3 lakhs. The patriarch, a landed moneylender, services about 30 cultivators with loans of up to Rs 20,000 on the basis of promissory notes and jewels, at 24 per cent interest. Three sons lend to a further 45 people. Their wives lend to about 30 women sums of up to Rs 200 on the security of household articles and at 60 per cent annual equivalent interest. Their sons lend small sums (up to Rs 500) on the same basis. All borrowers are described as 'friends'. Then there are two female moneylenders, plus a grocer and teashop keeper, who lend on the basis of watches, clocks, cycles and pledged ration cards, mainly to scheduled-caste borrowers, at an interest reflected in the discounted price of rationed commodities. Next there is one particular urban pawnbroker lending money at 24 to 36 per cent on gold and jewels, together with five urban paddy traders and rice millers who habitually service this village with preharvest advances of up to Rs 750 and repayment either in cash (at 24 per cent) or in kind (at an equivalent deduction). These, together with a large silk merchant and certain smaller ones, tie the loans to the purchase of agricultural inputs or groceries sold by particular urban traders. So there is a tight nexus of mercantile credit connected through interlocking triadic contracts. These lenders will also lend for the purchase of land

and other long-term purposes. These are the lenders who over the last decade have come to employ 'agents' to enforce repayment. The latter in turn use village elders and the authority of the village Panchayat to press threats. Farmers in nearby villages also lend, on bonds at 36 per cent, sums up to Rs 50,000 to the bigger farmers in Vinayagapuram. The latter lend onwards on the same terms and conditions to poorer borrowers for the expenses connected with paying labour, consumption, illness and death. Mercantile and agricultural money-lenders are all able and willing to take land in cases of default.

There are three seasonal rotating credit funds (*chit funds*) run by and for richer farmers in and near the village. There are two further chit funds for small peasants and weavers, one when the total take is auctioned at full moon and one at new moon. Scheduled-caste people have three chit funds: a dual-purpose one, the net interest of which maintains a temple, one for female agricultural labourers and a third which auctions up to Rs 20,000, run by a woman teacher. Two further chit funds are used to subsidize annual pilgrimages. A bunk shop owner organizes two more chit funds, one of which also fuels the ruling political party. Recently deceased are two important figures, a landed Brahmin money-lender who had his own scheduled-caste 'police force' and a Chettiar living nearby for whom moneylending started as a side business to carting paddy.

Here we see various axes of segmentation: gender, caste, locality and class. We find moneylending interlocked not with other 'markets' so much as with specific individuals operating in different markets. We find lending not only interlocked with product markets but also with redistributive activity connected with religious observances. We see 'access to urban credit' meaning access to specific urban intermediaries. We see an increasingly organized process of repayment, which is developing out of relations of authority based on threats to third-party interests into sets of physical enforcers who operate through local political parties as well. Money markets are interlocked with party politics. We see at least a dozen rotating credit funds, the striking feature of which is the social homogeneity of their membership.

1.4.2 *Nesal*

Nesal is a large, peri-urban, diversified village with a very unequal structure of property relations. Its system of grain traders' and silk merchants' lending and chit funds is similar to that of Vinayagapuram. Nesal has some unique features too. First there is an itinerant moneylender who arrives on Thursdays, a Gounder by caste, who lends to up to 150 people in Nesal petty sums below Rs 100. Interest of 3 per cent is deducted at source and a further 25 per cent interest has to be paid along with the principal over ten weeks – annualized at 140 per cent. This man prefers to lend to women, whom he reckons to be 'sober and compliant'. Two wives of major landholders lend foodgrains to landless women at 12 per cent. Three other female Yadhavas and Mudaliars (agricultural castes) specialize in *siruvadu* – small loans of up to Rs 300 with vessels, utensils and earrings as collateral, with annualized interest varying from 60 to 120 per cent and with the capacity to confiscate security. These women are said to have got their starting capital by diverting small streams of their husbands' loans from 'Operation Flood' from cattle-feed to chit funds. Another woman operates four different chit funds among female milkers of cows, whose 'takes' range from Rs 1,000 to Rs 10,000. Again she characterizes female borrowers as compliant and unviolent.

Although the survey data reported in the next section suggests that *women who are heads of households are at an extreme disadvantage as borrowers*, the material from Nesal suggests that *there is a concealed but thriving sector of petty borrowing which is gender-specific and female.*

1.4.3 *Veerasambanur*
Veerasambanur is a small, remote, undiversified, poor yet unequal village. The village is close to an active agricultural cooperative bank at Thaccambadi, the only formal-sector source of credit actually mentioned in the village diaries. In addition, the local Christian church provides grants of money for small livestock to a womens' group in the village.[30] There are three village moneylenders, none of whom has a reputation for force but all of whom have purchased land and invested in rice mills or other property as a result of moneylending. Then come two rural and two urban grain traders who work with promissory notes, thereby tying loans in kind to particular traders. A group of six peasants and two landless labourers operate a seasonal chit fund – *boga cheetu* – and among the caste households can be found another chit fund, the net proceeds of which maintain one of the four village temples. Four women pawnbrokers operate from the village and four specific pawnbrokers are patronized in town. In this way, quite poor peasants pawn brass vessels, silver anklets and such like for money to pay agricultural labour. Finally, there is *kanthu vaddi*, which is loosely translated as 'kicking in the back while running, and snatching away'. These lenders are outsiders and the arrangement is reported as comparatively new.[31] Their clientele is about 40 scheduled-caste agricultural labourers who borrow for routine lean-season and/or urgent and unforeseeable consumption purposes. Sums of up to Rs 200 are lent, 12.5 per cent being retained at the start and the rest repaid over ten weeks at interest which can be annualized (without risk of exaggeration) at 125 per cent, together with a deduction of up to a further 35 per cent on the prices of goods in kind, if payment is not in cash. Collateral takes the form of work pledges by female relatives. Debt levels of Rs 1,000 or more can build up quite quickly. When payment becomes irregular, durables are seized.

Here we see certain common patterns, including the high frequency of small loans and a classic, Bhaduri-style deployment of interest to bring about default.[32] We also find collaterals distinct from articles seized (and authority derived from the general reputation of kin rather than the personal particularities of the borrower), which we will try to explain later. In addition, we find general reputation (scheduled castes as drunkards; women as docile and biddable) powerful in the segmentation and fracturing of 'markets' in money.

Drèze Lanjouw and Sharma (1998a) argue that the key characteristics of village lenders are not their monopoly position so much as such attributes as wealth, caste, age, relative lack of education, the social authority to minimize default, the personal capacity to threaten, enforce interlocked contracts and seize collateral, shrewdness and finally the capacity adversely to affect the lives of borrowers. Our description falls in line with their argument, but with micromonopoly power added to the stew.

1.5 *Formal and informal credit*

Table 2 shows the percentages of households taking loans only from formal sources or from both (together with non-borrowing households). The picture is now very different from that implied by the history of overachievement of state-regulated credit, discussed at the start of this chapter.

While very few indebted households confine borrowing to the formal sector, 70 per cent of households borrow from non-state-regulated sources. Nesal has the highest proportion of households borrowing from informal sources (65 per cent) and the lowest proportion of households taking loans from both formal and informal institutions. Vinayagapuram has the highest percentage of unindebted households (37 per cent), while Veerasambanur has the largest percent-

TABLE 2 Summary of formal and informal credit

Village	Source of Credit				
	Formal only	Informal only	Both	No loan	Total
Nesal	2.77%	62.86%	9.85%	24.53%	100%
Vinayagapuram	–	47.24%	15.75%	37.01%	100%
Veerasambanur	6.94%	55.80%	19.61%	17.65%	100%
All Villages	2.56%	56.04%	13.74%	27.66%	100%

Note: 115 households (for a total of 230 observation and 200 new loans).

Formal, or institutional, sources of credit are: cooperatives, commercial banks, land development banks, IRDP and other govt sources.

Informal sources are: moneylenders and pawnbrokers, traders, silk merchants and weavers, friends and relatives, shopkeepers and others.

age of households borrowing from formal sources (20 per cent in conjunction with informal borrowing). However these shares are sensitive to the populations of the villages. In fact there are 13–14 people with formal loans in each village: every bit as though there were a standardized target. Although the percentages of households which do not borrow and which borrow from formal or informal institutions are not exactly the same between villages, debt relations follow a common pattern.[33] A very small percentage of households take loans from formal institutions alone, while the great majority of borrowing households only borrow from informal sources. Between 10 and 20 per cent of households take both formal and informal loans while, on average, 28 per cent of households do not borrow at all.

1.5.1 *The social profile of access to credit*

Table 3 maps access to credit onto the social characteristics of caste, gender and education (see chapters 1–4 and 1–5). About 78 per cent of scheduled-caste households (SCH) and about 67 per cent of those households whose head is illiterate (IH) are indebted. By contrast, more than half of the households headed by women (FHH) do not borrow at all. Not all FHH are poorly asseted; the richer minority may be self-sufficient non-borrowers rather than being excluded potential borrowers (which is what we suspect for the majority). *The access of all kinds of socially disadvantaged households to formal credit is extremely constrained.* FHH only borrow from informal institutions (moneylenders, friends and others). Only 2 per cent of SCH and 7 per cent of IH borrow from formal sources (either from only formal or from both), which contrasts very

TABLE 3 Social characteristics of borrowers: 3 villages

Social Characteristics	Source of Credit				
	Formal only	Informal only	Both	Loan	Total
Gender					
Female-Headed Hhs		44%		56%	100%
Male-Headed Hhs	3%	58%	16%	23%	100%
Caste					
Scheduled Caste	1.74%	74.19%	2.20%	21.87%	100%
All others	3.12%	43.88%	21.46%	31.54%	100%
Education					
Illiterate Hh head	0.96%	59.98%	5.91%	33.14%	100%
Literate Hh head	3.67%	53.32%	19.14%	23.88%	100%
All	2.56%	56.04%	13.74%	27.66%	100%

Note: 115 households (for a total of 230 observation and 200 new loans).

strikingly with the 25 per cent of households belonging to other castes and the 23 per cent of 'literate' households.[34]

Access to the formal sector varies directly with land holding, while the relation to the informal sector is inverse (see Table 4). While all households with over 5 acres are indebted, between 20 and 48 per cent of those with less than 5 acres, including the landless, did not borrow over the period of the survey. *Land secures access to the formal sector.* While 85 per cent of households with more than 5 acres get state-regulated loans, a mere 6 per cent of those with under 0.1 acre and 3 per cent of landless households do. *In fact, it is a threshold of 5 acres that enables access to the formal sector to approach an entitlement,* a factor masked in the land-holding classification of Hazell and Ramasamy (see Table 5) as well as in our cluster analysis (see Table 6).[35]

TABLE 4 Land holding and access to formal and informal credit

Land size groups		Source of Credit				
		Formal only	Informal only	Both	No loan	Total
Landless		1.9%	64.6%	2.5%	31%	100%
Marginal		–	67.8%	5.9%	26.3%	100%
	0.01–1 acres					
Small		2.7%	66.2%	10.9%	20.3%	100%
	1.01–2.50 acres					
Medium		6.2%	18.4%	32.4%	43%	100%
	2.51–5 acres					
Large		7.5%	7.5%	85.1%	–	100%
	>5 acres					
All		2.56%	56.04%	13.74%	27.66%	100%

Note: 115 households (for a total of 230 observation and 200 new loans).

TABLE 5 Access to formal and informal credit according to the landholding classification of Hazell and Ramasamy (1991)

Farm Size (HR)		Source of Credit				
		Formal only	Informal only	Both	No loan	Total
Large		7.2%	29.2%	44.9%	18.8%	100%
	>1 hectare					
Small		1.6%	68.1%	10.3%	20%	100%
	<1 hectare					
No farm		1.5%	56.9%	4.5%	37.1%	100%
All		2.56%	56.04%	13.74%	27.66%	100%

Note: 115 households (for a total of 230 observation and 200 new loans).

TABLE 6 Access to formal and informal credit by class

Cluster	Source of Credit				
	Formal only	Informal only	Both	No Loan	Total
Elite	7.9%	17%	56.5%	18.5%	100%
Middle with land	–	54.5%	19.7%	25.8%	100%
Middle landless	–	74.4%	–	25.6%	100%
Poor with land	5.2%	57.4%	12.5%	24.9%	100%
Poor landless	1.9%	62.2%	2.5%	33.4%	100%
All	2.56%	56.04%	13.74%	27.66%	100%

Note: 115 households (for a total of 230 observation and 200 new loans).

1.5.2 *Flows of money*

Formal credit had apparently shrunk as a proportion of total credit by 18 per cent over the decade from 1983–4. Despite decades of developmental offensives by state-regulated credit institutions, 61 per cent of money borrowed was 'informal' in 1993–4. Average formal loans varied from Rs 6,445 to Rs 8,769 according to the village, while informal loans varied from Rs 1,573 to Rs 3,832. Half the volume of informal credit emanated from agricultural product traders and silk merchants. It exceeded the volume from all state sources (see Table 7).[36] Credit relations were reverting to the forms taken in the first phase of the Green Revolution, while by the 1990s the wage labour force had been greatly expanded. This had the effect that a much larger proportion of the population was excluded from credit requiring land as collateral than was the case in the 1970s.

Village credit was strongly socially niched. *Female-headed households, which constitute 14 per cent of the sample,* only took 5.5 per cent of the total number and *1.8 per cent of the total volume of loans.* None of these loans came from formal sources. The average debt for a female-headed household was Rs 1,549, in contrast to Rs 7,766 for male-headed households. *Scheduled-caste households formed 40 per cent of the sample* and, although they borrowed a proportional number of loans, their share of the total flow of borrowings was only 13 per cent. The average size of formal loans did not differ by caste status, but *only 8.5 per cent of this credit* (whether in number or in volume) went to scheduled-caste households. The average loan size was much lower than that for households of other castes – at Rs 2,227 and Rs 11,061 respectively per borrowing household.

Considering literacy as a categorizing variable, *IH on average took lower and smaller loans.* Whether they were borrowing from formal or informal markets, the average size of loan was always lower than that taken by a literate household. Almost 90 per cent of the total amount of credit borrowed by illiterate

TABLE 7 Sources of money by social characteristics

| | Financial Sources | | | | Informal Institutions | | | | | All Sources |
| | Formal Institutions | | | | | | | | | |
	Co-Operatives	Com-mercial Banks	Land Develop-ment	IRDP	Money-lenders & Pawn-brokers	Traders	Silk Merchants & Weavers & Shop-keepers	Friends & Relatives	Other Informal	
GENDER										
Female Headed Hhs										
% tot.v.loans (row)					268			2908	278	1042
% n.loans (row)					7.73%			81.41%	10.87%	100%
% tot.v.loans (col.)					30.05%			29.17%	40.78%	100%
% n.loans (col.)					1.01%			16.08%	1.51%	1.83%
					6.89%			11.83%	10.07%	5.47%
Male Headed hhs	8813	5722	10636	4376	1937	1886	5643	2037	2033	3227
% tot.v.loans (row)	21.29%	11.98%	4.95%	1.10%	14.10%	10.11%	15.27%	7.93%	13.26%	100%
% n.loans (row)	7.79%	6.75%	1.50%	0.81%	23.48%	17.31%	8.73%	12.57%	21.05%	100%
% tot.v.loans (col.)	100%	100%	100%	100%	98.99%	100%	100%	83.92%	98.49%	98.17%
% n.loans (col.)	100%	100%	100%	100%	93.11%	100%	100%	88.17%	89.93%	94.53%
CASTE										
Schedule Caste	6653	19000		3000	871	1130	1222	731	798	1106
% tot.v.loans (row)	11.31%	10.71%		2.99%	20.48%	12.97%	2.82%	11.76%	26.96%	100%
% n.loans (row)	1.88%	0.62%		1.10%	25.99%	12.70%	2.55%	17.78%	37.37%	100%
% tot.v.loans (col.)	7.22%	12.15%		37.10%	19.53%	17.43%	2.51%	16.89%	27.20%	13.34%
% n.loans (col.)	9.56%	3.66%		54.12%	40.84%	29.08%	11.58%	49.44%	63.26%	37.46%

TABLE 7 (cont.):

Other Castes	**9041**	**5217**	**10636**	**6000**	**2479**	**2195**	**6222**	**3517**	**3679**	**4306**
% tot.v.loans (row)	22.37%	11.92%	5.61%	0.78%	12.98%	9.46%	16.87%	8.90%	11.10%	100%
% n.loans (row)	10.65%	9.84%	2.27%	0.56%	22.56%	18.55%	11.67%	10.90%	13%	86.66%
% tot.v.loans (col.)	92.78%	87.85%	100%	62.90%	80.47%	82.57%	97.49%	83.11%	72.80%	62.54%
% n.loans (col.)	90.44%	96.34%	100%	45.88%	59.16%	70.92%	88.42%	50.56%	36.74%	24.87%
EDUCATION										
Illiterate	**2896**	**6000**			**889**	**1062**	**3374**	**2218**	**1311**	**1629**
% tot.v.loans (row)	6.18%	6.19%			15.54%	6.92%	15.93%	27.79%	21.45%	100%
% n.loans (row)	3.48%	1.68%			28.48%	10.62%	7.69%	21.38%	26.67%	100%
% tot.v.loans (col.)	8.91%	21.54%			18.83%	11.81%	17.99%	50.71%	27.49%	16.94%
% n.loans (col.)	17.59%	38.19%			38.58%	20.97%	30.09%	51.24%	38.92%	32.30%
Literate	**8813**	**6325**	**13500**	**4376**	**2408**	**2104**	**6619**	**2163**	**2204**	**3812**
% tot.v.loans (row)	25.16%	12.90%	4.59%	1.30%	13.67%	10.54%	14.80%	5.51%	11.54%	100%
% n.loans (row)	10.88%	7.77%	1.30%	1.13%	21.63%	19.10%	8.53%	9.70%	19.96%	100%
% tot.v.loans (col.)	100%	91.09%	78.46%	100%	81.17%	88.19%	82.01%	49.29%	72.51%	83.06%
% n.loans (col.)	100%	82.41%	61.81%	100%	61.42%	79.03%	69.91%	48.76%	61.08%	67.70%
ALL	**8813**	**5722**	**10636**	**4376**	**1822**	**1886**	**5643**	**2140**	**1856**	**3107**
% tot.v.loans (row)	20.89%	11.76%	4.86%	1.08%	13.98%	9.93%	14.99%	9.28%	13.22%	100%
% n.loans (row.)	7.37%	6.39%	1.42%	0.76%	23.84%	16.36%	8.26%	13.48%	22.13%	100%
	100%	100%	100%	100%	100%	100%	100%	100%	100%	100%
	100%	100%	100%	100%	100%	100%	100%	100%	100%	100%

households came from informal sources, while literate households relied on formal institutions for 44 per cent of the total volume of loans they took.

1.5.3 *Economic characteristics of borrowers*

Credit is disproportionately concentrated among the asseted (see Table 8).[37] Here, of the total amount borrowed, *only 12 per cent goes to the third of households which are landless*. The debt of households with in excess of 5 acres is 10 times that of the landless. *Medium and large landholders* (more than 2.5 acres), accounting for *less than 20 per cent of the sample, obtain more than 50 per cent of the total volume available. The inequality is even more pronounced for formal credit.* Landless households and those with only a marginal extent of land (58 per cent), obtain less than 10 per cent of credit disbursed by formal institutions. More than 50 per cent of formal credit is taken by the 7 per cent of households holding above 5 acres of land. *The possession of a micro-holding (0.1 to 1.0 acre) enables households to double the size of their loans over those of the landless with equivalent incomes* (from Rs 1,225 and 2.5 months' income equivalent to Rs 2,700 and 6 months).

Friends and relatives are the only sources of money geared to the poor, but in contradictory ways. Some loans, at 22 per cent interest, are indistinguishable from commercial ones, others (at an annualized average of 6 per cent) operate according to a logic of reciprocity. Most of the debt of marginal and small peasants is from traders of one sort or another, such that kind repayment interlinks two 'markets'. *About half of the pawnbroking credit and three quarters of silk merchants' loans go to the agricultural and weaving households of the middle peasantry and 60 per cent of agricultural traders' credit goes to the agrarian elite.*

With the exception of IRDP, the retrogressive role of formal institutions is highlighted in Table 9.[38] Even the antipoverty IRDP loans[39] went to men, all to literates. Half the IRDP loans (but 37 per cent of the volume) went to scheduled castes. Two thirds of IRDP funds found their way to poor peasants with land. The exceptionally rare cornering of land development and cooperative credit by poor peasants was diverted by them for consumption. Again, *the possession of a small amount of land is seen to give poor peasants access to a wider range of state-regulated markets for money.* Commercial bank and cooperatives, which provide 85 per cent of all formal credit, supply their loans essentially to the rural elite, exactly as does the bulk of informal credit.

1.5.4 *The use of credit*

A third of the torrent of credit is for subsistence, 60 per cent for production and 7 per cent for refinance (see Table 10). Credit institutions allocate funds distinctively according to their intended purpose. *Formal credit is predominantly*

TABLE 8 Class, land holding and loan sizes

	Land holding					Cluster					Farm size		
	Landless	Marginal	Small	Medium	Large	Poor landless	Poor with land	Middle landless	Middle with land	Elite	No Farms	Small Farms	Large Farms
% of Households	36.01%	22.49%	21.92%	14.31%	5.26%	36.65%	20.71%	9.26%	23.43%	9.95%	46.17%	36.14%	17.69%
% of total borrowing households	34.4%	22.9%	24.2%	11.3%	7.3%	33.7%	21.5%	9.5%	24.0%	11.2%	40.2%	39.9%	19.9%
% of Total Loans: number	30.0%	22.5%	24.2%	12.1%	10.2%	28.6%	21.0%	11.0%	24.9%	14.5%	36.30%	38.65%	25.04%
% of Total Loans: volume	12.2%	19.8%	16.5%	15.9%	35.5%	11.3%	16.9%	9.3%	30.1%	32.4%	15.61%	34.17%	50.22%
Average Loan size (Rs)	1225	2731	2126	4085	10868	1231	2491	2630	3762	6938	1336	2747	6231
Formal Loans (Rs)	4792	4267	5810	4911	13926	4792	5425	.	5726	12103	5023	5204	8854
% of formal loan number within groups (col sum)	4.41%	5.06%	7.30%	58.81%	44.76%	4.79%	11.99%	.	29.07%	33.20%	7.6%	7.5%	41.0%
% of formal loan volume within groups (col sum)	17.26%	7.91%	19.95%	70.71%	57.36%	18.66%	26.11%	.	44.25%	57.91%	28.6%	14.2%	58.3%
% of formal loan number between groups (row sum)	8.6%	7.2%	11.1%	44.7%	28.5%	8.6%	15.8%	.	45.4%	30.2%	17.3%	18.2%	64.4%
% of formal loan volume between groups (row sum)	5.5%	4.1%	8.6%	29.2%	52.8%	5.5%	11.4%	.	34.5%	48.6%	11.6%	12.6%	75.8%
Informal Loans (Rs)	1061	2649	1836	2905	8389	1051	2091	2630	2957	4372	1032	2547	4408
% of informal loan number within groups (col sum)	95.59%	94.94%	92.70%	41.19%	55.24%	95.21%	88.01%	100%	70.93%	66.80%	92.4%	92.5%	59.0%
% of informal loan volume within groups (col sum)	82.74%	92.09%	80.05%	29.29%	42.64%	81.34%	73.89%	100%	55.75%	42.09%	71.4%	85.8%	41.7%
% of informal loan number between groups (row sum)	35.3%	25.5%	26.7%	5.9%	6.7%	32.4%	22.0%	13.1%	21.0%	11.5%	39.9%	42.5%	17.6%
% of informal loan volume between groups (row sum)	16.5%	29.7%	21.6%	7.6%	24.7%	15.0%	20.3%	15.2%	27.3%	22.2%	18.1%	47.7%	34.1%
% of Borrowing households	69.03%	73.72%	79.75%	56.96%	100%	66.60%	75.09%	74.39%	74.19%	100%	62.95%	79.98%	81.24%
Average Loan amount (per borr hh)	2527	6251	4951	10220	35291	2427	5679	7072	9066	20900	2810	6188	18284
Average Loan number (per borr hh)	2.1	2.3	2.3	2.5	3.2	2.0	2.3	2.7	2.4	3.0	2.1	2.3	3.0
Average Loan amount (per hh)	1779	4608	3949	5821	35292	1617	4264	5261	6726	17035	1769	4949	14855
Average Loan number (per hh)	1.5	1.7	1.9	1.4	3.2	1.3	1.7	2.0	1.8	2.5	1.3	1.8	2.4

Note: 115 households (for a total of 230 observation and 200 new loans).

TABLE 9 Sources of money by economic characteristics

Clusters	Financial Sources				Informal Institutions					All Sources
	Formal Institutions									
	Co-Operatives	Com-mercial Banks	Land Develop-ment	IRDP	Money-lenders & Pawn-brokers	Traders	Silk Merchants Weavers & Shop-keepers	Friends & Relatives	Other Informal	
Poor landless Peasants	5000		6000	3000	1083	1066	1222	1462	843	**1231**
% tot.v.loans (row)	5.88%		9.26%	3.53%	25.82%	7.83%	3.32%	18.27%	26.11%	100%
% n.loans (row)	1.45%		1.90%	1.45%	29.33%	9.04%	3.35%	15.38%	38.11%	100%
% tot.v.loans (col.)	3.18%		21.54%	37.10%	20.90%	8.93%	2.51%	22.28%	22.36%	11.32%
% n.loans (col.)	5.61%		38.19%	54.12%	35.16%	15.79%	11.56%	32.62%	49.23%	28.58%
Poor Peasants with land	6949	3000		6000	931	1405	4630	2492	2188	**2491**
% tot.v.loans (row)	17.01%	5.09%		4.01%	10.91%	6.72%	23.95%	19.84%	12.47%	100%
% n.loans (row)	6.10%	4.23%		1.67%	29.18%	11.91%	12.89%	19.83%	14.19%	100%
% tot.v.loans (col.)	13.74%	7.31%		62.90%	13.16%	11.42%	26.96%	36.07%	15.91%	16.87%
% n.loans (col.)	17.42%	13.93%		45.88%	25.76%	15.33%	32.65%	30.97%	13.50%	21.05%
Middle landless Peasants					1079	1000	14833	200	950	**2630**
% tot.v.loans (row)					15.76%	3.28%	70.49%	1.10%	9.36%	100%
% n.loans (row)					38.42%	8.64%	12.50%	14.52%	25.92%	100%
% tot.v.loans (col.)					10.50%	3.08%	43.76%	1.11%	6.59%	9.31%
% n.loans (col.)					17.73%	5.81%	16.66%	11.85%	12.89%	11%

TABLE 9 (cont.):

Middle Peasants with land

	4826	**4458**	**13500**	**4845**	**1291**	**3879**	**4295**	**1349**	**3762**
% tot.v.loans (row)	17.28%	14.30%	12.67%	22.36%	6.11%	13.32%	8.42%	5.55%	100%
% n.loans (row.)	13.47%	12.07%	3.53%	17.36%	17.80%	12.92%	7.38%	15.48%	100%
% tot.v.loans (col.)	24.91%	36.62%	78.46%	48.16%	18.52%	26.75%	27.32%	12.64%	30.12%
% n.loans (col.)	45.49%	47.01%	61.81%	18.11%	27.06%	36.91%	13.61%	17.40%	24.87%

Elite

	16287	**8214**		**4093**	**3040**		**2585**	**11291**	**6938**
% tot.v.loans (row)	37.55%	20.37%		3.15%	17.80%		3.79%	17.35%	100%
% n.loans (row.)	16%	17.20%		5.33%	40.64%		10.17%	10.66%	100%
% tot.v.loans (col.)	58.17%	56.07%		7.28%	58.05%		13.22%	42.49%	32.37%
% n.loans (col.)	31.48%	39.06%		3.24%	36.01%		10.94%	6.99%	14.50%

All Groups

	8813	**5722**	**10636**	**4376**	**1822**	**1886**	**5643**	**2140**	**1856**	**3107**
% tot.v.loans (row)	20.89%	11.76%	4.86%	1.08%	13.98%	9.93%	14.99%	9.28%	13.22%	100%
% n.loans (row.)	7.37%	6.39%	1.42%	0.76%	23.84%	16.36%	8.26%	13.48%	22.13%	100%
	100%	100%	100%	100%	100%	100%	100%	100%	100%	100%
	100%	100%	100%	100%	100%	100%	100%	100%	100%	100%

TABLE 10 Credit by intended purpose

Intended Purpose	Financial Sources					Informal Institutions						All Sources
	Formal Institutions											
	Co-Opera-tives	Com-mercial Banks	Land Develop-ment	IRDP	Total Formal	Money-lenders & Pawn-brokers	Traders	Silk Merchants & Weavers & Shop-keepers	Friends & Relatives	Other Informal	Total Informal	
Consumption	**6000**	**7467**	**6000**		**6830**	**791**	**2117**	**5942**	**2032**	**1246**	**1743**	**1935**
% n.loans (row)	0.64%	2.13%	0.99%		3.76%	27.05%	7.66%	7.82%	21.33%	32.38%	96.24%	100%
% tot.v.loans (row)	1.99%	8.22%	3.08%		13.28%	11.06%	8.38%	24.02%	22.41%	20.86%	86.72%	100%
% n.loans (col.)	4.76%	18.25%	38.19%		12.91%	62.08%	25.61%	51.83%	86.64%	80.09%	62.65%	54.72%
% tot.v.loans (col.)	3.24%	23.81%	21.54%		11.72%	26.95%	28.74%	54.58%	82.28%	53.76%	48.12%	34.07%
Production	**8953**	**5459**	**13500**	**4376**	**7834**	**3366**	**1783**	**3094**	**2837**	**4705**	**2827**	**4377**
% n.loans (row)	16.77%	10.25%	2.10%	1.83%	30.94%	19.23%	28.53%	7.76%	4.30%	9.23%	69.06%	100%
% tot.v.loans (row)	34.30%	12.79%	6.47%	1.83%	55.39%	14.79%	11.62%	5.49%	2.79%	9.93%	44.61%.	100%
% n.loans (col.)	95.24%	67.17%	61.81%	100%	81.24%	33.74%	72.96%	39.32%	13.36%	17.46%	34.37%	41.84%
% tot.v.loans (col.)	96.76%	64.09%	78.46%	100%	84.59%	62.33%	68.98%	21.56%	17.72%	44.26%	42.82%	58.94%
Refinance		**4747**			**4747**	**4678**		**15222**		**1500**	**7311**	**6565**
% n.loans (row)		29.10%			29.10%	31.13%		22.82%		16.95%	70.90%	100%
% tot.v.loans (row)		21.04%			21.04%	22.18%		52.90%		3.87%	78.96%	100%
% n.loans (col.)		14.59%			5.84%	4.18%		8.85%		2.45%	2.70%	3.20%
% tot.v.loans (col.)		12.10%			3.69%	10.73%		23.86%		1.98%	8.70%	6.76%
Multi Purpose							**3000**				**3000**	**3000**
% n.loans (row)							100%				100%	100%
% tot.v.loans (row)							100%				100%	100%
% n.loans (col.)							1.43%				0.28%	0.23%
% tot.v.loans (col.)							2.27%				0.37%	0.23%
All Groups	**8813**	**5722**	**10636**	**4376**	**7524**	**1822**	**1886**	**5643**	**2140**	**1856**	**2270**	**3107**
% tot.v.loans (row)	7.37%	6.39%	1.42%	0.76%	15.94%	23.84%	16.36%	8.26%	13.48%	22.13%	84.06%	100%
% n.loans (row)	20.89%	11.76%	4.86%	1.08%	38.59%	13.98%	9.93%	14.99%	9.28%	13.22%	61.41%	100%
	100%	100%	100%	100%	100%	100%	100%	100%	100%	100%	100%	100%
	100%	100%	100%	100%	100%	100%	100%	100%	100%	100%	100%	100%

supplied for productive purposes and essentially for agriculture. Although the average size of a loan does not vary much with its purpose, only 13 per cent of all formal loans are issued for consumption, and then mainly for the purchase of durable goods (usually for house purchase or renovation). Informal credit is less dedicated. Most informal sources give credit for subsistence, for the acquisition of durables, for the costs of health and education, and for ceremonial expenditure. Loans taken from friends and relatives are principally used for consumption (particularly for health and education). Moneylenders, pawnbrokers, silk merchants and master weavers also provide significant volumes for consumption. The difference in the average size of consumption loans between the two groups is partly explained by the fact that the former group of lenders gives a large number of small loans for domestic consumption to agricultural producers, while the latter mainly provides loans of larger size for durable goods and the consumption of weaving households.

Table 11 describes the use of funds according to the two classifications of land holdings and class clusters. The poorest peasants, landless households and those who do not cultivate their land use the great bulk of their borrowings (between 83 and 89 per cent of the number, and between 60 and 70 per cent of the volume, of loans taken) for consumption. A small sector of petty landed proprietors incur sizeable debts for refinance. To see the difference to credit behaviour made by a small quantity of land we can compare the poor landless and poor landed clusters. *The poor landed have double the debt of the landless and the proportion used for productive purposes rises from 24 per cent to 38 per cent of the volume, that is by nearly 60 per cent.* We see the same relation in the fine-grained land-holding classification: a rise from 26 per cent among the landless and marginal to 40 per cent among smallholders, itself an increase of 85 per cent. *The possession of one acre marks a significant change in the use of credit.* In contrast, the elite of the villages, the medium and large landowners, allocate most of the loans to production. Even so, when the elite borrows for consumption, the average loan is Rs 10,000, equivalent to twice the annual income of an agricultural labouring household. Credit is an income-smoothing insurance for those without assets, while it is a factor of production for the rural elite.

2. THE COLLATERAL QUESTION

Collateral is the means by which borrowers gain access to finance with which to create future wealth (even when used for smoothing contingent dips in income streams) and the means used by lenders to screen (so as to reduce default risks), to share risk and to compensate for default. But of course collateral is productive in its own right (though certain types of collateral are hardly ever

TABLE 11 Use of credit by economic characteristics

Actual Purpose	Household economic characteristics										Farm size		
	Landholding					Cluster							
	Landless	Marginal	Small	Medium	Large	Poor landless	Poor with land	Middle landless	Middle with land	Elite	No Farms	Small Farms	Large Farms
Consumption	976	2161	2976	3233	10000	871	2630	2655	2071	7936	1051	3000	5744
% n.loans (row)	46.72%	27.15%	16.55%	6.18%	3.40%	44.52%	21.39%	14.89%	13.54%	5.66%	58.75%	33.23%	8.02%
% tot.v.loans (row)	21.98%	28.27%	23.73%	9.63%	16.39%	18.69%	27.11%	19.05%	13.51%	21.64%	29.75%	48.04%	22.21%
% n.loans (col.)	82.74%	66.22%	37.61%	28.06%	18.42%	85.61%	55.85%	74.39%	29.91%	21.45%	88.93%	47.25%	17.61%
% tot.v.loans (col.)	65.92%	52.40%	52.64%	22.21%	16.95%	60.59%	58.98%	75.07%	16.47%	24.53%	69.94%	51.60%	16.24%
Production	2478	2346	1592	4378	11588	3257	2228	2560	3816	6834	3673	1920	6367
% n.loans (row)	10.80%	15.52%	36.44%	19.08%	18.16%	6.38%	22.08%	6.91%	37.83%	26.79%	5.80%	46.30%	47.90%
% tot.v.loans (row)	6.45%	8.77%	13.97%	20.13%	50.69%	5%	11.85%	4.26%	34.77%	44.11%	5.13%	21.41%	73.45%
% n.loans (col.)	14.18%	28.06%	61.43%	64.25%	72.93%	9.09%	42.76%	25.61%	61.99%	75.33%	6.51%	48.82%	77.95%
% tot.v.loans (col.)	28.68%	24.10%	45.99%	68.85%	77.75%	24.06%	38.24%	24.93%	62.87%	74.19%	17.91%	34.12%	79.65%
Refinance	2149	11231		4747	6650	3567	5000		9597	2500	3562	11231	5778
% n.loans (row)	23.59%	31.77%		22.98%	21.67%	37.34%	7.18%		49.71%	5.77%	40.80%	31.77%	27.43%
% tot.v.loans (row)	7.67%	54%		16.51%	21.81%	20.16%	5.44%		72.22%	2.18%	22%	54%	23.99%
% n.loans (col.)	3.08%	5.71%		7.69%	8.65%	5.29%	1.38%		8.10%	1.61%	4.56%	3.33%	4.44%
% tot.v.loans (col.)	5.40%	23.50%		8.94%	5.30%	15.35%	2.78%		20.66%	0.58%	12.15%	13.62%	4.12%
Multi Purpose			3000							3000	3000		
% tot.v.loans (row)			100%							100%	100%		
% n.loans (row)			100%							100%	100%		
% n.loans (col.)			0.97%							1.61%	0.60%		
% tot.v.loans (col.)			1.36%							0.70%	0.66%		
All	1225	2731	2126	4085	10868	1231	2491	2630	3762	6938	1336	2747	6231
% tot.v.loans (row)	31.03%	22.53%	24.18%	12.11%	10.15%	28.58%	21.05%	11%	24.87%	14.50%	36.30%	38.65%	25.04%
% n.loans (row)	12.24%	19.81%	16.54%	15.92%	35.50%	11.32%	16.8%	9.31%	30.12%	32.37%	15.61%	34.17%	50.22%
	100%	100%	100%	100%	100%	100%	100%	100%	100%	100%	100%	100%	100%
	100%	100%	100%	100%	100%	100%	100%	100%	100%	100%	100%	100%	100%

theoretically recognized as productive, because they take the form of poorly specified future promises or – like utensils – are productive in the unvalorized domestic sphere of the rural economy).

Land is found to be the most widespread form of collateral in the agrarian economy.[40] Land affects both the supply of, and the demand for, credit.[41] The collateral role of land may determine the supply of credit to its owner. Above a certain point, its collateral capabilities may be outweighed by the substitution effect on the demand for credit of income generated directly by it, after which point demand for credit is reduced.[42] For smallholders, land is a problematic collateral because: a) they have little; and b) they are risk-averse about what little they have because of its centrality to their livelihoods. So the collateral offered by smallholders also takes non-land forms: status in terms of access to water, commitments of future labour or crops, utensils, gold, third-party guarantees or reputation underwritten by kinship.[43] The fact that the formal sector discriminates against such collaterals restricts credit access by their owners to non-state-regulated lenders in the informal sector. Higher informal-sector interest both reduces supply because of the increased probability of default and reduces demand because higher-risk activity tends to be screened out.[44] Swaminathan (1991) discovered, however, that interest was not so much related to risk but instead was inversely related to the marketability of collaterals. Well-commercialized land was associated with lower informal interest. Gold and jewels were poorly commercialized and the highest interest was demanded on brass vessels and promissory notes, which were hardly commercialized at all.

If landless and currently marginal landholders were able to purchase land, their collateral base would broaden, enabling access to the formal sector, reducing interest rates on credit and redistributing a productive asset in conditions where the draconian preconditions to successful pro-poor land reform are absent.

2.1 *Collateral in the villages*

Over 75 per cent of the loans observed among the household borrowers surveyed were secured with some sort of collateral. Although based on a small sample of only 200 loans – which has to be treated with caution – Table 12 reveals patterns in the role of collateral.[45] Formal institutions rarely supply loans without collateral. Land and gold are the sort of collateral most commonly required by state-regulated cooperatives and commercial banks, although other types of collateral, such as future crops and bonds, are also accepted. Indeed, land was the basis for only half the formal loans. Loans offered by land development banks had been secured either with land (in 62 per cent of instances) or with personal

TABLE 12 Financial sources and collateral

| | Financial Sources | | | | | Informal Institutions | | | | | | All Sources |
| | Formal Institutions | | | | | | | | | | | |
Type of Collateral	Co-Opera-tives	Com-mercial Banks	Land Devel-opment	IRDP	Total Formal	Money lenders & Pawn brokers	Traders	Silk Mer-chant Weavers & Shop keepers	Friends & Rela-tives	Other In-formal	Total In-formal	
Total number of loans	16	13	3	2	34	42	36	16	29	43	166	200
Loans without				54.1%	2.6%	7.9%	13.9%	13.8%	52%	39.6%	25.1%	21.5%
obs				1	1	4	5	2	17	17	45	46
Loans with collateral	100%	100%	100%	45.9%	97.4%	92.1%	86.1%	86.2%	48%	60.4%	74.9%	78.5%
obs	16	13	3	1	33	38	31	14	12	26	121	154
of which:												
Gold & Silver	15.8%	18.2%			14.6%	15.3%					4.3%	6%
Land	48%	53%	61.8%		48.9%	2.3%					0.7%	8.4%
Crop	15.3%	6.9%			9.8%	3.1%					14%	13.3%
Bond	3.2%				1.5%	20.1%	55.2%	8.8%	2.6%	4.3%	20.3%	17.3%
Labour	7.3%				3.4%	1.7%	11.4%	6.6%	27.4%	27.7%	11.9%	10.6%
Personal	5.6%				8.2%	2.3%	10.9%	61.7%	6.6%	8.3%	7.6%	7.7%
Brass vessels							8.6%		11.4%	12.9%	1.2%	1%
Bond & jewels	4.8%	18.2%	38.2%	45.9%	9.5%					4.7%		13.3%
Loom						47.2%				2.5%	14%	0.7%
Other	3.7%	3.7%			1.5%			9.1%			0.9%	0.2%

reputation (for the other 38 per cent). By contrast, each informal source accepts a wide variety of forms of security. A quarter of the loans borrowed from the informal sector as a whole were not secured by any kind of collateral, while crops (14 per cent), labour (12 per cent), bonds and jewels (20 per cent) were the more generally accepted security for the other 75 per cent. It is quite striking that *although informal credit is biased towards the landed classes, land itself is used as collateral in less than 1 per cent of cases. Its role as collateral is confined to the formal sector.* Although types of collateral are not exclusively associated with types of lending institutions, there is a strong tendency towards segmentation. Pawnbrokers and moneylenders mostly accept gold and silver, bonds and other precious metals (jewels), and they rarely offer money without collateral. Traders secure more than 50 per cent of their loans not only on the future crop but also on pledges of labour, bonds and on personal reputation. Silk merchants secure their loans with labour. About 50 per cent of loans from friends and relatives were unsecured and another 10 per cent were based on personal assurance. Kin and friends, therefore, rely more on reputation.

Collateral is patterned by caste, gender and class. Female-headed (FHH), illiterate (IH) and scheduled-caste households (SCH) use bonds, jewels and personal reputation the most, while literate, male-headed households and those of other castes usually offer bonds, future crops and land as collateral. As Table 12 shows, land and crops are the kind of collateral most commonly used by elites. Landless households and marginal farmers, instead, have to rely on personal assurance, bonds, jewels and future labour agreements. It is noteworthy, however, that the percentage of loans secured by collateral is lower for the poorest households. This partly reflects the fact that poor households get fewer formal loans (which need to be secured by some form of collateral, although it often has to be land or gold) and partly may be explained by the fact that poor households have less collateral to offer, and of lower quality.

Tables 13 and 14 break down collateral in terms of the social status and class of borrowers. More loans are completely unsecured by lenders to FHH, IH and SCH than to male, literate caste borrowers. Bonds and reputation are prominent kinds of security for loans among the disadvantaged. For informal loans, land drops out completely as collateral for socially and economically advantaged households but remains important for a minority of FHH where gold and land secure them loans (which accentuates the difference between this group and SC, landless or poor labouring households). Distinguishing between poor landed and equally poor landless households (see Table 14), we see that only a tiny fraction of the collaterals of those small and marginal peasants with land is made up of land. *The possession of land broadens their access entitlements, but land is protected from exposure as a front-line collateral. Since the landed poor do* not use land as a collateral, the hypothesis which we started with, that the relationship between the value of land as collateral and the directly productive value of land alters through the land distribution, is not relevant. Instead we find that land in these villages is a prior screen of eligibility and is considered by lenders as a security of last resort. Other collaterals can be used because the borrower has land. Crop and labour are distributed as securities in opposite ways. Crops rise and labour pledges fall with increasing landholding size. Yet labour pledges *are* used as security even among the elite and reveal again the intense desirability to lenders of being able to interlink credit, product and labour 'markets' or arrangements.

2.2 Collateral and interest by source

Lenders accept a range of forms of security and appear to discriminate between collaterals in their interest charges (see Table 15). However, they rarely behave consistently across the board. *Bonds* (at 36–40 per cent from most sources) and *crops* (in a narrow band of interest around 20 per cent) are the exceptions and *by the criterion of interest behave most like an integrated market*. For the other kinds of collaterals there are mixes of high and low interest or none at all, suggesting either non-commercial exchanges or loans linked to returns on other markets, which coexist with commercial contracts. Interest at 60 per cent on the security

TABLE 13 Social characteristics and collateral

Type of Collateral	Gender		Caste		Education	
	Female Headed	Male Headed	Scheduled Caste	Other Caste	Literate	Illiterate
Total number of loans						
Loans without collateral obs	28.1%	21.1%	31.7%	15.4%	25.8%	19.4%
Loans with collateral obs	71.9%	78.9%	68.3%	84.6%	74.2%	80.6%
of which:						
Gold & Silver	9.93%	5.76%	1.45%	8.71%	1.68%	8.04%
Land	10.19%	8.25%	2.26%	12.01%	4.48%	10.21%
Crop		14.12%	6.63%	17.38%	1.36%	19.07%
Bond	26.21%	16.76%	15.01%	18.63%	19.27%	16.32%
Labour	8.03%	10.70%	9.47%	11.20%	15.80%	8.05%
Personal	17.49%	7.10%	14.81%	3.38%	13.55%	4.86%
Brass vessels		1.11%	0.94%	1.12%		1.55%
Bond & jewels		14.08%	17.14%	11.02%	18.09%	11.03%
Loom		0.79%		1.20%		1.11%
Other		0.25%	0.62%			0.35%

TABLE 14 Economic characteristics and collateral

Type of Collateral	Economic Characteristics												
	Land holding					Cluster					Farm size		
	Landless	Marginal	Small	Medium	Large	Poor NL	Poor L	Middle NL	Middle L	Elite	No Farm	Small	Large
Total number of loans						56	46	16	43	39			
Loans without collateral	28.1%	28%	13.3%	11.8%	17.5%	37.4%	16.4%	14.5%	15%	13.9%	37%	12.4%	12.9%
obs						22	9	3	6	6			
Loans with collateral	71.9%	72%	86.7%	88.2%	82.5%	62.7%	83.6%	85.5%	85%	86.6%	63%	87.6%	87.1%
obs						34	37	13	37	33			
of which:													
Gold & Silver	3.54%	5.26%	2.89%	13.71%	13.26%	5.75%	3.05%		12.07%	4.84%	6.45%	3.47%	9.21%
Land	4.81%	4.42%	4.88%	35.48%	18.57%	1.95%	6.99%		17%	14.48%	1.53%	4.19%	24.68%
Crop	18.80%	12.16%	26.89%	5.79%	18.85%	1.90%	12.48%	8.64%	19.69%	29.88%	16.18%	18.42%	24.87%
Bond	10.10%	16.46%	14.05%	21.93%	16.55%	20.94%	12.89%	8.64%	17.24%	23.03%	10.58%	16.89%	19.46%
Labour	18.50%	15.23%	14.26%		5.31%	9.09%	15.94%	16.97%	8.83%	3.72%	13.19%	15.98%	2.15%
Personal		4.40%	2.89%		2.30%	13.43%	4.71%	17.28%	2.80%	1.61%	1.92%	6.83%	0.93%
Brass vessels		4.65%					1.67%		2.80%			0.91%	
Bond & jewels	14.64%	8.10%	19.85%	11.32%	7.62%	9.60%	24.47%	29.78%	4.57%	6.94%	11.86%	19.56%	5.77%
Loom	1.48%	1.29%					0.58%	0.92%			1.26%	0.75%	
Other			0.97%							0.47%	0.60%	0.60%	

TABLE 15 Annualized interest by source and collateral

Interest Rates	Informal Institutions					
	Money-lenders & Pawn-brokers	Traders	Silk Merchant Weavers & Shop-keepers	Friends & Relatives	Other Informal	Total In-formal
Type of Collateral						
Total number of loans	40	32	15	29	39	155
Loans without collateral	24.4%	2.5%	0	6.6%	37%	18.5%
obs	4	5	2	17	14	42
Loans with collateral	37.3%	17.5%	7.7%	22%	31.6%	26.9%
obs	36	27	13	12	25	113
of which:						
Gold & Silver	29.4%					29.4%
Land	60%					60%
Crop	20%	18.8%	24%	0	0	16.9%
Bond	40%	26.4%	36%	38.6%	36.2%	36.5%
Labour	36%	0	0	0		1.9%
Personal	120%	24%		0	40.7%	35.4%
Brass vessels					60%	60%
Bond & jewels	34.9%				36%	35%
Loom			18.6%			18.6%

of land and at 120 per cent on personal security suggests that moneylenders exploit a degree of monopoly control where social factors permit no alternatives to borrowers. Madhura Swaminathan's hypothesis that interest reflects the marketability of collateral is confirmed here. Of the four common collaterals, crops at 19 per cent are by far the most easily commercialized. Gold (29 per cent) is more marketable than jewels (35 per cent). Brass vessels and bonds/promissory notes fetch 38–60 per cent, being hard to resell and harder to redeem in court. Unmarketable personal assurance tends to require 40–120 per cent. Of all the types of lender, specialized moneylenders most consistently discriminate interest according to the marketability of collateral.[49]

3. CONCLUSIONS

Even though most money-borrowers confine themselves to one or two sources of loans, there is a vast array of credit institutions servicing these villages. They range from state-managed credit and banking schemes (IRDP; land development banks and cooperative credit banks) through state-regulated private commercial and nationalized banks, to informal moneylending dynasties, pawnbrokers, grain traders, silk merchants and master weavers, shopkeepers, elite farmers, chit fund organizers (from farmer's wives to schoolteachers and shopkeepers) and itinerant moneylenders.

Formal – state-regulated and often state-owned – credit has been a major component in India's 'heavy agriculturalization', the initial phases of which were dominated by informal credit. Informal credit in northern Tamil Nadu tended to preserve smallholder agriculture and to slow – though not to halt – the pace of the process of landlessness. Even so, the proportion of the rural population which is landless has increased (in the three villages) by one third between 1983–4 to 1993–4.[50]

Despite two decades of targeted credit, with rates of achievements in priority sector lending in Tamil Nadu of 2.5 times the national average, by 1993–4 there were signs of a trend of reversion to forms of finance reminiscent of those of the 1970s, as a result of which formal credit does the exact opposite of its stated purpose of favouring marginal groups and supplementing private credit.[51] In practice, the two systems have developed as complements. The distribution of debt is more unequal than that of land and the distribution of formal credit is much more unequal than that of informal credit.[52] Despite the problems of extrapolation from the 11-village survey in 1983–4 to the 3-village one in 1993–4, formal state-regulated credit directed to agriculture seems to have shrunk in relative terms, the cooperatives shrinking at the expense of private commercial banks. Formal credit is the preserve of traders and of the rural elites from whom, according to the village credit profiles, we know it is lent onwards. It thus fuels informal financial arrangements. While the rural elite is not wealthy by local urban standards, these credit relations are differentiating.

The informal sector dominates rural credit, both in number of loans and in volume of money. Unlike the conclusion for 1983 and unlike findings elsewhere in India,[53] merchants' credit remains important, on a par with state-managed credit, reflecting the value to traders of interlinked contracts. Traders' credit in the *non-farm* economy now supplements that in agriculture proper. Our results are consistent with those of Reddy (1992), who finds these interlocked contracts to be prevalent in 'developed' and diversified rural regions of India, and of Janakarajan (1993) who found them in adjacent Chinglepet District. Loans repaid in kind do not necessarily signify backwardness. The fact of a contract does not indicate the role it plays. Interlocked contracts do, however, deprive the borrower of choice on two or three markets and, in so doing, they shape the distribution of the gains to production and trade, biasing it towards trade.

Informal money markets consist of sets of highly personalized arrangements in which specific kinds of lender are accessed by specific kinds of borrower for specific purposes with a great range of terms and conditions. These markets are fragmented. Interest-rate differences are most unlikely to be removed if risk could be factored in, though our data did not actually enable us to do this. Social relations and social status fragment these markets. While all classes can gain access to moneylenders and pawnbrokers, friends and relatives are key sources for the poorest borrowers while paddy and silk traders dominate loans to the rural elite. Being of scheduled caste and female is a formidable barrier to formal sector credit. Whatever they own, women who head households are effectively without acceptable collateral. They are constrained to borrow from friends and relatives.[54] Many of these loans are without interest and based on a non-market solidary logic of reciprocity associated with poor people. This category may include women-only chit funds. The village profiles revealed that both female heads of households and other women use a specific system of circulation of money, organized by and for women, but masked in the survey under the code 'friends and relatives'.

Illiteracy is almost as forbidding a barrier to access to credit as is being female. Scheduled-caste borrowers are also excluded from formal credit and, being for the most part landless, from traders' credit as well. Their loans are confined to scheduled-caste chit funds (of which there is a massive proliferation), moneylenders and pawnbrokers. From the latter sources, they can borrow only on a small scale and at high interest and their loans are strikingly for 'consumption' purposes. Consumption is the production of labour. It is of no concern to state-regulated credit, despite the fact that the difference in informal interest for production and consumption loans is not significant, which may indicate that moneylenders reckon that consumption loans are not significantly more risky.[55] None of the factors which structure *exclusion* from credit can be other than adversely affected by the social-sector cuts which form part of the paradigm of liberalization.

The least fragmented elements of credit relations, and ones in which 'markets' are beginning to be integrated, are those using bonds and crops as collateral – right across the informal sector – and the arrangements involving grain traders, silk merchants and professional moneylenders, where the borrowers tend to be the agrarian and rural elites.

Interest rates are subject to competing explanations. The *loan cost* argument, from which interest is predicted to be highest among the credit-starved poor, cannot account for the high frequency of loans to poor people at no interest. The interest rates in these villages do, however, reflect *transactions costs* in so far as transactions costs are found (with exceptions) to reflect the marketability of collateral.[56] Though lack of information on overdues and default stymied our analysis of risk, we do know that consumption loans are not charged higher interest than production loans once the source is factored out. Either risk is not a factor in interest or, as we suspect, consumption loans are not riskier than production loans since they 'produce' labour through which loans are repaid. Interest varies significantly with the *precise institutional source* from which loans are obtained – irrespective of the collateral offered and the social status of the borrower. *Pace* Drèze and colleagues (1998a), we have no evidence that formal-sector credit has by itself made informal credit more usurious. The fragmentation of informal credit with particular ranges of interest is of long standing.

Both land and livestock (but no other form of collateral) play contradictory roles in demand for credit. First, as collateral, they secure income-increasing loans. Second, as direct generators of income they reduce demand for loans. When these assets increase in value, then their role as income earners replaces that of collateral. Indeed we found that for informal loans, land drops out as a collateral as assets increase. Informal lenders accept labour and product pledges on a far wider scale than in the formal sector and from all classes of agrarian society. In both formal and informal sectors, significant amounts are lent unsecured by any collateral. The incidence of unsecured loans is higher for poorer households and landless borrowers, the reverse of what was expected. While these groups also pay higher interest on loans, lack of collateral was of no statistical significance in explaining these rates.

3.1 *Deregulation*

Credit relations are changing as the non-farm economy grows, creating demand for credit of a type (consumption and production) and in sectors (low-caste landless labour, women, agrarian weavers) ignored by the formal sector. If, as envisaged in the millennial budgets, credit is further deregulated (taking the form of 'detargeting', removing interest subsidies but without changing conventions on collateral), it is abundantly clear that the rural elites will continue to be the major beneficiaries. And the much wealthier urban *éminences grises* in silk manufacturing and paddy-rice trading (who routinely borrow from private commercial banks and who lend onwards in ways which personalize lending arrangements and which contractually lock two or more markets together) will benefit indirectly from the impact on rural elites. Though formal lending is retrogressive, further deregulation will not have redistributive outcomes. The state intervened in the first place for a set of reasons which are still valid. The state has proved unable to deliver equitable access, *but deregulated banking will further exacerbate the lack of equity in access.* The village of Veerasambanur shows that *cooperative credit can reach remote and poor villages.* Of the three villages studied, Veerasambanur had the most extensive and inclusive credit relations and the most active formal sector. Directed credit policy has a new opportunity to respond to the rapidly changing structures of rural credit. Through state credit, dependent out-working might be replaced by a non-agricultural form of petty production independent of mercantile control, an objective which the weavers with better assets are themselves trying to achieve.

3.2 *The collateral question*

The collateral of poor people – those with no land at all or micro-properties of 0.1 acres and below – needs not only increasing but also improving in quality. Land titling for male and female tenants and credit for the purchase of land are all consistent with the results of our research. Loans for land are the most practically and politically feasible.

But the collateral question is not quite so simple. In the formal sector, land is the most important single form of collateral. Land confers access rights to credit. Small-scale landholding enabled preferential access to the IRDP, to a wide range of formal and informal loans and thus to larger loans at lower interest than otherwise. In households with similar incomes, a micro-landholding of 0.1 to 1 acre enables a borrower to double the size of loan taken and to invest in production rather than consumption. These benefits are enough to justify loans for land. However, holdings below 5 acres in size do not confer working rights to *formal* credit. Only the agrarian elites have secure entitlements to state-regulated finance.

In the informal sector, the role of land is subtle. Land is rarely used as collateral for informal loans. Land ownership is a screening device. Other collaterals are then used for loans. Land is then a second-order collateral of last resort, activated only in cases of long default, when the first-order collateral has been relinquished by the borrower.

Rural credit policy has long been Janus-faced. State-regulated credit complements informal loans. Acting to preserve small-scale production (but not reaching it directly), the state subsidizes the agrarian elite, perhaps because they are unable to survive using capital-biased technology without subsidized credit, perhaps because production with wage workers is more costly per unit of output than that with family labour, but certainly as a differentiating service to capital and one which would be *more* differentiating if deregulated.

Yet the state has also preserved petty production, not only by tolerating onward informal lending by formal borrowers but also by its own assets-creating schemes (such as the IRDP) and by the successful penetration of remote villages by cooperative credit. At the very least, potential buyers of land ought not to be prevented from making their choice. *De facto* the lack of choice prevents scheduled-caste people from acquiring land. That the balance of these contrary policies currently favours the propertied elites is very clear from the expansion of the rural market for labour, most of which is of scheduled caste.

ACKNOWLEDGEMENTS

This chapter owes much to the comments on an early version by G S Bhalla, Venkatesh Athreya, Wendy Olsen, Neal Bliven and Judith Heyer. It is also indebted to two Oxford University masters' theses on credit in these villages: Paul Barbour, 1995, 'Rural Credit Markets in Tamil Nadu and the Role of Collateral', and Vishal Agarwal, 1997, 'Rural Credit Markets in India: Factors Affecting Access and Terms of Credit'; and, last but certainly not least, to the field notes of V Jothi, S Mariasusai and S Ramachandran.

Fertilizer Reforms and Nutrient Balances

BARBARA HARRISS-WHITE

1. BACKGROUND

THE heavily regulated, state-protected growth of the fertilizer industry has been India's biggest success as an upstream production link to agriculture. The watchword of fertilizer policy has been self-sufficiency, in order to wrench consumption from dependence on a volatile world market,[1] to contribute to self-sufficiency in grains and to provide essential agricultural commodities at low prices to urban and rural wage workers. Domestic production has seized the dominant market share, growing from 20 per cent of total fertilizer consumption in 1961 to 86 per cent by 1996.[2] From 3 kg per hectare in the 1960s, chemical-fertilizer use quintupled in the 1970s and has doubled every decade since then (to 75 kg/ha by 1995–6). The share in incremental agricultural production due to fertilizer has risen inexorably to become the most important component. It is a sobering fact, however, that the yield gap separating potential from actual incremental outputs has not declined over time. It has widened. Whereas one kg of fertilizer generated 5.7 kg of extra product over the decades of the 1960s and 1970s, it produced 4.1 in the 1980s and has declined further. This is odd when the history of HYV inputs responses, of producers' increasingly well-disseminated knowledge of fertilizer and of expansion in irrigation all suggest the opposite.[3]

Inequities are built into its use: 70 per cent of irrigated land is farmed with chemical fertilizer, but the proportion for rain-fed land on which pulses and oilseeds are grown is much lower. One fifth of India's districts consume one half of its fertilizer.[4] Despite the fact that fertilizer, along with water, is the leading component of the first-generation HYV package and that fertilizer has long been distributed through a plurality of institutions (markets, cooperatives, agriculture departments, trading corporations), non-price factors have been found to be considerably more important than price factors in determining fertilizer use.[5] The spatial distribution of these 'non-price' factors (irrigation, credit availability, marketing points, rainfall) explains the regional pattern of fertilizer use.[6] Whereas in the 1970s fertilizer was captured by the largest green revolutionaries, two decades later this was no longer the case. In the 1990s, there was thought to be little disadvantage in being a small peasant from the point of view of fertilizer use. National Council for Applied Economic Research (NCAER) data for 1988–9, for instance, show that chemical fertilizer was deployed on about three quarters of the cultivated surface area of small and marginal rice farmers and on 78 per cent of that of 'large farmers'. When it came to applications, marginal peasants (with 69 kg per ha in *kharif* and 103 in *rabi*) used fertilizer about 10 per cent more intensively than did large farmers.[7] Wastage and physical losses run high (about 60 per cent of nitrogen and 70–80 per cent of phosphorus being thought to be lost in application[8]), but not only in its final use. There are further suboptimalities in the domestic industrial production processes due to low capacity utilization and chronic energy losses.

Despite the high rhetorical priority to fertilizer-substituting biotechnologies on environmental grounds,[9] fertilizer *per se* is alleged not necessarily to cause environmental degradation. In defence of fertilizer, it is said that environmental damage can result from inadequate fertilizer use – from the overexpansion of area without land-augmenting technology.[10] So there is little doubt that the long-term project for Indian agriculture has a vast expansion in fertilizer use at its heart, if only to correct first-generation inequities and physical inefficiencies.

But by the time of the economic reforms of the 1990s, success had bred its own intractable problems. Fertilizer production was overcapitalized as a result of the production incentives established by the Retention Price Scheme (to guarantee the manufacturing companies a post-tax return of 12 per cent on net worth), which had been set in motion to break the destructive 'hog cycle' of the 1970s. Fertilizer production and distribution had become heavily dependent upon state transfers. Feedstocks, freight (for feedstock and for fertilizer from factory to field godowns) and imports were subsidized in such a way that final users received only about 48 per cent of the subsidy in the form of retail prices.[11] The Hamumantha Rao Committee reported that the structure of subsidies still offered perverse incentives, rewarding plants operating at low capacity utilization and higher than average costs and discouraging innovation or improvements in energy efficiency.[12] The annual subsidy had grown by a factor of five from 1981–2 to 1990–1. At Rs 4,389 crores, it was 1 per cent of GDP by the 1990s and, although it was not administered through the Agriculture Ministry, it was half of all government spending on agriculture.

A range of reform options was canvassed by various interests, ranging from phased decontrol (the Fertilizer Association of India, representing the industrial producers) through concessions on import duty (the Joint Parliamentary Committee in 1992), joint ventures abroad (Hanumantha Rao Committee in 1998), buffer stocks for phosphatic (P) and potassic (K) fertilizers controlled by parastatal corporations to stabilize prices prior to lifting price ceilings (Cabinet Committee on Economic Affairs, 1998) to a retail price reduction (Ministry of Agriculture), reflecting the need to increase agricultural production. Reviewing policy proposals, Vaidyanathan detected an 'obsession' with prices and subsidies which may have actually weakened incentives for efficient use and deflected attention away from other aspects of fertilizer policy. The latter include the need for synergy with rural electrification and irrigation, transport infrastructure, extension and information, agricultural credit and the social and site planning of dealers and agents for private and public sector retail outlets.[13] Although this list consists of so-called non-price policies, each has implications for coordination and expenditure, not only across several departments of government but also at its interfaces with banking and business.

 - In the event, policy-makers experimented. First, fertilizer subsidies were lifted in 1991 (keeping concessions for small and marginal farmers). These concessions were patchily implemented, were vulnerable to fraud and retrading and were abandoned the following year. Next, the subsidies on imported fertilizer were lifted and P and K were decontrolled.[14] Wholesale prices for imported P doubled and K trebled. Meanwhile, freight was subsidized and the price of urea produced by the subsidized domestic industry even declined by 10 per cent. Urea (nitrogen) is the biggest element in all fertilizers and the most important for agricultural yields.

While the reform period actually witnessed an *increase* in the fertilizer subsidy (Rs 5,600 crores in 1993 and Rs 8,350 by 1997–8[15]), it has fluctuated obstinately around 1 per cent of GDP. Policy changes by central government had a rapid impact on the agricultural micro-economy. The biggest two impacts were on fertilizer use and on nutrients balance. In a field project to evaluate the impact of the confused fertilizer policy on its use in an irrigated and dry village in Karnataka, Landy tracked a significant reduction in fertilizer use (responding to price increases).[16] He also found a deepening differentiation in fertilizer-based productivity along lines of class and agro-ecology, where small producers are increasingly disadvantaged by barriers to access to institutional credit and other kinds of transactions costs, and where dry regions are increasingly disadvantaged as fertilizer grows as a component of the costs of production nationally.

Balance in nutrients is thought to be achieved by two means. One is through price; but the importance of price is contested. On the one hand, Rao and Gulati argue that only international prices give the right incentives.[17] On the other, Vaidyanathan concludes that there is no evidence whatsoever to corroborate the inverse relation between the fertilizer–crop price ratio and fertilizer use per hectare.[18] The second means is through non-price factors, notably information: through soil testing and extension.[19] Thus we read that lack of nutrients balance is likely to be due to ignorance.[20]

Recently, it has been shown that the fertilizer policy has led to dramatic shifts in the nutrients ratios (see Table 1) in favour of the still-subsidized nitrogen (N).[21] The N:P:K ratio in the 1990s was in the region of 9:3:1, imbalanced towards nitrogen by a factor of two. From this trend, it would seem that price is more important than non-price factors in fertilizer allocation. So much so that the Government of India was forced to reintroduce concessional sales for di-ammonium phosphate and muriate of potash – 10 per cent of the total subsidy.

TABLE 1 Nutrient balances, India, Tamil Nadu and three villages

ALL INDIA	N	P	K
Desirable Ratio	4	2	1
Desirable Ratio for rice	2	1	1
1955–6	10.8	1.3	1
Actual Ratios pre-reform (1990–1)	6	2.4	1
Reform Period			
1991–2	5.9	2.4	1
1992–3	9.5	3.2	1
1993–4	9.6	2.9	1
1994–5	9	2.8	1
TAMIL NADU			
Pre-reform 1990–1	1.7	0.63	1
Pre-reform 1997	3	1	1
OLD NORTH ARCOT DT			
Recommended Ratio	2.5	1.05	1
Pre-reform 1990–1	2.2	1	1
Reform period			
1991–2	2.8	0.9	1
1992–3	2.9	1	1
1993–4	2.5	1	1
3 villages, TVM Dt (reform period 1993–4)			
chemical fertilizer	1.74	1.28	1
all fertilizer	1.22	0.81	1
chemical fertilizer – paddy	1.90	1.32	1
all fertilizer – paddy	1.40	0.87	1

Sources: Economic Survey, 1994–5; Govt of Tamil Nadu, Dept of Stats; Govt of Tamil Nadu, Dept of Agriculture, raw data field survey.

The constituent states have operated retail subsidies on a selective and ad hoc basis.[22]

We can use village-level evidence to review fertilizer policy in practice by assessing: i) the impact of nutrient balances on productivity; and ii) the social distribution of fertilizer use.

2. FERTILIZER USE IN THE OLD NORTH ARCOT DISTRICT, TAMIL NADU

While Hazell and Ramasamy recorded a six-fold increase in fertilizer use between 1965/6 and the early 1980s (associated with HYVs and with their season – *navarai*), on the eve of the economic reforms the old North Arcot District's agriculture presented a mixed picture. It was heavily dependent upon fertilizer, local average applications being four times the national average. Fertilizer use had tripled from 90 kg/ha to 270 kg/ha over the decade from 1980–1. North Arcot stood highest in the entire state, along with Madurai, Thanjavur and the Nilgiris.[23] But between 1980–1 and 1990–1 the area under HYVs had declined, at –0.46 per cent p.a., that under food crops shrank, at –0.37, and irrigation as a proportion of gross cropped area dropped, at -1.4 per cent p.a.

In this, North Arcot was by no means alone: 14 of the 20 districts of Tamil Nadu had registered a drop in the proportion of land under food crops. Five others in the central and southern littoral rice bowl had experienced a decline in the land down to HYVs and seven others throughout the state had reduced irrigation ratios.[24]

For the state as a whole, fertilizer consumption by districts over the period 1977–8 to 1990–1 was regressed against a vector of price and non-price factors. The results were very surprising: fertilizer use was negatively related to agricultural income, to the proportion of land irrigated and to rainfall. Such relationships could only be explained by the capture of a substantial portion of income by large farmers doing perennial cultivation,[25] but the evidence needed for this explanation is not very convincing.

The mix of chemical nutrients varied greatly within the state. It was characterized by an excessive and inefficient balance in the nutrients ratio. The pre-reform N:P:K ratio for the state was 1.7:0.63:1.0 (1990–1) against the all-India recommended ratio of 4:2:1, the recommended rate for rice of 2:1:1[26] and the recommended average rate for the state of 2.5:1.05:1.[27] In the region of the old North Arcot District there was a dramatic contrast between the new Ambedkar District in the north, where fertilizer consumption in 1990–1 reached 181 kg/ha with a nutrients ratio of 1.5:0.71:1.0, and Tiruvannamalai District (where the villages we studied lie), where fertilizer consumption was very much lower at 89.4 kg but where the ratio was tilted more towards nitrogen at 3.6:1.4:1.0. Table 1 shows that the North Arcot region has followed the all-India trend since decontrol, with a 20 per cent further shift towards nitrogen in the nutrients balance since 1991. By contrast, in the three villages, fertilizer for paddy was balanced, quite close to recommended levels and evidently not responsive to the relative prices of nutrients.

3. FERTILIZER IN THE VILLAGES

Fertilizer is applied in paddy cultivation by every paddy household at transplanting and afterwards in a series of top-dressings. In all three villages, the paddy area under fertilizer considerably exceeds that under irrigation. On the aggregate, while 57.4 per cent of the gross cropped area is irrigated, 96 per cent of it has fertilizer applied to it. All paddy producers use chemical fertilizer and 95 per cent of their plots are 'fertilized'. The situation is quite different for groundnut. While 55 per cent of the groundnut area is irrigated in the three villages, only 27 per cent of it gets chemical fertilizer. Although 72 per cent of households use fertilizer on groundnuts, only 27 per cent use *chemical* fertilizer, and this is less frequently applied on the plots of the poor than on those of the rich (19 per cent versus 56 per cent).

Fertilizer use is summarized in Table 2. Although a very small proportion of land is down to bananas and sugar cane, these crops, on average, absorb by far the highest input of fertilizer, paddy coming a poor third. Fertilizer is used more intensively on land of better quality, while it is hardly ever applied to rain-fed plots. Though the seasons are merging into one another, the sunny and hot *navarai* is the time of maximum expenditure on fertilizer. The local elite uses over 1.5 times the intensity of fertilizer compared to poor peasants. Finally, there is some marginal intervillage variation, expenditure in chemical fertilizer per cultivated hectare in Nesal and Veerasambanur being about two thirds higher than that in Vinayagapuram.

Much of the economic literature on fertilizer use works in monetary values – as we have done so far – or in unit weights of total fertilizer. The latter may not be helpful for three reasons. First, fertilizers contain different proportions of neutral filler. Second, each type contains different proportions of NPK. Third, in such studies *the role of organic manures is usually ignored*. 'Organic manure' is a blanket term for crop residues, composts, animal wastes, sludge and tank mud (see Appendix 1). A quintal of manure roughly equals 1 kg of chemical fertilizer.[28] Manure has had a chequered history and geography. Its use has declined most sharply in north-western India where agriculture has been most industrialized. Elsewhere, its use has declined relative to chemical fertilizer inputs in a way that suggests that organic and inorganic fertilizers are substitutes. They

TABLE 2 Value Rs of natural manure, commercial fertilizer and pesticides

	N	Manure		Fertilizer		Pesticides	
		Average value	Average Rs/ha	Average value	Average Rs/ha	Average value	Average Rs/ha
By village							
Veerasambanur	31	114.6	441.5	676.6	1630.1	79.8	191.4
Vinayagapuram	84	183.2	496.6	337.9	903.9	72.8	238.4
Nesal	70	178.3	223.9	1169.9	1666.6	232.2	327.4
By season							
Season 1	80	169.3	367.1	611.8	1010.3	116.9	201.4
Season 2	54	181.5	435.1	735.3	1437.9	110.9	260.6
Season 3	51	154.3	464.5	509.1	1389.1	122.8	327.6
By cluster							
Poor	51	97.3	434.9	322.9	1016.6	43.9	200.9
Middle	79	158.7	386.7	541.3	1225.1	85.4	207.5
Elite	55	286.5	439.9	1186.2	1581.2	275.8	415.3
By land type							
Nanjai	77	227.3	483.3	959.4	1729.4	170.5	320.5
Punjai w w	75	130.1	331	552.6	1207.5	113.1	284.8
Rainfed	33	131	456.7	27.5	84.2	5.9	31.2
By crop							
Paddy	107	178.9	490.5	801.8	1753.8	161.3	388.5
Groundnut	60	177.6	332.7	214.7	252.7	54.7	52.1
Sugarcane	7	91.3	117.3	1612.5	2390.2	33	55
Banana	2	–	–	2685	3310.7	–	–
Ragi	4	54.3	400.1	24.7	151.8	–	–
Cholam/GGram	1	100	125.1	–	–	300	375
Jowar	1	–	–	–	–	–	–
R.Gram	1	–	–	–	–	–	–
Casurina	2	–	–	–	–	–	–
TOTAL	185	169	413.9	622.2	1242.5	116.7	253.7

Note: Values are averages for all agricultural producers.

both certainly work within the same plant nutrient cycles, but manure has between 12 and 40 times the bulk of chemical fertilizer. Since the nitrogen content of farmyard manure is 0.5 per cent, its bulkiness makes it intensive in labour costs or labour time. According to Vaidyanathan, the increase in (implicit) labour costs of collection may have 'induced farmers to be more careful to collect dung and develop better techniques of composting to increase the nutrient content of manures. But we have little hard evidence of any of these issues'.[29] In addition to carrying nutrients, organic manure increases the water retention of the soil, provides conditions for the propagation of micro-organisms and furnishes organic acids that help to dissolve soil nutrients.

In our field research, the full range of manures was recorded in local volumetric units, which were converted first to weight equivalents and then to nutrients (see Appendix 1 for the factors used). Our data on fertilizer was detailed by type and enabled us to convert specific chemical-fertilizer brands and types into their constituent nutrients. From each and every plot, details on the use of chemical nutrients from both sources (chemical fertilizer and manures) by village, by irrigation status, by season and by socio-economic cluster are presented in Table 3. Here we see:

a) a relatively high level of nutrients application (135 kg of nutrients per acre cultivated, that is 336 kg nutrients per hectare);
b) a balance between nutrients from manures and fertilizer, the former providing as much as 45 per cent of total nutrients applied.

There is no significant variation in nutrients application between the three villages, although chemical fertilizer is more intensely adopted in Nesal and Veerasambanur than it is in Vinayagapuram. In the latter village, *natural manure counts for more than 50 per cent of total nutrients.* Twenty years earlier, it was observed by John Harriss in Nesal that a striking proportion of the expenditure

TABLE 3 Nutrients in paddy cultivation 1993–4 (av. kg/acre cultivated)

	Chemical			Organic			Total		
	N	P	K	N	P	K	N	P	K
Poor Peasants	31.08	24	18.62	23.04	13.43	26.87	54.04	37.10	45.09
Middle Peasants	30.74	21.96	18.26	21.65	12.75	25.37	52.24	34.66	43.48
Elite	32.94	23.45	28.43	21.36	12.51	25.21	54.30	36.33	53.70
Samba (1)	30.41	21.37	18.87	19.54	11.36	22.74	49.77	33.09	41.64
Navarai (2)	33.72	21.52	20.10	22.24	13.04	26.37	55.98	34.45	46.33
Sarnavari (3)	30.01	25.85	23.49	24.19	14.29	28.22	54.06	39.77	51.28
Nanjai	37.42	26.51	23.43	22.82	13.35	26.69	60.14	40.03	50.07
Punjai w w	26.03	19.83	18.79	20.70	12.18	25.26	46.63	31.74	42.78
Rainfed	12	9.33	6.67	30	17.33	36.67	42	27.33	42.67
Nesal	36.70	26.16	25.06	19.52	11.54	22.87	54.15	37.63	47.79
Vinayagapuram	26.31	19.51	17.91	26.11	15.30	30.78	52.34	34.78	48.46
Veerasambanur	42.09	28.33	22.87	12.80	7.40	14.47	54.69	35.75	37.33
ALL VILLAGES	31.37	22.91	20.82	21.98	12.89	25.77	53.26	35.77	46.41

N = Nitrogen
P = Phosphorus
K = Potassium

Source: Village data 1993–4.

of small and marginal peasants was on farmyard manure (see Table 4). He wrote that the heavy use of organic manure goes back well over a century and that, in the absence of local village-level manure, cow dung (in heavy demand for fuel), leaves, tank silt, and the folding of sheep or swine, farmers routinely purchased cartloads of organic refuse from the compost pits on the eastern edge of Arni and as far away as Vellore or Arcot.[30] What is sometimes called 'farmyard manure' is often a commercialized by-product of the urban economy (see Chapter 2–2).

Aggregating for the three villages, seasonality makes little difference to the intensity of fertilizer applications. Fertilizer use varies, instead, according to the quality of land. Chemical fertilizer is used three times as intensively on wetland as it is on rain-fed plots, while organic manure is 33 per cent higher on rain-fed land than it is on *punjai* land.

When the sample is disaggregated by agrarian class, we see that poor cultivators apply marginally lower doses of nutrients per acre than does the local elite and also that their husbandry differs. While the chemical-fertilizer applications per unit of land of poor producers are 85 per cent those of richer households, and more biased towards nitrogen, *total* fertilizer use by poor producers is 95 per cent that of rich households because of their heavier use of manures.

Comparing the total real Rs value of agrochemicals applications over the last 20 years (see Table 5), we see that fertilizer applications predated HYVs. There has been little real change in average real Rs fertilizer costs per unit area over the 13 years between 1981 and 1994, while the value of agrochemicals for pesticides

TABLE 4   Paddy production, by agrarian class, 1973–4 (Rs/acre)

	Traditional varieties		Total	High Yielding Varieties		Total
	F + AC	manure		F + AC	manure	
Capitalist farmers	112	22	134	244	11	255
Small capitalists	79	23	102	130	49	179
Marginal peasants	33	20	53	115	83	198

Source: JC Harriss 1982, table 5.3, p. 155.

Key: F + AC: Fertilizer and Agrochemicals

TABLE 5   Agrochemical uses, 1973–4 to 1993–4
HYV Paddy, Rs/ha, constant prices

	1972–3	1973–4	1981–2	1982–3	1993–4
Fertilizer	242	184	463	384	437
Pesticides	14	12	33	7	98.5

Note: The deflator is the CPIAL (see Chapter 1–1).

Sources: 1972–4, 1993–4 field survey 1981–3; Cost of cultivation of Principal Crops data, TNAU.

has greatly increased, tripling in real terms. The assumption made by policy-makers that price increases will feed their way back into increases in the unit costs of production does not operate for fertilizer.

4. THE RESPONSE OF PADDY PRODUCTION TO NUTRIENTS, ENVIRONMENTAL AND SOCIAL VARIABLES

Fertilizer is a means to an end. Its relevance lies in its impact on production. While the latter can be indicated by yield per unit cultivated, fertilizer can be described in terms of its Rs value, its total physical nutrients content, then disaggregated into chemical and organic components, and finally into individual nutrients. Following Sagar (1995), the effect of this key input can be placed in the context of other environmental, locational, price and social variables theorized as affecting productivity (see Appendix 2). Having tested for collinearity diagnostics, a stepwise regression model was run in non-linear, logarithmic form and compared with linear variables. The latter proved superior. With R-squareds varying, with one exception, between 0.82 and 0.84, the models seem reasonably well specified. Their results are given in Appendix 2, models 1 to 4.

In separate regressions, total nutrients, Rs value and total kilograms of nutrients from chemical fertilizer are significant as determinants of production, whereas organic manure is not. The chemical versions of nitrogen and potassium have a statistically significant impact on yields, while phosphorus and all forms of organic nutrients do not. Agrarian class is a significant determinant of response. Village variables are significant.[31] In Chapter 3–5 we find that the distribution of castes is likely to be the defining characteristic of significant village dummy variables. Season, price and the percentage of paddy land irrigated are not. We saw in Chapter 1–1 that paddy production with new generation HYVs is losing seasonality, so these results are consistent with a wider trend. The indifference of response to price is consistent with findings about supply response generally in Tamil Nadu and specifically in the northern region. The last result confirms the anomalous result found in the district-level analysis for the state as a whole by Srinivasan.[32] We have no explanation for it. It is *not* the case that most paddy land is irrigated and therefore that there is little variation to correlate: over 30 per cent of paddy is grown on unirrigated land.

4.1 *Nutrients balance*

Scatter plots and regression analysis showed there to be no significant relation between the ratios of chemical nitrogen to chemical phosphorus and potassium, on the one hand, and yields on the other.

4.2 *Factors affecting fertilizer use*

Potential determinants of chemical-fertilizer uptake were modelled after Sagar (1995) in the same way as yield (see Appendix 2, models 5 and 6). Models using total fertilizer quantity and value and per acre fertilizer quantity and value as dependent variables all had poor fit; season, class and price variables had persistently low significance. Models for the area of land under fertilizer and total chemical nitrogen had best explanatory power (r^2= 0.50 and 0.33 respectively). Significant village dummies once more confirm the idiosyncratic importance of locality; and irrigated land is the most significant scale variable associated with fertilizer use.

4.3 *Elasticities*

The elasticities of production with respect to plant nutrients are given in Table 6.

As expected, elasticities are highest for nitrogen. A 1 per cent increase in nitrogen elicits a 0.36 increase in production, holding other things constant. The production of poor peasants is more responsive to fertilizer than is that of elite households. The same is true but to a lesser degree with respect to the response to potassium. Production does not respond to organic manure, whose significance must be in retaining soil structure for chemical fertilizer.

5. CONCLUSIONS

Paddy yields are significantly dependent on chemical fertilizer. The nutrient composition for paddy is more balanced than that at the all-India level. It seems to be less biased towards nitrogen than is generally recommended for paddy production. This is in contrast with the local manifestation of the widely attested, price-driven All-India tilt towards urea. Even though price is far from being the sole factor determining use, we agree with Vaidyanathan that the scaling down of subsidies needs to be carefully balanced so as not to distort price incentives. Our work supports the argument that *non-price factors are important*

TABLE 6 Fertilizer nutrients elasticities–three-village pooled sub-samples–plot level

Production on:	all hh	elite hh	poor hh
Chemical Nitrogen	0.36	0.23	0.39
Chemical Phosphorus	0.07	0.12	0.04
Chemical Potassium	0.15	0.15	0.22
Nitrogen in Manure	0.004	0.007	0.004

in determining fertilizer balances. There are significant variations in nutrients use and production between agrarian classes and villages.

Plot size exerts an independent positive effect upon yields. The elasticity of production in relation to its most responsive nutrient (N) is 0.36. *The production of poor peasants is some 70 per cent more responsive to nitrogen than is that of richer households. Yet poor producers use chemical fertilizer at about two thirds the intensity of the local elites,* in stark contradistinction to what is by now the orthodoxy that they are no longer disadvantaged. Organic manure contributes as much as 46 per cent of nutrients in the paddy plots of small producers.

Even though fertilizer intensity is relatively high, yields in the three villages are low. We may be seeing the effect of the depletion of other production factors to which yields are elastic: notably micro-nutrients, soil structure, husbandry practices (which our research could not investigate) and water availability (see chapters 1–2 and 2–3). There is much potential in the recycling of urban waste, if the problem of its increasingly non-biodegradable components can be resolved. Since biofertilizer technology is still in the earliest infancy of its extension phase,[33] and although fertilizer policy focuses heavily on production, the research reported here suggests that market supply still needs to be shaped by agricultural planners if small/poor producers, remote villages and unfavourable hydrogeological endowments are to develop their higher productive response to fertilizers. A systemic and stable social and geographical targeting is still needed for this purpose. This has cost implications, not only for subsidies within the chain of fertilizer production, distribution and consumption but also for the information systems and personnel needed to reach disadvantaged producers with high potential responses. The elites show that they can take care of themselves.

ACKNOWLEDGEMENTS

With thanks to M V Srinivasan, Shukri Ahmed, Diego Colatei and Trevor Crowe for research assistance, to S Ramachandran, G Jothi and M Susai for field assistance, to S Janakarajan for direction of the fieldwork, to N Narayanan for official data and to S Panda and G Bhalla for discussants' comments at the 1996 workshop.

Appendix 1

1.1 *Units and weights*

Chemical Fertilizers Used:

50 kg bags	complex
	urea
	chloride
	ammonium
	potash
	ammonium sulphate
	mixture
	ammonium chloride
	dap

Manures Used:

cartloads	farmyard manure)	450 kg
	cow dung)	
	natural manure	200 kg
	groundnut plants	250 kg
ton	natural manure	ton = tonne
bundles	natural manure)	15–20 kg
	green manure)	
75 kg bags	oil cake	
50 kg bags	neem cake	
50 kg bags	goatskin	

1.2 *Nutrient content of common fertilizers and manures*

Fertilizer	Nutrient content (%)					Maximum retail price (Rs/t)
	N	P₂O₅	K₂O	S	Others	
Urea	46	–	–	–	–	2760
Ammonium Sulphate	21	–	–	24	–	1920
Ammonium Chloride	26	–	–	–	–	2000
Calciul Amm Nitrate	25	–	–	–	Ca	2000
Single Superphosphate	–	16	–	12	Ca 20%	decontrolled*
Potassium Chloride	–	–	60	–	Cl	–
Potassium Sulphate	–	–	50	18	–	–
Diammonium Phosphate	18	46	–	–	–	–
Urea Amm. Phosphate	28	28	–	–	–	–
Amm. Phos.Sulphate	16	20	–	15	–	–
Amm.Phos.Sulphate	20	20	–	15	–	–
Nitrophosphate	20	20	–	–	–	–
Nitrophosphate	23	23	–	–	–	–
Nitrophosphate	15	15	15	–	–	–
NPK Complex	12	32	16	–	–	–
NPK Complex	10	26	26	–	–	–
NPK Complex	17	17	17	–	–	–
NPK Complex	19	19	19	–	–	–
NPK Complex	14	35	14	–	–	–
Rock Phosphate	–	18–20	–	–	Ca	700
Gypsum (Agric Grade)	–	–	–	13	Ca 16–19%	varies
Phosphogypsum	–	–	–	16	Ca 21%	varies
Pyrites (Agric Grade)	–	–	–	22	Fe	varies
Magnesium Sulphate	–	–	–	13	MgO 16%	
Borax	–	–	–	–	B 10.5%	
Solubor	–	–	–	–	B 19%	
Copper Sulphate	–	–	–	13	Cu 24%	
Ferrous Sulphate	–	–	–	12	Fe 19%	
Chelated Iron as Fe-EDTA	–	–	–	–	Fe 12%	
Manganese Sulphate	–	–	–	15	Mn 30.5%	
Zinc Sulphate	–	–	–	1	Zn 21% or	
Chelated Zinc as Zn-	–	–	–	–	Zn 12%	
Farmyard Manure (FYM)	1	0.6	1.2			
Rural Compost	0.6	0.5	0.9			
Urban Compost	1.5	1	1.5			
Castor Cake	5.6	1.8	1			
Neem Cake	5.2	1	1.4			
Groundnut Cake	7	1.5	1.3			
Rapeseed Cake	5.1	1.8	1.1			
Dried Blood	10	1.2	0.7			
Bone meal steamed	1.5	25	–			
Sludge (activated)	58	3.2	0.6			
Night soil	13	0.9	0.4			

* Free market prices

Source: *Fertilizer Statistics*, FAI, 1993/1994; Tandon 1994.

Appendix 2

The Response of Paddy Production to Fertilizer Nutrients, Environmental, Economic and Social Variables

Fertilizer response depends on soil quality and fertility, the quantity of fertilizer applied, crop variety, seed quality, water availability and husbandry practices (particularly water, weed and pest management). Not all of these (soil fertility, seed quality, husbandry) can be easily modelled. Other factors can also be theorized as being influential in eliciting a yield response.

i) Season. Historically HYVs have required a package of assured water and sunlight in order to maximize fertilizer response, conditions best guaranteed during the minor seasons.

ii) Village. 'Villages' as a variable are a complex of physical access characteristics, rural assets structure, environmental and labour force characteristics. In this instance, physical accessibility can be expected to affect fertilizer use.

iii) Social class is another such component, indicating scale of production, access, formal education and specialized knowledge, with all of which yields are expected to relate positively.

Thus a yield function for paddy was set up as follows:

$$P_n = C\{F_t. \ P. \ I. \ S_1. \ S_2. \ V_1. \ V_2. \ C_1\}$$

where:

P_n: production per plot (kg) (YIELD)
P: price (Rs/kg) (PRICE)
I: irrigation dummy (0= not irrigated; 1=irrigated) (IRIG)
S_1: *samba* season dummy (SEASON1)
S_2: *navarai* season dummy (SEASON2)
V_1: dummy for Nesal village (VILLAGE1)

V_2: dummy for Vinayagapuram village (VILLAGE2)
C_1: dummy for agrarian class (0: poor; 1: elite) (CLUSTER)

C: constant

F_t: fertilizer.

Fertilizer in turn was modelled in four ways in separate exercises:

i) as total nutrients from all sources (NPKTOT);
ii) as two separate variables: total nutrients of fertilizer (NPKC) and of manure (NPKN);
iii) total Rs value (FERVALUE);
iv) all nutrients separately (NC,PC,KC; NN,PN,KN).

N: nitrogen; P: phosphorus; K: potassium
C: chemical; N: organic nutrients

FERTILIZER – YIELD RESPONSE

MODEL 1 Stepwise Regression of Yield on Total
Fertilizer (Total Physical Nutrients Content)
Dependent Variable = Yield

Variable	B	SE B	Sig T
Area	647	124.7	0
Price	108.8	163	0.5060
Season 1	−212.8	258.2	0.4118
Season 2	−30.8	248.9	0.9016
Village 1	1066	397.7	0.0086
Village 2	1010.8	391.7	0.0113
Cluster	611.4	219	0.0063
IRIG	25.5	229.9	0.9116
NPKTOT	10.6	1.2	0
(Constant)	−1439.2	722	0.0490

$r^2 = 0.29$

MODEL 2 Stepwise Regression of Yield on
Chemical (NPKC) and Organic (NPKN) Fertilizer

Variable	B	SE B	Sig T
Area	337.3	114.4	0.0040
Price	59.6	136.6	0.6632
Season 1	−120.5	216.4	0.5789
Season 2	60.8	208.6	0.7713
Village 1	450.1	345.5	0.1957
Village 2	258.2	347	0.4585
Cluster	348.1	187.5	0.0663
IRIG	−221.5	195.9	0.2609
NPKC	16.1	1.3	0
NPKN	1.7	1.7	0.3195
(Constant)	−371.2	625.2	0.5540

$r^2 = 0.84$

MODEL 3 Stepwise Regression of Yield on Total Rs
Value of Fertilizer

Variable	B	SE B	Sig T
Area	290.4	133.3	0.0318
Price	4	146.1	0.9780
NMVLU	0.7	0.3	0.0485
Fer Value	1.2	0.1	0
Season 1	−238.5	229.9	0.3021
Season 2	55.0	220.5	0.8033
Village 1	823.5	358.1	0.0236
Village 2	249.9	398.1	0.5315
Cluster	159.4	208.6	0.4466
IRIG	−230.9	205.6	0.2641
(Constant)	−107.5	696.5	0.8776

$r^2 = 0.82$

MODEL 4 Stepwise Regression on Individual Nutrients

Variable	B	SE B	Sig T
Area	350.5	114.3	0.0028
Price	75.7	134.2	0.5743
Season 1	−93.0	215.2	0.663
Season 2	44.1	205.1	0.8302
Village 1	492.3	341.1	0.1522
Village 2	187.9	349.5	0.5921
Cluster	357.4	184.2	0.0553
IRIG	−242.9	192.6	0.2103
KC	21.65	3.9	0
NC	16.02	3.4	0
PC	6.97	5.8	0.2337
PN	11.53	20.7	0.5799
(Constant)	−298.7	622.8	0.6326

$r^2 = 0.84$

MODEL 5 Factors Conditioning Fertilizer Use
Dependent variable: FERTAREA (area of land under chemical fertilizer)

Variable	B	SE B	Sig T
Village 1	−1.1	0.28	0
Village 2	−1.4	0.28	0
Season 1	0.2	0.23	0.31
Season 2	0.3	0.22	0.17
Price	0	0.14	0.64
Cluster	−0.07	0.19	0.70
IRIG	−0.36	0.22	0.09
(Constant)	2.01	0.59	0

$r^2 = 0.50$

MODEL 6 Factors Affecting Nitrogen Use

Variable	B	SE B	Sig T
Village 1	52.8	14.7	0
Village 2	23.1	14.8	0.12
Season 1	20.1	12.2	0.10
Season 2	16.4	11.5	0.15
Price	6.2	7.6	0.41
Farm Size	7.3	2.0	0
Cluster	7.6	10.3	0.46
IRIG	−14.7	11.6	0.20
(Constant)	−28.4	31.5	0.36

$r^2 = 0.32$

PART THREE

Social Welfare in the Villages

Introduction:
Village Studies and Welfare

I N Part 3 we turn to welfare. As with agriculture the agenda is complex, involving many departments of government, international, national and local politics. As with agriculture the real resources it receives shrank during the 1990s. The first three chapters do not follow the pattern of Part 2, in which policy agendas are compared with the experience of access. Instead, Chapter 3–2 is addressed to procedural aspects of policy while chapters 3–3 and 3–4 explore welfare issues which arose unexpectedly out of fieldwork, issues which are at the very foot of the policy agenda.

Chapter 3–2 is a critique of the concept of targeting, which has been built into agricultural planning ever since the Intensive Agricultural District Programme of the early 1960s and was revived in the 1990s as a response to debt-induced pressures to trim public expenditure. Targeting requires the labelling and identification of the poor (and hence of poverty lines). In this chapter the practical identification of poor households is investigated. A parsimonious set of predictors of poverty is developed using a new technique adapted from machine learning. Simulating the plight of an official responsible for targeting without inside knowledge or trust, another set of 'unfudgeable' poverty indicators is determined. With this technique, households plausibly exaggerating their income poverty to qualify as eligible can be identified.

Chapters 3–3 and 3–4 expose two development problems that are seriously neglected in development policy. The consequences of this neglect are examined and some policy instruments are justified. One of these problems is the growing differential in female life chances that accompanies the accumulation of property – even on a micro-scale (see Chapter 3–3). This is the only respect in which increasing wealth is associated with increasing deprivation in the villages we studied, but, by any definition of development, it is a very serious contradiction. The local state's policies on abandoned female babies and on incentives such as subsidies to poor parents of girl children confront social forces which are more powerful than the state. A state which cannot regulate ultrasound clinics (the 'market for sex-selective abortion') certainly cannot regulate neglectful post-natal health care, which was the means of culling girls in these villages. The second problem is the differentiating impact of preventable adult disability and incapacity in a society that depends on hard physical labour (see Chapter 3–4). The exclusion which results from the state's exiguous expenditure, and from a restrictive categorization of eligibility (derived from medical classifications of disability), is contrasted with the alternative of providing simple technical equipment, small loans for crises and mediated access to social security benefits that would help incapacitated people to be active in ways they themselves wish. The objectives of the disability movement involve goals of 'empowerment' and/or 'rehabilitation' that are at variance with the expressed needs of disabled, rural, labouring people.

The remaining chapters follow the method established in Part 2. In Chapter 3–5, the forces which have challenged the high priority given to food and nutrition in all aspects of the policy process are deconstructed and the role of public food provision in nutrition, the pattern of resource allocation and public access to the public distribution system and to the nutritious meal scheme are investigated. Despite leakages, these policies have allocated and redistributed resources in a way that is progressive if judged in terms of access for poor labouring households (though we have to note forms of access biased against girls where there was no bias ten years previously). New changes to the rules of access, in which the poor are first 'targeted' and then prevented from accessing affordable consignments, appear to be a deliberate political attempt to destroy the public distribution system and deny food security to the poor. The experience in implementing policy by state employees in Fair Price Shops and the noon meal scheme revealed something of the informal procedures through which grain and rents are reallocated within the bureaucratic system. We also explored another neglected development problem – policy on alcohol. This lies squarely outside the set of policies labelled 'nutritional' but has such a retrogressive impact on the poverty and nutrition of the most deprived households so significant that in 7 per cent of households the net outflow in tax on alcohol alone exceeded the inflow in food subsidies.

Whereas most social-sector policy is not coercive, education in most countries of the world is compulsory. Chapter 3–6 reveals India's exceptionalism in this regard. Education policy is non-mandatory and education is heavily 'supply-constrained' in terms of resources. State education reveals a state of last resort. Access is intensely structured by caste, class, village and gender. The policy *not* to educate the children of low-caste, poor, landless citizens is faithfully implemented in our villages. In the absence of procedural coercion, state incentives can only operate by lowering the direct costs of supposedly free public education and by policies which have an impact on 'demand' for education outside the education 'sector'. The most notable of these is the banning of child labour. But India had already 'structurally adjusted' her education policy long before the reforms and clearly has no intention of producing an educated workforce, apart from an educated elite (a significant proportion of which is now provided as a grant-in-aid to the rest of the world).

The fact that there is substantial room for manoeuvre in policy – even in an era when the state is under extreme pressure to deregulate, cut subsidies for production and trim expenditure on redistributive activity – is evident from social security policy (see Chapter 3–7). Calling the bluff of those who argue that, since social security is a luxury, all redistributive policy needs relabelling as social security, Tamil Nadu has implemented a skeletal security policy and even successfully exported its agenda and procedure to the central state. Access to social security makes for harrowing reading, shedding light on the way very poor, often elderly people are systematically excluded from the patronage networks mediating access to the state and on those whose access depends on bribes worth many multiples of their monthly benefit. At the same time, the harsh official procedure restricting eligibility has been informalized. While aid agencies have 'mainstreamed' gender, have 'labelled' women as poor and publicized the poverty of female-headed households, the most abject poverty is actually to be found in single-person households, the incidence of which is increasing.

It is very hard to detect what is *not* included in development policy for agriculture and social welfare. The lowest priority on the liberalization agenda is assigned – in the sector of production – to sanitation and drinking water infrastructure, organic fertilizer, credit for land purchase by landless producers and wage protection. The social welfare sector is lower in the ranking of policy priorities than is agricultural production. Ranked low in the scheme of priorities of the social sector are incapacity and disability, the devastation of alcohol, the life chances of girls, child labour and single-person households. These exclusions are not to be regarded as a complete list, since the means whereby they came to be noticed were not systematic. However, the policy sectors of least importance involve physical dirt, manual labour, ritual pollution, youth, old age and gender subordination. Quite how liberalization might do anything but intensify these neglects is not at all apparent.

Antipoverty Policy: Targeting and Screening for Eligibility

Ruhi Saith and Barbara Harriss-White

1. INTRODUCTION

In this chapter, we investigate a method of aiding and refining the criteria commonly used as part of antipoverty policy to target state transfers in India. In the 1990s, given the conditions of stabilization and structural adjustment, including stagnation in public expenditure on the social sector, targeting was stressed as the policy instrument which could ensure that the poorest, who are known to depend most on the state, were not the worst-hit.

Antipoverty policy (APP) in India has had close relationships on the one hand to research and on the other to surpluses of grain resulting from the 'green revolution', price stabilization and grain procurement policy. It has also been shaped by the urgency of electoral politics.

The first generation of research focused on the poverty line, on the number of poor people and their regional distribution and trends. It informed policy on public works and employment. The second phase of research drew attention to the persistence of poverty in regions of relatively advanced agriculture, and therefore to the social relations of work and the way poverty shaped other aspects of deprivation. It justified a basic-needs approach to redistribution. The third kind of research evaluated the raft of policies set up to address all the dimensions of backwardness which had been retrospectively labelled 'antipoverty policy'. The fourth has branched off in a number of directions exploring the complexity of poverty,[1] its implications for agency[2] and has experimented with participation and action research.[3]

APP in India has, however, also had a history unrelated to research, starting with positive discrimination for 'backward classes' (scheduled castes and tribes).

APP emerged as a label at the end of the 1960s when the capacity of growth to deal with poverty started to be doubted by the political elites. Indira Gandhi's Congress nationalized banks in 1969 and made the first attempts at targeted redistribution along the lines of basic needs. The needs in question were drinking water, education, health and sanitation. They were later transformed into a minimum-needs programme backed up by the public distribution system of food and basic wage goods and a host of nutrition and health interventions. At the same time, public resources were ploughed into production schemes for small and marginal farmers and later elaborated for hostile and backward agro-ecological regions (rain-fed agriculture, drought-prone areas, deserts etc.). The large buffer stocks resulting from the green revolution and from price support policies also made food for work schemes possible.

In the 1970s, APP was consolidated with the integrated rural development programme (credit for assets to selected households below the poverty line) and a national rural employment programme. At its apogee in the late 1980s, nearly 40 per cent of public sector plan outlays were in one way or another for APP.[4] Poor people have been targeted in elaborate ways: by region, holding size and type, by occupational status, caste, gender, sex, age, by physiological status and by income.

In the 1990s, given the pressure to reduce public expenditure, welfare transfer policy instruments refocused on targeting as though it were a novel procedure, in order to ensure the existence of a safety net for the poorest. The standard dimensions of poverty used in India for targeting are monetary, with households below a predefined income poverty line being considered eligible for a variety of social transfers.[5]

Values for private income (the monetary variable used in the analysis presented in this chapter[6]) may, however, often be under- or overstated by the respondent. Even if income were to be stated correctly and measured accurately for the year in question, households may well have moved in or out of poverty on a temporary basis.[7] When such information is used for purposes of targeting benefits, it can result in a certain proportion of quite poor households being classified as ineligible for benefits based on their declared income (this is the type I error or F mistake – i.e. the failure to cover all the target group[8]). On the other hand, a certain proportion of non-chronically poor households may be classified as being eligible for benefits based on their declared income (the type II error or E mistake – i.e. excessive coverage with interventions going outside the target group). Existing targeting criteria need refining to take such factors into account.

We attempt this using a multivariate method of analysis. Recently, some 'poverty status' analyses have begun to use a multivariate probit or logit framework. A dichotomous poverty variable is regressed on independent variables (such as region, household size and composition and assets ownership) and the relationship between a large number of household variables and income is expressed as a mathematical equation.[9] In this chapter, we use the technique of 'class probability trees' analysis (CPTA) to explore such relationships. This works by analysing data related to different classes of a poverty variable (e.g. 'above' and 'below' a poverty line, although more than two categories can be included). The pattern of variables characterizing each class is discovered. Complex interactions, including non-linear relationships between variables, are automatically taken into account and results are expressed as rules that are easy to understand and apply. We use the method to identify the pattern of features that characterizes and discriminates households with incomes declared as being 'above' and those declared as being 'below' the poverty line. The characteristic pattern can then be used to increase the reliability of private income as an indicator for targeting benefits.

Although the study focuses on exploring the relationship between income and a range of other variables, it does not follow that we accept income as the sole appropriate dimension that comprises poverty.[10] Rather, we use the available income-based data to introduce and explore the potential of a new method of analysis of screening criteria, a method which may find application in a range of other multidimensional policy-oriented poverty studies as well. This chapter is thus more a study of technique than of poverty. Our focus is on demonstrating the potential of the CPTA method. The results obtained are discussed for the general insights that the use of this methodology is able to provide and for its suitability for policy implementation, given the ease of interpretation of the results, rather than with a view to making specific policy prescriptions.

2. CLASS PROBABILITY TREES AND RULES

The CPTA method is a tool of multivariate analysis in which a large number of features can be analysed simultaneously. It is capable of capturing linear as well as non-linear relationships between features. Very importantly, results are expressed as rules and are easier to understand and apply than mathematical equations.

Tree techniques have earlier been explored successfully in such diverse analyses as guiding the landing of the Space Shuttle,[11] evaluating the credit-worthiness of clients applying for a credit card,[12] location of primary tumours[13] and guiding the selection of embryos in *in vitro* fertilization treatment.[14] It works by analysing data related to a sufficient number of cases. The cases belong to different classes or groups and the pattern of variables characterizing each class is discovered.[15] See the Appendix for a hypothetical example and details of tree and rule construction.

3. DATA

3.1 *Source of data*

The data used for this study are a subset of the 11-village census of 1993–4. Data for 2,057 households in 8 villages (Vegamangalam, Sirungathur, Duli, Vengodu, Vayalur, Meppathurai, Amudhur and Kalpattu) have been used. A pilot study investigating the feasibility of application of the class probability tree method for poverty analysis had been conducted earlier, on data for the three other villages of Nesal, Vinayagapuram and Veerasambanur.[16]

Data contained in this village census database are voluminous as the variables included were not selected with any one specific focus, being elements brought forward from the two previous rounds of village surveys. Variables were first selected for the 1972 census in these villages to give the best possible economic and social characterization of agrarian households.[17] The list of variables included in the census was modified ten years later to cope with the growing importance of the non-farm economy.[18] Other additions to the recent census in the 1990s included data related to social welfare, access to a range of state interventions, gender and water management.

This type of database typifies those of long-term village studies where the objects of research have had both a core of continuity and a periphery which has evolved over time.[19] The use of such a database to focus on poverty and to examine relationships between income and other variables characterizing households has the distinct advantage over previous studies of the incorporation of a large number of variables which have not been preselected.

3.2 *Variables*

The census data for the eight villages contains variables collected under ten different headings as shown in Table 1. A number of variables from under the different headings given in Table 1 were included in the analysis. These amounted to a total of 478 variables, relating to 2,057 cases.[20]

3.3 *Method of analysis*

The tree program See5 was executed under the Microsoft Windows 95 operating system. As with most tree-based analyses, it is capable of analysing data related to a large number of cases and including a large number of variables.[21]

Each household was classified as belonging either to the class of 'Income Poor' or to that of 'Income Non-poor' using a poverty line defined by the Government

TABLE 1 Groups of variables describing each household

No.	Group
1	Demographic and Occupational profile
2	Migration details
3	Housing condition
4	Welfare (education and reproductive health)
5	Land holding status
6	Cropping pattern, 1993
7	Agricultural assets
8	Irrigation status
9	Non-agricultural assets
10	Liabilities

of India.[22] A household was classified as 'Income Poor' if its per capita income per month was below the poverty line (defined at Rs 195.31) and classified as 'Income Non-poor' if the income was greater than or equal to this amount. Roughly half (1,033 households) were 'Income Poor' and the remaining half (1,024) 'Income Non-poor'. Class probability tree analysis was used to obtain rules giving the variables characterizing 'Income Poor' and 'Income Non-poor' classes.

3.3.1 *Training and test sets*
The data were split randomly into two groups. One group consisted of 1,500 cases (i.e. the 'training set') and the other (the remaining 557) comprised the 'test set'.[23] The training set is the sample from which sets of outcome-predicting rules are constructed. The test set is used to test these rules to see how well they predict the 'Income Poor'/'Income Non-poor' outcomes of a new set of cases. This is standard practice, adopted to evaluate the usefulness of such techniques.[24]

3.3.2 *Error rate of rules obtained*
The performance of a given set of rules derived from a class probability tree when classifying N cases can be summarized by a two by two table. This is shown in Table 2, together with the meanings of the entries. The entries have been labelled taking into account the context of our study in which the data simulate the scenario of a targeted antipoverty scheme. Such a scheme would involve 'beneficiaries' and 'non-beneficiaries' of benefits based on income that has been declared as being below or above the income poverty line – the former being labelled class 'Income Poor' and the latter class 'Income Non-poor'.

The declared class is the class to which a case belongs, i.e. the class assigned based on the income declared by the household. The predicted class is the class

TABLE 2 2×2 table

		Predicted Class		
		Income Poor	Income Non-poor	
Declared Class	Income Poor	CB	UB	N_1
	Income Non-poor	UN	CN	N_2
		N_3	N_4	N

CB = Corroborated Beneficiaries
UB = Uncorroborated Beneficiaries
UN = Uncorroborated Non-beneficiaries
CN = Corroborated Non-beneficiaries

assigned to a case by the program See5 based on the rule (i.e. the pattern of variables) it satisfies. Corroborated beneficiaries (CB) are the number of cases that declared themselves as having an income below the poverty line, i.e. being 'Income-Poor', and are assigned (i.e. predicted or classified by the rules) as such. Uncorroborated non-beneficiaries (UN) are the number of cases that declared themselves as having an income above the poverty line, i.e. 'Income Non-poor', that are classified by the rules as 'Income-Poor'. The pattern of variables characterizing these households thus resembles that of 'Income-Poor', although they have declared themselves as belonging to the 'Income Non-poor' class. Corroborated non-beneficiaries (CN) are the number of 'Income Non-poor' cases correctly classified as such. Uncorroborated beneficiaries (UB) are the number of self-declared 'Income-Poor' cases classified here as 'Income Non-poor'. The pattern of variables characterizing these households thus resembles that of 'Income Non-poor' although they have declared themselves as belonging to the 'Income-Poor' class.

N_1 (CB+UB) is the total number of cases that belong to the 'Income-Poor' class, i.e. those households that have declared their income as being below the poverty line. N_2 (UN+CN) is the number of cases that belong to the 'Income Non-poor' class, i.e. income declared as above the poverty line. N_3 (CB+UN) is the total number of cases classified by the rule set as 'Income-Poor' and N_4 (UB+CN) as 'Income Non-poor'. N gives the total number of cases in the training set. The error rate of the rules is then estimated by the fraction of cases incorrectly classified, that is (UB+UN)/N. This error can be compared with the error made by a very simple classifier which would predict that every new case would belong to the most common class in the training data. In this way, the rules' capacities to classify can be evaluated. Our training data of 1,500 cases had approximately 744 'Income-Poor' households and 756 'Income Non-poor' households. A majority classifier would thus classify any new case as 'Income Non-poor', i.e. as belonging to the most common class. Thus for the test set, which has 557 cases with 289 'Income-Poor' and 268 'Income Non-poor', the majority classifier would classify all cases as 'Income Non-poor'. 289 of these are however 'Income-Poor'. The predictive error rate of the classifier would thus be 52 per cent. The pattern of rules constructed by See5 would thus be judged by comparing their predictive error rate against the majority classifier error rate of 52 per cent.

3.3.3 *Tree and rule construction*
The data for the training set of 1,500 households with 744 belonging to the 'Income-Poor' class and 756 to the 'Income Non-poor' class were analysed using See5. The rules were obtained by analysing data related to 478 variables at default See5 settings.[25] Details of the tree construction process and that of converting the trees to rules (which indicate the variables characterizing and discriminating 'Income-Poor' households from 'Income Non-poor' households) are given by Quinlan (1993).

4. RESULTS AND THEIR INTERPRETATION

The results are presented in the following sequence. The predictive accuracy of the rule set obtained at default settings is estimated by a 'leave 10 out' cross-validation.[26] The 2 × 2 table representing this performance is given first (see Table 3). This is followed by a 2 × 2 table (see Table 4) representing the performance of the rule set on the test set of 557 households.[27]

The estimated predictive error at 24 per cent is significantly lower than that of the majority classifier error rate (52 per cent). The results also indicate that of the 744 households that declared their income as 'Income-Poor', 586 (79 per cent) are classified by the rules as 'Income-Poor'. This suggests that the pattern of variables characterizing these households is consistent with this low income. The remaining 158 (21 per cent) households, however, are classified by the rules as 'Income Non-poor'. The pattern of variables characterizing these households is more similar to the households which declared their income above the poverty line. Similarly, 73 per cent of the households of declared 'Income Non-poor' households are found to have a variable pattern consistent with their income, while 27 per cent are more similar to households that declared their income as being below the income poverty line.

These results are confirmed by using the previous rules to classify the remaining test data in which the corresponding results are 78 per cent for the

TABLE 3 'Leave 10 out' cross-validation 2 × 2 table on training set

		Predicted class		
		Income-Poor	Income Non-poor	
	Income-Poor	586	158	744
Declared Class				
	Income Non-poor	202	554	756
		788	712	1500

Notes:

Estimated predictive error of the rule set = (158 + 202)/1500 + 24%

The proportion of households declaring income so as to belong to class 'Income-Poor' and classified 'Income-Poor' i.e. Corroborated beneficiaries (CB) = 586/744 = 79%

The proportion declaring income so as to belong to class 'Income-Poor' and classified 'Income Non-poor' i.e. Uncorroborated beneficiaries (UB) = 158/744 = 21%

The proportion of households declaring income so as to belong to class 'Income Non-poor' and classified 'Income Poor' i.e. Uncorroborated Non-beneficiaries (UN) = 202/756 = 27%

The proportion declaring income so as to belong to class 'Income Non-poor' and classified 'Income Non-poor' i.e. Corroborated Non-beneficiaries (CN) = 554/756 = 73%

TABLE 4   2 × 2 table obtained on the test set

		Predicted Class		
		Income-Poor	Income Non-poor	
	Income-Poor	225	64	289
Declared Class				
	Income Non-poor	71	197	268
		296	261	557

Notes:

Estimated predictive error = (64 + 71)/557 + 24%

The proportion of households declaring income so as to belong to class 'Income-Poor' and classified 'Income-poor' = (CB) = 225/289 = 78%

The proportion declaring income so as to belong to class 'Income-poor' and classified 'Income Non-Poor' = (UB) = 64/289 = 22%

The proportion of households declaring income so as to belong to class 'Income Non-poor' and classified 'Income-Poor' = (UN) = 71/268 = 27%

The proportion declaring income so as to belong to class 'Income Non-poor' and classified 'Income Non-poor' = (CN) = 197/268 = 73%

corroborated beneficiaries, 22 per cent for the uncorroborated beneficiaries and 73 per cent for the corroborated non-beneficiaries and 27 per cent for the uncorroborated non-beneficiaries (Table 4).

The rule set characterizing 'Income-Poor' and 'Income Non-poor' households suggests that, of the 478 variables analysed, about 40 variables have a close relationship with the income of the household. As an illustration, 2 of the most reliable of the 26 rules are presented here.[28]

'Income-Poor' rule:
    If
        at least one (or more) female members is currently an agricultural labourer,
        the value of total land leased out is less than or equal to Rs 25,000,
        the gross overall production of all crops is less than or equal to 1.8 metric
            tonnes and
        the total amount of chit fund loans subscribed to is less than or equal to Rs
            15,000
    Then
        the probability of being 'Income-Poor' is 77 per cent and 'Income Non-poor'
            is 23 per cent.
        Class prediction is taken as *'Income-Poor'.*[29]

'Income non-poor' rule:
    If
        at most two male members are dependant,
        no male member is currently an agricultural labourer and
        the gross overall production of all crops is greater than 1.8 metric tonnes
    Then
        the probability of being 'Income Non-poor' is 94 per cent and 'Income Poor'
            is 6 per cent.
        Class prediction is taken as *'Income Non-poor'.*

These two rules demonstrate the manner in which the results of class probability tree analysis are expressed. The predictors identified show that, in rural households, poverty is still largely defined by reference to agriculture. 'Income-Poor' households include those with *female agricultural labourers, low value of total land leased out, low output of crops and a low amount of chit fund the household subscribes to.* This is supported by the cluster analysis of census data for the same period for three other villages in the region, showing the 'elite' cluster in all three villages to own, as well as operate, an average of at least six times more land than the 'peasant' cluster (see Chapter 1–4). The condition related to *leasing out land* (the value of total land leased out being equal to or under Rs 25,000) appears counterintuitive, as there is little tenancy at all in this region. Besides, it would be expected that most income-poor households would not own any land, let alone be capable of leasing out land. However, 'Income-Poor' households leasing out small amounts (up to a value of at most Rs 25,000) may be explained by 'reverse tenancy'. This is a contract where households with incapacitated members or small, dependent households (often with elderly women) are forced to lease out their land to others, usually more able-bodied. Janakarajan (see Chapter 1–2) discusses the impact of the changing irrigation scenario on land lease in the region. Lessors are found to be poor farm households who do not own wells or whose wells have dried up and who are forced by circumstances to lease out their own land to adjacent better-off well owners. The cluster analysis shows no land as being leased out by the 'elite' cluster for two of the villages, but average amounts of just 0.03 and 0.06 acres as leased out by the 'peasant' clusters. (In the third village, however, the average amount of land leased out by the 'elite' cluster [0.22 acre] is about twice that leased out by the 'peasant' cluster [0.13 acre].) The *chit fund* mentioned in the last condition (the total amount of chit fund share being equal to or under Rs 15,000) also needs some explanation. This is a rotating savings and credit association (ROSCA), common in the urban and rural informal finance sectors (see Chapter 2–4).[30] Although participation in chit funds is widespread, they are particularly common among the poor owing to their low transaction costs, which increase their accessibility.[31] At first glance, the limit of the chit fund identified in the rule as Rs 15,000 looks high for 'Income-Poor' households (being above the annual income at the poverty line of an average household of 4.5 members). But the condition also includes households which are not members of a chit fund. Of the 2,064 households in the data, only 259 households (13 per cent) participated in a chit fund. Of these, more than half had a total chit of less than Rs 15,000. About 60 per cent of households in this subgroup had a total chit fund amounting to less than Rs 5,000. About two thirds of this group with small-sized chits had the payment spread out over 20 or more instalments either seasonally or monthly (amounting to Rs 250 or less per month). When viewed in terms of instalments, therefore, it is entirely plausible for 'Income-Poor' households to be characterized either by non-participation in ROSCAs or by participation in ROSCAs with small funds spread out over many instalments.

The rule predicting cases as 'Income Non-poor' indicates the commonest combination of features found characterizing 'Income Non-poor' households. If a household has able-bodied and active workers with *two or fewer male dependent members* (i.e. aged either less than 15 or more than 64 years), with *none* of the males in the household being employed as *agricultural labourers*, and is landed with a *gross crop output* of at least 1.8 tonnes (or more), there is a high probability that the household has a declared income above the poverty line. These findings are also supported by the cluster analysis mentioned above (see Chapter 1–4), where the dependency ratio was found to be consistently higher for the 'peasant' group compared to the 'elite' in all three villages.[32] Further, 'Income Non-poor' households usually have a source of earned income (such as from wage work in the non-farm economy) other than from agricultural labour.[33] Normally, they also have higher gross agricultural production than 'Income-Poor' households.[34]

We will not go further into the relationships identified between income and other variables in the entire rule set comprising 26 rules, preferring to focus on the general pointers that can be obtained from results presented in this manner, irrespective of the specific variables used in the particular analysis. As the results presented in tables 3 and 4 indicate, such an analysis would be useful to identify households whose declared income results in suboptimal inclusion or exclusion with regard to the receipt of state welfare benefits. In the data analysed here, about 21 to 22 per cent of households fall in the box UB – those cases that declare income so as to belong to the 'Income-Poor' class but are predicted as 'Income Non-poor', i.e. show a pattern of variables similar to 'Income Non-poor' households. Similarly, about 27 per cent of cases fall in the box UN, i.e. declare income so as to belong to the 'Income Non-poor' class but are predicted as 'Income-Poor'. The possible reasons for the lack of corroboration of the declared incomes of almost a quarter to a fifth of cases are as follows:

1 . *Income distortion or mis-estimation or temporary alteration:*
   Some households might have deliberately declared their income as being much higher or lower than it is in reality, thus reducing the accuracy of predictions possible. It is also possible that the income may have been underestimated or overestimated by mistake, rather than deliberately. An example of the former is when any costly event such as medical treatment or ritual expenses is netted out of statements of income by a respondent. Further, evidence is emerging from panel studies that most houses move in and out of poverty (eg. Hyat's finding [2001], with the use of panel data for rural Pakistan, that nearly 80 per cent of households have moved in and out of poverty over a period of ten years). It is possible therefore that some of the households may have been going through temporary upward or downward mobility during the year for which the data was collected.
   A frequency distribution of our data does reveal that there is a slightly higher than expected frequency of individuals with incomes declared as being below the poverty line in an interval close to the poverty line.

2. *Mistakes:*
   There might be mistakes made in the entry of data, e.g., although the income

may have been declared by the household such that it belongs to the 'Income Non-poor' class, the house was wrongly classified as 'Income-Poor' or vice versa.

3. *Limits to predictability:*
The census data used in this study may not include all the appropriate variables. If some of the missing variables had been included in the census, it is possible that other patterns of variables characterizing households with an income below or above the poverty line would have been identified, resulting in their classification as such by the rules. Further, given the particular variables included in the analysis here, there may be certain limits to prediction as some of the variables themselves may be difficult to estimate and prone to errors. It is an entirely different point, confirmed with panel data for rural Pakistan by Hyat (2001) that returns to assets may be stochastic or heterogenous, implying that average relationships by themselves will be inadequate as predictors of income. Yet average relationships are all that the vast majority of surveys on poverty have generated. It is also possible that See5 is not capable of capturing all possible patterns that characterize the households belonging to the declared classes. Some outliers might thus have been left out and are classified as belonging to a class different to that declared by them.

Using the CPTA technique, it is not possible to distinguish between cases belonging to the three categories above. What can be concluded is that all cases that fall in the cell UB (i.e. cases that declare income so as to belong to the 'Income-Poor' class but are predicted as 'Income Non-poor') and vice versa (i.e. cases falling in the cell UN) would be worthy of further investigation to try and identify those that are eligible for any transfers.

5. FURTHER ANALYSIS

The extent to which the technique could be applied usefully would depend on the use of features that are easy to collect. We therefore repeated the analysis, restricting the variables included to 75 accessible variables identified from among the 478 variables included in the initial analysis. These 'easily accessible' or 'non-fudgeable' variables cover physical assets, caste status, demographic data and data on health, all variables which are most straightforwardly and visibly verifiable by an outsider.

When the analysis is restricted to the 'easily accessible' variables, the rule set obtained characterizing 'Income-Poor' and 'Income Non-poor' households suggests that, of the 75 variables analysed, about 36 have a close relationship with the income of the household. Two of the rules from the rule set obtained by the analysis of 'easily accessible' variables for the training data are presented illustratively here:[35]

'Income-Poor' rule:

> If
>> the household belongs to a scheduled caste,
>> the dependency ratio (dependants/working population) is greater than 0.6,
>> the estimated monetary value of electrical pump sets owned is at most Rs 6,668,
>> the estimated monetary value of oil engines owned is at most Rs 3,333,
>> the value of agricultural implements owned is at most Rs 350,
>> the estimated monetary value of buildings owned in the village is at most Rs 35,000 and the estimated monetary value of business assets owned in the village is at most Rs 1,000,
> Then
>> the probability of being 'Income-Poor' is 88 per cent and 'Income Non-poor' is 12 per cent.
>> *Class* prediction is taken as '*Income-Poor*'.

'Income non-poor' rule:

> If
>> the head of the household is male,
>> the number of female members in the working age group (aged between 15 and 64 years) is at most one,
>> and the dependency ratio (dependants/working population) is at most 0.6,
> Then
>> the probability of being Income Non-poor is 70 per cent and Income-Poor is 30 per cent.
>> *Class* prediction is taken as '*Income Non-poor*'.

We do not discuss the rules in detail but indicate below the main features identified in the full rule set as characterizing and discriminating 'Income Non-poor' and 'Income-Poor' households. Let us recall that these rules have been obtained by restricting the analysis to 75 'non fudgeable' variables. The rules presented earlier were obtained by analysis of the entire range of 478 variables.

5.1 *Caste status*

In the villages included here, households belonging to scheduled castes usually live in separate hamlets and are thus easily identified. Being scheduled caste is closely related to income poverty. The finding is supported by the cluster analysis of census data for the same period for the three other villages in the region, which shows that most (more than 80 per cent) scheduled-caste households belonged to the 'landless peasant cluster' (see Chapter 1–4 here). Further, there is also much evidence from other research in India confirming the high probability of income poverty among scheduled castes and tribes.[36]

5.2 *Gender of head of household*

The gender of the household head was found in our study to be an important discriminatory feature for 'Income-Poor' and 'Income Non-poor' households. Further, in Chapter 1–4 here it is shown that, although exceptions existed, female-headed households were most likely to be in the lower half of the asset distribution.[37] Households composed solely of female members were always found to belong to the poorest cluster. The relationship between the gender of the household head and monetary poverty is also well attested in the literature.[38]

5.3 *Demographic variables*

These include the type of family (nuclear or joint) and the gender and age distribution of household members, as having a close relationship with the income poverty status of the household.

5.4 *Illness*

The number of male and/or female members that are ill, handicapped or otherwise incapacitated from work matters in determining the 'Income-Poor' or 'Income Non-poor' status, a result confirmed both in National Sample Surveys[39] and in the study of disability here (Chapter 3–4).

5.5 *Assets*

Physical assets identified as being useful in discriminating between the 'Income Poor' and those who may in reality belong to the 'Income Non-poor' group are the possession of very low-value electrical pump sets, agricultural implements and oil engines. Low-value buildings and business assets possessed inside the village (so easily verifiable by observation) were also identified as important factors characterizing poor households.

5.6 *Variables describing the dwelling*

These include the material used for the construction of the floor, roof and walls of the dwelling, absence of an electricity connection, the kind of fuel used for cooking, the number of families occupying a single house and the village the family lives in. A similar use of the dwelling to identify those in most need of assistance has more recently been explored by Bliven and others, who find that the poorest families in North Arcot District were most likely to be residing in temporary shacks. Glaring differences in the kind of housing and electricity provision between the caste village and the Harijan (scheduled-caste) colony in Iruvelpattu village in South Arcot District, Tamil Nadu, were also reported by Guhan and Mencher.[40]

Given the relative ease of collection of information for the variables identified in the rule sets, results of such a nature are likely to be more practically useful for the identification and further investigation of households that may have been suboptimally included or excluded from benefits. Further, the accuracy of the results obtained by restricting the analysis to 75 'easily accessible' variables as determined by cross-validation, as well as testing on the 'test' set, were found to be largely similar to that of the previously discussed rule set that was obtained by an inclusion of all 478 variables in the analysis.

6. CONTRIBUTIONS AND SHORTCOMINGS

We have applied a method of multivariate analysis which takes into account non-linear relationships and the results of which are expressed as easily understandable rules. The CPTA method may be useful for the identification of households or individuals that have been wrongly included or excluded from the target group. Further, the easily interpretable rules by which the results are presented make the CPTA method particularly useful for field officials involved in the implementation of antipoverty policy and social transfers.

If the results of this kind of analysis are to be practically useful, however, it is essential that the variables used are reliable and easily accessible. Ideally, the rule set that helps identify the UB and UN as worthy of further investigation ought to be small, comprising just two to three rules and including as few variables as possible. The analysis thus needs to be refined towards developing simpler rules. Minimizing inclusion in the analysis of data related to households that deliberately or mistakenly under- or overestimate their monetary income, or temporarily have moved in or out of poverty, ought to contribute towards such refinement. This is possible by excluding from the analysis the grey zone of cases around the income poverty line, where it would be expected most such mistakes were likely to occur. If the data were restricted to households with incomes some distance away from the poverty line, then more accurate and tighter patterns of 'Income-Poor' and 'Income Non-poor' households could be obtained – and thus smaller trees and simpler rule sets. The rules so obtained may be simplified further by pruning so as to obtain the simplest possible set of rules, at the cost of minimally decreasing the accuracy of the results.[41]

Finally, while the method of analysis itself is inexpensive (requiring the purchase of particular software) and provides clear and easily interpretable results, any policy application of such an analysis – the purpose of which is to confirm the eligibility or ineligibility of households for receipt of benefits – would have to take into account the cost in time and resources required to: a) collect the key variables for analysis; and b) follow up and confirm if households identified as uncorroborated beneficiaries or non-beneficiaries are indeed ineligible or eligible for the receipt of benefits. Political, financial and social factors will bear on the relative desirability and the actual practicality of identifying and investigating such households.

ACKNOWLEDGEMENTS

The authors thank Mr N Narayanan, IAS, for his suggestions and support for the project in its embryonic form; Dr S Janakarajan and his team at the Madras Institute of Development Studies (MIDS), who collected the census data; Prof. S Subramanian (MIDS) for an updated poverty line; U Archana (MIDS) for answering queries related to the data; Dr Ashwin Srinivasan at the Oxford University Computing Laboratory for advice on the class probability tree analysis method and for very profitable discussions; Prof. Donald Michie for his incisive comments and pointers to the limits of the analysis; Susana Franco for most useful and pertinent observations; Diego Colatei for comments on the initial draft and computing assistance; Prof. Frances Stewart and Taimur Hyat for useful critical comments; and Prof. Quinlan for answering queries related to See5. Dr Saith was supported by DFID and a Wingate Scholarship.

Appendix

Details of Class Probability Tree Analysis

THE class probability tree analysis technique works by analysing data related to a sufficient number of cases. The cases belong to different classes or groups and the pattern of variables characterizing each class is discovered. Table 1 contains data related to cases belonging to two groups and described by four variables.

The pattern-class relationships are initially expressed as trees, which are then re-expressed as a set of easily understandable statements or rules. As can be seen in Fig. 1, the tree starts as a 'root node', with a set of cases that are to be used to construct outcome-predicting rules. In the example here, these are 100 households which are referred to together as the 'training set'.[1] These cases are known to belong to mutually exclusive classes (here the classes of 'Poor' and 'Non-poor'). Each training case of a known class is described by its variable values

TABLE 1 Example of cases for constructing a class probability tree

Case (household) nos.	Total area operated dependants	Nos. of male land (acres) dependants	Nos. of female	Cash balance (Rs)	Class
1	5	2	–	20,000	Non-poor
2	3	1	–	17,000	Non-poor
3	1	2	1	1000	Poor
4	2	4	3	200	Poor
5	10	3	1	40,000	Non-poor
. . .	. . .	. . .	. . .	. . .	. . .
100	18	2	1	10,000	Non-poor

[1] These cases are referred to as 'training' cases as the analysis programme 'trains' on the information provided by them and extracts patterns which can then be used to classify new cases.

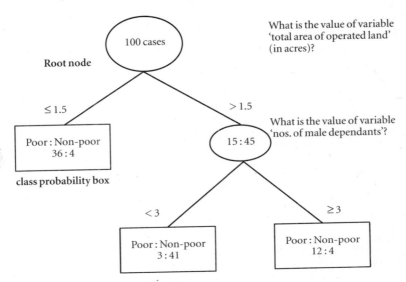

FIG. 1 Hypothetical class probability tree.

(here, four variables related to each household). The training data is analysed by the class probability tree programme and patterns of variables characterizing and discriminating the 'Poor' and 'Non-poor' classes are identified. The computer program used here to conduct this task is See5 (Quinlan 1998).

Details of tree-extraction methods are given in Quinlan 1993. Briefly, See5 looks at the root node to determine if all cases at this node belong to the same class. If they do not, as in the example in Fig. 1, it then grows 'branches' from this node using the variable that best sorts the households (here, variable 'total area of operated land' in Fig. 1) into distinct groups. The test that determines which variable is the 'best' considers the ability of the variable to sort into groups that contain a high proportion of households belonging to the same class. The ideal group has either an all 'Poor' or an all 'Non-poor' outcome. Here different values for the variable 'total area of operated land' (= 1.5 and > 1.5 acres) gave two groups. One clearly had a high proportion of batches belonging to the class 'Poor' (36 out of 40) and the other to the class 'Non-poor' (45 out of 60). Following the split at the root node, the resulting nodes are examined. Further splits may take place (e.g. 'nos. of male dependants' in Fig. 1) or the tree may terminate at a node. Termination happens in two situations. First, if all cases at a node belong to the same class and, second, if the test indicates that the gain by further splitting is unlikely to add to the overall discriminatory power (as here with the variable total area of operated land ≤ 1.5 acres). Such a terminal node is declared a 'leaf' or 'class probability' box. In Fig. 1 the proportion of cases belonging to each class in that box is shown. When used for outcome prediction, this box provides an estimated probability of whether a new household would be predicted as belonging to the class 'Poor' or 'Non-poor' (hence the name class probability trees). This is achieved for a new household by checking the condition at the top of the tree and working down the branches, depending on which branch its features satisfy, until a 'class probability' box is reached.

The variable pattern-class relationship can be written as a set of rules, as shown below:

RULE SET

Rule 1:
   If
      variable 'total area of operated land (acres)' has a value less than or equal to 1.5,
   Then
      the probability of being 'Poor' is 90 per cent (36/40) and the probability of being 'Non-poor' is 10 per cent (4/40).
      Class prediction taken as *Poor*

Rule 2:
   If
      variable 'total area of operated land' has a value greater than 1.5 acres and variable 'nos. of male dependants' has the value less than 3,
   Then
      the probability of being 'Poor' is 7 per cent (3/44) and probability of being 'Non-poor' is 93 per cent (41/44).
      Class prediction taken as *Non-poor*

Rule 3:
   If
      variable 'total area of operated land' has a value greater than 1.5 acres and variable 'nos. of male dependants' has a value greater than or equal to 3,
   Then
      probability of 'Poor' is 75 per cent (12/16) and probability of 'Non-poor' is 25 per cent (4/16).
      Class prediction taken as *Poor*

Each rule contains class probability estimates expressed as percentages. These have been obtained from the proportion of cases in each class in the 'class probability' box in the tree. In this example, the class label ('Poor' or 'Non-poor') attached to the rule is that of the class that has the higher probability. Note that each rule bases 'class prediction' on a majority-vote principle. That is to say, where less than 50 per cent 'Poor' is predicted, the class prediction is 'Non-poor', otherwise 'Poor'. The 50 per cent prediction criterion is convenient, particularly given the structure of the rule-building See5 package, but it is to a degree arbitrary.

For further details on the tree and rule construction procedure, the reader is referred to Quinlan 1993.

Life Chances: Development and Female Disadvantage

PAUL H L NILLESEN AND BARBARA HARRISS-WHITE

'Mortality which is based on ideas or on an ideal, is an unmitigated evil.'
D H Lawrence, *Fantasia of the Unconscious*, ch. 7.

1. INTRODUCTION

FROM Independence to 1997, India's birth rate dropped from 42 to 28 live births per thousand.[1] Such a decline in fertility is normally associated with a preceding decrease in the mortality rate. However, sex ratios for the Indian population suggest that this mortality decline has not occurred equally for both sexes. Table 1 shows the female–male ratios for India since the turn of the century. They are famously characterized by excess female mortality.

Excess relative female mortality refers to mortality that is a consequence of unequal treatment within the household. Equal treatment need not necessarily

TABLE 1 Female–male ratio for India, 1901–91

Year	Female–male ratio
1901	0.972
1902	0.964
1921	0.955
1931	0.950
1941	0.945
1951	0.946
1961	0.941
1971	0.930
1981	0.935
1991	0.927*
2001	0.933

Source: Kynch and Sen 1983; *Rajan, Mishra and Navaneetham 1991; Census of India, 2001.

imply identical quantities of treatment, rather that all members receive what, at least nutritionally and medically, they need.

Das Gupta and Mari Bhat argue that, as a result of the decline in fertility, women are better at controlling the gender composition of their family.[2] So, given a social preferences for males, the relative mortality rate of girls may actually increase. The mortality rate of a child is influenced, first, by exposure to life-threatening insults and, second, by the quantity and quality of resources allocated to it in its youth. Girls may routinely receive a lower quantity and quality of food or, at times of acute need, of medical care. Further, the selective and deliberate abortion of female foetuses or female infanticide has lately been reported as spreading.[3]

The literature discusses two alternative motives for the unsymmetrical intra-familial distribution of resources and care between children of different sex. First, the distribution is argued to accord with the standard economic principles of utility maximization.[4] This utility is some aggregated family utility function, which in turn depends on total household income. So resources are allocated according to the return a child generates. Second, the distribution of resources within a household reflects social and cultural norms, expressing male preference.[5] Kishor has attempted to test both explanations simultaneously.[6] However, although both economic and cultural factors are found to influence mortality rates, they do so to a differing extent in different classes of a population. It is now generally accepted by scholars, the public and politicians that dowry payments play an important role in the culling of girls. A poor household will not necessarily be as concerned with this as a wealthy family might be, since the poor household does not have any significant wealth to transfer and is compelled to make male and female family members labour, whereas a wealthy family will take intergenerational flows of capital into account when making allocation decisions. The argument is theoretically stylized: most families will have some assets and also engage in wage work.

We hypothesize first that the allocation of resources in poor households is governed by labour market considerations (the *wage effect*). Poor households derive most of their income from labour. Second, in households which have accumulated some property, the allocation of resources is expected to be governed by accumulation strategies, in turn depending on capital flows between generations (the *wealth effect*). These households will be more concerned with inheritance norms and marriage transfer payments (dowries) than poorer households which have fewer assets to transfer. The wage and wealth effects of the different classes will act in opposing directions (for reasons that are discussed later in this chapter), suggesting that increases in household income may increase, rather than decrease, the relative disadvantage of females in India.

Further, modernization[7] is commonly associated with 'Sanskritization', in which lower castes will try to emulate the cultural attributes of higher castes. So if, as we argue here, excess female mortality is associated with economic status, poor people will attempt to emulate the behaviour of the rich. 'Development' will then be accompanied by increased biases against females. Sex imbalances will be the product not of poverty but of wealth. *It is conceivable that a by-product of India's economic reforms will be greater, rather than reduced, female disadvantage.*

The possibility that wealth, rather than poverty, might be related to the deteriorating life chances of girls in India has been raised by Clark (1987) and by Heyer (1992). Subsequently, using data from northern Tamil Nadu, Sargent and colleagues (1996) and Harriss-White (1999a) found indications that wealthier, landed households have lower female–male ratios than poorer, landless households. It is urgent to know what is determining the sex ratios among the labouring peasantry and the capitalist elite. This will be done by dividing the data we use so as to separate out wage and wealth effects.

The chapter is ordered as follows. First, we give a brief and non-technical overview of the mechanisms through which resources are allocated within a household. Second, we examine in greater detail the case of Tamil Nadu and our sample, drawing upon the work of Sargent *et al.*, Harriss-White and Nillesen.[8] We then consider policy responses.

2. THEORIES OF INTRAHOUSEHOLD DISTRIBUTION

The way goods are distributed within a household has important implications for policy. Knowledge of the motivating factors behind a differential allocation of resources between boys and girls might allow a government, if it has the political interest, to alter the incentive structure faced by households and thus indirectly to influence relative mortality rates. There are two economic factors at work that influence the economic strategies of households: the labour market and norms of asset transfer. But these do not exhaust the determinants of sex bias. Culture is a social force which disadvantages women quite independently of their role in the economy. In 1983, Dyson and Moore identified a major subcontinental cultural faultline between the 'north' and the 'south'. The northern patriarchal kinship system features village exogamy; there is cooperation in production between male blood relatives; women are excluded from property ownership; there is higher fertility, relatively low age at marriage, relatively higher infant and child mortality and more masculine sex ratios. The south differs on all counts save that of patriarchy. Women are thought to have greater autonomy, even though autonomy is not an unambiguous indicator of advantage, from the point of view of welfare.[9] These culture regions have proved to be less distinct on the ground than in the model.[10] Harriss argues that the 'discriminatory practices of patriarchy may be unrelated to the wealth and economic status of the household'.[11] Further, Kapadia, examining gender inequalities in Tamil Nadu villages, finds it cuts across all classes and castes.[12] Male preference is ingrained, if only because men play an important religious role and are necessary for death rites. Culture influences the divine and moral aspects of the intrahousehold distribution of resources.[13]

Two types of economic model of distribution appear in the literature: unitary models, initially developed by Becker and Tomes; and bargaining models, initially developed by McElroy and Horney.[14]

2.1 *The unitary model*

Becker and Tomes argue that the household can be viewed as a single decision-making unit. Parents aim to maximize overall family utility, in which the income and wealth of the children are elements. By maximizing the utility function, parents invest so as to reinforce differences but compensate for this with transfer payments. The result is that if one child obtains a higher return from a given investment of resources than another, parents respond by allocating more resources to the first child *ex ante*. So, if a male has better employment and earnings prospects than a female, the family will allocate more resources to the male child. The result of fewer resources being allocated to the female child than she needs is likely to lead to a lower survival chance, if household resources are scarce.

Criticism of the unitary approach runs along four lines. First, perfect capital markets and information are assumed. Parents operate in a static environment where all decisions are made simultaneously and with all the necessary information about the future available. In practice, information is sure to be incomplete and imperfect and may be perceived differently according to the gender to which it relates.[15] If perceptions differ from reality, a bias will be introduced into the interpretation of the information and it becomes 'noisy'. If the information about female wages is less reliable than the information about male wages, for example, parents will be less responsive to wage changes when they occur for females than when they occur for males. In order to induce an identical decrease in mortality for both male and female children, the increase in wage or employment opportunities for females must then be substantially larger than that for males to compensate for the lower reliability of information about female wage increases.[16] Second, Foster and Rosenzweig suggest that the role of the daughter in agricultural production may be complementary to that of the son.[17] If the labour-market participation opportunities for women were to increase, the demand for a son may increase without it having any effect on the demand for girls. This increase in demand may then be reflected in the lower relative mortality of boys, widening – as opposed to closing – the survival differential. Third, an *ex ante* unequal concern for children of different sex, if found to exist for cultural reasons, will not generate a difference in the levels of return of the different sexes.[18] Fourth, Folbre argues that the unitary model is fundamentally misconceived.[19] In practice, households are sites of struggles over resources, and these struggles are simultaneously over socially constructed meanings and definitions. It is more realistic to see a household as consisting of individual agents, each attempting to maximize his or her utility, not some aggregate family utility function. This latter proposition is developed in bargaining models of intra-household allocation.

2.2 *The bargaining model*

Social status is determined not only by economic participation but also by control over resources, which in turn influences individual bargaining power in decision-making. In a bargaining model of marriage, it is theorized that the two agents maximize the product of each partner's utility gain from marriage. Two factors, the ability to earn income and the possibility of entering the 'remarriage market', have been argued to affect the distribution of resources within the household through their effects on the breakdown position. The breakdown position is the utility each agent achieves if not married.[20] Household distribution is determined by a Nash-bargained solution involving both partners and their respective breakdown positions.[21]

Bargaining models differ in two respects from unitary models. First, in unitary models income is pooled and therefore all that matters is total income. By contrast, in bargaining models it is the individual control over income that influences the distribution of resources within the household. Second, the Nash-bargaining model incorporates the opportunity cost of family membership on the distribution of resources within the family.[22] However, in wealthier families, as some feminists argue, women's bargaining power may be independent of the resources they control. It depends entirely on the institutional context. Further, as Sen points out, what determines bargaining power is not solely the contribution to the household, but rather the perceived contribution.[23]

So far we have discussed how households with male and female adult working members make allocative decisions. However, in rich Indian households women play a limited role both in the labour market and in the productive family labour force. Labour market considerations become less important when undertaking allocation decisions, and the logic shifts to keeping wealth within the family. Whereas the wage effect alters the marginal cost of having daughters, the wealth effect alters the fixed costs. The transfer of wealth is in turn influenced by society and culture, which we will now consider.

> In India, as in most other developing agrarian societies, kin relationships still constitute for the great majority of people the prime avenue of access to such scarce social resources as information, economic assistance, and political support.[24]

The kinship structure is vital to understanding economic decision-making in the longer run by wealthier households. In India, kinship is strongly patriarchal and the inheritance of property favours males over females.[25] Since girls migrate on marriage, the management of any property they inherit is made difficult. A propertied family will thus prefer sons, so as to keep control of the wealth within the family.[26] Although a married daughter may still have contact with her parents, she will not contribute to their income any longer.[27] Further, increasingly, the bride's family pays a dowry to the groom's family. Even though dowry payments are illegal, following the Dowry Prohibition Act of 1961, they are nevertheless increasing in prevalence and magnitude.[28] Heyer and Agnihotri both note that dowry is starting to colonize the south of India, where bride price or small mutual transfers on marriage existed previously.[29] Women have become agents in the display and transfer of wealth. Heyer argues that spending substantially on daughters' marriages and dowries confirms or raises a household's reputation.[30] The wealthy household faces two costs for its daughter. First, a dowry payment to the husband's family[31] and a stream of gifts subsequently, including loans at zero interest.[32] Second, a stream of income from labour is permanently lost. This income might be relatively small in monetary terms, but it covers the shadow benefits from having a cheap source of labour to work on the family land, especially in post-harvest processing and the work of domestic maintenance. So girls are associated with large outflows of capital, while boys are viewed as generating a large inward flow of capital upon marriage. The sex of a child at birth may have an immediate impact on household consumption and savings behaviour: the birth of a female child has been theorized to have the same effect as a negative shock on lifetime household wealth. Households with more female children will, *ceteris paribus*, reduce their expenditure and increase their savings to pay for a future dowry. Male preference is reinforced and the relative disadvantage of females is increased.[33]

Finally, the bargaining power of women may be eroded, rather than strengthened, in wealthy families. Wealthy households conventionally withdraw their women from participation in the labour market. Since housework is perceived as less valuable, the perceived contribution of women to the household will be lower. As a result, female bargaining power will be reduced. Further, if the family views women as agents in the transfer of wealth out of the family, their actual contribution will be negative and their breakdown positions may also be negative. So it is reasonable to test the idea that, with the wealth effect, women's bargaining power is inversely related to the wealth of their family.

3. INDIA AND TAMIL NADU IN THE 1990S

The probability of survival in India is cruelly influenced by location. Death rates for all ages are highest in rural areas and in North India. The all-India infant mortality rate in 1996 was 26 per thousand for rural India, compared to 14 per thousand for urban India.[34] In rural areas, the generally lower life chances are not equally shared by males and females. Table 2 shows the estimated age-specific death rates by sex for rural India for 1996. Up to age 30, female mortality is

TABLE 2 Estimated age-specific death rates by sex per thousand, rural India, 1996

Age Group	Total	Male	Female
Below 1	84.6	83.7	85.7
1–4	9.3	7.1	11.6
0–4	26.2	24.3	28.3
5–9	2.6	2.2	2.9
10–14	1.4	1.3	1.4
15–19	1.8	1.5	2.1
20–24	2.5	2	3
25–29	2.6	2.5	2.8
30–34	3.1	3.1	3.1
35–39	3.7	4.2	3.1
40–44	5.2	5.9	4.5
45–49	7	8.1	5.9
50–54	11.3	13	9.4
55–59	16.2	18.6	13.8
60–64	26.8	29.4	24.3
65–69	38	42.5	33.8
70–74	62.9	68.9	56.9
75–79	88.6	95.2	81.9
80–84	120.8	130.1	111.5
85+s	184.4	192.1	177
All age	9.7	9.8	9.6

Source: Sample Registration System Statistical Report, 1996 (excludes Jammu and Kashmir).

higher than male mortality. Especially for the 0–4 age bracket, the death rate is substantially higher for females than for males. Biologically, however, female infants have a higher resistance to infectious diseases than males, so we would expect to find their death rates to be lower, rather than higher. Table 3 shows the child and infant mortality rates for India for 1996, disaggregated by age. Again the rural mortality rates are substantially higher than the urban rates.

Tamil Nadu is a state (along with the deservedly more famous Kerala) where the status of women has been relatively high. It now seems to be a demographic microcosm of the subcontinent as a whole. Tamil Nadu's population was nearly 56 million in 1991. From 1981 to 1991, it experienced the second highest fertility decline of all Indian states. As a result of unequal mortality-rate decreases for males and females, sex ratios have converged with the national average. Das Gupta and Mari Bhat estimate that between 1981 and 1991 an additional 88,000 girls went 'missing' from the census in Tamil Nadu alone.[35] Table 4 reports the sex ratios for the juvenile population (0–10 years) of Tamil Nadu from 1941 to 2001.

The sex ratio for the population as a whole in Tamil Nadu, at 974 in 1991, was second highest to that of Kerala. But it hides the secular downward trend for the juvenile population (Table 4). *Between 1981 and 1991 the life chances of girl children in Tamil Nadu deteriorated at a rate 1.5 times the national average;* while between 1991 and 2001 the rate of deterioration, at 1.7 times the average, got worse. Is this deterioration of female life chances in Tamil Nadu linked to economic development and the accumulation of wealth? Will liberalization *worsen* female life chances?

4. THE EVIDENCE

National-level evidence lends increasing support to this hypothesis. In 1982, Rosenzweig and Schultz published an analysis of child survival data from a

TABLE 3 Child and infant mortality indicators, India, 1996

Indicators	Total	Rural	Urban
Child (<5yrs) Mortality Rate	24	26	14
Infant M.R	72	77	46
Neo-Natal M.R.	47	50	28
Early Neo-Natal M. R.	35	37	23
Late Neo-Natal M. R.	12	13	5
Post Neo-Natal M. R.	25	27	17
Peri-Natal M. R.	44	46	32
Still Birth Rate	9	9	9

Source: Sample Registration System Statistical Report, 1996 (excludes Jammu and Kashmir).

Table 4 Juvenile population sex ratios for Tamil Nadu and India, 1941–2001

	1941	1951	1961	1971	1981	1991	2001
Tamil Nadu	1010	999	995	984	974	948*	917
India	n/a	n/a	976	964	962	945*	927

Source: Chunkath and Athreya 1997, *(0–6 yrs); Athreya 2001b.

national sample of 1,331 rural households with results that did *not* corroborate it. Finding that children who are likely to be more productive economically receive a greater share of resources, they observed a general association between household wealth and improved female to male survival chances, which implies that greater equality was practised as household wealth increased. Their data are now one generation old. However, Murthi and colleagues used equally old data from 1981 for 296 districts throughout India which supported the hypothesis. They found a negative and statistically significant association between poverty and female disadvantage. They claim that:

> . . . variables reflecting the general level of development and modernisation (e.g. per capita expenditure, male literacy, urbanisation, and the availability of medical facilities) have a negative but comparatively weak impact on mortality and fertility levels, and, if anything, amplify rather than reduce the gender bias in child survival.[36]

Agnihotri has plotted state-level National Sample Survey data from 1991 for household expenditure (in the absence of that for wealth) against the sex ratio to test for a U-shaped, 'Kuznets curved' relationship and found ominously that in many states, Tamil Nadu included, there is either no upwards kink in the decline in the sex ratio with increasing private income, or that the upward turn is at income levels which will not be reached by other than a tiny minority in the foreseeable future.[37]

Regional evidence is increasingly supportive over time. Browning and Subramanian, using an ICRISAT Village-Level Survey panel data-set for Central India 1975–84, have found that households behaved as if there were a shock to their lifetime wealth following the birth of a girl.[38] Households with girls reduced total household expenditures and the other components of expenditure as well. By contrast, expenditures increased following the birth of a boy, with the exception of narcotics – a purely adult commodity. The authors reckon their findings corroborate anthropological evidence that the cost of marriage is an increasing function of wealth. The largest land-holding households incurred significantly higher marriage costs in the form of higher marriage expenses and dowries. This is a form of social signalling of the status of the household. Heyer, examining the accumulation of wealth in rural Coimbatore District in South India in the early 1980s, recorded significant (then recent) increases in dowry among the landed propertied classes, along with hypergamy (the practice of organizing the marriage of girls in an upward direction in status).[39] The dowry (no longer vested in the bride but in the groom's family) plus life-long and open-ended ceremonies connected with the girl's reproductive cycle were the means of expressing improved status and making advantageous connections in agriculture and trade. Heyer argues that the system is driven by brides' households. But within the class with land and non-land property, wealth is redistributed to households with higher ratios of sons to daughters. So daughters tend to be neglected.

George and others looked at 13 villages, covering some 13,000 people in KV Kuppam Block of North Arcot–Ambedkar District, very close to the villages we studied.[40] These villages have witnessed striking increases in their productive bases as a result of the Green Revolution. Female infanticide was discovered in six of these settlements, affecting 10 per cent of newborn girl babies. But no such practice was found in the other seven. Searching for explanations, they point to three: physical remoteness, villages with low levels of education, and villages where land ownership is dominated by the Gounder or Vanniar caste. Widespread and active land acquisition by Gounders over the last two decades of the Green Revolution[41] is quite likely to be accompanied by kinship relations ensuring at best the accumulation of more land, at least the retention of existing land. In the presence of dowries and patrilineal inheritance, it is thus increasingly advantageous to have sons rather than daughters.

4.1 *Ambedkar and Tiruvannamalai districts*

Sargent *et al.* and Harriss-White have provided further evidence that the accumulation of wealth may be causing the deteriorating life chances of girls.[42] They use data from the set of villages sampled and surveyed in the Ambedkar and Tiruvannamalai districts of Tamil Nadu.[43] Table 5 reports the infant mortality rates for the combined two districts. The village censuses were conducted in 1993 on three villages and in 1994 on the other eight by the MIDS team. Just over 2,000 households were surveyed – nearly 10,000 people (see chapters 1–1 and 1–3).

Sex-ratio data have been organized to examine the relation between caste, class and excess girl child deaths. The child sex ratios can be seen in Table 6. The overall sex ratio of 856 is much lower than the state average for the under-seven age group (946) and is similar to that of Salem and Madurai districts. The figure 750 for caste households is extremely low. If the data for the caste population are disaggregated further according to land-ownership status, the sex ratio of 730 is

TABLE 5 Gender-specific infant mortality rates per thousand for Ambedkar, Tiruvannamalai and Tamil Nadu, 1995

	Male	Female
Ambedkar	38.1	45
Tiruvannamalai	31.7	39.2
Tamil Nadu	36.9	44.3

Source: Chunkath and Athreya 1997.

TABLE 6 Child sex ratios in villages in Ambedkar and Tiruvannamalai districts (girls under 7 per thousand boys), 1993–4

Status	Sex Ratio
Aggregate	856
Scheduled Caste	886
Caste	750
Landless	952
Landed	730
Landed Caste	645

Notes: (i) the data have been tested for misreporting; (ii) it is assumed that the random error is insignificant; (iii) the average disaggregates will not equal the average total because of the category 'other' (Muslim, Christian etc.).

exceedingly low: on a par with the seventh lowest development block in the state as a whole and with the under-15 sex ratio for the business elite of the local town.[44] By contrast, for those households without land, the sex ratio of 952 is not much different from the state average of 946. The ratio for scheduled castes follows the state-level trend of being higher than that for the caste population.[45] *The lowest sex ratio for the under-seven age group is found among landed caste households – 645*: not very different from that found in Macdonald's Country Development Block (651) in Salem, the third lowest block-level sex ratio in Tamil Nadu. Excess girl-child mortality seems to have appeared most strikingly in a class-specific form among landed households – irrespective of caste – and not because of poverty or distress. *Land accumulation seems to have been accompanied by female disadvantage.*

Economic development and the associated accumulation of wealth appear to have lowered the relative probability of survival of girls. Further, the ratios suggest that the gender composition of poor landless households is motivated by different factors than in wealthy, asset-rich households. In order to examine the effect of wealth accumulation and its intergenerational transfer on the survival prospects of a girl child, the MIDS village-level data were truncated into landless and landed sections. By running individual regressions on the subsamples, we can identify whether certain variables influence household sex ratios differently according to the socio-economic status of the household. The next section reports the results.

4.2 *Ambedkar and Tiruvannamalai – poverty versus wealth*

Households in which there was at least one child under the age of nine were selected for analysis. Harriss[46] found that two thirds of female mortality occurs before the age of four; however, we chose a slightly broader age range in order to keep our sample size at a reasonable level, with a view to truncating it later. The final population size was 1,071 households. The household was defined as those sharing the same house. The average household size in the total sample was 4.9. The sex ratio of male to female children under 9 was 1.116 (896 in terms of females per thousand males). The sex ratio of 5–9-year olds in the USA in November 1998 was 1.05 (952).[47] Applying this ratio to our sample, a total of 59 girls are *missing* from our population.

Following Rosenzweig and Schultz (1982), a survival differential was calculated by taking the difference in the survival probability of a male and female child. Our data were limited, however, by the fact that only the total number of births by a woman in the family was reported, without indicating whether these births were male or female. We therefore divided the total number of births by two, assuming that there is a roughly equal probability of bearing a son as of bearing a daughter. Biologically, however, slightly more males are born than females everywhere and pre- and perinatal mortality is male-biased. Further, in India there is a tendency to underestimate female births because they are not considered as significant and hence may not be as easily remembered as male births.

To calculate the survival probability, the total number of children under nine was divided by half the total number of births:

$$\frac{m}{(B/2)}, \frac{f}{(B/2)}$$

where m, f are the total number of male or female children under nine years old in the family and B is the total number of births to the family. The survival differential, S, is then:

$$S = \frac{m}{(B/2)} - \frac{f}{(B/2)}$$

The probability of survival is thus the probability of a nine-year-old being alive in a family, given the number of births in that family. If the child has brothers, sisters or cousins older than nine, then his or her probability of survival will be lowered. It is likely that the more brothers, sisters or cousins a newborn child has in the family, the lower its chances of survival are. Female children's life chances have been found to diminish in the presence of sisters.[48] The average survival differential in our sample was 0.0584, indicating that the probability of a male child surviving is greater than the probability of a female child surviving.

The population was truncated according to land ownership, generating 347 landless households and 654 landed households. The under nine-year-old male to female sex ratio was 1.255 (797) for the landless households and 1.102 (907) for the landed households. Table 7 lists the variables used in the analysis and their sample means and standard deviations.

The variables and their expected signs are described in more detail below.

4.2.1 *Land holdings*
Land holdings were calculated by adding up the total land owned (in acres) outside and inside the village, irrespective of whether the type of land was wet (*nanjai*) or dry (*punjai*).[49] We have hypothesised that land holdings will decrease the survival differential. Landed households can provide more productive work and thus make girls more 'attractive' to the household by raising their implicit income potential.

4.2.2 *Land value, total wealth*
Total land value was calculated by summing the values for the different plots of land owned by a household. Total wealth includes total land value but also includes household gross income for 1992–3, total value of agricultural assets,[50] and total value of non-agricultural assets.[51] We expect that the value of a household's land holdings and total wealth will increase the survival differential and that this effect will be larger in the rich group, as a result of the wealth effect described earlier.

4.2.3 *Female and male labour-force participation*
Labour-force participation was calculated as the ratio of working men or women to the total men or women in the household at the time the census was conducted. We expect that female labour force participation will reduce the survival differential in poor households but have less effect in rich households. Rosenzweig and Schultz, and Kishor, have confirmed in their empirical work that female labour-force participation lowers relative female mortality.[52] Murthi and colleagues give five reasons why this might be the case:[53]

TABLE 7 Variable means and standard deviations, landed and landless households, Tamil Nadu, 1993–4

Variable	Total Mean	s.d.	Landless Mean	s.d.	Landed Mean	s.d.
Total Males <9yrs	.9785	.7857	1.0202	.7505	.9771	.8083
Total Females <9yrs	.8768	.8437	.8127	.7769	.8869	.8747
Total Children	1.8553	.8606	1.8329	.7943	1.8639	.9084
Total Births	4.6032	2.8410	3.7003	2.2788	5.0719	2.991
Male Surv. Prob.	.4856	.3972	.5754	.4075	.4452	.3770
Female Surv. Prob.	.4272	.4268	.4644	.4511	.3989	.4132
Survival Diff.	.0584	.6639	.1110	.6992	.0463	.6373
Electricity Conn. (dummy)	.5303	.5049	.3429	.4754	.6346	.4914
Gross Income 92–93/Rs	19,095.45	32,018.25	6,942.608	2,507.167	25,389.36	39,296.55
Total Value Agri Assets/Rs	26,824.71	56,390.01	2,983.436	1,0837.5	41,062.11	67,089.4
T. Val. Non-Agri Assets/Rs	26,966.72	82,262.68	4,012.272	8,584.53	41,119.41	102,333.3
Total Landholdings/acres	3.2411	5.9680	—	—	5.3077	6.8830
Value of Landholdings/Rs	73,667.3	176,933.4	—	—	120,638.7	213,592.1
Total Wealth/Rs	146,554.2	301,602.4	13,938.32	16,577.41	228,218.5	362,558.2
Ave. Ed. Adult Males	1.2673	1.0350	.8713	.9983	1.4602	.9995
Ave. Ed. Adult Females	.5923	.8067	.4755	.7800	.6490	.8190
Male L.F.P. Ratio	.5520	.2593	.5443	.2598	.5449	.2402
Female L.F.P. Ratio	.4740	.4099	.5077	.4144	.4660	.4093
Sample Size	1,071		347		654	

Note: Total Wealth equals Gross Income + Total Value Agric. assets + total value Non-Agric. assets + Total Land Value.

Source: Field survey, 1993–5.

i) female labour-force participation raises the returns to 'investment' in girls;

ii) it raises the status of women in society;

iii) it lowers dowry levels;

iv) it makes women less dependent on adult sons in old age; and

v) it raises the bargaining power of women.

Harriss-White (1999a) argues that the absence of property among the landless eliminates the problem of distribution at inheritance and that the necessary participation of landless women and girls in the wage labour force increases their relative economic status within the household over their status in households where women do not work for wages. However, it also depends on what type of jobs women are filling. If the work requires little or no education, then increased labour-force participation will give no incentive to 'invest' in girls. In this case, increases in labour-force participation may actually increase the survival differential because the mother is not present to take care of the children, leaving other family members to look after them. Male infants are likely to be taken to work by mothers, whereas female infants are more likely to be left at home and therefore breastfed less frequently. Further, as Foster and Rosenzweig (1999) argue, female labour-force participation may be complementary to a biased sex composition. As female labour-force participation increases, the demand for males increases and their relative mortality falls, widening the survival differential. We expect that male labour-force participation reduces the relative probability of a female surviving by raising male bargaining power and increasing the perceived expected returns from male children.

4.2.4 *Education*

Educational attainment was averaged across the adult household members.[54] Attainment was ranked from 0 to 4, where:

−0: illiterate;

−1: primary (up to seven years of age) or literate without formal education;

−2: middle (up to nine) or literate with formal education (of less than five years);

−3: secondary matriculation or HHS/pre-university or diploma (tech and non-tech);

−4: graduates and above.

Education is normally associated with lowering mortality. This will be the case for poor households, where we expect to find that male education increases the survival differential. Female education lowers the differential if employment prospects require it. We are led to expect, however, that female education will widen the survival differential in the rich group. An educated woman is better at controlling the mortality of her children, but also better at controlling her fertility and her family composition. Given son preference, this will increase the relative probability of a girl not surviving and thus the survival differential.[55] Further:

> . . . if gender bias is lower among poorer households, it would be quite possible, in principle, to find a positive bivariate association between parental literacy and gender bias (given the positive correlation between poverty and illiteracy), even if literacy reduces gender bias at any given level of poverty.[56]

So we expect the relation between the survival differential and female education to be positive in the rich group, but negative in the poor group. Male education will increase the rate of return to male children and, through higher earnings, will raise their relative bargaining power. This will have the effect of raising the survival differential in both groups. Table 8 summarizes the hypothesized effects on the survival differential.

Before proceeding to examine the truncated samples, a regression analysis was conducted on the whole sample. The model was estimated using total wealth instead of land value in order to make comparisons possible with the truncated samples.[57] Table 9 gives the results.

The land-holdings coefficient is consistent with the idea that landed households can provide more on-farm, non-wage work opportunities for girls and women, which make them valued. *Increases in wealth are associated with an exacerbation of the survival differential.* Richer households discriminate more against girls than poorer households. This is explained by the wealth effect where, in richer households, the transfer of wealth across generations plays an

TABLE 8 Summary of hypotheses

Variable	Wage Effect	Wealth Effect
Landholdings	–	–
Land Value	n/a	+
Wealth	n/a	+
Female L. F. P.	–/+	n/a
Male L. F. P.	+	n/a
Female Education	–	+
Male Education	+	0

Note: L. F. P. = labour force participation.

Source: Field survey, 1993.

TABLE 9 Ordinary least squares regression: survival differential total sample rural Tamil Nadu, 1993–4, with robust standard errors[58]

Variable	S
Constant	.5296***
	(.0829)
Landholdings	−.0108**
	(.0043)
Wealth	2.39e–07***
	(7.92e–08)
Male Ed.	−.0155
	(.0171)
Female Ed.	.0203
	(.0211)
Male L. F. P.	−1.2159***
	(.1274)
Female L. F. P.	.4273***
	(.0492)
R"	.3310

Note: * 10 per cent significance level; ** 5 per cent significance level; *** 1 per cent significance level; standard errors are shown in parentheses. L. F. P. = labour force participation. Ed. = education.

Source: Field survey, 1993.

important role in determining the direction and quantity of household resources allocated to different members.

The coefficients on the education variables were not statistically significant. However, the sign on the female coefficient suggests that a *rise in the average education of the adult females in a household exacerbates the survival differential.* Das Gupta also found this for the Punjab.[59] This supports the possibility of a positive relationship between education and gender bias.[60] The sign on the male coefficient suggests that a rise in male educational attainment reduces the survival differential. This contradicts our hypothesis but has potentially positive implications if we extrapolate from this cross-section data to processes over time.

The coefficients on male and female labour-force participation are both statistically significant. Male labour-force participation reduces the survival differential between boy and girls, which contradicts our a priori expectation. It might be the case that, with most men working, the mother gives more direct care to her children. But the result might also have been a spurious product of seasonal fluctuations in the data. Tamil Nadu is a state where female status was relatively high. If this has changed, it may be women, rather than men, who are driving it. Female labour-force participation results in the survival differential increasing. As was theorized earlier, increased participation in the labour market will reduce a woman's time at home and this might adversely affect the survival chances of her female children more than those of her male children. Mothers may also be more likely to engage in wage work if they have only daughters, whereas they may stay at home, or take the child with them, if they have sons. Daughters do the domestic work and it may be thought that they can take care of themselves, whereas a 'valuable' son cannot be left on his own. Alternatively, our findings provide support for the Foster and Rosenzweig (1999) hypothesis that the role of the female is complementary to the role of the son in an agricultural household. However, without further evidence it is not possible to distinguish between the effects of an increase in female mortality or a decrease in male mortality.

Running the same regression on landless and landed households separately gives the results shown in Table 10. The most striking result is the different effect that wealth has in both subsamples. *Total wealth reduces the survival differential in landless households but increases the survival differential in landed households.* This supports the contention that *prosperity reduces the life chances of girls only when this prosperity is in the form of land or other property.* Since the wealth of an

TABLE 10 Comparison of OLS results on landless and landed households, Tamil Nadu, 1993–4

Variable	S landless	S landed	S total
Constant	.5618***	.6101***	.5296***
	(.0946)	(.0681)	(.0829)
Total Landholdings	n/a	−.00988**	−.0108**
		(.0050)	(.0043)
Wealth	n/a	2.64e–07***	2.39e–07***
		(9.64e–08)	(7.92e–08)
Male L. F. P.	−1.2112***	−1.3586***	−1.2159***
	(.1224)	(.0845)	(.1274)
Female L. F. P.	.4518***	.4053***	.4273***
	(.0782)	(.0501)	(.0492)
Male Ed.	.0211	−.0216	−.0115
	(.0320)	(.0208)	(.0171)
Female Ed.	.0254	.0173	.0203
	(.0414)	(.0248)	(.0211)
R"	.3031	.3598	.3310
Sample Size	347	654	1,071

Source: Field survey, 1993.

agricultural household lies predominantly in the value of its land, then the direction and way this land is transferred across generations are on the way to being significant factors in determining the optimum sex composition of households so that the economic status of the family is maintained or increased.

The education coefficients were not found to be statistically different between the subsamples. This may have been caused by the high variance and low precision of the education coefficients, which increase the probability of committing a type II error: failing to reject the null hypothesis when there is actually a significant difference in the values. Nor were the coefficients on female labour-force participation statistically significant. On the face of it, though, the difference suggests that *labour-force participation by landless females exacerbates the survival differential more than participation by landed females does.* This might be due to the fact that the wage labour undertaken by landless females is not education-intensive and hence does not signal a greater return to female children. The only effect increased participation has is to lower the attentiveness of mothers to female children.[61]

We hope to have shown the determinants of excess female mortality rate in these villages. Class position is inversely related to the female mortality rate here. Different strata of a population need looking at separately, rather than in one large sample. Only through a stratified analysis can the roles of material factors in the differential allocation of resources be distinguished and this, in turn, may fine-tune policies intended to remove gender bias.

5. SO WHAT FOR POLICY?

Excess female mortality is a product of both poverty and of wealth. There is a dichotomy in explanations for the apparent gender bias: economic and cultural. There are also two opposing economic effects, one due to the labour market and the other to asset transfers. Our theoretical model has it that the poor and landless evaluate the gender of their children according to the returns from the labour market, as opposed to the rich and landed, whose logic follows from the transfer of wealth. In a society where wealth flows patrilineally, as here, the effect of an increase of wealth for a family is to encourage greater gender bias.

Factors motivating the life decisions of landed and landless households differ significantly. A structural break in the data between poor landless and rich landed households was confirmed using the Chow test. Failing to truncate a population when examining survival differentials will result in a misspecification error and possibly biased estimates.[62] We nevertheless found the following:

(i) Land ownership is reducing the survival differential of children, but at a diminishing rate. It has the greatest equalizing impact in households with little land.

(ii) Wealth increases the survival differential of children for rich landed households but reduces it in poor landless households.

Our results are consistent with those of the 2001 All-India Census, where the juvenile (under ten) and child (under seven) sex ratios – female to male – have registered the most staggering declines in the wealthiest states and most developed districts of North India.[63]

The Tamil Nadu Government has reacted in two ways to public outcry over the practice of gender cleansing. First, it set up a 'protection scheme for the girl child', whereby couples with one or more daughters get financial benefits if they are sterilized.[64] Second, it has established a 'cradle baby scheme', about which Basu reports:[65]

> . . . cradles have been placed outside selected primary health centres for parents to deposit unwanted girls for adoption, and [this] seems to be meeting with some success. The government has also announced a 1 per cent reservation in jobs for these 'cradle babies' when they grow up; while this may be a meaningless provision, the publicity it generates may be useful.[65]

However well intended, these schemes only attempt to address the *symptoms*, without altering *the causes* of excess female mortality. The status of women must be altered if excess female mortality is to be halted and reversed. India's policies to reduce the gender imbalance have largely been superficial. This is not for lack of laws and acts, but for lack of enforcement.

So we argue for the *enforcement of the Dowry Act* and the strict *regulation of amniocentesis*. Pending that, civil society stirs, in the form of social movements and projects by non-governmental organizations, with activities ranging from versions of travelling folk theatre (*kalai payanam*) replete with local idiom and local activists, through village debates about the ideology of patriarchy, to individual counselling of mothers and adolescent girls.[66] There is also room for the media shaming of the men of wealthy culling castes and classes. Such responses are generally made by dedicated individuals. They are aimed at both symptoms and causes; but they are drops in the ocean. *These demographic changes are a form of demographic 'structural adjustment' without precedent.* Any incentive or any movement to counter the social relations enforcing the combination of dowry and marriage patterns featuring consanguinity (to keep property within a tight circle of kin), exogamy (in which a bride's contact with her natal family – and her support – is minimized) and hypergamy (in which dowry compensates for the lower [sub] caste status of the bride) needs much more formidable backing – politically and culturally – than is currently available.

Indian development might draw investment away from land into more liquid forms, so that wealth and its transfer become less associated with males. More fundamentally, the role of patriarchy, the pattern of marriage and residence, and the perception of females in society need to change. Meanwhile, employment opportunities for females that require skills and take them out of their homes should be encouraged. This will raise the potential economic contribution that women can make and raise their bargaining power, their organizing power and their self-confidence. The dowry, which can be seen as a compensating payment for an economically unproductive person, might then become of less importance as women become more independent and economically valuable.

The social and cultural structure of Indian society influences the economic strategies pursued by households. The result of this structure, in combination with economic development, has been to increase female mortality as more families develop strategies to cover the transfer of wealth across generations. This research has shown that culture influences economic decisions. The question remains whether economic policy can influence the cultural fabric of Indian society and mitigate the evil of excess female mortality based on the 'idea or the ideal' of female subordination, one that D H Lawrence would have found as abhorrent as we do.

ACKNOWLEDGEMENTS

We are grateful to Judith Heyer, S Janakarajan, K Nagaraj, Jean Sargent, Rajesh Venugopal and the MIDS Jubilee conference participants for their constructive reactions.

Incapacity and Disability

SUSAN ERB AND BARBARA HARRISS-WHITE[1]

1. INTRODUCTION

IF measured by resources committed and by rhetoric, by the quality of analysis and by data availability, alleviating the condition of the disabled is the lowest priority on state welfare agendas in practically all underdeveloped countries, and arguably in all countries.

The 1993 Human Development Report of the United Nations Development Programme (UNDP) contains compendious data on all aspects of the human condition, with the exception of disability, on which there is nothing. Influential typologies of vulnerability ignore the disabled.[2] On the social welfare agenda of India, poverty, caste and gender push disability to the foot. This low priority can be explained by the political weakness of disabled people, by the high perceived economic costs and the low perceived political benefits of a state response to problems which are administratively anomalous. Such calculations (familiar from public-choice theory) could be expected to operate more powerfully on the welfare agendas of poor countries than they do on those of rich ones.

Intellectual neglect accompanies political neglect. Disability signifies what a person suffering impairment cannot be and cannot do. A K Sen's notion of development as the expansion of potential capabilities and actual functioning (what people can be or do) involves the exercise of positive and negative freedom.[3] But for certain disabled people, certain types of capability expansion and positive freedom are simply not possible. While, for a physically disabled person, remedial social technology ranges from porters and sedan chairs to motorized wheelchairs, there is no technical response at any price that can make some types of blind people see (even if there are means by which their environmental perceptions and capacities to communicate visually can be improved). If 'poverty (is) a deprivation of capabilities',[4] then disabled people are poor. Further, for an equal advance in the exercise of 'freedom to be and to do', a disabled person will have to use more commodities than an able-bodied person. The disabled person will be relatively less well-off as a result than the condition implied by their income alone. This is indeed a double whammy. Sen calls it a 'coupling of disadvantages'.[5] And, for most disabled people to experience, let alone expand, their positive freedom, both the capability to function and the negative freedom of *non*-disabled people may have to be constrained. At the macro level, society will have to divert resources with potential benefits to able-bodied people away from them and direct such resources towards disabled people. At the micro level, able-bodied individuals and differently disabled individuals must help disabled individuals to realize agency and, in so doing, they do *not* do something else. A reduction in the freedom of others is a precondition to the achievement by disabled people of equality in the list of otherwise 'basic capabilities'. These capabilities, which invariably include health, nutrition and education, are also denied to the entire set of poor people by the complex condition of poverty.

The third neglect interacts with the other two, granted that both theory and policy for social development is famously data-constrained.[6] This neglect is one of knowledge. Disability has received little attention from social scientists as a subject worthy of research and public action. Globally comparable data on disability do not exist. Country-specific information is more often than not out of date. The present body of literature addressing the economic and social experience of the disabled is: i) often highly aggregated; ii) approached through a clinical medical conceptual framework; and iii) dominated by justifications (often polemical) for therapeutic action by NGOs.[7] Non-clinical, field-based literature on this huge but virtually taboo subject is patchy and may be characterized, very understandably, by the same 'special pleading' that is visible in the much larger literature on social aspects of nutrition.

The depth of ignorance about disability and development is exposed when the well-established literatures on poverty, caste and malnutrition are related to the numbers of people estimated to be deprived in these dimensions. In India, about 332 million out of a population of 884 million in 1991 are thought to have existed below the official nutrition-based poverty line.[8] A different but overlapping population, some 270 million, belong to scheduled castes and tribes, collectively labelled as 'weaker sections'. Both socio-economic groups have long qualified for targeted development resources, the latter also for positive discrimination in education and employment. In comparison, the disabled population remains marginalized in terms of public policy action.

Even crude totals of disabled people are not known. The 2001 census was the first to count disabled people in detail, and the results are not yet available. The 1981 Census of India was the first and last twentieth-century census to enumerate disabled people. They were classified as 'blind', 'dumb' and 'crippled'. Extreme criteria of impairment were used: blindness required complete loss of sight in both eyes, dumb people were unable to speak and cripples had lost use of both arms and/or both legs. As a result, only 1.1 million were identified as disabled. The National Sample Survey Organization (NSS) also surveyed 'the disabled' in 1981 and subdivided them into four classes: visually handicapped, communication handicapped, locomotor handicapped and mentally handicapped. These were less restrictively defined than in the census,[9] although only marginally so. The census took no account of the mentally handicapped and neither the census nor the NSS estimated those afflicted with leprosy (see Table 1).

The figures given in Table 1 are great underestimates. From clinical evidence it is currently thought that 3.7 per cent of the total population suffers from locomotor, visual, communication-related disability or from mental retardation.[10] This is a larger proportion than that estimated as severely malnourished (2.7 per cent).[11] *So the number of people medically disabled is likely to have increased from 32 million in 1991 to 38 million in 2001.[12] The lives of their families, those people affected indirectly by disability, amount to perhaps four–five times as many: 190 million.*

Disability is also a state which affects all classes and ethnic groups. Its impact and the cost of the response to it vary not only according to the type, combination, severity and cause but also according to the social context and status of disabled people. In this chapter, we will explore the condition of disability through the social structures which shape its experience and then use a study of three villages, to examine the social and economic impact of adult incapacity, from

TABLE 1 Aggregate results of the NSS survey: number of disabled persons in India (millions) (1981–3)

Type	Total	Percent	Rural	Urban	Male	Female
Locomotor	5.4	40%	4.3	1.1	3.5	1.9
Visual	3.4	25%	2.9	0.6	1.4	2
Hearing	3	20%	2.4	0.5	1.6	1.3
Speech	1.7	12%	1.4	0.4	1.1	0.6
Physical*	11.9	n/a	9.6	2.2	7	5.1
%			81%	19%	57%	43%

* more than one of the 4 categories

Source: National Sample Survey Organization, 1981/1983.

which we extrapolate its impact on aggregate production and a number of suggestions for policy.

2. DISABILITY AND THE LIFE CYCLE

Globally, the prevalence of moderate to severe disability increases from 2 per cent in infancy to 55 per cent in the over-80 age groups. Thus increased life expectation carries with it the 'paradox' of increasing disability prevalence rates.

In India, while 6 to 10 per cent of all disabled people were born with their disability, children are especially vulnerable to disabilities resulting from malnutrition and communicable diseases. Children with disabilities are more likely to die young than they are in developed countries. So some forms of disability in India relate to age in a manner opposite to that of the global model. It has been estimated that 75 per cent of the mentally retarded, for instance, are under the age of 10 and only 4 per cent are over 20.[13] Dumbness behaves similarly. Other forms of disability, such as loss of aural and visual acuity, behave according to the global model and occur within the geriatric population with far greater frequency than in the general population.[14]

3. DISABILITY AND GENDER

The material and ideological subordination of women is so well documented that disabled women are expected to be severely socially disadvantaged. The disabled woman has been depicted in graphic terms as suffering 'multiple handicap'.

> Her chances of marriage are very slight, and she is most likely to be condemned to a twilight existence as a non-productive adjunct to the household of her birth . . . (she may be) the object of misplaced [*sic*] sympathy . . . or she may well be kept hidden in order not to damage the marriage prospects of siblings; alternatively she may be turned out to beg.[15]

Yet World Bank evidence for India shows female survivors as having a 10 per cent lower disease burden and losing fewer disability-adjusted life years from disability than do males.[16] Disability-related mortality may be higher among girl children and women than it is among men. Anyway, this female 'advantage' is not distributed evenly across clinical disabilities. The 1981 disability ratio was highest at 1,789 males per thousand females for locomotor disability and 1,788 for speech disability; it was 1,211 for the hearing-disabled and only 699 for visual disability where (despite the fact that over three times more men than women are born blind) the sex bias is antifemale.[17] Female advantage may thus be translated into female disadvantage by socialization and discrimination.

4. DISABILITY AND POVERTY

Disability and poverty are closely related. In OECD countries, for instance, disability causes poverty.[18] In a country with mass poverty, poverty also causes disability.[19] The mechanisms include malnutrition, inadequate access to inadequate preventive and curative medical care, and risks of accident or occupational injury. Poverty interacts simultaneously with caste, family size and the quality of parental or adult care to create the condition of *simultaneous deprivation*. Sen (1992) finds that simultaneous deprivation is further compounded by a syndrome composed of ideological reinforcement, punitive experience, psychological extinction, stimulus deprivation and a cognitive and verbal development which especially affects what is beautified as the 'participation' in the economy of low-caste groups: the terms and conditions on which they are forced to labour. This syndrome sets up barriers to the participation of all types of disabled people, but especially mentally disabled people and especially girls. The positive association between disability and poverty is confirmed in the three villages of our resurvey (see Table 2).

Working with people's own definition of chronically sick and disabled, between 17 and 30 per cent of households had at least one chronically sick or disabled member – there being wide intervillage variation. A slightly higher proportion of these households were below the income poverty line and had assets under Rs 5,000 than households without disabled members and lower percentages of households with incapacitated members were in the top assets category. Chronic sickness and disability seem to affect both short-term and long-term poverty. Households with chronically sick and disabled people

TABLE 2 Households with and without disabled members, Tamil Nadu, 1993–4

	Village 1		*Village 2*		*Village 3*	
	a	*b*	*a*	*b*	*a*	*b*
No of Households	270	75	217	45	96	41
Av income Rs/yr	12400	7650	13500	11300	9500	7000
% of Households below Poverty Line*	51	54	36	60	51	62
% of Households with under Rs 5,000 assets	31	35	26	47	24	30
% of Households with greater than Rs 100,000 assets	20	10	2	3	25	15

* computed at Rs 6,000 for a household of 4 members
a = without chronically sick or disabled members
b = with chronically sick or disabled members

Source: Field survey, 1993.

tended to have smaller family sizes, smaller operational land-holding sizes, lower grain consumption from own production and greater market dependence for food. Working members put in fewer days on average into their own agricultural production and more in non-agricultural production than did 'healthy' households. Those with sick and disabled members had livestock of lower value than those without, and higher levels of debt.

But others argue an inverse relation between income poverty and the prevalence of disability on grounds that mortality from disability is greatest among the poor. There is evidence for a *disability transition* during which disabilities due to malnutrition and infectious/contagious disease are eradicated. However, they are more than offset by reduced mortality rates, the increased survival of para- and quadriplegics and by increases in disabilities due to trauma and old age, such that the total incidence of disability increases.[20] There is international evidence for the inverse relationship.[21] This latter evidence, however, is no excuse for non-interventionism just because raised levels of mortality result from the economic incapacity of poor families to sustain the lives of disabled members.

5. DISABILITY AND THE ENVIRONMENT

Two aspects of the environment seem to be important. The first is that factors in the physical environment may predispose towards disability. The second is that the social, spatial environment may predispose towards disability.

With respect to the first aspect, the National Sample Survey's 36th Round in 1981 showed that certain states (Bihar and West Bengal in the north; Maharashtra, Andhra Pradesh and Tamil Nadu in the south) have much higher than average concentrations of disabled people.[22] The prevalence of locomotor handicap is strongly associated with agriculturally advanced regions; that of deafness and dumbness with northern regions and Himalayan valleys. The incidence of leprosy is strongly concentrated in tribal regions of Bihar and West Bengal, as well as in Tamil Nadu and Andhra Pradesh in the south.[23]

Research on the 1981 census data for Uttar Pradesh confirms that disabilities have strong environmental geographies. The state was classified into contiguous regions of high, medium and low prevalence. High-prevalence regions had over 14 times the state's average prevalence. This concentrated distribution is attributed to environmental factors (lack of iodine), diseases (poliomyelitis and lathyrism), social and economic factors (low levels of urbanization, high levels of food insecurity, poverty and 'criminal offences' which incapacitate victims).[24]

With respect to the social environment, it has been argued that the prevalence of disability is higher in urban than in rural areas. But while the rate of urbanization is 25 per cent in Uttar Pradesh, 9 per cent of disabled people were urban in location.[25] In Uttar Pradesh, highly urbanized districts had the lowest prevalence of the censused disabilities, the lowest incidence of poverty and the highest incidence of health care infrastructure.[26]

So disability identifies a big social category, like poverty does. But complexity is central to disability and this medicalized social condition cannot be reduced to one criterion for evaluation in the way that until recently poverty has been appraised and evaluated for policy purposes – however crudely and controversially – by income. Just as social factors – such as gender, age (and caste) – and economic factors – such as poverty – condition disability (sometimes in opposite ways to those which have been modelled), so environmental factors – such as the disease ecology and physical resources – and political factors – such as the distribution and type of health care – play a spatial role in the creation and perpetuation of disabilities.

6. THE RESPONSE OF THE STATE

India serves as an apt example of a country which has all but ignored the economic, social and political rights of its disabled citizens. Historically, the Constitution offers no comprehensive or specific legislation ensuring the rights of the disabled Indian.[27] In India, disabled people are given concessions in two sectors of the economy: education and employment. The legal justification for such reservation is beyond controversy, however there is no direct provision in the Constitution conferring a legal entitlement to such reservation on disabled people. Disabled people's 'rights' are instead protected by a class of administrative procedure called the Office Memorandum, which has no significance in law.

The development of procedure to reserve employment for disabled people has been slow and piecemeal, lagging far behind that for scheduled castes and tribes. From 1957 to 1965 a 'sympathetic attitude' to disabled people was encouraged by government order. Employment concessions were introduced in 1965, reservations in the lower levels of central government service and in public-sector enterprises from 1977 to 1978 and discretionary 'preference' in upper levels in 1986. Promotion between the lowest two groups in government service had to wait until 1989.[28]

Formal sector reservation is not guaranteed by the Indian Constitution, but 1 per cent of category C and D public-sector employment (clerk, assistant, orderly, peon) is allotted to blind, deaf and locomotor-disabled people. While most states strain to comply with this reservation, in Tamil Nadu this quota is as much as 3 per cent and there is also a 3 per cent quota in all professional and technical institutions.

No evaluation of the system of reservations for disabled people has been found. It is said that reservations are not monitored, that quotas are not filled. In such conditions, the practice of reservations and concessions for disabled people is putting the cart before the horse, since there is no congruence between resources and the population eligible for them. It is also argued, usually by non-beneficiaries, that rather than reducing disadvantage, such positive discrimination actually reinforces it by the intensely political focus given to labelling and eligibility.

Procedural aspects of policy for disabled people suffer from being low-status, arbitrary and the result of a reactive politics. The Constitution, under Article 41, envisages a comprehensive social security system which enables the lives of disabled people to be fulfilled. This constitutional responsibility is currently realized only in a weak reservations policy which does not guarantee entitlement. According to the Supreme Court, which has the power to set binding precedents through judgements, 'it is not possible to compel the state through the judicial process to make provision by statutory enactments or executive fiat for assuring the basic essentials which go to make up a life of human dignity'.[29]

The needs of the disabled are then compartmentalized under the Government of India's Ministry for Social Welfare. Resources have always been meagre.[30] In 1988–9, for instance, the central Government of India's Ministry of Welfare allocated the sum of Rs 960 lakhs for disability-related programmes. This sum was less than the budget for a medium-sized municipality. It was less than the short-term cooperative credit for a small district. It was less than what neighbouring Sri Lanka spent on disability in a population under 2 per cent of that of India's.[31] In the 1990s, resources began to be expanded.[32]

In principle, the state finances on a means-tested basis the purchase of artificial limbs (both orthopaedic and prosthetic) for physically disabled people, the purchase of Braille kits and tape recorders for blind people and corner seats and prone boards for people with spastic limbs.[33] As of 1990, access to 100 per cent subsidies on goods and services up to Rs 3,600 required disabled people to have a monthly income below Rs 1,200. Access to 50 per cent subsidies was limited to those with monthly incomes between Rs 1,201 and 2,500. In practice, these funds are severely rationed, both to voluntary agencies and to individuals. While it may be argued that people with disabilities use 'ordinary' state services, the National Sample Survey reported that over half the disabled people they identified had never seen a qualified physician for any purpose.[34]

So far, the Indian State has failed to create a coherent agenda for disabled people, a legal frame of obligation and an institutional means whereby needs can be translated into practical claims. The resources devoted to alleviating disabilities, to which a tiny fraction of those needing support actually gain access, are on a trend of decline in real terms. The state also fails to regulate both the private sector and NGOs with any consistency. For the mass of disabled people, the state does not exist.

Despite favourable cost–benefit ratios, the costs of training, education, care and assistance are left to NGOs which themselves are only able to reach an alleged 3 per cent of the disabled population, predominantly in urban locations.[35] This tendency has been compounded by the historical legacy of religious missions assuming responsibility for organizing both segregated institutional care and community outreach programmes for disabled Indians; resulting in the heavy reliance on voluntary non-governmental services to marginalized groups, rather than use of more formal, state-operated and funded services which would provide a mechanism through which disabled people could claim constitutional rights (albeit vaguely specified ones).[36] The vast majority of disabled Indians are 'socially excluded' from official provision.

We sought to use village studies to answer three questions: i) what do disabled adults do in a rural society depending on hard physical labour; ii) what are the costs and economic impact of disability; and iii) what do disabled adults need? We used a social model of disability in which incapacity is related to environments and social situation and which seeks to discover the causes and effects of incapacity in an open way.

7. INCAPACITATION IN THE RURAL ECONOMY

The 1993 census of the three villages found an average of 19 per cent households declaring that at least one member was chronically sick (CS) or disabled (D). Acknowledging fatigue among our respondents, it was decided to explore the issue further in three other villages close by, between Walajabad and Kancheepuram in Chinglepet District. These are villages where an NGO has been active in the causes of i) countering violence against scheduled-caste women, ii) education, and iii) the organization of claims to economic and social rights. The field work reported here, in the nature of a pilot project, was carried out over four months in 1995 by an anthropologist (Susan Erb) with language assistance and logistical support from the NGO (but without specialized medical input).

The three villages (Thammanur, Kalur and Vitchanthangal–TKV) each comprised caste settlements with separate scheduled-caste hamlets ('colonies'): totalling 540 households (1,753 adults). Half of the households are landed and the majority depend to some extent on agricultural wage labour. Five per cent of households with land and looms control 48 per cent of the total income, while 43 per cent, mainly labouring households, account for 18 per cent of the total income of these three villages. The scheduled-caste population amounted to 23 per cent. Some 15 per cent of households, none of which were scheduled-caste, worked in the non-farm economy (mainly in silk saree weaving and in its ancillary industries). The latter activities accentuate economic inequality.

8. INCIDENCE, TYPES AND CAUSES

While disabled children were very rare,[37] some 8.5 per cent of adults – 156 people – described themselves as disabled/incapacitated, and practically all in adulthood (see Table 3). Their incidence was evenly distributed across the genders (47 per cent male and 53 per cent female) but biased towards the caste population (86 per cent were from the 68 per cent of the total population who are caste Hindus, with only 16 per cent of scheduled-caste adults admitting incapacity). However, the lower incidence of disability in the 'colonies' was due to the different social context of landlessness and poverty in which disabilities have to be much more severe to be publicly recognized as such. Within the caste settlements, disability occurred in proportion to the distribution of intravillage castes, reflecting no type of caste bias. Most disability encountered was mild to moderate in form and the result of old age, occupation-related diseases and accidents and illness. The range of disabilities affecting rural workers was vast. Conditions which would not be deemed disabling according to Western medical definitions were seen to result in disability owing to indigenous definitions of health/ill-health and/or inability to work productively in an agrarian society heavily dependent on physical vitality.

Almost all disabled people were physically impaired, having visual loss, orthopaedic disorders and hearing impairments. Mental disability went practically unnoticed in women, a comment on the nature of the work they are required to do. Old age tends to be defined by the onset of incapacitating conditions rather than by years alone. But many of the conditions which incapacitated people from work were the product of occupation-related diseases, conditions and accidents. Since the landless agricultural labour force spends years staring at the

TABLE 3 Rural adult disability 1995: populations

	Total		Disabled	
	Male	Female	Male	Female
Thammanur				
Village	358	347	35	48
Colony	169	157	9	4
Kalur/Vitchanthangal				
Village	239	237	22	26
Colony	162	84	8	4
TOTAL	928	825	74	82

reflection of the sun in flooded paddy fields, as they tend seedlings in nurseries, transplant and weed, it is hardly surprising that such workers suffer sight impairment in early middle age.[38] The public space of villages without electricity supplies is dark and dangerous at night and roots, unembedded water pipes, rutted pathways and holes in the ground can damage limbs with consequences on work that we will track. Silk looms are installed in huts which, in an effort to keep out heat, are not only poorly ventilated but also very poorly lit. Conditions not disabling according to Western medicine can be incapacitating in the universe of rural work, notably because they make sustained physical effort painful: sterilization was quoted several times in this regard (medical treatment is regarded as potentially disabling); ulcers and other causes of chronic stomach pain; deep-seated warts (disabling pain in the foot); asthma (and other causes of dizziness) etc.

Disability, chronic sickness and pain were seen to elide. In these villages, then, 'disability' is an affliction, usually physical in nature, which results in the partial or complete incapacitation of a household member. The moderate nature of most impairments means that even if incapacitated people could gain access to treatment, their condition denies them eligibility for state and NGO facilities, which tend to be complements to, rather than substitutes for, one another and are confined to severe cases.

9. THE SOCIAL CONSTRUCTION OF DISABILITY

Gender, caste and class condition the perception of incapacity and a household's response to it.[39] While slightly more women than men acknowledge themselves as disabled, domestic work hides both the condition and its impact. Women's domestic work is a compulsory prior which is difficult to negotiate. We might infer from the social relations behind these village statistics that considerably more women may be disabled than are men but that fewer may be able to declare themselves incapacitated. Fieldwork showed that women also recognize themselves to be disabled at a more advanced stage of incapacity than do men. Even when forced to withdraw from agricultural labour, half of the disabled women continue to perform domestic work. There is no relaxation in the domestic division of labour.

In a similar way, scheduled-caste people have to be more severely disabled than inhabitants of the caste settlement before they will publicly acknowledge their infirmity.

Class also determines the type and intensity of work, exposure to environmental hazards, poverty and the capacity to 'come out' as disabled. By and large, landed disabled people are less severely incapacitated than landless agricultural labourers. Not only is the latter's work more energy-intensive and hazardous, but their work hours are longer.[40]

10. TREATMENT AND RESPONSE

While 53 per cent of caste males seek and obtain some kind of treatment for their condition, only 11 per cent of (more severely disabled) SC females can do this. In this region, treatment is always sought from the public and private allopathic systems. In both cases, since the public health system is de facto substantially privatized (through rents, payment for prescriptions and private referrals[41]), payments are involved. There is a huge variation in access and in the type, cost and competence of the clinical response (see Table 4). Clinic visits usually result in the provision of analgesics, and of spectacles for those who are partially blind and who can afford to pay. The entire process of 'care' is also socially constructed and extremely male-biased (Table 5). As regards women, 26 per cent fewer (more severely incapacitated) caste women get any kind of treatment and their care is 75 per cent less costly on the average than that of men. Only men had treatment involving surgery. Among scheduled-caste people, even though their economic participation rates are much more gender balanced, 80 per cent fewer women than men get access to treatment. The seasonality of visits to clinics does not relate to the timing of onset of an incapacitating condition, rather it reflects labour demands and the prior compulsions of wage work. Treatment is more frequent in the agricultural slack season and is usually part of a multipurpose journey.

TABLE 4 The cost of treatment of disability (1995)

Types of Treatment	Clinic Visit (with medication)	Spectacles	Hearing Aid	Orthopaedic Aid	Surgery
Cost	Rs 75–150	Rs 150	Rs 750	Rs 500–10,000+	Rs 2,000–15,000+

TABLE 5 Services received by gender (1995)

	Males			Females		
	Main Settlement	Colony	Total	Main Settlement	Colony	Total
Total Disabled	57	16	73	74	9	83
Total Treated	30	9	39	29	1	30
Percentage of all Disabled Adults Receiving Treatment	53%	56%	53%	39%	11%	36%

The costs of being disabled have three components: i) the direct costs of treatment, including the costs of travel and access; ii) the indirect costs to those who are not directly affected (called 'carers' in the West); and iii) the opportunity costs, the income foregone from incapacity. The direct annual costs of incapacitation vary staggeringly from the equivalent of three days' work to that of two years' work for an average household of able-bodied agricultural labourers with two adults and two children (ALHH) in which a male income averaged Rs 3,000 and a female one Rs 1,800 per annum. Direct costs depend on the type and severity of the incapacity. The average annual direct costs, Rs 1,200 in 1995, are equal to three months' income for an ALHH. The average orthopaedic treatment amounts to five months' labour for an ALHH. Added to this are opportunity costs, totalling an average of Rs 1,800, that is four months' income for an ALHH. The average direct and opportunity costs of incapacity for a woman are 25 per cent of those of a disabled man. This gender difference in the treatment of disability is due to: i) gender ideologies expressed in gendered differences in the evaluation of severity; ii) biased access in treatment and social response; iii) gender roles stressing the subservience of woman; iv) differences in earnings from gendered labour markets and contractual arrangements; and v) the dominant role of unwaged female labour in the indirect cost component.

Indirect costs to 'carers' arise in only 4 per cent of cases, where the disabled person cannot complete his or her daily living tasks unaided. None of those who help with these personal tasks have ever earned wages. Yet this addition to their domestic work burden has effectively excluded all of them from 'participation' in the labour market. All the 'carers' are female and one is disabled herself. It is not uncommon in these admittedly rare instances to find a girl removed from school for such work, in which case she is denied future returns to education. We have not attempted to compute this income stream foregone.

11. THE IMPACT ON HOUSEHOLDS AND ON THE RURAL ECONOMY

For half the incapacitated men and two thirds of the women, the costs of treatment prohibit any treatment at all. Most of these people continue to work more or less dysfunctionally in the agricultural labour market and in their homes. Others interpret the treatment improperly, do not complete it or share prescriptions – practices which lower both the direct cost of the response and its therapeutic impact. Even so, such households tend to be dosed with debt and make strong efforts to minimize the economic dependence of disabled members.

In these villages, being incapacitated does not seem to affect social standing:

disabled people are not socially excluded or ostracized on account of disability, almost certainly because of its onset during adulthood. But disabled people have fewer days of employment and lower wages when they work. Sight is more important than hearing to casual agricultural labour. An inability to contribute to the household economy definitely affects social status (hence there is a double incentive to minimize economic dependence – loss of status and avoidance of debt). Status is of particular importance in the lives of elderly, incapacitated men.

The onset of disability is an economically disabling event for the entire household. The loss of a complete male income pitches an ALHH without savings immediately into debt. The loss of a complete female income leads to an income loss such that an average ALHH cannot feed itself adequately (assuming expenditure on calories amounts to 85 per cent of the reduced income). In over half the cases of male disability and over a third of those of female disability, households are set on a track of downward economic mobility as a result of the loss of earnings of the incapacitated person.

The sequence of coping and survival tactics bears a strong family resemblance to those modelled for the process of famine (see pp. 433–5):

i)   drawing down of savings;
ii) incurring of emergency debt – typically in the region of Rs 500 – from local neighbours;
iii) increased debt from moneylenders and pawnbrokers;
iv) female assets (jewels) disposed of before male assets (land/house site);
v)   begging from neighbours (and therefore caste folk).

In this process of destitution, blind, landless widows without supportive children are the worst off.

We have attempted to summarize and stylize the evidence given us so as to calculate the likely costs of disability to a household and to the rural economy (see tables 6 to 8). Table 6 uses the evidence on the numbers of adults involved, their gender and socio-geographical origins given in Table 3 to compute the proportions of disabled adults incurring the three types of cost due to disability and the estimated average direct, opportunity and indirect costs for the year 1995. In Table 7, the impact of the full cost of an average disabled person has been estimated for two types of households, the first simulating the mass of the labouring population and the second simulating the loom-owning agrarian elite. Here our data begin to come to life. They show how an agricultural labouring household cannot bear the full costs of a disabled male without being plunged into considerable debt, while the full costs of a disabled man or woman in a loom-owning household are a substantial drain while not threatening its elite status.

TABLE 6 Costs of disability to a household, 1995

Costs	% of disabled people affected	Rs
Direct:		
men	57%	1,200
women	36%	864
Opportunity:		
men	47%	3,900–12,000[1] av: 7545
women	35%	1,800
Indirect	4%	1,800

1 the average is weighted according to estimated differences in incomes before and after disablement in actual occupational distribution of disabled men (0.39 agriculture + 0.44 agricultural labour + 0.15 silk + 0.03 other (mill work) = (2613+2451+1800+324)

TABLE 7 Differentiating impact of disability: full costs, 1995

	Rs
Agricultural labouring household income	5,700
with disabled male	−6,900 = −1,200
with disabled female	−4,464 = 1,236
Silk weaving household income	36,000
with disabled male	−15,000 = 21,000
with disabled female	−4,464 = 31,536

TABLE 8 Costs of disability to rural economy, 1995 (based on TKV villages and colonies)

	n	%	av income (Rs)	total income (Rs)	%
a) RURAL ECONOMY					
Landed agricultural hh	251	48	9,200	2,309,200	33
Ag. Wage Lab + Millwork	18	3	12,600	266,800	3
Agriculture plus looms	10	2	27,500	275,000	39
Landless Agric labour hh	228	43	5,7000	1,299,600	18
Loom owning hh	18	3	36,000	648,000	9
	525			4,758,600	
b) SOCIAL COSTS OF DISABILITY					
Direct costs		males	(d.p. × 0.57)	49,932	
		females	(d.p. × 0.36)	25,816	
Opportunity costs		males	(d.p. × 0.47)	258,869	
		females	(d.p. × 0.35)	52,290	
Indirect costs			(d.p. × 0.04)	11,232	
				398,139	

c) LOSS TO RURAL ECONOMY 8.4%

The income gap between labouring and elite households (a factor of at least 6 in the absence of disability) rises to a factor of 25 for disabled adult women and towards infinity for men because of negative income streams in the poor household. *Disability is the more serious an economic shock the poorer the household in the first place and it is economically differentiating.*

In Table 8 there is an estimate of the social costs of disability to a rural economy, simulated by data aggregated for the three caste villages and three scheduled-caste colonies.

Set against this simulated economy we see in Table 8 an estimate of the economic losses from locally defined disabilities. The largest components of the social losses are those pertaining to men. *The direct and opportunity costs of disabled women are one quarter those of disabled men*; this is due, first, to gender ideologies leading to the undervaluation of the severity of female disabilities, second, to gender roles stressing subservience and support and, third, to gender differences in wages in the labour market. In addition, the small component of indirect cost is borne by women and girl children. *The cost to society of disability which directly affects 8 per cent of adult men and 10 per cent of adult women and which indirectly affects the lives of a third of the rural population, connected by ties of close kinship and living in the same households, is about 8 per cent.*[42] This can be read in several ways. There are those who would read this as a small loss. Disability does not stop rural Indians from working. Disability is not much of a development problem. It is perfectly reasonable then that disability should be outcast from the social welfare agenda as it operates in practice, even if it is included in policy rhetoric.

The value of micro-level village research lies in its capacity to provide an alternative interpretation and one that we believe is more reasonable. First, it is a development problem: a proportion of gross product needing to be reduced. *Losses to incapacity are twice the estimates of current productivity losses due to undernutrition, losses interpreted as 'huge'.*[43] Second, it is a partial and underestimated representation of the social costs of incapacity due to the important invisible contributions made by women in not acknowledging their own impairments in the first place, by their unwaged reproductive domestic contribution to the economy and by their unwaged care for disabled relatives. Third, this 8 per cent can be read as underestimated because so many disabled scheduled-caste and caste men from landless households and from households with hardly any land are actually coerced by poverty into continuing to labour for wages. Fourth, the loss of productive income due to disability and incapacity reflects the low wages paid to both male and female agricultural labour – and thus the low opportunity cost of the agricultural income foregone.

Irrespective of the exact type of disability (and many disabled people have moderate-degree combinations of impairments which confound the notion of type), there are social rules regulating the relations between impairments, work compulsions, expert treatment, social assistance and domestic care. These rules work through land relations and control over productive resources, through caste, gender and household composition. These rules further lead to a distribution of costs due to disability which are highly unequal and in which those most dependent upon the labour market for income, those anyway most socially discriminated against, and those who are gender-subordinated, work without social acknowledgement until they are much more severely impaired than others. Landless scheduled-caste women are particularly more vulnerable to exclusion from any treatment. Their household poverty is then exacerbated by the heavily male-biased recourse to narcotics and/or alcohol for the relief of pain and of feelings of guilt, a form of therapy which can cost a labouring household between 10 and 40 per cent of its income. This cost was not included in the calculation of the costs of disability to the rural economy. Nor were the opportunities and incomes foregone by child substitute labour. Nor was the invisible, unwaged household productive and reproductive work of disabled women. Nor was their unwaged work as carers, except for the tiny minority of women caring for completely dependent disabled people. All these costs are unknowable, but they are not trivial. If included, they might more than double the social costs of disability.

However this statistic is interpreted, the needs of disabled rural people are worth listening to. For the first type of interpretation, it is necessary to understand ways of increasing the physical efficiency by which disabled people participate in the economy, for the second, to distinguish male and female needs, for the third, to establish the rights of the disabled poor to social security and their real access to it and, for the fourth, to look at ways of creating livelihoods, improving the terms and conditions of employment and fighting for what the International Labour Office (1999) calls 'decent work' for disabled people.

12. DISABLED PEOPLE'S NEEDS

The fieldwork reported here has several implications for any polity concerned with rural poverty and distress. First, there is a need for schemes to increase the physical ease of economic participation. In 2 of the 156 households with disabled people, the trend to downwards mobility had been bucked and income has *risen* as a result of a transformation of the terms of participation in the economy of the disabled person. In one case of a well-landed household with 8 acres, a new buffalo milk business was set up for a deaf landowner, whose son took over his supervisory role and who was replaced in the fields by a hired labourer.

In another case, a blind woman had started trading in leaf plates, although this had the adverse indirect effect of her daughter's being withdrawn from school to take over the domestic reproductive burden.

Male and female needs can then be distinguished. Disabled women need access to treatment, pure and simple. Women did not receive treatment for four reasons. First, the costs of restorative equipment and clinical consultations were considered prohibitive. Second, the treatment of women's disabilities was perceived as a very low domestic priority. Thus, even when households did have access to liquid cash, it was used preferentially for agricultural investment or debt repayment. Also, if a disabled woman were to seek treatment, an adult would be subtracted from child care and domestic chores, leaving responsibilities unfulfilled unless there were other women to replace her – a complaint repeatedly voiced by male household heads. Third, many women appeared unaware of how to gain access to restorative equipment. Finally, there appeared to be a strong mistrust of allopathic medical practitioners regarding surgical treatment. Cataract operations had been recommended to four visually disabled individuals who were unwilling to invest either time or money in the surgery due to the demonstration effect of the failure of such surgery on neighbours. To these rural people, *medical treatment itself runs a high risk of being a disabling activity.*

Both men and women need *simple restorative equipment* (spectacles, crutches, hearing aids: see Table 9). For most poorly sighted people, their visual disability was too mild to qualify them for any government schemes enabling free access to ophthalmic tests, spectacles and facilities for the repair and maintenance of restorative equipment. It is altogether another matter that most had no idea such schemes existed or that they might have rights of access to them. The provision of spectacles would have allowed them to undertake household or agricultural chores with greater ease and efficiency and, in more than one household, might have allowed them to return to wage work and to participate more fully in domestic and social life.

The second need was for *short-term assistance in the form of loans or grants* to cover access to health care or equipment: up to Rs 500 in 1995 prices. Disabled people are more vulnerable to shocks and to costlier 'wear and tear' in day-to-day living. This expressed need is also a disguised plea for better public health care. Conditions which incapacitate workers are poorly recognized and treated. Private health care is much preferred, even by the poor. Inappropriate medicine may be prescribed; half-prescriptions obtained because of the poverty of patients; medication is often shared between people with the same condition. Poverty leads to quackery by doctors being to some extent matched with delinquency by patients. By the standards of micro-finance such loans would be

TABLE 9 Treatment and restorative aids sought by disabled adults, 1995

Services Wanted	Thammanur				Kalur/Vitchanthangal				Average Cost of Restorative Aids and Surgery (As Reported by Villagers)
	Main Settlement		Colony		Main Settlement		Colony		
	M	F	M	F	M	F	M	F	
Visual:	5	9	2		1	6			Rs 150 per pair of spectacles
Spectacles									
Cataract	6								Rs 600+
Surgery & Specs	1								
Eye Surgery									unknown
Ortho: Prostethics									
Hospital Care	1								
Aural: Hearing Aid									Rs 800–2,000
Surgery	3	3	1	1		1	1		Rs 6,000
Surgery:		1							unknown
Uterine									
Clinic Care: Medication for									Rs 75–100
Pain Relief	2	5							
Pension:		1							
Handicapped									
Widow's		4						1	
Assistance with Medical Expenses:									Rs 600+
for Operations		2		1					
for Medication and	3	5**							Rs 50–Rs 100 per visit
Consultations									
Medical Cards	1	1							no cost

** one woman sought help with paying her son's school fees, since money set aside for that was spent on medical expenses.

extremely small and pose acute problems, not of default but rather of administration costs.

The third need was for *information, bureaucratic transparency and intermediation*, most specifically for access to social assistance entitlements which most commonly take the form of a pension of Rs 75, 4 kg of rice per month, plus an annual allotment of two sets of new clothing a year (see Chapter 3–7). These pensions can be for disabled, destitute, widowed or elderly individuals. Most commonly, disabled people gain access to old age and widow's pensions.

Our research showed that the eligibility criterion for a pension for disability is extremely harsh (again, see Chapter 3–7 for similar evidence for old age and widow's pensions). For disabled people who are unable to bring an income into the household, a pension can be a valuable social and economic asset. The government pension form is a standard document requiring information on the individual seeking the pension and details of their disability or their specific social, age and health status. Access to state pensions requires both a birth certificate and the signature of a doctor supporting the applicant's claim. Because the majority of disabled villagers did not fulfil the official conditions for 'handicapped pensions', they were often compelled to pay medical doctors large bribes to secure their support and signatures for other kinds of pension or benefit (which they saw as interchangeable). These bribes varied from two weeks' to seven months' worth of a female agricultural labourer's income. However, given that the pension is equivalent to two thirds of a woman's income, *the bribe might be as much as the equivalent of 14 months' worth of pension payments*: another swingeing indirect cost of disability which we did not include in our calculation of social costs.

In these three villages, 34 women had secured a widow's pension with payments of bribes ranging from Rs 50 to Rs 1,000. *There were no individuals in the settlements who were receiving 'handicapped pensions'.* A profile of a woman applying for the handicapped pension highlights some of the difficulties in gaining access to state provision.

Manjula is a 23-year-old woman who contracted typhoid fever at age 2, at which point government doctors diagnosed her as also having 'dwarfism' accompanied by '100 per cent weakening' in all four limbs. She was then and there declared fully handicapped by the government doctors and given a letter certifying her as such. She is immobile, unable to care for her daily living needs and has never contributed to household maintenance. She currently lives with her mother, two sisters and cousin. The household subsists entirely on the eldest sister's income from teaching of Rs 300 per month (less than the average income of a male agricultural labourer) and the mother's widow's pension of Rs 75. However, the household finds it virtually impossible to support five people on this sum and frequently takes out small loans from neighbours to pay for daily living expenses. Receipt of the handicapped pension would increase the household's monthly income by 20 per cent. There is no question of institutional care for Manjula.

In February 1995, a petition was delivered to a local official by Manjula's sisters with a bribe of Rs 500. However, the petition was returned with the explanation that Manjula is too young to receive a pension and, as a result, the official was unwilling to take the appeal further. On a charitable construction of such behaviour, this example of social exclusion is the product of bureaucratic ignorance.[44] According to government rules, Manjula *is* eligible for disability benefit. She is fully disabled, dependent on her family members for care and unable to earn an income. However, because the family cannot pay large enough bribes, the application will never be filed.

13. PUBLIC ACTION

In the introduction to this chapter, we outlined the roles of NGOs and the state. In this section, we chart the roles of these institutions in the region studied. NGO activity is thin on the ground. One Christian charitable organization provides shelter and a peaceful environment for disabled women. Certain medical doctors with a philanthropic disposition give free treatment for incapacitation (just as they do for other conditions). The international business-cum-philanthropic organizations (Lions and Rotary Clubs) set up peripatetic eye camps providing cataract surgery, eligibility for which is determined by the rural social networks of the largely urban professional and businessman members. Of the concerns of the literature on disability and development: one, income generation, is not seen by respondents as relevant to them and the second, empowerment, is seen as a problem of governance rather than of local social and political attitudes. Of the concessions for disabled people in education and employment, there was of course no sign in these villages, not so much because of the dereliction of duty by the state as because so few of the rural incapacitated were eligible through their medical and educational status and their age. Depending on the type of disability, between 1 and 3 per cent of medicalized and therefore severely disabled people have access to either an NGO or the state.

Incapacity and disability in these rural areas are dangerous to the individuals concerned and to their households. They cause efficiency losses in the economy and are the object of egregious neglect. It is argued that structural adjustment, in its reductions of public expenditure, places a disproportionate compensatory burden on women and in the domestic arena.[45] With respect to rural incapacity and disability, this process of cuts in public expenditure has been by-passed, for there was no public expenditure in the first place.

14. CONCLUSION

Evidence from the research area shows that medicalized and state-legitimated definitions of disability are but one way in which societies understand the concept of disability. The people we studied do not recognize or experience disability in terms of the classifications or severity categories of the medical model. Policy based on the medical model overlooks the large number of mild to moderately disabled rural adults incapacitated from rural work.[46] Conditions not disabling according to rigid medicalized definitions *do* result in disability according to local understanding and experience of health, ill-health and well-being. For individuals living in a society where economic productivity depends on physical stamina and manual dexterity, even a small loss of these skills can result in downward mobility. For the disabled people in the region we studied, social and economic standing is measured against capacity to work. Disability is predominantly defined according to the dual compulsions of household maintenance and the labour market. It is anything that prevents men and women from being part of the social reproduction of a labour process producing paddy, groundnuts and silk sarees.

Types, combinations and intensities of disability have a varying social impact on the disabled individuals and their household in light of age, gender, household status, class and wealth, caste and existing state provisions in terms of rights and social welfare assistance. The majority of adults in these villages were only mildly to moderately afflicted according to medical parameters. The ramifications for access to service provision for this doubly marginalized population is their exclusion from both private voluntary sector and government programmes intended to improve their standard of living. Until voluntary and government service providers modify their perception of who the disabled are and what their needs are, the costs of disability will remain high.

Caste and gender remain highly significant determinants of disability. Women, especially scheduled-caste women, receive low priority for treatment. Identity as a disabled woman or as a disabled 'colony' inhabitant indicates a much higher degree of physical debilitation than is the case for disabled caste men. For women, this is the result of prevailing social perceptions that, even when women are unable to earn an income due to incapacitation, they are still required to carry out domestic work.

The lower incidence of disabilities in the 'colonies' results from the different social context of landlessness, poverty and the compulsions of work in which disabilities have to be much more severe to be publicly recognized as such. Not only does the condition of disability cause poverty by means of direct, indirect and opportunity costs, but impoverished households are fundamentally more susceptible to disabling circumstances via malnutrition, defective access to preventative and curative medical care, exposure to disabling disease and an increased risk of occupation-related accident. Disability combines with poverty to create situations of downward mobility which are more strongly experienced within scheduled-caste households. Caste, family size and reduction in economic opportunity converge with disability to create a condition of simultaneous deprivation. Disability is differentiating.

It is society which is disabling rather than people who are disabled. Development indicates the social change which weakens the forces 'disabling people', households and classes. If gender and environment can become intellectual paradigms, why not also disability, which raises fundamental questions about human welfare?

Disability, like gender, is a cross-class phenomenon, even if relations of disability manifest themselves differently by class. Like gender, the relations of disability are reinforced by social divisions of labour and by ideologies which appear natural but are in fact historically constructed and which in practice are remarkably similar to gender-based ideologies of subordination. Like environmental issues, disability has a weak constituency. Like caste, ethnicity and old age, disability is a distinct kind of passport to exclusion, intensified with poverty, but cutting across poverty. Like poverty, disability entails political remoteness, but the second deprivation cuts across the first.

Gender and the environment have become influential development narratives not only because of the work of new social movements but also because of the impacts made by feminist and environmental professionals – and of social movements created and/or sustained by them in *developed* countries – upon international development institutions. Their current priority is the result of institutional engineering. The same constellation of forces is needed for disability, yet the constraints on disabled people as activists are far greater and more debilitating than those which curb the opportunities of women. The support of non-dominating professionals, the local state and even international aid agencies is the more necessary.

Disability is a highly varied condition. Complexity is key to understanding its social consequences. It should not be and cannot be reduced to a single criterion for the purposes of policy formulation. By doing the latter, the specific needs of individuals may be overlooked in favour of policy transfers from the West addressing the perceived needs of crudely categorized, severely disabled people.[47] As important as the provision of restorative equipment is to disabled rural

Indians, so also are small loans and access to social assistance and, last but not least, the improvement of rural health care and access to it.

ACKNOWLEDGEMENTS

We are very grateful to the people of the villages of Thammanur, Kalur and Vitchanthangal, to GUIDE (Gandhian Unit for Integrated Development Education), and especially to R Vasantha and Chitra whose help was essential to the fieldwork, to Drs Maya Thomas, Michael Miles, Karen Moore and Emma Haynes who read drafts, and to participants at the MIDS workshop, in particular Dr K John and R Vasantha, for their discussants' comments.

Food, Nutrition and the State in Northern Tamil Nadu

Barbara Harriss-White

1. THE POLICY IMPASSE

MODERN Tamil Nadu has placed food and nutrition first on its social wel-fare agenda. Since 1981–2, the state's current outlays for this purpose increased by a factor of 100 to stand at Rs 388 crores in 1994–5. Its outlay speci-fically on nutrition alone is the highest in India and greater than that of all other states put together. A review of food and nutrition policy in the state identifies and traces the historical development of the political forces which now chal-lenge this prioritization.[1] There are three types of food politics.

The first has been international. In the 1960s, in response to the discovery that Tamil Nadu ranked exceedingly low on average calorie availability,[2] USAID funded an ambitious survey into diet and nutrition, as a result of which the weaning stage of human growth was recognized as critical for nutritional dis-advantage and the lowest two deciles of the income distribution were identified as the most vulnerable. As a result, Tamil Nadu was made a 'policy laboratory', funded by the IDA/IBRD, in which the largest donor-aided nutrition scheme in the world was implemented, supported by interests pleading for highly targeted nutrition investment as a cost-effective element of the World Bank's lending for the development of human capital. The Tamil Nadu Integrated Nutrition Pro-gramme (known as TNIP) was set up in 1980 with the goal of reducing mal-nutrition by 50 per cent through a sophisticated mixture of voluntary weighing and anthropometric monitoring of children targeted at under 36 months, nu-tritional supplementation (with relapse treatment) for growth faltering and the centralized feedback of information. Implemented first in a few pilot districts, it was intended to be run state-wide, with World Bank funding phased out over time in favour of state funding. This did not happen. The project has also always relied heavily on a voluntary element.

By the time the TNIP pilot stage had expired, according to its in-house evaluation, malnutrition had been reduced by 29 per cent – just over half its target. However, while severe malnutrition had been eliminated, the proportion of young children in moderate conditions of malnutrition had actually increased. The relapse rate was high at 30 per cent. But the programme has been generalized and has its own 'vested' interests, ranging from its cadre of village workers to technical policy advisers in the World Bank, concerned with leavening the bank's neoliberal adjustment policies by measures to improve 'human capital'.

The second political forces are local and state-level. Shortly after TNIP had been set in motion, but with a long political tail (dipped in the waters of mass mobilization, mass redistribution and a rhetoric of mass risk reduction),[3] the Anna Dravida Munnetra Kazagam (the ADMK party, led by M.G. Ramachandran) assumed power, relaxed prohibition[4] and introduced the chief minister's nutritious meal scheme (NMS). This is a midday school-meal scheme aimed originally at children between 5 and 14 years[5] and justified not only as a nutrition intervention but overtly as a gesture of political patronage, employment creation and social welfare.[6] Heavily criticized at the time by development professionals as not scientifically sound, the project was 20 times larger than that of the World Bank. Rejected by the Planning Commission, it has required the imaginative mobilization and deployment of the state's own funds. While the scheme remains heavily politically personalized, the Dravida Munnetra Kazagam (DMK led by M. Karunanidhi) opposition wasted no time in embellishing it when finally in power, with foods (a fortnightly egg) which make no sense in terms of nutritional cost-effectiveness. In the 1990s, when the All-India Anna Dravida Munnetra Kazagham (the AIADMK party, led by J Jayalalithaa) was returned, soya and corn flour were added for meals in school holidays along with sweet *pongal* to celebrate the birthdays of ADMK party leaders and luminaries.[7] Despite widening the target, participation declined from the later part of the 1980s (see Table 1). Evaluations during the 1990s show i) a general improvement in nutritional status, but ii) a gap in malnutrition opening up between the genders for the first time in this part of India (see Table 2), and iii) a secular shift in diet against coarse grains and towards rice. The latter trend was already set by the late 1970s[8] and is likely to have been further affected by the composition in the form of rice of the noon meal and the public distribution system. From Rs 3.4 crores in 1981–2, the NMS cost Rs 388 crores in 1995–6 (within which delivery charges – 5 per cent at the start – rose inexorably to 29 per cent).[9] Salaries are the bulk of this cost component. About 100,000 people are employed as cooks and helpers. Formal preference is given to employees who are low-caste/destitute

TABLE 1 The noon meal scheme in Tamil Nadu, 1982–3 to 1990–1

	TAMIL NADU			NORTH ARCOT		
	Centres	Bene-ficiaries (lakhs)	Em-ployees ('ooo)	Centres	Bene-ficiaries (lakhs)	Employees ('ooo)
1982–3	27,846	22.5	83.4	n.a.	n.a.	n.a.
1983–4	61,675	64.2	61.6	n.a.	8.9	6.3
1984–5	63,582	83	n.a.	n.a.	9.5	n.a.
1986–7	63,502	83	n.a.	4,900	9.8	n.a.
1987–8	63,913	85	n.a.	6,600	9.7	n.a.
1988–9	63,861	79	n.a.	6,600	8.9	n.a.
1990–1	66,231	77	n.a.	6,700	9.4	n.a.

Note: Publicly available data on this scheme is characterized by constantly shifting classifications and level of disaggregation such that the little that can be inferred about time trends is the material presented here.

Source: *Tamil Nadu Statistical Handbook*, relevant years (1982–3 to 1990–1).

TABLE 2 Malnutrition by sex over time (%)

a) Madurai District

Nutritional Status	BLS T-NIP-1 (1982)		End of T-NIP-1 (1986)		BLS T-NIP-2 (1992)	
	Boys	Girls	Boys	Girls	Boys	Girls
(Normal + Grade I)	69.9	55.7	68.5	53.2	80.5	61.6
Grade II	23.1	31.3	26.8	36.2	14.6	30.7
Grade III + IV	7	13	4.7	10.6	4.9	7.7

b) Ramanathapuram District

Nutritional Status	BLS T-NIP-1 (1982)		End of T-NIP-1 (1986)		BLS T-NIP-2 (1992)	
	Boys	Girls	Boys	Girls	Boys	Girls
(Normal + Grade I)	62.3	50.8	64.7	52.6	76.8	58.7
Grade II	26.2	31.5	28.2	35.4	17.5	31.1
Grade III + IV	11.5	17.7	7.1	12	5.7	10.2

Note: BLS = Base Line Survey.

Source: Narayanan 1996a, using T-NIP data.

widows/women, and at the start there was a certain amount of success with this positive discrimination. As is evident below, this has been diluted over time. Aside from its high visibility in public opinion, the intervention has built a decentralized and entrenched set of 'bureaucratic' interests in its perpetuation.

The third political force is both local and national (and has also been influenced by the Washington consensus). From the era of droughts in the 1960s, Tamil Nadu has controlled marketing and procurement (particularly in the Kaveri delta) in pursuance of a food policy objective of self-sufficiency (which it has never reached, being heavily dependent on imports from North India through the public distribution system [PDS]) (see Table 3). The Indian PDS covers about 10 per cent of foodgrains' distribution.[10] In Tamil Nadu, people's entitlement to PDS quotas of rice at controlled prices fluctuates, is politically controlled and has become ruralized as part of a more generalized political response to agrarian voters. In 1993–5, entitlements were widespread and hardly targeted (Table 4). The rises in the issue prices of ration (PDS) grain implemented by the Government of India in 1991 and again in 1994 as one prong of its agricultural reform policy were almost entirely absorbed by the Government of Tamil Nadu, in an act of political resistance to New Delhi. In Tamil Nadu, the real subsidies on the PDS and NMS to maintain stable food prices for poor adults and children *doubled* over five years, amounting to Rs 1,157 crores in 1995–6. While this exceeded the deficit on the state's revenue account,[11] both schemes have been politically rock-solid. In 1992, the Government of Tamil Nadu attempted to target the PDS to the poor but had to retract within four

TABLE 3 Public distribution system, Tamil Nadu, 1980–91 (lakh tonnes)

Year	Procurement	Offtake	
		Total	Rice
1980	1.62	6.6	3
1981	1.82	11.7	7.9
1982	5.95	12.5	8.1
1983	4.27	15.8	9.4
1984	7.31	16.1	9.7
1985	8.07	21.5	13.6
1986	9.5	16.9	11.8
1987	8.87	16.9	15.1
1988	5.64	17.4	15.7
1989	7.55	20.5	17.9
1990	9.5	17.1	15
1991	8.98	n.a.	n.a.

Sources: Indian Agriculture in Brief, 24th and 22nd editions.

TABLE 4 Fair Price Shop entitlements under Essential Commodities Act and prices 1983–4 to 1992, rural North Arcot, Tamil Nadu

	Rice			Oil		Kerosene	
	Entitlement	Prices Rs/Kg		Entitlement	Prices Rs/Kg	Entitlement	Prices Rs/Lt
		coarse	good				
1983–4	6kg/m/card	1.75	2.15	–	9	3 Lt/m	1.88–2.17
1984–5	4kg/m/person (max 20kg/hh)	1.75		1kg/m	10.55	10 Lt/m	2.37
1986–7	4kg/adult/m 2kg/child/m (max 12kg/hh) for hh with monthly income <Rs 1,000	1.75	2.5	–	11.20	3 Lt/m	2.53
1987–8	" -	"	"	–	13.65	"	"
1988–9	" -	"	"	–	16–17.5	"	2.28 -2.53
1990–1	4kg/m/person	2	–	3.50	13.65	"	2.95
1991–2		2	–	3.25			

Sources: Tamil Nadu Statistical Handbook, relevant years (1983–4 to 1992).

days. In 1995, Fair Price Shop workers were given permanent status as employees at a time when the state government was under intense pressure to shed staff.

Tamil Nadu, like Andhra Pradesh, is running a politics of opposition to staple food policy reforms about which there is a wide professional consensus.[12] Johl is typical:

> It would be prudent to target the priorities of the PDS to the really needy and vulnerable sections of society... Unless the PDS is rationalised to contain its requirements within reasonable limits, catering only to the exigencies of natural calamities... and for supply only to the vulnerable sections of the society, in addition to building reasonable levels of stocks for food security, the vicious circle of escalating needs for higher procurement targets and the accompanying market and price distortions will continue to play havoc to the farm economy which acts at cross purpose with the development of a free and competitive market.[13]

This minimalist formulation, the orthodoxy of the food policy high command, has been reinforced by canon from New Delhi: orders from the central government's Finance Commission to reduce subsidies on staple food. In 1992, New Delhi attempted geographical targeting on individuals in deprived regions and slums. New Delhi has found the PDS very difficult to reform, even as its control over food security to states like Tamil Nadu has increased. At the all-India level, despite the hikes in the issue price, food subsidies actually increased in the early reform period while PDS offtake declined (from 16.6 m tonnes in 1991–2 to 12.6 m tonnes in 1994–5).[14] In 1997, the PDS was targeted at households below an income poverty line and entitlements to the rest of the population were modified, greatly reduced or withdrawn.[15] Since political resistance is straining at its fiscal limits, states like Tamil Nadu with low debt–service ratios must borrow to maintain their food subsidies. Such borrowing is still regulated by the central government, which puts the policy ball back in New Delhi's court. The Tenth Finance Commission provided a blueprint for the reduction in food and electricity subsidies in the second half of the 1990s. Resistance to these recommendations by such states as Tamil Nadu involves a trade-off between on the one hand employment, expenditure on welfare schemes and developmental investment (all of which would need cutting) and on the other hand the raising of local tax revenue and plugging of tax loopholes – both of which are exceedingly difficult. To understand this resistance it is worth knowing the extent and character of nutritional vulnerability, the social profile of access to these nutrition interventions and the management of delivery systems. In addition, it is possible to compare and contrast food and nutrition in northern Tamil Nadu over a period of 20 years, when technical change in agriculture has affected both income distribution and crop prices and therefore the prices of the essential commodities which constitute a high proportion of the diet. These are the objectives of this chapter.

2. RURAL NUTRITION IN TIRUVANNAMALAI DISTRICT OF NORTHERN TAMIL NADU OVER TWO DECADES

Details of food consumption for 1993–4 were obtained for the sample of 128 households.[16] Four classes were distinguished as a basis for analysis to incorporate both agrarian and non-farm activity, exchange relations and demographic factors (see Chapter 1–4): i) poor non-agricultural households; ii) poor peasants with land; iii) poor landless households; and iv) elite households. Land holdings vary within these classes and overlap between them.[17]

This is a finer-grained classification than that used by Hazell and Ramasamy for 1982–4 (henceforth HR91),[18] but a rigorous comparison is precluded in any case by the smaller survey domain in 1993–4 and by the fact that 1982–3 was the second year of severe drought, while a follow-up survey in 1983–4, the year of recovery, was confined to a subset of those villages which had suffered most during the drought. So far as possible, however, the methodology followed by Pinstrup-Andersen and Jaramillo (1991) is used here so that a rough comparison may be attempted. In what follows, we have to make two rather heroic assumptions. One is that the 1993–4 data for the 3 villages are not wildly different from what those for the 11 villages would have been. The second is that the class of poor farmers proxies the category of the 'small farmer' of 1982–4 (with under 1 ha) and that of the elite households proxies that of 'large farmers' with more than 1 ha of operational holding in 1982–4. Table 5 presents details of these classes (and may be compared with HR91, table 5.1, p. 87, reproduced here as Appendix 1, Table 1). While between 1973–4 and 1982–3 the average size of landless households had risen from 3.6 to 4.4, that for small farmers from 5.1 to 5.6 and that for large farmers from 6.2 to 7.2, in 1993–4 family sizes in the subset of villages were smaller: 4 for landless households, 4.8 for poor households and 5.2 for elite households.

2.1 *Incomes and food expenditures*

Real incomes and expenditures have been deflated using the Consumer Price Index for Agricultural Labour (CPIAL) for the adjacent and quite similar district of South Arcot (in the absence of a district-specific CPIAL for the districts of North Arcot or Tiruvannamalai). These are presented in Table 6 (and see Appendix 1, Table 2, for the period 1973–4 to 1982–3). The income data for the

TABLE 5   Characteristics of study households (1993–4)

	Per H-H Family Composition			Operated Farm Size (ha)	
	Sample Size	Av. Persons	Adult Equiva-lent	In Village	Outside Village
VINAYAGAPURAM					
Richer H-H	9	4.89	4.12	0.37	—
PP-Landed	17	4.53	3.86	0.64	0.06
PP-Non-Landed	10	4.10	3.24	—	—
VEERASAMBANUR					
Richer H-H	7	5.86	4.61	0.92	—
PP-Landed	6	5.33	4.43	0.65	—
PP-Non-Landed	9	4	3.18	—	—
P-HH Non-Ag.	3	4	3.37	0.02	—
NESAL					
Richer H-H	15	5.07	4.35	1.25	0.46
PP-Landed	14	5.07	4.38	0.53	0.53
PP-Non-Landed	27	3.96	3.33	—	—
Rich Non-Ag.					

Note: 1 adult equivalent = 1 man older than 14 years old = 2.94 babies < 1 year old = 1.69 children 1–5 years old = 1.27 girls and women > 5 years old = 1.09 boys and men 6–14 years old.

Source of adult equivalence scale: Hazell and Ramasamy 1991, p. 87.

1982–3 period is biased severely downwards as a result of two years of severe drought, such that the best comparison skips a decade to 1973–4. Although there are wide intervillage variations (see Table 6),[19] *real* per capita incomes have increased over the two decades by a factor of 2.8 for landless agricultural labour households (Rs 885), 4.5 for small paddy producers (Rs 1,749) and by 6 for richer households (Rs 4,433). Despite the rise in absolute real incomes throughout the rural class structure, and in contrast to the conclusions drawn for the decade 1973–4 to 1983–4 (namely that income inequality was declining), relative income inequality is increasing. This is a result of investment in the non-farm economy by the agrarian elite, most notably in so-called informal financial institutions: transport, construction and rice milling (see Chapter 1–4). A similar trend (and likewise a conclusion different from that of the first decade) is evident in total real per capita consumption expenditure,[20] which has increased by a factor of 2.2 for landless labour (Rs 714), by 2 for poor producers (Rs 693), but by 3.2 for richer households (Rs 1,758).

While in 1982–4 food expenditures amounted to 70–80 per cent of total expenditure throughout the expenditure distribution, conditions were radically changed by the 1990s. Only among landless labourers in Veerasambanur and

TABLE 6 Annual consumption expenditure, income and food as percentage of total expenditure (in 1974 Rs per capita)

	Income Rs per person	Expenditure Rs per person	Income Rs per adult equiv.	Expenditure Rs per adult equiv.	Food Expenditure % of Total Exp.
VINAYAGAPURAM					
Richer H-H	1385.05	784.02	1643.90	930.54	54.12
PP-Landed	2119.11	871.64	2486.93	1022.93	51.30
PP-Non-Landed	897.68	871.19	1135.95	1102.43	48.71
Rich Non-Ag.					
VEERASAMBANUR					
Richer H-H	1845.65	526.90	2346.09	669.77	57.22
PP-Landed	537.69	373.40	646.92	449.26	66.36
PP-Non-Landed	809.50	517.43	1017.53	650.40	77.13
Rich Non-Ag.	1208.90	721	1434.89	855.79	67.23
NESAL					
Richer H-H	7471.94	2917.96	8708.67	3400.93	26.69
PP-Landed	1820.25	609.77	2107	705.83	73.83
PP-Non-Landed	906.83	655.13	1078.39	779.08	70.27
Rich Non-Ag.					

Deflator: 0.249 = 1973–4 constant prices with a rice price deflator.

Nesal does the relation remain. In other agrarian classes and villages the ratio is 50–60 per cent. Among the agrarian elite of Nesal it has actually fallen to 27 per cent, similar to average food-expenditure patterns of developed countries such as France and Italy.[21] Again we find a recent, strong, growing social differentiation in expenditure relations and a social and geographical transition in expenditure patterns within and between villages.

The cost of the diet (measured as the cost per 1,000 calories and deflated to 1973–4 prices) had increased during the first decade faster than had the general consumer price index (Appendix 1, Table 3); the average real cost of the diet increased by 50 per cent. Real food prices had increased and yet dietary diversification towards more expensive calories had also taken place. This was attributed to the income effect of the new agricultural technology. In 1993–4, the real cost of the diet per caput per day ranged inversely with class between Rs 0.13 and 0.3 (see Table 7). Over the second decade, it declined by an average of about 65 per cent.[22] The decline in costs can also be observed from the real price of rice per kg in 1993–4, which ranged greatly from Rs 0.77 to 2.14 per kg (in 1973–4 prices) with a median 11 per cent below that of 1983–4. By and large, the cost per calorie varied directly with class, elites eating more costly, fine-quality raw rice

TABLE 7 Rice prices and the calorie cost of the total diet (1993–4)

	Curr Rice Price/Kg	*Cost Curr/ 1000 cal.*	*Rice Pr./Kg. 1973–4 Pr.*	*Constant Cost/ 1000 cal.*
VINAYAGAPURAM				
Richer H-H	5.17	0.67	1.29	0.17
PP-Landed	5.20	0.68	1.29	0.17
PP-Non-Landed	5.02	0.70	1.25	0.17
Rich Non-Ag.				
VEERASAMBANUR				
Richer H-H	4.31	0.84	1.07	0.21
PP-Landed	3.08	0.79	0.77	0.20
PP-Non-Landed	3.71	0.71	0.92	0.18
P-HH Non-Ag.	6.18	0.59	1.54	0.15
NESAL				
Richer H-H	8.58	0.57	2.14	0.14
PP-Landed	5.74	0.54	1.43	0.13
PP-Non-Landed	8.17	1.19	2.03	0.30
Rich Non-Ag.				

Deflator = 0.249 = 1973–4 constant prices with a rice price deflator.

and poor households eating coarse-quality parboiled rice. The decline in rice prices will be affected directly by the supply of rice at heavily subsidized administered prices through the PDS but also by the deflationary effect of the PDS on open-market rice prices.

2.2 *Household energy and protein consumption*

Food consumption in 1993–4 was reported in quantities for a preceding month. Conversion to nutrients made use of the factors in Platt's classic food composition tables.[23] Conversion of household members by age and sex to male adult equivalents used the standard consumption coefficients specified in HR91 (Table 5, p. 87). While between 1973–4 and the recovery year of 1983–4 average calorie consumption per person increased in about two thirds of cases, the gap between small and large farmers narrowed, while that between small farmers and the landless widened. Average daily energy consumption per adult equivalent was about 1,900 calories in 1973–4, consistent with other estimates for the period and region.[24] By 1983–4, it was reckoned to be about 2,500 (Appendix 1, Table 4), but by 1993–4 it was 2,186 in the three villages. Table 8 updates the evidence. Over the second decade, daily calorie consumption had settled back: from 2,884 to 2,231 per capita for richer households and from 2,606 to 1,877 for poor peasant households. Calorie consumption in these households is very

TABLE 8 Daily energy and protein consumption (1993–4)

	Total Consumption Per Person	Calorie Per Day Per Adult =	Total Consumption Per Person	Protein Per Day Per Adult =
VINAYAGAPURAM				
Richer H-H	1815.62	2154.95	39.30	46.65
PP-Landed	2021.43	2372.30	43.82	51.42
PP-Non-Landed	1840.99	2329.65	41.54	52.57
Rich Non-Ag.				
VEERASAMBANUR				
Richer H-H	2468.37	3102.70	53.31	67.01
PP-Landed	1661.69	1999.28	35.53	42.75
PP-Non-Landed	1481.73	1883.50	33.84	43.01
P-HH Non-Ag.	2129.03	2527.03	49.75	59.04
NESAL				
Richer H-H	2338.76	3407.34	41.13	47.93
PP-Landed	1795.39	2078.22	16.93	19.60
(PP-Non-Landed	2890.70	3437.59	28.27	33.62)
Rich Non-Ag.				

Note: () queriable results, see note 25.

similar to that calculated for 1973–4. In many households, apparently low calorie consumption may not necessarily be want-induced. In landless labourer households, mean calorie consumption p.c.p.d. has increased from 1,642 to a weighted average of 1,700 – a 4 per cent increase over the decade. This is less than income and expenditure trends, but at variance with that of other classes.[25]

With increases in real incomes, an increase in protein consumption could be expected. But, with the exception of landless households which register a slight increase, these remain roughly constant and considerably below the (differentiated) levels registered throughout all social classes by Ryan and others in the late 1970s for four regions in South and Central India.[26]

In the first decade from 1973–4 the share of rice in total calories dropped by 25 to 50 per cent from three quarters to two thirds. Pinstrup-Andersen and Jaramillo argue that the absolute amount of rice consumed changed little but was complemented by a more diversified diet. Table 9 shows that rice still provides two thirds to three quarters of total calories. The shares of calories from rice have risen across villages and classes. Table 10 breaks energy down according to its food origins (and may be compared with Appendix 1, Table 5). Here, intervillage variation in the type and extent of diversification is more strikingly apparent than is social differentiation in diet. Whereas *ragi* and pulses provide 21 to 28 per cent of calories in Vinayakapuram, and while the diets of Veerasambanur are

TABLE 9 Energy obtained from rice consumption (1993–4)

	Total Calorie Consumption Per Person	From Rice Per Day Per Adult =	Rice Calorie Cons. as % of Tot. Cal. Cons.
VINAYAGAPURAM			
Richer H-H	1229.94	1459.81	67.74
PP-Landed	1278.24	1500.11	63.26
PP-Non-Landed	1142.08	1445.23	62.04
Rich Non-Ag.			
VEERASAMBANUR			
Richer H-H	1911.01	2402.11	77.42
PP-Landed	1356.01	1631.50	81.60
PP-Non-Landed	1067.02	1356.34	72.01
P-HH Non-Ag.	1643.50	1950.74	77.19
NESAL			
Richer H-H	1606.59	1625.05	68.69
PP-Landed	1214.59	1405.93	67.65
PP-Non-Landed	1776.60	2112.71	61.46
Rich Non-Ag.			

much more widely diversified than 20 years ago but still dominated by rice, in Nesal fruits and vegetables, and to a lesser extent groceries and dairy products, contribute materially to calorie consumption. This intervillage variation in dietary composition of nutrition is even more pronounced when protein is examined (see Table 11). In particular, in Nesal, negligible shares of protein appear to come from rice (2 per cent contrasted with 60 to 70 per cent in the other two villages). This may be a result of the 'festival bias' discussed in note 25.

2.3 *Energy deficiencies*

Malnutrition is a phenomenon most accurately ascertained at the individual level by anthropometric measurement and by clinical signs and symptoms. Food and nutrients supplies at the household level at a single point in time are only the roughest of indicators of household nutritional stress, let alone individual malnutrition. Nutritional stress may also occur in households without apparently low supplies owing to intrahousehold allocative inequities.[27]

In a separate study of the nutrition of households with children under ten years of age in Veerasambanur and Dusi villages in North Arcot, carried out in 1983–4 as part of an evaluation of the PDS and NMS, comparisons were made between energy intakes at the household level and energy requirements.[28] The notion of requirement is controversial for four reasons:

TABLE 10 Mean daily energy consumption by food items (*percentage of total calories consumed, 1993–4*)

	Rice	Wheat	Ragi	Pulses + Veget (Lentil + Veget)	Grocery	Meat + Fish	Dairy + Egg	Fruit	Sugar+ Sweets	Other Food
VINAYAGAPURAM										
Richer H-H	67.74	–	21.12	3.98	3.63	0.13	0.29	0.17	2.93	–
PP-Landed	61.01	0.52	28.19	3.50	1.91	0.41	0.17	0.26	2.77	1.25
PP-Non-Landed	62.04	–	24.78	4.73	4.21	0.02	1.28	0.18	2.77	–
Rich Non-Ag.										
VEERASAMBANUR										
Richer H-H	72.01	0.95	3.52	3.45	2.65	1.48	0.67	7.54	3.87	3.84
PP-Landed	81.60	2.60	4.03	2.25	1.60	0.54	0.06	4.46	2.06	0.81
PP-Non-Landed	77.42	1.30	6.47	2.03	2.08	1.25	0.09	6.30	1.61	1.46
P-HH Non-Ag.	77.19	0.90	2.65	5.53	2.41	0.56	0.98	5.31	3.30	1.16
NESAL										
Richer H-H	54.96	0.52	1.47	5.88	6.90	1.68	2.15	17.89	3.83	4.72
PP-Landed	67.65	0.63	3.93	5.24	2.98	0.85	1.15	14.20	2.63	0.74
PP-Non-Landed	61.46	–	1.22	4.02	3.83	1.32	1	19.50	2.64	5.01
Rich Non-Ag.										

TABLE 11 Mean daily protein consumption by food items (*percentage of total protein consumed, 1993–4*)

	Rice	Wheat	Ragi	Pulses + Veget (Lentil + Veget)	Grocery	Meat + Fish	Dairy + Egg	Fruit	Other Food
VINAYAGAPURAM									
Richer H-H	63.31	–	17.32	12.42	5.25	0.60	1.02	0.08	–
PP-Landed	56.95	0.76	23.09	11.37	2.76	2.74	0.54	0.12	1.68
PP-Non-Landed	55.62	–	19.49	15.05	5.84	0.08	3.85	0.08	–
VEERASAMBANUR									
Richer H-H	63.80	1.32	2.74	11.12	3.63	10.28	1.80	3.21	2.11
PP-Landed	77.21	3.87	3.34	7.50	2.34	2.79	0.16	2.02	0.77
PP-Non-Landed	72.52	1.91	5.31	6.76	3.01	6.64	0.24	2.83	0.77
P-HH Non-Ag.	66.84	1.23	2.01	17.92	3.22	3.66	2.55	2.21	0.35
NESAL									
Richer H-H	1.61	1.17	1.91	31.13	15.35	18.47	9.93	12.35	8.08
PP-Landed	2.96	2.14	7.62	40.71	9.90	11.52	8.37	14.62	2.16
PP-Non-Landed	2.59	–	2.28	28.95	12.26	15.64	6.98	19.36	11.94
Rich Non-Ag.									

i)   Requirement levels established from reference populations seem to be set high in relation to energy consumed by them.
ii) Standard alterations to Western requirements to cater for body weights, work and activity, pregnancy and climate in tropical conditions seem to result in exaggeratedly high norms.
iii) There is interindividual variation in requirements.
iv) There may also be intra-individual variations in requirements. It is hypothesized that the human body adjusts its efficiency of energy metabolism in a benign, autoregulatory manner over a range of levels of energy supply. Adjustment may also take physiological and/or behavioural forms.[29]

The choice of requirement is therefore somewhat arbitrary. The advantage of setting a 'low' requirement lies in its diagnostic accuracy. It is the more likely that nutritional stress will be felt by most or all members of households below a low requirement level.[30] We have used two concepts of requirement. The first is nutritional: 1.2 times the basal (resting) metabolic rate (BMR) for adults (calculated per kg of body weight) for the average body weight of an adult male in Tamil Nadu. This is 1,700 calories. This can then be used as a standard by which to evaluate the energy supply of each household (once its members have been converted to adult equivalents). It can also be used to compare the results of the 1993–4 surveys with those of the survey of Veerasambanur and Dusi in 1983–4.[31] Second, in order to compare our results with those of Pinstrup-Anderson and Jaramillo, we use their higher 'economists' standard of 80 per cent of the recommended daily allowance (RDA) for an adult man, 2,400 calories (HR91, p. 94). This is 1,920 calories. The results are presented in tables 12 and 13 respectively.

2.3.1 $1.2 \times BMR$

In 1982–3, 7 per cent of elite households and 55 per cent of poorer landed and non-landed households were estimated as having energy supplies below 1,700 per day per consumption unit. Table 12 for 1993–4 shows that one richer household in Nesal still falls into this category and the weighted intervillage average for richer households is half that of ten years earlier. Between 17 and 35 per cent of poor peasant households have low energy supplies (the weighted average being 27 per cent), while 25 per cent of agricultural labourers fall into this category. A weighted average of 26 per cent of all types of poor household risks energy stress.[32] The combined effects of real income increases, lower real food prices and access to the public distribution scheme have halved apparent nutritional stress between 1982–3 and 1993–4.

2.3.2 80 per cent RDA

In 1973–4, two thirds of small farmers, 56 per cent of agricultural labour

TABLE 12 Undernutrition and food stress, 1993–4

% households consuming less than 1,700 cals/day/adult equivalent			
	Elite	*Poor Landed*	*Poor Landless*
Nesal	7.5	23	23
Vinayagapuram	–	35	20
Veerasambanur	–	17	30
% households consuming less than 80% of Energy RDA			
Nesal	–	42	40
Vinayagapuram	–	47	22
Veerasambanur	–	33	40

Note: RDA = 2,400 cals/day/adult equivalent.

TABLE 13 Poverty and alcohol consumption

Village	*Sample Size*	*% sample hh drinking*	*Av. income of drinking hh, Rs/m*	*% of drinking hh*			
				<1 lt./m		*>1 lt./m*	
				>PL	*<PL*	*>PL*	*<PL*
Nesal	53	51	3,250	11	7	37	44
Vinayagapuram	37	27	2,400	60	10	30	–
Veerasambanur	23	65	1,900	33	20	20	27

Note: PL = poverty line = Rs 820 per average household of 4.2 people per month @ Rs 195.3 per person per month (see Chapter 3–2, note 22).

households and 39 per cent of richer households consumed less than this requirement level. Agricultural labour households were better off nutritionally than were small producers. By 1982–3, the proportion of small farm households in apparent energy stress had dropped to 56 per cent and those in the other two groups remained about constant.[33] In 1993–4, 38 per cent of poor peasant households were below 80 per cent RDA while 35 per cent of landless labour households suffered such stress. We see that much (about one third) of the energy stress identified by the less strict second criterion is of shallow intensity and is excluded by the use of the first. The shallower energy stress of poor peasants and landless labour appears to have dropped by about 35–40 per cent over the last ten years.

3. THE IMPACT OF CHANGE IN INCOMES, PRICES AND HOUSEHOLD FACTORS ON FOOD CONSUMPTION

In this section we examine the impact of income and price on nutrition. After Pinstrup-Andersen and Jaramillo, we modelled nutrition as a function of a vector of household, income and price variables and the analysis was disaggregated for two pooled subsamples, that of poor landed households and another of landless agricultural labour households.[34]

In each case we modelled nutrition in two ways:

i) as total daily calorie consumption per adult equivalent (LCALPAD);
ii) as daily calories obtained from rice per adult equivalent (LRCALPAD).

Independent variables were:

i) household size (PERS);
ii) monthly income per adult equivalent (LY_PMPAD);
iii) prices in Rs per kg of the principal food items:
    rice (LRICEPR)
    ragi (LRAGIPR)
    vegetables (LVEGPR)
    meat (LMEATPR)
    groceries (LGROCPR).

For the analysis of the nutrition of landless households, the last two items were excluded, as not only did they prove insignificant in a trial but also they reduced the explanatory power of the regression (judged by R squared and F statistics). A logarithmic transformation provided superior fits (see Appendix 2).

3.1 *Poor landed peasants (see Appendix 2, Tables 1 and 2)*

Income has little effect on total calorie consumption: the income elasticity of demand for total calories was 0.03 and income was insignificant as a determinant. By contrast, it was highly significant for rice consumption, with an elasticity of −0.26. A 1 per cent rise in income leads to a drop in rice calories of 0.26 per cent as consumers diversify their diets. Ten years previously income elasticities were calculated as much higher (that for total calorie consumption being 0.72 and for rice 0.9). There are two possible explanations for this phenomenon. One is that both total calories and rice consumption reach the flat part of the Engels curve. The second is that PDS supplies neutralize the effect of income, which is an important feature of a successful rationing system.

The rice price elasticity of total calorie demand was −0.48, emphasizing the sensitivity of rice consumption to prices. Other products – *ragi*, vegetables, meat and groceries – all had positive price elasticities and all, except that for meat, were above unity and highly significant. While *ragi* and vegetables had negative cross-price elasticities, groceries had a positive coefficient, showing that *ragi* and vegetables are substitutes and groceries are complements to rice consumption.

Household size has a positive but insignificant impact on calorie consumption. The explanatory power of the models is high and significant.

3.2 *Landless agricultural labouring households*
(see Appendix 2 and Tables 3, 4)

The same cannot be said of the model for landless labour, where almost all the variables are insignificant and the R squareds and F statistics are low. For what they are worth, the income elasticity of demand for total calories is 0.16 and for rice 0.09, which contrasts strikingly with the respective coefficients for 1983–4 – 0.78 and 0.87. The various price elasticities of demand for total calories were generally below unity and highest for vegetables. Unlike for the landed households, the cross-price elasticity of rice consumption and vegetable price is above unity (1.25) such that vegetables are a complement to rice while that for *ragi* is negative, *ragi* being a substitute, as it is for landed households. Household size exerts no effect on consumption, perhaps because it has reached a low limit, with little demographic variation in this class.

Income is thus only of significance to calories from rice in the class of poor peasants, while *rice consumption in both sets is sensitive to rice prices.*[35] *If income and prices are not very significant influences on total calorie availability at the household level, then something else must be. We suggest that this is the public distribution system, to which we now turn.*

4. THE ROLE OF THE PUBLIC DISTRIBUTION SYSTEM IN NUTRITION

Almost every household has access to the PDS both in entitlement and in practice (93 per cent in Nesal and the entire sample elsewhere[36]).[37] The Fair Price Shops from which rice is retailed at controlled prices also sell sugar and kerosene at controlled prices and under ration. Details of access are presented in Appendix 3. Rice consumed varied from 122 kg (in the households of poor peasants in Nesal) to 30 kg per household per year (richer households in Vinayagapuram). By and large, this was lower than the PDS consumption ten years previously and well under the quota everywhere (Appendix 3, Table 1). While quotas were underutilized to the same extent by all social classes in Veerasambanur, in the other two villages the richer households made less use of the PDS than did the poor. There was very considerable intervillage variation in access: Nesal, the most unequal, diversified and accessible village (with half the households in our sample), cornered no less than 86 per cent of the rice distributed in the three villages.[38] The PDS played a far less important dietary role among the other half of our sample in the other two villages, where the bias was less markedly pro-poor. On average, then, PDS rice made up 22 per cent of total calories and 35 per cent of calories from rice in the diets of richer landed households. It con-stituted 27 per cent of total calories and 39 per cent of rice calories in the diets of poor peasant households and 50 per cent of total calories[39] and 72 per cent of rice calories in the diets of landless agricultural labour. Here we have the ex-planation for the lack of effect of income and prices on nutrition. The subsidy was progressive: both absolutely and relatively less in the richer households than in the poor ones, where it represented a transfer of Rs 200–350 per year.[40] The bulk of the subsidy went to the most developed and unequal village, where it was heavily biased in favour of the poorest households (see Appendix 3, Table 2).

The PDS was evaluated by its users, as it was ten years previously (see Ap-pendix 3, Table 3). The system has not changed much. Employees are not sub-stantially more manipulative than a decade earlier. Outside scarce periods, self-sufficient households may donate their ration cards to poor/client house-holds. Only one household owned up to pledging its card to a shopkeeper in return for a loan. Interviews with PDS employees, however, revealed that pledg-ing is common. In 1994, one village grocery shop had ten cards from scheduled-caste households to which the shopkeeper had paid Rs 25–50 per card. That shop owner then purchased goods on ration (this time up to the full quota, which would be four times the actual average offtake per household) and retailed them at open-market prices. In all three villages, there were complaints from cardholders about poor quality and about tricks with weights and meas-ures. Other problems (adulteration in one, the sales of ration rice at open-market prices) were not so widespread. In addition to rectifying these faults, people asked for higher quotas not only for rice but for other commodities traded under the Essential Commodities Act. They revealed the political sensi-tivity of reductions in entitlement. Furthermore, certain other 'Essential Com-modities' are also diverted for trade. Subsidized kerosene is resold from ration shops to substitute for diesel (the price of which is three times the price of kerosene) in oil engines, a process which damages them.

The experience of PDS employees was juxtaposed. By social background all were male, from landed, caste Hindu households where agriculture was the main source of income. They had a higher social status than the bulk of their clients. One of three had paid a bribe to obtain the job. Supplies to their shops were timely but tended to be short, except for kerosene which was both delayed and short. Their own admitted chicanery with weights and measures was justi-fied as compensating for transit losses or theft of rice by Civil Supplies Corpor-ation employees, typically of 5 kg per 75 (or around 6 per cent). This is quite high, but very similar to leakages reported ten years earlier.[41] The sale of PDS rice at open-market prices at the month end also helps Fair Price shopkeepers to 'recoup losses'.

The delivery system of the PDS has not deteriorated noticeably and it remains a redistributivist measure, important in the calorie base of the poor.

5. ACCESS TO THE NUTRITIOUS (NOON) MEAL SCHEME

While a total of 78 children from 40 per cent of the households sampled ate the meals, our survey captured no pensioners taking this part of their pension entitlement. Access was gendered against girls throughout the age distribution but maximized in two physiologically sensitive age ranges: first, in the preschool cohort, where half as many girls as boys ate the meal; and second, in adolescence, when two young women ate the meal for every three young men who did. Access was biased in favour of the assets-poor and low-caste in all villages. No children from weaving households had access to the scheme because they were hard at work instead of at school. While 55 per cent of children from landless agricultural households took the meal, just 25 per cent of children from elite households did (see Appendix 4, Table 1). Although intended as a universal entitlement, the nutrition scheme turned out to be broadly socially redistributive. Holding class constant, the households where children ate the school meal (the calories from which were not included in the calculation of household consumption) had a lower average total calorie consumption than those where children were excluded. As was the case with the PDS, the subsidy on the NMS was progressive. It amounted to between Rs 45 and 57 per month for poor landed or landless households: the equivalent of twice or thrice the actual Rs benefit of the PDS and half the cash benefit of a pension. Depending on the number of children participating, it supplied an additional 740–939 calories to poor households. In proportional terms, the bulk of the subsidy went to the poorest, most remote village – thereby complementing rather than supplementing the distribution of the PDS (see Appendix 4, Table 2).

The NMS was evaluated for us by parents of its users (see Appendix 4, Table 3). It is hard to summarize the wide variety of responses. The noon meal ought to supplement food eaten at home. This was only the case (according to parents) in Veerasambanur, while in the other two villages parents said it substituted for meals at home. An important proportion of poor households reported the NMS as enabling families to improve school attendance. In Vinayagapuram and Veerasambanur, parents in exactly those poor households where food was most needed reported low quality or quantity: 'very bad food', 'worms and weevils in food' and 'no vegetables or green food'. Caste discrimination and the appropriation of food by cooks was a quite common complaint – along with demands for improvements in quality and quantity, for monitoring by state officials and for the involvement of parents in advising on recipes.

Employees of the NMS described their experience of the scheme. Unlike ten years ago, they are now 90 per cent caste Hindus, half from land-owning families in which their income was a minor element and half from landless households where this income mattered. They report caste interdining as a major achievement of the NMS. However they face systematic problems with raw materials. Supplies are fixed not on the enrolment record but on 90 per cent of enrolment on school days and two thirds during holidays. This is intended to dam leakages, but it means short supplies on occasions of complete enrolment when the 'feeding strength' increases. Over and above this, there are shortages in supplies at the point of offtake from the Civil Supplies depots. One estimate was Rs 250 per month, once more recouped by reducing the entitlement per person. Other problems for the smooth running of the NMS were the cash allocation for cooking fuel and for vegetables, the poor quality of the ingredients supplied and poor storage conditions – with rats a menace. Further problems for the organizers included delayed payments of salary.

The inspection of accounts, stocks and food quality is regular, politicized, but, unlike ten years previously, apparently no longer lubricated by any 'commissions'. However, while older employees generally did not secure their posts corruptly, this is no longer always the case and bribes as high as Rs 7,000 were mentioned. Corruption is far from expunged from the system.

A second group of nutrition workers managed to combine the work on the Tamil Nadu Integrated Nutrition Programme or TNIP (described at the start of this chapter and covering children aged from six months to three years) with that on the nursery/*balwadi* sector of the noon meal scheme (for children aged two–five years). Their comments on raw materials entirely confirm those made by the noon meals organizers attached to schools.[42] By contrast, the one TNIP organizer interviewed is well motivated and also describes a well-functioning system of monitoring and supplementation devoid of problems of corruption, theft, shortages and low quality.

The noon meals scheme could be improved, according to those who run it, if the supply irregularities could be reformed. This however points not only to a lack of permanent incentives but also to criminal or corrupt transactions in the urban or non-local economy, which are by no means confined to the Civil Supplies Corporation but generalized (see Chapter 3–8). No single institution of the state could easily be 'cleaned' or keep itself clean thereafter in isolation from others.

6. ENERGY FROM ALCOHOL

The consumption of alcohol is generally excluded from nutrition. Calories from alcohol are 'empty' of other nutrients. They are also expensive and confined to adult men. Their consumption is reputed to be a vice of low castes, a vice moreover in which the state has a keen interest since it generates a reliable current of revenue. In Tamil Nadu, this amounted to Rs 319 and Rs 413 crores in 1994–5 and 1995–6 respectively.[43] In earlier research, we learned that drinking was not simply a low-caste practice but was widespread. It also added to, or created, food stress. In 7 per cent of households the outflow to the state in alcohol tax exceeded the subsidy from the state in PDS/NMS. In all food-stressed households, if the expenditure on alcohol had been diverted to the cheapest sources of calories and allocated to all family members according to requirements, food stress could have been eradicated.[44]

In 1993–4, while about half the households had a drinker (see Table 13), the proportions varied from one third among landless labour to two thirds among the rich. While there is wide intervillage variation in the social distribution of light drinkers (those known as 'drinkards' who consume less than one litre of spirit [arrack] per month), of the 42 per cent of drinkers whose households are below the poverty line, some three quarters consume more than one litre per month.[45] *All the food-stressed households* (those in which calorie consumption per adult equivalent was under 1,700 calories [1.2 BMR] per day) *had drinkers,* including five richer households in Veerasambanur. If the cost of this habit is added to total food expenditure, we find that alcohol made up 22 per cent of the total food-and-drink budget in food-stressed landless households, 26 per cent in poor peasant households and 33 per cent in (admittedly unusual) rich, food-stressed households. In household with drinkers but not in food stress, the respective proportions were much lower – 7 and 6 per cent – excepting rich households where they averaged 44 per cent owing to heavy consumption (> 59 millilitres/day over the long term in two cases). If the average expenditure on alcohol in food-stressed households were translated into the cheapest source of calories from foodgrains, an additional 20 person-days of energy would be released. Among poor landed and landless drinking households the outgoings to the state in tax on alcohol (estimated at Rs 35/month) cut the net subsidy on the noon meal by two thirds.

7. CONCLUSIONS AND POLICY IMPLICATIONS

While real incomes increased over the two decades (by a factor of 2.8 for landless agricultural labour, 4.5 for poor peasants and 6 for richer households), they also became more highly unequal. In the richer group, dominated by the village of Nesal, this growing inequality led to a massive decline in the proportion of expenditure on food and was coupled with dietary diversification. Non-food disposable income will have increased in both absolute and relative terms because the cost of the diet, of calories from rice, and real rice prices have all dropped over the last decade by a factor slightly greater than their rise in the previous decade, leaving calorie costs at about their 1973–4 level. Calorie consumption has followed the same trend, except for that of landless agricultural labourers (apart from those of Nesal), whose calorie consumption has gone up by 4 per cent.

Nutritional vulnerability (very low calorie supplies) has declined by a third over the last decade. Yet among the classes of poor households it averages 26 per cent.[46] Alcohol consumption exacerbates food stress and eats into the net subsidies from the PDS and NMS.

It is argued that a state verging on bankruptcy cannot justify the maintenance of food subsidies when real agricultural wages are rising.[47] We found that income and prices are only significant determinants of calorie consumption for poor landed peasants and not for other groups of poor households or for landless labour, whose food consumption is significantly affected by the PDS. The PDS works in a socially redistributive way and protects the food security of poor peasants and agricultural labour households. It provides 39 per cent of the rice calories for poor peasants and 72 per cent for agricultural labourers. On the other hand, these social benefits are disproportionately captured by one of the three villages – the largest, most accessible, most diversified village. And, through 'leakages', the mortgage of cards, sale of ration rice at open-market prices etc., there is a non-trivial upwards and sideways redistribution of rice. The quality of the PDS and NMS has not improved, but it has not markedly deteriorated either. The interventions are themselves the targets of a multiplicity of interested attention (from theft, amounting to 6 per cent of grain and borne ultimately by the official 'targets', to bribes for employment, of up to Rs 7,000).

The public distribution system needs to be protected, since poor agrarian classes use it to an extent that confounds the relationships between income and consumption. If finer targeting were forced upon the Government of Tamil Nadu, then to entitle the landless (who are more visible and conspicuous for targeting) to the neglect of the hardly landed, would, on these results and on strictly nutritional grounds, be inequitable. Targeting raises the costs of delivery. In addition, there are many other costs of targeting, listed by Swaminathan:[48] errors of exclusion, the distortion of information, the stigmatization of the eligible, loss of quality and the erosion of budget support. In a further longitudinal study of village evidence from Maharashtra, Swaminathan and Misra found that, as targeting has intensified, both the E errors (of inclusion of the ineligible) and the F errors (of exclusion of the eligible) are on the increase.[49] In addition, food and 'freedom from hunger' is a right,[50] best guaranteed by the state with minimal targeting.

As for reform in the direction of self-selection (which is known to minimize both administration costs and F errors), the state, by its choice of rice for procurement and distribution, and 'the market', by the convergence of prices of superior and inferior grains, have forfeited the possibility of targeting by means of inferior, coarse grains.

To raise the entitlements of income-poor households by doubling the ration to 20 kg while not allowing poor households to purchase less than the stipulated consignment, as happened in 2000–1, is not only inequitable and inefficient, it is an act of political vandalism on the PDS itself. The much criticized operating costs, unprecedented levels of stockpiling of foodgrains and rank waste are the consequence of an antisocial issue policy combined with the political need for incentive pricing to producers of marketed surplus in NW India.

Although reform to the PDS needs to protect the consumption of poor people and although consumption of poor landed producers does not seem to have increased over the long term, real trends in incomes and prices suggest room for modest upwards adjustment of PDS issue prices.

If, as has been suggested, costs are to be reduced by targeting preschool nutrition along the lines of TNIP-2 (the World Bank's project) or by engineering some convergence between the NMS and PDS,[51] the special nutritional position of girls, which is deteriorating, may be rendered even more vulnerable. Preschool girls may not be brought for nutrition monitoring; take-home food supplements are, once there, subject to social norms or allocation sometimes at variance with those advised by the state.

The Government of Tamil Nadu could protect the PDS as presently implemented by preserving a socially inclusive entitlement and only the crudest of targeting. However, to do so, it would have to look at ways of reducing tax evasion on those revenue heads which it controls so as to preserve or increase its revenue base.

ACKNOWLEDGEMENTS

I am grateful to Dr S Janakarajan and the MIDS field team for the data, to Aziz Arya for research assistance, to N Narayanan, discussant at the MIDS workshop in 1996, who also helped with data and evaluated our material on bureaucratic delivery and whose report on food and nutrition policy in Tamil Nadu (Narayanan 1996a) is summarized in the first section, and to Dr A Khati for her constructive comments at the MIDS workshop.

Appendix 1:

Nutrition Data 1973–4 to 1982–4

TABLE 1 Characteristics of study households

	Per Household Family Composition			Operated Farm Size (ha)
	Sample Size	Persons	Adult Equivalents[a]	
1973/74 (resurvey villages)				
Small paddy farmers[b]	15	4.7	4	0.62
Large paddy farmers[b]	5	5.6	4.8	1.48
Landless labourers	17	4	3.4	
1982/83 (resurvey villages)				
Small paddy farmers	23	5.7	4.9	0.57
Large paddy farmers	41	7	5.8	2.75
Landless labourers	44	4.8	4	
1983/84 (resurvey villages)				
Small paddy farmers	11	4.5	4	0.50
Large paddy farmers	22	6.5	5.5	2.87
Landless labourers	23	5.1	4.2	
1973/74 (all villages)				
Small paddy farmers	31	5.1	4.2	0.58
Large paddy farmers	22	6.2	5.2	2.42
Landless labourers	48	3.6	3	
1982/83 (all villages)				
Small paddy farmers	72	5.6	4.7	0.59
Large paddy farmers	89	7.2	6	2.76
Landless labourers	114	4.4	3.7	

Notes:
[a] 1 adult equivalent = 1 man older than 14 years old = 2.94 babies <1 year old = 1.69 children 1–5 years old = 1.27 women > 5 years old = 1.09 men 6–14 years old.
[b] A small paddy farmer is defined as one who operates 1 hectare or less. Large farmers operate more than 1 hectare.

Source: HR91, table 5.1, p. 87.

TABLE 2 Total annual consumption expenditures and incomes (1974 Rs/capita)

	Resurvey Villages			All Villages	
	73/74	82/83	83/84	73/74	82/83
Expenditures					
Small paddy farmers	250	318	743	293	350
Large paddy farmers	395	513	828	435	541
Landless labourers	254	295	580	304	316
Average paddy farmers[a]	311	412	784	352	442
Incomes					
Small paddy farmers	264	237	535	386	320
Large paddy farmers	525	431	657	770	578
Landless labourers	261	214	443	311	206
Average paddy farmers[a]	374	330	594	547	444

Notes: The expenditures and incomes figures above are not directly comparable. Incomes were calculated with farm-gate prices, while the value of the own-production share of expenditures was calculated with consumer prices. This explains why expenditures are greater than incomes in some cases.

Deflated using the CPI for Kunnathur village in Chingleput District.

[a] Weighted average using the weights given in HR91, chapter 3.

Source: HR91, table 5.2, p. 88.

TABLE 3 Rice prices and the calorie cost of the total diet

	Resurvey Villages			All Villages	
	73/74	82/83	83/84	73/74	82/83
Small paddy farmer (current Rs)					
Consumer rice price per kg	1.32	2.18	2.96	1.31	2.24
Cost per 1,000 calories	0.45	0.87	1.51	0.45	0.92
Small paddy farmers (1974 Rs)					
Consumer rice price per kg	1.32	1.19	1.47	1.31	1.21
Cost per 1,000 calories	0.45	0.47	0.75	0.45	0.49
Large paddy farmers (current Rs)					
Consumer rice price per kg	1.36	2.10	2.88	1.30	2.14
Cost per 1,000 calories	0.50	0.90	1.37	0.50	0.94
Large paddy farmers (1974 Rs)					
Consumer rice price per kg	1.36	1.14	1.43	1.30	1.16
Cost per 1,000 calories	0.50	0.49	0.68	0.50	0.51
Landless Labourers (current Rs)					
Consumer rice price per kg	1.27	2.11	2.76	1.28	2.14
Cost per 1,000 calories	0.46	0.87	1.35	0.48	0.88
Landless labourers (1974 Rs)					
Consumer rice price per kg	1.27	1.14	1.37	1.28	1.16
Cost per 1,000 calories	0.46	0.47	0.67	0.48	0.48

Source: HR91, table 5.4, p. 89.

TABLE 4 Daily energy and protein consumption

	Resurvey Villages			All Villages	
	73/74	*82/83*	*83/84*	*73/74*	*82/83*
Calories/person					
Small paddy farmers	1,386	1,494	2,606	1,592	1,602
Large paddy farmers	1,724	1,848	2,884	1,759	1,924
Landless labourers	1,426	1,495	2,154	1,604	1,642
Average paddy farmers[a]	1,528	1,664	2,739	1,662	1,756
Grams of protein/person					
Small paddy farmers	29	32	64	34	34
Large paddy farmers	37	40	69	37	42
Landless labourers	28	34	57	33	36
Average paddy farmers[a]	32	36	66	35	37
Calories/adult equivalent					
Small paddy farmers	1,630	1,729	2,953	1,893	1,882
Large paddy farmers	2,053	2,218	3,456	2,085	2,270
Landless labourers	1,673	1,783	2,572	1,919	1,962
Average paddy farmers[a]	1,807	2,407	3,194	1,973	2,068
Grams of protein/adult equivalent					
Small paddy farmers	34	37	73	40	40
Large paddy farmers	44	48	82	44	39
Landless labourers	33	40	67	39	43
Average paddy farmers[a]	38	42	77	42	44

[a] Weighted average using the weights given in HR91, chapter 3.

Source: HR91, table 5.5, p. 91.

TABLE 5 Mean daily energy consumption, resurvey villages (percent of total calories)

Commodity	1973/74			1982/83			1983/84		
	Small Paddy Farmers	Large Paddy Farmers	Landless Labourers	Small Paddy Farmers	Large Paddy Farmers	Landless Labourers	Small Paddy Farmers	Large Paddy Farmers	Landless Labourers
Rice	76.5	72.3	74.6	66	61.9	62.1	42.6	50.5	38.1
Ragi	20.6	19.5	22	17.4	18.7	22.2	12.7	11.6	17.2
Wheat	–	–	–	–	0.2	0.1	3.6	2.3	4.5
Other cereals	0.2	–	–	2.6	2	3.4	3.3	2.5	3.8
Grams	1.3	2.6	0.8	2.5	3.1	2	6	5.4	4.7
Dairy products & eggs	0.1	2	1.1	0.5	1.5	0.1	4.4	5.6	5.2
Meats	0.3	0.2	0.4	0.4	0.3	0.9	1.4	1.1	1.9
Vegetables	–	–	–	3.3	2.8	3.1	7	4	6.4
Fruits	–	–	–	0.2	0.5	0.1	2	1.6	2
Oils	0.6	1.8	0.9	5	5.9	4.9	8.6	7.1	6.8
Other foods	0.4	1.4	0.1	2	3.2	1	8.5	8.1	9.3
Total calories per capita	1,386	1,724	1,426	1,494	1,848	1,495	2,606	2,884	2,154

Source: HR91, table 5.7, p. 93.

Appendix 2:

Income, Prices and Household Factors in Household-level Calorie Availability, 1994

A. LANDED POOR PEASANTS

TABLE 1

		Dependent Variable:		*LCALPAD = Total Calories*		
PERS	LY_PMPAD	LRICEPR	LRAGIPR	LMEATPR	LVEGPR	LGROCPR
Multiple R		0.99475		R Square		0.98953
Adjusted R Square		0.91624		Standard Error		0.03959
Analysis of Variance						
	DF		Sum of Squares			Mean Square
Regression	7			0.14814		0.02116
Residual	1			0.00157		0.00157
F =	13.50163	Signif F =		0.2066		
Variables in the Equation						
Variable	B		SE B	Beta	T	Sig T
PERS	0.06		0.02	0.61	3.72	0.1673
LY_PMPAD	0.03		0.10	0.11	0.35	0.7877
LRICEPR	−0.49		0.46	−0.34	−1.06	0.4816
LRAGIPR	1.20		0.28	11.11	4.36	0.1436
LMEATPR	0.03		0.10	0.05	0.29	0.8232
LVEGPR	2.26		0.61	2.44	3.72	0.1674
LGROCPR	16.80		3.70	12.22	4.54	0.1381
(Constant)	−24.87		6.26		−3.98	0.1569

Marginal Propensity of Consumption

$$\text{M.P.C.} = \frac{0.0341(3.29)}{2.796} = 0.04$$

Average Propensity of Consumption

$$\text{A.P.C.} = \frac{3.29}{2.796} = 1.177$$

TABLE 2

PERS	LY_PMPAD	Dependent Variable: LRICEPR	LRAGIPR	LCALPAD = Rice Calories	LVEGPR	LGROCPR
Multiple R		0.77870		R Square		0.60637
Adjusted R Square		0.46745		Standard Error		0.12603
Analysis of Variance						
	DF		Sum of Squares			Mean Square
Regression	6			0.41594		0.0.6932
Residual	17			0.27000		0.01588
F =	4.36471	Signif F =		0.0076		
Variables in the Equation						
Variable	B		SE B	Beta	T	Sig T
PERS	−0.04		0.02	−0.33	−0.197	0.0660
LY_PMPAD	−0.27		0.09	−0.63	−0.302	0.0078
LRICEPR	−		0.38	−	0.01	0.9948
LRAGIPR	−0.04		0.03	−0.20	−1.27	0.2218
LVEGPR	−0.02		0.32	−0.11	−0.62	0.5432
LGROCPR	0.22		0.10	0.34	2.17	0.0445
(Constant)	3.83		0.35		10.84	−

$$\text{M.P.C.} = \frac{-0.265(3.12)}{2.833} = 0.29$$

$$\text{A.P.C.} = \frac{3.12}{2.833} = 11$$

B. LANDLESS AGRICULTURAL LABOURERS

TABLE 3

PERS	LRICEPR	*Dependent Variable:*		*LCALPAD = Total Calories*		
		LRAGIPR	*LVEGPR*	*LY_PMPAD*		
Multiple R		0.56435		R Square		0.31849
Adjusted R Square		0.19679		Standard Error		0.18267
Analysis of Variance						
	DF		Sum of Squares			Mean Square
Regression	5			0.43661		0.08732
Residual	28			0.93428		0.03337
F =	2.61702	Signif F =		0.0461		
Variables in the Equation						
Variable	Elasticity B		(SE B)	(Beta)	T	Sig T
PERS	–		0.02	0.03	0.21	0.8392
LRICEPR	0.30		0.29	0.17	1.03	0.3108
LRAGIPR	−0.14		0.06	−0.37	−2.22	0.0347
LVEGPR	0.87		0.76	0.19	1.14	0.2655
LY_PMPAD	0.16		0.11	0.23	1.41	0.1696
(Constant)	2.40		0.57		4.19	0.0003

Marginal Propensity of Consumption

$$\text{M.P.C.} = \frac{0.16121(3.336)}{2.445} = 0.22$$

Average Propensity of Consumption

$$\text{A.P.C.} = \frac{3.336}{2.445} = 1.364$$

Social Welfare in the Villages

TABLE 4

PERS	LRICEPR	Dependent Variable:		LCALPAD = Rice Calories	
		LRAGIPR	LVEGPR	LY_PMPAD	
Multiple R		0.54507		R Square	0.29710
Adjusted R Square		0.17159		Standard	0.23955
Analysis of Variance				Error	
	DF	Sum of Squares			Mean Square
Regression	5			0.67917	0.13583
Residual	28			1.60678	0.05739
F =	2.36704	Signif F =		0.0653	

Variables in the Equation

Variable	B	SE B	Beta	T	Sig T
PERS	−0.34	0.03	−0.25	−1.48	0.1488
LRAGIPR	−0.16	0.08	−0.32	−1.90	0.0688
LRICEPR	0.31	0.38	0.14	0.81	0.4245
LVEGPR	1.25	0.99	0.22	1.25	0.2205
LY_PMPAD	0.09	0.15	0.10	0.62	0.5410
(Constant)	2.36	0.75		3.14	0.0040

$$\text{M.P.C.} = \frac{0.0928(3.142)}{2.445} = 0.119$$

$$\text{A.P.C.} = \frac{3.142}{2.445} = 1.285$$

Appendix 3:

The Public Distribution Scheme (PDS)

TABLE 1 Average monthly offtake from the PDS

	Sample Size	Rice from PDS Kg/M	Sugar from PDS Kg/M	Kerosene from PDS Kg/M	Oil from PDS Kg/M	Av. Prop. of total calories per month per adult from PDS Rice	Av. Prop. of total rice calories from PDS Rice
VINAYAGA-PURAM							
Richer HH	10	2.47	0.95	1.90	–	0.05	0.07
PP Landed	17	5.82	1.17	2	–	0.09	0.14
PP Non-Landed	10	7.40	1.03	1.87	–	0.11	0.18
VEERASAM-BANUR							
Richer HH	7	5.93	0.67	1.19	–	0.10	0.13
PP Landed	6	5.56	0.67	1.11	–	0.10	0.14
PP Non-Landed	8	4.67	0.42	0.83	–	0.05	0.08
PP Non-Agricultural	3	5.56	0.78	1.33	–	0.10	0.12
NESAL							
Richer HH	14	8.29	1.86	3	–	0.44	0.72
PP Landed	13	10.15	1.69	3	–	0.60	0.84
PP Non-Landed	26	8.77	1.31	2.47	–	0.60	0.8

Kg/M = kilograms per month.

TABLE 2 Average monthly PDS subsidy on rice per HH, 1993–4

	Subsidy on Rice Rs/Month
VINAYAGAPURAM	
Richer HH	7.40
PP Landed	17.47
PP Non-Landed	22.20
VEERASAMBANUR	
Richer HH	17.79
PP Landed	16.67
PP Non-Landed	14
PP Non-Agricultural	16.67
NESAL	
Richer HH	24.86
PP Landed	30.46
PP Non-Landed	26.31

TABLE 3 Qualitative data analysis of PDS

	Sample Size	% of HH Pawning card	% of HH Pledging card	Problems with PDS				
				% 11	% 3	% 8	% 9	% 2
VINAYAGAPURAM								
Richer HH	10	—	—	40	30	10	—	
PP Landed	17	—	—	47	12	—	—	
PP Non-Landed	10	—	—	20	30	—	10	
VEERASAMBANUR								
Richer HH	7	—	—	—	14	—	—	43
PP Landed	6	—	—	16	—	—	—	33
PP Non-Landed	8	—	12	12	—	—	—	25
PP Non-Agricultural	3	—	—	33	33	—	—	33
NESAL								
Richer HH	14	—	—	—	28	—	28	—
PP Landed	13	—	—	—	38	—	—	—
PP Non-Landed	26	—	—	—	61	—	7.7	—

Problems faced with the PDS:-

Urban bias-1; adulteration-2; poor quality-3; discrimination in queue for poor or low-caste-4; mortgage of card-5; theft or loss of card-6; bribes and delays to replace card-7; ration rice sold at open-market prices-8; tricks with weights and measures-9; unannounced closures-10; short weighment-11; low quantity-12.

TABLE 3 (*cont.*):

	Suggestions for Improving PDS						
Codes	% 1	% 2	% 3	% 5	% 6	% 8	% 9
VINAYAGAPURAM							
Richer HH	20	10	10	10	10	–	–
PP Landed	23	6	–	6	12	–	–
PP Non-Landed	30	10	–	–	20	–	–
VEERASAMBANUR							
Richer HH	14	57	57	–	–	14	14
PP Landed	–	50	66	–	–	–	50
PP Non-Landed	–	50	75	–	–	–	25
PP Non-Agricultural	–	33	100	–	–	33	33
NESAL							
Richer HH	36	14	–	–	–	–	–
PP Landed	15	23	–	–	–	–	–
PP Non-Landed	11	42	–	–	–	–	–

Codes for suggestions for improving PDS:-

Good quality with correct measurements-1; good quality-2; ration items should not be sold outside at higher prices-3; frequent inspection-4; supply of more kerosene & more edible oil-5; quantity of rice supply should be increased-6.

Appendix 4:

Noon Meal Scheme (NMS)

TABLE 1 Total number of children participating in noon meal scheme, 1993–4

	Age Sample Size	Particip. HH No.	<=5		6–10		>10		>65	
			M	F	M	F	M	F	M	F
VINAYAGAPURAM										
Richer HH	9	4	—	1	3	2	—	—	—	—
PP Landed	17	6	3	—	2	2	3	1	—	—
PP Non-Landed	10	9	2	1	3	6	1	2	—	—
VEERASAMBANUR										
Richer HH	7	2	2	—	2	2	—	—	—	—
PP Landed	6	4	1	—	2	3	—	—	—	—
PP Non-Landed	8	6	—	2	4	4	—	—	—	—
PP Non-Agricultural	3	—	—	—	—	—	—	—	—	—
NESAL										
Richer HH	14	2	—	—	1	1	—	—	—	—
PP Landed	12	3	—	—	1	1	—	1	—	—
PP Non-Landed	27	10	2	1	7	7	5	2	—	—

Note: Data from Field survey, 1993–4.

TABLE 2 Nutritional effects of NMS and monthly government subsidy for participating HHs

	Av. Daily NMS Cals. Per Part. HH (1)	Av. Monthly Rs NMS Subsidy Per HH (2)	Av. T. Cal. Cons for All HH/D/ACU (3)	Av. T. Cal. Non-Part. HH/D/ACU	Av. T. Cal. Participating HH/D/ACU
VINAYAGAPURAM					
Richer HH	740	45	2154.95	2011.32	2343.96
PP Landed	885	55	2372.30	2676.20	2016.79
PP Non-Landed	816.67	50	2329.65	2444.48	2314.85
VEERASAMBANUR					
Richer HH	1430	90	1883.50	1623.59	2412.10
PP Landed	740	45	1999.28	2113.04	1939.33
PP Non-Landed	816.67	50	3102.70	3315.34	2837.41
PP Non-Agricultural	–	–	2527.03	–	–
NESAL					
Richer HH	765	45	3407.34	2798.70	2244.40
PP Landed	850	50	2078.22	2064.79	2113.04
PP Non-Landed	939	57	(3437.59)	2191.53	2133.47

Notes: 1. Part. HH= participating household
2. Monthly subsidy is in current prices of 1993–4
3. Average total calorie consumption does not include the calories from NMS
4. ACU = adult consumption unit
   () = queriable data, see note 25

TABLE 3 Qualitative data for NMS, percentage of participating HHs

	Use of NMS		Changes to NMS			School Attendance	
	Supplem. %	Substit. %	Quality poor %	Qty Shrunk %	No Diff. %	No Effect %	Improved %
VINAYAGAPURAM							
Richer HH	–	100	75	–	–	50	50
PP Landed	–	100	33	33	16	66	16
PP Non-Landed	–	89	22	55	11	66	22
VEERASAMBANUR							
Richer HH	100	–	100	–	–	50	–
PP Landed	100	–	100	–	–	–	100
PP Non-Landed	83	16	100	–	–	–	100
PP Non-Agricultural	–	–	–	–	–	–	–
NESAL							
Richer HH	–	100	–	–	–	50	–
PP Landed	33	66	–	–	–	33	66
PP Non-Landed	30	70	–	–	–	40	40

Note. Data from File [SWS10.WK1].

No End to the Betrayal?
Primary Education in its Social Context:
Evidence from Rural Tamil Nadu

LISA GOLD AND BARBARA HARRISS-WHITE

'*Education sharpens Man's intellect, making it glitter like a diamond*'
Government of Tamil Nadu, 2001

INDIA's education system is top-heavy, producing more scientists than any-where else. The Indian State also subsidizes a massive brain drain. Even so, India's technologists and engineers number only half those of South Korea. China and Indonesia have more technologists and engineers per unit of popu-lation than does India. India actually lags behind in technological and industrial learning.[1]

If this were not enough of a developmental problem, Article 45 of the Indian Constitution states: 'the state shall endeavour to provide within a period of ten years from the commencement of this Constitution (1950) for free and compul-sory education for all children until they complete the age of 14'.

1. EDUCATION POLICY

In India, education has been recognized as a right ever since Independence. But it is a 'right' that has never achieved mandatory status nor is it enforceable in law. Under pressure from a public campaign triggered by Myron Weiner's book[2], the Government of Tamil Nadu was the first to commit itself to this goal (1993). A bill for the compulsory education of children aged 6 to 11 years was passed by the Tamil Nadu State Assembly in May 1994, but it still awaits Presidential assent.[3] Compulsory primary education is the policy instrument by which the Indian states could effectively remove children from the labour market, thereby not only educating them but also protecting children against both their parents and their employers. In India, investment in primary education is much more modest in scope either than what was envisaged in the Constitution or than what has been achieved in other developing countries.[4] Primary education receives 25 per cent of the education budget, compared with 45 to 60 per cent in countries such as Kenya, Tanzania, Indonesia, Sri Lanka and China. Yet although tertiary education in technology-related subjects is an integral part of *industrial policy* in the East Asian developmental states, *most of the measurable private and social benefits of education are obtained from the basic literacy and numeracy skills imparted during the first five years.* It is in the marketplace that the diamonds from primary education begin to glitter. Private benefits include measurable increases in employment, income and productivity.[5] They include operational rights of citizenship and rights of access to the state.[6] Social benefits in health, nutrition and fertility, in increasing political awareness of rights and in intergenerational mobility accrue when a large mass of a population (in particular a majority of women) complete primary education. Primary education is thus a crucial instrument for development.

When parental assets, income and education and the probability of children completing primary education are closely related, then education restricts its private and social benefits to an elite, creates a major fault line in the labour market and reinforces social and economic stratification.

India saw a spectacular quantitative expansion in education after Independence. Primary schools expanded from 210,000 in 1950 to 520,000 in 1984.[7] Yet regional variations in levels of educational deprivation are such as to suggest – as Majumdar puts it – 'different realities . . . on different planets'.[8] Scheduled-caste (SC) rural women in Rajasthan are four times as educationally deprived as urban caste men in Kerala. Poor rural women in Uttar Pradesh are six times worse off educationally than rich urban men in Kerala. In the ranking of states according to the uptake of education, Tamil Nadu is generally placed third after Kerala and Maharashtra, though it drops one further place when ranked on the educational deprivation of SC women and one more for SC men.[9] Tables 1 and 2, drawn from Majumdar's data,[10] show how rural location, poverty, scheduled-caste status and gender interact to structure educational advantage in Tamil Nadu. At the extreme, rural SC women had 0.22 years of schooling, while rich urban men had nearly 9 years – a factor 40 advantage!

At an all-India level, attempts were made to 'supply' primary education and by 1986 all urban and 95 per cent of rural children were within one km of a primary school.[11] Fees (already very low in the state sector) were abolished in 1990, leaving 'only' the costs of books, uniform, travel and examination fees to be met by parents. Even though education is not compulsory, if it had been supply-constrained then it would be reasonable to have expected equality of access and universal completion once the infrastructure of primary education had been

TABLE 1 Mean years of schooling, Tamil Nadu, 1981–7

| | Caste | Status | Income | |
	Non SC/ST	SC/ST	Top 20% Income Distribution	Bottom 20%
Rural				
Male	8.1	1.4	4.9	2
Female	0.97	0.22	2.9	1
Urban				
Male	6.7	3.6	8.7	3.2
Female	3.5	1.2	6.9	2.2

Source: Majumdar 1999, pp. 294–5, Tables 9A–1 and 9A–2 from Census Reports (1981) and NSSO (1989).

TABLE 2 Relative educational deprivation in Tamil Nadu, 1981–7

| | Caste | Status | Income | |
	Non SC/ST	SC/ST	Top 20% Income Distribution	Bottom 20%
Rural				
Male	0.52	0.73	0.37	0.57
Female	0.80	0.93	0.19	0.44
Urban				
Male	0.28	0.51	0.57	0.74
Female	0.52	0.77	0.27	0.57

Note: The index of deprivation is a composite index constructed using the adult literacy of people over 15 and mean years of schooling of people over 25. 0= undeprived; 1= completely deprived.

Source: Majumdar 1999, pp. 274–5, Tables 9.2 and 9.3 from Census Reports (1981) and NSSO (1989).

provided and fees abolished. But this has not happened. Literacy rose from 17 per cent in 1951 to a mere 36 per cent by 1981. Despite high and inaccurate enrolment rates, actual attendance was estimated at 55 per cent for rural boys and 35 per cent for rural girls of primary age in 1988[12] and the all-India drop-out rate between years one to five was 47 per cent for boys and 50 per cent for girls.[13] In Tamil Nadu as late as 2000, although progress appeared to have been made in primary enrolment (which had officially increased to 94.4 per cent for girls and 98.5 per cent for boys), the aggregate primary completion rate was still only 44 per cent of enrolment.[14] When buildings exist but lack teachers and equipment, education remains supply-constrained.[15]

It has been well established – and fully corroborated in this book – that the poor are most dependent upon public-sector social expenditure. The poorer states also have the poorest records on social spending, but even the states with better rankings have experienced cuts in social-sector expenditure due to structural adjustment.[16] Between 1985 and 1992, the share of total educational expenditure allocated to the elementary sector fell in 8/15 states. That in Tamil Nadu fell from 52 per cent to 49 per cent, where it remained up to 1994 – our latest figures.[17] There is a general consensus among development policy analysts that it ought to be at 60 per cent to stand a chance of coping with universal primary education. There is also a consensus that the poor should be protected from cuts in sectors on which they are demonstrably most dependent. Food is one; primary education is clearly another. There is also a consensus that the states, like Tamil Nadu, with relatively high social-sector spending are the most 'vulnerable to adjustment related stress'.[18] The supply of primary education is not only of poor quality but also budget-constrained and vulnerable to cuts.

We can see the consequences of these 'supply' factors at work in the three villages. Two schools, one state and one Catholic, provide primary education in Nesal and enable caste and scheduled-caste children to be educated – and fed – quite separately. The Catholic school educates between 30 and 50 scheduled-caste children in each year group, with an antifemale sex ratio of 0.75. The spacious state school has year groups of between 40 and 70 caste children and a better sex ratio of 0.88. Along with the noon meal infrastructure, the schools generate a significant amount of employment in the village: 15 teachers and assistants and 3 workers to organize and provide meals. During the time of our survey, these schools seemed comparatively well run. By contrast, the state school in Vinayagapuram was running half staffed and with low standards of competence and motivation. To quote from the village diary: 'The standard of education is low and not much has been done by government officials about this, nor are the villagers bothered. Boys and girls of the fourth and fifth class stop their schooling to go as apprentice labour to the weavers.' Ten children, including scheduled-caste children, journey to a neighbouring village to attend a Christian school. The state elementary school in Veerasambanur is also understaffed (by a third). It caters to a grand total of 80 children, with an antifemale gender bias among them of 0.76. In 1993, it was open for 220 days. Like Oxford University, but for different reasons, it had short terms. There was no drinking water, no latrines (children dirtied the playground), no cleaner or caretaker and inadequate furniture and equipment. Between 15 and 20 per cent of pupils drop out from each year of primary education. Despite the incentive of the noon meal, children leave school 'to guard goats and cattle, help with irrigation and ploughing, carry food from farm to field, perform wage work in agriculture, care for younger children and help with water, cooking and cleaning'.

2. FACTORS AFFECTING A CHILD'S EDUCATION

If we turn to demand for primary education, education policy disappears. The finger is often pointed at apathy and lack of aspiration as the causes of lack of demand. De and Noronha report:

> In its golden-jubilee analysis of India's failure to achieve universal elementary education, the *Times of India* (15th August, 1997, p. 37) confidently asserts that 'illiterate and semi-literate parents see no reason to send their children to school'.[19]

Here, however, we will examine the structural factors at work. The decision to educate a child is an economic one taken by its elders. The factors affecting that decision and the process of learning resulting from it will be of two kinds (see Fig. 1). One kind is *proximate* (set ii). In turn, there are two types: first, attributes of the individual child (gender, age, health, ability) and, second, the social and economic institutions conditioning the returns to education and its direct and opportunity costs. The second kind is *structural* (set i), consisting of three types of elements: first, household characteristics (size, composition and birth order); second, economic (relating to the class position of the parents); third, social (both ascribed factors such as caste and acquired factors such as parental education). Here, we will discuss those for which we have evidence from the three villages.

With a rapid rise in educational provision, we expect older people to have lower achievement rates because of constraints on the supply of educational facilities in the past. The relation between *age* and education is complicated in Tamil Nadu by the special incentive of the noon meals scheme (NMS), which was set up in 1982 and is sited in schools. The education of people up to the age of

(i)	(ii)	(iii)	(iv)
Background	*Individual*	*Cost: benefit*	*Demand*
Education/ Income/ Wealth of Parents	Gender/ Age/ Health Market- & Non-Market Returns to Education		
Caste/ Religion	Child Ability	Perceived Benefits of Education	Parental Demand for Child's Education
Household Size/ Composition	Opportunity cost of Education	Perceived Costs of Education	
Birth Order of Child, Sibling Sequence	Direct cost of Education Noon Meal Incentives		

FIG. 1 Factors affecting the social background to primary education.

20 may well have been affected by a nutrition intervention which at its inception was *also* justified as an intervention to enhance education, rural employment and socialisation between castes.[20]

Health and disability may screen the access of children owing to social prejudice or socially conditioned lower returns to the economic activity of chronically sick or disabled people (for which there is much evidence; see Chapter 3–4 in this volume).[21]

Several aspects of the proximate factors affecting primary education are gendered (where *gender* is a screen): most notably lower returns and constrained access by women to credit and product markets as well as in the labour market (see chapters 1–5 and 2–4). The exploitation of female labour operates both through discrimination in wage rates for similar tasks and through differential returns to tasks made gender-specific by the division of labour. Then the quality of education may discriminate against girls by means such as the quality of teachers' time, gendered access to materials and the content of textbooks. The domestic opportunity costs of a daughter's labour (in childcare, fuel and water gathering, in agricultural and non-agricultural household production) may cast the *cost–benefit equation* against primary education, even in cases where the activity is uncosted (set iii, Fig. 1).[22] The long-term benefits to education will be experienced by the son-in-law's household rather than the natal one (especially where *sibling sequence and household composition* mean that the exchange of brides is not symmetrical). The practice of assortative marriage alliances and hypergamy means that female education is associated with an increase in the dowry, while male education both attracts an increased dowry and imports a person with a beneficial impact on household welfare.

The balance of costs and benefits in the education of a child will be affected by the *size and composition of the household*. Where old age is defined not by years but by the onset of disability or chronic sickness, domestic reproductive requirements may not be easy to 'plan' and may result in the dropping out of children in order to cover the costs of care, the costs of substituting for the lost work of an elder and household maintenance (see Chapter 3–4).

Education also depends on *wealth and class position*. While the opportunity cost of child labour in a poor household may be lower than that of a wealthy household, it is not the absolute returns from child labour which count, it is their relative contribution to the household resource base. Not all of this is valorized. Much is directly for use and unresponsive to prices. Here, poverty is critical to the domestic 'priors' because it will assign a high implicit value to a household's 'discount rate'. Among the rural elite, while the opportunity cost of a household's child labour is the current rate for a child substitute, a different calculation involving future income streams at lower 'discount rates' may be made. The immediate cash costs of education will also be absolutely and relatively less of a barrier.

Parental education, class and caste status can affect the returns to education irrespective of education and ability, by means of 'socially inefficient' discrimination in access to assets and occupations.

Child ability will be positively associated with educational achievement, as more able children complete any given level more easily than less able children. The relation between socio-economic status and ability has not been proved to be genetically determined. It is much more likely to work through socialization, nutrition, health and the domestic resources supporting education.

3. EDUCATION IN THE VILLAGES

In the three villages, primary schools offering education up to grade five appeared (well before the first survey) in the 1960s. Veerasambanur (though the most isolated village) has a mission school close by. The nearest secondary schools are in the local town of Arni. A further education college eventually appeared there, but well after our field survey. Here we examine the relation between the completion of primary education in 1993–4 and those variables for which data were obtained from the village censuses: economic status (cluster); distance (from urban labour markets proxied by village dummies); social status (caste and parental education); and individual attributes (age and gender).

It is a shocking fact that, despite decades of welfarist politics and two generations of children brought up with schools in their villages, on aggregate only 33.4 per cent of men and 15.3 per cent of women have completed 5 years of primary education by the age of 12 and above.

First, let us examine *village-specific influences* on the probability of completing primary education. Village-specific differences arising from differential returns to education may be due to relative access to secondary education as much as to differences in wage rates, employment opportunities and access to wages and employment of the nearest towns. If village accessibility and employment opportunities positively affect education, we would expect Nesal to have the highest primary completion attainment figures. This is not borne out for men but does appear to hold for women. The differential between male and female primary completion rates also varies across villages (see Table 3).

TABLE 3 Completion of primary education, by village

	Nesal		Vinayagapuram		Veerasambanur	
	Men	*Women*	*Men*	*Women*	*Men*	*Women*
Primary Completion Rate	33.3%	18.4%	31.7%	11.75%	37.4%	13.5%

3.1 Caste

The population of the three villages consists mainly of six castes, all officially listed as 'Backward' or 'Other Backward' castes: relatively underprivileged and entitled to positive discrimination in public-sector employment. In addition, one third are scheduled castes, entitled by the Constitution to further positive discrimination in public-sector education and employment. Table 4 shows the varied distribution of village populations across castes. Nesal has the largest caste diversity, with scheduled castes forming one third of the population but with the higher-ranking cultivating caste of Agamudaiyan Mulaliars also numerous. Vinayagapuram, by contrast, has a dominant caste of working peasant Vanniars (70 per cent of the population). Veerasambanur has the highest proportion of scheduled castes (48 per cent of the population), together with 'poor, would-be seigneurial landholders'[23] (Agamudaiyan Mudaliars).

Although caste is a fundamental social attribute, it determines and restricts economic or educational status in complex ways which cut across wealth and income and which cannot be read off from one another. Tables 5 and 6 show

TABLE 4 Distribution of village populations across castes

Caste	Code	Nesal	Vinaya.	Veeras.	Total
Agamudaya Mudaliar	AM	362	–	212	574
Naidu	NAI	49	–	–	49
Vanniar	VAN	4	806	69	879
Yadava	YAD	285	–	–	285
Scheduled-Caste Harijan	SC-H	513	232	4	749
Scheduled-Caste Christian	SC-C	113	6	272	391
Other	OTH	223	101	21	345
Total	TOT	1549	1145	578	3272

TABLE 5 Caste and household income and land holding

Caste	Household Income (Rs)		Landholding Value (Rs)	
	Mean	Standard Deviation	Mean	Standard Deviation
AM	18,580	18,901	60,863	1,13,648
NAI	12,582	14,428	10,915	4,738
VAN	13,438	13,303	76,849	92,488
YAD	16,242	21,366	64,449	62,711
SC-H	6,655	4,986	20,170	19,936
SC-C	8,327	10,796	9,147	20,935
OTH	10,590	9,087	74,606	1,74,186

TABLE 6 Caste and educational achievement among workers

	Illiterate		Literate and Completed Primary Education		Completed Middle School		Completed Secondary School		Higher Secondary Pre-Univ and above		Total Numbers	
	M	F	M	F	M	F	M	F	M	F	M	F
Caste												
Agamudaya Mudaliar	14	51	43	31	24	13	11	4	8	1	182	127
Naidu	30	62	38	15	23	23	8	–	8	–	13	13
Vanniar	33	80	38	15	15	5	8	0.03	5	–	291	257
Yadava	37	82	38	12	14	6	10	–	1	–	94	66
Scheduled Caste	46	79	34	13	11	6	7	0.5	1.5	–	197	189
Scheduled-Caste Christian	38	78	30	12	22	6	2	1.2	7	2	86	83
Other	24	60	39	25	25	12	8	3	4	1.5	100	69
Total	32	73	38	17	17	7	8	1	5	0.06	964	804

Source: Jayaraj 1996b, tables 6 to 10, based on 1993–4 village survey data.

the variation in household income,[24] land-holding values[25] and educational attainment levels[26] respectively for the seven caste categories.[27] Analysis for each separate village finds similar levels of intercaste variation.

Classifying the population into relatively homogenous socio-economic classes is increasingly difficult as the economy diversifies. In the 1993 resurvey, cluster analysis was used to identify households of similar socio-economic status.[28] If socio-economic status is related to educational attainment, we should see a strong link between class/cluster and the probability of completing primary education. The proportion of each class not completing primary education is shown in Table 7. There are systematic class differences in the population completing primary education with *as small a minority completing primary education among the poor as those failing to complete it among the elite.*

3.2 Parental education

The impact of parental education can be studied only for a more restricted sample consisting of those individuals over the age of 12 where data are available for at least one parent. From a total population of 3,272 and an over-12 population of 2,307, there are 656 individuals for whom we have some information and 529 persons for whom we have data on both parents' education (see Table 8). Numbers in parentheses represent the observations on which the percentages are

TABLE 7 Agrarian class and educational achievement in the over-12 population (% *not* completing 5 years)

	Nesal	*Vinayaga-puram*	*Veera-sambanur*
Number	1,101	816	390
Poor, agricultural	77%	82%	80%
Poor, non-agricultural	–	95%	–
Elite	20%	55%	78%

TABLE 8 Probability (%) of completing primary education, parents' education

		Father's Education			
		Illiterate	*Literate*	*Primary*	*>Primary*
Mother's Education	Illiterate	45 (296)	53 (49)	71 (69)	82 (38)
	Literate	40 (296)	83 (6)	86 (7)	70 (10)
	Primary	71 (7)	100 (8)	67 (9)	100 (13)
	>Primary	–	–	–	86 (7)

Note: numbers are bracketed.

based and illustrate the problem of small sample size, due especially to the low variation in the educational attainment of mothers.

One consequence of restricting the sample is that proportionate educational attainment levels are now higher than those seen before. This is because a sample with information on people with living parents must be a young sample in relation to the population as a whole, and younger age groups have higher primary completion rates. In addition, as women tend to leave the natal household on marriage, the older part of our restricted sample is dominated by men (as no data are available on wives' parents). Requiring information on parents restricts us to a sample in which 62.65 per cent of observations are of men, as compared to 49.7 per cent in the whole population, 49.2 per cent in the over-12 population and 49.4 per cent in the 12–30 population as a whole. There appears to be a systematic relationship between parental and child education.

However, the problem with looking at single-factor distributions is that excluded factors are not accounted for. Location, caste, class and parental education may capture some important social and economic influences on educational attainment, but individual attributes are factors which have even clearer effects. Figure 2 gives an age–sex distribution of the total population[29] and shows the numbers completing less than, or at least, primary education. Male advantage in the probability of primary completion compounds the age effects seen here.

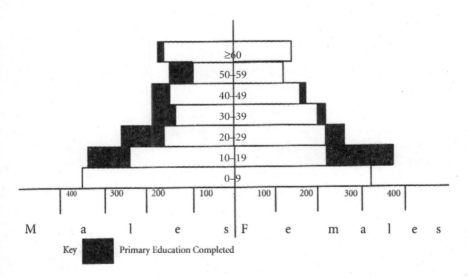

FIG. 2 Age–sex distribution for total combined population.

3.3 *Other factors*

Both *age and gender* have strong influences on the probability of a person hav-ing at least primary-level education. *The noon meals scheme may be associated with the age effect. Meals at school have accompanied an increase in the schooling of children of all backgrounds since 1982* (i.e. those aged up to 20 in 1993–4). Girls are half as likely as boys to complete primary education and working women are twice as likely as men to be illiterate (see Tables 3 and 6 above).

So the relationships described here confirm the theoretical arguments. Pri-mary completion rates *are* higher for younger age groups, for males and for children of higher socio-economic/more educated backgrounds; location also appears influential, especially for females. However, to be able to draw conclu-sions about the relative power of various influences on educational attain-ment, we examine these relationships in the holistic setting of an econometric model.

4. A MODEL OF PRIMARY COMPLETION

We are interested in the importance of completing primary education for the capture of private and social educational benefits. Educational data in the 1993–4 resurvey are discrete, so completed primary education is modelled as a discrete dependent variable. The classical regression model has problems with such variables, so maximum likelihood estimation is used for a non-linear probit model.[30]

The discrete outcome of primary completion reflects the unobserved contin-uous process of parental demand for a child's education. Demand for educa-tion, D_i, is the latent variable underlying the probit model, determined by some process:

$$D_i = \delta X_i + \varepsilon$$

If educational demand is above some critical level, κ, the child will complete primary education:

$$CP_i = 1 \text{ if } D_i > \kappa$$
$$CP_i = 0 \text{ if } D_i \leq \kappa$$

So: $\quad \Pr(CP_i = 1) = \Pr(D_i > \kappa)$

and: $\quad \Pr(CP_i = 1) = F(\beta X_i)$

We cannot observe D_i, only $CP = 1$ or $CP = 0$. However, we know which independent variables (X_i) are likely to affect educational demand and we can observe many of these.

We have investigated links between some of these explanatory variables and educational attainment in the study area and can guess the sign and magnitude of the effects of several variables from this, as well as from theory. However, in some cases, the characteristics of our restricted sample of 529 children for which data are available for both parents and 656 children for which data on the educational achievement of one parent are available will be different from those of the full or over-12 population. One difference already seen is in the proportion completing primary education. Another change is in the completion rate differentials, shown in Table 9, especially the lack of differential between the sexes in the pooled restricted sample.

4.1 *Data*

The data from the 1993–4 resurvey provide the explanatory variables. *Age* is used both in its normal continuous form and in interaction with an NMS dummy for people under 20. *Gender* is given by a dummy variable for males, which in turn allows us to differentiate other explanatory variables by gender. Another dummy variable represents the small number of *disabled*. In the pooled full sample, *location* is given by village dummies for Vinayagapuram and Veerasambanur, given separately for men and women; Table 9 suggests the magnitude and direction of effects here. *Household size* and the *number of younger siblings* are continuous variables, with dummy variables for being the first-born child and for the presence of grandparents also used for household composition. Household variables were used both differentiated by gender and non-differentiated by gender.

Household *income* estimates for 1993–4 are available for all but 14 individuals in the sample and are used as a continuous variable indicating economic status. *Caste* is included as numerically ordered variable (from 1 [Agamudaiya

TABLE 9 Primary completion rates across the 3 villages (restricted sample plus total population over 12 years)

| | % Completing Primary Education | | | | | |
| | Sample | | | Over-12 Population | | |
	Men	Women	All	Men	Women	All
Nesal	55.8	61.7	58	33.2	18.4	25.7
Vinayagapuram	46.2	42.3	44.9	31.7	11.75	21.9
Veerasambanur	55.4	44.7	50.5	37.4	13.5	24.6
Total	52.1	52.2	52.2	33.4	15.3	24.2

Mudaliar] to 7 [other]), and in dummy-variable formulation.[31] *Cluster* (class) is included as dummies for elite and poor clusters. Family *educational background* is presented in levels split as in Table 8, with dummy variables used to show the influence of parental literacy, primary completion and above-primary completion (relative to illiteracy)[32] on child educational attainment.[33]

To estimate a model of completion of primary education in the study area as a whole we use the pooled sample of 656 individuals, with village dummies. A summary of the main variables is given in the Appendix.

4.2 Discussion

The preferred model combines a subset of significant variables operating at a variety of levels on the probability of a young person's completing primary education (see Table 10).[34]

Turning first to variables found to be insignificant in trial models,[36] gender proved not to be a significant determinant of primary completion. Age and participation in the NMS had a positive but insignificant impact on primary

TABLE 10 Significant individual, family and structural factors affecting primary completion[35]

Variable	Coefficient	z	P(z)
age	−0.0411	−3.430	0.001
veef	−0.5648	−2.695	0.007
dis	−1.4719	−2.462	0.014
scc	0.4953	2.485	0.013
van	−0.3505	−2.863	0.004
hinc	0.0000093	2.687	0.007
f1	0.2788	1.668	0.096
f2	0.72407	4.471	0.000
f3	0.7625	3.464	0.001
m2	0.8712	3.039	0.002
constant	0.8488	2.242	0.023

642 observations
Log-likelihood = −388.526
Chi-sq (10) = 112.64
Pseudo-Rsq = 0.1266

Notes: age: age in years; veef: dummy for females in Veerasambanur village; dis: dummy for disabled people; scc: scheduled-caste Christian; van: Vanniar caste; hinc: household income; f1: father literate; f2: father had primary education; f3: father had some secondary education; m2: mother had some secondary education.

education. The addition of social characteristics to the model rendered all but one village dummy insignificant, suggesting that 'villages' connote differentials in the distribution of castes. Dummies for class had expected signs but were also insignificant and so were dropped from the final specification to avoid the statistical effects of multicollinearity.

A mix of individual and structural factors are at work in stigmatizing access to education. The age variable reveals that younger people are significantly more likely to have completed primary school. The location variable shows girls at a significant educational disavantage in the remotest village, despite a Catholic mission school being sited on its boundary. Being disabled significantly lowers the chance of primary completion. The Vanniar caste appears significantly not to value primary education. The caste-specific access to silk weaving, in which Vanniars are concentrated, may explain early withdrawal of children from school (see Chapter 1–6 here). By contrast, scheduled-caste Christians are significantly likely to complete primary education. Last but not least, household income and the educational background of parents have a powerful impact on the primary educational achievements of their children.

5. CONCLUSIONS

There are shamefully few glittering diamonds and far too many rough ones in these villages. Despite some recent improvements in early schooling, socioeconomic status has a substantial influence on educational attainment. *Household income and parental education are the structural factors positively and significantly related to primary completion by children.* This means that children of economically – and educationally – poorer households are still restricted from acquiring the private benefits of education and that the social benefits of education, far from being maximized, are instead stratified. These socially inefficient and inequitable outcomes perpetuate an educational elite (though hardly one that challenges those of the East Asian 'Tigers') and reinforce social and economic exclusion.[37] The preferential access to handloom weaving of the Vanniar caste appears to have had a significant negative impact on the probability of their children completing primary education.

The implications for policy are significant and wide-ranging. Our evidence for 'supply side' variables revealed understaffing and opportunistic behaviour by teachers. If the quality of schooling were improved – for instance by more motivated teachers, more classroom materials, a content for literacy and numeracy that is relevant to social contexts and the appropriate timing of classes – then education would become accessible in ways other than purely geographical and its benefits might become more obvious.[38] The latter need to exceed the social costs of education. To increase primary completion rates, the noon meal scheme, though important, is not enough of an incentive.

The state also needs to direct its efforts towards the factors restraining children's access to education: first and foremost, low income levels which compel parents to force children to work (see chapters 1–1 and 1–6 for discussion of child labour). Day-care facilities for young children might liberate girls for school. But government primary schooling is not without direct costs. One estimate for North Indian conditions in 1996 was Rs 18 per child per year in fees and Rs 315 in non-fee costs (including the uniform).[39] These entry barriers need to be lowered. A wide variety of *non*-educational policies affect the opportunity cost of education and therefore of educational achievement. These range from policies banning child labour to those focusing on improving access to (and rates of return from) work, especially for women and for lower-ranking castes. Poor parental education is likely to be reproducing the effects of poverty where education and income levels are positively related. But insofar as the educational poverty of parents implies differences in parental attitudes to the education of children, our results add weight to the argument that adult literacy campaigns would generate important multiplier effects on poor children.[40]

In the current political economy, how a state might respond to caste discrimination, to prejudice against disabled children, to intervillage variation in access to (gendered) employment and occupations and to the intergenerational reinforcement of low parental education (identified in the model of individual and structural influences on primary completion developed here) is hard to see. *Making primary education mandatory would of course cut through the bewildering indeterminacy of 'policy choice' at a stroke.*[41] The point is the more important in the context of economic reforms when experience elsewhere has shown that those already vulnerable – rural people, women and girls and the poor – are those most likely to lose out. Despite India's poor comparative record in the production of the highly skilled technologists required for successful late industrialization, *the retrogressive subsidies to secondary and tertiary education*[42] *need reallocating to free primary education.*[43] If necessary, user fees for secondary and tertiary education need introducing.

As Manabi Majumdar commented on the draft of this paper:

> What is required in the education sector is to bring the state back in with a big bang and big bucks. By big bang I mean mandatory primary education and big bucks to substantially increase public expenditure on the non-salary sectors of elementary education.

We could not agree more. Tamil Nadu is an educationally advanced state, and one in which the political nettle could be most easily seized.

Acknowledgements

We are grateful to Drs S Janakarajan and D Jayaraj for managing the survey and for designing the coding and formatting of the village census data; P J Krishnamurthy for translating the village diaries; the field team; and Drs M Majumdar and Sharmista Pal for their thorough comments.

Appendix:

Summary Statistics for Probit Model Variables

Variables	#Obs	Mean	Std. Devin	Min	Max	Notes
ed	656	0.5213	0.4999	–	1	
age	656	19.5854	4.4873	13	30	
nms	656	0.6646	0.4725	–	1	if age <21 = 1
male	656	0.6265	0.4841	–	1	
caste	656	3.7652	1.9808	1	7	
am	656	0.2179	0.4132	–	1	aga.mudaliar
nai	656	0.0229	0.1496	–	1	naidu
van	656	0.2744	0.4465	–	1	vanniar
yad	656	0.0808	0.2727	–	1	yadava
sch	656	0.1859	0.3894	–	1	sc-harijan
scc	656	0.1006	0.301	–	1	sc-christian
vin	656	0.3598	0.4803	–	1	
vinf	656	0.1189	0.3239	–	1	vin* (1-male)
vinm	656	0.2409	0.4279	–	1	vin* male
vee	656	0.157	0.3641	–	1	
veef	656	0.0716	0.2581	–	1	vee* (1-male)
veem	656	0.0854	0.2796	–	1	vee* male
dis	656	0.0107	0.1028	–	1	if disabled = 1
hsize	656	5.2787	2.0608	2	17	
ysib	656	1.3735	1.2365	–	1	
gp	656	0.1845	0.3881	–	1	grandparents
bo	642	0.5396	0.4988	–	1	1st born
hinc	656	15964.21	177277.6	–	1	
clpo	656	0.1265	0.3327	–	1	clusters < main
clri	567	0.1845	0.3881	–	1	clusters > main
f1	567	0.1287	0.3352	–	1	
f2	567	0.1587	0.3657	–	1	father primary
f3	567	0.1199	0.3252	–	1	father > primary
m1	618	0.0583	0.2344	–	1	mother literate
m2	618	0.0663	0.2491	–	1	mother primary
m3	618	0.0113	0.1059	–	1	mother > primary

Computed Variable	Description	Min	Max
agenm	age*nms	–	20
ysibf	ysib* (1-male)	–	1
ysibm	ysib* male	–	1
fbo	bo* (1-male)	–	1
mbo	bo* male	–	1
naif	nai* (1-male)	–	1

Socially Inclusive Social Security: Social Assistance in the Villages

Barbara Harriss-White

Rights to social security have often been concluded to be a luxury India cannot afford to generalize. In this chapter, we use village studies to examine the case for a more 'socially inclusive' policy on social security. This is not as anomalous as it seems at first encounter since in the mid-1990s, on the crest of the neoliberal wave when social sector budgets were being threatened, and with regressive consequences, the enabling legislation for social assistance was put through the Indian Parliament. The case for state-provided 'protective' social security rests residually on the poor record of 'promotive' social security in reaching the weakest members of Indian society. Promotive social security is a concept covering that set of development, 'antipoverty' and welfare policies seeking to expand people's capabilities;[1] the act of relabelling policy suggests that protective social security is unaffordable. Yet promotive social security has been criticized as being ineffective at reaching those poor people who are incapable of work. The lowest percentiles of the income distribution are known to have a high incidence of individuals with special needs as a result of advanced age, disability and sickness (including mental illness), destitution and abandonment. We have encountered such needy people already in this book. They live in the shattered, dependent households and the female households discovered in chapters 1–4 and 3–2; they belong to households with disabled members (Chapter 3–4).

A reappraisal of protective social security resulting from threats to welfare budgets is therefore very timely. Protective and promotive security do not operate independently. The two forms are interrelated. For one example, with the increased incomes derived from promotive social security, social insurance may become more feasible and protective social security less necessary. For a second example, there are 'negative externalities' emanating from promotive social security because extended life expectation increases the need for protective social security. In this chapter we examine the roles of the state, of policy regulating market provision and of the household in protective social security. We then show what light a village-level study can shed on the implementation of social assistance targeted to the neediest people.

1. STATE-MEDIATED PROTECTIVE SOCIAL SECURITY

Protective social security, as implemented in contemporary India, covers by means of social assistance the territories of unemployment benefit (on an insurance basis), medical care, sickness and maternity benefit, family benefit, injury benefit, invalidity and disability benefits, old age pensions and survivor benefit.

If we consider India as a whole, it is now well established that protective social security is restricted to employees in the organized sector – at most 12 per cent of the workforce. Within the organized sector, 'public employees are served best, or rather have ensured that they are best served'.[2] It was the great majority, not some marginalized minority, that was – and is – effectively socially excluded, thereby making the concept, in its original European incarnation, inappropriate. Even so, the legal access to social protection of workers in the organized industrial sector is defective, not least because of the widespread evasion of their obligations by employers. Furthermore, state insurance benefits (e.g. survivor benefit and old age pensions) are often inadequate, illiberal in their qualifying criteria and delayed in timing. For the vast mass of the Indian population in the 'unorganized' and self-employed sectors (i.e. the 'real' Indian economy), state social insurance institutions are non-existent for they have no enforceable rights to work, at work or to social security. These workers tend to have multiple simultaneous social security needs somewhat distinctive from those of organized (corporate and public-sector) workers. They give high priority to housing, maternity and child care, survivor benefit on the death of the main earner, wage protection for sickness, occupational accidents and incapacity. Those most vulnerable are those without work, even though work does not entitle workers to social security. In India, social assistance is confined to means-tested old age pensions (in every state), provisions for destitute widows and physically disabled people (in some states) and survivor benefit for death from certain specified occupational hazards (in a few states). Old age pension coverage – the most quantitatively important of the provisions – covers under 20 per cent of those eligible below the poverty line, though there are significant differences in coverage between states.[3]

The Planning Commission was unforthcoming about reform of protective social security, and the silence was filled by Guhan,[4] who proposed a series of reforms to existing protective policy to make it more socially inclusive and cost-effective. Because of confident predictions of declines in social welfare as a result of the reforms,[5] if equity were high on the developmental agenda it would be necessary during an era of general expenditure cuts to *increase* expenditure in this area. A reformist agenda for social security legislation would concentrate on developing those entitlements depending on the discharge of employers' liabilities. Employee injury benefit (an acute problem for construction workers), maternity benefit and retrenchment benefit might be converted to payments via insurance so that compensation to employees is not delayed because of enforcement difficulties.

In the unorganized sector, the development of institutions for the payment (through sales taxes and cesses) of premiums for insurance protection against occupational disease risks is ripe for experimentation. Mutual benefit societies, trades unions and workers' cooperatives have started to organize in order to claim social protection and to argue for appropriate social protection. Of top priority for women are maternity protection, crèches for children, funeral expenses, access to preventative health care and insurance against losses in riots, floods and drought.[6] It has been suggested that occupational groups should finance social security through resources mobilized in appropriate ways (for example 'dedicated' cesses levied on agricultural employers at harvest). Currently, an arbitrary subset of occupations, with a range of modes and rates of tax, are entitled to benefits focused on health, housing and education. They include workers in mining, *beedi*-rolling, cinema, dock and construction workers – all in subsectors where such 'tax' collection is most feasible. Even here, social security provision is exiguous; home-based workers and agricultural workers have proved almost impossible to reach.[7] So a *core of protective social assistance cannot be avoided*, particularly for the needs of old age and death. The state could rationalize this provision. In particular, survivor benefits (so that household members can cope with the death of the household head) need supplementation by lump sum arrangements for the funeral costs of poor people and for the rehabilitation of the bereaved family, given the close relation between widowhood and intense poverty.[8]

Far from being exorbitant, the costs of a minimalist protective programme for income-poor households are quite modest. The Working Group on Social Security of the Economic Reforms Commission in 1984 proposed a package of OAP and survivorship benefit which would be 1 per cent of GNP and less than 4 per cent of combined central and state revenue. In 1989, Tamil Nadu initiated a set of social assistance schemes covering pensions for old age, for widows and deserted wives, agricultural labourers and physically handicapped people; survivor benefit; maternity assistance; marriage grants and accident reliefs amounting to 1.5 per cent of state revenue expenditure and administered through pre-existing channels. While the costs of such a combination of maximum feasibility and minimum benefit are accommodable, the benefits are of a mass nature.[9] An evaluation of this scheme forms the burden of this chapter.

In the 1995–6 central government budget, the Congress Party, appreciating the vote-pulling potential of such benefits (and largely as a result of the experience in Tamil Nadu which we will describe later), set in place the enabling laws for a national social assistance programme which would enable states to increase their paltry social security coverage, although at the cost of central government 'interference'. An optimist would call this scheme a goal for mobilization. It consists of a Rs 75 per month pension for destitute people over the age of 65, a national maternity benefit fund disbursing Rs 300 to poor women for their first two live births, and a national family benefit fund giving Rs 5,000 to poor households on the death of their primary breadwinner if within the age band 18 to 64. The central government's financial obligation would be capped at a sum determined by the proportion in each state below the 1987–8 poverty line and applied to the proportion of the population estimated as being over 65 in the 1995 Sample Registration Survey projection.[10]

2. PROTECTIVE SOCIAL SECURITY AND THE MARKET

Protective social security is almost always a mixture of state and market provision. In India, the market component consists of large-sized organizations, which help to minimize covariate risks. It is also heavily regulated by the state. Social insurance normally involves a tripartite involvement of employers, employees and the state. That of the state is extensive. The Employees Provident Funds Act of 1952 was extended in 1971 to cover provision for whole families of contributors. Later the Government of India set up a special group life insurance for agricultural labour under the auspices of the Integrated Rural Development Programme, together with a rural hut insurance scheme in 1988–9 for fire damage. The nationalization of insurance has led to improved schemes for survivor benefit, accidents, health, crop and cattle insurance on a voluntaristic, commercial basis, with the additional possibility of subsidized low-cost group insurance for certain occupations. There is hardly any actuarial relationship between contributions and benefits, nor is there much adjustment of premiums to accommodate variations in risk.

Nevertheless the highly regulated 'market' achieves very low coverage; only 8 per cent of lives. While life insurance is also urban-biased, crop insurance is regressive and has made heavy financial losses. Group insurance schemes have low rates of adoption because of poor information and inadequate benefits.

There is room for manoeuvre in composite combinations of social insurance, state assistance and voluntary insurance where premiums might cross-subsidize benefits to the poorest. Large groups reduce problems of adverse selection or moral hazard and have lower per unit administrative costs. State governments or cooperatives might sell wholesale insurance, with or without cross-subsidies. Group life insurance can be devised so that contributions from state and central government augment those from beneficiary households.

3. PROTECTIVE SOCIAL SECURITY AND THE HOUSEHOLD

For most Indians, security is not social; it is household. A good example of how households struggle against the contingencies which are considered in policy discourse as warranting social security responses is seen in Chapter 3–4. There, work incapacity – frequently provoked by occupation-related diseases and accidents and taking forms classified as irrelevant to official medical conceptions of disability or taking mild to moderate forms ineligible for benefit – is seen to have a considerable impact on aggregate production and to trigger downwards mobility and debt in the households affected. It imposes costs, some with long-term implications, not only on the incapacitated person but also on other family members, particularly girls and women. The major contingencies which have been studied at household level are of a different nature, however, involving the differentiated impact of regional contingencies: drought, scarcity of food and famine.[11] Though famine itself is subject in principle to pre-emptive state intervention, drought can affect households year on year. Droughts lead to a decline in, or failure of, irrigation and crop protection, whose impact on the area and yield of crop production will depend on the season of occurrence. Failure of production leads to failure of entitlements and the trapping of numerically large sectors of rural society in a price scissor. The productivity of land and livestock all usually decline. As a result, demand for labour drops and wage rates collapse, as do the prices of non-food rural products (especially of livestock unable to withstand harsh conditions), while the prices of food and other consumer goods rise.

Households react by changing their behaviour in order to *cope* and – if that fails – further adapting in order to *survive*. Such changes in behaviour are sequenced and patterned in ways specific to local areas.

Coping involves shifts in time allocations and increases in work burdens. Women and children forage and glean. Common property resources become disproportionately important at the very moment at which they are themselves under moisture stress, often leading to conflicts. Changes take place in the caste connotations of work and people take on demeaning and polluting occupations. Unless state relief work can compensate, victims of drought at this stage may migrate. The increased needs for consumption credit stretch patronage relations, especially as small patrons may themselves be 'coping'. Obligations to distribute may be reduced, gifts denied and the terms of credit tightened. The relationship of patronage may snap altogether. Here the generational durability of the mutual relations of patronage and clientelage is thought to be of great significance, because market-based credit relations are the first to fail. Group sharing arrangements break down and access to state credit and state relief becomes increasingly differentiated.

Consumption drops in a sequence in which non-food items are jettisoned first. Grains substitute for protective foods, calories substitute for other nutrients and cheap calories substitute for expensive ones. Access to state distribution outlets are increasingly taken up.

Marked changes in intrahousehold relations disfavour women, children and the aged. Assets are protected at the expense of (food) consumption. Asset disposal is sequenced and gendered when consumption can no longer protect assets. Non-productive assets and consumer durables are usually shed first, while productive assets are retained. Usually, the disposal rights of the first assets and durables to be shed are in the hands of women. The sequencing of productive assets begins with those which are the responsibility of women but whose rights of disposal are in male hands; assets owned and disposed of by men are the last to be shed.

Resistance to such long-term ratchets may take many forms: from joint family arrangements for investments in water and in agricultural intensification to group resistance to the physical export of food from villages.

If coping fails, survival strategies may result in the disintegration of the household as an economic unit. Individual disadvantage at such a stage has varied through history and regionally. It is now thought that women and children are most vulnerable. Their survival strategies require prostitution, destitution and beggary to stave off death. There is debate over why a household will disintegrate. On the one hand, it is argued that the male head has to exclude the least valued members, so that the legitimacy of women's moral claims breaks down in the face of the moral responsibility of the male head to continue his line. On the other hand, it is argued that the weaker bargaining position of women leads to household disintegration when the female bargaining position collapses completely. These two positions have different implications for policy, the former requiring the economic empowerment of the male household head and the latter requiring the strengthening of the economic position of women prior to household destitution.[12] Such state action is easier said than done, because intrahousehold allocation is based not on market relations or on legally enforceable concepts of fairness but instead on customary enfranchisement and gender-specific notions of just deserts. Yet in the intimacy of poor households, state intervention is crucial. The state alone has authority to sidestep relations of market and custom and the capacity to pre-empt the slide into destitution.

4. SOCIAL SECURITY AND STRUCTURAL ADJUSTMENT IN TAMIL NADU

There is no national consensus about the form to be taken by social security, apart perhaps from the enduring notion that it is a luxury item. It comes under the responsibilities of the constituent states rather than the central government of India. Nimble policy footwork has been necessary in the fiscal stresses of the 1990s to keep it on policy agendas at all.[13] The central government made no effort to assist states in the management of their finances during the early reform period and left states to their own devices. In 15 major states, from 1991 to 1996, social spending declined – from 40 to 36 per cent of revenue expenditure.[14] Tamil Nadu's form of 'market socialist' development (also widely regarded as a form of populism which pendulums competitively between the two Dravidian parties) has involved the creation and piecemeal embellishment of a rudimentary welfare state. In 1993–4, total expenditure on social services (including health and education) amounted to 41 per cent of the state's total expenditure.[15] Before and throughout liberalization, Tamil Nadu had the highest outlay on social security of any state in India. Tamil Nadu, along with Orissa and Bihar (which have low outlays), were the only states not to reduce real outlays.[16] Tamil Nadu's high outlays contributed to a growing revenue deficit.[17] Social-sector spending and food and electricity subsidies were maintained by ever heavier levels of debt.

In 1989, under the DMK government and before the reforms, Tamil Nadu created a system of pensions (for old age, disability and widows of whatever age) and maternity benefits for the poor. Although there was no (internationally endorsed) template for the social sector under adjustment[18] nor any domestic consensus, despite one of the worst fiscal situations (see chapters 2–1 and 3–5), without consulting the central government and with no detailed thought as to its financing, this state was quick off the block in 1992–3 to protect its politically visible spending priorities and counter the anticipated, perceived and predicted adverse effects of structural adjustment on the poor. The Finance Minister announced 'highest priority in safeguarding the position of the poor and underprivileged. We have organised a comprehensive safety net which will ensure that no person in Tamil Nadu suffers from want and deprivation'.[19]

The 'safety net' in India is an *ex post facto* relabelling of a set of policies on which Tamil Nadu has long placed emphasis. It is comprehensive, for it involves food security and nutrition, the public distribution system (whose prices are fixed by the central government, leaving a small discretionary role and the burden of subsidy to each state) and the state-financed noon meal scheme (see Chapter 3–5), primary and public health, and drinking water (see Chapter 2–2), housing, shelter and employment and special programmes for the weaker sections.[20] The latter kind of programmes are financed by the central government. Despite the fact of increasing central government involvement in the social sector generally, they had already been cut back by the time of fieldwork. In any case, they had been non-existent in the three villages. Social security is a non-universal element of this 'social safety net' so, being already highly targeted, was not included in the debate on finer targeting. It is also a small component – about 10 per cent – of the 'net', with pensions as its main element. The eligibility criteria are age and poverty, defined as follows: no age threshold for physically handicapped people, widows or deserted wives; age 65 for old age pensions (reduced to 60 for people with certain handicaps and for agricultural labourers). This age threshold screens out all but the hardiest of poor people. Poverty is reduced to destitution, a condition in which people have 'no means of subsistence and no relatives bound to them by custom or usage to support them'. Evidence of destitution in the mid-1990s would be a house worth less than Rs 1,000 and jewels worth less than Rs 5,000.

The number of pensioners covered increased from 392,600 in its first year of operation in 1989 to 602,100 in 1995.[21] The pension had indeed been protected, meagre as it was (Rs 50 per month, increased to Rs 75 in 1992 and Rs 100 in 1995, when maternity benefit was also increased from Rs 200 to Rs 300). With a 50 per cent increase in coverage and a doubling of outlays, even this small component is difficult to maintain and is under pressure from efforts to reduce expenditure. In this situation, the significance of the central government's scheme mentioned earlier is threefold. First, it is an endorsement of Tamil Nadu's approach. Second, it is a declared obligation that states may claim in future. Third, since the central government will contribute to its funding, state fiscal burdens might be eased, even though the central funding of the social sector has been criticized by the National Development Council as an illegitimate encroachment on state sovereignty.

In the rest of this chapter, we deconstruct what the reduction of want and deprivation means to the local bearers of state power and what social security means to the deprived.

5. SOCIAL ASSISTANCE IN THE THREE VILLAGES

Pensions and other social security benefits are sanctioned at *taluk* level by the revenue inspector (RI) based on applications certified as 'verified' by village administrative officers (VAOs). The cash element is then sent monthly by post as a money order. But pensions also have an important kind element, pensioners being entitled to the noon meal cooked at the local school or 4 kg of rice supplied monthly and free of charge from the local Fair Price Shop, together with two *dhotis* or sarees per year supplied free at festivals. A variety of encounters with the state (village and local revenue officials, postmen, Fair Price shopkeepers and noon-meal cooks) is involved in the access by the poorest rural people to social assistance. The interface is subject to temptations of patronage and rent-seeking.

In telling the story of social assistance we will focus on pensions and maternity assistance, since there were no recipients of family benefit in these villages. The two most important aspects of this form of assistance are: i) targeting and the eligibility of pensioners; and ii) their need. Our evidence comes from three sources. First, the village censuses canvassed in 1993 in which beneficiaries identified themselves. Second, a more detailed survey of beneficiaries in 1995. Since 15 months had elapsed between the census and sample in which new pensioners might have succeeded in gaining access to the 'welfare state', this 1995 survey is best regarded (and has been treated here) as a set of case studies. Third, official data on beneficiaries in each village. This shows further discrepancies. Table 1 includes the official record of coverage, while Table 2 shows the population of elderly in the villages according to our census and survey.

5.1 *Pensions*

With an official record of 26 pensioners in Nesal, 7 in Vinayagapuram and 2 in Veerasambanur, 7, 13[22] and 2 respectively were caught in our sample. With extremely few exceptions, pensions date from 1989, the period of establishment of the social security scheme targeted at poor people. The sources of information about rights (village officers, the Panchayat president, teachers, postmen and political party workers) were all local. The time taken to arrange the posting of pensions varied hugely: from 3 to 18 months, averaging 9, in Nesal; from 1 to 12 months, averaging 4, in Vinayagapuram; and from 2 weeks to 12 months in Veerasambanur. There were extremely few cases which did not need bribes: to VAOs, revenue inspectors, the *tehsildar*, to primary-health centre doctors and, later on, universal Rs 3 tips to the postmen who deliver the pension. The bribes also varied (from Rs 150 to 300 in Nesal and from Rs 25 to 300 – averaging Rs 145 – elsewhere). Bribes and other transactions costs could amount to three months'

TABLE 1 Estimated coverage of old age pensions

	Total Popu- lation	65+ Popu- lation	65+ Population in needy and neediest categories	65+ Population in neediest categories	OAP cases (in official records)
1. Nesal	1551	94	56	34	26
Proportion of OAP cases (per cent)	1.7	27.7	46.4	76.5	
2. Vinayagapuram	1153	63	37	19	7
Proportion of OAP cases (per cent)	0.6	11.1	18.9	36.8	
3. Veerasambanur	578	25	21	14	2
Proportion of OAP cases (per cent)	0.3	8.0	9.5	14.3	
4. All three villages	**3282**	**182**	**114**	**67**	**35**
Proportion of OAP cases (per cent)	1.1	19.2	30.7	52.2	

Source: Survey data, 1995.

TABLE 2 Demographic position of the 65+

Village	Male Population	Female Population	Total Population
Nesal	764	787	1551
of whom 65+	47	47	94
proportion of 65+ (per cent)	6.2	6	6.1
Vinayagupuram	584	569	1153
of whom 65+	34	29	63
proportion of 65+ (per cent)	5.8	5.1	5.5
Veerasambanur	284	294	578
of whom 65+	14	11	25
proportion of 65+ (per cent)	4.9	3.7	4.3

Source: Village Census schedules.

pension payments. There had been one case of a two-month hitch in 1995 because of the parlous state of depletion of state finances, about which there was universal complaint. Otherwise pensions were delivered in a timely and regular fashion. Despite their economic vulnerability, since all beneficiaries lived alone (except the plainly fraudulent – two, of whom more anon), none of the pensions were diverted to others.

While the Sample Registration Survey tables for 1992 for rural Tamil Nadu give the proportion of the population over the age of 65 as 4.2 per cent for men and 4.3 per cent for women, those declared for Nesal (6.2 per cent men and 6 per cent women) and Vinayagapuram (5.8 per cent and 5.1 per cent) are unusually high, while the figures for Veerasambanur (4.9 per cent men and 3.2 per cent women) is closer to the state average but more gender-biased against women (see Table 2). It is likely that the first two villages are further advanced in their demographic transition than the average for the state. It is also just possible that age was exaggerated in the expectation of entitlements from the impact of our research. But that does not explain the case of Veerasambanur.

5.1.1 *Eligibility and targeting*

In Nesal, six of the seven pensioners were 'not eligible' (three being disqualified by age and three by having income), but the stories of their ineligibility are still ones of intense poverty. Their other sources of income vary from Rs 900 per year (from agricultural labour) to Rs 2,520 (from trade in *dosas* [rice pan-cakes]). There is one case of outright fraud, in which the vice-president of the Ambedkar Iyakkam (a local NGO for scheduled castes) procured a pension for his father-in-law, who lives in a household of seven people with two incomes and a far from substantial but disqualifying income of Rs 5,700.

In Vinayagapuram, by 1995, 13 people had pensions while 7 were off-record and 9 were able to be evaluated. Eight of the nine are strictly ineligible. In three cases of destitution and complete dependence on the pension and on charity, the age criterion was flouted. In five households, the family income ranges from Rs 1,440 from agricultural labour to Rs 2,264 (from another household member's job as a noon-meals cook). Of the two successful receipts of pensions in Veerasambanur, one is eligible: a deaf and blind man, aged 75 and living alone, for whom the pension is his sole income. The other is not technically needy, being the village barber whose wife is the village midwife. Together, they have a subsistence income of paddy provided collectively by the village.

5.1.2 *Eligible non-beneficiaries*

In Nesal, there are ten people who are either destitute and/or unsupported or in receipt of extremely low incomes, meagre and irregular support from sons and/or disabled. They exist in acute poverty with paltry sums to eke out their existence, unable to afford the bribe to render them officially eligible. In Vinayagapuram, three otherwise eligible non-beneficiaries sell milk, work in the fields and get family support of a meagre Rs 500 to 2,520 per year. In Veerasambanur, each case of three eligible non-beneficiaries gets family support of up to Rs 600 per year.

Clearly, the official definition of eligibility is highly restrictive and local interpretations of neediness prevail more often than not. Since the criteria of eligibility, one aspect of targeting, is not set in tablets of stone, it is worth examining 'need' more carefully.

5.1.3 *Old age and need*

Need can be proxied by an income threshold since the census data for village households contain estimates for private incomes. On the basis of an already restrictive subsistence poverty line of Rs 150 per adult in 1993–4[23] and half – Rs 75 – per dependent child, an annual private 'subsistence income estimate' (SIE) has been calculated for each household with at least one member aged 65 or over on the basis of the household size and composition given in the village census schedules. People over 65 in households above the SIE are classed as 'not needy' (although the threshold is conservative and there is no knowing the 'fairness' of individual allocations). Those in households between 0.5 and 1.0 SIE are classed as 'needy' and those in households under 0.5 SIE are 'neediest' (see Table 3 for household and Table 4 for individual data). Within the latter category there are two kinds of household. One is 'collapsed' or shattered, consisting of old individuals or couples (these are prima facie the most deprived and destitute), and the other contains old people living with younger relatives.

In Nesal, some 60 per cent of households with old people are under the SIE and 37 per cent of households (with 36 per cent of the elderly) are in the neediest category. Of the latter, one third are collapsed households close to destitution. The three old couples are in each case supported from agricultural labouring by the wife which brings in annual incomes in the region of Rs 900–960. Of the individuated households, that of the scheduled-caste male aged 85 depends on his light casual work uprooting paddy seedlings, plus family support totalling Rs 600 a year from two sons who are agricultural labourers. The other six neediest elderly people are single women. The kind of work they are able to do includes collecting and drying cow dung and gleaning. They subsist on petty remittances from relatives and on local charity. Only 3 of the 13 most destitute households receive a pension. In one case, where a husband has a pension, his wife is also eligible but excluded. Eight people would be ineligible even though extremely needy because of meagre transfers of money within their families. Indeed, in two cases their applications for pensions had been rejected on these grounds. In a further case, an eligible person cannot afford the bribe and transactions costs of Rs 300 necessary to gain access to the pension.

In Vinayagapuram, 59 per cent of both the households and the population over 65 are beneath the SIE and 30 per cent (17 households) are in the neediest category, in which 4 are individuated or are elderly couples. Two of these destitute households receive, and depend utterly on, their pensions. The other two receive petty support from sons and small localized acts of charity. In Veerasam-

TABLE 3 Household composition and extreme poverty

	Number of Households (% in brackets)			
	Not Needy	Needy	Neediest	Total
Nesal				
All households (%)	157	116	72	345
	(45.5)	(33.6)	(20.9)	(100)
HHs with 65+	32	19	30	81
	(39.5)	(23.5)	(37)	(100)
HHs with children	61	39	24	124
under 5	(49.1)	(31.5)	(19.4)	(100)
Vinayagapuram				
All households (%)	149	70	43	262
	(56.9)	(26.7)	(16.4)	(100)
HHs with 65+	23	16	17	56
	(41.1)	(28.6)	(30.3)	(100)
HHs with children	60	28	10	98
under 5	(61.2)	(28.6)	(10.2)	(100)
Veerasambanur				
All households (%)	60	37	40	137
	(43.8)	(27)	(29.2)	(100)
HHs with 65+	4	7	13	24
	(16.6)	(29.2)	(54.2)	(100)
HHs with children	22	16	11	49
under 5	(44.9)	(32.7)	(22.4)	(100)
All three villages				
All households (%)	366	223	155	744
	(49.2)	(30)	(20.8)	(100)
HHs with 65+	59	42	60	161
	(36.6)	(26.1)	(37.3)	(100)
HHs with children	143	83	45	271
under 5	(52.8)	(30.6)	(16.6)	(100)

TABLE 4 Old age and poverty

Category	Nesal		Vinayagapuram		Veerasambanur	
	HH	People	HH	People	HH	People
Not needy	32	38	23	26	4	4
Needy	19	22	16	18	7	7
Neediest	30	34	17	19	13	14

Source: Village census schedules, 1993.

banur, as many as 84 per cent of households contain old people and are below the SIE and 55 per cent (13 households) are among the neediest. In five households, elderly people live alone. Two are above the level of need, but levels of support in the other three – in the absence of the pension – amount to Rs 600 per year.

Those receiving old age pensions are 19.2 per cent of the population above the age of 65. Pensions are 31 per cent of the total in the 'needy' category and 52 per cent of those who are the neediest. *The number of pensions would need to be doubled to cover the total population of neediest and trebled to cover them together with the merely 'needy'.*

If strictly applied, the official eligibility criterion is very restrictive (see Table 5). People over the age of 65 are ineligible if they have any relatives bound by custom or usage to support them, regardless of the actual availability, extent and regularity of such support, or however meagre their own earnings. As actually applied, 20 per cent of old age pensions have leaked out of both the age and eligibility criteria and 60 per cent of the pensioners are ineligible on one or other count. Age is being interpreted in an elastic way. Support is being interpreted quantitatively and not in terms of legal entitlement or availability. The arbitrariness of this kind of implementation is reflected in the refusal of applications from needy elderly people.

5.2 Widows' pensions

Some scheduled-caste widows came to know about the existence of a pension and their rights to it via the Ambedkar Iyakkam, others through the Panchayat president and village officers. The access lag was six months on average. Bribes of Rs 1–300 were involved in over four fifths of cases. Once in receipt of pensions, all recipients had control over its disposition.

TABLE 5　Analysis of cases of old age pension

Village	Eligible Cases	Ineligible Cases			
		Ineligible	On account of age	On account of income	On account of both age and income
1. Nesal	1	6	3	3	2
2. Vinayaguparam	1	8	4	4	–
3. Veerasambanur	1	1	1	1	1
4. All three villages	3	15	8	8	3

Source: Survey data, 1995.

In Nesal, of the 12 beneficiaries sampled, only 2 are eligible, a woman living alone aged 70 and a disabled scheduled-caste widow aged 40, also living alone. Nine however (75 per cent) are not strictly eligible according to official criteria because they receive support or earn income. Examples: i) a 12-year-old son who brings in Rs 1,200 a year as a weaving assistant; ii) incomes from agricultural labouring of Rs 400 to Rs 1,800 a year; iii) the collection and sale of firewood amounting to Rs 3,260 a year. There is one clearly ineligible case, fraudulently obtained through the Ambedkar Iyakkam for a woman whose husband is still living. In Vinayagapuram, there is one widow – pensioner: a woman aged 30 with 0.1 acre of land who needed to give a bribe of Rs 100 and to wait for 6 months to obtain her pension. In Veerasambanur, one of the two pensioners is actually ineligible on grounds of support. The other, a widow aged 60, also gets Rs 1,400 as an agricultural labourer.

Of the 15 widows' pensions, only 2 are strictly eligible, yet, except for one case of fraud, all the rest have gone to people under the SIE.

One case of a pension for a physically handicapped person was mentioned for Nesal but no further details had been provided.

5.3 *Maternity assistance*

This is a lump sum of Rs 300, only obtained by mothers in Nesal and Vinayaga-puram who had been informed of their entitlement by village health workers. Seven instances in Nesal had taken an average of five months and a bribe of Rs 50 (a sixth of the benefit) to activate. The two cases in Vinayagapuram had been much faster in the coming (two months) but required bribes of Rs 30–50. In one case, the money was used productively to help buy a goat and, in the second, to buy vegetables and medicines.

CONCLUSIONS

Tamil Nadu's 'social safety net' is actually being implemented in terms of *need* rather than of strict *eligibility* in these villages (see Table 6). Although 14 of the 18 pensions have gone to the neediest (those in households with under half a very conservative SIE) and a further 3 to needy people (with 0.5 to 1.0 the SIE), of the 24 elderly people who live alone (36 per cent of the total elderly), 22 of whom are needy, only 7 are eligible and only 5 (21 per cent) get the pension.

Entitlements are not well known. Wide and sustained publicity is necessary to increase knowledge of the existence of such schemes. Procedures need to be as simple as possible and the application forms more widely available.

The rationale for screening by 'destitution' rests on three factors: first, a

TABLE 6 Analysis of old age pension cases according to eligibility and need

	Not needy	Needy	Neediest	Total
Eligible (all three villages)	–	–	3	3
1. Nesal	–	–	1	1
2. Vinayaguparam	–	–	1	1
3. Veerasambanur	–	–	1	1
Ineligible (all three villages)	1	3	11	15
1. Nesal	1	1	4	6
2. Vinayaguparam	–	1	7	8
3. Veerasambanur	–	1	–	1

Source: Survey data, 1995.

budget constraint that is deteriorating; second, the argument that the pension should supplement and not displace informal social security from the family; and third, the strong possibility that broader targeting may increase leakages and capture by those at the upper end of the distribution of those entitled (as happened with IRDP).[24] It is clear that current eligibility criteria are excessively restrictive. Selection needs reforms which are practical, unlikely to increase leakage or fraud, and do not put intolerable pressures on the budget. A proactive and rational selection procedure for pensions would involve the following.

i) Targeting all single-member households and couples aged over 65 living alone with income from all sources of less than Rs 600 (so that the SIE would be reached using transfers or earnings plus the pension).

ii) Targeting all the neediest first: households with income of less than half the SIE. If this still threatens state budgetary resources, then those with the highest dependency ratios among the neediest could be targeted first.

Income estimation is always subject to abuse, especially if it is known to be related to pension provision (see Chapter 3–2). Household types (such as individuated households or ones composed of couples over 65) are non-income and non-fudgeable means of refining income estimates of eligibility. Other leakages might be staunched by cross-checking the income estimates against lists of land/assets holdings (subject to other kinds of time and transactions costs) and by collective action: screening by publishing the draft lists of beneficiaries and making implementation subject to collective approval.

The amount of the pension is extremely low. Many recipients, when their opinions were canvassed in our survey, wanted it increased to Rs 200 (£3) per month. But in the absence of an increase in the state budget, there will be a trade-off between coverage and quantity. At the least, the pension needs to track inflation.

There are other problems with the administration of social assistance. While the official norm for approval of applications is 3 months, most instances here took 6 to 18 months. Further, the transactions costs (including travel, a photograph and the dominant element, bribes) amounted to three–four months' benefit, with significant monthly tips thereafter to the postmen who delivered it. For such 'retail' corruption to be corrected, punitive action on corrupt low-level officials by those further up the system is an unlikely scenario,[25] or likely only to be translated into extortion. In its absence, pressure from below can only be applied by the Panchayat or by local NGOs where they exist. But NGOs are not particularly superior, either as intermediaries or as publicizers of rights. The Ambedkar Iyakkam in Nesal has been instrumental in getting benefits for scheduled castes but has not eliminated the need for bribes and has acted as facilitator in cases of gross errors of ineligibility. A foreign NGO in Vinayaga-puram dropped its support for a vulnerable person without arranging any kind of substitute or a state pension for which this woman is eligible.

Last, social assistance is gently politicised (see Table 7). The scheme was brought in under the DMK government and, when we studied it, was being administered by the AIADMK. In the set of recipients willing to state their affiliation, 80 per cent of the pensions had been distributed to open supporters of the ruling party.

TABLE 7　Political affiliation of beneficiaries

	Nesal	*Vinakapuram*	*Veerasambanur*
Old Age Pensions			
AIADMK	4	9	1
DMK	–	1	2
No allegiance	3	2	1
Widow's Pension			
AIADMK	6		
No allegiance	6		
Maternity Benefit			
AIADMK	1		
DMK	1		
No allegiance	5		

ACKNOWLEDGEMENTS

The empirical part of this chapter keeps close to 'Social Assistance in the Three Villages', a set of comprehensive notes and tables compiled from the social security field schedules made by the late S Guhan in 1996 at the Madras Institute of Development Studies, Chennai. Guhan also made extensive comments on social security at the workshop on Adjustment and Development at the MIDS in 1996, as did A Dayal and N Narayanan IAS, to whom I am very grateful.

So What for Policy?
Rural Development in a Poor State

Barbara Harriss-White

1. POLICY CONCLUSIONS

IN this book, we have kept watch on a set of policies on production and welfare and charted their roles in the lives of rural people in South India. Policies often have very different effects from those imagined by policy-makers. There are patterned disjunctures in policy priorities between centre and state. In the case of rural *electricity*, for example, bound up inextricably with the regulation of *groundwater* for agriculture, the 'distant' agenda in New Delhi concerns the administrative separation of generation and transmission and their privatization under a deliberately loose and non-mandatory regulative framework. Policy in Chennai, on the other hand, has been frozen for a decade since the DMK government made agricultural electricity free. We found that its huge subsidy has led to a highly differentiating and inefficient use of electricity (now 18 per cent of the true social cost of agricultural production). Production is sited on the outer wastes of the 'production function' where the returns to water are far below their imputed marginal social costs. The subsidy has invited an accelerated plundering of groundwater which has reached an environmentally critical point. It is clear that electricity can and ought to be used to regulate groundwater extraction. The consequences of reintroducing a significant cost component (not only into paddy production but also into that of groundnuts, vegetables, sugar cane and banana) during an era of cost-price squeezing would require two conditions to be met: first, the creation and acceptance of an environmental rationality in a highly socially differentiated system of production and, second, the careful calibration of subsidy removal with the procurement prices of agricultural products, targeted at small producers if they are not to go to the wall.

Similarly with *fertilizer*. In New Delhi, the agenda concerns balances. One balance is between the manufacturing, trading and agricultural beneficiaries of the fertilizer subsidy. The other is between subsidy removal and efficiency in the use of chemical nutrients when the price elasticities of yields are actually declining. In Tamil Nadu, if small producers, those in remote locations and/or with less favourable hydrogeological endowments are to develop what still appears to be their higher productive response to fertilizer, then fertilizer distribution needs state support for extension work and non-market targeting.

State-managed credit was a major prong of heavy agriculturalization. New Delhi is intent on unravelling targeted credit and deregulating cooperative, nationalized and commercial bank lending practices (especially uncapping interest rates and freeing up sectoral conditions for loans). Our research showed that the regulation of credit has resulted in increasingly unequal access and in capture of formal credit by traders and rural on-lenders. Some formal credit feeds into a highly complicated informal sector where markets are fragmented, personalized and exclusive. The development of the non-farm economy is shaped by mercantile lenders through interlocked contracts which shape the distribution of gains. Deregulation will now increase their power. Chit funds represent one important response by the mass of small borrowers who are excluded from state-regulated credit. Meanwhile the credit policy issue completely ignored by New Delhi but of importance for poor rural people concerns loans to landless borrowers for small quantities of land. We found that such micro-property is acceptable collateral for formal credit and is a prior screening device for informal loans. There is thus still plenty of scope for a developmental state when it comes to credit policy.

New Delhi clearly wishes to phase out the *public distribution system* (PDS) of essential commodities, most notably foodgrains. To have doubled the quota of grain to which households below an increasingly politically determined 'poverty line' are entitled (to 20 kg a month in 2000, and later to 35 kg) while not allowing poor people to buy consignments *less* than this entitlement is condemning the poor to exclusion, since they can only buy what they can afford out of their daily wages. It also artificially condemns the PDS to unprecedented levels of cost and waste. In Chennai, the PDS and *noon meal scheme* (NMS) are being *protected* because they are socially redistributive and accessible to the most disadvantaged people and – we think – not solely because they are voters. If PDS targeting is necessary, then we found that small landed households are only slightly less nutritionally vulnerable than landless agricultural labour.

Further, the state alone is in a position to offer resources to protect the deteriorating position of girls and women (manifest in life chances, school attendance, access to the noon meal, access to credit, not to mention wages and access to the non-farm economy). Other institutions cannot protect girls and women. The village is still the unit for the female sector of the 'labour market' and it discriminates against women. The Tamil Nadu Government has responded to deteriorating *female life chances* by creating state orphanages and guaranteeing reserved jobs for unwanted babies and social security incentives to protect girl children. It is not simply an irony of development that the acquisition of property makes its inheritance matter so much that girls are culled, it is a tragedy. The spread of dowry southwards from North India and outwards in society converts girls into liabilities in a way never previously experienced in Tamil Nadu. As long as the state honours in the breach the Enforcement of Dowry Act of 1961 and fails to regulate sex-selective abortion, the policy of greatest importance to female status is public-sector employment for women, not only those from backward and scheduled castes but also even for educated women.

In New Delhi, policy on *primary education* focuses on hand-wringing over the 'brain drain' and educational quality and on a long debate over the chicken-and-egg issues arising from the sequencing of the abolition of child labour and of mandatory primary education.[1] Primary education is superceded on the policy agenda by issues such as language (demand for English), public subsidies to private education, the Indian State's commitment to tertiary education, and the returns to public versus private provision. In Chennai, progress was made in 1993 with a commitment to mandatory primary education, but this has been honoured in the breach. The local agenda also concerns quality, the reduction of the opportunity costs of schooling and the spread of adult literacy to change parental attitudes. The state has provided unprecedented incentives – a meal, uniforms, shoes and equipment – to reduce the direct and opportunity costs of school attendance, to little avail. Primary completion is 44 per cent. Educational deprivation is still being faithfully reproduced across the generations, reflecting income, caste and class and the disadvantages of disability and gender.

For people *incapacitated* for work in adulthood by health conditions and accidents, many of which are work-related, the state is necessary to provide remedial equipment and the small loans needed at times of distress, on terms and conditions which do not trigger downward mobility. Access to the social security benefits to which poor disabled people are entitled needs improving. We saw that this *social security system* is correctly targeted on elderly people, although the age threshold is punitively high for rural labourers. Households with members over 65 are poorer than those with children under 5, especially households consisting only of members over 65. Pensions currently operate according to need rather than the state's eligibility criteria, which are highly restrictive. But – in implementation – the system is stingy and therefore arbitrary and prone to political patronage. To cover people in households that are somehow getting by on *half* a conservative local poverty line – *half* an estimated subsistence minimum – state resources for these pensions would need to be *doubled*. To cover those merely under the subsistence minimum, resources would have to be *trebled*.

A flaw in considering policy issue by issue, sector by sector, as we have done in these village studies, is that their political synergy is obscured. Free electricity, subsidized fertilizer and credit are all captured by the agricultural elite. Although welfare is not captured by this class, even so girl children, shattered families, scheduled-caste and disabled people tend to be excluded. Policy also slips and is transformed in implementation. Apparently unintended consequences are routine (e.g. the impact on yields of suboptimal fertilizer use following the partial lifting of subsidies; the impact on grain stocks of increased quotas of food staples for poor people [which they are too poor to lift]; the capture of targeted credit). Our research has revealed political resistance to economic reforms (e.g. the deregulation of credit; the lifting of subsidies on electricity and food). It has revealed lack of coordination (physical infrastructure); lack of consultation (social security targeting, appropriate disability benefits); neglect (primary education, incapacitated people); and outright vulnerability faced with powerful social forces (corruption, the increasing domination of patriarchal ideology). Neither village-level evidence on its own nor a sectoral approach to policy analysis reveals the beneficiaries of this synergy: respectively fertilizer manufacturers, grain traders, asseted debtors, large farmers, contractors, private-sector substitutes for public provision, rent-seekers in markets as well as in the state – sectors in which low-caste people, wage labour and women are rarely found.

Three themes emerge from these conclusions. All are out of fashion. It has been said that the fashions of one era are scarcely intelligible to the next, but in this case it is the fashions of Chennai that are scarcely intelligible to the policy elite in New Delhi and the needs of villages that are obscure in Chennai.

The first unfashionable theme is the importance of votes as a means of protecting structures of rents and of distribution which transfer resources to poor people (e.g. the public distribution system, the noon meal scheme, the social security system). This is not to argue that votes are always the currency of progress: the case of the electricity subsidy is relevant as a counter-example, not only because it is a widespread cost concession to agricultural producers but also because of its differentiating and destructive economic and environmental impacts. Nor is it to argue that votes ought to be the prime regulator of policy priorities (there are no votes in primary education). But it is to recognize that electoral democracy, whatever its intrinsic value, is also instrumentally crucial to wide-based development. It is necessary, but it is not sufficient, as we shall see later in this chapter.

The second unfashionable theme concerns the case for (means-tested) targeting as an effective way to achieve accuracy and cost-effectiveness in redistributive social transfers. The unfashionable conclusion from our research is that this is undesirable. First, the information required for targeting is costly. Our work on *poverty* and on *social security* shows that poverty lines can create distorted incentives favouring underdeclaration of income. In the households studied here, potentially 20–25 per cent of households over the poverty line underdeclared (see Chapter 3–2). Local knowledge enables access to be captured. Without local knowledge, non-fudgeable indicators of eligibility can be used with good predictive powers (e.g. for poor people: caste, a female household head, the presence of one or more people incapacitated from work, households consisting of people over 61, the construction of the dwelling – mud and thatch – etc.). Second, the use of even proxy indicators like these involves a trade-off between errors of inclusion (of the ineligible) and those of exclusion (of the eligible). We consider the latter the worse error. Third, targeting also increases delivery costs. Fourth, it stigmatizes those eligible. Last of all, it turns rights – which have had to be fought for in order for them to be institutionalized – into discretionary awards in a context when budgetary support for all kinds of downwards redistribution is under pressure of cuts.[2]

It is the third theme, however, that will be elaborated in this final chapter. It is the crucial importance of the state as the only social instrument potentially capable of declaring universal obligations, implementing them, instituting claims, adjudicating disputes and enforcing redress and accountability. The state is therefore central to development.

The alternatives to the state are said to be markets and 'civil society'. But markets in theory have another objective altogether – the efficient allocation of resources through the linking of supply and demand. It is well known that this task is consistent with any income distribution. In practice in this project we have vivid evidence of the differentiating consequences of markets, even when average real incomes for labour have risen, and especially when these markets are poorly regulated by the state. The chapter on *credit* shows the staggering extent to which commercial credit is captured by the rural elite. The chapter on *water* markets reveals the increasingly unequal outcomes resulting from interlocked triadic contracts involving grain, water and money. The evidence on *labour* shows how labour markets differentiate particularly against low-caste workers and women. The chapter on the *non-farm economy* shows how scheduled-caste people are severely disadvantaged in their access to the best-paid segment of the rural labour market.

Positioned research on 'civil society' and the work of NGOs attributes to them an importance as a mechanism of political agency and social redistribution which does not correspond to their real resources and which is inconsistent with the evidence of their potential – especially when it is the regional economy rather than the groups themselves that is the focus of the story. In our research, NGOs, however worthy their objectives and however committed their workers, are seen to have small resources, arbitrary projects, varying competence and limited accountability (see especially the chapter on *disability*). As intermediaries acting on behalf of people making claims on the state, they are not above the occasional act of fraud (see the chapter on *social security*). Where they are most successful, as the Catholic and Protestant churches are in the provision of *education*, their spread effect may not extend as far as an adjacent village. They are another form of private development, even if they do not necessarily practise market exchange. A politics of redistributivist development has no option but to be state-centred.

2. POLICIES AND POLITICS

Tamil Nadu's political culture is perhaps unusually supportive of redistributivist state intervention. It has been described as both clientelist and populist. In and out of power, both the two main Dravidian nationalist parties subvert state resources and institutions to their own ends. Party allegiance and rewards to political clients have distinctive characters. In the All-India Anna Dravida Munnetra Kazagam (the AIADMK, created by the film star M G Ramachandran and run after his death in 1987 by his former political and dramatic partner), patronage has been dominated by J Jayalalithaa. As Chief Minister in the first half of the 1990s, she was said to be remote and to have relied on her direct appeal to the masses. Over the duration of our field project she operated a politics of tribute-raising and of distribution of spoils marked by a culture of submission, unsymmetrical benefits, discretion and authoritarianism. In 2000 she was convicted and sentenced in two cases of corruption, but she has returned to power.[3] In contrast, the Dravida Munnetra Kazagham (DMK) under M Karunanidhi has operated with less charisma, using the patriarchal idiom of a family and attempting to form a dynasty. Through a cascade of cadres, the party is thought to be somewhat more meritocratically structured than is the AIADMK; local leaders can be more independent and the principles governing the distribution of spoils are thought to be more systematically applied. However, allied with the coalition led by the Bharatiya Janata Party (BJP) at the centre, it has been unable to contain an upsurge of casteist politics in the state and a proliferation of caste-based parties with which the DMK aligned itself in the 2001 elections.

The parties' approaches to public policies are often said to be significantly different. The DMK's has an urban centre of gravity and has been focused on the rectification of long-standing caste injustices through the most generous policies of positive discrimination in the subcontinent: '*reservations*' in education and public-sector employment. The AIADMK's is, if anything, rural-biased and based on an ambivalent policy on alcohol[4] and on the biggest nutrition scheme in the world – the noon meals programme – which embraces all preschoolers, school-going children and old age pensioners and other recipients of social security benefit below the poverty line (see Chapter 3–5). Largesse is also periodically distributed to the poor (e.g. kits of clothes on the party leader's birthday), but in the idiom of charity rather than entitlement. So while the DMK makes appeal to 'low caste people', the AIADMK appeals to 'the masses', and particularly to women.[5] It has to be said that, when power swings like a pendulum, neither party can undo its opponent's populist practices and that, when in power, each tends to add marginal endorsements in order to trawl for loyalties (e.g. the DMK added a fortnightly egg to the AIADMK's noon meal – which out of office it had criticized for profligacy; and the AIADMK refused to contemplate lifting the DMK's 100 per cent subsidy on electricity).

The focus on competitive distributive politics obscures the facts: first, that there is no hard and fast division between distribution and production (food subsidies, for instance, lower the costs of the production of labour); and, second, that the biggest subsidies (electricity and fertilizer) are openly for production and are not progressive. Even so, these kinds of political arrangements, combining clientelism and populism, are structurally among the most stable in India when it comes to resistance to the lifting of subsidies, the downsizing of public employment and expenditure and privatization, which are central themes of structural adjustment and liberalization. The point is not simply that this kind of state puts up vigorous resistance to external pressure to reduce its scope. There are also two further important aspects to policy for the early part of the twenty-first century. One is state capacity. The second is the politics of capital, a far less visible kind of politics which meshes with party politics, and its conspicuous politics of distribution. Using our field material, we will discuss each in turn.

3. STATE CAPACITY, LOCAL-LEVEL GOVERNANCE AND INSTITUTIONAL SCARCITY

What does this state look like from the perspective of the villages we studied? The general administration has two wings at the local level, developmental and revenue. State performance is illuminated through the life histories of 35 local officials which we collected, roughly half in each wing, operating at village, block and *taluk* level. Development officials tend not to live in the villages they administer, but in town. All those interviewed were male caste Hindus: of higher caste status than the majority of the rural population. Eighty per cent owned land and of these half received more income from land than they did from their employment in the state. So, for nearly half the employees interviewed, their salaries from state employment provided a supplement rather than a main income.

At the level of the local block administration, duties were described as being vulnerable to political interference, particularly those involving scarce resources, which were routinely rationed according to political considerations. Not only did party politics structure the queues for access of rural supplicants, it also structured administrative responses and careers. Two in every five officials admitted to having paid a bribe to obtain state employment or to shape his postings. This may be an underestimate.

Resource scarcity was reflected in levels of pay. Despite the fact that the state is in certain ways a progressive employer (with higher proportions of women and of scheduled castes, and with a more egalitarian aggregate pay structure than in the private sector), for low-ranking officials pay is much lower than for commensurate work in the private sector.

Targeting has long been a pervasive feature of performance at this level of government. In the policy literature, as we have already seen, targeting is presented as a necessary response to resource scarcity, with states under intense pressure to fine-tune. In practice, it is used coercively within the administration both to induce and to monitor performance. Twenty years ago, the date for acceptance of high-yielding rice varieties (HYVs) was distorted by achievement targets imposed on agricultural officials. The practice persists. Low-level officials have diverse administrative responsibilities, which, if conscientiously performed, amount to a heavy load, and many of them are subject to achievement targets.[6] The *grama sevak* (village worker) for instance administers (at least) small savings schemes and IRDP loans and their recovery, unemployment schemes, biogas and smokeless stove programmes, eye camps and streetlights, as well as the chores connected with drinking water: maintenance of hand pumps and overhead tanks. In the absence of administration by means of incentives[7] or of work loads which could be negotiated, the practice of imposing performance criteria across a range of responsibilities deforms performance. We came across a number of cases of money borrowed individually and privately in order to achieve official targets incommensurate with public resources. In two cases, the money was needed for the officials' transport to villages. In another case, a large private payment was made to the police to encourage them to investigate a theft of state property. In a fourth case, private funds were being used to rent a store for the safekeeping of state property. Accessible parts of the informal economy have also been plundered for private funds so as to achieve state objectives (e.g. illegal industrial units are threatened with sanctions by the district collector unless they fund and maintain a sterilization ward in the local hospital).

Resource scarcity in these low levels of the state results in public action and reaction. Long before 'structural adjustment' and pressures to downsize the state, the state had in effect already transferred responsibility for the maintenance of much of its rural property onto 'the community', but not through user fees and not in a formal, legally defined manner. The ad hoc 'collective' maintenance of infrastructure such as water supply has proved ineffective and inequitable, leading to frequent conflicts and disputes. The alienation of 'beneficiaries' or participants was reported. Officials gave examples of the low quality of the information they must screen and of a high rejection rate for routine claims of various sorts. The lack of cooperation of intended beneficiaries also results in the misuse of state funds and in poor responses, performance and recovery of funds. It also gives rise to frequent conflict in the long queues for access, which officials declare they are powerless to resolve. While an alienated civil society sees itself forced to respond collectively to the scarcity of state resources and personnel, the latter see it in terms of defiance by village collective institutions, which appear to them as both informal and non-democratic. Both sides report increasing conflict over public utilities between these ad hoc village-level institutions of collective response (organized on gender, caste and class lines) and the 'proper' jurisdiction of the state. Downsizing by itself is no solution to such politicized administrative relations, for collective, so-called communitarian institutions exacerbate deeply institutionalized conflicts, while the state's capacity to regulate conflict is seriously compromised.

The second arm of local government is concerned with revenue and registration. This group differs from those in the development wing in respects other than their job description. Of them, 45 per cent were of scheduled castes. A much greater proportion, over half, had paid bribes for their posts and 20 per cent admitted to paying regular commissions. Those admitting to paying bribes were at the foot of the bureaucratic ladder. The bribes were considerable, ranging from Rs 1,200 to Rs 12,000. Continual tributes (commissions) were paid on a monthly basis to patrons by a few of them. As with the development administration, three quarters had land. Of these, half (i.e. over a third of the total) had a greater income from land than from their public employment.

The experience of this slice of the bureaucratic hierarchy complements what we learned about the operation of the development wing. At each level of the bureaucratic hierarchy, there is considerable local variation in the objectives and content of posts, exacerbated by a mismatch in the specification of content and load. The revenue wing is suffused with political interference. Private party-political allegiance is a determinant of performance and of career. Since authority is increasingly derived from party-political patronage, state officials face resistance to regulation and taxation. Their weak capacity to target has a more complex derivation, taking both technical and political forms. Technically it is found to be difficult, first, to administer targeting criteria with effectiveness and, second, to meet targets which are not customized to local conditions. Politically it is difficult to weed out and differentiate among the poor in a neutral manner and to cope with pressures to determine eligibility according to party-political allegiance. As a result, these officials lose authority as representatives of the state.

The state actually generates informal activity in response to its failures and incapacities. It is common that state duties are a risk-averting residual income source (for example, the Agriculture Department official whose main income is derived from exports of pickles). A bureaucratic niche is no doubt also important for its private returns. When bribery screens entry, the subsequent postings are required to make returns on the initial investment. More insidiously, it has been found that state effectiveness increasingly depends on the private ascribed status of public officials – on their class background, their caste and their gender.[8] The latter can be said to permeate the state and to blur the boundary between state and society.[9]

3.1 A local-level example: private status and the depletion of municipal finance

Private status can be seen at work in the case of the market town of Arni, which 'serves' the three villages. Its impact on developmental resources is far-reaching and dire. (see Table 1).

For nine years (from 1987 to 1996), local municipalities were not democratically managed; instead they were run by political appointees from the state capital. There was a brief interlude of democratic governance between 1986 and 1991. During this period, inflation and a tax revaluation greatly increased *potential* municipal revenue. Table 1 shows selected elements of local revenue and expenditure. Under democratic rule, revenue from property taxes and from the tax on municipal market traders increased, as did expenditure on salaries.[10] Under the undemocratic and politicized rule of the early 1990s, duties on property transfers were better enforced than they were under the elected local government. Throughout the period for which we have data, 1983–4 to 1992–3, professional tax paid by the local elite fluctuated wildly; but the trend was towards the evasion of payments. The contribution to local revenue by citizens with taxable property and incomes fluctuated significantly but rose in absolute

TABLE 1 Municipal receipts and expenditure[1]

Source	1983–4	1984–5	1985–6	1986–7	1987–8	1988–9	1989–90	1990–91	1991–2	1992–3
Total Receipts[2]	77.9	102.2	94.8	166.7	139.3	133.3	190.6	180.1	165	199.9
of which:-										
Fees, rents and income from services	8	7.1	8.1	11.8	20.6	19.5	18.9	21.8	24.1	29.8
Taxes from Propertied Classes:-										
Property	7.4	8.8	9.1	9.8	13.3	19.3	17.5	18.8	22.4	22.4
Professional	1.1	1.5	1.2	2	1.2	0.8	0.9	0.7	3.6	0.8
Duties on Property Transfers	2.5	2.5	2.5	5.4	5.5	5.9	6.4	6.9	11.5	16
% of total receipts	14	12.5	13.5	8.6	14.3	19.5	13	11	22	19.6
Taxes and levies from Poorest Traders:-										
Municipal Market	2.3	2.4	2.5	4.7	11.5	11.8	11.5	12.1	11.5	15
Cart Stand	1.4	1.5	1.8	2.8	2	2.6	2.5	3.3	2.4	3
Fines on Encroachment	0.2	0.2	0.2	0.2	0.1	0.1	0.1	0.1	0.1	0.1
Slaughter House Fees	0.1	0.1	0.1	0.3	0.1	0.2	0.2	0.8	0.3	0.2
% of total receipts	5	4.1	4.8	4.7	9.8	11	7.5	9	8.6	9
Total Expenditure of which:-	62.2	99.9	102.6	105.1	119.1	128.7	205	183.6	164.2	201.3
selected staff[3]	19.8	22.1	27	29.8	31.7	44.8	108	87.7	85.5	96.2
% of total exp	32	22	26	29	27	35	53	47	52	48
Total			1950777				4116731			

Notes:
[1] Arni Municipality, current Rs lakhs.
[2] Major sources of revenue are regular Government of Tamil Nadu allocations, deficit grants, loans and advances.
[3] Staff of Municipal Office, tax collectors, public works, water supply, public health, sanitation and inspection, market and cart-stand management, urban lighting and town planning.

Source: Raw data provided by Commissioner, Arni Municipality.

current terms by a factor of 3.5 from 1983–4 to 1992–3, while their proportional share of revenue increased by 35 per cent. More significantly for our argument, the very poorest firms in the municipal markets, 'platform' traders doing business at the entrance of established shops or from mobile stalls, or those with wares displayed on gunny bags and sacking beside the roads (with typical gross outputs per firm well under 0.5 per cent of those of the 15 top firms), contributed 4.5 times more in absolute terms by the end of the period than they did at the start. Their share in the municipality's total revenue doubled. The municipality proved to be better at taxing people earning less than its own employees than it was at taxing the elite.[11] The entire municipal budget for 1993 equalled the declared gross output of just one of the most substantial businesses in town. Three interpretations suggest themselves: i) a class conspiracy (between officials and the commercial elite) to exploit other classes; ii) a class battle, given the political weakness of local government in the face of the local elite (since the tax collectors have lower social status than those being taxed); and iii) lack of state legitimacy (tax evasion representing a 'principled protest' by the elite at the high spend on salaries and the low spend on infrastructure). The last set of circumstances is likely to be self-perpetuating.

While the town has been upgraded as a first-class municipality for tax purposes, for other purposes it has not. Its population figures, conditioned by an increasingly irrelevant administrative boundary, are a severe underestimate. This anomalous situation prevents the appointment of officials by the Public Service Commission, with the result that the entire staff of the local state consists of appointees of the Special Officer (from the time of direct rule) or the Commissioner (democratically elected since 1996). So most of the appointees are said by key informants to be the clients of local economic notables, through their influence with one or other of these two officials.

4. CORRUPTION

The fact of bribery has seeped into this chapter and this book. Quite humble positions in the state require bribes of up to one and half year's returns from them. Of lower orders of magnitude are the cost–benefit relations of a pension for disability or old age (three to six months' worth of benefit). Even the postman delivering the pension gets a small, regular kickback. So why is it surprising that corruption is the 'great black hole of development economics and public policy'?[12] As Leys pointed out long ago, there is a 'widespread feeling that the facts cannot be discovered or that if they can, they cannot be proved, or that if they can be proved, the proof cannot be published' for reasons either of research diplomacy or of social-science conventions about validity.[13]

This means that the theorization of corruption has had a field day unpolluted by much empirical material. Orthodox corruption theory cannot explain the immense proliferation of corruption over the period when reforms supposed to quash it have taken effect. In the new political economy, corruption is theorized as the development of property rights over (subsidized) public goods rights, resources, positions and promotions in conditions of institutional scarcity, the venal official being placed centre stage.[14] This is easily generalized to the 'private interest state', the case against which accompanies the case for 'the market'. While the soft policy options following from such theories form a lengthy agenda,[15] the hard option is less contested and involves deregulation to remove sites for rent-seeking.[16] In this approach, the social relations in which corrupt transactions are 'demanded' (or funds for corruption are 'supplied') by the (non-bureaucratic) party to the corrupt contract are neglected. Talk of corruption as 'the market clearing response to the inefficient distribution of free public goods'[17] both obscures the mechanisms by which there is a 'market' in the first place and assumes that there is only one form taken by (and only one logic for) the corrupt exchange.

Bureaucratic corruption is defined and well understood in India to be '*all forms of improper or selfish exercise of power and influence attached to a public office or to the special position one occupies in public life*'.[18] The way it may become politicized over time, such that patrons become clients and vice versa as the balance of power between them alters, can be illustrated with the case of bus transport in and around the villages we studied. Bus routes should be allocated bureaucratically according to closed tender proceedings and bus fares are capped by administrative fiat. Administrative corruption has over time ensured a 'clearing response' allocation of routes which maximized returns, net of wear and tear. However, this administrative exercise of rent-seeking discretion has been subject to political capture. Politicians have inserted themselves as regulators and fund collectors. Routes are doled out periodically in a 'public' meeting of politicians and bus owners according to the latter's *individual* roles in electoral and party-political funding. The political executive comes both to command the administration and to capture the formerly private rents they gathered. Even more recently, the *collective* political investments of bus owners themselves have fetched returns in the form of discriminatory policy changes timed to disadvantage the state's own public-sector bus transport and to advantage private owners. This is a simple illustration both of the role of corruption in development policy paradoxes and of more subtle forms of corruption[19] in which the state subverts its popularly mandated development project on behalf of powerful interests in society. It yields the rents it needs for distribution to other sections of society to classes whose power is derived from the further rents they create and protect in markets. Corruption is part of a broader institutionalized process of upwards redistribution and accumulation.

Flows of money up and down political networks solidify relations of tribute and political patronage which run closely parallel to those of state revenue and development. Political campaigning may devour funds raised lawfully and create an appetite for funds raised corruptly. The distribution of gains from political corruption is central not only to party politics but also to forms of the state. Under one regime, funds originating mainly in the commercial economy may flow upwards, be centralized and subsequently redistributed to the mass of potential voters in the form of money as pre-election sweeteners.[20] Whether this is generalized to patrimonial, populist or clientelist forms of state politics depends on the relative status of the bribers and those collecting bribes and on the need to buy votes. Centralized funds may also be privately appropriated and used for conspicuous consumption, or re-allocated, semi-legitimized, into forms of politicized bureaucratic provision or commercial investment. Under circumstances of corrupt accommodation, there may be extensive political (or political-cum-administrative) leakage (either privately appropriated or partly redistributed downwards) at every stage of the upward and downward trajectory of money. Further, political corruption may bypass the bureaucracy entirely, the implementation of reciprocal favours from corrupt alignments being administered by officials according to political command.

5. POWERFUL CLIENTS AND THE LOW-PROFILE POLITICS OF LOCAL CAPITAL

Local businesses fund political parties in a risk-minimizing, opportunistic way. They can put pressure on the police and the judiciary. With and without bribery, they lobby systematically to protect business from state regulative and fiscal policy. Until very recently, local business politics has operated not in the discursive and procedural spheres of policy-making but in the process of implementation. In the town servicing the three villages we studied, collective institutions such as trade associations appear superficially as regulatory bodies to whom disputing parties would be expected to turn. They can establish norms of conduct for transactions and for the adjudication of dispute. These associations also defend members from threat – from organized labour or the government. They can and do organize collective bribes in the general interest of members. They exclude entrants into business. They also perform small acts of redistributive charity. On closer inspection, many are tight networks of interest cemented by caste and kin. Institutions such as kinship and caste are put to new economic uses. The Chamber of Commerce is also maturing as a political force, organizing collective protest, petitions, non-compliance and *bandhs* (strikes) in order to challenge state taxes on entry into business and local business taxes, the regulation of packaging and branding and the provision of improved infrastructure.[21]

While bureaucratic earnings are comparatively low (and low-risk), long and extremely costly waits are accepted by the local commercial elite in order to lodge kin in the bureaucracy, for the state has high economic and non-economic entry barriers. Bribes are investments (made with funds derived from forms of accumulation in which fraud, economic crime and the oppressive exploitation of labour play their part) yielding returns (derived from corruption). Symbiotic economic relations then develop between business, the administration and the ruling political party. Thus politics and administration become commercialized and oriented to commercial interests. That the main focus of economic 'reform' is cutting public expenditure rather than fiscal compliance (irrespective of how tax regimes may also be in the process of being reformed) is eloquent testimony to the power of this 'reversed' clientelism.

6. TAX EVASION

Widespread, large-scale tax evasion is entrenched in India. As long ago as the early 1980s, it was estimated that 41–58 per cent of potentially taxable income from all sources escaped taxation and, that in specific instances of commercial taxation on agricultural products, non-compliance could amount to 80 per cent of potential revenue.[22] There is a trade-off between the costs of, and returns to, tax collection which creates incentives to organize production and commerce in units below the various thresholds. Above these thresholds, the art of avoidance and the craft of evasion are practised, often using corrupt transactions. Much business politics grows out of fraud. In the local business economy, all but the pettiest of commercial firms had net returns before tax above the income tax threshold of Rs 45,000 p.a. Little tax is paid as a matter of pride. Bus companies keep no accounts at all and the income tax of the owners is collectively negotiated. Commercial taxation is avoided and evaded. The first is instanced by the burgeoning scrap-metal sector, where commercial taxes are levied only on the 'first purchase'. The sector is structured around a sizeable number of independent small wholesalers whose gross output is beneath the commercial tax threshold and who sell to a small number of large wholesalers (whose 'second purchases' are therefore tax-exempt). In practice, all the apparently independent small wholesalers are completely financed by the large wholesalers and are really not very well disguised wage labour. Evasion is illustrated by groundnuts, which are subject to cascading taxes at every stage. These taxes are extensively evaded by means of verbal, spot contracts with immediate cash payment. So a striking paradox is arrived at: the only commodity whose conditions of transaction remotely resemble those of perfect competition (groundnuts) assumes this particular and rare contractual form specifically to evade its share of the collective tax burden.

Tax evasion fuels a black economy characterized, first, by the informal privatization of local government services and, second, by pervasive relations of corruption. Third, a large black financial sector composed of funds not declared to the tax authorities – which nonetheless must be invested and/or banked – reinforces tendencies to unproductive investment, oppressive labour relations in the informal economy and short-term finance and investment. Roy has convincingly shown that the great bulk of black income is due not to corruption but to the lack of capacity of the Indian state to tax effectively; these are 'primarily areas of petty bourgeois activity – the domain of the trader, contractor and (real) estate agent. This points to the build-up of a significant wealth owning and wealth generating constituency *outside* the dominant coalition identified by Bardhan'.[23] (Bardhan's coalition is of big business, agrarian capital and the big bureaucracy.) The mechanisms are underdeclaration of receipts, undervaluation of assets and exaggeration of expenses. The form of black wealth is not cash (the medium of corruption), it is real estate, trade stocks and precious metal.[24] Leakages due to corruption from the private and public sectors amount to a quantity one twentieth as large as those due to tax evasion. All of these practices were in evidence in our study, becoming ever more widespread and significant over the decades.[25]

7. STRUCTURAL ADJUSTMENT AND THE PARADOX OF CORRUPTION

Even within the stylized world of corruption theory, there are several reasons why the prediction that deregulation will reduce corruption may be confounded. First, partial changes in ownership may multiply sites for corruption by complicating lines of accountability and by diluting enforcement capacity. Second, even if ownership changes, from public to private, the state will still have to regulate conduct. The regulatory responsibilities of the state may remain substantial, while central bureaucratic controls over the behaviour of state officials can remain weak. Then some business interests may use corrupt means to maintain access to resources or exemptions, while other interests will bribe to enforce deregulation and increase the territory of market exchange. Lastly, officials may seek bribes against promises of future economic rents, given that their tenure outlives that of politicians. Outside this stylized theoretical hothouse, a ganglion of relations of black economy, economic crime and – during our research – increasingly political and mafianized corruption set the conditions for its own perpetuation and created obstacles for reforms in the directions suggested by corruption theory. Structural adjustment did not take the form expected by macro-economic policy-makers. The real reforms to the state have been proceeding apace from much earlier than 1991 and are due to scarcities of resources and the scarcity of appropriate institutions. Further deregulation could even strip the state of its residual capacity to regulate markets and curb corruption.

8. REAL STRUCTURAL ADJUSTMENT AND THE INDIAN BUREAUCRACY

The scarcity of resources and personnel symptomatic of state decay have had a profound impact on the capacity and the legitimacy of the state. The discretionary powers of officials rise, but so too do those of their patrons and minders in civil society. Understaffing is selective and often politicized.[26] The pattern of staff vacancies is less and less due to the difficulty of filling reserved posts[27] and more and more due to intense pressure from civil social organizations for preference in recruitment. Lines of accountability suffer havoc because lay-offs are not systematic, which reduces the capacity to enforce regulative, developmental and distributive policies. The Departmental memory is relocated to low-ranking officials who tend to stay put. The terms and conditions of bureaucratic service deteriorate, raising incentives to moonlight and to supplement salaries. The quality of goods and services supplied deteriorates, encouraging private or black alternatives. As queues lengthen, so incentives to 'exit' increase. Those left in queues are only the neediest clients. The overall result is that the state tends to be aggravating inequality, the very opposite of its constitutional mandate.

As the state becomes weaker, rights in the state's political transactions proliferate as elements in the state attempt to buy off powerful challenges from the informal economy. Politicians have long realized this and inserted themselves as brokers, paid by powerful interests in the economy to *prevent* regulation and taxation, and paid by officials to shape their transfers and promotions. The latter set of incentives leads to an acceleration in the velocity of postings and a 'spinning' senior administration.[28] In India as a whole, in the late 1990s, half the IAS officers were transferred within 12 months of posting.[29] This 'spinning state' has a severe impact on economic regulative activity, which Robert Chambers has dubbed a 'slipping clutch'.[30] The costs in travel and in the loss of quality of administration are not negligible. Incompetent post-holding increases, if only because the time needed to acquire informal knowledge and to develop the informal relations which make institutions work exceeds the time allowed in specific postings; but also because of corrupt preferment. This leads in turn to acts of passive resistance from subordinates. Since the quality of supervision declines, other kinds of disruption are possible. Disincentives to innovate are built in. State capacity to achieve goals slows down as the velocity of transfer speeds up. Time-bound planned projects are subject to time and cost over-runs. Information to the public is less systematic and abundant. Poor-quality, easily sabotageable law raises questions about the intentions underlying the law and the possibility of corrupt coalitions between law officials, the administration and the judiciary. The prevalent lack of experience of legislators suggests incompetence rather than conspiracy. But the skeins of corruption which result satisfy a broad set of interests so effectively that the consequences of incompetent law-making are indistinguishable from those of a conspiracy. As the state loses legitimacy, tax compliance weakens and the contradiction between rights, obligations and resources intensifies. This is hardly what is envisaged in the World Bank's demands for good governance.[31]

9. WHAT IS TO BE DONE?

This is what the state of Tamil Nadu (which is far from being the poorest in the Indian rankings and is one known for its combination of populism, caste advancement and clientelism) looks like through the eyes of people in at least three villages and a local town when the politics of business is added to the other ingredients of policy analysis. Off the conventional development policy agenda lies an even more intractable problem: one of accountability. Lack of accountability shapes lack of tax compliance and oppressive labour relations every bit as much as it does the behaviour of the state and its redistributive reach. In their edited collection on *Corruption in India: an Agenda for Action*, S Guhan and S Paul set out a series of constructive suggestions to combat corruption and increase accountability. At first sight, these seem very far removed from the policy agendas we have examined in this book. In fact, they are a response to the regulative conditions and political culture in which these village economies are enmeshed. They are summarized here in the box. We finish by trying to relate these suggestions to the rural economies we have described.

SUMMARY OF THE PUBLIC AFFAIRS CENTRE'S AGENDA TO COUNTER CORRUPTION[32]

Reform to the Indian State

1. Politics
- stop criminals from entering party politics;
- enforce accounting discipline and transparency in political parties; set up an Ethics and Conduct Committee for Parliament;
- reform compensation and privileges of politicians; stop discretionary allocations (telephone and gas connections, petrol-pump allotments); end MPs' and MLAs' immunity from the Prevention of Corruption Act and their non-declaration of assets and income;
- reform election funding (the state should fund elections; there should be ceilings on election expenses, a ban on donations from big business and the elimination of rigging);
- Commissions of Inquiry must ensure political accountability.

2. Bureaucracy
- reorganize anticorruption vigilance;
- slow the velocities of transfer, especially of top officials;
- facilitate whistle-blowing;
- systematize ombudsmen (Lok Ayukt and Lok Pal) with a constitutional status, independent staff and juridical personality;
- create Civil Service Tribunals with inquisitorial procedure to hear appeals of departmental abuse against civil servants.

3. Regulative law
- deregulate in a partial fashion, not necessarily so as to dilute the regulative function of the state but to eliminate incentives for corruption;
- prioritize deregulation by the extent of opportunity for the control of corruption;
- develop detailed parametric instructions for discretionary decisions;
- strengthen an independent Central Vigilance Commission, supported by the Central Bureau of Investigation and to be given a nation-wide jurisdiction and statutory base to facilitate coordination, prevent political interference and the pooling of intelligence pertaining to corruption.

Reform to Society

1. Social empowerment
- reduce the culture of secrecy and limit the power of public-service providers with a reform to the Official Secrets Act based on defence of the public interest; introduce a Freedom of Information Act;
- institute a system of bureaucratic standards and norms ('mission statements');
- decentralize resource allocations and service delivery;
- strengthen the morals and resolve of the '85 per cent of the public abhorring corruption', starting with the young.

2. Popular regulation
- involve NGOs, religious groups and research bodies to publicize, intermediate and aid complaint;
- encourage the press to investigate and publicize;
- engage lawyers in public-interest litigation and judicial activism;
- challenge business lobbies to suggest specific measures to stop corruption between business and government.

Guhan and Paul's agenda assumes that corruption is top-heavy and that reform begins at the apex rather than the base. It ignores the problems of administrative and institutional scarcity and of the fiscal crisis. It assumes that these reforms can be expedited on the basis of rhetorical appeals urging their necessity and it externalizes their costs. Its position on the economic forces we have identified as powerful and complicitous partners in the struggle for control over rents in markets as well as in bureaucracies is to ask poachers to turn gamekeepers. Is this enough? Who will gain from resisting such reforms? Is the democratic deficit to be reduced by broadening clientelist politics or by eliminating it? How is anticorruption vigilance to be developed? By what factors *other* than by the potential for controlling corruption should deregulation be sequenced? How would they be traded off? How can decentralized governance be protected from powerful economic 'clients'? How can young people be educated in public ethics through school when schooling is still frequently caste-segregated and when primary completion is under half? How would the power relations between parties, the state and the interest groups which might act as popular regulators or watchdogs be likely to evolve under conditions of clientelist politics? Are there better alternatives to this agenda? Are there supplements? The answers are as relevant to the social impact of changed fertilizer subsidies or the regulation of groundwater as to the protection of young girls or the struggle for education of low-caste children. In the search for them, an even more ambitious project of local-level and rural research emerges, as does an even greater challenge to longitudinal field studies of villages and rural regions.

ACKNOWLEDGEMENTS

I am grateful to Shapan Adnan, Mushtak Khan, P J Krishnamurthy, C T Kurien, Colin Leys, N Narayanan, Wendy Olsen, John Rapley, Rathin Roy and the late S Guhan and Gordon White for their helpful reactions to earlier incarnations of this chapter, but I am responsible for its inadequacies.

Notes

Endnotes (Preface)

1. Farmer (ed.) 1977; B Harriss 1981c; J Harriss 1982; Hazell and Ramasamy (with others) 1991; Bliven, Ramasamy and Wanmali 1997. On nutritional and health issues in subsets of the villages and ones nearby from field projects closely interconnected with our research see: B Harriss 1991c; Gillespie and McNeill 1992; and Erb and Harriss-White 2002.

2. See Harriss and Harriss 1984; B Harriss 1991d; Nagaraj, Jayaraj, Janakarajan and Harriss-White 1996a; and Basile and Harriss-White 1999a.

3. Which might have happened of course without selection as a 'model village'.

4. See Chinnappa 1977.

5. Maddumma Bandara 1977.

6. Chinnappa, op. cit.

7. Hazell *et al.* 1991a.

8. Hazell *et al.* 1991c.

9. J Harriss 1991a and 1991b.

10. Hazell, *et al.* 1991b.

11. Hazell, *et al.* 1991d.

12. Analysed in detail in Cassen, Joshi and Lipton (eds.) 1995.

13. Thereby fulfilling Hazell and Ramasamy's prediction that rice prices would be (long term) stable.

14. See particularly Lanjouw and Stern (eds.) 1998.

15. And not because of the ammonia in fertilizer. . .

16. Janakarajan, 1996a.

17. Palaskas, and Harriss-White 1997.

18. Nagaraj *et al.* 1996a. See also Harriss-White 2003.

19. IDS Bulletin, 1996, vol. 27, no. 2 on *Liberalisation and the New Corruption*, co-edited with Gordon White.

20. And see his Festschrift: Harriss-White and Subramanian (eds.), 1999, *Illfare in India: Essays on India's Social Sector in Honour of S. Guhan*, Sage, New Delhi.

21. Some of the themes we had intended to include but which are neglected in this book are migration, factor productivity and its implications for *reverse* land reformism: the lifting of ceilings for (corporate) capital, the changing role of the pastoral economy, health (apart from incapacity), reservations policy and the impact of ceremonial expenditure on the household economy.

Endnotes (1–1)

1. Farmer 1977; Vaidyanathan 1994.
2. Vaidyanathan op. cit., table 2, p. 68.
3. Palmer-Jones and Sen (2001), however, have recently shown that in half the agrocli-matic regions of India, agro-ecological conditions have played a more important role than has development expenditure, irrigation infrastructure or technology in determining the level of rural poverty in India. It is interesting to note that, in their analysis, the state of Kerala (considered to be so highly distinctive as to constitute a development model) is seamlessly part of a west coast zone.
4. For later events, see Swaminathan 2000a.
5. Vaidyanathan op. cit.; Rogaly *et al.* 1999.
6. Rao and Gulati 1994; Johl 1995b.
7. Cassen, Joshi and Lipton 1993.
8. Dobb 1975.
9. These involve free electricity to producers, a minimally targeted public distribution system, a comprehensive school meals nutrition scheme, a social security system for poor people and the most inclusive reservations system for backward and scheduled castes and scheduled tribes.
10. See Farmer (ed.) 1977 and Hazell and Ramasamy 1991. Three of these villages were taken for intensive study in 1993–5. They are Veerasambanur, Vinayagapuram and Nesal.
11. Janakarajan 1998 and see Chapter 1–2.
12. See Maddumma Bandara 1977, p. 325.
13. Chinnappa 1977, p. 93.
14. Though these had sometimes, as in the case of IR20, been based on South Indian genetic material.
15. For the rice equivalent a rule of thumb is to multiply by 0.66.
16. See J Harriss 1977.
17. Hazell and Ramasamy op. cit., p. 14.
18. See Hazell and Ramasamy op. cit., p. 32.
19. Ibid. and p. 26.
20. A revolutionary change in agricultural production should be marked not only by changes in growth but also by lower per unit costs of production; but real, per unit weight, costs of production have increased by 63 per cent – see the section on 'production' in this chapter.
21. See Hazell and Ramasamy op. cit., pp. 13–18.
22. Op. cit., pp. 31–5.
23. Op. cit., p. 13.
24. See J Harriss 1982, 1991c.
25. In the current period we sumarize accounts given in detail elsewhere in this book and present in fuller detail the elements of the story not appearing later. The 1996 workshop papers are available from Queen Elizabeth House, Oxford.
26. This statement is based mostly on data in the Tamil Nadu Economic Appraisal. It has

to be said that in certain years the published data are greatly at variance with those available locally in the Department of Statistics, Tiruvannamalai (the district's headquarters), and the Regulated Market Annual Report at Arni (the local administrative centre). It is possible that the declining quality of public service has resulted in a deterioration of data quality. However official data on agricultural production twenty years before were also of low quality (see Chinnappa 1977, pp. 93–100). We have to take them at face value.

27. While the potential is 7 tph.
28. This is in fact a long historical process, noted by Chen Hang Sen in the early 1930s (in Thorner [ed.] 1996, p. 139). See also Janakarajan (1993a and Chapter 1–2 here) for more evidence concerning the Palar Basin.
29. Govt of India 1989.
30. These data are not for the region surveyed in our project but from seven villages in the Vaigai Basin in southern Tamil Nadu (Janakarajan 1998).
31. See Janakarajan, Chapter 1–2 here.
32. Govt of Tamil Nadu 1994b, table 3.39, p. 379.
33. From this point onwards in this account, 'survey data' for 1993–4 refers to that for Nesal, Vinayagapuram and Veerasambanur villages. 'Census data' refers to the recensused 11 villages.
34. J Harriss 1977, 1982, 1991c; Chambers and Harriss 1977.
35. *Ineqfac*, the STATA ado-file used for the analysis, provides an exact decomposition of the inequality of total assets value into inequality contributions from each of the factor components of total assets: value of land, value of other agricultural assets and value of non-agricultural assets (see S P Jenkins, http://ideas.uqam.ca/ideas/data/Softwares/bocbocodeS366003.html).
36. So the trend of greatest concentration in the poorest villages between 1973 and 1983 is the opposite of what is seen in this truncated sample of villages (see J Harriss 1991a).
37. Op. cit., p. 55.
38. Ibid., p. 53.
39. Nesal and Vinayagapuram had both been classified as rich villages by Hazell and Ramasamy (1991). Although Gini coefficients by village had not been reported by the previous research, we can nevertheless compare the coefficients computed with 1993 data with those calculated for 1973 and 1983 for the rich villages. The zero values in Table 6 refer to landless and assetless households. In Nesal 208 households are landless, 11 of which do not own any other asset. The first columns under each village report Gini coefficients for land and asset value distributions only for landed households and those owning some assets. Second columns, instead, refer to Gini coefficients for all households.
40. Bliss and Stern 1982.
41. Using the distribution of land ownership among Nesal farmers by size categories reported by J Harriss (1991c, p. 116), a Gini coefficient is computed of 0.75.
42. Hazell and Ramasamy, op. cit.
43. In the remaining eight villages which were recensused, the proportion of farmers

with less than one hectare increased from 52 per cent in 1982–3 to 64 per cent in 1995 (see Srinivasan, Chapter 1–3 here).

44. A similar classification where '*punjai* with wells' is replaced by garden land was used by John Harriss in a detailed analysis of Nesal. In his categorization of the land of 'Randam' (Nesal), Harriss (1982, p. 65) adopted the classification used by the revenue authorities for *wetland* (or *nanjai*), as the '. . . low-lying areas commanded by tanks' and for *dryland* as the area above and between the tanks. He also recognized the existence of a third category of land use. This is the '. . . garden land irrigated from wells, though is not distinguished in the revenue classification because of the policy . . . of exempting private land improvement from additional taxation'.

45. John Harriss (1982) reported the following percentages: wetland 21.8 per cent, dry land 62 per cent and garden land 16.2 per cent. However, we should take account of the fact that 36.5 per cent of the total land reported in that period was dry land owned outside the village. Although a great amount of this land has been sold to a prominent family of Muslim sweet-sellers in Arni over the years, the problem of under-reporting, especially for land owned outside the village, makes comparisons difficult. Nevertheless, changes in the proportions of land types, and specially an increase of garden land at the expense of dry land, do also appear when we concentrate the analysis on the land owned inside the village. From Harriss's data: wet 26.8 per cent, dry 50.3 per cent, garden 22.9 per cent. From 1992–3 census data: wet 29.3 per cent, dry 32.5 per cent, *punjai* with wells 38.2 per cent.

46. See Haggett 1965.

47. Chapman and Harriss 1984.

48. See J Harriss 1977, p. 126.

49. See Hazell and Ramasamy 1991, p. 34.

50. Of course local farmers may have better knowledge about varieties than agriculture department officials and may have good reasons for rejecting official advice, but we have no evidence about this.

51. Harriss-White, Crowe and Janakarajan 1996.

52. See Appendix 2, Table 3.

53. The cost of production has been calculated, comparably to Hazell and Ramasamy's set, as the total paid-out costs for seed, manure, fertilizer, pesticides and seed treatment, hired labour (including payment for the animals that accompany ploughing labour) and other costs. The latter include diesel/electricity (the latter being free in 1993–4), other hired-in equipment, fodder and veterinary expenses and costs of maintenance of other implements. Left out of the calculation were the depreciation of farm implements, land rent, interest on loans and any imputed cost of family labour. Prices are at the 'farm gate' and returns exclude those from by products.

54. If electricity were charged, it is estimated it would amount to 18 per cent of the costs of production (see Chapter 2–4).

55. The Hazell and Ramasamy classification, proxying for class, is being used for consistency: small farms are below 1 ha, 'large' farms above 1 ha.

56. See Harriss-White, Crowe and Janakarajan 1996.

57. In 1973, small farms were 25 per cent more labour-intensive than large ones.
58. Attached labour is permanently employed by one particular farmer, therefore such labourers do all kinds of work and are paid partly in kind. Attachment ranges from bondage to seasonal contracts.
59. See Tables 17 and 20 on costs of production.
60. Marked gender bias in access to the noon meals scheme has appeared in the last decade (see Table 2 in Chapter 3–5).
61. Bryceson 1995.
62. Visaria 1995.
63. Mellor 1976.
64. In Mellor's original formulation, it does not matter how this increased income is distributed, but later on Mellor used the argument to justify a post-green revolution income distribution more biased than before towards large farmers (see B Harriss 1987a and Hart 1996 for critical treatments of this justification).
65. Mellor 1976; Bell *et al.* 1982; Hazell and Ramasamy 1991.
66. We offered a critique of this part of the argument with reference to the development of the regional rural *and urban* economy of North Arcot over the decade from 1973–4 in B Harriss 1987b.
67. Visaria 1995, pp. 402–3.
68. Vaidyanathan 1986; Bhalla 1999; Jayaraj 1996a.
69. B Harriss *et al.* 1984.
70. B Harriss 1987a.
71. Hart 1996.
72. Jayaraj 1996a.
73. Visaria 1995, p. 408.
74. 1994 data; Harriss-White, Janakarajan and Legassick 1996.
75. See Nagaraj *et al.* 1996a for evidence and discussion.
76. At the base of each village is a cluster (varying between 5 and 12 per cent of households) with less than Rs 10,000 assets. Much above this, in two of the three villages, is the mass (60–80 per cent) of households averaging Rs 60,000. But in one village, this mass is twice as wealthy. In two villages, the small elite which dominates the village economy does so with assets worth Rs 3–6 lakhs. But in Nesal this wealth category denotes an intermediate elite comprising a third of households. The latter's elite is five times wealthier. The wealthiest and poorest household studied differ by a factor of 2,250; see Chapter 1–4.
77. The sample survey did not pick up beggars, who comprise about 3 per cent of the original village census.
78. The 43rd NSS round for 1987–8 estimated that 2.4 million male workers and 151,000 female workers residing in rural locations commute to work, *but also* that 590,000 male and 109,000 female workers commuted from urban locations to rural ones for work (Visaria 1995, p. 399).
79. There is no implication that these dual flows of investment have to be equal.
80. We assume that institutional finance either is sited or flows outside villages, that the

samples' rice mills are outside (which we know is the case); and we include the land and irrigation investments which we know lie in village territories outside those studied.

81. Nagaraj *et al.* 1996a, follow this argument in relation to the diffusion into villages of silk handloom weaving.

82. Ellis 2001, pp. 160–78.

83. Jayaraj 1996a; Harriss-White, Gold and Janakarajan 1996.

84. Piecework glove sewing had spread 30 km south of its epicentre to reach a young, home-bound, female *Agamudaiyar Mudaliar* labour force in Arni in 1994. Also see Kennedy 1999.

85. See *www.tn.gov.in/economy/eco-sep-b,2000* and *www.tn.gov.in/economy/eco-band. htm*, 2001.

86. Lipton 1994.

Endnotes (1–2)

1. For a detailed discussion on this aspect and for more statistical information pertaining to tanks in Tamil Nadu and North Arcot District, see Bandara 1977, MIDS 1983, Janakarajan 1986, and Vaidyanathan and Janakarajan 1989.

2. For a historical account of the discussion on the deteriorating condition of tanks and the legislative measures attempted to revamp the tank irrigation system in the then Madras Presidency, see Krishnaswami 1947, Saradaraju 1941 and Baliga 1960. See also Cox 1895.

3. Krishnaswami 1947, p. 438.

4. For more details see Vaidyanathan and Janakarajan 1989. See also J Harriss 1982 and Bandara 1977.

5. Janakarajan 1993b.

6. Bandara 1977, pp. 337–8.

7. Chinnappa 1977.

8. For details of the survey and the methodology, see Janakarajan 1996b. For details of the original survey and the first resurvey, see Farmer (ed.) 1977 and Hazell and Ramasamy (eds.) 1991 respectively.

9. The Brahmin landlords' interest in the tank may be judged from the fact that they possessed 5 out of 18 shares of the fishery rights (*machcha maghasul*) as per the village 'A' Register.

10. According to J Harriss (1982), there were ten divisions.

11. J Harriss 1982, p. 126.

12. Vaidyanathan and Janakarajan 1989; Janakarajan 1993a.

13. J Harriss 1982, pp. 71–2.

14. Ibid., p. 130.

15. This has happened in the other parts of the district as well as the state (Vaidyanathan and Janakarajan 1989; see also Janakarajan and Vaidyanathan 1996).

16. See Janakarajan and Vaidyanathan 1996.

17. However, the possibility of errors in our data which might have caused such a big

difference in the yield level between Veerasambanur and the other villages cannot be ruled out.

18. For a detailed discussion of this issue see Jayaraj 1996b.
19. Nagaraj *et al.* 1996b.
20. Ibid., pp. 67–9. The other major non-farm employment which was virtually non-existent in 1973 is the significant numbers of rice mill *coolies* (scheduled-caste workers) and hulling merchants in Nesal (Agamudaya Mudaliars who commute to Arni every day) and female twisting factory workers in Veerasambanur (who commute to the town of Devikapuram).
21. Janakarajan 1996b.
22. See Janakarajan 1992.

Endnotes (1–3)

1. Dasgupta 1975.
2. Aziz 1989.
3. Chambers and Harriss 1977.
4. Jodhka 1998.
5. Rudra 1992.
6. Dasgupta 1975; B Harriss 1992.
7. Aziz 1989.
8. The villages in alphabetical order are Amudur, Duli, Kalpattu, Meppathurai, Nesal, Sirungathur, Vayalur, Veerasambanur, Vegamangalam, Vengodu and Vinayagapuram.
9. See Farmer (ed.) 1977 for details.
10. See Chambers and Harriss 1977, J Harriss 1991b and Dasgupta 1975.
11. Chambers and Harriss 1977.
12. J Harriss 1991b.
13. See Dasgupta 1975.
14. See Chambers and Harriss 1977.
15. Information given by village administrative officers.
16. This village revealed higher literacy rates than all the other villages from both census and survey. It has a higher proportion of scheduled castes (SC) than other villages and is located remote from the nearby urban centre (Kaveripakkam). It has two primary schools – one for scheduled castes and the other for non-scheduled castes – which may be the reason for the higher literacy. Having separate schools for SCs, undisturbed by the caste–Hindu local elite, might have contributed to higher literacy rates. In Tamil Nadu, prior to the late 1980s, primary schools were functioning under local panchayats which were under the control of local elites. However this is not to argue that there should be two schools to improve literacy (see Chapter 3–6).
17. Sargent *et al.* 1996.
18. In Vayalur as many as 7.7 per cent of households were tenant cultivators.
19. Hazell and Ramasamy 1991.
20. From the late 1980s, the Government of Tamil Nadu provided power to farmers virtually free of cost. This led to a sudden increase in applications for power connections.

In some areas, farmers waited for more than ten years to get them. Recently the state government announced an immediate power supply to those who pay a deposit of Rs 10,000. But political and technical turmoil over this issue prevented the implementation of this scheme.

21. Hazell and Ramasamy 1991.
22. See Janakarajan 1996a.
23. We found that a few public works contractors from Cheyyar engage workers from Sirungattur colony on a long-term basis. In the same manner, owners of brick-kilns in Vegamangalam employ local labourers on a regular basis. This could be one of the reasons the workforce tends towards non-farm jobs there.
24. Nanjamma *et al.* 1977, p. 216.
25. J Harriss 1991b.
26. See Srinivasan 1997 for details on agricultural minimum wages in Tamil Nadu.
27. But see Chapter 2–4, where barriers to their access are revealed.
28. The interpretation for the factor matrix or factor loadings is similar to that for standardized regression coefficient in the multiple regression equation, with the original variable as the dependent variable and the factors as the independent variables. If the factors are not correlated, the values of the coefficients are not dependent on each other. In short, the factor loadings represent the unique contribution of each factor and are the correlations between the factors and the variables. When we judged how well the four-factor model described the original variables, the table revealed that all the variables were explained by more than 30 per cent. Except for six variables, the model explains all the other variables by more than 50–99 per cent.
29. Though many variables other than non-farm employment are influenced by this factor, it influenced positively the area under groundnut and negatively male agricultural labourers and male non-farm workers.

Endnotes (1–4)

1. Olsen 1996, p. 55.
2. See Hazell and Ramasamy 1991 and Hazell *et al.* 1991b.
3. Janakarajan 1986, 1993c.
4. Bhaduri 1983; Sarap 1991.
5. See Majid 1994 and the discussion in Sharma and Drèze 1998, pp. 471–5.
6. Swaminathan 1988; Olsen 1996.
7. Patnaik 1976; B Harriss *et al.* 1984; Bhattacharyya, 2003.
8. Patnaik 1987.
9. J Harriss 1982; Athreya *et al.* 1987.
10. Olsen 1996.
11. See for example the discussion in J Harriss 1982, chapter 5.
12. Scott 1976.
13. Cain 1981.
14. Attwood 1979.
15. Bhaduri *et al.* 1986.

16. See Rogaly *et al.* 1999, p. 15 ff.
17. See Olsen 1996.
18. Chandrasekhar 1993; Nagaraj *et al.* 1996b; and see chapters 1-3, 1-5 and 1-6.
19. Razavi 1992.
20. Kydd 1982.
21. Pryer 1990.
22. Everitt 1974.
23. The comparative advantages of these techniques are as follows. In the hierarchical analysis, clusters are formed by grouping cases into bigger and bigger groups until all cases become members of a single cluster. This method can be seen as a stepwise progression in which cases and/or clusters are combined together. At the beginning of the analysis, each observation is considered as a unique cluster and the number of clusters g equals the number of observations n. At the first step, the two most similar observations are merged into a new cluster, so that there will be g = n-1 groups. At the second step, either a third observation joins the cluster formed in the previous step or two other cases are linked into a new cluster and the number of groups will be g + n-2. At every following step, either single cases are added to existing clusters or new clusters are created or existing clusters are merged. As a result of this fusion process, more and more observations are linked together, and clusters with dissimilar characteristics are aggregated. A limit of this technique is that clusters, once they have been formed, cannot be split. So cases which have been assigned to specific clusters cannot be separated from them and relocated to others.

    A k-means cluster analysis, also called optimization-partitioning or iterative relocation, is also used for clustering large number of cases. The numbers of groups, however, have to be specified in advance. It is therefore supposed that the researcher already knows, or can make reasonable assumptions about, the actual number of clusters which are expected from the analysis. Thus once it has been assumed, for example, that the original data can be reduced into k groups, the analysis starts with k initial cases selected either randomly or in a way to maximize the initial distances between cluster. The observations will be then relocated between groups through iterations in order to minimize the variability within clusters and to maximize the variability between clusters. In general, the k-means method will produce exactly k clusters of greatest possible distinction, although the results will be sensitive to the selection of the initial clusters.
24. See Thorner 1982.
25. Kydd 1982; Everitt 1974.
26. Norusis 1994. Such a procedure is based on the proposition that, at any stage in the analysis, the loss of information which results from grouping entities into clusters can be measured by the total sum of squared deviation of every point from the mean of the cluster to which it belongs. For each cluster, the means of all variables are therefore calculated. For each case, then, the squared Euclidean distance to the cluster means is estimated. These distances are summed for all of the cases. At each step, the union of every possible pair of clusters is considered and the two clusters whose

fusion results in the minimum increase in the overall sum of square distances are combined, until all observations become members of the same cluster.

27. It is recognized that seasonality of agricultural operations will make the choice of one month somewhat arbitrary, but this has to be traded off against respondents' capacities to recall under census field conditions. The census was undertaken during the main growing season of the agricultural year – November–December 1993 – so the data concern busy times in the agricultural calendar.

28. Variables 10, 12 and 14 can be considered as indicators of rural diversification, although non-agricultural work is only to a limited extent substituteable with agricultural work. Occupation data, which would denote diversification more precisely, were in a categorical form incompatible with the classificatory technique adopted in the analysis, as were data on caste.

29. Certain household groups could be qualitatively very interesting but quantitatively less important than others (Kydd 1982). If we find, for example, that a relatively small group of households is characterized by some strongly atypical attribute, this group will most probably remain distinct until the latest stages of the fusion process. It might therefore happen that bigger and different clusters are linked together only because the degree of dissimilarity between these large groups is lower than the degree of dissimilarity between them and the small cluster. Although qualitatively interesting because of its peculiarity, the latter is quantitatively less important than the former and bigger clusters. If we are concerned with the less sharp differences which distinguish subgroups of households among the bulk of the population, we will then have to define a classification of households based on a higher number of clusters. But we do not know whether strongly atypical groups, and clusters constituted by a high proportion of households, are encountered or not in the hierarchical progression unless we analyse the results for the different cluster solutions.

30. Hazell and Ramasamy 1991, p. 30.

31. In set C) of Table 1 we can see that, in Veerasambanur, the average income of the elite is 1.85 times the average village income, while in Vinayagapuram and Nesal the average income of the elite is 3.55 and 4.93 times the respective village average. In Veerasambanur, the extent of landholding operated by the elite is 2.38 times the village average. In Vinayagapuram and Nesal, instead, the elite's landholding size is 4.63 times and 6.44 times their respective village average size. The value of assets owned by the elite in Veerasambanur is 2.24 times higher than the village average, while in Vinayagapuram and Nesal it is 4.37 times and 6.05 times the respective averages.

32. This is a strongly atypical cluster for the fact that its discriminating variable (dependency ratio) shows values (infinite) highly different from those of any other cluster.

33. To be precise, the results show that household members are employed as occasional workers. In Nesal, one household is engaged in a relatively small amount of own non-agricultural activity; while three households hire labour out either in agricultural or in non-agricultural activities. One household in Vinayagapuram works in own agriculture and four households occasionally hire out agricultural labour. In

Veerasambanur, only one of the eight dependent households occasionally hires out agricultural labour.

34. However, if we look carefully at the results presented in Table 2 it seems that a class of households hiring in labour for non-farm activities also exists in Nesal (Elite 1) and Veerasambanur (Elite 2). Not only is this group in the elite of these villages and thus much richer in terms of land, assets and income, but it also deploys a great amount of both own and hired-in labour in agriculture.
35. Fuller 1996; Janakarajan 1996; Bliss *et al.* 1998.
36. K Bardhan 1993.
37. Basile and Harriss-White 1999b.
38. Since strongly atypical clusters are likely to remain distinct until the latest stages of the fusion process, and given that neither a 6- nor a 10- nor a 15-clusters solution gave evidence of any quantitatively significant household group that is highly village-specific (apart from the households hiring in non-agricultural labour in Vinayaga-puram), it follows that no big cluster will be village-specific. This consolidates the impression that intervillage variation is better captured in terms of differences between similar groups than not: by looking for some other peculiar characterization of local society. It cannot be denied, however, that household groups with extraordinary village-specific attributes might appear from a more careful and in-depth analysis, although almost certainly they will be of a relatively small size.

    Elsewhere in this book (Chapter 3-5), the castes have been grouped and ranked.
39. Olsen 1996.
40. Miller 1981; P Bardhan 1974; B Harriss 1993.
41. Agnihotri 2000.
42. Chunkath and Athreya 1997.
43. Saradamoni 1994.
44. These also 'conform to the most common perception of female-heading' (Louat, Grosh and van der Gaag 1993).
45. Rosenhouse 1990.
46. See the review in Harriss-White 1999a.
47. On the threat to authority caused by incapacity of the elderly, see Chapter 3–4 here.
48. See the chapters on intervillage variation (1–3), on labour (1–5), on credit (2–5), on fertilizer (2–6), food and nutrition (3–5), education (3–6) and social assistance (3–7).
49. Cahill 2001.

Endnotes (1–5)

1. Beteille 1974; K Bardhan 1973, 1977a, b, c and 1984; Bhalla 1976; Binswanger and Rosenzweig 1984; Harriss-White and Gooptu 2000; Kapadia 1993; Rogaly 1994; and Rudra and Bardhan 1983.
2. Rudra 1982; Rogaly 1994.
3. Mendelssohn 1993; Panini 1996.
4. Basile and Harriss-White 1999b, Harriss-White, 2003.

5. Ramamurthy 1993.

6. See the review in Jackson and Palmer-Jones 1998.

7. J Harriss 1982; Ryan and Ghodake 1984; Mencher 1985; Ramachandran 1990; Ramamurthy 1993.

8. Jackson and Palmer-Jones 1998.

9. Kapadia 1993.

10. Kapadia 1993; Ramamurthy 1993.

11. Ryan and Wallace 1986; Rosenzweig 1978; Ryan and Ghodake 1984.

12. Mencher 1985.

13. G Sen 1982; Ryan and Ghodake 1984; see also Chapter 2-4 here.

14. Gibbs 1986; Gillespie 1989; Samuels 1989.

15. Samuels 1989.

16. J Harriss 1991a; B Harriss 1993.

17. Mencher 1985.

18. Ramachandran 1990; Ramamurthy 1993.

19. B Harriss 1981c; J Harriss 1982; Mencher and Saradamoni 1982.

20. J Harriss 1992.

21. Ghodake and Ryan 1981. See Chapter 1-1, Appendix 1, and Chapter 1-4 for details of sample selection and classification into clusters or 'classes'.

22. The Chi-Squared test showed intervillage variation in the organization of production is highly significant, with $P<0.005$.

23. These differences are statistically significant: Nesal ($P=0.007$); Vinayagapuram ($P=0.02$); Veerasambanur ($P<0.005$).

24. Hazell and Ramasamy 1991.

25. For example, see Mencher 1985.

26. Table 16 in Chapter 1-3 shows that in the other 8 villages, while the male kind wage has increased by 163 per cent over the 20-year period, the female kind wage increased by only 44 per cent.

27. The intervillage and intercluster variations have low statistical significance. In Chi-Squared tests, for intervillage variation for poor peasants, $P=0.07$, for females $P=0.298$.

28. J Harriss 1991b. The method of data collection and entry in 1983 resulted in inaccurate readings for the proportion of both non-farm wage and agricultural labour days and earnings.

29. Asadullah 2000.

30. Reported 'in the last month'.

31. B Harriss 1991a.

32. Gillespie 1989.

33. In two of the other eight villages where casual agricultural wage work has been more feminized than in these three cases, real wage rates for women have declined.

34. See also Rudra 1982.

35. Razavi 1998.

Endnotes (1–6)

1. Employment means an occupation or an activity pursued by individuals and not necessarily wage employment.
2. Saith 2001.
3. See, for example, Krishnamurthy 1972 and 1973, Basant and Kumar 1989 and Visaria 1994. I do not go into this literature in detail since the issue of the magnitude or extent of diversification is not the primary focus of my research.
4. These studies include Rangarajan 1982, Hazell and Roell 1983, Ahmed and Herdt 1984, Rao 1985, Vaidyanathan 1986, Bhatty and Vashistha 1987, B Harriss 1987a, 1987b, Mahendradev 1989, Unni 1991, Jayaraj 1992 and 1994, Chandrasekhar 1993 and Shukla 1994.
5. See Bell, Hazell and Slade 1982.
6. Chandrasekhar 1993.
7. See Mellor 1976, Chuta and Liedholm 1979, Ellis 2001 and Vaidyanathan 1986, and the critique in B Harriss 1987c.
8. Vaidyanathan 1986.
9. Ellis 2001.
10. This section draws very heavily on Jayaraj 1994.
11. See Sanghera and Harriss-White 1995.
12. It appears that the empirical studies that emphasize agricultural growth-induced linkages as the engine for growth of employment in the rural non-farm sector implicitly assume: a) the existence of surplus labour in the rural area (Rao 1985); and b) underemployment/disguised unemployment to be a feature of the agricultural sector alone (Mellor 1976). See also Rangarajan 1982, Hazell and Roell 1983, Ahmed and Herdt 1984, Rao 1985, Vaidyanathan 1986, Bhatty and Vashistha 1987, B Harriss 1987a, Mahendradev 1989, Shukla 1994, Jayaraj 1992 and Chandrasekhar 1993.
13. Kuznets 1966.
14. McGee 1971. The term surplus labour is used to connote labour released from the agricultural sector which seeks employment in the non-farm sector and does not imply the existence of labour in the farm sector whose marginal productivity is necessarily zero.
15. Thorner and Thorner 1962, Chattopadhyay 1985.
16. Kuznets 1966.
17. Growth of irrigation, particularly well irrigation, is an example of a technical change that is productivity-raising and labour-absorbing (see also Walker and Ryan 1990).
18. Mellor 1976, Chuta and Liedholm 1979, Vaidyanathan 1986.
19. B Harriss 1987a.
20. Srinivas 1962.
21. Jayaraj 1992.
22. B Harriss 1987a and UNRISD, 1994.
23. See Vaidyanathan 1986, B Harriss 1987a and Setty 1991.
24. For workers who report their primary occupation to be household chores or pensioner, her/his secondary occupation is considered to be the primary occupation.

25. The index of excess land is constructed as follows:

    i) for land: as the difference between the proportionate contribution of each caste to the number of households having access to land and its proportionate contribution to the total number of households expressed as a percentage of the latter;

    ii) for non-agricultural employment among households with access to land: as the difference between the proportionate contribution of each caste to number of households with access to both land and non-agricultural employment and its proportionate contribution to the total number of households with access to land expressed as a percentage of the latter;

    iii) for non-agricultural employment among landless households with at least one agricultural labour: as the difference between the proportionate contribution of each caste to number landless households with access to employment in both agricultural and non-agricultural sectors and its proportionate contribution to the total number of landless households with at least one member working as agricultural labour expressed as a percentage of the latter; and

    iv) for households with no connection to agriculture: as the difference between the proportionate contribution of each caste to number of households with access to only employment in the non-agricultural sector, and its proportionate contribution to total number of households expressed as a percentage of the latter.

26. See Janakarajan 1986, 1993a.
27. Nagaraj, Janakarajan, Jayaraj and Harriss-White 1996b.

Endnotes (2–1)

1. Cowen and Shenton 1996; Kitching 1982; Leftwich 2000; Leys 1996; Rapley 1996.
2. Pedersen 2000.
3. Ferguson 1990, pp. xiv–xv.
4. Policy analysis leads to 'decisions which are impartial, taken in a technical sound fashion' (Timmer, Falcon and Pearson 1983).
5. Schaffer 1984.
6. Apthorpe 1997.
7. *Mutatis mutandis*, this framework could be applied to policy-making in other institutions which govern development, for instance (qua)NGOs and multi-national corporations (MNCs), though to my knowledge it has not to date.
8. Ferguson parallels Schaffer's earlier insights in his compelling analysis of aid and development policy in Botswana as being an *Anti-Politics Machine*.
9. See Ram 1995 on the media and 'hunger' in which he shows that extreme events are publicized, but routine chronic malnutrition is screened out.
10. See B Harriss 1981a for cases of intraparty contradiction in Tamil Nadu on the subject of the regulation of markets.
11. Wood (ed.) 1985.
12. Codification is frequently not specified sufficiently to enable a breach of policy to be

identified, which is the case with many conventions on economic and social rights (see Alston 1994).

13. Von Benda Beckmann and van der Velde 1992; von Benda Beckmann 1994; Ghai *et al.* 1987.

14. Trubeck and Galanter 1974.

15. Shore and Wright 1997, pp. 6–7.

16. Mooij 1999a.

17. After Hirschman 1970.

18. Chambers 1997; and see Mosse 1993 for a critique.

19. The phrase is Sudipta Kaviraj's (1988). Subir Sinha illustrates this point by showing how scientific research and institutions, the mini-narratives and unsustainable resources of aid donors contrive with local power relations to construe 'watershed development' *not* as collective activity around soil and moisture conservation but as a form of village-level development including seasonal employment, diversification, productive activities 'labelled' for children and women (Seminar: 'Watershed Development and Rural Transformation in India', Queen Elizabeth House, Oxford, 2001).

20. Wood 1984. Among these possibilities are those of the social regulation of markets in the mass interest, of the collective provision of 'equity' and of the operationalization of rights, all of which were given a mandate in India's Constitution.

21. See Mooij 1999b for a reflection on field methods.

22. Mooij 1999a; B Harriss 1991a.

23. There are, for instance, four separate regulative frameworks governing domestic financial institutions (industrial development banks) and two regulating corporate governance.

24. For a fourth, well resourced and written in the language of management studies in which 'participation' has been further transformed into a mode of access of corporate capital to 'small farmers', see www.natp.org.

25. Randhawa 1994, pp. 353–78.

26. Pedersen 2000.

27. Interviews in *Frontline*, 18/3 (Feb 3–16 2001), pp. 112–20. The M S Swaminathan Institute has also generated a powerful agenda involving decentralized food security.

28. See also CPM Rajya Sabha member Biplab Dasgupta's accounts of structural adjustment and the environment, 1998, chapters 3 and 5.

29. Government of Tamil Nadu (GoTN), 1994 to 1997, *Policy Notes on Agriculture, 1994–5 to 1997–8.*

30. Taking Ellis 1992 as a good example of the latter's scope.

31. Table 3 also shows that all state subsidies on electricity and the social sector increased from 1991 to 1996.

32. For instance, selective subsidies are given for well boring and digging, while participative water management groups are organized and surface water resources are said to be exhausted (GoTN 1996, p. 64; 1997, p. 78).

33. GoTN 1996, pp. 16, 46; GoTN 1997, p. 96.

34. GoTN 1997, pp. 68–78, 96.
35. It was not possible to study how the Department of Agriculture's agenda is implemented in villages because our funded project had not anticipated such a radical policy disjuncture, being led by the national-level policy literature in economics and by the themes acceptable to DFID, one of which was structural adjustment.
36. Srivastava 1998, pp. 224–5.
37. Tamil Nadu's noon meal scheme was justified not only as a nutrition intervention but also as an education, employment and social welfare intervention (B Harriss 1991a).
38. www.tn.gov.in/economy/eco-may.htm, 2001.
39. Randhawa 1994; Patnaik 2001.
40. Bardhan 1998.
41. Pedersen 2000.
42. Jenkins 1999.
43. Bardhan 1998, p. 128; see also Corbridge and Harriss 2000, p. 284.
44. Hazell and Ramasamy 1991; Harriss-White and Saigal 1996b.
45. Mishra and Chand 1995; Rao and Gulati 1994; Johl 1995a.

Endnotes (2–2)

1. For Nairobi, see Werna 1993; for Los Angeles, Davis 1990.
2. Werna 1993.
3. Muraleedharan 1993, p. 1,296.
4. See Kennedy 1999 and Kjellborg and Banik 2000 for evidence of the polluting impact on drinking water of untreated effluents from leather tanneries, silk and cotton textiles dyeing units in the Palar Basin.
5. Appasamy 1993, pp. 203–8.
6. World Bank 1994.
7. Govt of India 1992a, p. 16. Our study on drinking water, refuse, sanitation and security at the microlevel thus examines infrastructure in a way complementary to the major IFPRI study carried out in North Arcot District in 1990–1, where the emphasis was on spatial access to hard physical infrastructure, and soft infrastructure in the form of education, health, housing, banking, transport and trading 'services': in all, public and private, 140 goods and services (Wanmali and Ramasamy [eds.] 1994).
8. Mohan 1992. See also Shaw 1996 for analysis of attempts since Independence to effect this.
9. Wanmali and Ramasamy 1994, pp. 14–20.
10. Wanmali and Islam 1994, p. 170.
11. Kothari and Kothari 1993, p. 465.
12. See Banerji 1993 for evidence pertaining to health.
13. Mehta and Mehta 1991, p. 1,108.
14. Op. cit., p. 1113.
15. Including Kothari and Kothari 1993, Appasamy 1993 and Wanmali and Ramasamy 1994.

16. Kothari and Kothari 1993, p. 476.
17. An American expression for a 'Not In My Back Yard' form of politics.
18. E.g. in Nairobi, while it is important for sewerage and water, it is less so for health and garbage (see Werna 1993).
19. A public good is non-withholdable and its consumption does not reduce the stock available. Many goods provided by the state are not pure public goods but are either provided in this way as the result of a social consensus or because their quality or availability would be compromised under private provision (see Batley 1992).
20. The case material is from Nairobi (Werna 1993).
21. Baru 1993, pp. 966–7.
22. Werna 1993.
23. Bagchi 1992, p. 1,779.
24. The section is written using evidence from the random sample survey of households in the three villages, together with detailed notes on village infrastructure compiled by the field research staff.
25. Wanmali and Ramasamy 1994, p. 53.
26. Ibid., p. 47.
27. An average of three days is reported for breakdowns to be repaired.
28. In Kalpattu village, another in the original sample, our census enumerator noted that 10 per cent of households have private latrines but that these private facilities tend to follow the pattern of public ones. Only one third of households with latrines use them.
29. As are women at night.
30. Residents, especially parents of female children, are acutely aware of the location of the government college that was awarded to the successful politician representing Cheyyar, a much smaller settlement at some distance from Arni (and which also boasts – for the same reason – a court and a modern rice mill).
31. Wanmali and Islam 1994, pp. 144–54.
32. Govt of Tamil Nadu 1982, p. 16.
33. Ibid., p. 12.
34. Wanmali and Ramasamy 1994, table 3.3, p. 47.
35. Arni had a population of 9,300 in 1901.
36. Not every member of this labour force can gain access to supplementary income, however.
37. Arni Municipal Abstract, 1993–4.
38. Beal 1997, Harriss-Whit, 2003, chapter 8.
39. Wanmali and Ramasamy 1994, pp. 191, 208.
40. Government of India, 1992a, *Eighth Five Year Plan*, chapter 14, p. 380.
41. This is happening on a grand scale in the UK in the (privatized) utilities and in health (publicly provided but with an internal market) and education (in the public sector, increasingly differentiated by quality from that of the private sector).
42. E.g., *inter alia*, see Rao and Gulati 1994, Wanmali and Ramasamy 1994.
43. See Basile and Harriss-White 1999b.

44. Govt of India 1992a, pp. 390–86.
45. Kumar and Mukherjee 1993, p. 774.

Endnotes (2–3)

1. Pursell and Gulati 1993.
2. Government of India's *Report of the Committee on Pricing of Irrigation Water*, 1992b, pp. ii–iii.
3. Government of India 1999a.
4. Government of Tamil Nadu 1997a.
5. Taking the lowest ranks are states such as Bihar (82 units), West Bengal (87 units) and Assam (90 units).
6. CMIE 1997a.
7. Ishiguru and Akiyama 1995.
8. TERI 1999, p. 78.
9. Gross power is total power generated and purchases made from other states.
10. One paise is one hundredth of a rupee.
11. TERI 1999.
12. Reddy and Sumithra 1997.
13. TERI 1999, p. 152.
14. Government of Tamil Nadu 1995–6.
15. See also Janakarajan 1996c, 1997.
16. Lindberg 1996.
17. See also Janakarajan 1997a, b.
18. See note d) to Table 5 for details of the imputing of electricity consumption. See Chapter 1–3 for discussion of gross irrigated acreage.
19. Janakarajan and Vaidyanathan 1997.
20. See Bandara 1977; Dhawan 1991; Rao 1993; Moench 1992; Bhatia 1992; Dinesh and Patel 1993; Janakarajan 1993a, 1997a, 1997b; Janakarajan and Vaidyanathan 1997; Vaidyanathan 1996.
21. Janakarajan 1997a, 1997b.
22. Janakarajan and Vaidyanathan 1997.
23. Janakarajan and Vaidyanathan 1997.
24. Janakarajan, forthcoming.
25. Ibid.
26. Ibid.
27. Janakarajan and Vaidyanathan 1997.
28. Janakarajan and Vaidyanathan 1997; Janakarajan, forthcoming.
29. Government of India 1999b, p. 131.
30. Gurumurthy 1997.
31. CMIE 1997, p. 53.
32. TERI 1999.
33. *The Hindu*, 9 September 1999.

34. More or less on similar lines, the SEBs of Andhra Pradesh, Orissa and Karnataka have been restructured.
35. Moench 1995b; Malik 1995; Shah 1993; Janakarajan, forthcoming.
36. Shah 1993, p. 93.
37. Narayanamurthy 1997.

Endnotes (2–4)

1. The informal sector is a catch-all category comprising village or 'local' moneylenders, pawnbrokers, friends and relatives, landlords and traders, typified by personalized contacts and by the lack of bureaucratic procedures and written agreements other than written bonds or 'promissory notes', which are unstandardized but stamped documents hovering between the formal and informal sector because they can be brought to court within three years of the latest date (Olsen and Rani 1997, p. 19). It is also termed 'non-institutional credit' (Janakarajan 1986). Formal credit (institutional credit) is based upon impersonal written documents accepted in a court of law and used by commercial banks, land development banks and cooperative societies.
2. Sarap 1991, Kohli 1999.
3. Copestake 1992.
4. Kohli 1999.
5. This information is from the RBI reports summarized in Olsen and Rani 1997. According to Hanumantha Rao, this expansion was led by the commercial banks, which increased their share of the formal rural credit market at the expense of the cooperative network (Rao 1994, p. 307). According to NSS data, by 1981 the share of moneylender credit was as low as 16 per cent, but the estimate is disputed (Bell 1990, quoted in Binswanger and Khandker 1995, p. 257). This argument about one form of private moneylending deflects attention from the quantitative importance of the informal sector as a whole.
6. Gadgil 1992.
7. Hoff and Stiglitz 1990.
8. Rao 1994, pp. 307–8; Olsen and Rani 1997; Drèze, Lanjouw and Sharma 1998a.
9. Kohli 1999.
10. Binswanger and Khandker 1995, pp. 253, 258.
11. Swaminathan 1991.
12. Sarap 1991. A large literature reviewed by Olsen and Rani (1997) concludes consistently that small farmers have been excluded from formal credit. With rare exceptions in cases where state credit reduced the inequality of control over resources – as in West Bengal (Bhattacharyya, 2003) – state-directed credit was doing the opposite of what was stated to be intended.
13. Rao 1994, p. 307.
14. Binswanger and Khandker 1995, p. 257.
15. Rao 1994, p. 310.
16. Ibid.
17. Desai 1996; Rao 1994, p. 337.

18. Rao 1994, p. 308.
19. Kohli 1999.
20. Johnson 1999.
21. J Harriss 1982.
22. B Harriss 1981c.
23. J Harriss 1991a.
24. Interest rates in the informal sector were a 'modest 24 per cent'. A minimum of 12 per cent was 'not at all unusual', while the maximum, 60 per cent, was exacted from small loans using vessels or jewellery as collateral and pledged for short periods to village moneylenders (J Harriss 1991a, p. 77).
25. Also manifested in electricity, the public distribution system and Fair Price Shop network, the noon meal scheme and the IRDP (J Harriss 1991a, p. 78).
26. We are not examining moneylending within these villages.
27. Indian Bank 1992, p. 1.9.
28. Kohli 1999.
29. Indian Bank, op. cit., p. 2.6.
30. It also operates a food-for-work scheme giving labourers food in return for well deepening and desilting of channels.
31. *Kanthu vaddi* is also known in Vinayagapuram.
32. Bhaduri 1983.
33. The Pearson tests of independence for a two-way contingency table, in this case equivalent to the test of homogeneity of rows, could not be rejected.
34. i) Of course not all members of households with a literate head are to be presumed literate; ii) this contrasts with Olsen and Rani's research (1997, p. 36) nearby, where they found that caste was not a good predictor of access.
35. Similar findings are reported by Sarap (1988, 1991) Rao (1994).
36. This contradicts J Harriss's conclusion (1991a) that the balance had shifted to the state but is consistent with estimates for the relative roles of a formal and informal credit in rural Andhra Pradesh by Olsen and Rani (1997, pp. 25–6).
37. Similar findings have been reported by Drèze *et al.* (1998a), Sarap (1988, 1991) and Rao (1994).
38. Drèze *et al.* (1998a) conclude similarly for Palanpur.
39. For cattle, carts and land improvement (well-digging).
40. See Jodha 1971; Binswanger and Rosenzweig 1986; Sarap 1990.
41. Higher informal-sector interest may have less to do with collateral than to spill-over from rationed supply in the formal sector (Acharya and Madhur 1983), or alternatively from the abundance of formal credit which shifts the high-cost/high-risk borrowers, concentrating them in an increasingly residualized informal sector (Drèze *et al.* 1998a).
42. Bhende 1986; Swaminathan 1991.
43. Janakarajan 1986; Sarap 1988.
44. Braverman and Guasch 1986.
45. All of the 32 loans from cooperatives, commercial and land development banks were

secured by collateral. There were three IRDP loans, one of which was given to a poor landless peasant without collateral in order for him to purchase a ploughing bullock (although the loan was actually used for consumption and to repay a previous debt).

[?? page-55 missing footnote number 46 to 48]

49. See Agrawal 1997.
50. From a weighted average for the three villages of 25 per cent in 1973 to 30 per cent in 1983 to 40 per cent in 1993–4 – using our field survey data plus data in Hazell and Ramasamy 1991, pp. 68, 111.
51. Kohli 1999.
52. Half all formal credit is taken by the 7 per cent of borrowers with more than 5 acres of land, while the landless and those with micro-holdings – 58 per cent of borrowers – gain access to less than 10 per cent.
53. J Harriss 1991a; Sarap 1990.
54. We do not know whether loans from friends and relatives form part of the tribute from wife givers to wife receivers (Drèze *et al.* 1998a). Certainly these loans flow inside the villages, which was not the case in Palanpur; but the South Indian kinship system (being jettisoned for North Indian elements by the dominant agrarian castes while low-caste people are increasingly 'Dravidianizing' themselves [Harriss-White 1999a]) features cross-cousin marriages, which are frequently *within* villages.
55. Though there are other explanations for interest-rate variation than risk, as we see below.
56. Otherwise the transactions costs of getting loans are much lower than those for social security benefit (see Chapter 3–7).

Endnotes (2–5)
1. Though the unstable demand from India and China still by and large determines the fluctuations in international prices.
2. Landy 1997, p. 15.
3. Vaidyanathan 1993, pp. 242–3.
4. CMIE 1992.
5. NCAER 1978; Srinivasan 1993; Vaidyanathan 1993.
6. The literature exploring demand for fertilizer resembles that on the determinants of the marketed surplus in being individualized, most studies using non-comparable subsets of variables theorized as affecting use. For irrigation, see Mohanan 1990. For credit, see NCAER 1978, Desai 1986 and Raju 1990. For physical infrastructure, see Parthasarathy and Chinna 1986; Ramasamy *et al.* 1986.
7. Vaidyanathan 1993, p. 249.
8. CMIE 1992.
9. Govt of Tamil Nadu 1994.
10. Rao and Gulati 1994, pp. 10, 21.
11. CMIE 1992. Even so, Indian rice production was one of the most highly taxed in Asia.

12. Kumar 1999.

13. Vaidyanathan 1993, pp. 238–9; see also B Harriss 1981c and Landy 1997.

14. Johl 1994, p. 186; Landy 1997, pp. 26–8.

15. Kumar 1999.

16. See Landy 1997.

17. Rao and Gulati 1994, p. 24.

18. Vaidyanathan 1993, p. 240.

19. See Rao and Gulati 1994. And other factors such as credit availability and reductions in the transactions costs of access.

20. Bliss, Lanjouw and Stern 1998, p. 273.

21. See also Gulati and Bhide 1995.

22. Govt of Tamil Nadu 1994, p. 19; Landy 1997, p. 27.

23. Contrasting with the figure for Tirunelveli – 33.5 kg/ha. While Madurai and Thanjavur are rice bowls, fertilizer use in the Nilgiris supported intensive horticulture and plantation agriculture.

24. Data given in Srinivasan 1993.

25. Srinivasan 1993.

26. Tandon 1994.

27. Govt of Tamil Nadu 1994, p. 19.

28. Sagar 1995.

29. Vaidyanathan 1993, p. 241.

30. J Harriss 1982, p. 84.

31. Hazell and Ramasamy 1991; Harriss-White and Saigal 1996a; Landy 1997; Vaidyanathan 1993.

32. Srinivasan 1993.

33. 1,000 tonnes of biofertilizer (Azospirillum, rhizobium and blue green algae) are manufactured in four locations in Tamil Nadu and distributed at block level but on an extremely small scale at present. (Government of Tamil Nadu, 1994, p. 3; and personal communications with Dt Agricultural Officer, Tiruvannamalai, and Block Development Officer, Arani, 1994, 1995.)

Endnotes (3–2)

1. Ruggeri Laderchi 1997.

2. Sen 1999; Saith 2001a.

3. Chambers 1992, 1997.

4. Guhan and Harriss 1992.

5. Two methods commonly used in developing countries to compute poverty lines are: (a) the food energy intake method; and (b) the cost of basic needs method (Wodon 1997a). In the former, the level of consumption or income at which households would be expected to satisfy the normative nutritional requirement is calculated. Poverty lines are set taking this computation into account (Dandekar and Rath 1971; Greer and Thorbecke 1986; Paul 1989). Under the cost of basic needs method, in addition to the cost of a food basket that enables the household to meet the normative

nutritional requirement, an allowance for non-food consumption is taken into consideration. Poverty lines are set taking into account this combined computed cost (Ravallion and Bidani 1994; Ravallion and Sen 1996). Although consumption expenditure is largely accepted as being a better monetary indicator of poverty than private income, we do not have access to this information in the census data used for analysis in this chapter. The analysis has therefore been carried out using information related to private income.

6. In the poverty literature, consumption is the standard measure, being the most reliable estimator. The village census used here canvassed private income rather than consumption. Additionally, the Government of India still uses an income-based poverty line and income-based targeting.

7. Hyat 2001.

8. Cornia and Stewart 1995.

9. See Gaiha 1988; Glewwe and Kanaan 1989; Ruggeri Laderchi 1997; Wodon 1997b; see also the studies referred to in Baulch and McCulloch 1998.

10. Poverty is now generally accepted as a multidimensional concept involving aspects as varied as income or consumption (recently reviewed by Ruggeri Laderchi [2000]), 'social exclusion' (recently reviewed in Saith 2001b), powerlessness, deprivation of 'functionings' (Sen 1985; also recently reviewed in Saith 2001a), vulnerability and livelihood unsustainability (Maxwell 1999) and people's own perceptions (Chambers 1997; also in a recent review in Ruggeri Laderchi 2001).

11. Michie 1984.

12. Michie 1988.

13. Clark and Niblett 1989.

14. Saith *et al.* 1998.

15. Note that the word 'class' throughout this chapter is used in the statistical sense of the word, rather than to mean 'class' as used in social sciences.

16. Saith 1996.

17. Farmer *et al.* 1977.

18. Hazell and Ramasamy 1991.

19. See Harriss-White and Harriss 2003.

20. Data were available for 2,067 households. Seven households for which the income variable was not available were however excluded. In addition, three households that showed an income of zero despite the possession of own land, raising the possibility that the income may have been entered as zero by mistake, were also excluded.

21. Details can be found in Quinlan 1998.

22. For the different methods that may be used to obtain poverty lines and the advantages, disadvantages and problems associated with these or the different poverty indices used to aggregate information, see Lipton and Ravallion 1995. In the Indian context, the poverty line is either that decided on by the central Indian Government's Planning Commission or one announced by state governments. In this study, the poverty line along the lines recommended by the central government of India was used. The poverty line for rural Tamil Nadu for 1973–4 in terms of monthly per

caput consumption expenditure is Rs 45.09 per caput (Government of India 1993). This had to be updated to 1992–3 prices as household income data collected in the census pertained to 1992–3. Subramanian (Personal Communication 2001) updates this as follows. The Consumer Price Index of Agricultural Labourers (CPIAL – available in issues of the *Indian Labour Journal*) for Tamil Nadu for 1992–3 with 1973–4 as base was calculated to be 424.38. (The 1992–3 CPAL for Tamil Nadu with 1960–61 as base is 1027, while for 1973–4 it is 242. Implicitly therefore, the CPIAL Index for 1992–3 with 1973–4 as base is 1027/242 = 4.2438.) Tamil Nadu's rural poverty line at 1992–3 prices was then estimated to be Rs 195.31 per month (= 45.09 * 4.2438). This is 30 per cent higher than the restrictive 'subsistence income estimate' used by Harriss-White in Chapter 3–7 here.

23. The split was done by using a computer program written by Dr Ashwin Srinivasan, such that the proportion of 'Income-Poor' and 'Income Non-poor' households within the training and test sets were similar to that in the full data set of 2,057 households, i.e. approximately 'Income-Poor': 'Income Non-poor' = 50:50.

24. Quinlan 1998.

25. We have used the default settings which are expected to give a reasonably low error rate. Obtaining the lowest possible error rate would however require experimentation with a systematic variation of the parameter settings. Some researchers have investigated methods to do this (see, e.g., Kohavi and John 1995).

26. An estimate of the predictive error can be obtained by using the rules to classify new data, i.e. the test set. For this estimate to be reliable, however, a large number of cases are essential in the 'training' and 'test' sets. Since our data set is not very large, an alternative procedure to obtain an unbiased estimate of predictive accuracy is the procedure of cross-validation (see Weiss and Kulikowski 1991). In this procedure, the training set (N) is divided so that a few cases (k) are 'left out'. This subset serves the role of new data. The rules obtained by training on the remaining cases (N-k) are tested for their classification ability on this subset, also referred to a test set. This procedure is repeated by 'leaving out' a different group of k cases each time most of the cases are used for training. The estimate of predictive error of the rule set obtained by training on all the cases is then the average of the predictive error for each subset sample calculated from a 2 × 2 table similar to that shown in Table 2 here. Consider, for example, a training set with N cases (usually two thirds of data available). The test set (remaining one third of the data) will have less than N cases. In cross-validation, a number of subsets play the role of the 'test' set. Each of these subtests is smaller than a single test set. As different parts of the training data are sequentially used as 'test' set, however, the effect is that of using a test set of size N.

27. If adequate data are available, a further (in addition to the cross-validation) and independent, unbiased estimate of predictive error may be obtained when the rule is used to classify a separate test set of new cases drawn from the same data source. This is not essential and just helps to confirm the estimate obtained by cross-validation results, which were subsets of the training data itself.

28. The full rule set comprises 26 rules. Of these, 10 rules characterize 'Income-Poor'

households and 16 rules 'Income Non-poor' households. Only one rule in each group has been presented in the results section as an illustration. The factors taken into consideration when selecting one representative rule for each class were a combination of the following.

A) **Cover:** This indicates the number of cases in the training set that are characterized by the pattern of features presented in the rule. The higher the number of cases covered, the higher the likelihood of finding cases with similar features in new data. Besides, the higher the number of cases covered by the rule, the more statistically reliable the probabilities of prediction (i.e. B below) associated with each rule are likely to be.

B) **Accuracy:** This is the probability of each case covered by the rule, belonging to a class the same as that indicated by the rule. The higher the value, the more accurately would the rule be expected to predict new data.

It would thus be reasonable to expect the value of A*B to be a good judge of the overall performance of the rule – the higher the value, the better. When the A*B for two rules is similar or very close, the ease of interpretation of the rules may be used as an additional factor in judging the rule performance. The 'Non-poor' rule presented above had the highest A*B value of the ten Non-poor rules. Among the 'Income-Poor' rules, two rules with the highest A*B values had very close values. The rule with the slightly higher value was more complex (with 12 conditions) than the rule presented here (which was simpler with just 4 conditions).

29. The class label ('Poor' or 'Non-poor') attached to the rule is that of the class that has the higher probability. Note that each rule bases 'class prediction' on a majority-vote principle. That is to say, where less than 50 per cent 'Poor' is predicted, the class prediction is 'Non-poor', otherwise 'Poor'. The 50 per cent prediction criterion is convenient, particularly given the structure of the rule-building See5 package, but it is to a degree arbitrary.

30. Calomiris and Rajaraman (1998, p. 208) define a ROSCA as follows:

> . . . a voluntary grouping of individuals who agree to contribute financially at each set of uniformly-spaced dates towards the creation of a fund, which will then be allotted in accordance with some prearranged principle to each member of the group in turn. Allotment is either through lottery (random ROSCAs) or auction (bidding ROSCAs).

The chit fund referred to here is a bidding ROSCA. The total amount of money to be put in, the amount in each instalment, the number of instalments and interval of payment are all predecided. At each payment round, people who need money put in a bid for it. The bids are slightly lower than the total amount. The person with the lowest bid gets the money but continues to pay all the instalments.

31. For a discussion, see Calomiris and Rajaraman 1998 and Ardener 1995.

32. The dependent age group in the cluster analysis was considered to be less than 15 or more than 60 years of age. This definition of dependence is a product of the age categories used for the data. The result confirms the general conclusion of Lipton and

Ravallion (1995). Other studies, however, find reduced dependency among the poor rather than the non-poor: see Ramu 1988; the review in B Harriss 1992; and Rodgers's conclusion that the relations between demographic or economic dependence and poverty in rural South Asia are 'weak' (1989, p. 15).

33. See Jayaraj 1992 and Chapter 1-6 here.

34. Harriss-White and Janakarajan 1997. The support provided by the findings of the cluster analysis showing the relationship between the average amount of land operated by households in the 'peasant' and the 'elite' groups has been mentioned earlier.

35. The procedure used to obtain the rule set is the same as that used for the analysis including the 478 variables. The criteria for selection of these two 'best' rules for illustration are also similar to those described earlier: i.e. rules with the highest Accuracy X Cover value.

36. E.g. Drèze and Sharma 1998, in Palanpur; and elsewhere as reviewed in Agnihotri 2000.

37. In the cluster analysis, Colatei and Harriss-White (see Chapter 1-4 here) take the gender of the respondent to indicate the gender of the head of the household. In the analysis conducted by us, the head was considered female in the following circumstances: (a) households with only female members; (b) households with male and female members, but with only females in the working age group (15–64). The head of the household was assumed to be male in all other households.

38. See Drèze, Lanjouw and Sharma 1998b, for evidence of downward economic mobility among widows living without an adult male.

39. Subramanian and Harriss-White 1999.

40. See Bliven *et al.* 1997; Guhan and Mencher 1983.

41. Quinlan 1993.

Endnotes (3–3)

1. Pai Panandiker 1998.

2. Das Gupta and Mari Bhat 1997.

3. Athreya and Chunkath 1996; Chunkath and Athreya 1997; George *et al.* 1992.

4. For example: Becker and Tomes 1976; Behrman *et al.* 1982; Browning and Subramanian 1994.

5. See, for example, Clark 1983, Dyson and Moore 1983, Caldwell and Caldwell 1987, and Heyer 1992.

6. Kishor 1993.

7. Modernization here refers quite specifically to a release from the deterministic association of caste with a certain occupation.

8. Sargent *et al.* 1996; Harriss-White 1999a; Nillesen 1999.

9. Factors affecting the capacity of women to control, decide and act for themselves do not relate without contradiction. Muslim women, for instance, may be less educated than Hindu women, but village studies show that they have less dowry. They migrate shorter distances, yet they have less contact with their natal home than do Hindu women (see discussion in B Harriss 1993, pp. 25–7).

10. Caldwell and Caldwell 1987.
11. See B Harriss 1991b.
12. Kapadia 1997 (reported in Sundari Ravindran 1999). However, she notes that women's status is steadily falling, especially in the castes that have bettered themselves economically.
13. B Harriss 1991b.
14. Becker and Tomes 1976; McElroy and Horney 1981. Many more models of intra-household distribution can be found in the literature, such as for example the Behrman *et al.* (1982) Separable Earnings-Transfers model. However, they can all be sorted into one of the above categories.
15. Kynch and Sen 1983: 'In dealing with within-family distribution, the perception of reality – including illusions about it – must be seen as an important part of reality'.
16. Nillesen (1999), using the Lucas supply function framework, found that, if the mortality rate of children depends on the wage rate and the information about the wage rate, the mortality rate is inversely related to the variance of the error in the wage determination equation.
17. Foster and Rosenzweig 1999.
18. This can be modelled explicitly using the Behrman *et al.* (1982) Separable Earnings-Transfers Model.
19. Folbre 1986.
20. The breakdown position is also known as the threat point.
21. See McElroy 1990.
22. Known as extra-household parameters, such as divorce laws or lone parent benefit.
23. Sen 1990b.
24. Dyson and Moore 1983.
25. Agarwal (1998) quotes a study by Marty Chen of rural widows in seven states, where only 13 per cent of the daughters of land-owning fathers inherited any land and even fewer effectively controlled any.
26. However, the preference depends on the liquidity of the assets. If land is at stake, dividing it between many sons is likely to be undesirable, whereas if jewellery is at stake it can easily be divided between daughters.
27. In poorer households, kinship may be structured so as to prevent the dissipation of resources. In South India a model of kinship involves cross-cousins, to keep resources tightly controlled.
28. See Heyer 1992.
29. Heyer 1992; Agnihotri 2000.
30. See, for instance, Bloch, Rao and Desai 1998.
31. This dowry payment need not be a one-off payment and may involve the daughter's family being required to supply a flow of gifts.
32. Drèze and Sharma 1998.
33. Browning and Subramanian 1994.
34. Source: Sample Registration System Statistical Report, 1996 (excludes Jammu and Kashmir).

35. See Das Gupta and Mari Bhat 1997.

36. Murthi *et al.* 1995.

37. Agnihotri 1997, 2000.

38. See Browning and Subramanian 1994.

39. Heyer 1992.

40. George *et al.* 1992.

41. See Janakarajan 1986.

42. Sargent *et al.* 1996; Harriss-White 1999a.

43. Vegamangalam, Sirungathur, Duli, Vengodu, Vayalur, Meppathurai, Amudhur and Kalpattu.

44. Harriss-White 2001.

45. Sundari and Thombre 1996.

46. See B Harriss 1991b.

47. Source: US Bureau of the Census.

48. Das Gupta 1987.

49. *Nanjai* and *punjai* are old classifications used for land revenue purposes by the British. *Nanjai* was referred to as wet land, i.e. land irrigated by tank, and *punjai* was dry land. With the passage of time and the increase in well-based irrigation this classification has lost its meaning as a result of both the productivity and the value of the lands converging.

50. This includes the value of wells, electric pump sets, oil engines, tractors, power tillers, sprays, traditional bullock carts, agricultural implements, plough bullocks, milch animals, sheep, goats and others.

51. This includes the value of homestead land inside and outside the village, buildings inside and outside the village, business assets inside and outside the village, jewellery and cash balance.

52. Rosenzweig and Schultz 1982; Kishor 1993.

53. See Murthi *et al.* 1995.

54. I.e., those over 18 years.

55. Das Gupta 1987.

56. Murthi *et al.* 1995.

57. Total wealth is highly correlated with land value but presents a more general picture of the financial status of a household.

58. The model was tested for the presence of heteroskedasticity using the Cook-Weisberg X'' test; using fitted values of survival: $X''(1)=16.81[0.0000]$). It was found that the null hypothesis of homoskedasticity was rejected at the 5 per cent level (using Best Linear Unbiased Estimators), therefore the model was run using robust standard errors.

59. Das Gupta 1987.

60. Murthi *et al.* 1995.

61. However, there is the possibility of a sample selection bias in our population as a result of endogeneity. There may be a correlation between the characteristics that influence the mortality rate and our explanatory variables. It is plausible that

the gender composition of a household itself influences the wealth accumulation and land-holding strategies in a family, as Browning and Subramanian (1994) argue.

62. Certainly in India one has to be cautious with birth figures, in view of the gender bias. Further, using cross-sectional data raises problems with heteroskedasticity. This was accounted for using heteroskedasticity consistent standard errors, but we might be interested in the actual pattern and location of the heteroskedasticity.

63. The child sex ratios of Punjab, Haryana, Delhi and Himachal Pradesh have dropped from 875, 879, 915 and 951 in 1991 to 793, 820, 865 and 897 respectively in 2001 (Census of India, 2001, pp. 92, 94; quoted in Premi 2001, p. 1876).

64. Harriss-White 1999a.

65. Basu 1999.

66. Athreya and Chunkath 1996, 1997.

Endnotes (3–4)

1. This is an abridged version of our book: see Erb and Harriss-White 2002.

2. E.g. Cornia, Jolly and Stewart 1985.

3. The concept of capability has been developed from a critique of income and of utility as indicators of well-being. In the ferment of refinement and criticism following Sen's formulation, disability has been used to exemplify types of limit to functioning and capability; or easily identified 'targets' who cannot cheat or manipulate their eligibility for welfare (Sen 1999, pp. 133, 326). The limits to functioning are significant. Disabled people in the USA and the West suffer higher unemployment, lower pay and higher rates of part-time employment than do able-bodied people. In the USA, while 82 per cent of non-disabled people of working age have a job, 29 per cent of disabled people have jobs and only 11 per cent of severely disabled people have jobs. Disabled people are three times more likely to be poor (29 per cent against 10 per cent) and are discriminated against at work or sacked from work more often (Russell 2001). Positive freedom is freedom to be and do; negative freedom is freedom from external control, hindrance or coercion.

4. Sen 1999, p. 20.

5. Ibid., p. 88.

6. See for example UNDP 1993; McGillivray, Pyatt and White 1995.

7. See Culshaw 1983, Desai 1990, Narsing Rao 1990, Sen 1992 and WHO 1980.

8. B Harriss *et al.* 1992.

9. 'The visually disabled' cannot count the fingers of a hand correctly from a distance of 3 metres in good daylight. 'The dumb' suffer voice defects. 'The deaf' were categorized as moderate, severe or profound. Locomotor disability is the lack or loss of the moral ability of an individual to move himself and objects. It was recognized to have several causes: paralysis, deformity, amputation and joint dysfunction. 'Hunchbacks' and 'dwarfs' were included among the locomotor disabled (NSS 1983).

10. Thomas 1993a.

11. Subbarao 1992.

12. Thomas 1992a; Helander 1993; Athreya 2001a.

13. Sen 1992, p. 255.

14. Jackson 1988; Desai 1990; ISS 1988, pp. 15–18.

15. Coleridge 1993, p. 154.

16. World Bank 1993.

17. ISS 1988, pp. 14, 16.

18. Barnes 1991; Hammerman and Maikowski 1981.

19. Narsing Rao 1990.

20. Mohan 1988.

21. Helander 1993.

22. ISS 1988, p. 20.

23. Ibid., pp. 14–17, 19.

24. Shukia 1990.

25. Krishnaswamy 1990.

26. Shukia 1990.

27. Bajpai 1991.

28. Ram and Harriss-White 1995.

29. In the case of Bandhu Mukji Morcha (Ram and Harriss-White 1995).

30. It is very difficult to find comprehensive data about government resources for disabled people and policy on disability. Data are out of date and decentralized. The constituent states also spend revenue on disability: see Erb and Harriss-White 2002.

31. Badrinath 1994.

32. See Lang 2000.

33. Culshaw 1983.

34. Sen 1992, p. 63.

35. Thomas 1992a.

36. Mallory 1993.

37. Either children are not disabled or they do not survive.

38. This is not to argue that vitamin A deficiency does not also play a part in causing such blindness.

39. Harriss-White 1999b.

40. Jackson and Palmer-Jones 1998.

41. Muraleedharan 1998.

42. 5.8 per cent of production is not a minor problem. Von Oppen's three-state spatial equilibrium simulation of gains to trade and liberalization in agriculture in India gave the result that complete free trade increased gross production by (only) 2–3 per cent (von Oppen 1978).

43. Lawrence Haddad, IFPRI, pers. comm, 2001. See Gillespie and Haddad 2001 for Pakistan and Vietnam. Estimates of GDP lost by protein-energy malnutrition, iodine and iron deficiencies vary from 2.4 to 4 per cent, effectively halving growth rates.

44. There is no age threshold for the receipt of a handicapped pension (Guhan 1996).

45. Elson 1992.

46. The medical model also focuses on the individual rather than the social and physical environment and on the body rather than the social being (Lang 2000).
47. For a critique of the latter, see ibid.

Endnotes (3–5)

1. Narayanan 1996a.
2. Despite the existence of 25 types of nutrition scheme already in the state, beset by patchy coverage, idiosyncrasy and food substitution rather than supplementation.
3. The Congress party leader, Kamaraj had piloted a midday meal as early as 1956 (*Frontline*, 6 October 1995).
4. Thereby releasing revenue resources via duties and taxes on alcohol.
5. But rapidly extended to age 2 and upwards, and to pensioners aged 65 and over, and to certain other non-age-specific categories such as destitute widows and disabled people.
6. The latter by means of different castes being encouraged to eat meals together, and by quotas for low-caste and female staff. See B Harriss 1991a.
7. Social Welfare Dept data, 1994.
8. B Harriss 1981b.
9. Narayanan 1996a.
10. See Olsen and Rani 1997, Mooij 2000, and Swaminathan 2000a and b for in-depth, critical analyses of the PDS. While, by 2001, its national subsidy had swollen to Rs 10,000 crores, it was not swingeing in comparative, international terms, nor was it absolutely so huge that its removal would put paid to the budgetary deficit.
11. Narayanan op. cit.
12. And, according to Mooij (2000), this is true to a lesser extent in the other two southern states, Karnataka and Kerala.
13. Johl 1995a, p. 478. But see also Rao and Gulati 1994, p. 3; Bhalla, ed., 1994, pp. 132–78; Pursell and Gulati 1995.
14. Swaminathan (2000b) finds that if food subsidies are calculated as a share of GDP they were practically unchanged over the decades of the 1980s and 1990s and have declined since the late 1970s.
15. Swaminathan 2000a.
16. Consumption includes that from own production and purchases, including those from the PDS; but it excludes the food intake of children from the NMS. Expenditure therefore is not confined to cash/expenditure but includes the imputed value of own production, estimated at average prices for the relevant social group and village.
17. Not all these classes were found in each village. Poor non-agricultural households were confined to Veerasambanur. Richer households were dominated by those in Nesal. Those in Vinayagapuram have a non-land assets base.
18. I.e. Hazell and Ramasamy 1991.
19. Low outliers being the landed poor in Veerasambanur and the richer households in Vinayakapuram (perhaps fallen on hard times between the household census in

September 1993 and the expenditure and consumption survey six months later?); high outliers comprising the richer households in Nesal village.

20. While 10 and 20 years previously this was obtained on a monthly basis, in 1993–4 it was collected for one month for each of the three seasons and multiplied up accordingly. It is just possible that the relatively low expenditure of poor landed households is a result of this method.

21. In Britain, with its industrial food culture, the proportion is even lower.

22. All intervillage averages in this chapter are weighted by relative subsample sizes.

23. Platt 1957.

24. See B Harriss 1979, 1991a, for reviews of evidence.

25. The statistic for landless labour excludes the results for Nesal, about which we have reservations that have not been resolvable (see Table 8). Total calorie consumption there is 2,891, 60 per cent of which is not from rice (see Table 9). Either this staggering increase is strongly influenced by dependence on the PDS which liberates income for fruit (see Table 10), and/or the data for this class are in error, and/or this is the result of a survey during exceptional times of feasting for agricultural labour (a fact confirmed retrospectively by field investigators).

26. In Veerasambanur and Nesal it appears that poor landed households consume less than landless labour households, while common convention and the evidence for 10 and 20 years before suggests otherwise; it is possible that consumption from own production was not correctly estimated in these villages. For detailed data on which a comparison of class-specific protein consumption can be based, see Ryan *et al.* 1984, pp. 97–120.

27. B Harriss 1991b.

28. B Harriss 1991a.

29. Payne 1994.

30. But we have not been able to examine seasonal nutritional stress.

31. B Harriss 1991a, pp. 43–7.

32. This statistic excludes Nesal. See note 25.

33. B Harriss 1991a.

34. Owing to insufficient degrees of freedom and incomparable characteristics in the richer strata across villages, richer households were dropped.

35. The reduced seasonality of prices has stabilized open-market prices over the two decades: see Chapter 1-1.

36. However, one ration shopkeeper gave evidence that 15 per cent of families in his ward were without cards.

37. Swaminathan (2000a), following Parikh, finds that PDS coverage (1986–7) was 87 per cent in Kerala, 55–60 per cent in Andhra Pradesh and Tamil Nadu, but 2 per cent in Uttar Pradesh and Bihar.

38. And with very similar trends for sugar and kerosene too.

39. Excluding Nesal: see note 25.

40. This was based on the fact of the issue price for common parboiled rice being Rs 2.5 in 1994, while a local (Arni Regulated Market) average open-market price was Rs

5.50. Other estimates suggest that rice prices averaged Rs 1.50 higher than this, in which case the subsidy was accordingly greater.

41. In a careful study of the PDS in Karnataka, Mooij (2000) put the systemic losses at about 10 per cent.

42. As did those of the five cooks, helpers, ayahs etc.

43. Government of Tamil Nadu 2001a.

44. B Harriss 1991a, pp. 53, 82.

45. The village diaries tell us that liquor is sold in the villages illegally but openly. In 1993, a litre of arrack cost Rs 12. Arrack was commonly diluted with water (three parts to one) and sometimes adulterated (e.g. with 'chloride hydrate') 'for kick'. Liquor is also smuggled from Andhra Pradesh in 100 ml cellophane packets via a marketing system in which fines on traders and bribes to the Excise Department and the police are institutionalized. Ex-servicemen and 'professionals' (teachers and officials) prefer Indian-made foreign liquor (IMFL), which is purchased (in local towns) for consumption and onward trade in the villages. Toddy is also tapped and fermented in local villages and plays an important role in village festivals and death ceremonies. In one of the three villages there is also an illicit still, working at high capacity.

46. The figure of 35 per cent is consistent with the state-wide head-count estimate of poverty (based on a nutritional poverty line) for 1993–4: 33 per cent (Government of Tamil Nadu, website, 2001b).

47. Narayanan 1996a.

48. Swaminathan 2000a.

49. Swaminathan and Misra 2001.

50. Alston 1994.

51. Narayanan 1996a, p. 35.

Endnotes (3–6)

1. Lall 2000.

2. Weiner 1993.

3. www.tn.gov.in/economy/eco-may.htm 2003.

4. India allocates a lower proportion of GNP to education than other developing countries (3.6 per cent as compared with 6.7 per cent (Kenya) 4.3 per cent (Tanzania) and 7.8 per cent [Malaysia]). In 1966, the Kothari Commission suggested a 6 per cent target. This has been revived most recently in the Eighth Plan of 1992.

5. Psacharopoulos 1988; Datta 1998. See Cotlear 1990 for an agricultural context. Education is related to access to higher-paid segments of the labour market, with or without a screening effect. However, the low *quality* of education in much of India may prevent a strong relationship between education and employment (see for instance Bliss *et al.* 1998, pp. 265–7).

6. See respectively Majumdar 1999 and Lockheed and Verspoor 1991.

7. World Bank 1989.

8. Majumdar 1999, p. 274.

9. Educational deprivation is derived from a composite index of adult literacy and

mean years of schooling in which 0 is undeprived and 1.0 is completely deprived (Majumdar 1999, pp. 270–2, 290–5).

10. Ibid., pp. 274–5, 294–5.
11. Kingdon 1994, 1996.
12. World Bank Country Study 1991.
13. *Economic and Political Weekly* (30 October 1993).
14. *http://www.tn.gov.in/policy/schedu2.htm;p1.*
15. Drèze and Sharma (1998, pp. 64, 73) make the points: i) that even with teachers and equipment education will be supply-constrained if the context and manner of delivery discriminate against castes and genders; and ii) that the defective 'supply' of education provokes no collective response from parents – perhaps not unconnected with i).
16. Ravallion and Subbarao 1992; Prabhu and Chatterjee 1992; Prabhu 1994.
17. Prabhu and Chatterjee 1992, p. 50; Prabhu 1994, p. 40.
18. Ravallion and Subbarao 1992, p. 30.
19. De and Noronha 1998. This kind of reasoning about the reasoning of the poor is also discussed in Majumdar 1999, pp. 282–3, and in Lanjouw and Stern 1998, pp. 63–5. A strand of policy debate not covered here, because not relevant to conditions in these villages, is demand for private elementary education. De and Noronha (op. cit.) reveal that private education in 1997 cost Rs 1,047 per year, against Rs 333 per child in a government school. Even for government schooling, these costs are high entry barriers and no guarantee of significant improvements in quality.
20. Harriss 1991a.
21. See also Helander 1993; Harriss-White 1996b.
22. B Harriss 1991a.
23. Hazell and Ramasamy 1991.
24. 1993 household income data are available for 98.2 per cent of the population (owing to missing values in the data).
25. Data on value of land owned are available for the 63.3 per cent of the population that own land.
26. Educational attainment data are given for the over-12s only, as this is a better representation of the final education level obtained.
27. Income and land data are continuous, educational attainment data are discrete and not numerically ordered, such that it could meaningfully be given in mean/standard deviation format.
28. See Chapter 1-4 here.
29. Village-specific distributions are very similar so are not shown here.
30. The probit model is based on the standard normal distribution:

$$E(CPi) = \Phi(\alpha + \beta X_i)$$

where $E(CP_i) = Pr(CP_i = 1)$ is the probability of completing primary education, $\Phi(.)$ is the cumulative density function and $\alpha + \beta X_i$ the set of independent or explanatory variables.

31. However, caste will not perform well since, due to the inclusion in 'OTH' (other

castes) of highest-ranked Brahmins along with lower-ranking minor castes and Muslims, it is not an accurate scale ordering of 'high-caste' to 'low-caste'.

32. Parental education was also defined to measure the marginal contributions of each higher education level, but the results proved very similar.

33. Obviously, there are several variables suggested by theory on which we have no satisfactory available data. These include non-income components of household wealth, measures of parental attitudes and child ability, and intervillage differences in a range of variables from employment opportunities to school quality. For this study we can only acknowledge the possible shortcomings of the model and assume that the variables we have used (of household income, village dummies etc.) will capture much of the influences of the omitted variables.

34. Note that m3 is rejected as a variable because there are too few non-zero variables. The fit is much improved from the first model but is still very low. Although goodness-of-fit measures are generally weak for probit models, having a low goodness of fit is a widespread problem in cross-sectional econometric studies (i.e. in studies using linear [OLS etc.] and non-linear [logit/probit] models).

35. All models are of probit estimation of ED on variables shown using STATA programme; z and P(z) show the individual significance of explanatory variables.

36. Fully described in Gold *et al.* 1996.

37. The unexpected result that gender is not a significant determinant of the probability of children completing primary education comes clearly from the particular characteristics of our restricted sample and would not be likely to hold if we could include data on the parents of females.

38. See the discussion of the social uses of literacy and oral culture in Kumar 1993.

39. De and Noronha 1998, p. 8.

40. Athreya 1995, 1999.

41. And be as radical as credit for land purchase!

42. Exposed by Kingdon and Murammil, 2003.

43. This is not exactly an original conclusion. It supports that of Prabhu and Chatterjee (1992, p. 42) and Ravallion and Subbarao (1992), among other analysts of structural adjustment and social expenditure.

Endnotes (3–7)

1. Drèze and Sen 1991.
2. Guhan 1992, p. 288.
3. Jhabvala and Subrahmanya 2000.
4. Guhan 1992, 1994.
5. J Harriss *et al.* 1992.
6. Swaminathan 2000c; Chen 2000; Bhatt 2000.
7. See the many cases in Jhabvala and Subrahmanya 2000.
8. Chen and Drèze 1992.
9. Guhan 1994.

10. Narayanan 1996b.
11. But see Chapter 3–4 here for the contingency of disabling incapacity.
12. Agarwal 1991.
13. Prabhu 1998.
14. Along with decline in quantity, state-provided social services are recognized to be low in quality and wasteful, yet they are accessed disproportionately by poor people (Prabhu 1997; Drèze and Sharma 1998, pp. 180–211).
15. Narayanan 1996b, p. 32.
16. Prabhu 1998.
17. The revenue deficit increased from 11.2 per cent in 1989–90 to 15.7 per cent in 1994–5 (Narayanan 1996b).
18. J Harriss *et al.* 1992; Prabhu 1997.
19. Narayanan 1996b.
20. Ibid., p. 31.
21. Ibid., p. 39.
22. Our field investigator found many more pensioners in fact than there were on the record.
23. Based in turn on the official poverty line of Rs 118 per adult in 1987–8, assuming 5 per cent inflation, then rounding down from Rs 158 to Rs 150 (and assuming a dependent child is 0.5, or Rs 75 [Guhan 1996]).
24. Copestake 1992.
25. Guhan and Paul (eds.) 1997.

Endnotes (3–8)

1. The cases for female primary education – instrumentalist, transformative and rights-based cases – reek of a paternalistic appropriation of discourse.
2. See Swaminathan 2000a.
3. Ram 2001. In 2001 Tamil Nadu's distinctive political pendulum swung once more and Jayalalithaa became Chief Minister, even though her several applications to stand for election had been refused under an Election Commission order of 1997 disqualifying those convicted of crimes, even those under appeal.
4. Alcohol creates a notorious tension in public policy, being a heinously polluting activity associated with low castes in the eyes of upper castes (who nevertheless do not desist from drinking), associated too with domestic violence against women and with the private appropriation of resources that could have been consumed much more equitably in the form of food, but also recognized to be a powerful antidote to hours of drudgery and – more to the point – a habit which can yield a flow of tax to the state amounting to up to 10 per cent of its total revenue (see Chapter 3–5).
5. Widlund 2000, pp. 345–80.
6. Contrast this with village menials in the Revenue Department, better paid and with the vaguest of job descriptions.
7. See Ramasundaram 1993 for details of reforms in the administration of sterilization

based upon incentives rather than targets, a kind of reform which may have much wider relevance.

8. Sengupta 1998.

9. See Harriss-White 2003.

10. These data are incomplete because the municipality does not account separately for salaries. The headings aggregated here are those categories indicated by the Municipal Commissioner as being dominated by the salary component. They show how salaries are protected in the structure of expenditure.

11. The Jha Committee (Govt of India 1983) reports that, with the efforts of 95 per cent of staff in the Revenue Department, a mere 5 per cent of income tax is collected, disproportionately from the lowest and most numerous category of assessees, mainly in the salariat.

12. Jagganathan 1987, p. 116.

13. Leys 1965.

14. Wade 1985; Jagganathan 1987.

15. Increase information to curb rent-seeking; use law to restrict the activities of those most prone to rent-seeking; raise bureaucrats' salaries, tax rent-seeking activities and use rent-seeking status to prioritize deregulation (Jagganathan 1987; Grindle and Thomas 1991; Nelson 1990; and Ades and di Tella 1995).

16. Krueger 1974; Buchanan 1980; Basu 1991. See also the critical discussion in Grindle and Thomas 1991.

17. Jagganathan 1987, p. 110.

18. This definition was given by the then influential Santhanam Report on the prevention of corruption (Government of India 1964).

19. Theorized in an original manner by Khan and Jomo (2000).

20. Wade (1988) described similar relations for village councils and the irrigation bureaucracy.

21. This politics is examined in detail in Basile and Harriss-White 2000.

22. Goswami *et al.* 1991; B Harriss 1984. Goswami *et al.* (op. cit.) estimate that only 7 million out of 1,000 million Indians pay income tax. This does not mean that 993 million people evade tax. It simply points to the fragility of this element in the tax base. The number who ought to pay income tax is unknown. By 2001, the number of income-tax payers had been revised to 12 million. Whether these income-tax payers are compliant is another question.

23. Roy 1996, tables and quotation, pp. 28–9. A questionnaire supplied to all income tax commissions as part of the last report on *Aspects of the Black Economy in India* (Government of India 1985a) is the source of Roy's data on the origins of black income.

24. The significance rating of gold is lower than these other forms of wealth.

25. B Harriss 1981c.

26. Exacerbated by increasing velocities of transfer (Noorani 1997; Banik 1999).

27. In 1999, a Special Commission of the Government of Tamil Nadu exposed the lie that the supply of suitably qualified candidates for reserved posts was in any way constrained (Ramakrishnan 1999).

28. The most extreme case is Uttar Pradesh, where between 1977 and 1999 there have been 13 governments interspersed with President's Rule. The six-monthly rotation of the BSP and BJP in 1997–8 led to over 1,000 transfers in the Uttar Pradesh cadres of the IAS and IPS. Under Mayavati, transfers ran at an average of seven per day. Under Kalyan Singh they had risen to 16 (Banik 1999, pp. 34–5, footnotes 69, 70).

29. Ibid.

30. *World Development Report*, World Bank 1997.

31. Guhan and Paul 1997.

References

Acharya, S, and Madhur, S, 1983, 'Informal Credit Markets and Black Money: Do They Frustrate Monetary Policy?', *Economic and Political Weekly*, 18 (18 October 1983), pp. 1751–6.

Adams, D, and Graham, D, 1981, 'A Critique of Traditional Agricultural Projects and Policies' *Journal of Development Economics*, 8, pp. 347–63.

Ades, A, and di Tella, R, 1995, 'Competition and Corruption', *Applied Economics Discussion Paper 169*, Institute of Economics and Statistics, Oxford University.

Adnan, S, 1997, 'Class, Caste and *Shamaj* Relations among the Peasantry in Bangladesh', in J Breman *et al.* (eds.), *The Village in Asia Revisited*, New Delhi, OUP, pp. 277–310.

Agarwal, B, 1991, 'Social Security and the Family: Coping with Seasonality and Calamity in Rural India', in Ahmed *et al.* (eds.), pp. 171–244.

—— 1998, 'Disinherited Peasants, Disadvantaged Workers: A Gender Perspective on Land and Livelihood', *Economic and Political Weekly*, 33/13, (26 March–3 April).

Agnihotri, S B, 1997, 'Sex-Ratio Imbalances in India – A Disaggregated Analysis,' Ph.D. thesis, School of Development Studies, University of East Anglia.

—— 2000, *Sex Ratio Patterns in the Indian Population: A Fresh Exploration*, New Delhi, Sage.

Agrawal, V, 1997, 'Rural Credit Markets in India: Factors Affecting Access and Terms of Credit', M.Sc. thesis, QEH, Oxford.

Ahmed, C S, and Herdt, R W, 1984, 'Measuring the Impact of Consumption Linkages on the Employment Effects of Mechanisation in Philippine Rice Production', *Journal of Development Studies*, 20/2.

Ahmed, E, Drèze, J, Hills, J, and Sen, A K, 1991, *Social Security in Developing Countries*, Oxford, Clarendon.

Alston, P, 1994, 'International Law and the Right to Food', in B Harriss-White and R Hoffenberg (eds.).

Appasamy, P P, 1993, 'The Linkage between Urbanisation and Environment in India', *Madras Institute of Development Studies Bulletin* (April), pp. 200–13.

Apthorpe, R, 1997, 'Writing Development Policy and Policy Analysis Plain or Clear: on Language, Genre and Power', in Shore and Wright (eds.), pp. 43–59.

—— and Gasper, D (eds.), 1996, *Arguing Development Policy*, London, Cass.

Ardener, S, 1995, 'Women Making Money Go Round: ROSCAs Revisited', in S Ardener and S Burman (eds.), *Money-Go-Rounds, The Importance of Rotating Savings and Credit Associations for Women*, Oxford/Washington DC, Berg Publishers Limited.

Arni Municipality, 1994, *Municipal Abstract, 1993–4*, Arni.

Asadullah, M, 2000, 'Gender Discrimination in the Intra-Household Allocation of Educational and Medical Expenditure: Evidence from Rural India', M.Sc. thesis, Oxford University.

Athreya, V, 1995, 'The Evaluation of National Adult Literacy in India', Bharathidasan University, mimeo.

—— 1999, 'Adult Literacy in India Since Independence: Policy and Practice', in Harriss-White and Subramanian (eds.), pp. 227–64.

Athreya, V B, 2001a, 'Census 2001: Some Progress, some Concern', *Frontline*, 18/8, pp. 14–17.

—— 2001b, 'Census 2001', *Frontline*, 18/8 (27 April), pp. 107–10.

—— and Chunkath, S R, 1996, 'Fighting Female Infanticide', *The Hindu* (17 March).

Athreya, V, Djurfeldt, G, and Lindberg, S, 1990, *Barriers Broken: Production Relations and Agrarian Change in Tamil Nadu*, New Delhi, Sage.

Attwood, D, 1979, 'Why Some of the Rich get Poorer', *Current Anthropology*, 20/3, pp. 495–516.

Aziz, A, 1989, 'Social and Economic Change in a Karnataka Village', *Pondy Papers in Social Sciences*, no. 3 (June), Department of Social Sciences, French Institute, Pondicherry.

Badrinath, K, 1994, 'Ethics and Society', *Frontline*, 11/5, pp. 117–18.

Bagchi, A, 1992, 'Riding the Free Rider: A Lesson from Barrackpore', *Economic and Political Weekly*, 27/34, pp. 1778–80.

Bajpai, 1991, 'The Disabled and the Law', *Action Aid Disability News*, 2/2, pp. 23–5.

Baker, C J, 1984, *An Indian Rural Economy 1880–1955: The Tamil Nadu Countryside*, Delhi, Oxford University Press.

Baliga, B S, 1960, *Studies in Madras Administration*, Volume 3, Government of Madras.

Bandara, C M M, 1977, 'Hydrological Consequences of Agrarian Change', in B H Farmer (ed.), *Green Revolution? Technology and Change in Rice Growing Areas of Tamilnadu and Sri Lanka*, London, Macmillan, pp. 323–39.

Banerji, D, 1993, 'Simplistic Approach to Health Policy Analysis: World Bank Team on Indian Health Sector', *Economic and Political Weekly*, pp. 1207–10.

Banik, D, 2001, 'The Transfer Raj: Indian Civil Servants on the Move', *European Journal of Development Research*, 13/1, pp. 104–32.

Barbour, P, 1995, 'Rural Credit Markets in Tamil Nadu and the Role of Collateral', M.Sc. thesis, QEH, Oxford University.

Bardhan, K, 1973, 'Factors Affecting Wage Rates for Agricultural Labour', *Economic and Political Weekly*, 8.

—— 1977a, 'Rural Employment, Wages and Labour Markets in India: a Survey of Research', *Economic and Political Weekly*, 12, pp. A34–A64.

—— 1977b, 'Rural Employment, Wages and Labour Markets in India: a Survey of Research II', *Economic and Political Weekly*, 13, pp. 1062–74.

—— 1977c, 'Rural Employment, Wages and Labour Markets in India: a Survey of Research III', *Economic and Political Weekly*, 13, pp. 1101–1118.

—— 1984, 'Work Patterns and Social Differentiation: Rural Women of West Bengal', in

H Binswanger and M Rosenzweig (eds.), *Contractual Arrangements, Employment and Wages in Rural Labour Markets in Asia*, London, Yale University Press.

—— 1993, 'Social Classes and Gender in India: the Structure of Differences in the Condition of Women', in A Clark (ed.), *Gender and Political Economy*, pp. 146–78.

Bardhan, P, 1974, 'On Life and Death Questions', *Economic and Political Weekly*, 9.

—— 1989a, 'A Note on Interlinked Rural Economic Arrangements' in P Bardhan (ed.), *The Economic Theory of Agrarian Institutions*, Oxford, Oxford University Press.

—— (ed.) 1989b, *Conversations Between Economists and Anthropologists: Methodological Issues in Measuring Economic Change in Rural India*, Delhi, Oxford University Press.

—— 1998, *The Political Economy of Development in India* (expanded edition), Delhi, Oxford University Press.

Barnes, C, 1991, *Disabled People in Britain and Discrimination: A Case for Anti Discrimination Legislation*, London, Hurst and Co.

Baru, R V, 1993, 'Inter-regional Variations in Health Services in Andhra Pradesh', *Economic and Political Weekly*, pp. 963–7.

Basant, R, and Joshi, H, 1994, 'Employment Diversification in an Agriculturally Developed Region: Some Evidence from Rural Kheda, Gujarat', in P Visaria and R Basant (eds.).

—— and Kumar, B L, 1989, 'Rural Non-Agricultural Activities in India: A Review of Available Evidence', *Social Scientist*, 17/1–2.

Basile, E, and Harriss-White, B, 1999a, 'Accumulation and Corporatist Capital in a South Indian Town', *www.qeh.ox.ac.uk:* working paper no. 34.

—— 1999b, 'The Politics of Accumulation in Small Town India', *Inst. of Development Studies (IDS) Bulletin*, 30/4, pp. 31–8.

—— 2000, 'Corporative Capitalism: Civil Society and the Politics of Accumulation', *QEHWP 38*, www.qeh.ox.ac.uk.

Basu, A M, 1999, 'Fertility Decline and Increasing Gender Imbalance in India, including a Possible South Indian Turnaround', *Development and Change*, 30, pp. 237–63.

Basu, K, 1991, *Economic Graffiti*, New Delhi, Oxford University Press.

—— (ed.), 1994, *Agrarian Questions: Themes in Economics*, New Delhi, Oxford University Press.

Batley, R, 1992, 'Co-operation with Private and Community Organisations', *Institutional Framework of Urban Management Working Paper 6*, Developing Areas Group, School of Public Policy, Birmingham University.

Baulch, B, and McCulloch, N, 1998, 'Being Poor and Becoming Poor: Poverty, Status and Poverty Transitions in Rural Pakistan', *Poverty Research Programme Working Paper 79*, Institute of Development Studies, Sussex University, Brighton.

Beal, J, 1997, 'Household Livelihoods and the Urban Environments: Social Development Perspectives on Solid Waste Management in Faisalabad, Pakistan', Ph.D. thesis, London School of Economics.

Becker, G S, and Tomes, N, 1976, 'Child Endowments and the Quality of Children', *Journal of Political Economy*, 84/4, pp. S143–62.

Beede, D N, and Bloom, D E, 1995, 'The Economics of Municipal Solid Waste', *World Bank Research Observer*, 10/2, pp. 113–50.

Behrman, J R, 1988, 'Intrahousehold Allocation of Nutrients in Rural India: Are Boys Favoured? Do Parents Exhibit Inequality Aversion?', *Oxford Economic Papers*, 40, pp. 32–54.

—— 1993, 'The Economic Rationale for Investing in Nutrition in Developing Countries', *World Development*.

—— 1997, 'Intrahousehold Distribution and the Family', in M Rosenzweig and O Stark (eds.), *The Handbook of Population and Family Economics*, North Holland.

Behrman, J, and Srinivasan, T N (eds.), 1995, *Handbook of Development Economics*, Vol. 3, Elsevier Science B.V., Netherlands.

Bell, C, 1990, 'The Extent and some Effects of the Expansion of Institutional Credit Agencies in Rural India', *World Bank Economic Review*.

—— Hazell, P, and Slade, R, 1982, *Project Evaluation in Regional Perspective*, Baltimore, Johns Hopkins University Press.

Benewick, R, Blecher, M, and Cook, S, 1999, 'Politics in Development: Essays in Honour of Gordon White', *Special Issue of the IDS Bulletin*, 30/4.

Bernstein, H, and Woodhouse, P, 2001, 'Telling Environmental Change Like it is? Reflections on a Study in Sub-Saharan Africa', *Journal of Agrarian Change*, 1/2, pp. 283–324.

Beteille, A, 1974, *Studies in Agrarian Social Structure*, Delhi, Oxford University Press.

—— 1996, 'Caste in Contemporary India', in C Fuller (ed.), *Caste Today*, New Delhi, Oxford University Press.

Bhaduri, A, 1983, *The Economic Structure of Backward Agriculture*, London, Academic Press Inc.

—— 1983, *The Structure of Backward Agriculture*, London, Academic Press.

—— Raman, H Z, and Arn, A L, 1986, 'Persistence and Polarisation: A Study in the Dynamics of Agrarian Contradiction', *Journal of Peasant Studies*, 13/3, pp. 82–9.

Bhalla, G S (ed.), 1994, *Economic Liberalisation and Indian Agriculture*, New Delhi, Institute for Studies in Industrial Development.

—— (ed.), 1995, *Economic Liberalisation and Indian Agriculture*, New Delhi, Institute for Studies in Industrial Development.

Bhalla, S, 1999, 'Liberalisation, Rural Labour Markets and the Mobilisation of Farm Workers', *Journal of Peasant Studies*, 26, 2/3.

—— 1976, 'New Relations of Production in Haryana Agriculture', *Economic and Political Weekly*, Review of Agriculture.

Bhatia, B, 1992, 'Lush Fields and Parched Throats: Political Economy of Groundwater in Gujarat', *Economic and Political Weekly*, 27/51 and 52 (December), pp. 19–26.

Bhatt, E, 2000, 'Foreword', in R Jhabvala and R K A Subrahmanya (eds.), *The Unorganized Sector: Work Security and Social Protection*, New Delhi, Sage.

Bhattacharyya, S, 2003, *Rural Credit and Class Differentiation: West Bengal under Left Interventionist Regime*, Kolkata, K P Bagchi & Co.

Bhatty, I Z, and Vashistha, 1987, 'Structure of Rural Non-Farm Sector and Stages of Economic Development in India', in R H Syed (ed.).

Bhende, M, 1986, 'Credit Markets in Rural South India', *Economic and Political Weekly*, 21/38/39, pp. 119–24.

Binswanger, H P, and Khandker, S R, 1995, 'The Impact of Formal Finance on the Rural Economy of India', *Journal of Development Studies*, 32/2, pp. 234–62.

Binswanger, H, and Rosenzweig, M, 1984, *Contractual Arrangements, Employment and Wages in Rural Labour Markets in Asia*, London, Yale University Press.

Binswanger, H P, and Rosenzweig, M, 1986, 'Credit Markets, Wealth and Endowments in Rural South India', *World Bank Discussion Paper, Report Number ARU* 59, Washington, World Bank.

Bliss, C, and Stern, N, 1982, *Palanpur: The Economy of an Indian Village*, Oxford, Oxford University Press.

—— Lanjouw, P, and Stern, N, 1998, 'Population Growth, Employment Expansion and Technological Change', in Lanjouw and Stern (eds.), pp. 243–312.

Bliven, N, Ramasamy, C, and Wanmali, S, 1997, *Developing Policies to Help the Poor in South India*, Washington, DC International Food Policy Research Institute.

Bloch, F, Rao, V, and Desai, S, 1998, 'Wedding Celebrations as Conspicuous Consumption: Signalling Social Status in Rural India', *Working Paper 98 06*, Population Studies Training Center, Brown University.

Bossiere, D, Knight, J, and Sabot, J, 1985, 'Earnings, Schooling Ability and Cognitive Skills', *American Economic Review*.

Braverman, A, and Gausch, J, 1986, 'Rural Credit Markets and Institutions in Developing Countries: Lessons for Policy Analysis From Practice and Modern Theory', *World Development*, 4/10/11, pp. 253–1267.

—— and Srinivasan, T S, 1981, 'Credit and Sharecropping in Agrarian Societies', *Journal of Development Economics*, 9, pp. 289–312.

Breman, J, 1997, 'The Village in Focus', in J Breman *et al* (eds.), *The Village in Asia Revisited*, New Delhi, Oxford University Press, pp. 15–76.

—— Kloose, P, and Saith, A, 1997 (eds.).

Browning, M, and Subramanian, R, 1994, 'Gender Bias in India: Parental Preferences of Marriage Costs?', Centre of Research into Industry, Enterprise, Finance and the Firm, University of St Andrews.

Bryceson, D F, 1995, 'De-agrarianisation in Sub-Saharan Africa: Development or Depletion of Rural Economic Potential?', in *Agrarian Questions: the Politics of Farming Anno 1995*, Wageningen, Netherlands, Agricultural University.

Buchanan, J M, 1980, 'Rent Seeking and Profit Seeking', in J M Buchanan, R D Tollison and G Tullock (eds.), *Toward a Theory of the Rent Seeking Society*, Texas A and M University Press.

Cahill, J, 2001, 'To What Extent Does Caste Affect Occupation in India? An Analysis of Occupational Mobility in North Arcot District, Tamil Nadu', M.Sc. thesis, Oxford University.

Cain, M, 1981, 'Risk and Insurance: Perspectives on Fertility and Agrarian Change in India and Bangladesh', *Population and Development Review*, 75, pp. 435–74.

Caldwell, P, and Caldwell, J, 1987, 'Where There is a Narrower Gap Between Female and

Male Situations: Lessons from South India and Sri Lanka', paper to the American SSRC Workshop on Differential Mortality and Healthcare in South Asia, Dhaka, Bangladesh.

Calomiris, C W, and Rajaraman, I, 1998, 'The Role of ROSCAs: Lumpy Durables or Event Insurance?', *Journal of Development Economics*, 56, pp. 207–16.

Cassen, R, and Joshi, V, 1995, *India: the Future of the Economic Reforms*, New Delhi, Oxford University Press.

——, —— and Lipton, M, 1993, 'Stabilisation and Structural Reform in India', *Contemporary South Asia*, 2/2, pp. 165–98.

——, ——, —— (eds.), 1995, *India: the Future of Economic Reform*, New Delhi, Oxford University Press.

Census of India Reports: Social and Cultural Tables, 1981, various volumes, Government of India.

CMIE, 1992, *Fertiliser Pricing: Extracts from the Report on the Joint Committee for Fertiliser Pricing, Government of India*, Centre for Monitoring the Indian Economy (CMIE), Economic Intelligence Service, New Delhi.

Chambers, R, 1982, *Rural Development: Putting the Last First*, Harlow, Longman.

—— 1992, 'Poverty in India: Concepts, Research and Reality', in Harriss, Guhan and Cassen (eds.), pp. 301–32.

—— 1997, *Whose Reality Counts? Putting the First Last*, London, Intermediate Technology Publications.

—— and Harriss, J, 1977, 'Comparing Twelve South Indian Villages: In Search of Practical Theory', in Farmer (ed.), pp. 301–22.

Chandrasekhar, C P, 1993, 'Agrarian Change and Occupational Diversification: Non-Agricultural Employment and Rural Development in West Bengal', *Journal of Peasant Studies*, 20/2.

Chapman, G, and Harriss, B, 1984, 'Crop Production and Market Involvement: a Combinatorial Analysis', in B Harriss, pp. 86–125.

Chattopadhyay, M, 1985, *Condition of Labour in Indian Agriculture: Apparent and Real*, K P Bagchi & Company.

Chen, M A, 2000, 'Indian Widows: In Search of Dignity and Identity', in Jhabvala and Subrahmanya (eds.), pp. 146–60.

—— and Drèze, J, 1992, 'Widows and Well-being in Rural North India', *Discussion Paper 40*, STICERD, LSE, London.

Chinnappa, B N, 1977, 'Adoption of the New Technology in North Arcot District', in Farmer (ed.), pp. 92–123.

Chunkath, S R, and Athreya, V B, 1997, 'Female Infanticide in Tamil Nadu: Some Evidence', *Economic and Political Weekly* (26 April), pp. WS21–8.

Chuta, E, and Liedholm, 1979, 'Rural Non-Farm Employment: A Review of the State of the Art', *MSU Rural Development Paper*, No. 4, Department of Agricultural Economics, Michigan State University, East Lansing, Michigan.

Clark, A W, 1983, 'Limitations on Female Life Chances in Rural Central Guajarat', *Indian Economic and Social History Review*, 20/1, pp. 1–25.

Clark, A, 1987, 'The Social Demography of Excess Female Mortality in India: New Directions', *Economic and Political Weekly*, 22/17 (25 April), Review of Women's Studies.

—— (ed.), 1993, *Gender and Political Economy: Explorations of South Asian Systems*, New Delhi, Oxford Univ. Press.

Clark, P, and Niblett, T, 1989, 'The CN2 Algorithm', *Machine Learning*, 3, pp. 262–83.

Clay, E, and Schaffer, B (eds.), 1984, *Room for Manoeuvre: an Exploration of Public Policy in Agriculture and Rural Development*, London, Heinemann.

CMIE, 1997a, *Economic Intelligence Service: Draft Approach Paper to Ninth Five Year Plan, 1997–2002*, Bombay, Planning Commission, Reprint Document.

—— 1997b, *Profiles of States* (March), Bombay.

—— 1997c, *Draft Approach Paper to Ninth Five Year Plan – 1997–2002*, (reprint) Bombay.

—— 1999, *Economic Intelligence Service*, 'Energy', March–April, Bombay.

Coleridge, P, 1993, *Disability, Liberation and Development*, Oxford, Oxfam.

Copestake, J, 1992, 'The Integrated Rural Development Programme: Performance during the Sixth Plan, Policy Responses and Proposals for Reform', in Harriss, Guhan and Cassen (eds.), pp. 209–30.

Corbridge, S, and Harriss, J, 2000, *Reinventing India*, London, Polity.

Cornia, G A, and Stewart, F, 1995, 'Food Subsidies: Two Errors of Targeting', in F Stewart (ed.), *Adjustment and Poverty*, London and New York, Routledge.

——, Jolly, R, and Stewart, F, 1985, *Adjustment with a Human Face*, Oxford, Oxford University Press.

Cotlear, 1990, 'The Effects of Education on Farm Productivity', in Griffin and Knight, *Human Development and the International Development Strategy for the 1990s*.

Cowen, M, and Shenton, R, 1996, *Doctrines of Development*, London, Routledge.

Cox, A F, 1985, *North Arcot District Manual*, Madras Presidency, Madras, Government Press.

Culshaw, M, 1983, *It Will Soon be Dark . . .*, Delhi, National Council of Churches, Litehouse Publications.

Da Corta, L, and Venkateshwarku, D, 1999, 'Unfree Relations and the Feminisation of Agricultural Labour in Andhra Pradesh, 1970–95', *Journal of Peasant Studies*, 26/2–3, pp. 71–139.

Dandekar, V M, and Rath, N, 1971, *Poverty in India*, Indian School of Political Economy, Poona.

Dasgupta, B, 1971, 'Socio-Economic Classification of Districts: A Statistical Approach', *Economic and Political Weekly* (August 14), pp. 1763–74.

—— 1975, 'A Typology of Socio-Economic Systems from Indian Village Studies', *Economic and Political Weekly* (special issue, August), pp. 1395–1414.

—— 1998, *Structural Adjustment, Global Trade and the New Political Economy of Development*, London, Zed Press.

Das Gupta, M, 1987, 'Selective Discrimination Against Female Children in Rural Punjab, India', *Population and Development Review*, 13/1, pp. 77–100.

—— and Mari Bhat, P N, 1997, 'Fertility Decline and Increased Manifestation of Sex Bias in India', *Population Studies*, 51, pp. 307–15.

Datta, R C, 1998, 'Human Capital, Performance and Earnings Connection – A Firm Level Study', paper to symposium on 'Reforming India's Social Sectors: Strategies and Prospects', Department of Economics, University of Mumbai, Platinum Jubilee Celebrations.

Davis, M, 1990, *City Of Quartz: Excavating the Future in Los Angeles*, London, Vintage Publishers.

De, A, and Noronha, C, 1998, 'Parental Motivation and Private Schooling', paper to symposium on 'Reforming India's Social Sectors: Strategies and Prospects', Department of Economics, University of Mumbai, Platinum Jubilee Celebrations.

Desai, A N, 1990, *Helping the Handicapped: Problems and Prospects*, New Delhi, S B Nangia, for Ashish Publishing House.

Desai, B M, 1996, 'Wither Rural Financial Institutions?', *Economic and Political Weekly*, 3 Aug.

Desai, M G, 1986, 'Fertiliser Use in India: The Next Stage in Policy', *Indian Journal of Agricultural Economics*, xll3, pp. 248–70.

Dhawan, B D, 1991, *Studies in Minor Irrigation with Special Reference to Groundwater*, New Delhi, Commonwealth Publications.

Dinesh, K, and Patel, M, 1993, 'Depleting Groundwater and Farmer Response: A Case Study of Villages in Kheralu Taluka of Mehsana, Gujarat', paper presented in a workshop on 'Water Management: India's Groundwater Challenge', organized by VIKSAT and Pacific Institute, 14–18 December, Ahmedabad (mimeo).

Djurfeldt, G, and Lindberg, S, 1995, 'Coming Back to Thaiyur – Health and Medicine in a Twenty-Five Year Perspective', paper contributed to workshop 'The Village in Asia Revisited', India, Trivandrum, 26–28 January.

——, —— and Rajagopal, A, 1997, 'Coming Back to Thaiyur: Health and Medicine in a Twenty-five Year Perspective', in Breman *et al.* (eds.), pp. 175–98.

Dobb, M, 1975 (1946), *Studies in the Development of Capitalism*, London, Routledge.

Drèze, J, and Sen, A K, 1991, 'Public Action for Social Security: Foundations and Strategy', in Ahmed *et al.* (eds.), pp. 3–40.

—— and Sen, A (eds.), 1991, *The Political Economy of Hunger, Volume I*, Oxford, Oxford University Press.

—— and Sharma, N, 1998, 'Palanpur: Population, Society and Economy', in Lanjouw and Stern (eds.), pp. 3–113.

——, Lanjouw, P, and Sharma, N, 1998a, 'Credit', in P Lanjouw and N Stern (eds.), pp. 506–83.

——, ——, —— 1998b, 'Economic Development in Palanpur, 1957–93', in P Lanjouw and N Stern (eds.), pp. 114–234.

——, Sen, A K, and Hussain, A (eds.), 1995, *The Political Economy of Hunger: Selected Essays*, Oxford, Clarendon.

Dyson, T, and Moore, M, 1983, 'On Kinship Structure, Female Autonomy, and Demographic Behaviour in India', *Population and Development Review*, 9/1, pp. 35–60.

Economic and Political Weekly 1992 (4 April), 'Education for All, the Financing Problem'.

Economic and Political Weekly 1993 (30 Oct), 'Structural Adjustment and Education'.

Elango, R, and Ramachandran, S, 1993, *The Urban Environment of Thanjavur Town*, Annamalai University.

Ellis, F, 1992, *Agricultural Policies in Developing Countries*, Cambridge, Cambridge University Press.

—— 2001, *Rural Livelihoods and Diversity in Developing Countries*, Oxford, Oxford University Press.

Elson, D (ed.), 1992, *Male Bias in the Development Process*, Manchester University Press.

Erb, S, and Harriss-White, B, 2002, *Outcast from Social Welfare: Adult Disability and Incapacity in Rural South India*, Bangalore, Books for Change.

Everitt, B, 1974, *Cluster Analysis*, London, Heinemann.

Fairhead, J, and Leach, M, 1996, 'Rethinking the Forest-Savanna Mosaic: Colonial Science and its Relics in West Africa', in M Leach and R Mearns (eds.).

Farmer, B H (ed.), 1977, *Green Revolution? Technology and Change in Rice Growing Areas of Tamil Nadu and Sri Lanka*, London, Macmillan.

——, Madduma Bandara, C M, Shanmuga Sundaram, V, and Silva, W P T, 1977, 'Setting the Stage', in B H Farmer (ed.) *Green Revolution? Technology and Change in Rice-growing Areas of Tamil Nadu and Sri Lanka*, Macmillan, London and Basingstoke.

Ferguson, J, 1990, *The Anti-Politics Machine: 'Development', Depolitisation and Bureaucratic Power in Lesotho*, Cambridge, Cambridge University Press.

Fertiliser Association of India (FAI), 1994, *Handbook on Fertiliser Usage*, 7th edition, FAI, New Delhi.

Folbre, N, 1986, 'Hearts and Spades: Paradigms of Household Economics', *World Development*, 14/2, pp. 245–55.

Food and Agriculture Organization (FAO), 1995, *Fertiliser Statistics (1993–4)*, FAO, New Delhi.

Foster, A D, and Rosenzweig, M R, 1999, *Missing Women, the Marriage Market and Economic Growth*, Philadelphia, University of Pennsylvania.

Fuller, C (ed.), 1996, *Caste Today*, New Delhi, Oxford University Press.

Gadgil, M V, 1992, 'Future of Institutional Credit in India: Likely Impact of Narasimhan and Khusro Committee Reports', *Indian Journal of Agricultural Economics*, pp. 47, 2, 255–65.

Gaiha, R, 1988, 'On Measuring the Risk of Rural Poverty in India', in T N Srinivasan and P K Bardhan (eds.), pp. 219–61.

George, S, Rajaratnam, A, and Miller, B, 1992, 'Female Infanticide in Rural South India', *Economic and Political Weekly*, 27/2 (30 May), pp. 2253–6.

Ghai, Y, Luckham, R, and Snyder, F (eds.), 1987, *The Political Economy of Law: A Third World Reader*, Delhi, Oxford University Press.

Ghodake, R D, and Ryan, J G, 1981, 'Human Labour Availability and Employment in Semi-Arid Tropical India', *Indian Journal of Agricultural Economics*, 36/4.

Gibbs, C, 1986, 'Characteristics of Household Expenditure in a Tamil Village in South India', B.A. thesis, Newnham College, Cambridge University.

Gillespie, S, 1989, 'Social and Economic Aspects of Malnutrition and Health Among South Indian Tribal Groups', Ph.D. thesis, University of London.

Gillespie, S, and Haddad, L, 2001, *Attacking the Double Burden of Malnutrition in Asia*, Washington DC, IFPRI.

—— and McNeill, G, 1992, *Food, Health and Survival in India and Developing Countries*, Delhi, Oxford University Press.

Glewwe, P, and Jacoby, 1992, 'Estimating the Determinants of Cognitive Achievement in Low-Income Countries', World Bank LSMS #91.

—— and Kanaan, O, 1989, 'Targeting Assistance to the Poor: A Multivariate Approach Using Household Survey Data', *Development Economics Research Centre, Discussion Paper 94*, Warwick University.

Godbole, M, 1997, 'Corruption, Political Interference and the Civil Service', in Guhan and Paul (eds.), pp. 60–87.

Gold, L, Harriss-White, B, and Janakarajan, S, 1996, 'No End to the Betrayal? Primary Education in Social Context: Evidence from Tamil Nadu', paper presented at the dissemination workshop for the ODA funded project between Queen Elizabeth House, Oxford and Madras Institute of Development Studies, Madras, 27 March.

Goswami, O, Sanyal, A, and Garg, I N, 1991, 'Taxes, Corruption and Bribes: A Model of Indian Public Finance', in Roemer and Jones (eds.), pp. 201–13.

Government of India 1964, *Report of the Committee on the Prevention of Corruption* (Santhanam Report), Ministry of Home Affairs, New Delhi.

Government of India 1982, *All-India Debt and Investment Survey*, New Delhi.

Government of India 1983, *Jha Commission Report*, New Delhi (RR).

Government of India 1985a, *Aspects of the Black Economy in India*, New Delhi.

Government of India 1985b, *Minor Irrigation Census*, New Delhi.

Government of India 1989, *Report of the Working Group on the Major and Medium Irrigation Programme for the Eighth Plan*, New Delhi.

Government of India 1991, *Indian Agriculture in Brief 1990–1*, New Delhi.

Government of India 1992a, 'Eighth Five Year Plan, 1992–7', Planning Commission, New Delhi.

Government of India 1992b, *Report of the Committee on Pricing of Irrigation Water*, Union Planning Commission, New Delhi.

Government of India 1993, *Report of the Expert Group on Estimation of Proportion and Number of Poor*, New Delhi.

Government of India 1996, *Sample Registration System Statistical Report*, Registrar General, New Delhi.

Government of India 1999a, *India 1999, A Reference Annual*, Research, Reference and Training Division, New Delhi.

Government of India 1999b, *Economic Survey*, Ministry of Finance, New Delhi.

Government of Tamil Nadu 1982, *Arni Plan*, Dept. of Town Planning, Madras.

Government of Tamil Nadu 1982–3 to 1990–1, *Tamil Nadu Statistical Handbook*, Chennai.

Government of Tamil Nadu 1994a, *Materials for Collectors' Conference, 1994*, Social Welfare and Nutritious Meal Programme Department, Chennai.

Government of Tamil Nadu 1994b, *Tamil Nadu – an Economic Appraisal 1993–4*, Evaluation and Applied Research Dept, Madras.

Government of Tamil Nadu 1994 to 1997, *Policy Notes on Agriculture, 1994–5 to 1997–8*, Madras, Department of Agriculture.

Government of Tamil Nadu 1996, *Budget Speech of the Finance Minister*, Chennai.

Government of Tamil Nadu 1997a, *Ninth Five Year Plan, 1997–2002: An Outline*, State Planning Commission, Chennai.

Government of Tamil Nadu 1997b, *Tamil Nadu – An Economic Appraisal*, Chennai.

Government of Tamil Nadu 2001a, 'Prohibition and Excise: State Excise Policy Note 2000–1', *http://www.tn.gov.in*.

Government of Tamil Nadu, 2001b, website, *www.tn.gov.in/economy/eco-may.htm*.

Government of Tamil Nadu 2001c, 'School Education Policy Statement, 2000–1', *www.tn.gov.in/policy/*.

Government of Tamil Nadu (various years), *Season and Crop Report*, Chennai.

Greer, J, and Thorbecke, E, 1986, 'A Methodology for Measuring Food Poverty Applied to Kenya', *Journal of Development Economics*, 24, pp. 59–74.

Grindle, M, and Thomas, J W, 1991, *Public Choices and Policy Change: The Political Economy of Reform in Developing Countries*, Baltimore, Johns Hopkins.

Guhan, S, 1992, 'Social Security in India: Looking one Step Ahead', in Harriss, Guhan and Cassen (eds.), *Poverty in India*.

—— 1994, 'Social Security Options for Developing Countries', *International Labour Review*, 133/1, pp. 35–53.

—— 1996, 'Social Assistance in the Three Villages', paper to the workshop on 'Adjustment and Development', Madras Institute of Development Studies, Chennai.

—— and Bharathan, K, 1984, 'Dusi: A Resurvey', *MIDS Working Paper 52*, Madras Institute of Development Studies, Madras.

—— and Harriss, B, 1992, 'Introduction' in Harriss, Guhan and Cassen, *Poverty in India*.

—— and Mencher, J, 1982, 'Iruvelipattu Revisited', *MIDS Working Paper 42*, Madras Institute of Development Studies, Madras.

—— 1983, 'Iruvelipattu Revisited', *Economic and Political Weekly*, 18/23, p. 1013; 18/24, pp. 1063–74.

—— and Paul, S (eds.), 1997, *Corruption in India: an Agenda for Action*, New Delhi, Vision.

Gulati, A, and Bhide, S, 1995, 'What do the Reformers have for Agriculture', *Economic and Political Weekly* (6 May).

Gurumurthy, 1997, *Dinamani*.

Gutkind, P, and Wallerstein, I (eds.), 1979, *The Political Economy of Contemporary Africa*, Beverley Hills, Sage.

Haggett, P, 1965, *Locational Analysis in Human Geography*, London, Arnold.

Hammerman, S, and Maikowski, S (eds.), 1981, *The Economics of Disability: International Perspectives*, Rehabilitation International, New York, UN.

Harriss, B, 1979, *Paddy and Rice Marketing in Northern Tamil Nadu*, Madras, Sangam for MIDS, pp. 291–237.

—— 1981a, 'Agricultural Mercantile Politics and Policy: a Case Study from Tamil Nadu', *Economic and Political Weekly*, 16/10–12, pp. 441–58.

Harriss, B, 1981b, *Coarse Grains, Coarse Interventions*, UNRISD, Geneva.

—— 1981c, *Transitional Trade and Rural Development*, New Delhi, Vikas.

—— 1984, *State and Market*, New Delhi, Concept.

—— 1987a, 'Regional Growth Linkages from Agriculture and Resource Flows in the Non-Farm Economy', *Economic and Political Weekly*, 22, pp. 31–46.

—— 1987b, 'Regional Growth Linkages from Agriculture: A Critique', *Journal of Development Studies*, 23/2, pp. 266–89.

—— 1987c, 'Regional Growth Linkages from Agriculture: A Critique', *Journal of Development Studies*, 23/3, pp. 114–28.

—— 1991a, *Child Nutrition and Poverty in Southern India*, Concept, New Delhi.

—— 1991b, 'The Intra-family Distribution of Hunger in South Asia', in Drèze and Sen (eds.), pp. 351–424.

—— 1991c, *Poverty and Child Malnutrition in South India*, New Delhi, Sage.

—— 1991d, 'The Arni Studies', in Hazell and Ramasamy (eds.), *The Green Revolution Reconsidered*.

—— 1992, 'Rural Poverty in India: Micro-level Evidence' in B Harriss, S Guhan and R H Cassen (eds.), *Poverty in India: Research and Policy*, New Delhi, Oxford University Press.

—— 1993, *Differential Female Mortality and Health Care in South Asia*, Monograph no. 1, Centre for the Study of Relief Administration, New Delhi.

—— and Harriss, J, 1984, 'Generative or Parasitic Urbanism?', in J Harriss and M Moore (eds.), *Development and the Rural Urban Divide*, London, Cass.

—— *et al.*, 1984, *Exchange Relations and Poverty in Dryland Agriculture*, New Delhi, Concept.

——, Guhan, S, and Cassen, R H (eds.), 1992, *Poverty in India: Research and Policy*, New Delhi, Oxford University Press.

Harriss, J C, 1977, 'The Limitations of HYV Technology in North Arcot District: the View from a Village', in Farmer (ed.), pp. 124–42.

—— 1982, *Capitalism and Peasant Farming: Agrarian Structure and Ideology in Northern Tamil Nadu*, New Delhi, Oxford University Press.

—— 1991a, 'The Green Revolution in North Arcot: Economic Trends, Household Mobility and the Politics of an "Awkward Class"', chapter 4 in P Hazell and C Ramasamy (eds.), *The Green Revolution Reconsidered*, London, John Hopkins University Press.

—— 1991b, 'Population, Employment and Wages: A Comparative Study of North Arcot Villages, 1973–1983', chapter 6 in P Hazell and C Ramasamy (eds.), *The Green Revolution Reconsidered*, London and Baltimore, John Hopkins University Press.

—— 1991c, 'Employment, Economic Mobility and the Politics of an Awkward Class', in P Hazell and C Ramasamy (eds.),

—— 1992, 'Does the Depressor Still Work?: Agrarian Structure and Development in India – A Review of Evidence and Argument', *Journal of Peasant Studies*, 19/2.

Harriss, J, and Chambers, R, 1977, 'Comparing Twelve South Indian Villages: In Search of Practical Theory', in Farmer (ed.), pp. 301–22.

——, Desai, M, Sen, P, and Harriss, B, 1992, *Economic Reforms in India: Potential Impact on Poverty Reduction and Implications for Social Policy*, DESTIN, London School of Economics, for ODA, London.

—— and B Harriss-White, 2004, 'The North Arcot Papers on Agrarian Change', chapter 1 in B Harriss-White and J Harriss, 2004, eds, *Green Revolution and After: Studies in the Political Economy of Rural Development in South India*, London, Anthem Press.

Harriss-White, B, 1994, 'Notes on the Classification of Village Households', Adjustment and Development Working Paper #7, QEH, Oxford.

—— 1996a, 'Liberalisation and Corruption: Resolving the Paradox (A Discussion based on South Indian Material)', in B Harriss-White and G White (eds.)

—— 1996b, 'The Political Economy of Disability and Development with Special Reference to India', *UNRISD Discussion Paper no. 73*, UNRISD, Geneva.

—— 1998a, 'On Power in Peasant Markets', in B Harriss-White (ed.), pp. 261–86.

—— (ed.), 1998b, *Agricultural Markets from Theory to Practice: Field Experience in Developing Countries*, London, Macmillan.

—— 1999a, 'Gender Cleansing: The Paradox of Development and Deteriorating Female Life Chances in Tamil Nadu', in Sunder Rajan (ed.), pp. 124–53.

—— 1999b, 'Onto a Loser: Disability in India', in B Harriss-White and Subramanian (eds.).

—— 2001, 'A Note on Male Governance of South Indian Family Businesses and its Implications for Women', *Indian Journal of Gender Studies*, 8/1, pp. 89–96.

—— 2003, *India Working: Essays on Economy and Society*, Cambridge, Cambridge University Press.

—-- and Gooptu, N, 2000, 'Mapping India's World of Unorganised Labour', in Panitch and Leys (eds.), pp. 89–118.

—— and Hoffenberg, R (eds.), 1994, *Food: Multidisciplinary Perspectives*, Oxford, Blackwells.

—— and Janakarajan, S, 1996a, 'Agricultural Yields and Rural Development in North Arcot Villages, 1973–4 to 1993–4', paper to the workshop on Adjustment and Development, MIDS, Madras.

—— 1996b, 'Rural Class and the Microeconomics of the Marketed Surplus', paper to the workshop on Adjustment and Development: Agrarian Change, Markets and Social Welfare in South India 1973–93, Madras Institute of Development Studies (and Queen Elizabeth House, Oxford).

—— 1997, 'From Green Revolution to Rural Industrial Revolution', *Economic and Political Weekly*, 32, p. 25.

—— and Saigal, H, 1996a, 'Agricultural Policy for the Reform Period and the Supply Response from Tamil Nadu', paper to the workshop on Adjustment and Development, Madras IDS, Madras.

—— 1996b, 'Agricultural Prices, Infrastructure and Performance in Tamil Nadu and North Arcot District, 1973–93', paper to the Workshop on Adjustment and Development: Agrarian Change, Markets and Social Welfare in South India 1973–93, Madras Institute of Development Studies (and Queen Elizabeth House, Oxford).

Harriss-White, B, and Subramanian, S (eds.), 1999, *Illfare in India: Essays on India's Social Sector in Honour of S. Guhan*, New Delhi, Sage.

—— and White, G (eds.), 1996, *Liberalisation and the New Corruption*, special issue, 27/2 of *Institute of Development Studies (IDS) Bulletin*.

——, Crowe, T, and Janakarajan, S, 1996, 'Rural Class and the Micro-economics of the Marketed Surplus', paper to the workshop on Adjustment and Development: Agrarian Change, Markets and Social Welfare in South India 1973–93, Madras Institute of Development Studies (and Queen Elizabeth House, Oxford).

——, Gold, L, and Janakarajan, S, 1996, 'No End to the Betrayal? Primary Education in Social Context: Evidence from Tamil Nadu', paper to the workshop on Adjustment and Development: Agrarian Change, Markets and Social Welfare in South India 1973–93, Madras Institute of Development Studies (and Queen Elizabeth House, Oxford).

——, Janakarajan, S, and Barbour, P, 1996, 'Rural Credit and Collateral Questions', paper to the workshop on Adjustment and Development: Agrarian Change, Markets and Social Welfare in South India 1973–93, Madras Institute of Development Studies (and Queen Elizabeth House, Oxford).

——, Janakarajan, S, and Legassick, L, 1996, 'Plus ça change, plus c'est la même chose: The More Things Change the More They Don't: Rural Gender Relations', paper to the Workshop on Adjustment and Development: Agrarian Change, Markets and Social Welfare in S. India 1973–93, Madras Institute of Development Studies (and Queen Elizabeth House, Oxford).

Hart, G, 1996, 'Regional Growth Linkages in the Era of Liberalisation: a Critique of the New Agrarian Optimism', unpublished paper, Berkeley, University of California.

Hazell, P B R, and Ramasamy, C, 1991 (eds.), *The Green Revolution Reconsidered: The Impact of High-Yielding Rice Varieties in South India*, Baltimore, Johns Hopkins University Press.

—— and Roell, A, 1983, 'The Rural Growth Linkages: Household Expenditure Patterns in Malaysia', *Research Report 41*, IFPRI, Washington DC.

Hazell, P, Ramasamy, C, Rajagopalam, V, Aiyasamy, P, and Bliven, N, 1991a, 'Economic Changes among Village Households', chapter 3 in P Hazell and C Ramasamy (eds.), *The Green Revolution Reconsidered*, London, John Hopkins University Press.

Hazell, P B R, Ramasamy, C, Rajagopalam, V, and Bliven, N, 1991b, 'A Social Accounting Matrix of the Regional Economy, 1982–3', chapter 7 in P Hazell and C Ramasamy (eds.), pp. 127–52.

Hazell *et al.*, 1991c, 'An Analysis of the Indirect Effects of Agrarian Change on the Region Economy', chapter 8 in P Hazell and C Ramasamy (eds.), *The Green Revolution Reconsidered*.

—— 1991d, 'Conclusions and Policy Implications', chapter 11 in P Hazell and C Ramasamy (eds.), *The Green Revolution Reconsidered*.

Helander, E, 1993, *Prejudice and Dignity: An Introduction to Community Based Rehabilitation*, New York, United Nations Development Programme.

Heyer, J, 1992, 'The Role of Dowries and Daughters' Marriages in the Accumulation and

Distribution of Capital in a South Indian Community', *Journal of International Development*, 4/4, pp. 419–36.

Hirschman, A O, 1970, *Exit Voice and Loyalty: Responses to Decline in Firms, Organisations and States*, Cambridge, Harvard University Press.

Hoff, K, and Stiglitz, J, 1990, 'Introduction: Imperfect Information and Rural Credit Markets: Puzzles and Policy Perspectives', *The World Bank Economic Review*, 4/3, pp. 235–50.

—— Braverman, A, and Stiglitz, J (eds.), 1993, *The Economics of Rural Organisation: Theory, Practice and Policy*, Oxford, Oxford University Press.

Hyat, T, 2001, 'Essays on Poverty and Consumption Mobility: A Micro-econometric Approach', D.Phil. thesis, Oxford University.

Indian Bank 1992, *Annual Credit Plan 1992–93 Tiruvannamalai–Sambuvarayar District*, Tiruvannamalai.

Institute of Social Sciences (ISS), 1988, *The Situation of the Handicapped in India with Special Reference to Andhra Pradesh, Bihar, Maharashtra, Tamil Nadu and West Bengal*, New Delhi, Manuscript Report no. 1 – ISS–MR/1–1988, ISS.

International Labour Office 1999, *Decent Work*, Geneva, ILO.

International Rice Research Institute (IRRI), 1985, *Women in Rice Farming*, Manila, Gaver Pulishing Co./IRRI.

Ishiguru, M, and Akiyama, T, 1995, 'Energy Demand in Five Major Asian Developing Countries', *World Bank Discussion Paper No. 277*, Washington DC.

Jackson, C, and Palmer-Jones, R, 1998, 'Work Intensity, Gender and Wellbeing', *UNRISD Discussion Paper 96*, Geneva, United Nation Research Institute for Social Development.

Jackson, H, 1988, 'Approaches to Rehabilitation of People with Disabilities: A Review', *Journal of Social Development in Africa*, 3/1, pp. 39–53.

Jagganathan, V, 1987, *Informal Markets in Developing Countries*, Delhi, Oxford University Press.

Jamison and Lockheed, 1987, 'Participation in Schooling: Determinants and Learning Outcomes in Nepal', *Economic Development and Cultural Change*.

Janakarajan, S, 1986, 'Aspects of Market Interrelationships in a Changing Agrarian Economy: A Case Study from Tamil Nadu', Ph.D. thesis, University of Madras.

—— 1992, 'Interlinked Transactions and the Market for Water in the Agrarian Economy of a Village in Tamil Nadu', in Subramanian (ed.).

—— 1993a, 'In Search of Tanks: Some Hidden Facts', *Economic and Political Weekly*, Vol. 28, No. 26, 26 June.

—— 1993b, 'Economic and Social Implications of Groundwater Irrigation: Some Evidence from South India', *Indian Journal of Agricultural Economics*, 48/1 (Jan–March).

—— 1993c, 'Triadic Exchange Relationships: An Illustration from South India', *Bulletin, Institute of Development Studies*, 24.3, pp. 75–82.

—— 1996a, 'Complexities of Agrarian Markets and Agrarian Relations: A Study of Villages in Northern Tamil Nadu', paper presented at the workshop for the ODA funded project between Queen Elizabeth House, Oxford and Madras Institute of Development Studies, Madras, 27 March.

Janakarajan, S, 1996b, 'Consequences of Aquifer Over-Exploitation: The Case of Prosperity and Deprivation', paper prepared for the Silver Jubilee Conference of the MIDS, 4–7 April, Madras.

—— 1996c, 'Ecological Crisis and Agrarian Distress? The Tale of Irrigation Development in Northern Tamil Nadu', paper presented in a workshop on 'Adjustment and Development: Agrarian Change, Markets and Social Welfare in South India, 1973–1993', jointly organized by QEH and MIDS, 27–29 March, Chennai.

—— 1997a, 'Consequences of Aquifer Over-Exploitation: Prosperity and Deprivation', *Review of Development and Change*, 2/3 (Jan–June).

—— 1997b, 'Conflicts Over the Invisible Resource: Is There a Way Out?', in Moench, M. and Ajaya, D., (eds.), *Rethinking the Mosaic: Investigations into Local Water Management*, First Report of Collaborative Research funded by International Development Research Centre, Canada (mimeo).

—— 1997c, 'Village Resurveys: Issues and Results', in Breman *et al.* (eds.), pp. 397–428.

—— 1998, 'Consequences of Aquifer Over-exploitation: the Case of Prosperity and Deprivation', *Review of Development and Change*.

—— forthcoming, 'Groundwater Drawdown: Socio-economic and Policy Implication' (draft), Madras Institute of Development Studies, Chennai.

——, and Vaidyanathan, A, 1996, 'Aspects of Groundwater Irrigation in the Vaigai Basin: A Village Level Analysis', report submitted to the Planning Commission, Government of India.

—— 1997, *Conditions and Characteristics of Groundwater Irrigation: A Study of Vaigai Basin in Tamil Nadu*, a study sponsored by the Union Planning Commission (mimeo).

Jayaraj, D, 1992, 'Determinants of Rural Non-Agricultural Employment: A Village-Level Analysis of the Data for Tamil Nadu', in S Subramanian (ed.), *Themes in Development Economics: Essays in Honour of Malcolm Adieseshiah*, Delhi, Oxford University Press.

—— 1994, 'Determinants of Rural Non-Agricultural Employment', in P Visaria and R Basant (eds.), *Non-Agricultural Employment in India: Trends and Prospects*, New Delhi, Sage Publications.

—— 1996a, 'The Evolution of the Non-Farm Economy in northern Tamil Nadu: the Impact of Sociological Factors', paper to the workshop on Adjustment and Development: Agrarian Change, Markets and Social Welfare in South India 1973–93, Madras Institute of Development Studies (and Queen Elizabeth House, Oxford).

—— 1996b, 'Structural Transformation of the Rural Workforce in Tamil Nadu: An Analysis of the Impact of Sociological Factors', paper prepared for the dissemination workshop Adjustment and Development: Agrarian Change, Markets and Social Welfare in South India 1973–1993, 27–29 March, organized by QEH and MIDS, Madras.

Jayaranjan, J, 1993, 'A Village Economy in Transition: A Study of the Process of Change in Iluppakkorai, Tamil Nadu, 1960–1985', Ph.D. thesis, University of Madras.

Jenkins, R, 1999, *Democratic Politics and Economic Reform in India*, Cambridge, Cambridge University Press.

Jhabvala, R, and Subrahmanya, R K A (eds.) 2000, *The Unorganized Sector: Work Security and Social Protection*, New Delhi, Sage.

Jodha, N, 1971, 'Land-based Credit Policies and Investment Prospects for Small Farmers', *Economic and Political Weekly*, 6/4, pp. A143–A148.

Jodhka, S, 1998, 'From 'Book View' to 'Field View': Social Anthropological Constructions of the Indian Village', *Oxford Development Studies*, 26/3, pp. 311–32.

Johl, S S, 1994, 'Agricultural Technology Policy in India: the Challenges Ahead', in Bhalla (ed.), pp. 179–241.

—— 1995a, 'Agriculture Sector and New Economic Policy', *Indian Journal of Agricultural Economics*, 50/3, pp. 473–87.

—— 1995b, 'Presidential Address: India's Economic Reforms and Agricultural Development', *Indian Journal of Agricultural Economics*.

Johnson, S, 1999, 'The Local Level Financial Market', Finance and Development Research Programme, Centre for Development Studies, Bath University.

Kapadia, K, 1993, 'Mutuality and Competition: Female Landless Labour and Wage Rates in Tamil Nadu', *Journal of Peasant Studies*, 20/2, pp. 296–316.

Kapadia, 1997

Kennedy, L, 1999, 'Co-operating for Survival: Tannery Pollution and Joint Action in the Palar Valley (India)', *World Development*, 27/9, pp. 1673–92.

—— 1999, 'Competing for Survival: Tannery Pollution and Joint Action in the Palar Valley (India)', *World Development*, 27/9, pp. 1673–92.

Khan, M, and Jomo, K S, 2000, *Rents, Rent Seeking and Economic Development*, Cambridge, Cambridge University Press.

Khusro, A M, 1993, *Review of the Agricultural Credit System in India: A Report of the Agricultural Credit Review Committee*, Bombay, Reserve Bank of India.

Kingdon, G, 1994, 'An Economic Evaluation of School Management Types', D.Phil. thesis, Oxford University.

—— 1996, 'Private Schooling in UP; Its Size, Nature and Equity Effects', *Economic and Political Weekly*.

Kingdon and Muzammil, 2003, *The Political Economy of Education in India*, Oxford, Oxford University Press.

Kishor, S, 1993, '"May God Give Sons to All": Gender and Child Mortality in India', *American Sociological Review*, 58/2, pp. 247–65.

Kitching, G, 1982, *Development and Under Development in Historical Perspective*, London, Methuen.

Kjellborg, and Banik, D, 2000, 'The Paradox of Pollution Control: Regulation and Administration in a South Indian State', *Research Report No. 2*, Dept of Political Science, University of Oslo.

Knight, J, and Sabot, 1990, 'Education, Productivity and Inequality'.

Kohavi, R, and John, G H, 1995, 'Automatic Parameter Selection by Minimizing Estimated Error', in A Prieditis and S Russell (eds.), *Machine Learning: Proceedings of the Twelfth International Conference*, San Francisco, CA, Morgan Kaufmann Publishers.

Kohli, A, 1987, *The State and Poverty in India: The Politics of Reform*, Cambridge, Cambridge University Press.

Kohli, R, 1999, 'Rural Bank Branches and Financial Reform', *Economic and Political Weekly* (16 Jan), pp. 169–82.

Kotaiah, P, 1998, 'Policy on Institutional Credit to Generate Employment and Marketing Skills – Indian Experience', Centre for Integrated Rural Development for Asia and the Pacific, Dhaka.

Kothari, M, and Kothari, A, 1993, 'Structural Adjustment versus Environment', *Economic and Political Weekly*, 28/11, pp. 473–7.

Krishnamurthy, J, 1972, 'Working Force in 1971 Census: Some Exercises on Provisional Results', *Economic and Political Weekly*, 7/3 (15 January).

—— 1973, 'Working Force in 1971 Census: Unilluminating Final Results', *Economic and Political Weekly*, 8/31, 32 and 33 (29 August).

Krishnaswami, 1947, *Rural Problems in Madras: Monograph*, Madras, Government Press.

Krishnaswamy, S, 1990, 'Role of Development in the Aid of the Handicapped', *Indian Journal of Social Work* 11/1, pp. 165–75.

Krueger, A, 1974, 'The Political Economy of a Rent Seeking Society', *American Economic Review*, 64.

Kumar, A K S, and Mukherjee, V N, 1993, 'Health as Development: Implications for Research, Policy and Action', *Economic and Political Weekly*, 28/16, pp. 769–74.

Kumar, K, 1993, 'Market Economy and Mass Literacy: Revisiting Innis's Economics of Communication', *Economic and Political Weekly* (11 December), pp. 2727–34.

Kumar, S, 1999, 'New Fertiliser Policy, A Practical Approach', *Economic and Political Weekly*, 34/1–2, pp. 57–63.

Kundu, A, 1991, 'Micro-Environment in Urban Planning: Access of Poor to Water Supply and Sanitation', *Economic and Political Weekly*, pp. 2167–71.

Kurien, C T, 1989, *Dynamics of Rural Transformation: A Study of Tamil Nadu 1950–1980*, Madras, Orient Longman.

Kuznets, S, 1966, *Modern Economic Growth: Rate, Structure and Spread*, Newhaven (Conn), Yale University Press.

Kydd, J, 1982, 'Improving the Classification of Rural Populations for Planning Purposes: A Report on a Cluster Analysis of an Agro-economic Sample Survey in the Area of the Phalomne Rural Development Project, Malawi', Dept of Economics, Chancellor College, Zomba, Malawi.

Kynch, J, and Sen, A K, 1983, 'Indian Women: Well-Being and Survival', *Cambridge Journal of Economics*, 7, pp. 363–80.

Lall, S, 2000, 'Skills, Competitiveness and Policy in Developing Countries', QEH Working Paper Series 46, *www.qeh.ox.ac.uk*.

Landy, F, 1997, 'Fertilisers, Structural Adjustment and Food Policy', *Pondy Papers in Social Sciences: 25*, French Institute, Pondicherry.

Lang, R, 2000, 'Perceiving Disability and Chastising Community Based Rehabilitation: A Critical Examination with Case Studies from South India', Ph.D. thesis, University of East Anglia.

Lanjouw, P, and Stern, N (eds.), 1998, *Economic Development in Palanpur over Five Decades*, Oxford, Clarendon Press.

Leach, M, and Mearns, R (eds.), 1996, *The Lie of the Land: Challenging Received Wisdom on the African Environment*, Oxford, James Currey.

Leftwich, A, 2000, *States of Development: On the Primacy of Politics in Development*, Cambridge, Polity Press.

Legassick, L, 1995, 'Rural Labour Market Heterogeneity and Female Subordination in Northern Tamil Nadu', M.Sc. thesis, Oxford University.

Leys, C, 1965, 'What is the Problem about Corruption?', *Journal of Modern African Studies*, 3/2, pp. 215–30.

—— 1996, *The Rise and Fall of Development Theory*, Oxford, James Currey.

Lindberg, S, 1996, 'While the Wells Went Dry – Tragedy of Collective Action among Farmers in South India', chapter in the anthology *From Wild Pigs to Foreign Trees* (mimeo).

Lipton, M, 1994, 'Food Production and Poverty', in B Harriss-White and R Hoffenberg, pp. 130–56.

—— and Ravallion, M, 1995, 'Poverty and Policy', in J Behrman and T N Srinivasan (eds.), chapter 41.

Lockheed, M E, and Verspoor, 1991, *Improving Education in Developing Countries*, Washington DC, IBRD.

Lockwood, M, 1989, 'The Economics of Fertility and the Infertility of Economics: Theory and Demographic Reality in Africa', *Development Studies Working Papers no. 12*, Luca D'Angliano Centre, Turin, and Queen Elizabeth House, Oxford.

Louat, F, Grosh, M E, and Gaag, J van der, 1993, 'Welfare Implications of Female Headship in Jamaican Households', *World Bank, LSMS Working Paper, no. 96*, Washington DC, World Bank.

Maddumma Bandara, C M, 1977, 'Hydrological Consequences of Agrarian Change', in Farmer (ed.), pp. 323–39.

Madras Institute of Development Studies (MIDS) 1988, *The Tamil Nadu Economy*, Madras.

Mahendradev, S, 1989, 'Some Aspects of Non-Agricultural Employment in Rural India', *Economic and Political Weekly*, 25/28 (14 July).

Majid, N, 1994, 'Contractual Arrangements in Pakistani Agriculture: A Study of Share Tenancy in Sindh', D.Phil. thesis, Oxford University.

Majumdar, M, 1999, 'Exclusion in Education: Indian States in Comparative Perspective', in B Harriss-White and Subramanian (eds.), pp. 265–302.

Malik, R P S, 1995, 'Electricity Prices and Sustainable Use of Groundwater: Evaluation of Some Alternatives for North-West Indian Agriculture', in M Moench (ed.), *Electricity Prices: A Tool for Groundwater Management in India?*, VIKSAT and Natural Heritage Institute, Ahmedabad.

Mallory, B L, 1993, 'Changing Beliefs About Disability in Developing Countries: Historical Factors and Sociocultural Variables', in D E Woods (ed.), *Traditional and Changing Views of Disability in Developing Societies: Causes, Consequences, Cautions*, IEEIR Monograph 53, University of New Hampshire, pp. 1–24.

Maxwell, S, 1999, 'The Meaning and Measurement of Poverty', *ODI Poverty Briefing*

Series, Overseas Development Institute, London. Also available at http://www.oneworld.org/odi/briefing/pov3.html.

McElroy, M B, 1990, 'The Empirical Content of Nash-Bargained Household Behaviour', *Journal of Human Resources*, 25/4, pp. 559–83.

McGee, T G, 1971, rpt. 1975, *The Urbanization Process in the Third World: Explorations in Search of a Theory*, London, G Bell & Sons Ltd.

McGillivray, M, Pyatt, G, and White, H, 1995, 'What Can We Tell from Social Indicators That GDP Doesn't Already Tell Us?', paper to ESRC Development Economics Research Group Annual Conference on Social Development, Leicester University, March.

Mehta, M, and Mehta, D, 1991, 'Housing Finance System and Urban Poor', *Economic and Political Weekly*, pp. 1107–14.

Mellor, J W, 1976, *The New Economics of Growth: A Strategy for India and the Developing World*, a Twentieth Century Fund Study, Ithaca and London, Cornell University Press.

Mencher, J P, 1985, 'Landless Women Agricultural Labourers in India: Some Observations from Tamil Nadu, Kerala and West Bengal', in *IRRI, Women in Rice Farming*, International Rice Research Institute, Gower Publishing Co. Ltd.

Mencher, J, and Saradamoni, K, 1982, 'Muddy Feet, Dirty Hands: Rice Production and Female Agricultural Labour', *Economic and Political Weekly*, Review of Agriculture, 17/52, pp. 149–67.

Mendelssohn, O, 1993, 'The Transformation of Power in Rural India', *Modern Asian Studies*, 27/4, pp. 805–42.

Michie, D, 1984, *Quality Control of Induced Rule Based Programs: The Fifth Generation*, The GS Institute, London.

—— 1988, 'Personal Models of Rationality', *Journal of Statistical Planning and Inference*, 25, pp. 381–99.

MIDS 1993, *Tank Irrigation in Tamil Nadu: Some Macro and Micro Perspectives*, Madras.

Miles, M, 1989, 'Disability and Dependency', in L Barton (ed.), *Rehabilitation Development in South West Asia: Conflicts and Potential*, London, The Falmer Press, pp. 110–26.

Miller, B, 1981, *The Endangered Sex: Neglect of Female Children in Rural North India*, Ithaca, Cornell University Press.

Mishra, S, and Chand, R, 1995, 'Public and Private Capital Formation in Indian Agriculture: Comments on Complementarity Hypothesis and Others', *Economic and Political Weekly*, 30/25 (24 July).

Moench, M, 1992, 'Chasing the Water Table: Equity and Sustainability in Groundwater Management', *Economic and Political Weekly*, 27 (December).

—— 1995a, *Groundwater Policy: Issues and Alternatives in South Asia*, Natural Heritage Institute, San Francisco, CA.

—— 1995b, *Electricity Prices: A Tool for Groundwater Management in India?*, VIKSAT and Natural Heritage Institute, Ahmedabad.

—— and Dixit, A (eds.), 1997, *Rethinking the Mosaic: Investigations into Local Water Management*, IDRC, Canada.

Mohan, D, 1988, 'Aids for the Disabled – A Technology Assessment', New Delhi, Centre for Biomedical Engineering, IIT.

Mohan, R, 1992, 'Housing and Urban Development: Policy Issues for the 1990s', *Economic and Political Weekly*, pp. 1990–96.

Mohanan, T C, 1990, 'Determinants of Fertiliser Use in Tamil Nadu: An Analysis', *Agricultural Situation in India* (Sept), pp. 387–94.

Mooij, J, 1999a, *Food Policy and the Indian State: The Public Distribution System in South India*, Delhi, Oxford University Press.

—— 1999b, 'Public Food Distribution and the Black Box of the State: Studying the Politics of Food Distribution', in B Harriss-White, (ed.).

—— 2000, *Food Policy and the Indian State*, Delhi, Oxford University Press.

Mosse, D, 1993, 'Authority, Gender and Knowledge: Theoretical Reflections on the Practice of Participatory Rural Appraisal', *ODI Network Paper 44*, London, ODI.

Mukhopadhyay, S, and Lim, C P (eds.), *Development and Diversification of Rural Industries in Asia*, Asian and Pacific Development Centre, Kuala Lumpur, Malaysia.

Muraleedharan, V R, 1993, 'When is Access to Health Care Equal? Some Public Policy Issues', *Economic and Political Weekly*, pp. 1291–6.

—— 1999, 'Technology and Costs of Medical Care: Some Emerging Issues' and 'Policy Imperatives' in Harriss-White and Subramanian (eds.), pp. 113–34.

Murthi, M, Guio, A C, and Drèze, J, 1995, 'Mortality, Fertility and Gender Bias in India', London School of Economics, Sticerd Discussion Paper Series Dep. 61.

Nagaraj, K, *et al.*, 1994, 'Borewell Failure in Drought-Prone Areas of Southern India: A Case Study', *Indian Journal of Agricultural Economics*, 49/1 (January–March).

——, Janakarajan, S, Jayaraj, D, and Harriss-White, B, 1996a, 'The Development of Silk Weaving in Arni Town and its Environs', paper to the workshop on Adjustment and Development: Agrarian Change, Markets and Social Welfare in South India 1973–93, Madras Institute of Development Studies (Queen Elizabeth House, Oxford).

—— 1996b, 'Socio-economic Factors Underlying the Growth of Silk Weaving in the Arni Region – A Preliminary Study', paper prepared for the dissemination workshop Adjustment and Development: Agrarian Change, Markets and Social Welfare in South India 1973–1993, 27–29 March, organized by QEH and MIDS, Madras.

Nanjamma, B, Chinnappa and Silva, W P T, 1977, 'Impact of High Yielding Varieties of Paddy on Employment and Income', in Farmer (ed.), *Green Revolution?*

Narasimhan, M, 1991, *Report of the Committee on the Financial System*, Bombay, Reserve Bank of India.

Narayan, S, 1990, 'Community Based Rehabilitation for the Mentally Handicapped – a Model', *Indian Journal of Social Work*, 51/1, pp. 157–64.

Narayanamurthy, A, 1997, 'Impact of Electricity Tariff Policies on the Use of Electricity and Groundwater: Arguments and Facts', *Artha Vijnana*, 39/3.

Narayanan, N, 1996a, 'Food and Nutrition in Tamil Nadu: Public Policy Options in a Federal State', paper for the South Asia Day South Asia Research Group, Hilary Term workshop, Queen Elizabeth House, Oxford University.

—— 1996b, 'The Social Safety Net in Tamil Nadu during the Structural Adjustment

Process', paper to the workshop on 'Adjustment and Development', Madras Institute of Development Studies, Madras.

Narsing Rao, M, 1990, 'Integrating the Disabled – a Reality?', *Indian Journal of Social Work*, 51/1, pp. 149–57.

National Council for Applied Economic Research (NCAER) 1978, *Interim Report: Fertiliser Demand Survey*, NCAER, New Delhi.

National Sample Survey Organization (NSSO), 1989, *Participation in Education: All-India and Major States, 1986–7*, New Delhi, Government of India.

National Sample Survey Organisation (NSS) 1983, *Sarvekshana*, New Delhi, 7/1–2.

Nelson, J M, 1990, *Economic Crisis and Policy Choice*, New Jersey, Princeton University Press.

Nillesen, P H L, 1999, 'Is Excess Female Mortality the Product of Poverty or of Wealth? An Examination of Rural Tamil Nadu, India', M.Sc. thesis, Queen Elizabeth House, University of Oxford.

Noorani, A G, 1997, 'Lok Pal and Lok Ayukt', in Guhan and Paul (eds.), pp. 189–217.

Norusis, M J, 1994, *SPSS Advanced Statistics*, 6.1 Manual SPSS Inc.

Oben, W K, 1998, 'Paradigms in the Analysis of Credit: Structures and Discourses in South Indian Banking', *Methodology Working Paper no. 5*, Graduate School, University of Bradford.

Olsen, W K, 1996, *Rural Indian Social Relations*, New Delhi, Oxford University Press.

—— 1998, 'Village Level Exchange: Lessons from South India', in B Harriss-White (ed.), pp. 40–86.

—— and Rani, U, 1997, '*Preparing for Rural Adjustment*', Research Monograph no. 2, Development Project and Planning Centre, University of Bradford.

Pai Panandiker, V A, 1998, 'The Political Economy of Centre-State Relations in India', in A Isher and I M D Little (eds.), *India's Economic Reforms and Development: Essays for Manmohan Singh*, New Delhi, Oxford University Press.

Palaskas, T, and Harriss-White, B, 1997, 'The Evolution of Wholesale Price Behaviour in Tamil Nadu 1973–93', *Journal of International Development*, 9/1, pp. 101–115.

Palmer-Jones, R, and Sen, K, 2001, 'What Luck has Got to Do with it. A Regional Analysis of Poverty and Agricultural Growth in Rural India', paper for the workshop on Social Relations and Well-being in South Asia, March, 2001, School of Development Studies, University of East Anglia.

Panini, M N, 1996, 'The Political Economy of Caste', in M N Srinivas *Caste: Its 20th century Avatar*.

Panitch, L, and Leys, C (eds.), 2000, *Working Class: Global Realities*, Socialist Register 2001, London, Merlin Press.

Parthasarathy, G, and Chinna, Rao B, 1986, 'Determinants of Fertiliser Use in Andhra Pradesh', *Agricultural Situation in India* (Oct), pp. 535–9.

Patnaik, P, 2001, 'Poverty of Theory', *Frontline* (30, March), 18/6.

Patnaik, U, 1976, 'Class Differentiation within the Peasantry; an approach to the Analysis of Indian Agriculture', *Economic and Political Weekly*, 11/39, Review of Agriculture, pp. A83–101.

—— 1987, *Peasant Class Differentiation; A Study in Method with Relation to Haryana*, Delhi, Oxford University Press.

Paul, S, 1989, 'A Model of Constructing the Poverty Line', *Journal of Development Economics*, 30, pp. 129–44.

Payne, P R, 1994, 'Not enough Food: Malnutrition and Famine', in B Harriss-White and R Hoffenberg (eds.), pp. 77–101.

Pedersen, J D, 2000, 'Explaining Economic Liberalisation in India: State-society Perspectives', *World Development*, 28/2, pp. 265–82.

Pinstrup-Andersen, P, and Jaramillo, M, 1991, 'The Impact of Technological Change in Rice Production on Food Consumption and Nutrition', in Hazell and Ramasamy (eds.), pp. 85–104.

Platt, B S, 1957, *Tables of Representative Values of Foods Commonly Used in Tropical Countries*, Medical Research Council Special Report Series no. 253, London, HMSO.

Prabhu, K S, 1994, 'Impact of Structural Adjustment on Social Sector Expenditure: Evidence from Indian States' (Dept of Economics, Univ. of Bombay), paper to seminar 'Structural Adjustment and Poverty in India: Policy and Research Issues', The Hague, Netherlands.

—— and Chatterjee, S, 1992, 'Social Sector Expenditures and Human Development: a Study of Indian States', *Devt.Res.Gp Study no. 6*, Bombay, Reserve Bank of India.

Prabhu, S, 1997, *Structural Adjustment and Human Development: a Study of Two Indian States*, UNDP/CDS, Thiruvananthapuram.

—— 1998, 'Social Sectors during Economic Reforms: the Indian Experience', Department of Economics, University of Mumbai.

Premi, M K, 2001, 'The Missing Girl Child', *Economic and Political Weekly* (26 May), pp. 1875–80.

Pryer, J, 1990, 'Socio-economic Aspects of Malnutrition and Ill-health in an Urban Slum in Khulna, Bangladesh', Ph.D. thesis, LSHTM, University of London.

Psacharopoulos, G, 1988, 'Education and Development – A Review', *World Bank Research Observer*, 3/1.

Puhazhendi, V, and Janakarajan, B, 1999, 'Rural Credit Delivery: Performance and Challenges before Banks', *Economic and Political Weekly*, (16 Jan), pp. 183–94.

Purkayastha, P, 1995, 'Infrastructure Sector and Withdrawal of the State', *Economic and Political Weekly*, (26 Aug), pp. 2114–18.

Pursell, G, and Gulati, A, 1993, 'Liberalising Indian Agriculture: An Agenda for Reform', *Working Paper 1172*, The World Bank, Washington DC.

—— 1995, 'Agriculture and the Economic Reforms', in Cassen and Joshi (eds.).

Quinlan, J R, 1993, *C4.5 Programs for Machine Learning*, San Mateo, CA, Morgan Kaufmann Publishers.

—— 1998, *See5: An Informal Tutorial*, notes accompanying the See5 software: http://www.rulequest.com/see5-win.html.

Rahman, M M, and Schendel, W van, 1997, 'Gender and the Inheritance of Land: Living Law in Bangladesh', in Breman *et al.* (eds.), pp. 237–76.

Rajan, S I, Mishra, U S, and Navaneetham, K, 1991, 'Decline in Sex Ratio: An Alternative Explanation?', *Economic and Political Weekly*, 26/51, pp. 2963–4.

Raju, S, 1990, 'Determinants of Fertiliser Use', *Agricultural Situation in India* (April).

Ram, N, 1995, 'An Independent Press and Anti-hunger Strategies: the Indian's Experience', in Drèze, Sen and Hussain (eds.), pp. 178–223.

—— 2001, 'Politics after Disqualification', *Frontline*, 18/10, (12 May)

Ram, R, and Harriss-White, B, 1995, 'Public Sector Employment and the Constitutional and Legal Vulnerability of the Physically Disabled in India', *Disability News* (June).

Ramachandran, V K, 1990, *Wage Labour and Unfreedom in Agriculture: An Indian Case Study*, Oxford University Press.

Ramakrishnan, V, 1999, 'Standing up for a Right', *Frontline*, 16/22.

Ramamurthy, P, 1993, 'Patriarchy and the Process of Agricultural Intensification in South India', in A Clark (ed.), *Explorations of South Asian Systems*, Delhi, Oxford University Press.

Ramasamy, C, Chandrasekharan, M, and Prabhakaran, R, 1986, 'Sustaining Rapid Growth in Fertiliser Use in Rice Regions', *Indian Journal of Agricultural Economics*, 41/4, pp. 503–10.

——, Hazell, P, and Aiyasamy, P K, 1991, 'North Arcot and the Green Revolution', in P Hazell and C Ramasamy (eds.), pp. 11–28.

Ramasundaram, S, 1993, *Demand for Family Planning – a Special Campaign in Tamil Nadu, India, to Study the Program Implications of Easterlin's Cost of Regulation Factor*, Collectorate, Vellore (and Dept of Health and Family Welfare, Madras).

Ramu, G N, 1988, *Family Structure and Fertility*, New Delhi and London, Sage Publishing.

Randhawa, N S, 1994, 'Liberalisation and Implications for Agricultural Policy', in Bhalla (ed.), pp. 353–78.

Rangarajan, C, 1982, 'Agricultural Growth and Industrial Performance', *Research Report 33*, IFPRI, Washington DC.

Rao, B S, 1985, 'Rural Industrialisation and Rural Non-Farm Employment in India', in S Mukhopadhyay and C P Lim (eds.)

Rao, C H H, 1994, 'Policy Issues Relating to Irrigation and Rural Credit in India', in Bhalla (ed.), pp. 287–352.

—— and Gulati, A, 1994, *Indian Agriculture: Emerging Perspectives and Policy Issues*, ICAR, New Delhi, and IFPRI, Washington DC.

Rao, D S K, 1993, 'Groundwater Over-Exploitation Through Bore Holes Technology', *Economic and Political Weekly*, 38, (25 December).

Rapley, J, 1996, *Understanding Development: Theory and Practice in the Third World*, Boulder/London, Lynne Reiner.

Rath, N, 1987, 'Agricultural Growth, Investment and Credit in India', S A Ramasamy, Mudalier Endowment Lecture, 14th August, University of Kerala, Trivandrum, India.

Ravallion, M, and Bidani, B, 1994, 'How Robust is a Poverty Profile?', *World Bank Economic Review*, 8, pp. 75–102.

—— and Sen, B, 1996, 'When Method Matters; Toward a Resolution of the Debate about Bangladesh's Poverty Measures', *Economic Development and Change*, 44, pp. 761–92.

—— and Subbarao, K, 1992, 'Adjustment and Human Development in India', Washington DC, IBRD (mimeo).

Razavi, S, 1992, 'Agrarian Change and Gender Power: A Comparative Study in Southeastern Iran', D.Phil. thesis, Oxford University.

—— 1998, *Gendered Poverty and Social Change: an Issue Paper Discussion*, Paper 94, Geneva, United Nations Research Institute for Social Development.

Reddy, 1992, *Journal of Peasant Studies*, p. 41.

Reddy, A K, and Sumithra, G D, 1997, 'Karnataka's Power Sector: Some Revelations', *Economic and Political Weekly* (22 March).

Rodges, G, 1989, ed., *Urban Poverty and the Labour Market: Access to Jobs and Incomes in Asian and Latin American Cities*, Geneva, International Labour Office.

Roemer, M, and Jones, C (eds.), 1991, *Markets in Developing Countries: Parallel, Fragmented and Black*, Harvard Institute for International Development/Institute for Contemporary Studies Press, San Francisco.

Rogaly, B, 1996, 'Rural Labour Arrangements in West Bengal, India', D.Phil. thesis, Oxford University.

——, Harriss-White, B, and Bose, S (eds.), 1999, *Sonar Bangla? Agricultural Growth and Agrarian Change in West Bengal and Bangladesh*, New Delhi, Sage.

Rosenhouse, P, 1990, 'Identifying the Poor; Is 'Headship' a Useful Concept?, *World Bank*, *LSMS* Working paper no. 58, Washington DC, World Bank.

Rosenzweig, M, 1984, 'Determinants of Wage Rates and Labour Supply Behaviour in the Rural Sector of a Developing Country', in Binswanger and Rosenzweig (eds.), pp. 211–41.

—— and Schultz, T P, 1982, 'Market Opportunities, Genetic Endowments and Intra-Family Resource Distribution: Child Survival in Rural India', *American Economic Review*, 72/4, pp. 803–15.

Roy, R, 1996, 'State Failure in India: Political-fiscal Implications of the Black Economy', *IDS Bulletin*, 27/2, pp. 22–30.

Rudra, A, 1982, *Indian Agricultural Economics: Myths and Realities*, New Delhi, Allied Publishers.

—— 1992, *Political Economy of Indian Agriculture*, Calcutta, K P Bakshi and Company.

Rudra, A, and Bardhan, P, 1983, *Agrarian Relations in West Bengal: Results of Two Surveys*, Bombay, Somaiya Publishers.

Ruggeri Laderchi, C, 1997, 'Poverty and its Many Dimensions: The Role of Income as an Indicator', *Oxford Development Studies*, 25/3, pp. 345–60.

—— 2000, 'The Monetary Approach to a Survey of Concepts and Methods', QEH Working Paper 58, QEHWPS58, www2.qeh.ox.ac.uk.

—— 2001, 'Participatory Methods in the Analysis of Poverty: A Critical Review', QEH Working Paper 62, QEHWPS62, www2.qeh.ox.ac.uk.

Russell, M, 2001, 'Disablement, Oppression and Political Economy', *Journal of Disability Policy Studies* (Fall).

Ryan, J G, and Ghodake, R D, 1984, 'Labour Market Behaviour in Rural Villages in South India: Effects of Season, Sex, and Socio-economic Status', in Binswanger and Rosenzweig (eds.).

Ryan, J G, and Wallace, T D, 1986, 'Determinants of Labour Market Wages, Participation and Supply in Rural South India', Economics Program, Patancheru, ICRISAT.

—–, Bidinger, P, Prahlad, R, and Pushpamma, 1984, *Determinants of Individual Diets in the Semi Arid Tropics*, Economics Programme, ICRISAT, Patencheru.

Sagar, V, 1995, 'Fertiliser Use Efficiency in Indian Agriculture', *Economic and Political Weekly*, 30/52, (30 Dec.), pp. A160–A180.

Saith, A, 1992, 'The Rural Non-Farm Economy: Processes and Policies', *ILO*, World Employment Programme, Geneva.

—— 2001, 'From Village Artisans to Industrial Clusters: Agendas and Policy Gaps in Indian Rural Industrialisation', *Journal of Agrarian Change*, 1/1, pp. 81–123.

Saith, R R, 1996, 'The Practical Identification of Poor Households: a Decision Tree Analysis of Village Census Data in Northern Tamil Nadu: Preliminary Results', *Adjustment and Development Project*, Working Paper 38, Queen Elizabeth House, Oxford.

—— 2001a, 'Capabilities: The Concept and its Operationalisation', QEHWPS66, *www2.qeh.ox.ac.uk*.

—— 2001b, 'Social Exclusion: the Concept and Application to Developing Countries', QEH Working Paper, QEHWPS72, www2.qeh.ox.ac.uk.

—–, Srinivasan, A, Michie, D, and Sargent, I L, 1998, 'Relationships between the Developmental Potential of Human In-vitro Fertilization Embryos and the Features Describing the Embryo, Oocyte and Follicle', *Human Reproduction Update*, 4/1.

Samuels, F, 1989, 'Changes in Female Income and Status in Rural Rajasthan: A Survey of 3 Villages', M.Sc. thesis, Oxford University.

Sanghera, B S, and Harriss-White, B, 1995, 'Themes in Rural Urbanisation', Open University, Development Policy and Practice Working Paper No. 27.

Saradamoni, K, 1994, 'Women, Kerala and Some Development Issues', *Economic and Political Weekly*, 29/9, pp. 501–10.

Saradaraju 1941, *Economic Conditions in the Madras Presidency, 1800–1850*, University of Madras.

Sarap, K, 1988, 'Transactions in Rural Credit Markets in Western Orissa, India', *Journal of Peasant Studies*, pp. 83–107.

—— 1990, 'Factors Affecting Small Farmers' Access to Institutional Credit in Rural Orissa', *Development and Change*, 21, pp. 281–307.

—— 1991, *Interlinked Agrarian Markets in Rural India*, New Delhi, Sage.

Sargent, J, Harriss-White, B, and Janakarajan, S, 1996, 'Development, Property and Deteriorating Life Changes for Girls in India: A Preliminary Discussion with Special Reference to Tamil Nadu', paper presented at the Dissemination Workshop for the ODA funded project between QEH, Oxford and MIDS, Madras, 27 March.

Satyamurthy, T V (ed.), 1998, *Industry and Agriculture since Independence*, Delhi, Oxford University Press.

Schaffer, B, 1984, 'Towards Responsibility: Public Policy in Concept and Practice', in Clay and Schaffer (eds.), pp. 142–90.

Schultz, 1988, 'Education Investments and Returns', in Chenery and Srinivasan, *Handbook of Development Economics*.

Scott, J, 1976, *The Moral Economy of the Peasant: Rebellion and Subsistence in South East Asia*, New Haven, Yale University Press.

Sen, A, 1985, *Commodities and Capabilities*, Amsterdam, Elsevier Science Publishers.

—— 1992, *Mental Handicap among Rural Indian Children*, New Delhi, Sage.

—— 1990a, 'Development as Capability Expansion', in K Griffin and J Knight (eds.), *Human Development and the International Strategy for the 1990s*, Macmillan.

—— 1990b, 'Gender and Cooperative Conflicts', in I Tinker (ed.), *Persistent Inequalities: Women and World Development*, New York, Oxford University Press, pp. 123–49.

—— 1999, *Development and Freedom*, Oxford, Clarendon Press.

Sen, A K, and Sengupta, S, 1983, 'Malnutrition and Rural Children and the Sex Bias', *Economic and Political Weekly*, 18/19,20,12, pp. 855–64.

Sen, G, 1982, 'Women Workers and the Green Revolution', in Lourdes Beneria (ed.), *Women and Development*, Geneva, International Labour Office.

Sengupta, A, 1998, 'Embedded or Stuck? The Study of the Indian State, its Embeddedness in Local Institutions and State Capacity', M.Phil. thesis, Queen Elizabeth House, Oxford University.

Setty, E D, 1991, 'Rural Industrialization, Small-Scale and Cottage Industries in Asia', *UNCRD*, Working Paper No. 91–2.

Shah, A, 1999, 'Institutional Change in India's Capital Markets', *Economic and Political Weekly* (16 Jan), pp. 183–94.

Shah, T, 1993, *Groundwater Markets and Irrigation Development: Political Economy and Practical Policy*, Delhi, Oxford University Press.

Sharma, N, and Drèze, J, 1998, 'Tenancy', in Lanjouw and Stern (eds.), pp. 462–99.

Shaw, A, 1996, 'Urban Policy in Post Independent India', *Economic and Political Weekly* (27 Jan), pp. 224–8.

Shore, C, and Wright, S, 1997, *Anthropology of Policy: Critical Perspectives on Governance and Policy*, London, Routledge.

Shukia, R K, 1990, 'Disabled Population – A Spatial Analysis of U.P.', *Deccan Geographer*, 28/2–3, pp. 683–99.

Shukla, V, 1994, 'A Regional Model of Rural Non-Farm Activity: An Empirical Application to Maharastra', in P Visaria and R Basant (eds.), *Non-Agricultural Employment in India: Trends and Prospects*, New Delhi, Sage Publications.

Singh, A K, 1994, 'Changes in the Structure of Rural Workforce in Uttar Pradesh: a Temporal and Regional Study', in P Visaria and R Basant (eds.), *Non-Agricultural Employment in India: Trends and Prospects*, New Delhi, Sage Publications.

Singh, K S, 1995 (2nd revised edition), *People of India*, National Series, Volume II, Anthropological Survey of India, Delhi, Bombay, Calcutta, OUP.

SPSS/PC+ V3.0, *Advanced Statistics Update Manual*, for the IBM PC/XT/AT and PS2, 1988, SPSS Inc., Chicago.

Srinivas, M N, 1962/1970, *Caste in Modern India and Other Essays*, New York, Asia Publishing House.

—— 1977, *Social Change in Modern India*, New Delhi, Orient Longman.

—— (ed.), 1996, *Caste: Its 20th Century Avatar*, Delhi, Viking.

Srinivasan, M V, 1993, 'Fertiliser Demand Scenario and its Influencing Factors in Tamil Nadu', M. Phil. thesis, Madras Christian College, Madras.

—— 1997, 'Minimum Wages in Agriculture: An Analysis of Secondary and Village Survey Data', *Indian Journal of Labour Economics*, 40/4, pp. 743–52.

Srinivasan, T N, and Bardhan, P K (eds.), 1988, *Rural Poverty in South Asia*, New Delhi, OUP.

Srivastava, R, 1997, 'Change and Resilience in Producer Strategia in Uttar Pradesh Agriculture', in Breman *et al.* (eds.), pp. 199–236.

—— 1998, 'Processes: an Analysis of Some Recent Trends', in Satyamurthy (ed.), pp. 219–47.

Subbarao, K, 1992, 'Interventions to Fill Nutrition Gaps at the Household Level: A Review of India's Experience', in B Harriss, S Guhan and R Cassen (eds.), *Poverty in India: Research and Policy*, New Delhi, Oxford University Press, pp. 231–58.

Subramanian, S (ed.), 1992, *Themes in Development Economics: Essays in Honour of Malcolm Adiseshiah*, New Delhi, OUP.

—— and Harriss-White, B, 1999, 'Introduction', in B Harriss-White and S Subramanian (eds.), *Illfare in India: Essays on India's Social Sector in Honour of S. Guhan*, New Delhi, Sage, pp. 17–43.

Sundari Ravindran, T K, 1999, 'Female Autonomy in Tamil Nadu: Unravelling the Complexities', *Economic and Political Weekly*, 34/16 and 17.

Sundari and Thombre, M, 1996, 'Declining Sex-Ratio: an Analysis with Special Reference to Tamil Nadu State', *Indian Economic Journal*, 43/4, pp. 30–47.

Sunder Rajan, R (ed.), 1999, *Signposts: Gender Issues in Post-Independence India*, New Delhi, Kali for Women.

Swaminathan, M, 1988, 'Inequality and Economic Mobility: An Analysis of Panel Data from a South Indian Village', D.Phil. thesis, Oxford University.

—— 1991, 'Segmentation, Collateral Undervaluation and the Rate of Interest in Agrarian Credit Markets: Some Evidence from Two Villages in South India', *Cambridge Journal of Economics*, 15/2, pp. 160–78.

—— 2000a, *Weakening Welfare: The Public Distribution of Food in India*, New Delhi, Leftword Press.

—— 2000b, 'Consumer Food Subsidies in India: Proposals for Reform', *Journal of Peasant Studies*, 27/3, pp. 92–114.

Swaminathan, Mina, 2000c, 'Worker, Mother or Both: Maternity and Childcare Services for Women in the Unorganised Sector', in Jhabvala and Subrahmanya (eds.), pp. 122–38.

Swaminathan, M, and Misra, N, 2001, 'Errors of Targeting: a Case Study of the Public Distribution of Food in a Maharashtra Village, 1995–2000', Mario Einaudi Centre for International Studies, Cornell University.

Syed, R H (ed.), *The Rural Non-Farm Sector and Process of Economic Development*, Association of Development Research and Training Institutes of Asia and the Pacific, Kuala Lumpur, Malaysia.

Tamil Nadu Electricity Board (various years), *Tamil Nadu Electricity Board Statistics at a Glance*, Chennai.

Tandon, D R, 1994, *Fertiliser Guide*, Fertiliser Development Consultation Organization, New Delhi.

Tata Energy Research Institute (TERI) 1999, *TERI Energy Data Directory and Year Book, 1998–99*, New Delhi.

Thomas, M, 1992a, 'Community Based Rehabilitation in India – an Emerging Trend', *Indian Journal of Paediatrics*, 58, pp. 401–6.

—— 1992b, 'The Action Aid Disability Programmes: Experiences in Early Identification and Early Intervention', *Indian Journal of Paediatrics*, 59, pp. 697–700.

—— 1993a, 'Disability and Rehabilitation – the Emergence of the Community Based Approach in India', paper presented at a conference on 'Asia in the 1990s: Meeting and Making a New World', 29–31 October 1993, Kingston, Ontario, Queen's University, pp. 1–13.

—— 1993b, 'Programme Planning and Implementation of Community Based Rehabilitation', India, ActionAid, pp. 1–20.

Thorner, A, 1982, 'Semi-feudalism or Capitalism?', *Economic and Political Weekly*, 17/4, pp. 1961–8; 17/11, pp. 1993–9; 17/18, pp. 2061–8.

Thorner, D (ed.), 1996, *Ecological and Agrarian Regions of South Asia circa 1930*, Karachi, Oxford University Press.

—— and Thorner, A, 1962, *Land and Labour in India*, Bombay, Asian Publishing House.

Tilak, J B G, 1986, *Education and Regional Development*, Paris, UNESCO.

Timmer, C P, Falcon, W, and Pearson, S R (eds.), 1983, *Food Policy Analysis*, Baltimore, John Hopkins for the World Bank.

Trubeck, D M, and Galanter, M, 1974, 'Scholars in Self-estrangement: Some Reflections on the Crisis of Law and Development Studies in the US', *Wisconsin Law Review*, pp. 1062–1102.

UNDP 1993, *Human Development Report*, New York, UNDP/OUP.

Unni, J, 1991, 'Regional Variations in Rural Non-Agricultural Employment: an Explanatory Analysis', *Economic and Political Weekly*, 26/3 (19 January).

UNRISD 1994, *Gender and Agriculture: with Special Reference to Bangladesh, Indonesia, Uganda and South Africa*, Geneva.

Vaidyanathan, A, 1986, 'Labour use in Rural India: a Study of Spatial and Temporal Variations', *Economic and Political Weekly*, 21/52, Review of Agriculture, (27 December).

—— 1993, 'Fertilisers in Indian Agriculture', *Bulletin, Madras Development Seminar series*, 22/5–6, pp. 236–52.

—— 1994, 'Performance of Indian Agriculture since Independence', in Basu (ed.), pp. 18–74.

—— 1996, 'Depletion of Groundwater: Some Issues', *Indian Journal of Agricultural Economics*, 51/1 and 2 (Jan–June).

—— and Janakarajan, S, 1989, 'Management of Irrigation and its Effect on Productivity under Different Environmental and Technical Conditions: A Study of Two Surface Irrigation Systems in Tamil Nadu', Research Report to Planning Commission, Government of India, New Delhi.

Visaria, P, 1994, 'The Sectoral Distribution of Workers in India, 1961–91', in P Visaria and R Basant (eds.), *Non-Agricultural Employment in India: Trends and Prospects*, New Delhi, Sage.

—— 1995, 'Rural Non-Farm Employment in India: Trends and Issues for Research', *Indian Journal of Agricultural Economics*, 50/3, pp. 398–409.

—— and Basant, R (eds.), *Non-Agricultural Employment in India: Trends and Prospects*, New Delhi, Sage Publications.

Von Benda Beckmann, F, 1994, 'Good Governance, Law and Social Reality: Problematic Relationship', *International Journal of Knowledge Transfer and Utilisation*, 7/3, pp. 55–67.

—— and van der Velde, M, 1992, 'Law as a Resource in Agrarian Struggles', *Wageningse Sociologische Studien no. 33*, Agricultural University, Wageningen.

Von Oppen, M, 1978, 'Agricultural Marketing and Aggregate Productivity: a Dimension to be Added to Agricultural Marketing Research', Economics Program Discussion Paper no. 3, ICRISAT, Hyderand.

Von Pischke, J, Adams, D, and Donald, G (eds.), 1983, *Rural Financial Markets in Developing Countries*, Johns Baltimore University Press, Hopkins.

Wade, R, 1985, 'The Market for Public Office: Or Why India is not Better at Development', *Journal of Development Studies*, 13/4, pp. 467–97.

—— 1988, *Village Republics*, Cambridge, Cambridge University Press.

Wai, U T, 1957,

Walker, T S, and Ryan, J G, 1990, *Village and Household Economies in India's Semi-Arid Tropics*, Baltimore and London, Johns Hopkins University Press.

Wanmali, S, 1991, 'Changes in the Provision and Use of Services in the North Arcot Region', in Hazell and Ramasamy (eds.), pp. 213–37.

—— and Islam, Y, 1994, 'Rural Infrastructure, Settlement Systems and Service Provision in North Arcot in 1990–91', in Wanmali and Ramasamy (eds.), pp. 132–78.

—— and Ramasamy, C (eds.), 1994, *Developing Rural Infrastructure for Poor People: Studies from North Arcot, Tamil Nadu, India*, ICAR, New Delhi and IFPRI, Washington DC.

Weiner, M, 1991, *The Child and the State in India*, New Delhi, OUP.

Weiss, S M, and Kulikowski, C A, 1991, *Computer Systems that Learn: Classification and Prediction Methods from Statistics, Neural Nets, Machine Learning and Expert Systems*, San Mateo, CA, Morgan Kaufmann Publishing.

Werna, E, 1993, 'Social Differentials in the Provision of Urban Services in Nairobi: Comments on Urban Management and Poverty Alleviation', Development Studies Association Conference Paper/London School of Hygiene and Tropical Medicine, London.

White, G (ed.), 1993, The Political Analysis of Markets, *Special Issue of the IDS Bulletin*, 24/3.

WHO, 1980, *International Classification of Impairments. Disabilities and Handicaps: A Manual of Classification Relating to the Consequence of Disease*, Geneva, World Health Organization.

Widlund, I, 2000, 'Paths to Power and Patterns of Influence: The Dravidian Parties in

South Indian Politics', D.Phil thesis, Dept of Government, University of Uppsala, Sweden/Stockholm, Elanders Gotab.

Williams, G, 1979, 'Taking the Part of Peasants', in Gutkind and Wallerstein (eds.). *The Political Economy.*

Wodon, Q, 1997a, 'Food Energy Intake and Cost of Basic Needs: Measuring Poverty in Bangladesh', *Journal of Development Studies*, 34/2.

—— 1997b, 'Targeting the Poor using ROC Curves', *World Development*, 25/12.

Wood, G, 1984, 'Bernard Schaffer, 1925–1984', *Public Administration and Development*, 14/3, p. 00.

—— (ed.), 1985, *Labelling in Development Policy*, London, Sage.

—— 1999, 'From Farms to Services: Agricultural Reformation in Bangladesh', in Rogaly *et al* (eds.), pp. 303–28.

World Bank 1986, *Financing Education in Developing Countries*, IBRD, Washington DC.

—— 1988, *Education in Sub-Saharan Africa. World Bank Policy Study*, IBRD, Washington DC.

—— 1993, *World Development Report 1993: Investing in Health*, Oxford, Oxford University Press.

—— 1994, *World Development Report: Infrastructure for Development*, Washington DC, IBRD.

—— 1997, *World Development Report: The State in a Changing World*, Washington DC, IBRD.

World Bank Country Study 1989, *India: Recent Developments and Medium-Term Issues*, IBRD, Washington DC.

—— 1991, *Gender and Poverty in India*, IBRD, Washington DC.

Index